RENEWALS 458-4574

DATE DUE

DEC 13			
NOV 15			
DEC 03			
NOV 05			
DEC 21			
MAR 20			
APR 03			
GAYLORD			PRINTED IN U.S.A.

CARE OR CUSTODY?

CARE OR CUSTODY?

*Mentally Disordered Offenders in the
Criminal Justice System*

JUDITH M. LAING

OXFORD
UNIVERSITY PRESS

OXFORD
UNIVERSITY PRESS

Great Clarendon Street, Oxford ox2 6DP

Oxford University Press is a department of the University of Oxford.
It furthers the University's objective of excellence in research, scholarship,
and education by publishing worldwide in

Oxford New York

Athens Auckland Bangkok Bogotá Buenos Aires Calcutta
Cape Town Chennai Dar es Salaam Delhi Florence Hong Kong Istanbul
Karachi Kuala Lumpur Madrid Melbourne Mexico City Mumbai
Nairobi Paris São Paulo Singapore Taipei Tokyo Toronto Warsaw

with associated companies in Berlin Ibadan

Oxford is a registered trade mark of Oxford University Press
in the UK and in certain other countries

Published in the United States
by Oxford University Press Inc., New York

© J. M. Laing 1999

The moral rights of the author have been asserted
Database right Oxford University Press (maker)

First published 1999

All rights reserved. No part of this publication may be reproduced,
stored in a retrieval system, or transmitted, in any form or by any means,
without the prior permission in writing of Oxford University Press,
or as expressly permitted by law, or under terms agreed with the appropriate
reprographics rights organization. Enquiries concerning reproduction
outside the scope of the above should be sent to the Rights Department,
Oxford University Press, at the address above

You must not circulate this book in any other binding or cover
and you must impose this same condition on any acquirer

British Library Cataloguing in Publication Data

Data available

Library of Congress Cataloging in Publication Data
Laing, Judith M.
Care or custody?: mentally disordered offenders in the criminal
justice system/Judith M. Laing.
p. cm.
Includes bibliographical references and index.
1. Insanity—Jurisprudence—Great Britain.   2. Mentally
handicapped offenders—Legal status, laws, etc.—Great Britain.
3. Insane—Commitment and detention—Great Britain.   I. Title.
KD7897.L35   1999
345.41'03—dc21   99–16147
ISBN 0–19–826818–1

1 3 5 7 9 10 8 6 4 2

Typeset in Times by
Cambrian Typesetters, Frimley, Surrey

Printed in Great Britain
on acid-free paper by
Biddles Ltd., Guildford and King's Lynn

Preface

Culminating in the 1990s, the 1979–97 Conservative Government introduced a series of measures aimed at diverting mentally disordered offenders from various stages of the criminal justice system. These measures emphasized the need for mentally disordered offenders to receive treatment from the health and social services wherever possible, and in particular, provided that this should take place by virtue of inter-agency diversion schemes operating at courts and police stations across the country. This explicit diversion policy has been embraced by the new Labour Government, which has affirmed its continued support and commitment to such measures. This book examines the treatment of mentally disordered offenders in this context. It also includes an empirical study which evaluates how far a group of court diversion schemes operating in West Yorkshire enable this diversion and treatment to take place, thereby promoting inter-agency working, facilitating diversion, and providing lasting treatment and support.

The book considers how mentally disordered offenders are problematic as they fall between the realm of differing disciplines, principally the law and psychiatry; the main difficulty is whether the emphasis should be upon their mental illness and providing timely and appropriate care and treatment, or whether they should be treated primarily as offenders and be made subject to the normal operation of the criminal law. The book attempts to demonstrate that mentally disordered offenders need special care and treatment, access to the health and social services wherever possible, and that this has been a desirable goal for many decades, but that previous attempts have been thwarted due to the lack of adequate funding and facilities and the absence of inter-agency co-operation between the different agencies involved. The arguments in favour of this approach and some of the problems surrounding the treatment of mentally disordered offenders are outlined in Ch. 1. In particular, the evident difficulties in achieving inter-agency co-operation are discussed, and it is argued that in order to achieve diversion and appropriate disposals, increased co-operation and collaboration is central to the diversion process. It will be shown that diversion is an inherently offender-oriented process, its primary focus being his or her needs, and that there is therefore a danger that other principles within the criminal justice system, such as respect for public safety and the rights of victims, may be jeopardized in the diversion process. Chapter 1 also considers the implications of diversion for mentally disordered offenders in these respects and examines whether it can be made to fit into the overall mould of the criminal justice system.

The remainder of Part I of the book outlines the national dimension and considers the origins, introduction, and implementation of diversion policy on a national basis. Having outlined the basic principles in Ch. 1, Ch. 2 briefly considers the historical origins of diversion, which largely stem from the Mental Health Act 1959 and which have greatly influenced the current legislation and provisions. Some of the difficulties encountered in the past are considered, with their undoubted influence and impact upon the implementation and future of diversion policy. In particular, the difficulties in achieving inter-agency co-operation and the lack of adequate funding and facilities for this category of offender are discussed. Chapter 3 considers the mechanisms that already exist to divert mentally disordered offenders, primarily under the Mental Health Act 1983 and related provisions. It argues that the intention inherent in these provisions, namely to ensure access to appropriate health care, has not been fully realized. It shows that by the end of the 1980s, there was growing concern about the high number of mentally disordered offenders still inappropriately finding their way into the penal system. The 1979–97 Government was called upon to take action to remedy the deficiencies and its response provides the origins of diversion policy and inter-agency assessment and diversion schemes. The introduction and implementation of what has emerged will be considered fully in Ch. 4.

Part II of the book is based upon an empirical study of a group of diversion schemes operating at magistrates' courts within West Yorkshire and is an evaluation of how far these schemes are able to provide mentally disordered offenders with access to lasting health care and treatment, and to what extent this has been facilitated by increased collaboration and co-operation. Ch. 5 includes an evaluation of the *process* of diversion schemes. It outlines the entire process of establishing and implementing them and considers the difficulties encountered therein. In particular, assessment is made of the degree to which the barriers traditionally operating between the law and psychiatry have been overcome and inter-agency working has been achieved. It also considers how far the principles of the criminal justice system outlined in Ch. 1 are respected in the diversion process. The methodology of the empirical study and the formulation and operation of the data collection process are also outlined in this chapter. The empirical study is concluded in Ch. 6, which is an evaluation of the *impact* of the diversion schemes and considers how far they actually enable mentally disordered offenders to be given access to appropriate health and social services care, and to what extent this is valued by the professionals and individuals concerned.

The book is concluded in Ch. 7, which discusses some overarching observations and draws upon the findings of the previous chapters. It also suggests possible future directions for research and considers what the future may hold for diversion policy in the light of past experiences. It is concluded that a degree of inter-agency working can be achieved which facilitates diversion attempts and that it is worthwhile and valued greatly by those involved. The case for special treatment is, it is submitted, clearly made out, but in general it is concluded that unless and until central Government places such decisions and the responsibility for them on a firm statutory footing with permanent funding arrangements and massive improvements in the provision of appropriate services and facilities, the future of the current initiatives hangs in the balance. This is a fitting conclusion for, ultimately, diversion policy, the treatment of mentally disordered offenders, and the provision of funding and facilities are political issues, which are entirely dependent upon political will.

I would like to express my gratitude to all the court diversion Community Psychiatric Nurses and Social Workers in West Yorkshire who have assisted with the research study—Ms Ruth Noonan, Mrs Gilly Speakman, Mr Stephen Flay, Mr Adrian Hill, Mr Patrick Darkwa, and Mr Ralph Firth (and latterly Belinda and Joann Gibson). They made the study possible by allowing access to records, providing information, allowing me to use the data and accompany them to court on innumerable occasions. I am especially grateful to all those who assisted me by agreeing to talk about their experiences and participate in the interviews. Without their co-operation much of the study would not have been possible. Thanks are also due to the police, and probation and court staff at the magistrates' courts who spoke with me about their experiences. I would also like to thank Mr Les Moss, Mr Terry Myers, and Dr Imogen Brown (West Yorkshire Probation Service), Mr Mike Farrar (NHS Management Executive), Inspector Andy Roughton, Mr Dermot Boyle, Mr Dave Mercer, Dr Keith Rix, Mrs Dorothy Tonak, and Ms Marion Bullivant for their assistance and information.

This book is based upon research conducted for my Ph.D. which was awarded by the University of Leeds in July 1996. I am grateful to my former Ph.D. supervisors Professor Clive Walker and Mr Ian Brownlee for all their comments and advice, to my Ph.D. examiner Professor Ronnie Mackay for his input, and to many of my colleagues at the University of Liverpool, in particular Professor Dominic McGoldrick, Dr Faye Boland, and Mr Steve Cooper for their practical assistance and support. A final massive thank you to my husband, Rob Laddle, and my family and friends for all their encouragement and support.

J.M.L.

Liverpool
May 1999

Contents

List of Figures

List of Tables

Abbreviations

ACOP	Association of Chief Officers of Probation
All ER	All England Law Reports
Am J of Psych	*American Journal of Psychiatry*
ASW	Approved Social Worker
BMJ	*British Medical Journal*
Brit J Criminology	*British Journal of Criminology*
Brit J Psych	*British Journal of Psychiatry*
Bull Am Acad Psych & Law	*Bulletin of the American Academy of Psychiatry and Law*
Bull RC Psych	*Bulletin of the Royal College of Psychiatrists*
Camb L Rev	*Cambridge Law Review*
CLP	*Current Legal Problems*
CPN	Community Psychiatric Nurse
CPS	Crown Prosecution Service
Cr App R	Criminal Appeal Reports
Crim Beh & Ment Health	*Criminal Behaviour and Mental Health*
Crim Law	*Criminal Lawyer*
Crim LR	*Criminal Law Review*
DoH	Department of Health
HMCIP	Her Majesty's Chief Inspector of Prisons
HMIP	Her Majesty's Inspectorate of Prisons
HO	Home Office
How J of Crim Just	*Howard Journal of Criminal Justice*
Int J Law & Psych	*International Journal of Law and Psychiatry*
J Com & App Soc Psych	*Journal of Community and Applied Social Psychiatry*
J For Psych	*Journal of Forensic Psychiatry*
J Law and Soc	*Journal of Law and Society*
JP	*Justice of the Peace*
J Prison & Jail Health	*Journal of Prison and Jail Health*
JSWL	*Journal of Social Welfare Law*
KCLJ	*King's College Law Journal*
LASSL	Local Authority Social Services Letter
Law Soc Gaz	*Law Society Gazette*
The Mag	*The Magistrate*
Med, Sci & Law	*Medicine, Science and Law*
MHAC	Mental Health Act Commission
MH Adv. Com.	Mental Health Advisory Committee

MISG	Mental Illness Specific Grant
MLR	*Modern Law Review*
NLJ	*New Law Journal*
ONS	Office of National Statistics
PMS	Prison Medical Service
PO	Probation Officer
Prison Serv J	*Prison Service Journal*
Probat J	*Probation Journal*
Psych Bull	*Psychiatric Bulletin*
Psychol Medicine	*Psychological Medicine*
QBD	Queen's Bench Division
RHA	Regional Health Authority
SLT	*Scots Law Times*
Web JCLI	*Web Journal of Current Legal Issues*
WLR	*Weekly Law Reports*
WYPS	West Yorkshire Probation Service

List of Cases

List of Statutes

PART I

1

The Basic Principles

The management, care and support of mentally disturbed people, whether they are offenders or not, will continue to raise difficult issues of public attitude, treatment methodology, resources and location of facilities. There are no quick or easy solutions.[1]

1.1. INTRODUCTION

This book is concerned with the treatment of mentally disordered offenders in the criminal justice system. In particular, it investigates the diversion of mentally disordered offenders from the criminal justice system and into the health and social services. So the first step is to identify precisely who mentally disordered offenders are and how they should be treated. This chapter will also consider what is meant by diversion in this context and how it fits in with treatment and with the criminal justice system as a whole, and the many difficulties which surround the treatment of mentally disordered offenders will be identified.

The problems are particularly acute given that the mentally disordered offender falls within the realm of two differing disciplines—the legal and medical professions—both of which have contrasting and often conflicting views and approaches towards treatment. This has a grave effect upon diversion, as its successful implementation is dependent upon the close and successful collaboration and co-operation of those disciplines and professionals involved in dealing with and caring for such people. The impact of these difficulties upon the trend to divert mentally disordered offenders from the criminal justice system will be considered.

Initially this chapter will consider the nature and meaning of 'mental disorder', and it will be shown that the definitions as to who is mentally disordered or insane are often vague and uncertain. Much difficulty and conflict has arisen between the legal and medical professions as to how best to treat these people because of this, and it will be illustrated how this has produced differing approaches towards the treatment of the mentally disordered offender. This, in turn, will highlight the difficulties faced in diverting mentally disordered offenders from the criminal justice system, as they are not often easily identified or placed.

The second half of this introductory chapter will be concerned with determin-

[1] *Report of an Interdepartmental Working Group of Home Office and DHSS Officials on Mentally Disturbed Offenders in the Prison System in England and Wales* (DHSS 1987) para. 8.2.

ing precisely what is the best approach towards this group of people. Should they be treated primarily as offenders and, therefore, be punished according to the law and their treatment motivated primarily by principles of justice and equality? Or should the emphasis be placed upon their mental disorder and their treatment motivated by humanitarian concerns according to the medical model by medical personnel? The answer to this difficult question will form the basis for the discussion in subsequent chapters.

1.2. WHO ARE MENTALLY DISORDERED OFFENDERS?

1.2.1. The Nature and Meaning of Mental Disorder

At present, the consolidating Mental Health Act 1983 is the main provision in force governing people with mental disorders. Not only does it concern the treatment of mentally disordered offenders,[2] but it also governs all aspects of the control of mentally disordered people, from their care and treatment to the management of their property and a variety of other related matters.[3]

This statute is therefore vital when considering the fate of people with mental disorders. However, before their plight can be addressed, it is imperative to ask exactly what do the words 'mental disorder' mean, and what is its precise definition and nature in the eyes of the law? The Mental Health Act provides a useful starting point, a helpful definition of 'mental disorder' in the eyes of mental health law. And it is essentially the treatment of offenders suffering from mental disorder within the meaning of the Act that will be considered. Whilst the book is primarily concerned with mentally disordered offenders as defined under the mental health legislation, in some cases mental disorder has a much broader definition. It will become evident in subsequent chapters, and especially in relation to the emergence of inter-agency diversion schemes, that the category of mentally disordered offenders can also include those who are suffering from mental health problems of a less serious nature, such as stress/anxiety, which would not warrant in-patient admission, as well as those suffering from a drug/alcohol problem which may be linked to an underlying mental illness. However, the definition of mental disorder within the meaning of the mental health legislation will initially be considered here, as it also serves to highlight how problematic this area of the law can be.

1.2.2. The Statutory Definition of Mental Disorder

Within the Act, the term 'mental disorder' is defined as any one of four specific categories identified. So the provisions of the Act must only be used with respect

---

[2] Mental Health Act 1983 pt. III.
[3] See Mental Health Act 1983 s. 1(1).

to people suffering from this legally recognized form of 'mental disorder'.[4] It is defined in section 1(2) of the 1983 Act and encompasses 'mental illness, arrested or incomplete development of mind, psychopathic disorder and any other disorder or disability of mind'.

The four specific categories of mental disorder include mental illness (discussed at 1.2.2.1); psychopathic disorder (discussed at 1.2.2.2); and 'arrested or incomplete development of mind', which includes most any kinds of mental handicap or subnormality, ranging from mental impairment to severe mental impairment (discussed at 1.2.2.3). The definition is wide, and residually includes 'any other disorder or disability of mind' (discussed at 1.2.2.4).

This is the basic definition of mental disorder in English law. It is, in fact, in line with the definition advocated in other jurisdictions, as other Commonwealth countries such as Australia and New Zealand adopt analogous terminology in their mental health legislation.[5] The British definition can also be said to be compatible with the European Convention on Human Rights' definition of persons of 'unsound mind' (Article 5(1)(e)).[6]

However, legal definitions are not always uncontentious, no matter how universal and widespread their application, and although in theory the definition may seem clear, the situation in practice is, in fact, very different. The definitions have attracted much criticism on a number of grounds, particularly from legal commentators.[7] Reasons for such criticism will now be explained.

1.2.2.1. Mental Illness

The first subcategory is mental illness, which has been left undefined in the 1983 Act because, as noted by Hoggett, the Government at the time believed 'that

---

[4] See *Kynaston* v. *Secretary of State for Home Affairs* (1981) 73 Cr App R 281.

[5] e.g. The New South Wales statute governing this area is the Mental Health Act 1990, where mental illness means a 'condition which seriously impairs; either temporarily or permanently, the mental functioning of a person' (Schedule 1); The Western Australia Mental Health Act 1962 (s. 5) and the Tasmanian Mental Health Act 1963 (s. 4) where 'mental illness' is defined as being 'any mental illness, arrested or incomplete development of mind, psychopathic disorder or any other disorder or disability of the mind'; and the New Zealand statute, the Mental Health Act 1969, where 'mental disorder' is defined as 'where a person is suffering from a psychiatric disorder/other disorder, continuous or episodic, as substantially impairs mental health, so that the person belongs to one or more of the following classes: (a) Mentally Ill; (b) Mentally Infirm and/or (c) Mentally Subnormal'. See further L. Crowley-Smith, 'Intellectual Disability and Mental Illness: A Call for Unambiguous and Uniform Statutory Definitions' (1995) 3 *Journal of Law and Medicine* 192–201.

[6] See further L. Gostin, 'Human Rights, Judicial Review and the Mentally Disordered Offender' [1982] *Crim LR* 779–93. This Article concerns the lawfulness of the detention and treatment of 'persons of unsound mind'. In the leading British case in this area *X* v. *UK* (1982) 4 EHRR 188 neither the Court nor the Commission questioned directly the compatibility of UK law with the Convention's definition of 'unsound mind'. Thus it is assumed that the definition of mental disorder and 'unsoundness of mind' are satisfactory in the European context. See further P. Van Dijk and F. Van Hoof, *Theory and Practice of the ECHR* (Kluwer 1990), 265.

[7] B. Hoggett, 'The Mental Health Act 1983' [1983] *Public Law* 172–90, 179–81; see also D. Carson, 'Mental Processes: The Mental Health Act 1983' [1983] *JSWL* 195–211, 195–8.

there is little evidence that the present lack of definition of mental illness leads to any particular problems'.[8]

It has been acknowledged in Parliament that 'mental illness is extremely hard to define',[9] thus a wide definition was preferable, given 'the difficulties of producing a definition which would be likely to stand the test of time'.[10] This has generated a great deal of controversy, however, due to the fact that it is so open-ended and the consequences of suffering from mental illness are severe and can result in compulsory hospitalization under other sections of the Mental Health Act.

In 1975 a Committee was appointed to conduct a meticulous review of the law relating to mentally disordered offenders, and its recommendations were based upon a wide definition of mental illness.[11] And an earlier 1957 Royal Commission, which considered the law relating to mental illness, had adopted a similar stance, recommending the use of broad terms without trying to describe medical conditions in detail.[12] As noted by Hoggett, this is regarded as the 'lay-view' of mental illness[13] and has received support from the Court of Appeal in *W v L*.[14] Lord Justice Lawton stated that the words 'mental illness' are 'ordinary words of the English language. They have no particular medical significance. They have no particular legal significance.'[15]

The court should therefore construe them 'in the way that ordinary sensible people would construe them'. Brenda Hoggett has subsequently described this approach as 'the man must be mad test',[16] as an ordinary person would say 'Well, the fellow is obviously mentally ill' and is therefore mentally ill in the eyes of the law! This is the very point that attracts the criticism, however. It is regarded as unacceptable, as the consequences of suffering from a mental disorder are serious and therefore should not be dependent upon 'any common person's misinformed view of behaviour which is perhaps only eccentric, non-conforming or anti-social'.[17]

---

[8] DHSS, *Review of the Mental Health Act 1959* (1978) Cmnd. 7320 para. 1.17.

[9] Session 1982–3 vol. XI col. 213 Special Standing Committee Mental Health (Amendment) Bill *per* M. Thomas MP.   [10] Ibid.

[11] The Butler Committee in its *Report on Mentally Abnormal Offenders* (1975) Cmnd. 6244 para. 1.13 (henceforth Butler Report). Its terms of reference were to consider to what extent and on what criteria the law should recognize mental disorder or abnormality in a person accused of a criminal offence as a factor affecting his liability to be tried or convicted, and his disposal; and to consider what, if any, changes are necessary in the powers, procedure, and facilities relating to the provision of appropriate treatment, in prison, hospital, or the community, for offenders suffering from mental disorder or abnormality, and to their discharge, and aftercare; and to make recommendations.

[12] The 'Percy Commission'—*Royal Commission on the Law Relating to Mental Illness and Mental Deficiency* (1957) Cmd. 169 para. 357. Its full terms of reference were to inquire, as regards England and Wales, into the existing administrative machinery governing the certification, detention, care, . . . absence on trial or licence, discharge and supervision of persons who are alleged to be suffering from mental illness or mental deficiency (other than Broadmoor patients); to consider, as regards England and Wales, the extent to which it is now, or should be made, statutorily possible for such persons to be treated as voluntary patients, without certification, and to make recommendations.

[13] B. Hoggett, *Mental Health Law* (Sweet & Maxwell 1996), 32–4.

[14] [1974] QB 711 C A; see also R. Jones, *Mental Health Act Manual* (Sweet & Maxwell 1996), 16.   [15] Ibid. 719.   [16] Hoggett, *Mental Health Law* (1996), 32.

[17] Hoggett, *Mental Health Law* (1990), 48.

Michael Cavadino has also criticized the term's very lack of definition, and particular objections have been aimed at this lay-view approach.[18] He stresses that this dependence upon the abilities of ordinary, sensible laypeople unanimously to define mental illness is highly suspect and 'far from satisfactory, especially in an area of the law where the liberty of the citizen is at risk'.[19] Consequently, he advocates that some form of official guidance should be provided—it need not be over-precise, but should be incorporated within the Code of Practice accompanying the Act.[20]

A revised Code of Practice accompanying the Act was issued in 1993, but was silent on the issue of the definition of mental illness. The only current official guidance is contained in the Memorandum to the Act which was revised in 1998 by the Department of Health. However, it merely states that the 'operational definition and usage is a matter for clinical judgement in each case',[21] and 'the one decided case on the subject serves mainly to confuse'.[22] Much, then, is left in the hands of the psychiatric profession to decide who is and who is not mentally ill, and this has caused much controversy, which will be further discussed below.

1.2.2.2. Psychopathic Disorder

The second subcategory is psychopathic disorder, which is defined in the Act as 'a persistent disorder/disease of the mind which results in abnormally aggressive/seriously irresponsible conduct on the part of the person concerned'.[23] The Butler Committee also highlighted the problems with regard to this concept, devoting an entire chapter to consider this contentious subcategory and concluding that 'it is no longer a useful or meaningful concept'.[24]

It is an unhelpful definition in many respects, as it does not specify the nature of the disorder or disability of mind, other than it must be 'persistent'.[25] In particular, the fact that it is associated with antisocial and violent behaviour has been greatly criticized, especially in relation to criminal offenders.[26] The definition is 'logically defective'[27] as it is a circular argument to say that a person is disordered because s/he commits crimes, but to conclude that the disorder should then

---

[18] M. Cavadino, 'Mental Illness and Neo-Polonianism' (1991) 2 *J For Psych* 295–304.
[19] Ibid. 299.   [20] Ibid. 302.
[21] DoH/Welsh Office, *Mental Health Act 1983: Memorandum on Parts I to VI, VIII and X* (HMSO 1998) para. 8.   [22] M. Cavadino, 'Mental Illness', 298.
[23] Mental Health Act 1983 s. 1(2). It is acknowledged here that the term psychopathic disorder is regarded as being unhelpful and stigmatizing, and that the term personality disorder is generally preferred. However, the term psychopathic disorder is adopted throughout this book as it is still used in the mental health legislation.
[24] *Butler Report* para. 5.23; see also R. Jones, *Manual*, 18–19.
[25] Mental Health Act 1983 s. 1(2); see also L. Gostin, *Mental Health Services: Law and Practice* (Shaw & Sons 1986) ch. 9.
[26] See A. Ashworth and J. Shapland, 'Psychopaths in the Criminal Process' [1980] *Crim LR* 628–40.   [27] *Butler Report* para. 5.20.

excuse these crimes.[28] As Baroness Wootton has observed, the definition is 'tautological'—'The psychopath's mental disorder is inferred from his anti-social behaviour while the anti-social behaviour is explained by mental disorder.'[29] Most of the criticism surrounding the general definition has been aimed at the psychopathic disorder element of it.[30] This can be seen from the Government reports and parliamentary debates that preceded the mental health legislation in 1959 and 1983[31]—'Not surprisingly, the issue of whether the psychopaths should be included in the 1959 Mental Health Act . . . became one of the most frequently debated aspects of the proposed changes in legislation.'[32]

The 1957 Percy Commission, which adopted a humanitarian approach, recommended the term's inclusion,[33] and the Government agreed. Ultimately it was felt that, despite the serious doubts as to the susceptibility to treatment, this group should be included within the scope of the Act, as the possibility of a future cure should not be ruled out. Furthermore, 'if deleted from the Bill, the result would be that these unfortunate individuals would be left to carry on their irresponsible behaviour until such time as they landed in prison'.[34]

As already noted, the Butler Committee devoted much of their report to this issue, as they regarded it as 'one of the most perplexing questions'[35] given the 'multiplicity of opinions as to the aetiology, symptoms and treatment of psychopathy'.[36] It has, in fact, been a source of contention from the moment that it was first diagnosed: 'For 150 years, science has known of the psychopath's existence, for at least 140 years scientists have quarrelled over the definition of his disorder.'[37] And the main problems relate not only to this lack of a clear definition, but also to the lack of suitable methods of treatment. The medical profession has produced a wealth of literature testifying to such difficulties.[38] This is felt to be so largely due to the nature of the disease itself, as one of the main symptoms is a lack of display of normal feelings of guilt or remorse. As noted by

[28]   See further B. Wootton (assisted by V. G. Seal, and R. Chambers), *Social Science and Social Pathology* (Allen & Unwin 1959).

[29]   B. Wootton, *Crime and the Criminal Law* (Stevens 1981), 90.

[30]   D. Chiswick, 'Managing Psychopathic Offenders: A Problem that Will Not Go Away' (1987) 295 *BMJ* 159–60, 160—'The very existence of psychopathic disorder as one category of mental disorder in the Mental Health Act has attracted fierce debate for decades.'

[31]   e.g. the White Paper, *Better Services for the Mentally Ill* (1975) Cmnd. 6233, stated that there was considerable uncertainty regarding psychopaths and the extent to which they could be helped by the health services (paras. 1.11–1.12). For a detailed account see S. Ramon, 'The Category of Psychopathy: Its Professional and Social Context in Britain', in N. Rose and P. Miller (eds.), *The Power of Psychiatry* (Polity 1988), 228–38.   [32]   Ibid. 226.

[33]   Percy Commission para. 357, as 'the lack of knowledge about the nature and causes of particular forms of disorder does not mean that they cannot be recognised and successfully treated in individual cases'.

[34]   Session 1958–9 Vol. IV col. 44 Standing Committee E Mental Health Bill *per* Sir H. Lucas-Tooth MP.   [35]   *Butler Report* para. 5.1.   [36]   Ibid. para. 5.2.

[37]   W. McCord, and J. McCord, *The Psychopath: An Essay on the Criminal Mind* (Insight 1964), 2.

[38]   A. Lewis, 'Psychopathic Personality: A Most Elusive Category' (1974) 4 *Psychol Medicine* 133–40; R. Cope, 'A Survey of Forensic Psychiatrists' Views on Psychopathic Disorder' (1993) 4 *J For Psych* 227–9; P. Collins, 'The Treatability of Psychopaths' (1991) 2 *J For Psych* 103–10.

Ramon, this lack of response of the patients inevitably results in the fact they appear as if they are not actually suffering themselves and are therefore less likely to evoke sympathy.[39] Many psychiatrists claim that psychopaths are 'unrewarding and unthankful patients . . . often biting the hand that tries to feed [them]'.[40] More recently, the case of Beverley Allitt, the serial child-killer, has provoked further controversy in this area.[41]

Moreover, there is evidence to suggest that most psychopaths do not respond to psychiatric treatment in hospital and can be the most difficult patients.[42] As noted by Hoggett, if there is no hospital bed available it is likely that the courts will impose a longer prison sentence, since 'by definition, [psychopaths are] more than usually dangerous'.[43] In fact she states that there is even evidence to suggest that very few hospitals are willing to admit psychopaths at all. In the case of *R.* v. *Thornton*[44] for example, the defendant was diagnosed as having a psychopathic disorder, and the medical evidence indicated that some treatment might help his condition, however no psychiatric hospital would accept him, so the judge was forced to impose a prison sentence. It seems therefore that this category is highly contentious and unsatisfactory.[45]

It is also interesting to note that this category is not used in mental health legislation in Scotland or Northern Ireland.[46] The Butler Committee preferred the use of the term 'personality disorder', which would be left undefined in the same way as 'mental illness' presently is.[47] It could be argued however, that this is just as vague and controversial. And it has been suggested that lawyers who found the Mental Health Act definition of 'psychopathic disorder' vague, would 'throw a fit when faced with this lot'![48]

Despite the doubts expressed regarding this category, successive Governments have continually refused to change their position. In the 1978 Review of the Mental Health Act the Labour Government announced that it had no plans to change the categorization, as 'the possibility of some future advance in treatment should not be ruled out and . . . it would not be right to deny all possibility of compulsory hospital treatment to psychopaths as an alternative to

---

[39] Ramon, *Category of Psychopathy*, 226.
[40] M. Craft, 'Should One Treat or Gaol Psychopaths?' in M. Craft, and A. Craft (eds.), *Mentally Abnormal Offenders* (Balliere 1984), 384.
[41] See *The Times,* 7 December 1993, p. 8, 'Child-killer Allitt exploited system to stay out of jail: Psychopaths such as Beverley Allitt should not serve sentences in the comfort of a hospital, a consultant claims'; *Daily Telegraph,* 19 May 1993, p. 17, 'Mad or Bad?'.
[42] See N. D. Walker and S. McCabe, *Crime and Insanity in England Volume* ii. *New Solutions and New Problems* (Edinburgh University Press 1973) chs. 6–8.
[43] Hoggett, (1996), 36.　　　　　　　　　　　　　　　[44] [1975] *Crim LR* 51.
[45] Joint DHSS/HO Consultation Document, *Offenders Suffering from Psychopathic Disorder* (HMSO 1986) para. 12.
[46] See Mental Health (Scotland) Act 1984 s. 1, and art. 3 of the Mental Health (NI) Order 1986.
[47] *Butler Report* para. 5.24.
[48] R. Fox, 'Butler on Sickness and Crime' [1975] *Crim LR* 683–7, 684.

prison'.[49] And again, in 1981, the 1979–97 Conservative Government stated that 'The weight of current medical opinion is that most psychopaths are not likely to benefit from treatment in hospital . . . but that there are some persons suffering from psychopathic disorder who can be helped by detention in hospital. For this reason, this category is not excluded from the Act.'[50] As one commentator has observed 'the psychiatric profession seems to continue to struggle and fail with the ambiguities inherent in the concept of psychopathy and in methods of intervention for so-called psychopathy. Nevertheless, *no one within the camp of psychiatry has expressed the view that this category has no place within psychiatry.*'[51]

The 1979–97 Conservative Government did, in fact, eventually give consideration to this category of offender. Due to public concern over the release of several dangerous psychopaths, a joint Consultative Document was published in August 1986[52] aimed at achieving greater public safety. The document acknowledged that the problems regarding the releases stemmed from the uncertainties surrounding the concept of psychopathic disorder itself and the questionable effects of treatment upon it. The recommendations were dropped following considerable discussion,[53] but at least attention had been drawn to the complexity of the issues involved. This was taken further by a recent comprehensive review of the arrangements and services for mentally disordered offenders.[54] This 'Reed Committee' report will be discussed at length at a later stage; however, it appointed a special working group to consider the issues raised by psychopathic disorder. It noted the continued lack of agreement about its diagnosis and treatment and recommended the need for further research and improvements in services for this category of offender.[55]

Indeed, such has been the depth of concern that there are now proposals from the Labour Government which will make specific provision for the management, care, and treatment of this particular category of offender-patient.[56] The Government has announced that it intends to 'improve the way that people with a severe personality disorder are managed', particularly where 'they present a grave risk to the public'.

---

[49] DHSS (1978) para. 1.24.

[50] DHSS, *Reform of Mental Health Legislation* (1981) Cmnd. 8405 para. 12; And in the words of Kenneth Clarke, then the Minister for Health, speaking at the Special Standing Committee of the Mental Health (Amendment) Bill 'the problems of definition have never been easy' but the term is 'workable in practice'. Session 1981–2 Vol. XI col. 212.

[51] Ramon, *Category of Psychopathy*, 234 (emphasis supplied).

[52] DHSS/Home Office (1986) *supra* n. 45.

[53] See further J. Peay, 'Offenders Suffering from Psychopathic Disorder: The Rise and Demise of a Consultation Document' (1988) 28 *Brit J Criminology* 67–81; see also A. Ashworth, 'Dealing with Mentally Disordered Offenders Classified as Psychopathic' [1986] *Crim LR* 705–7 (Editorial).

[54] DoH/HO, *Review of Health and Social Service for Mentally Disordered Offenders and Others Requiring Similar Services* (HMSO 1992) Cm. 2088.

[55] Ibid. Overview para. 9; DoH/HO, *Report of the Department of Health and Home Office Working Group on Psychopathic Disorder* (DoH/HO 1994).

[56] DoH, *Modernising Mental Health Services: Safe, Sound and Supportive* (1998) para. 4.31–4. These proposals form part of a comprehensive review and reform of the mental health service which is being conducted by the Government and will be considered in more detail in Ch. 4.

Consideration is therefore being given to the possibility of introducing a new form of 'reviewable detention' for this category of patient which would require the development of specialist programmes and interventions and a completely new and separate regime of management, treatment, and release into the community.

Indeed, in February 1999 the Home Secretary announced that the Labour Government intends to introduce legislation which will enable the courts to order the indeterminate reviewable detention of dangerous people with a severe personality disorder.[57] It is envisaged that these powers would be exercised where the individual concerned is suffering from a severe personality disorder and poses a serious risk to the public. Moreover, these powers would be applicable, irrespective of whether or not the individuals concerned have been found guilty of a criminal offence. A recent Inquiry into allegations of mismanagement at Ashworth Special Hospital recommended, *inter alia*, the introduction of a reviewable sentence, but that was in relation to *offenders* suffering from a personality disorder.[58] However, it recognized that the Government may also wish to consider introducing legislation based on this principle for other types of offender, especially in circumstances when prisoners who 'are still considered to possess a substantial risk of causing harm to others have to be released'.[59] The Government has indeed taken note, and would appear to have gone a stage further, as the new proposals could apply to dangerous and seriously disordered people who may never have come into contact with the criminal justice system at all. Undoubtedly, the prospect of indefinite detention, particularly in the absence of the commission of a criminal offence, is highly controversial and raises serious civil liberties implications and any new legislation will be required to comply with the Human Rights Act 1998, which incorporates international human rights law into the United Kingdom legal system. Consequently, the Government has announced that it intends to conduct an in-depth consultation process before the new measures will take their place on the statute book.

The precise scope of the proposed reforms is not yet known and it is likely that they will be introduced in the foreseeable future. In the light of the controversy and complexity which has surrounded the treatment and management of patients with personality disorder, reform in this area must surely be welcomed. However, the Government has made it clear that the prime concern is the safety of the public[60] and it is therefore highly questionable to what extent the reforms will represent a shift to a more humane and enlightened approach towards this particular category of offender-patient. It would seem that the reforms are, in reality, being driven by a desire to protect the public, as is evident from the language used by the Home Secretary when he announced in Parliament that the new measures are necessary 'in order further to protect the public from dangerous people in our society'.[61]

---

[57] HO Press Release 056/99, 'New Measures to Protect the Public from Dangerous People'; Session 1998–9 HC Debs, 15 February 1999.

[58] *The Report of the Committee of Inquiry into the Personality Disorder Unit., Ashworth Special Hospital* (HMSO 1999) Cm. 4194.   [59] Ibid. para 7.3.5.

[60] As n. 57.   [61] Session 1998–9 HC Debs, 15 February 1999.

1.2.2.3. Mental Impairment

The term 'mental impairment' has also attracted criticism. The Act distinguishes between 'mental impairment' and 'severe mental impairment'.[62] 'Mental impairment' encompasses a 'significant' as opposed to a 'severe' impairment of intelligence or social functioning. Again here, there are difficulties, as the differences between the conditions have not been made clear. No specific guidance is provided and in the case of *R. v. Hall*[63] it was decided that the terms should be construed as ordinary people would construe them. It has already been found however, that this 'lay' approach does not necessarily shed any further light on the situation. In order to alleviate some of the confusion, the Code of Practice accompanying the Act states that '[t]he identification of an individual who falls within these legal categories is a matter for clinical judgement, guided by current professional practice',[64] and provides guidance by setting out the 'key components' of the condition. But again, this places great discretion in the hands of the medical profession and causes further controversy due to the fact that the consequences of suffering from the condition are severe and can result in compulsory hospitalization.

Further criticism has been aimed at the fact that the term is said to include mental handicap. Many opinions have been expressed that mental handicap should be totally removed from the scope of the Act, given that the compulsory hospitalization powers can apply to this specific disorder, and strong representations have been made by both MENCAP and MIND as to its exclusion. During the debates prior to the 1982 legislative amendments, these mental health organizations campaigned vigorously for it to be taken out of the Act altogether and the Special Standing Committee received much evidence from a variety of bodies to this effect. The Royal College of Psychiatrists firmly opposed the new category of mental impairment as, by definition, it would 'confuse the patients, unjustifiably, with those suffering from psychopathic disorder'.[65] MIND concurred, stating that 'The term mental impairment brings with it the dangers of prejudice, alienation and rejection.'[66] And MENCAP and the Royal College of Nursing expressed similar views.[67]

The 1978 and 1981 White Papers which preceded the 1983 Act broached this issue, and ultimately concluded that it should be retained within the scope of the Act, given that 'The weight of professional opinion is that there is a very small minority of mentally handicapped people, without any other mental disorder, who do need to be detained in hospital—usually for their own safety.'[68] Despite the

---

[62] Mental Health Act 1983 s. 1(2); see R. Jones, *Manual,* 17; Hoggett, *Mental Health Law,* 37–9.

[63] *R. v. Hall (John Hamilton)* (1988) 86 Cr App R 159.

[64] DoH/Welsh Office, *Mental Health Act* 1983 *Revised Code of Practice* (HMSO 1999), para. 30.5.

[65] Session 1981–2 Vol XI col 63 Special Standing Committee Mental Health (Amendment) Bill.

[66] Ibid. col 144.   [67] Ibid. col 85.   [68] DHSS (1981) para 9.

'weight of opposition',[69] the Government felt that 'In the absence of anything better; this narrow and rather neutral phrase, with clear definitions attached to it by the Bill, is the one that should be allowed to stand.'[70]

The association with mental illness is further criticised as many believe that mental handicap cannot be cured in the same way that other psychiatric disorders can be. Mental handicap and learning difficulties are invariably present since birth, and are not generally regarded as being responsive to treatment. People suffering from mental handicap will usually do so for their entire life, so if such patients are committed to hospital they will find it much more difficult to be released.[71]

A further reason for their exclusion is that some believe that the mentally handicapped should actually be prosecuted and held responsible for their crimes where responsibility exists. David Carson firmly advocates this approach claiming that 'Much harm can be done under the guise of being kind. It is often considered to be a kindness not to prosecute people with mental handicaps for their crimes.'[72] But he believes that 'being kind has been cruel', as such people with learning disabilities should be held responsible and not subjected to the traditional methods of treatment, as mental handicap is no longer regarded as a disease or illness capable of being cured. Accordingly, the preferable approach is to 'advocate responses that . . . provide learning opportunities'.[73] Being prosecuted and held publicly and formally responsible for one's actions is regarded as part of this learning process.

The Butler Committee in 1975, however, recommended that they did not want to deny this group the chance of a therapeutic disposal, and the DHSS concluded that handicapped non-offenders still need to be compelled to hospital to be protected from exploitation.[74] Surely the same can be applied to handicapped and impaired offenders; they also need this therapeutic care and treatment, albeit that they cannot be cured in the same way. A prison sentence will not normally guarantee them this degree of therapy and is therefore inadequate. Prison is also notorious for being the place where those who are most vulnerable and unable to adequately defend themselves are most likely to be exploited. Those suffering from mental illness are clearly prime targets, thus every possible step should be taken to ensure that they are not put in that position, where they may be abused and exploited.

---

[69] Session 1981–2 Vol. XI col. 220 Special Standing Committee Mental Health (Amendment) Bill.

[70] Session 1981–2 Vol. XI col. 226 Special Standing Committee Mental Health (Amendment) Bill *per* Kenneth Clarke, Minister for Health.

[71] See e.g. the evidence of the Boynton Report of the *Review of Rampton Hospital* (1980) Cmnd. 8073 para. 15.6.7, where it was noted that some mentally handicapped persons had been on the hospital discharge waiting list for over two years. Hoggett, *Mental Health Law*, 37–40.

[72] D. Carson, 'Prosecuting People with Mental Handicaps' [1989] *Crim LR* 87–94, 87.

[73] Ibid. 91.   [74] DHSS (1976) app. III para. 5.

1.2.2.4 Any Other Disorder or Disability of Mind

Finally, the residual category of 'any other disorder/disability of mind' must be considered.[75] This category has also been left undefined, but was intended to cover 'the sort of disorders and disabilities which would not be covered by any of the other categories'.[76] As noted in the parliamentary debates, for example, it would include disorders arising from head injuries, encephalitis, or mental enfeeblement as a result of mental illness. In practice however, Gostin suggests that it could encompass individuals displaying an extremely broad range of unstable behaviour.[77] However, s. 1(3) of the Act specifies that a person is not to be classed as mentally disordered under the legislation solely by reason of odd or abnormal behaviour.[78] These elements must be accompanied and supported by other independent medical evidence.[79]

It is maintained, in view of the fact that these terms have been deliberately left undefined, that they should be construed as such. It has already been noted, however, that to many this can result in far too wide an application of the wording and is unsatisfactory. It has been suggested by some commentators that the current practice seems to be that the doctors recommend that a person or an offender is mentally disordered under this head if s/he is suffering from a disease which has already been identified and described by psychiatrists and appears in their textbooks.

1.2.3. Summary

The evidence above indicates that the definition of 'mental disorder' is problematic. On the one hand, generous and open wording is advocated, as it does not exclude certain categories and therefore they are not denied access to treatment. But on the other hand it is strongly criticized as being too open-ended and vague and thereby giving too much scope to the medical profession. NACRO recently identified these issues and recommended that current definitions of mental disorder should be reviewed.[80] In particular, this was felt necessary as many people diagnosed as having personality disorders are considered untreatable and consequently are

---

[75] See further R. Jones, *Manual*, 17; Hoggett, *Mental Health Law*, 40.

[76] Session 1958–9 Vol. IV cols 65–6 12 February 1959: the Minister, Mr Derek Walker Smith, speaking at the Committee stage of the Mental Health Bill—House of Commons Official Report of Standing Committee E.

[77] Gostin, *Mental Health Services*, ch. 9.

[78] Ibid. For example promiscuity, immoral conduct, sexual deviancy, or dependency on alcohol or drugs.

[79] See *R. v Mental Health Review Tribunal ex p. Clatworthy* [1985] 3 All ER 699, where the only evidence of mental disorder was repeated and persistent sexual offending, so the patient was found not properly to be suffering from psychopathic disorder; see also *R. v Mental Health Commission ex p. W.* (1988) *The Times*, 27 May, where evidence of sexual deviancy alone was not sufficient for a finding of mental disorder.

[80] *The Resettlement of Mentally Disordered Offenders* (NACRO 1991), 20 Recommendation 3; see also NACRO, *Risks and Rights* (NACRO 1998).

refused access to health service care. As outlined earlier, it would seem that this has at last been recognized at an official level and there will be some reform in the near future in recognition of this with the possible introduction of a new regime for people suffering from personality disorder.[81] However, it simply further serves to underline the complexities and uncertainty which surround the definition and identification of mental disorder.

The above analysis of mental disorder has identified in general who offenders suffering from mental disorder are, and it is primarily the treatment of this category of offender-patient which this book will examine. However, in practice the category may also extend to include those suffering from less serious forms of mental disorder but who are also in need of treatment and care, and this broader category will also be considered in subsequent chapters. The discussion above, however, has also revealed that, as a result of the often vague and unhelpful legal definitions, much is left dependent upon what is generally regarded as 'well-founded medical opinion'. Psychiatrists therefore play an important role in this decision-making process. However, this is precisely where further complexity and confusion has arisen, and it will be outlined below how the definition and differing concepts of mental disorder have caused much tension between the legal and medical professions who are both involved with the management of mentally disordered offenders. This has significant consequences for diversion, as successful implementation of diversion policy relies upon the full co-operation and mutual understanding of those professionals involved. Consequently, the role which psychiatry plays in the treatment of mental disorder, and mentally disordered offenders in particular, will now be considered.

1.3. WHAT ROLE DOES PSYCHIATRY PLAY IN THE TREATMENT OF MENTAL DISORDER?

1.3.1. 'Legalism' or 'Professional Discretion'?

One of the first areas of conflict between the differing groups involved in the treatment of mentally disordered offenders is the tension between what has been termed 'legalism' and 'professional discretion'.[82] The historical treatment of mentally disordered people has reflected society's attitudes and approaches towards them, and the development of mental health legislation has been described by some commentators as a 'pendulum swinging between two opposing schools of thought', those of 'legalism' and so-called 'welfarism' or

---

[81] See further 1.2.2.2 above and DoH, *Safe, Sound and Supportive*, paras. 4.31–4; see also HO, Press Release 056/99; Session 1997–8 HC Debs, 15 February 1999 *per* Home Secretary.

[82] For a discussion of such competing views in the context of mental health legislation, see further T. Mason and L. Jennings, 'The Mental Health Act and Professional Hostage Taking' (1997) 37(1) *Med, Sci & Law* 58–68.

'professional discretion'.[83] The current legislation, namely the Mental Health Act 1983, at the time of its introduction, was intended to represent a 'new legalism', under which approach, decisions about mental disorder are questions for the courts, as the treatment of the mentally disordered is a legal matter, for lawyers to decide and define, and not a medical one.[84] If this was the intention, then the legislation has, to an extent, been unsuccessful, and this is where the tension exists between the medical and legal professions. It has been noted by several commentators that the Act was intended to represent such a legalistic approach, requiring explicit legal definitions which are construed, understood, and applied by lawyers, but, in practice categorization has largely been a matter for medical opinion,[85] due to the imprecise nature of the legal definitions. Indeed, as stated earlier, the Department of Health Memorandum to the Mental Health Act 1983 states that the operational definition of 'mental disorder' is 'largely a matter for *clinical* judgement in each case'.[86]

In practice, therefore, there appears to prevail the alternative socio-medical approach of 'professional discretion' towards the legislation and the diagnosis and treatment of mental disorders whereby professional medical and social-work personnel are given broad discretionary powers to decide the fate of patients.

1.3.2. 'Orthodox Psychiatry'

Linked to this dichotomy is the persistent tension that has existed within and between all professions and experts in this field. That is between an 'orthodox traditional psychiatric' approach towards the treatment of the mentally ill, which is strongly held,[87] and the opposing views of the 'critical anti-psychiatrists'.[88]

The traditional orthodox view is regarded as the 'medical model of mental illness' and regards mental illness as an illness just like any other, which should be treated as such. Accordingly, the medical profession has a rightful role to play in its diagnosis, treatment, and cure.[89] The role of the medical profession is justified because it possesses the relevant skills to treat mental disorder. As noted by Cavadino, doctors and psychiatrists are primarily motivated by the humanitarian concern to relieve suffering, thus, the rightful role of mental health legislation is for its therapeutic provisions to apply when doctors decide this is necessary. It is

---

[83] See L. Gostin, 'Contemporary Social Historical Perspectives of Mental Health Reform' (1983) 10 *J Law & Soc* 47–70.

[84] C. Unsworth, *The Politics of Mental Health Legislation* (Clarendon 1985) ch. 10.

[85] Ibid.

[86] DoH/Welsh Office, *Mental Health Act 1983: Memorandum* (1998) para. 8 (emphasis supplied).

[87] A. Colombo, *Understanding Mentally Disordered Offenders: A Multi-Agency Perspective* (Ashgate 1997), 53.

[88] M. Cavadino, *Mental Health Law in Context; Doctor's Orders?* (Gower 1988) ch. 1.

[89] D. Ingleby, 'Mental Health and Social Order' in S. Cohen, and A. T. Scull, *Social Control and the State* (Blackwell 1985), 142.

only right that doctors make the decision, as mental illness is a medical concern.[90] The Percy Commission advocated this approach in 1957, and asserted that 'disorders of the mind are illnesses which need medical treatment'.[91] This 'medical model' was advocated and followed by the Mental Health Act 1959, which accepted that it should be doctors who take the decisions on whether patients needed to be treated and detained. The current 1983 Act also seems in practice to be applied in this way, despite its legalistic pretensions. This medical viewpoint has been advocated by numerous commentators, such as Kathleen Jones and Nikolas Rose, who have championed the medical profession's cause and cast doubts upon the claims of the opposing beliefs of anti-psychiatry. They fully endorse the medical profession's involvement in the treatment of mental illness, as its role is, in their view, both necessary and desirable. These views will be considered in detail below.

1.3.3. Anti-Psychiatry: The Main Accusations

In complete contrast to this, however, is the advent of the anti-psychiatry views. They emerged during the 1960s and 1970s, and are still highly regarded by many, particularly in the USA. It is a strong indictment of the orthodox view, and is associated with the writings of Ronald D Laing,[92] Thomas Szasz,[93] Thomas J Scheff,[94] Erving Goffman,[95] and Michel Foucault.[96] The following discussion will endeavour to provide an overview of some of their main accusations and challenges to the medical profession.

The writings of these authors consist of a collection of similar accusations,[97] the gravest of them being that the best mode of treatment and approach is to keep people with mental disorders away from psychiatrists and doctors—'the domination of the medical profession is neither warranted nor desirable'.[98] In general it is claimed that psychiatric treatment is bad for you, particularly with regard to mentally disordered offenders who are removed from prisons and detained, the better to be treated (or so it is intended and believed), in secure psychiatric hospitals.[99] Part of the critique holds that the psychiatric system is no better than the prison, it is still a horrifyingly inhumane 'total institution'.[100] One is still incarcerated, the only difference being the four walls that surround one! This was the main thrust of Erving Goffman's writings. He conducted a period of fieldwork at

---

[90] Cavadino, *Doctor's Orders?*, ch. 1. [91] *Percy Commission*, para. 5.
[92] *The Divided Self: An Existential Study of Insanity and Madness* (Penguin 1990).
[93] *The Myth of Mental Illness: Foundations of a Theory of Personal Conduct* (Paladin 1972).
[94] *Being Mentally Ill: A Sociological Theory* (Aldine 1984).
[95] *Asylums: Essays on the Social Situation of Mental Patients and Other Inmates* (Penguin 1968).
[96] *Madness and Civilisation: A History of Insanity in the Age of Reason* (Tavistock 1971).
[97] See e.g. D. Ingleby (ed), *Critical Psychiatry: The Politics of Mental Health* (Pantheon 1980; Penguin 1981) for a collection of writings from the anti-psychiatry perspective.
[98] Ingleby, 'Mental Health and Social Order', 143.
[99] See Scull's account of the takeover of the asylums by the 'mad-doctors' in *Museums of Madness: The Social Organisation of Insanity in Nineteenth Century England* (Allen Lane 1979).
[100] Goffman, *Asylums*, 15.

a mental hospital and his findings formed the basis for his ideas on the debilitating and destructive effects of institutional life. His analysis however was not exclusively concerned with asylums as the title of his work would suggest, but is an examination of many other similar kinds of 'total institution'—prisons, boarding schools, and military bases for example—all of which share characteristics which are common to institutional life:'their encompassing or total character is symbolised by the barrier to social intercourse with the outside and to departure that is often built right into the physical plant, such as locked doors, high walls, barbed wire, cliffs, water, forests or moors'.[101] Upon entrance to such an establishment, each inmate will suffer a total 'mortification of the self'[102] whereby one's identity is routinely stripped away by the formal admission procedures.[103] Goffman describes the life of the inmate in terms of being subjected to a constant stream of violations and invasions of personal privacy. Life in such a 'total institution' simply provokes a 'sense of injustice, bitterness and alienation'.[104]

Particularly with regard to mental institutions, he charts the 'moral career of the mental patient' and describes the 'degrading conditions of the hospital setting'.[105] Inmates are subjected to constant indignities and mutilations and, in his opinion, they are forced into a totally 'anti-therapeutic experience', whereby their lives are cramped by the routines and procedures of institutional life: 'In the mental hospital, the setting and the house rules press home to the patient that he is, after all, a mental case who has suffered some kind of social collapse on the outside, having failed in some over-all way, and that here he is of little social weight, being hardly capable of acting like a full-fledged person at all.'[106]

To other anti-psychiatrists, psychiatry is perceived as being an agent of the state—a method of social control. Its activities are perceived to be 'an illegitimate expansion of the coercive authority of the state' whereby 'psychiatrists were engaged in a moral enterprise of social control, rationalised and legitimised through the appeal to a specialist body of esoteric knowledge'.[107] This implies, therefore, that all social control is a bad thing or, at least, that even when it is justified, psychiatrists should not play a part in it.[108] Furthermore, psychiatrists' claims to provide effective treatment are unjustified, particularly in view of the history of harsh treatments such as purges, floggings, and more recently the practice of ECT and lobotomies.[109] Finally, it is maintained that no one should ever be subjected to compulsory psychiatric hospitalization and treatment.[110] In fact, according to Szasz it is the 'gravest crime against humanity'.[111] He further argues that 'mental illness is a myth'.[112] He believes that it is merely an acceptable name

---

[101]   Goffman, *Asylums*, 158.   [102]   Ibid. 30.   [103]   Ibid. 24, 29.
[104]   Ibid. 70.   [105]   Ibid. 142.   [106]   Ibid. 140.
[107]   N. Rose, 'Law, Rights and Psychiatry', in N. Rose and P. Miller, *The Power of Psychiatry* (Polity 1988), 179.
[108]   N. Walker, *Sentencing: Theory, Law and Practice* (Butterworths 1985) para. 21.84.
[109]   Ibid. para. 21.87.
[110]   As is presently found in certain provisions of the Mental Health Act 1983 (e.g. ss. 2, 3, 4, 36, 37, 38).   [111]   Szasz, *Myth of Mental Illness*.   [112]   Ibid. 269.

for 'problems in living' to which we are all susceptible. Psychiatrists are therefore not concerned with studying, diagnosing, and treating mental illness; consequently, he opines that the assumption that they have something to offer is both 'worthless and misleading'.[113]

Scheff states that it is the labelling of people as being mentally ill that causes them to be mentally ill in the eyes of society—i.e. that the label is self-fulfilling.[114] He has been regarded as the foremost proponent of the 'labelling theory' in the field of mental illness, and his work has been extremely influential.[115] In particular, he perceives the mental health legislation and compulsory admission mechanisms to be a legal weapon of social control.

However, one of the most influential 'anti-psychiatrists' was Michel Foucault who charted the 'Great Confinement' of mad people in institutions in seventeenth-century Europe.[116] Sarup has provided a useful account of Foucault's writings and she notes that he describes how the mentally ill, poor, and unemployed were regarded as a 'social problem' which was the responsibility of the state.[117] He argues that leprosy disappeared from the Western world during the sixteenth century, and attitudes towards lepers were instead directed at the insane. Consequently they were subjected to social exclusion and sought solace in the countryside. From the middle of the seventeenth century however, 'madness becomes material for neither tragedy nor comedy, but for confinement'.[118] The insane, disabled, poor, sick, and unemployed were increasingly confined to institutions due to their inability to work: 'In the classical age, for the first time, madness was perceived through a condemnation of idleness and in social immanence guaranteed by the community of labour. This community acquired an ethical power of segregation, which permitted it to eject, as into another world, all forms of social uselessness.'[119] Consequently, the 'great confinement' of the mentally ill took place, and it is from this stage in history that hundreds of public mental hospitals/asylums evolved. As noted by Sarup, this confinement was huge and the insane inmates were forced to work:[120] 'The new meanings assigned to poverty, the importance given to the obligation to work, and all the ethical values that are linked to labour, ultimately determined the experience of madness and inflected its course.'[121]

By the end of the eighteenth century, however, it became clear that this 'great confinement' had been counter-productive in the sense that the unemployed were herded into the institutions and forced to work, but, as a result, there was less

[113] Ibid. [114] Scheff, *Being Mentally Ill*, 58–9.
[115] For a discussion of Scheff's claim that mental illness is a label which acts as a 'conceptual dustbin' see Cavadino, *Doctor's Orders?*, ch. 4; see also Walker, *Sentencing*, para. 21.80–3.
[116] See Foucault, *Madness and Civilisation*.
[117] See M. Sarup, *An Introductory Guide to Post-Structuralism and Postmodernism* (Harvester Wheatsheaf 1988) ch. 3, for a full and detailed account of Foucault's views in this respect.
[118] Ingleby, 'Mental Health and Social Order', 146.
[119] Foucault, *Madness and Civilisation*, 56.
[120] Sarup, *Introductory Guide*, 67, 'labour was instituted as an exercise in moral reform'.
[121] Foucault, *Madness and Civilisation*, 64.

work available in the neighbouring regions, so unemployment increased.[122] So these institutions began to disappear at the beginning of the nineteenth century, to be replaced by lunatic asylums, and the legislation at that time was targeted at such segregation. Foucault is highly sceptical of the claim that these actions led to a more humanitarian approach in the treatment of the insane, however.[123] He outlines how the confinement of the mad resulted in the rise of the medical men; the doctor gained a prominent status in these institutions and the mentally ill patients 'surrendered' to them.[124] Foucault strongly criticizes this new approach: ' [it] substituted for the free terror of madness the stifling anguish of responsibility . . . The asylum no longer punished the madman's guilt . . . it did more, it organized that guilt.'[125]

These practices led to 'a gigantic moral imprisonment'. The previous methods were perceived as inappropriate, and were replaced by what Foucault terms as 'moral treatment'. He maintains that although physical constraint was largely abolished, it was substituted by mental and moral controls of self-restraint.[126] He argues that throughout the eighteenth and nineteenth centuries, attitudes and approaches towards the insane changed dramatically, and indeed for the worse. As noted by Sarup, in Foucault's eyes the mentally ill have been released from the physical chains, but mental ones have taken their place.[127] He therefore perceives psychiatrists to be harmful and, to him, they are essentially a control mechanism whose sole function is to identify and isolate deviant behaviour.

Andrew Scull has adopted a similar perspective in his account of the English situation. He attributes the segregation of the insane to practical and economic reasons, 'a cost cutting exercise'[128] which formed part of a general change in society's response to deviance. This led to 'the rise of centralized, highly organized state control, increasing segregation of deviants from the normal population'.[129] The insane were therefore segregated into asylums, whereupon proceeded the 'medical capture of insanity' and they 'found themselves incarcerated in a specialized, beauracratically organized, state supported asylum system which isolated them both physically and symbolically from the larger society. And within this segregated environment . . . their condition had been diagnosed as a uniquely and essentially medical problem. Accordingly, they had been delivered into the hands of a new group of professionals, the so-called "mad-doctors".'[130]

Scull is critical of this rise of the psychiatric profession and their dominance

---

[122] Sarup, *Introductory Guide*, 66–71.　　　　　[123] Foucault, *Madness and Civilisation*, 250.
[124] This was also perhaps characterized by the rise of such notable medical scientists as Freud and Jung who became extremely influential in this field of psychiatry.
[125] Foucault, *Madness and Civilisation*, 247.　　　　　　　　　　　[126] Ibid. 254.
[127] Sarup, *Introductory Guide*, 69.
[128] P. Bean, 'Social Control and Social Theory in Secure Accommodation' in L. Gostin (ed), *Secure Provision* (Tavistock 1985), 305.
[129] Ingleby, 'Mental Health and Social Order', 150.
[130] Scull, *Museums of Madness*, 14.

in the treatment of the mentally ill in these asylums—the 'museums of madness'. He questions the ability of the psychiatric profession, and he firmly believes that the 'efficacy and reliability' of their claims and diagnoses are highly 'suspect'.[131] The reason for this is the fact that the psychiatric profession simply took their place in the asylums and laid claim to the treatment of the mentally ill: 'By 1845 the medical profession had secured powerful support for the proposition that insanity was a disease, and thus was naturally something which doctors alone were qualified to treat.'[132]

1.3.4. The Contemporary View

These views and theories are vital background when considering the value of diverting mentally disordered offenders out of the prison detention system and into the health and social services sector.[133] The main aim of this book is to analyse the development and assess the efficacy of the trend towards diversion into the psychiatric hospitals and psychiatric care in the community.[134] But diversion is of little value if one accepts the anti-psychiatrist critique which casts doubt upon the benevolence of psychiatry and considers that hospitals are in fact no better at all than the prisons and prison life.

Whilst recognizing that the powerful anti-psychiatrist views do have great value and express legitimate concerns, it is argued that, in general, they are not an accurate portrayal of contemporary English and Welsh law and practice and are more appropriate descriptions of practices in other societies and bygone eras.[135] Several commentators have cast doubts upon their arguments in this respect.[136] For example, Philip Bean believes that Foucault's contentions are more relevant to nineteenth-century than present psychiatry, as few modern psychiatrists would defend the earlier practices and classifications.[137] It is accepted here, therefore, that the traditional orthodox approach is far more relevant, thereby acknowledging that it is necessary to identify and 'label' the mentally ill. They are a group of individuals who are vulnerable and require care and treatment, and in order to provide them with the degree of therapeutic care and treatment desired, it must be known as precisely as possible for whom this care should be provided. As noted by Cavadino, the 'labelling of patients and their illnesses—diagnosis—is desirable in order to apply the treatment which will cure or alleviate the illness and so make matters better'.[138]

---

[131] Ibid. 238.   [132] Ibid. 164.

[133] See *Provision for Mentally Disordered Offenders,* Home Office Circular 66/90, esp. para. 2; see further ch. 4.   [134] Ibid.

[135] See P. Sedgwick, 'Anti-Psychiatry from the Sixties to the Eighties' in W. R. Gove (ed), *Deviance and Mental Illness* (Sage 1982) 213: 'Anti-psychiatry has lost the theoretical and political initiative, and has failed to renew its ideas or its audience'.

[136] See e.g. M. S. Moore, 'Some Myths about Mental Illness' (1975) 32 *Archives of General Psychiatry,* 1483–97; K. Jones, 'Scull's Dilemma' (1982) 141 *Brit J Psych* 221–6.

[137] Bean, 'Social Control', 294.   [138] Cavadino, *Doctor's Orders?*, 26.

It is acknowledged, however, that labelling people as mentally ill can result in much stigma and prejudice. Concerns have also been expressed that in some cases, due to the desire to protect the safety of the public, receiving a therapeutic restriction order disposal can result in disproportionately long periods of detention.[139] Labelling people as criminals can also result in stigma. This is not an attempt to examine, challenge, or overturn labelling theory and the anti-psychiatry critique, but it is accepted that in the majority of cases, despite the body of literature which exists to the contrary, the benefits of labelling someone as mentally ill outweigh the disadvantages. It is necessary and desirable to provide relief from the distressing and disabling conditions of mental illness. If people are left unidentified and untreated, for whatever reason, even more tragic consequences may result. The daily newspapers are full of examples where this has been the case and mentally ill people, or in some cases their victims, have died because, for whatever reason, they have not received the care and treatment that they needed.[140]

Kathleen Jones is a prominent supporter of the medical model and has cast doubts upon the claims of the anti-psychiatrists, notably Andrew Scull's account of the rise of the mad-doctors and the terrors of institutional care, and his subsequent account of the inadequacies of community care provision.[141] Indeed, she appropriately terms her critique 'Scull's Dilemma', asserting that his analysis inevitably begs the question, 'if it is wrong to get patients out of the mental hospitals and wrong to keep them in, what are we to do with them?'[142]

Many of the traditional studies of psychiatry focus upon the rise of the asylum and the subsequent incarceration—the 'great confinement'—of the mentally ill.[143] Such criticisms are no longer relevant to the modern practice of psychiatry, as what is termed as 'community psychiatry' has come to the forefront, replacing previous methods of institutional psychiatry. As a result of the 1979–97 Conservative Government's emphasis upon care in the community, increasing numbers of mental institutions are disappearing. Their previous inhabitants have been redirected into the community to receive the medical care and treatment that they need to help them live as normal a life as possible. This is, therefore, a much more enlightened approach.[144] The doubts cast by Goffman and Foucault are less compelling as community psychiatry gains increasing prominence. Moreover, the criticisms targeted at the standard and quality of life in mental institutions are also open to

---

[139] See e.g. L. Gostin, 'Towards the Development of Principles for Sentencing and Detaining Mentally Abnormal Offenders' in Craft and Craft (eds.) *Mentally Abnormal Offenders* , 229–35; R. Henham, 'Dangerous Trends in the Sentencing of Mentally Abnormal Offenders' (1995) 34 *How J of Crim Just* 10–18.

[140] See e.g. 'Bible man mauled in zoo lion's den' *Daily Telegraph,* 13 September 1994, p. 5; 'The gentle son who met a violent death' *Daily Telegraph,* 14 July 1995, 9; 'Mentally sick could kill again says campaigning widow' *The Times,* 25 February 1994.

[141] Scull, *Museums of Madness*; id., *Decarceration Community Treatment and the Deviant: A Radical View* (Polity 1984). [142] K. Jones, 'Scull's Dilemma' 221.

[143] Foucault, *Madness and Civilization*; Goffman, *Asylums;* Scull, *Museums of Madness.*

[144] See D. Bennett, *The Drive towards the Community* in G. E. Berrios, and H. Freeman (eds.), *150 Years of British Psychiatry 1841–1991* (Gaskell 1991).

objection. For example, a survey was conducted into mental patients' views of mental hospitals which has questioned those qualitative studies that have portrayed a bleak picture of such hospitals.[145] Anonymous questionnaires were completed and favourable responses were received in 69 per cent of cases. The research concluded that 'The facts concerning patients' degree of favourableness towards mental hospitals do not coincide with the myth about patients' attitudes.'[146]

Similar viewpoints have been expressed in many recent tragic cases, such as the killing of Jonathan Zito, both by the offender him/herself and by his/her family.[147] Due to the inadequacies in the provision of community care many claim that the best place to receive care and treatment is in hospital and so many such offenders and their families have expressed favour towards adequately resourced contemporary hospital care.[148] Indeed, the value of providing a wide range of hospital-based and community psychiatric support and treatment has recently been recognised by the Labour Government. In December 1998 it launched a new strategy—its 'third way for mental health' which outlines its proposals for introducing a network of assertive outreach teams, more hospital beds, and more secure facilities for the mentally ill.[149]

The orthodox reaction to the critical views is, therefore, extremely compelling and it is maintained that

to implicate the form of modern society in the determination of mental illness is childlessly wishing away unpleasant facts of life . . . [T]o question the motives behind treatment, as wilful obstruction of the relief of suffering, show[s] a callous indifference to the plight of the mentally ill . . . [and] to challenge the powers of the medical profession is seen as irresponsible meddling with justified authority, inviting a return to the eighteenth-century barbarism in the treatment of the insane.[150]

So to advocate the anti-psychiatry approach completely would invite a return to the 'eighteenth-century barbarism'[151] which is clearly undesirable and unwanted, and these issues will be further considered below in the discussion of how mentally disordered offenders should be treated.

1.3.5. The Battle in Practice

1.3.5.1. Law v. Psychiatry

The conflicting attitudes that have been outlined above can still be clearly seen and felt today. Eminent lawyers and distinguished psychiatrists have frequently

---

[145] R. M. Weinstein, *The Mental Hospital from the Patient's View* in W. R. Gove (ed) *Deviance and Mental Illness*.   [146] Ibid. 142.

[147] See e.g. the comments of Jonathan's widow, Jayne Zito, at the ISTD Annual Residential Conference in April 1995, in J. Braggins and C. Martin (eds.), *Managing Risk: Achieving the Impossible: Report of the ISTD Annual Conference 1995* (ISTD 1996), 68–74.

[148] These issues are further discussed in ch. 4.

[149] DoH, *Safe, Sound and Supportive*. These proposals will be discussed at length at a later stage, esp. in ch. 4.   [150] Ingleby, 'Mental Health and Social Order', 143.

[151] Ibid.

noted this persistent tension between the legal sphere and the world of modern psychiatry as to the treatment of mentally disturbed offenders. Richard Smith[152] in his account of insanity and responsibility in Victorian trials has documented the heated disputes between lawyers and doctors. He argues that where questions of mental abnormality and criminal responsibility are concerned, inevitably both disciplines overlap and this has formed a 'protracted struggle'. At trials where medical evidence is in issue, the 'battle of the experts' is often visible in the courtroom.[153] Lord Mustill has observed how the 'diversity of aim' of the legal and medical professions has produced an endemic conflict: 'the professional aims, training and philosophies of the persons in these two groups have nothing in common, and are in some respects antithetical . . . it is not surprising that where their fields of activity overlap there is a confusion of purpose; a degree of mutual incomprehension; and friction'.[154]

Nigel Walker has also highlighted this dissonance in his historical account of crime and insanity in England.[155] In particular, he notes that at the heart of the contention is the principle that there should be only two alternative verdicts in the field of criminal law, Guilty or Not Guilty.[156] Psychiatrists perceive most mental disorders in degrees, and thus find it difficult to reconcile the two stark extremes demanded by the criminal law. The criminal law on the other hand prefers to deal simply in black and white. The accused must therefore be either liable to punishment or not liable, i.e. guilty or not. It is only when the sentencing stage has been reached can differences of degree be taken into account.

Indeed, this hypothesis has been supported from a medical perspective. Legal notions, such as responsibility, are extremely difficult for medical professionals to grasp. From this medical viewpoint, it is asserted that 'A doctor should never be asked to speak on matters of responsibility: these are matters for the judge. A doctor should confine himself to diagnosis, prognosis and treatment.'[157]

Both disciplines are highly critical of each other,[158] and there is certainly

---

[152] R. Smith, *Trial by Medicine: Insanity and Responsibility in Victorian Trials* (Edinburgh University Press 1981), 4.

[153] J. E. Hall Williams, 'Legal Views of Psychiatric Evidence' (1980) 20 *Med Sci & Law* 276–82; see also P. Gerber, 'Psychiatry in the Dock—A Lawyer's Afterthoughts' in Craft and Craft (eds.) *Mentally Abnormal Offenders*.

[154] Lord Mustill, 'The Mentally Disordered Offender: A Call for Thought' (1992) 3 *KCLJ* 1–28, 5.

[155] *Crime and Insanity in England* i. *The Historical Perspective* (Edinburgh University Press 1968), 244.

[156] Walker argued that even a finding that is obviously of a third kind, such as the special verdict of insanity, must be disguised as one or the other. From 1800 to 1883 it was disguised as an acquittal; from 1883 to 1964 it was a conviction; and now it is again disguised as an acquittal.

[157] A. Samuels, 'Mental Illness and Criminal Liability' (1975) 15 *Med, Sci & Law* 198–204, 203; see also J. R. Hamilton, 'Diminished Responsibility' (1982) 138 *Brit J Psych* 434–6.

[158] See e.g. J. Gunn, 'The Trials of Psychiatry: Insanity in the Twentieth Century' in K. Herbst and J. Gunn (eds.), *The Mentally Disordered Offender* (Butterworth Heinemann 1991).

evidence of the degree of misunderstanding that exists.[159] Clearly, therefore, there is much evidence of the long battle which has been taking place and is continuing to do so between the lawyers on the one hand, and the physicians on the other. Such diverse approaches and attitudes and the definitional problems which have been identified, all serve to highlight the distinct lack of communication and absence of a mutual understanding between these professions. This aspect will be vital when considering the new multidisciplinary and diversionary approaches[160] which are being encouraged and developed nationwide, in response to the problems posed by the mentally disordered offender. Indeed, it serves to emphasize the need for a certain degree of discretion and collaboration in order to temper the system, as no one side is certain. Inter-agency diversion allows this degree of flexibility and modification to take place and is therefore worthwhile. But it also leaves open the issue of which side is to 'lead' the partnership, and this will be discussed further in Chs. 4 and 5.

1.3.5.2. Integrating Law and Psychiatry

The discussion above has served to highlight the need for a better mutual understanding, a united and comprehensive approach and increased collaboration between all the different professions and agencies involved. As Sir Roger Ormrod noted in an address to the Annual General Meeting of the Institute for the Study and Treatment of Delinquency, 'one of the most striking developments in recent years has been the realisation among scientists themselves of the importance of co-operation between different scientific disciplines in the solution of common problems'.[161]

1.4. HOW SHOULD MENTALLY DISORDERED OFFENDERS BE TREATED?

1.4.1. Mad or Bad?

Having established as precisely as possible in the eyes of the law who mentally disordered offenders are, and that psychiatry has a valuable and legitimate role to play in the treatment of mental disorder, the next issue to consider is, in principle, how mentally disordered offenders should be treated. Should the emphasis be upon their early treatment and humane approaches or should the legalistic approach prevail and their rights be fully protected as they are subject to the

---

[159] See M. Weller and A. Somers, 'Differences in the Medical and Legal Viewpoint Illustrated by *R. v Hardie*' [1984] (1991) 31 *Med, Sci & Law* 152, where it is alleged that the judgment can be challenged on a number of medical grounds, particularly as the judges completely 'misunderstood the pharmacological effects of valium'; see also LCJ Goddard's inaccurate translation of *dementia praecox* in his otherwise carefully prepared judgment on Rivett's appeal *R. v Rivett* (1950) 34 Cr App R 87.   [160] See further ch. 4.

[161] R. Ormrod, 'The Developing Relations between the Law and the Social Sciences' (1964) 4 *Brit J Criminology* 320–31, 320.

ordinary operation of the criminal law? Furthermore, having accepted that psychiatry has a role to play, should mentally disordered offenders be treated in prison or in hospital? These issues will now be considered below.

One of the main difficulties in this area is whether mentally disordered offenders should be treated as mad, or bad, or both. In the infamous words of Herschel Prins—are they 'Offenders, deviants or patients?'[162] and this is the main dilemma surrounding the treatment of mentally disordered offenders—as they fall within the penal and psychiatric systems, both of which, as has already been identified, have opposing aims and functions. In the words of Lord Longford, "We punish lawbreakers; we do not punish sick people—we try to heal them, but the mental offenders . . . fall on both sides of the line. We search in vain for the perfect way to deal with them. The problem will never go away.'[163] Henry Rollin argues that a man can be both mad and bad, and that to suggest otherwise is 'arrant nonsense'. He gives the example of the insane individual who is as 'acquisitive, as aggressive or as sexually perverse as his mentally "normal" brother'—'Indeed, . . . because he is insane he may lose some or all of his inhibitory control and the more readily therefore commit crimes in one or other or all of these spheres.'[164]

Much controversy exists about the link between crime and mental illness,[165] however, it is accepted here that mentally disordered offenders are presumed to be both mad and bad and can be helped by the medical profession and at the same time processed through the criminal justice system. Given therefore that a person can be both mad and bad, the answer to how best s/he should be treated is a complex one which is linked closely to the issues which have already been discussed as to whether the medical profession has a rightful role to play.[166] It is argued here that at least the principal disorders are amenable to objective identification, and that the treatment of those persons who are suffering from and exhibiting those symptoms is preferable to their incarceration, whenever they engage in criminal behaviour. It is firmly acknowledged that this is highly contested, however, and whilst this book does not seek to provide a detailed examination of opposing arguments, some of these issues and the differences between this approach and others will now be explored.

[162] H. Prins, *Offenders, Deviants or Patients? An Introduction to the Sudy of Socio-Forensic Problems* (Tavistock 1980).

[163] Session 1984–5 HL Debs Vol. 458 col. 351 *per* Lord Longford; see also Lord Longford, *Prisoner or Patient?* (Chapmans 1992), 169.

[164] H. Rollin, *The Mentally Abnormal Offender and the Law* (Pergamon 1969), 119.

[165] H. J. Eysenck, and G. H. Gudjonsson, *The Causes and Cures of Criminality* (Plenum 1989), 217–19, suggest that the relationship between mental illness and crime is a complex one and there are many studies which support either view as to whether or not there is a link between the two. See also H. Prins, 'Mental Abnormality and Criminality: An Uncertain Relationship' (1990) 30 *Med, Sci & Law* 247–57; S. Wessely, and P. J. Taylor, 'Madness and Crime: Criminology versus Psychiatry' (1991) 1 *Criminal Behaviour and Mental Health* 193–228.

[166] See further P. Fennell, 'Law and Psychiatry: The Legal Constitution of the Psychiatric System' (1986) 13 *J Law* and *Soc* 35–65.

1.4.2. The Liberal Approach

It is argued here that the medical profession has a role to play in treating mental illness and alleviating its symptoms. However, there are many who would contest this assumption and who believe that the emphasis should not be upon early treatment but rather upon protecting the rights of mentally disordered offenders, in the way that the rights of all human beings are accorded protection. Accordingly they should be held responsible for their crimes, have the right to be treated equally, and be punished just like everyone else. Thus, the emphasis should be upon treating mentally disordered offenders in a just and equitable manner.

This is indeed part of the legalistic approach to the treatment of the mentally disordered as it is further argued by this rights-based approach that the law should take an active role in the treatment of mental illness by controlling the activity of the caring medical profession. Thus the emphasis is upon the legal profession injecting safeguards to ensure that the civil liberties and human rights of the mentally ill are fully protected.

One of the most prominent advocates of this rights-based approach is Larry Gostin who, during his period as Legal Director of MIND, campaigned vigorously for increased rights and safeguards for the mentally ill.[167] He is an American lawyer who has been influenced strongly by the mental health rights movement in the USA. Indeed, rights strategies have 'won significant victories' on that side of the Atlantic, as numerous court cases during the 1960s, the result of growing concern, led to the introduction of many procedural and substantive rights for mental patients.[168] Gostin supports the view that the law has a positive role to play in curbing the power of psychiatry, injecting increased legal safeguards, and bolstering the rights of people suffering from mental disorder. He maintains that legal rules protect the mentally ill from 'indiscriminate medical decisions'. Much emphasis has been placed upon the UK's obligations under International and European Declarations and Conventions, given the absence of any written constitution or Bill of Rights laying down the state's obligations with respect to its citizens.[169] With regard to mentally disordered offenders, Gostin

---

[167] L. Gostin, *A Human Condition* i. *The Mental Health Act 1959–1975*, ii. *The Law Relating to Mentally Abnormal Offenders* (MIND 1975; 1977), id., 'The Ideology of Entitlement: The Application of Contemporary Legal Approaches to Psychiatry' in P. Bean (ed), *Mental Illness: Changes and Trends* (John Wiley 1983).

[168] N. Rose, 'Law Rights and Psychiatry' in P. Miller and N. Rose (eds.), *Power of Psychiatry*, 177–8.

[169] This is particularly significant now in view of the introduction of the Human Rights Act 1998, which incorporates international human rights law into the United Kingdom legal system. This means that legislation in this country will be required to emphasize and protect individual rights, in accordance with the obligations under European and International Human Rights Conventions. Specifically, under s. 19 of the Act, there is an obligation to ensure that any future legislation conforms with the European Convention on Human Rights. In the context of the detention of the mentally ill, any legislation must be read in the light of and comply with Article 5 of the Convention which safeguards against the arbitrary deprivation of liberty (see further J. Wadham and H. Mountfield,

believes that they have the right to be held responsible and punished for their crimes, for a period justified by the gravity of the crime committed. Accordingly, they should be dealt with by the legal and penal system. That is not to say that they should not receive treatment for their disorder whilst being punished however: 'when a mentally disordered person has been convicted of a criminal offence, society is justified in protecting itself by holding him in custody for a period proportional to the gravity of his offence. During that period, society should do all that it can to rehabilitate him by offering treatment in a psychiatric hospital whenever possible'.[170]

Philip Bean also supports this liberalist approach. He is highly critical of medical paternalism, and believes that 'groups with power, and especially power to detain people against their will, must *always* be subject to scrutiny'.[171] To him, the rights-based approach has several advantages. It enables people suffering from mental disorder to be perceived in a different light, as being more than just 'the aggregate of their symptoms', and further, it 'impresses upon us that mental patients are actually capable of making their own decisions'. The legalistic and rights-based approach therefore 'protects their self and their essential human-ity'.[172] Furthermore, 'It controls, or exerts pressure on the maverick psychiatrist bringing him into line with more realistic psychiatric thinking.'[173] He therefore maintains that when professionals are given such extensive powers to determine compulsory hospitalisation, the law should lay down strict criteria and procedures for the exercise of such powers.

This has been one of the main strands of attack upon the alternative medical treatment model. As outlined above, the psychiatric profession has been widely criticized, not least by some of its own members, notably Szasz and Laing when it became clear to them that the 'apparent benevolence of psychiatry could now be construed as illusory, its treatments harmful, and its institutional regime degrading, dehumanizing and damaging'.[174] Accordingly, they demanded the introduction of legal rules to control the doctors in order to protect mentally disordered people.

Michael Cavadino also advocates this liberal model which places important values on the liberty of the individual.[175] He contends that the present Mental Health Act is inadequate in this respect, the definitions too wide, ambiguous, and

---

Blackstone's Guide to the Human Rights Act 1988 (Blackstone 1999)). This has also been recognized in the recent edition of the *Mental Health Act Code of Practice* issued in March 1999. One of the guiding principles contained in the Code is the need to recognize the basic human rights and needs of patients (DoH/Welsh Office, *Mental Health Act 1983 Revised Code of Practice*, para. 1.1).

[170] Gostin, *A Human Condition*, ii. 96; see also Unsworth, *Politics of Legislation*, 19, 33, 80.

[171] P. Bean, *Mental Disorder and Legal Control* (Cambridge University Press 1986), 14 (emphasis supplied).   [172] Ibid. 181.   [173] Ibid.

[174] Rose, 'Law, Rights and Psychiatry', 179.

[175] Cavadino, *Doctor's Orders?*, chs. 11, 12; see also id., 'A Vindication of the Rights of Psychiatric Patients' (1997) 24 *J Law & Soc* 235–51, where he examines the need for due process and restrictive criteria in the context of the Mental Health Act 1983, which is taken a step further in relation to the application of the Mental Health (Patients in the Community) Act 1995.

contested, and the criteria for detention and compulsory treatment too vague to satisfy this model: 'The Act leaves it entirely open to the professionals to operate on the basis that the patient's therapeutic interests (as perceived by professionals) are paramount.'[176] This is evident from the discussion of the definition of mental disorder earlier in this chapter. Cavadino believes it to be an extremely dangerous position as the medical professionals place too much faith in their ability to effect a cure and their judgement is clouded by their inflated beliefs in their own expertise: 'medical training and experience tends to lead doctors to have strong faith in their own diagnostic and predictive powers to an extent unsupported by empirical research into those powers'.[177] Thus he argues that mentally ill people should enjoy at least the same rights as suspected offenders and does not unquestionably accept that merely by calling something 'treatment' it is rendered harmless and preferable.

These are indeed compelling and forceful arguments, which are accepted as legitimate concerns; however, there are several objections to this predominantly legalistic rights-based approach, which will be outlined below. Indeed, even Cavadino acknowledges that there are some medical conditions so bizarre and extreme as to be obviously 'real' to almost everyone. Accordingly, given that they are illnesses, they should be treated as such.

1.4.3. The Treatment Approach

What is termed here as the 'treatment approach' maintains that the emphasis should be upon treating mentally disordered offenders with dignity and humanity and they should not be unnecessarily subjected to the detrimental effects of custodial sentences and penal sanctions. That is not to say that the rights of the mentally ill should not be protected, there should be a minimum level of intervention in that respect, but the emphasis should be upon ensuring that they receive treatment and support in the appropriate setting at the earliest possible opportunity. It will be shown here that this treatment approach is far preferable, and some of the counter-arguments to the liberal approach will now be considered and the claims of the treatment-based approach further explored.

1.4.3.1. The Disadvantages of Legalism and the Law

Those advocating the treatment model argue that the law has no place in treating and caring for those suffering from mental illness. The legal approach is inappropriate, as 'there is little in the traditions, training or experience of judges or members of the legal profession to commend them in preference to professionals traditionally associated with humanism'.[178] This view is supported by Professor John Wood who maintains that the emphasis that has been placed upon the ability

---

[176] Cavadino, *Doctor's Orders?*, 150.   [177] Ibid. 152.
[178] Gostin, 'Contemporary . . . Perspectives . . . on Reform', 28.

of the law to intervene by providing improved safeguards is aimed at elevating the position of the mentally ill. However, 'it is very naïve indeed to believe that 'the law', despite its majesty, does not inevitably have its own weaknesses and creates, in turn, its own problems'.[179] He further emphasizes that the law is not particularly suited to the task in hand. The adversarial model in place in the British criminal justice system creates greater 'tensions and distortions', as lawyers consequently tend to regard each problem as having two sides and will build up the conflicting and often contradictory case for each side. This antagonistic approach is not more congenial in the intricate web of mental health service and provision; 'especially where sensitive social relationships are concerned, it also tends to hinder the settlement of problems'.[180]

These arguments are extremely compelling as mental health matters are delicate and highly emotive, and so the law should not take the lead role in dealing with them. This has already been seen with regard to matrimonial and divorce issues, which are equally sensitive and complex. The legal profession is not particularly sympathetic to the difficult and distressing situation posed by a marriage break-up, hence the image that has been conjured of the 'gladiatorial divorce lawyer'. And once the case comes to court, the adversarial nature of the system simply makes matters worse: 'Once the powerful machinery of divorce was set in motion, husband and wife became insignificant figures crushed under a weighty legal process which ground along under its own momentum, with apparently little concern for those whose lives it was reshaping drastically.'[181] Accordingly, calls for a more conciliatory and mediatory administrative system (without the prominent involvement of lawyers) have been constantly heard.[182]

The same argument has been applied to childcare law, another sensitive area where vulnerable individuals are involved. The adversarial nature of the legal system was also regarded as highly unsatisfactory in this area; consequently, the Children Act 1989 was passed to reduce the tension and friction by focusing more upon the interests of the child him/herself than the interests of others involved in the proceedings.[183] The same should be applied to those suffering from mental disorder. Rather then focusing on the interests and rights of others, e.g. the state's right to punish the mentally disordered offender, more emphasis should be placed upon the offender him/herself, and upon providing timely and appropriate treatment and care for his/her mental condition.

Nikolas Rose also believes that there should be less emphasis upon the legal

---

[179] Prof. Sir John Wood, *Future Directions for Mental Health Law* in W. Watson, and A. Grounds (eds.), *The Mentally Disordered Offender in an Era of Community Care: New Directions in Provision* (Cambridge University Press 1993), 24.   [180] Ibid.

[181] L. Parkinson, *Conciliation in Separation and Divorce* (Croom Helm 1986), 14.

[182] Ibid. 30.

[183] i.e. the 'welfare principle' whereby the child's welfare is the court's paramount consideration, Children Act 1989 s. 1(1). See further J. Bridge, S. Bridge and S. Lake, *Blackstone's Guide to the Children Act 1989* (Blackstone 1990); see the dicta of the House of Lords in *Gillick v West Norfolk & Wisbech Area Health Authority and the DHSS* [1986] AC 112; [1985] 3 All ER 402.

profession in the care and treatment of the mentally ill.[184] He asserts that the shift to judicial and legal forums advocated by the proponents of the legalistic approach has, to an extent, already taken place with the establishment of Mental Health Review Tribunals under the Mental Health Act 1983. Their function is to provide an arena for the periodic review of those detained under the Act, thereby scrutinizing the powers of the medical profession. In practice however, evidence shows that their decision-making tends to be influenced by therapeutic goals rather than by the application of legal rules.[185]

Philip Bean has acknowledged that the liberal approach does have certain limitations, because as much reliance will be placed upon the integrity of those enforcing the rules, and lawyers do not possess a completely unblemished and unscrupulous reputation. Indeed, he goes so far as to say that mental health issues have suddenly become fashionable and questions the role of the legal profession within it: 'Fashions tend, however, to be unstable. Might it not be that lawyers, finding few commercial rewards in mental health, depart for more lucrative pastures?'[186] And even though it can be argued that this is itself not a significant justification for denying that the law has a useful to role to play, it is still an important factor to be considered in conjunction with all the other arguments.

Adopting this perspective, it follows that a completely liberal and legalistic approach is inappropriate.[187] This is particularly so when considering the old Victorian lunacy legislation which was based exclusively upon such principles and has been noted by Kathleen Jones in particular. Placing fetters on the exercise of the discretion of the medical profession, it was concerned more with safeguarding the rights of the general public to prevent their wrongful detention than with the actual care and rights of mental patients themselves![188] Legalism's concerns for the mentally ill are misplaced in this respect, and the traditional legalism of the lunacy legislation and the so-called modified 'new legalism'[189] can be further criticized in this vein. Its preoccupation with safeguarding civil rights and injecting tighter legal controls on the exercise of medical discretion, intending to better the lot of the mentally ill, can indeed have the adverse effect, by hindering their care rather than helping it. It has been observed that increasing the protection for the civil liberties of the mentally ill by tightening admission and treatability criteria can, in fact, lead to the denial of that treatment for mentally

---

[184] 'Legal arguments, techniques and functionaries have generally been regarded as inimical to the sensitive and humane operation of welfare services, decreasing flexibility . . . introducing unhelpful adversarialism': Rose, 'Law, Rights and Psychiatry', 192; see also id., 'Unreasonable Rights: Mental Illness and the Limits of the Law' (1985) 12 *J Law & Soc* 199–217.

[185] Rose, 'Law, Rights and Psychiatry', 197.   [186] Bean, *Mental Disorder*, 195.

[187] See in particular the arguments of Kathleen Jones. She believes that legalism has been tried and failed, and now 'The need is not for increased legal formalism, but for human compassion and professional skill': 'The Limitations of the Legal Approach to Mental Health' (1980) 3 *Int J Law & Psych* 1–15, 14; see also id., 'The Wrong Target in Mental Health?' (1977) *New Society* 3 March 438–40; id., *A History of the Mental Health Services* (Routledge & Kegan Paul 1972).

[188] K. Jones, *Asylums and After: A Revised History of the Mental Health Service* (Athlone 1993), 113–14.   [189] See further Gostin, 'Contemporary . . . Perspectives . . . on Reform'.

disordered offenders. This practice has been termed 'defensive psychiatry'.[190] By tightly controlling the amount of psychiatric intervention, the medical profession will be able to alleviate the suffering of fewer and fewer patients, fewer will consequently be classified as mentally disordered and susceptible to treatment, and so increasing numbers will inevitably end up untreated, and may ultimately go to prison. This has been noted by many commentators,[191] particularly in America, where one has likened the debate to the scenario of either 'dying with your rights on' or 'living with your rights off'![192] Adopting the former approach simply results in 'pyrrhic victories where a demand for narrow legal rights has resulted in persons not being treated and dying as a result'.[193]

Rose has further dismissed the liberalist claims, as he believes that these theories of rights have many 'wrongs', and traditionally have a limited part to play in the UK: 'Legal mechanisms and concepts of rights have a very different role in the British political context from that which obtained in the USA, where the legal environment provides encouraging conditions for rights strategies. ... The British environment is considerably less favourable to rights campaigns'.[194]

John Monahan casts further doubt upon the claims of the liberalists. Civil libertarians often cite John Stuart Mill as one of the main thrusts of their critique of the psychiatric system and their opposition to compulsory hospitalisation of the mentally ill.[195] He was highly critical of state paternalism and maintained that the only legitimate exercise of state power is in order to prevent harm to others:

the only purpose for which power can be rightfully exercised over any member of a civilized community, against his will, is to prevent harm to others. His own good, either physical or moral, is not sufficient warrant. He cannot rightfully be compelled to do or forbear because it will be better for him to do so, because it will make him happier, because in the opinions of others, to do so would be wise, or even right.[196]

Therefore, according to the liberalists, the compulsory treatment of people suffering from mental disorder who pose no danger or threat of harm to others is illegitimate. However, serious doubt has been cast upon this statement as a basis of

---

[190] H. Prins, 'The Diversion of the Mentally Disordered: Some Problems for Criminal Justice, Penology and Health Care' (1992) 3 *J For Psych* 431–43, 433.

[191] In the UK, Nikolas Rose argues that legal formalities can hinder the early treatment of mental disorder, which can exacerbate the damage done by allowing the illness to remain untreated and possibly to worsen. If the legalistic approach were completely implemented it 'would deny patients access to the treatments they need to help them recover, condemning them to lives of suffering outside the hospital if not admitted, or to long-term segregation within it if admitted and not treated', 'Law, Rights and Psychiatry', 200.

[192] A. Hoffman, 'Living with Your Rights Off' (1977) 5 *Bull Am Acad Psych & Law* 18; see also P. S. Appelbaum, *Almost a Revolution: Mental Health Law and the Limits of Change* (Oxford University Press 1994) 215: 'an excessive regard for such rights should not be allowed to impede unduly the process of providing care and treatment'.

[193] H. J. Steadman, 'Attempting to Protect Patients' Rights under a Medical Model' (1979) 2 *Int J Law & Psych* 185–97, 187.   [194] Law, Rights and Psychiatry', 191.

[195] J. S. Mill, *On Liberty* (Penguin 1985).   [196] Ibid. 22.

the libertarian claims. John Monahan[197] argues that it has been taken out of context, and that elsewhere Mill expressly excluded from these considerations those 'in a state to require being taken care of by others' and who were lacking 'in the ordinary amount of understanding'. Consequently he asserts that 'It is, perhaps, hardly necessary to say that this doctrine is meant to apply only to human beings in the maturity of their faculties'.[198] Monahan argues that such exceptions include 'in short, those who today would be regarded as mentally ill'[199] and that 'Use of the partial citation to the contrary is historically inaccurate.'[200]

1.4.3.2. The Advantages of the Treatment Approach

> The developments in these fields [neurobiology, psychopathology, and genetics] has led to advances in validity and reliability of diagnoses and to a strengthening of the evidence for biological factors in the aetiology of mental illness, both contributing to the redefinition of the traditional 'medical' model as being relevant to psychiatry.[201]

Michael Cavadino, whilst supporting the liberal model, also acknowledges that psychiatry can be valuable in helping people with some mental illnesses because the criteria for diagnosing mental illness can be standardized and applied consistently, particularly in relation to schizophrenia, the most common of all mental illnesses.[202] Thus doubts can be cast upon the claims of Thomas Szasz, who argued, with regard to schizophrenia, that since there was no agreement on the causes of the condition or its definition, it was not a real disease but a myth. This view is now open to objection. Gostin who has also campaigned so vigorously for increased legal formalism acknowledges that 'There is [now] a common sense acceptance that *madness is not a myth* invented by medicine. Moreover, one is aware that 'crazy behaviour' or extreme feelings of emotion can cause grave suffering to individuals and their families which sometimes can be *alleviated by medical, nursing or social support*'.[203] It is now generally conceded (although not unanimously agreed) that mental illness is not a figment of the imagination, but an illness just like any other, that can and should be treated by medical professionals. Their therapeutic and beneficial involvement should not be delayed or denied by strict legal controls as, in the view of one proponent of the treatment model, 'Neglect of [the] needs [of the mentally ill], whether in institutions or in the community, is the final betrayal of their human and civil rights.'[204]

---

[197] J. Monahan, 'John Stuart Mill on the Liberty of the Mentally Ill: A Historical Note' (1977) 134 *Am J of Psych* 1428–9.   [198] Mill, *On Liberty*.

[199] Monahan, 'J. S. Mill on Liberty', 1429 (emphasis supplied).

[200] Ibid.   [201] Gove (ed.), *Deviance and Mental Illness*, 188.

[202] Cavadino, *Doctor's Orders?*, 38–9.

[203] Gostin, 'Contemporary . . . Perspectives . . . on Reform', 37–8 (emphasis supplied); see also Janet Daley, *The Times*, 21 April 1994, p. 6: 'denying the reality of madness [is] just another way of denying responsibility for people in distress'.

[204] P. Steghart (ed), *Human Rights in the United Kingdom* (Pinter 1988), 39.

Cavadino further refutes the claim that because it is not 'real' like physical illness, mental illness is a myth. Cavadino asserts that this is a 'naïve preconception' as the label of myth could be equally applicable to physical illness, for example, migraine or pre-menstrual tension. Such conditions as SAD and ME are increasingly recognized as being physical illnesses. They do, in fact, produce many distressing physical symptoms that can be treated, but many argue that they are simply 'all in the mind' and not physical illnesses at all.[205] Indeed, many would contend that such conditions are simply theoretical, but nevertheless they have been recognized as being a treatable branch of physical medicine. Therefore, although Cavadino advocates the liberalist stance and the need for due process and restrictive criteria, he is also sympathetic to the psychiatric point of view, acknowledging that 'there are indeed mental illnesses which are undesirable states of mind which disable the sufferer and which can be effectively treated'.[206] And on the basis of his research at Fardale hospital, he concluded that 'patients are not imprisoned and tortured, but on the contrary are freely accepting medical advice and assistance because they believe it will do them good, as in physical medicine'.[207]

It is therefore suggested that the medical profession are well placed to make decisions about the mentally ill as they are trained, qualified, and experienced, and are traditionally regarded as a 'caring' profession, in the sense of treating patients with the aim of enriching their lives. Although lawyers also care, they care about different values and principles, such as public safety, due process, and retribution. These values are not best suited to the care and treatment of those suffering from mental illness, therefore lawyers are not appropriately placed in adopting primacy in managing the mentally ill. Cavadino acknowledges that psychiatrists are capable of making better decisions than laypeople. Research shows that lay members of tribunals are much more cautious about discharging patients from detention, and thereby prolong it, despite libertarian concerns that people are being detained against their will. He suspects that 'this is because psychiatrists are often more aware of the limitations of psychiatry then many lay people are'.[208]

Kathleen Jones argues that the 'Law cannot cure the mentally ill . . . cannot fully protect the mentally ill'[209] and that fears, particularly those entertained by civil rights lobbyists, that the mentally ill are always inhumanely treated and particularly, that the medical profession abuses its powers are, to a large extent exaggerated: 'The horrifying abuses which come to light in mental hospitals have not occurred primarily because there were brutal members of staff who ought to be restrained by law . . . Abuses have occurred because deteriorating morale and conditions of work in mental hospitals have facilitated the development of a vicious sub-culture.'[210]

---

[205] Ibid. 41–2; see also ' "All in mind" ruling angers ME victims' *Sunday Telegraph,* 20 November 1994, 1, 2.   [206] Cavadino, *Doctor's Orders?*, 14.
[207] Ibid. 90.   [208] Ibid. 153.   [209] K. Jones, 'Limitations', 13.
[210] Ibid. 14.

So, abuses have taken place as a result of 'squalid conditions', lack of guidance, and 'inadequate provision for secure accommodation'. This is further supported by the evidence and conclusions of a succession of official reports, which were published during the 1970s, into allegations of ill-treatment at several psychiatric institutions. The reports of the inquiries into allegations of abuse at Whittingham,[211] Ely,[212] and Farleigh[213] Hospitals identified mismanagement, overcrowding, understaffing, dilapidated buildings, and insufficient facilities as central causes of the problems. Such ill-treatment incidents were not generic, however, but were isolated instances, concerning specific wards and particular staff.[214] The Committee conducting the Whittingham inquiry acknowledged that the majority of wards were 'well run and provided a high standard of care'.[215] And the Ely Hospital Committee were impressed with the 'real concern' shown by the majority of staff, and expressed genuine sympathy with them given the 'difficult job' they did which undoubtedly placed 'great strain upon them'.[216] More recently, an official inquiry was launched in the wake of concerns about patient care at Broadmoor Special Hospital; however, the report concluded that the overall standard of patient care at the hospital was acceptable.[217]

1.4.3.3. The Notion of Responsibility

Further rationale for adopting the treatment-based approach with regard to mentally disordered offenders is the notion that within the British criminal legal system 'liability is based upon the concept of moral responsibility or culpability',[218] so those not fully responsible for their actions by reason of their mental illness should not be held fully liable.[219] Indeed, 'For a variety of different reasons, retributive, deterrent, protective and rehabilitative, the criminal law holds certain persons responsible for their deeds, others it excuses in whole or in part. The criminal law is based on the model of the reasonable, normal person.'[220] It is accepted here, as H. L. A. Hart has stated in his substantial contribution to the theories of punishment and study of the legal criteria of responsibility, the law of most countries provides

---

[211] *Report of the Committee of Inquiry into Whittingham Hospital* (1972) Cmnd. 4861 paras. 58, 70, 106.

[212] *Report of the Committee of Inquiry into Allegations of Ill-Treatment of Patients and other Irregularities at the Ely Hospital, Cardiff* (1969) Cmnd. 3975 Paras. 338, 345, 408, 481, 504, 520, 521.

[213] *Report of the Committee of Inquiry into Farleigh Hospital* (1971) Cmnd. 4557 paras. 174, 178, 179.

[214] See further comments of K. Jones, *The Culture of the Mental Hospital* in G. E. Berrios, and Freeman, H. (eds.), *150 Years of British Psychiatry 1841–1991* (Gaskell 1991), 27.

[215] *Report . . . Whittingham Hospital,* para. 30.

[216] *Report . . . Ely Hospital,* para. 481.

[217] DoH Press Release 97/084, 'Report of Broadmoor Review Published'.

[218] Samuels 'Mental Illness and Criminal Liability', 198.

[219] This issue will not be considered here in great detail, but see further R. D. Mackay, *Mental Condition Defences in the Criminal Law* (Clarendon 1995).

[220] J. E. Hall Williams, 'Legal Views', 276–82, 282.

that the person liable to be punished should at the time of his crime have had the capacity to understand what he is required by law to do, and to control his conduct in the light of such decisions. Normal adults are generally assumed to have these capacities, but they may be lacking where there is *mental disorder* or immaturity, and the possession of these normal capacities is very often signified by the expression 'responsible for his actions'.[221]

Accordingly, when people are suffering from mental disorder and commit offences while partly or fully lacking in these normal capacities, they should not be held fully responsible for their actions.

1.4.3.4. The Minor Nature of the Offending

This argument can be taken further when the nature of the offences of this category of offenders is considered. The majority of mentally disordered offenders commit relatively minor offences, whereby their criminality is typically symptomatic of their mental illness.[222] They are not wilful and hardened criminals; in the words of one commentator, 'although mentally disordered offenders have the capacity to commit the most serious offences, the frequency and regularity with which they do is minimal in comparison with other forms of offending. Indeed, *they are much more likely to kill themselves than others*'.[223]

Serious and violent offences committed by mentally ill offenders are the exception rather than the rule and there is a tendency on the part of the media to publicize and dramatize the isolated cases when they commit serious, violent, and dangerous offences.[224] But this is a distortion of the facts as the majority are ordinarily 'low level offenders'[225] whereby their mental disorder diminishes their guilt and culpability and therefore calls for specialized treatment. This further reinforces support for the treatment model, as 'The experience of the police and others involved with mentally disturbed offenders suggests that many mentally disturbed offenders commit 'nuisance' offences, often with an expressed intention to obtain the shelter, warmth, food and so forth which results from being

---

[221] H. L. A. Hart, *Punishment and Responsibility: Essays in the Philosophy of Law* (Oxford University Press 1968), 218 (emphasis supplied).

[222] See F. Watt, *et al.,* 'The Prevalence of Psychiatric Disorder in a Male Remand Population: A Pilot Study' (1993) 4 *J For Psych* 76; see also the study conducted at Winchester prison which shows that the majority of offences committed by the mentally disordered are relatively minor and are often associated with a need to obtain food or shelter: J. Coid, 'Mentally Abnormal Prisoners on Remand: Rejected or Accepted by the NHS' (1988) 296 *BMJ* 1779–84.

[223] J. Peay, 'Mentally Disordered Offenders' in M. Maguire, R. Morgan and R. Reiner (eds.), *The Oxford Handbook of Criminology* (Oxford University Press 1994), 1150 (emphasis supplied).

[224] See e.g. 'Schizophrenic's knife attack was predictable,' *Independent*, 17 January 1995, p. 3; 'Psychopathic killer of lonely hearts GP is sentenced to life', *The Times*, 9 September 1994, p. 6; see further H. Prins, *Dangerous Behaviour, the Law and Mental Disorder* (Tavistock 1986).

[225] Lord Mustill, 'Call for Thought', 24; see also R. Berry, 'Police Contact with Mentally Disordered Persons in the Northumbria Force Area' (1996) 69 *Police Journal* 221–6, where the author conducted a study of police contact with the mentally ill and concluded that the vast majority of offending was minor and involved offences against public order and acquisition, such as shoplifting; see also 'Mentally ill guilty of fewer murders', *Independent*, 6 January 1999.

detained in police custody and, indeed, in prison.'[226] The petty nature of the offences of this group therefore implies that 'More often than not, the offender, before he/she commits the crime, has been crying out for help from a society too deaf to hear.'[227]

On the basis of the discussion and arguments which have been presented, the medical profession should be responsible for ensuring that this help is provided. It is suggested that the medical profession is skilled and experienced in providing care, treatment, and often cure which enables those suffering from mental disorder to live fulfilling and worthwhile lives. The doctors and nurses are not therefore simply using their skills as a device to get such people out of the way, but to try to enable them to lead their own lives. The focus on the medical profession is appropriate since it emphasizes care and support for the sake of the patient, rather than punishment for the sake of society.

1.4.3.5. The Lack of Adequate Funding and Facilities

It must be noted here, finally, that many of the problems in this area, and in particular the difficulties identified at 1.4.3.2 have stemmed from the general lack of adequate financial provision and resourcing in this area. Mental health service provision and care has always been regarded as the 'Cinderella of the Health Services of this country'[228] and this is a fundamental issue which is central to the treatment of mentally disordered offenders and will be examined throughout the book. The funding issue, however, is one about which everyone agrees: 'regardless of revised patients' rights codes, the political process still controls the purse strings and the treatment to which patients are entitled costs money'.[229] Furthermore, 'all the watchdogs in the world, all the fine legal safeguards, will not prove a substitute for the resources so often found wanting in this field'.[230] Even Philip Bean admits that the rights-based movement 'cannot protect patients from government decisions to close mental hospitals, from providing too little money for the psychiatric services'[231]—it 'hardly touches questions relating to patient care, of its quality and extent'.[232] The medical profession can at least be said to be aiming to provide this patient care, and goes some way towards healing the wounds caused by mental illness. The liberalists are preoccupied with safeguarding rights at the cost of providing treatment and care, which, ultimately, is what people suffering from mental disorder require. What is the point in providing increased rights and safeguards if the recipients are in such a state of pain and despair as not to appreciate what they are being given? The ability to

---

[226]   NACRO MH Adv. Com., *Community Care and Mentally Disturbed Offenders*, Policy Paper 1 (NACRO 1993), 15.

[227]   Lord Longford, *Prisoner or Patient?*, 72.

[228]   Session 1953–4 HC Debs Vol. 523 col. 2352 *per* Dr A. Broughton MP; Session 1997–8 HC Debs Vol. 302 col. 1269.

[229]   Steadman, 'Attempting to Protect', 197.

[230]   H. Prins, 'Attitudes towards the Mentally Disordered' (1984) 24 *Med, Sci & Law* 181–91, 190.

[231]   Bean, *Mental Disorder*, 183.   [232]   Ibid. 182.

appreciate fully what rights are and why they are given to us may not materialize until healing, care, and treatment has been provided. That is not to say that such rights should be totally abrogated, but that the emphasis should be upon providing *timely care and treatment* as opposed to bolstered legal safeguards.

1.4.4. Penal Sanctions or Therapeutic Intervention?

Given that the treatment model is espoused, it follows that mentally disordered offenders should be given access to therapeutic care wherever possible and should not be unnecessarily subjected to the prison environment and penal sanctions. Although the majority of offences are relatively minor in nature, some offenders may be at risk of a remand in custody or custodial sentence as they are facing multiple charges or have previous convictions or loose community ties. It is the author's view that, whilst such offenders may be prosecuted, they should not be unnecessarily subjected to the prison regime. There is indeed a wealth of evidence to this effect and there are constant reminders that prison is not the place for those suffering from mental illness: 'Prisons can never be anything other than prisons. One cannot graft a therapeutic regime on to a punitive one. . . . Disordered people . . . should be in hospital. . . . Prisons exacerbate mental disorder.'[233]

1.4.4.1. The General View

Throughout the history of prison medicine, it has been constantly stated that prison is 'a system intentionally organized for the purpose of inflicting deterrent punishment and suffering on its inmates'.[234] Joe Sim's account of the birth and growth of the prison medical service has highlighted its tainted history in this respect. Given its place within the penal system and the disciplined prison regime, the history of the Prison Medical Service (PMS—now known as the Health Care Service for Prisoners) has emphasized control and discipline as opposed to therapeutic intervention and treatment.[235] Thus any attempts to carry out rehabilitative and therapeutic treatment there will be frustrated and hampered. From the turn of the century, Prison Commissioners were urging that mentally ill prisoners should be transferred to a more appropriate therapeutic environment. This was echoed in a string of annual reports, particularly in the 1912–13 report, which identified the need to purge the prisons of the mentally ill 'which are more fitly the subject of medical care and attention than of penal discipline' thereby enabling the prisons to 'fulfil the purpose for which they exist, viz. the due punishment of fully responsible persons; sane in body and mind'.[236] And again,

---

[233] Bean, *Mental Disorder.* 90.

[234] J. Gunn, *et al.*, *Psychiatric Aspects of Imprisonment* (Academic Press 1978), 9.

[235] J. Sim, *Medical Power in Prisons: The PMS in England 1774–1989* (Oxford University Press 1990).

[236] *Report of the Commissioner of Prisons and the Directors of Convict Prisons 1912–1913* (1914 Cd. 7092) para. 89.

in 1927, many prison medical officers stressed the undesirability of imprisoning the mentally ill: 'The need for the provision of some means of permanent detention for these mentally unstable prisoners other than prison [was] pointed out by various Medical officers in their annual reports to the Commissioners.'[237]

More recently, the annual reports of the Chief Inspector of Prisons have identified the inadequacy of the PMS in terms of the inappropriate facilities for and the treatment of mentally disordered offenders.[238] And both Houses of Parliament have, on several occasions, acknowledged that the prison environment and punitive sanctions are not appropriate for mentally disordered offenders. It is regarded as 'totally intolerable for mentally ill people to be put in prison. That is not the place for them. In prison they cannot receive the kind of care or treatment that they deserve and need and to which they are entitled. . . . It is a national scandal that we should allow ourselves to put sick people into prison.'[239] Indeed, research conducted by the Home Office into suicide attempts in male prisons found that the mental health of prisoners is greatly influenced by the prison regime and staff attitudes, and that the prison environment does have an adverse and detrimental effect upon the prisoners' mental health.[240]

Many prison reformers would claim that prisons today are in such a sorry state due to severe overcrowding and mismanagement that they are no longer even suitable places for the confinement and rehabilitation of ordinary offenders.[241] If this is so, then surely there is very little hope of a mentally disordered offender being successfully treated and rehabilitated there! Reformers have widely acknowledged that this is indeed the case, and that, sadly, too many men and women are already in prison who should be receiving care and treatment elsewhere.[242]

This argument is further reinforced by a study conducted by NACRO. It analysed staff and prisoner perceptions of one particular penal establishment— HMP Birmingham—and concluded that, like most prisons, it is not organized for

---

[237] *Report of the Commissioner of Prisons and the Directors of Convict Prisons—year ended 31 March 1927* (1928–9 Cmd. 3292), 32.

[238] See e.g. Session 1991–2 HC 54 *Report of HM Chief Inspector of Prisons 1990–1991* paras. 4.24–8; Session 1992–3 HC 203 *Report of HM CIP 1991–1992* paras. 4.13–18; Session 1994–5 HC 760 *Report of HM CIP1994–95* ch. 5; Session 1995–6 HC 44 *Annual Report of HM CIP 1995–1996* 22–4; see also HM IP England and Wales, *Patient or Prisoner? A New Strategy for Health Care in Prisons: A Discussion Paper* (Home Office 1996).

[239] Session 1978–9 HC Debs Vol. 963 col. 693 *per* R. Kilroy-Silk MP; see also Session 1976–7 HC Debs Vol. 928 col. 864: 'It is not part of a civilised policy to put the mentally ill in prison and make prison the receptacles of those whom no other agency in society will accept', *per* Minister of State for the Home Office; Session 1985–6 HC Debs Vol. 101 cols 1146–54; Session 1992–3 HC Debs Vol. 210 col. 364 'Imprisonment is not appropriate for the mentally disordered' *per* Minister of State for the Home Office; Session 1992–3 HL Debs Vol. 542 col. 743 *per* Lord Henderson; Session 1987–8 HL Debs Vol. 501 cols 487–94 *per* Lord Longford; Session 1996–7 HC Debs Vol. 288 cols 51, 52, 56.

[240] A. Liebling and H. Kramp, *Suicide Attempts in Male Prisons*, Research and Statistics Department Research Bulletin, 36 (Home Office 1994), 38–43.

[241] V. Stern, *Imprisoned by our Prisons* (Unwin Paperbacks 1989) ch. 2.

[242] Lord Longford, *Punishment and the Punished* (Chapmans 1991), 169.

dealing appropriately with mentally disturbed prisoners. Furthermore, the prison hospital is no more than a sick bay, staff are not trained to deal with mentally disturbed prisoners, and the prison routine tended to manage rather than treat them, providing palliative care only.[243] Thus, an overwhelming majority of the staff and prisoners interviewed strongly endorsed the view that prison is not appropriate for mentally disturbed offenders. This has been echoed by another research study into psychiatric services at HMP Bullingdon. The findings simply confirm the poor standard of psychiatric services that are provided to the vast majority of prisoners.[244]

1.4.4.2. The Arguments in Favour of Medical Care in Therapeutic Settings

Philip Bean has highlighted some of the main issues in this area. Psychiatry is concerned with treating the mentally disordered offenders according to the 'medical paradigm', whereas the law is concerned with 'inflicting suffering according to principles of retribution or deterrence'.[245] Accordingly, prison is not the place for those suffering from mental illness:

> It is not even in accordance with traditional theories of punishment that the mentally disordered should justifiably be placed in prison. *Retribution* based on deserts cannot apply; mentally disordered people cannot be said to deserve punishment if they lack the necessary responsibility to be aware of their crime. Similarly, *individual deterrence* cannot apply; mentally disordered people are not responsible for their actions whilst they remain disordered. *Rehabilitation* will not apply either, for the Prison Medical Service . . . cannot provide the necessary treatment.[246]

Consequently, the ultimate goal should be rehabilitation by psychiatric treatment in appropriate facilities and not retribution or deterrence by way of penal sanctions. This issue was discussed earlier in this chapter.

As will be shown in the following chapter, a succession of governmental and official reports throughout the latter half of this century have also emphasized the need to treat mental illness just like any other illness, with care and compassion,[247] and particularly with regard to mentally disordered offenders, that they should be treated and cared for by the health and social services and not subjected to the adverse effects of punitive sanctions and the prison regime.[248] Furthermore, many aspects of penal policy generally at present places the emphasis upon

---

[243] NACRO, *Mentally Disturbed Prisoners at Winson Green* (NACRO 1993), 5–6.

[244] J. Reswick, 'Waiting for Treatment: An Audit of Psychiatric Services at Bullingdon Prison' (1995) 6(2) *J For Psych* 305–16.   [245] Bean, *Mental Disorder*, 87.

[246] Ibid. 92 (emphasis supplied).

[247] Percy Commission, para. 5; 1978 White Paper Cmnd. 7320 Note 1, p. v.

[248] See e.g. *Butler Report* para. 3.22–3: 'hospital is generally a preferable disposal for mentally disordered offenders . . . [as] conditions in prisons are not favourable for the identification and treatment of mental disorder'; *Report of an Interdepartmental Group of Home Office and DHSS Officials on Mentally Disturbed Offenders in the Prison System in England and Wales* (HMSO 1987) para. 4.19–20; *Report of a Review by HM Chief Inspector of Prisons on Suicide and Self-harm in Prison Service Establishments in England and Wales* (1990) Cm. 1383 para. 3.78 (Tumim Report).

community-based penalties as opposed to custodial sentences.[249] Accordingly, the treatment of mentally disordered offenders should follow the same vein.

Many liberals and legalists would argue that mentally disordered offenders should be treated primarily according to principles of equality and justice, and therefore be subject to the same penal sanctions as ordinary offenders. Should they require medical treatment whilst in custody or serving a term of imprisonment, it should be given to them by the prison medical service, just like those offenders who suffer from physical illnesses whilst in prison. Whilst prisons do provide a medical service, the current prison medical service psychiatric facilities are in no way comparable to those provided by the NHS psychiatric hospitals.[250] A string of official reports have recently condemned the quality and standard of psychiatric care provided by the Health Care Service for Prisoners, expressing grave concerns that the standards of service are totally incomparable to NHS standards, nor does the service satisfy the requirements of the Patients' Charter.[251] The majority of prisons are ill-equipped to deal with prisoners suffering from mental illness and cannot provide an adequate level of care and commitment or a therapeutic environment in which to rehabilitate the offender. A Social Services Select Committee on the PMS, which reported in 1986, was extremely perturbed about the level of psychiatric assessment and treatment provided in the prisons: 'Only 40% of medical officers have some qualification in psychiatry. A considerable number of psychiatric reports are prepared by doctors who are not psychiatrists. ... Without doubt prisons are not the best place to assess the psychiatric state of a person: there must be a risk that diagnosis will in some cases be distorted by the fact of imprisonment.'[252] Moreover, the prisoner is also still being subjected to the prison regime, and it is this which can have such a detrimental effect upon a person's mental health: 'The regime for prisoners ... is so deprived that in my opinion unless a man has considerable mental resilience when he comes in he will deteriorate.'[253]

J. H. Orr, during his period as Director of the PMS, voiced his belief that 'The mentally disordered offender cannot cope with [prison] routine and with prison

[249] e.g. the provisions of the Criminal Justice Act 1991 place greater emphasis upon punishment in the community as opposed to imprisonment, and custodial sentences are reserved for the most serious crimes. This philosophy is also evident in some of the more recent criminal justice reforms, such as the Crime and Disorder Act 1998. The current Government has stated that it is of the opinion that 'imprisonment is the right response for serious offenders', but that 'a more flexible approach is required for more minor offenders', and many such crimes can be 'adequately punished by fines and community penalties'. See Home Office, *Annual Report 1998: Government's Expenditure Plans 1998–1999* Session 1997–8 Cm. 3908 para. 4.17.

[250] See further HMIP, *Patient or Prisoner?*

[251] See e.g. *Annual Report of HMCIP1995–6* Session 1996–7 HC 44 pp. 22–3 and HMIP, *Patient or Prisoner?*, 1, 4, 7.

[252] Session 1985–6 HC 72 paras. 55, 56, Social Services Select Committee, *Third Report*.

[253] The chaplain of one prison giving evidence to the Tumim Report, 19; see also research conducted in 1998 on suicide in prisons which identified that the environmental factors such as prison regimes and staff attitudes have a significant impact on suicide rates—G. T. Towl, *et al.*, 'Suicide in Prisons in England and Wales from 1988–1995' (1998) 8 *Crim Beh & Ment Health* 184–92.

discipline . . . prisons can offer little more than custody to the mentally disordered'.[254] A recent report into the prison Health Care Service conducted by HM
Inspectorate of Prisons stated that there is a

particularly urgent need for increased provision for the care of those with mental health
problems, who make up a larger proportion of the prison population than they would of
any other group in the community. What is more, unless proper care is provided, prison
can exacerbate mental health problems, which has a long term impact on the individual
concerned and the community into which he or she may be released.[255]

Some would argue that the preferable solution would be to improve the health
care services provided in prison. A recent Efficiency Scrutiny into the Prison
Medical Service recommended that prisons should contract-in local NHS health
care for the prisoners.[256] This has been supported and encouraged by HM Chief
Inspector of Prisons[257] and the Health Advisory Committee of the Prison
Service.[258] This is indeed a valid argument, and a highly desirable goal, as some
mentally disordered offenders will still slip through the net or develop mental
illness once in prison and so they will require proper care until they can be transferred to the appropriate health care facility. However, such wholesale improvement of the standards and facilities will require massive injections of money and
take a great deal of time, and very little development has taken place in this
respect since the Efficiency Scrutiny recommendations. Indeed, a discussion
document was issued in 1996 which made similar recommendations to ensure
that prisoners are given access to the same quality and range of health care
services as the public receives from the NHS.[259] It was hoped that the paper
would 'soon lead to full, frank and meaningful discussions between all
concerned in the National Health and Prison Services . . . to ensure the delivery
of urgently required, genuine and lasting improvement as soon possible'.[260]
Unfortunately, progress has not been as rapid as the discussion document envisaged and the Health Care Service for Prisoners is still operating independently
of the NHS. However, it is now encouraging to note that the discussion document has, at least, succeeded in prompting discussions and a joint DoH/Prison
Service Working Group on Prison Health was subsequently appointed to explore
the possibilities for such arrangements.[261] The Working Group produced its

---

[254] J. H. Orr, 'The Imprisonment of Mentally Disordered Offenders' (1978) 133 *Brit J Psych*
194–9, 198.   [255] HMIP, *Patient or Prisoner?*, 23.
[256] *Review of Health and Social Services for Mentally Disordered Offenders and Others
Requiring Similar Services* (Reed Report) (1992), Cm. 2088, para. 11.84.
[257] HMIP, *Patient or Prisoner?; Annual Report* of *HMCIP 1995–1996* Session 1996–7 HC 44 p.
23; see also 'NHS should cover prisons', *The Times*, 22 October 1996.
[258] *Annual Report of the Director of Health Care 1996–1997* (Home Office 1998), 6; Home
Office, *Annual Report 1998: Government's Expenditure Plans 1998–1999* Session 1997–8 Cm. 3908
para. 12.39.   [259] HMIP, *Patient or Prisoner?*   [260] Ibid. Foreword.
[261] *Annual Report of the Director of Health Care 1996–7*; Health Advisory Committee for the
Prison Service, *Commentary of the Annual Report of the Director of Health Care 1996/97* (Feb.
1998).

report in March 1999, and it reinforced the discussion document by recommending a partnership between the Prison Service and NHS for the provision and delivery of prison health care. The Government has, fortuitously, accepted this recommendation and responded by setting up a Joint Task Force to conduct a needs assessment and take forward the process of change.[262] This is undoubtedly a major step in the right direction, and it can only be hoped that the rhetoric will become a reality. The process of change is likely to take a considerable amount of time, however, and until such concrete developments take place, the health care service for prisoners will continue to be a cause for concern.

Furthermore, no matter how many improvements take place, it is argued that the prison regime will still operate and the prison environment still be present, and it is this which is so damaging to the mental health of prisoners.[263] The ethos of punishment is still present and cannot be obviated. As has already been outlined, 'a therapeutic regime cannot be grafted onto a punitive one',[264] and the courts have ruled that prison medical officers are first and foremost prison officers and so the emphasis will inevitably be upon control and discipline.[265] Finally, those individuals who are seriously mentally ill, are uncooperative, and lack insight into their condition cannot be forced to take medication against their will in prison[266] and this may be a major obstacle to ensuring their treatment, care, and possible recovery.

Similar concerns have been expressed in America and research was conducted investigating the perceptions of correctional officers towards mentally ill inmates. The study found that mentally disordered offenders were viewed less favourably than other inmates and the majority of officers who participated in the study felt that they could not cope with the mentally ill in the prison.[267] This reinforces the view that mentally disordered offenders are not best placed in the prison environment.

Professor Gunn argues that there is no place at all for psychiatrists within the prison service as this may actually encourage society and its courts to direct more mentally abnormal offenders into prisons[268]—places where, in his view, they clearly should not be. Further, psychiatric assessments taking place in prison are likely to have a detrimental effect, as they will inevitably bias medical reports to prison disposals. The conditions in prisons for the treatment of people suffering from mental disorder are unsatisfactory, and, echoing Joe Sim's analysis, one commentator has noted that 'the history of psychiatric penality has been one of

---

[262] DoH/HO, *Joint Prison Service/NHS Executive Working Group Report on the Future Organisation of Prison Health Care* (DoH/HO 1999); DoH, *The Future Organisation and Delivery of Prison Health Care* HSC 1999/077 (DoH 1999); DoH, Press Release 1999/0181 (DoH 1999).

[263] See Liebling and Kramp, *Suicide Attempts*.

[264] R. Smith, 'Disorder, Disillusion and Disrepute' (1983) 287 *BMJ* 1522–5, 1786–8, 1787.

[265] *Freeman* v. *Home Office* [1984] 2 WLR 130–45, 802–14 *per* McCowan J, 143–4.

[266] Ibid.

[267] P. Randall Kropp, *et al.*, 'The Perceptions of Correctional Officers toward Mentally Disordered Offenders' (1989) 12 *Int J Law & Psych* 181–8.

[268] J. Gunn, *The Role of Psychiatry in Prisons* in M. Roth and R. Bluglass (eds.), *Psychiatry, Human Rights and the Law* (Cambridge University Press 1985), 146; see also 'Psychiatry and the Prison Medical Service' in L. Gostin (ed), *Secure Provision* (Tavistock 1985).

unfulfilled promise'.[269] Psychiatry has, therefore, an extremely limited role in prisons, and there is very little scope for helping mentally disordered prisoners: 'assessment and categorization is *seldom* followed by special psychiatric treatment'.[270]

Gunn has further developed this argument. Together with his colleagues he conducted a study of the psychiatric population in two prisons—Grendon (a therapeutic community), and Wormwood Scrubs (a local remand prison). Not surprisingly, they found that there were immense benefits in treating the mentally ill at Grendon, and most prisoners at Wormwood Scrubs who suffered from mental illness complained that there was too little psychiatry available to them. The study demonstrated that there are high levels of psychiatric disorder in prisons, which has also subsequently been identified elsewhere. However, in conclusion, Gunn believes that the solution to these problems is not to expand psychiatry in prisons, but to develop it elsewhere

One of the greatest problems facing psychiatric treatment in prison is precisely that, it is in prison. Many of the advances of modern psychiatry are related to the de-institutionalising of psychiatric care. Modern psychiatry . . . has fully grasped that community care embracing sheltered accommodation, sheltered work, day care and out-patient care are the essentials of good treatment. Prisons are set apart from society, they have few or no links with local communities. In such a setting it is extremely difficult, if not impossible, to practise good modern psychiatry, especially the psychiatry of chronic disorders such as most neurotic prisoners present.[271]

It is therefore maintained that prisons have very little to offer the mentally disordered offender as the medical facilities provided by them are generally regarded as inadequate.[272] Ian Bynoe, the Director of MIND recently compared the standards of psychiatric treatment within the prison and the hospital, and concluded that no such comparison can be made, given the massive gulf that exists. For mentally disordered offenders sentenced to a term of imprisonment, 'compared to even the worst psychiatric facilities in the National Health Service, the physical environment, staffing resources and practices devoted to meeting these needs can render the experience of prison treatment for this group almost wholly different from what would be felt in hospital'.[273] He states that the Government has even acknowledged that there are serious limitations for a prison medical service, which is perpetually 'starved of essential resources and operating within a penal system paralysed by a constant state of crisis'.[274] Even the courts have stated that the standard of medical facilities in prison is significantly lower than in other hospitals, thus, ideally, prisoners should receive treatment for

[269] P. Carlen, *Psychiatry in Prisons* in Rose and Miller, *Power of Psychiatry*, 258.
[270] Ibid. 248; see further R. Smith, *Prison Health Care* (BMA 1984) (emphasis supplied).
[271] J. Gunn, *et al., Psychiatric Aspects*, 258.
[272] R. A. H. Washbrook, 'The Psychiatrically Ill Prisoner' (1977) 1 *The Lancet* 1302–3: 'Prison hospitals are generally no more than sick bays'.
[273] I. Bynoe, 'The Prison Medical Wing: "A Place of Safety" ?' (1990) 1 *J For Psych* 251–7, 251.
[274] Ibid.

mental disorder in hospitals.[275] Therefore, to imprison the vast majority of mentally disordered offenders would clearly be an affront to principles of humanity, and 'to permit the mentally sick within prisons would be to put the clock back 100 years'[276]—a state of affairs that would be undesirable, as revealed by Joe Sim in his account of the brutality of treatment in prisons in Victorian England.[277]

1.5. WHAT IS DIVERSION?

1.5.1. The Meaning of Diversion

Having considered how mentally disordered offenders should be treated and why they should be directed out of the prison/penal system, the final preliminary issue that must be considered here is precisely what is meant by diversion in this context and how it fits into the principles outlined above. In recent years the 1979–97 Conservative Government introduced an explicit policy of diverting mentally disordered offenders from the criminal justice system, which has also now been embraced and supported by the new Labour Government. The genesis, evolution, and implementation of this policy will be further discussed in the following chapters; however, it is first necessary to define exactly what is meant by the diversion of mentally disordered offenders.

'Diversion' is used to describe a process of decision-making at various stages of the criminal justice system whereby certain offenders are not prosecuted, or not imprisoned, or not punished, but are identified and treated in a different way. This approach, whereby juvenile defendants have been referred to multi-agency panels and been cautioned or given non-custodial penalties wherever possible,[278] has taken place with regard to young offenders for many years. In the case of mentally disordered offenders, diversion will normally be to the health and social services, and away from prosecution, custody and/or penal disposals. Thus 'The aim of diversion is to reduce the role of the criminal justice system and increase that of the health system.'[279]

---

[275] *Knight v Home Office* [1984] 1 All ER 1036; see further P. Fennell, 'Diversion of Mentally Disordered Offenders' [1991] *Crim LR* 333–48, as to the controversies regarding psychiatric treatment in prison and also R. Rogers and M. R. Bagby, 'Diversion of Mentally Disordered Offenders: A Legitimate Role for Clinicians?' (1992) 10 *Behavioural Sciences and the Law* 407–18, where it was stated that correctional facilities are ill-equipped to provide adequate medical care for mental illness, and that such institutions simply provide an environment in which psychiatric patients are viewed negatively and are highly vulnerable to abuse.

[276] P. D. Scott 'Punishment or Treatment: Prison or Hospital' (1970) 2 *BMJ* 167–9, 168.

[277] Sim, *Medical Power.*

[278] See e.g. NACRO Young Offenders Committee, *Diverting Young Offenders from Prosecution*, Policy Paper 2 (NACRO 1992); J. Mott, 'Police Decisions for Dealing with Juvenile Offenders' (1983) 23 *Brit J Criminology* 249–62; see also G. Dingwall and C. Harding, *Diversion in the Criminal Process* (Sweet & Maxwell 1998) esp. ch. 6.

[279] S. Blummenthal and S.Wessely, 'National Survey of Current Arrangements for Diversion from Custody in England and Wales' (1992) 305 *BMJ* 1322–5, 1322.

The diversion of a mentally disordered offender can be achieved in many ways. Firstly, in the narrowest possible sense, what is being achieved is simply diversion from custodial measures—the offender is still prosecuted and in contact with the criminal justice system at an early stage, but is subsequently diverted into health care and not necessarily subjected to a penal or custodial remand/sentence. However, in the broadest sense possible, diversion can mean complete diversion from the criminal justice system altogether, whereby the offender is diverted at the outset and will not be prosecuted at all, but is directed into health and social services care immediately. This may be achieved in a variety of ways. For example the police may decide not to take any formal action and refer the offender directly to the health services, or s/he may be admitted to the relevant health service facility under s. 136 of the Mental Health Act which is discussed fully in Ch. 3. Alternatively, the CPS may decide to discontinue the case on the basis of the medical evidence, and so the offender may then be directed into appropriate health care. Diversion can also take place when an offender is still processed within the criminal justice system in court but is remanded into hospital care or given medical treatment as a condition of bail as opposed to being remanded into custody. Finally, diversion can occur when a charge is reduced or the court imposes a therapeutic disposal so that custodial penalties are avoided. Diversion can therefore take place at various stages in the criminal justice process, be it at the point of arrest, the police station, at court at first appearance, or at the sentencing stage. Diversion therefore ranges from broad to narrow depending on the stage in the criminal justice system at which it occurs. In relation to mentally disordered offenders, the level of diversion is clearly dependent upon what is most appropriate in any given situation, in view of the nature of the disorder and the circumstances of the offence.

Mechanisms do already exist, primarily within the Mental Health Act 1983, which enable diversion to take place. They will be considered in detail in Ch. 3; however, essentially they are therapeutic remand and disposal powers which enable mentally disordered offenders to be given access to hospital care and treatment during the prosecution process. These powers largely enable diversion in its narrowest sense to be achieved. However, during the 1980s it was perceived that these powers were not being used adequately, and so the 1979–97 Conservative Government introduced an explicit diversion policy in 1990 to urge their more effective and increased use. It also described that this could best be achieved by the establishment of psychiatric assessment diversion schemes at police stations and courts throughout the country. It is evident that the diversion of mentally disordered offenders is compatible with the approach adopted in this book, as it seeks to increase the role of the health and social services and to ensure that appropriate therapeutic, as opposed to penal, disposals take place. In Chs. 5 and 6 therefore, an analysis of diversion in West Yorkshire will be conducted to assess and evaluate the level of diversion which is taking place and whether the diversion schemes in operation are achieving these aims.

1.5.2. Diversion within the Context of the Criminal Justice System

Because it is largely motivated by humanitarian concerns, it must be asked how diversion fits in with the criminal justice system as a whole, which, as noted previously, has differing aims and ideals as it is traditionally concerned with establishing guilt, prosecution, and punishment.[280] Andrew Ashworth has identified certain values and principles, which must be respected if there is to be a coherent framework within the criminal justice system.[281] He identifies the need to preserve the rights of victims, ensure proportionality, accountability, and access to information about decisions. It must therefore finally be considered how diversion fits in with these values and whether it is compatible with these aims.

Ashworth has expressly considered the notion of diversion in the context of the criminal justice system and suggests various ways in which it can be made to fit into this overall 'framework of values'.[282] He maintains that diversion decisions should ensure that the offender's decision to accept is 'free and informed' and that there should be access to legal advice and a court hearing if guilt is in issue. Further, the diversion system should not compromise the victim's right to compensation, for example under the Criminal Injuries Compensation Scheme, and that there should be a sense of proportionality between the seriousness of the offence and that which the offender is asked to agree to as the condition of diversion. Provided such measures are taken and adopted, then diversion decisions can be made to fit into the overall framework of the criminal justice system and dispositive values are preserved: 'There are good arguments in favour of the diversion of non-serious offenders from the criminal courts, but this should be done at the least possible cost to the rights of victims and of defendants.'[283]

With regard to the diversion of mentally disordered offenders, however, Ashworth further maintains that fairness and protection of the vulnerable are also important values to be respected within the criminal justice system. Included within this consideration are the mentally ill, who are especially vulnerable and in whose cases there should be favourable discrimination and additional protection and support.[284] And so, the diversion of the mentally ill can be said to fit in with the overall framework, as mentally disordered offenders are being given special protection.[285] But this must not be at the expense of other values, such as accountability, public safety, and the interests of victims. In theory, therefore, it is suggested that the diversion of mentally disordered offenders can be made to fit into the overall mould of the criminal justice

---

[280] See N. McKittrick and S. Eysenck, 'Diversion: A Big Fix?' (1984) 148 *JP* 377–9, 393–4, for an analysis of the main issues.
[281] A. Ashworth, *The Criminal Process: An Evaluative Study* (Oxford University Press 1998) ch. 2.
[282] Ibid. 33–7.   [283] Ibid. 172.   [284] Ibid. 58–9.
[285] Ibid. 166–8.

system, and this will be further explored below. But in Chs. 4 and 5 it will be
also be considered in further detail whether this compatibility in theory extends
to the actual practice of diversion.

1.5.2.1. What about the Victims and the Safety of the Public?

Particular concern has been expressed, notably by Herschel Prins[286] that more
emphasis should be placed upon the views and needs of the victims of the crimes
committed by the mentally ill. He implies that their feelings are not considered
when decisions about diversion are taken. Adrian Grounds has also expressed similar concerns: 'Whilst the broad policy of diversion is widely agreed, it also requires
some critical scrutiny . . . it has to be recognized that diversion effectively removes
a category of offender from the operation of the criminal justice system, and as a
corollary removes a category of victims from the operation of the criminal justice
system too'.[287] This is indeed an extremely valid issue, inherent in any diversion
decision,[288] and one which the Reed Committee in its recent review of services for
mentally disordered offenders acknowledged in its *Report*.[289] It is particularly relevant in view of the recent increasing emphasis being placed upon the role of the
victim in the criminal justice system. The British criminal justice system has traditionally been criticized for paying too little regard to the victims of crime. In 1990,
however, the 1979–97 Conservative Government produced the Victim's Charter,[290]
which provided for increased attention to be paid to the views of the victims of
crime. It has subsequently been revised and a second edition was published in June
1996, which gives improved rights and access to information for victims.[291] The
revised charter gives them the opportunity to explain how the crime has affected
them and describes how this will be taken into account, as well as ensuring that they
receive information about the progress of their case. Indeed, the revised Charter
places direct responsibility for keeping victims informed onto the police, as they are
perceived to be the single point of contact who will provide victims with all the
relevant information as to the charges, trial date, and final outcome of the case.
They are the 'One Stop Shop' who are able to receive, channel, and communicate
the necessary information.[292] This has been taken a step further by virtue of Home

---

[286] H. Prins, 'Is Diversion Just a Diversion?' (1994) 34 *Med Sci & Law* 137–47; see also id.,
Offender-Patients: The People Nobody Knows in Watson and Grounds, (eds.), *Mentally Disordered
Offender: New Directions*; P. Joseph, 'The Diversion of the Mentally Disordered: Some Problems for
Criminal Justice, Penology and Health Care (1992) 3 *J For Psych* 431–43.

[287] A. Grounds, *Mental Health Problems* in S. Cassale and E. Stockdale (eds.) *Criminal Justice
under Stress* (Blackstones 1993), 297.

[288] McKittrick and Eysenck, 'Diversion: Big Fix?'   [289] Cm. 2088 paras. 4.18–19.

[290] Home Office, *Victim's Charter: A Statement of the Rights of Victims of Crime* (1990); see
further A. Ashworth, 'Victim Impact Statements and Sentencing' [1993] *Crim LR* 498; D. Tucker,
'Victim's Rights?—Wrong' (1991) 141 *NLJ* 192, 194; M. Wright, 'Victims, Mediation and Criminal
Justice' [1995] *Crim LR* 187.

[291] Home Office Press Release 177/96, 'New Charter for Victims of Crime'.

[292] See further C. Hoyle *et al.*, *Evaluation of the 'One Stop Shop' and Victim Statement Pilot
Projects* (Home Office 1998), ch. 6.

Office Circular 55/98, which serves as a timely reminder to the police of their obigation to keep victims informed of the developments in their case. The Circular reaffirms that 'The Government wants the criminal justice system as a whole to do more to recognize, and be sensitive to, the needs of victims'.[293] The CPS has also recently stated that it is committed to providing a high standard of service to victims and witnesses,[294] and the former DPP announced that the Crown Prosecution Service will now routinely take account of the views of victims of violent crime in assessing the public interest element in prosecution.[295] Indeed, the revised Code for Crown Prosecutors expressly states that consideration must be given to the victims of crime in the decision whether or not to prosecute an offender: 'Crown Prosecutors must always think carefully about the interests of the victim, which are an important factor, when deciding where the public interest lies.'[296]

The current Labour Government has also announced its commitment to improving the treatment of victims in the criminal justice system.[297] Helping victims of crime and reducing witness intimidation are regarded as a 'high priority'; accordingly a range of measures have been taken to further these aims.[298] The Government has increased the grant, which is made available to Victim Support as well as launching a major interdepartmental review into the treatment of victims and vulnerable witnesses in the criminal justice system.[299] The review has resulted in the introduction of a new Youth Justice and Criminal Evidence Bill.[300] It contains a number of new measures, which are designed *inter alia* to protect victims of rape and other vulnerable witnesses in criminal trials. It is evident that the victims of crime, especially serious and violent crime, are gaining increasing prominence within the British criminal justice system, and this is therefore an important consideration for diversion, as the decision to divert an offender will undoubtedly impact the victim of his/her offence. Indeed, the revised Code of Practice which accompanies the Mental Health Act 1983, and which was published in March 1999 makes express reference to the need to respect the rights of victims when decisions about mental health care are being

---

[293] HO Circular 55/1998, *Keeping Victims Informed of Developments in their Case* (HO 1998), para. 2.   [294] *CPS Annual Report 1996–1997* Session 1997–8 HC 68 p. 16.
[295] 'Victims of violent crime to be asked for views on cases' *The Times*, 22 February 1995, 6; B. Mills, 'Victims' Influence on the Criminal Justice System' (1995) 51 *The Mag* 83, 99.
[296] *CPS Annual Report 1996–1997* Session 1997–8 HC 68, Code for Crown Prosecutors para. 6.7.
[297] Session 1997–8 HC Debs Vol. 301 col. 1091 *per* Secretary of State for Home Department.
[298] Home Office, *Annual Report 1998: Government's Expenditure Plans 1998–1999*, Session 1997–8 Cm. 3908 para. 10.1; see also Session 1996–1997 HC Debs Vol. 301 cols 1089–93; Session 1996–7 HC Debs Vol. 299 cols 341–57 *per* Secretary of State for Home Department.
[299] Ibid. para. 10.2; see also Home Office, *Speaking up for Justice; Report of an Interdepartmental Working Group on the Treatment of Vulnerable and Intimidated Witnesses in the Criminal Justice System* (Home Office 1998); Home Office Press Releases 012/97, 'Procedures for Vulnerable Witnesses to be Reviewed' and 211/98, 'Victims and Witnesses to Get a Greater Say'.
[300] 'Youth Justice and Criminal Evidence Bill—To Modernise Youth Courts and Protect Vulnerable Witnesses' Home Office Press Release 480/98, 4 December 1998.

made. One of the guiding principles enshrined in the new Code is the need for health care professionals, who are involved with patients detained under the criminal provisions of the Act, to be alive to 'the benefits of enabling some information to be given . . . to victims, within the spirit of the Victim's Charter'.[301] This must be done at the least possible cost to the offenders' right to confidentiality, and will 'enable victims and victims' families to be informed about progress'.[302] Accordingly, mental health professionals have also been reminded and advised of the requirements in the Victim's Charter.

However, the crimes of mentally disordered offenders are frequently minor disturbances, largely summary offences, not serious violent crimes[303] thus one could argue that in such circumstances the rights of victims are not accorded such primacy and that the safety of the public will not be endangered. The harm and suffering caused by the majority of mentally disordered offenders is not extensive, serious, or personal, thus, the rights of victims may yield to the welfare of the offender.

Moreover, it would seem that with many assessment and diversion schemes (as will be revealed in Ch. 4), in the majority of cases where diversion takes place, the prosecution will still proceed but some form of medical or social supervision and care is additionally arranged. Thus, more often than not, it is simply a narrow form of diversion which is achieved—the mentally disordered offenders will still be prosecuted and a fine or other minor non-custodial penalty, such as a probation order, imposed. So diversion schemes are not just about diverting offenders out of the criminal justice system altogether, thus completely escaping prosecution, but are also a mechanism for providing quicker and easier access to the health and social services. This is an extremely vital consideration, so it is important to remember that diversion and discontinuance are not synonymous. In some cases discontinuance may clearly be desirable and appropriate, given the nature of the charge and the degree of mental illness. However, in the majority of cases the 'rights' of the victims are not totally abrogated, and the offender is invariably still prosecuted, thus, from the victim's perspective, justice is still being seen to be done and compensation claims will not be thwarted. At the same time the mentally disordered offender is being given access to therapeutic care and treatment. Thus principles of humanity, care, retribution, and punishment are not necessarily mutually exclusive. But a person's mental disorder is clearly an important mitigating factor and mentally disordered offenders should have access to the relevant services to be given appropriate treatment and support.

As noted above, heinous and seriously violent crimes committed by the mentally ill are exceptions to the rule: 'The cases of mentally disturbed individuals charged with capital crimes . . . represent only the tip of the iceberg. These are

[301] DoH/Welsh Office, *Mental Health Act 1983 Revised* Code of Practice, para. 1.9.

[302] *Mental Health Act 1983 Revised.*

[303] K. Potter, 'Cries for Help' (1995) *Police Review,* 10 February 24–5, 'The vast majority of crimes [mentally disordered offenders] commit are more to do with survival, such as shoplifting or stealing milk from doorsteps. Any aggression is usually to do with frustration and can be seen as a cry for help.'

unusual examples because most mentally ill are not likely to attempt to assassinate a public figure or hijack an airplane.'[304] Most of the available evidence indicates that mentally disordered offenders are far more likely to harm themselves than others.[305] In many such cases however, it is not just the victims of the crime who suffer, but the mentally disordered offenders themselves are also victims—casualties of the failure to provide adequate care, as the tragic life of Christopher Clunis portrays. Failed by the system, he had been in and out of prison and left to cope on his own in the community. This he clearly could not do and the tragic consequence of this was the death of Jonathan Zito at his hands on a tube station platform in London.[306] The attitude of his murder victim's widow, Jayne Zito, bears testimony to this, as she does not blame Christopher Clunis for what he did, but rather pities him and blames the Government for its failure in adequately implementing and financing community care policies. Clunis was left alone in the community without treatment and support, which led to a deterioration in his condition resulting in Jonathan Zito's death. Her concerns do not lie with seeking retribution and punishment for Christopher Clunis, but she now campaigns vigorously to ensure better and improved care and supervision for the mentally ill.[307] That is not to say that such violent mentally disordered offenders do not deserve punishment—but that they also need care. This type of offender would not be regarded as a suitable candidate for discontinuance or diversion to a community penalty under such schemes, but would need to be diverted in the narrowest possible sense to secure hospital care. His or her mental disorder may be of such a degree that it may warrant some form of therapeutic disposal such as a restriction order at the sentencing stage, thereby ensuring both public protection and individual treatment.

Despite such tolerant and sympathetic attitudes, however, in view of the increasing emphasis being placed upon the views of victims of crimes, it may be necessary, as the Reed Committee identified, 'that the police should be reminded to inform victims of the reasons why an offender is cautioned rather than prosecuted. Such advice is equally important if a mentally disordered offender is diverted from the criminal justice system or a medical disposal is likely.'[308] Such

---

[304] R. Sommer and H. Osmond, 'The Mentally Ill in the Eighties' (1981) 10 *Journal of Orthomolecular Psychiatry* 193–201, 199.

[305] S. Wessely, 'Crime and the schizophrenic—mentally ill are no more likely to murder than other people are' *The Times,* 18 August 1994.

[306] See the *Report of the Inquiry into the Care and Treatment of Christopher Clunis* (HMSO 1994).

[307] See J. Zito, 'Learning the Lessons' in J. Braggins and C. Martin (eds.) *Managing the Risk: Achieving the Possible. Report of ISTD's Annual Conference 1995* (ISTD 1996), 68–74; 'Overdue reforms welcomed as long as the funding follows' *The Times,* 30 July 1998, p. 4; *The Times,* 25 February 1994. In fact, her campaign for such improvements has gathered such momentum that the Zito Trust was established in July 1994. It is a charitable organization aimed at influencing policy and providing support in the field of community care for the mentally ill. See *Monitor:* the journal of the Zito Trust, ed. M. Howlett and A. Lloyd.

[308] Cm. 2088 para. 4.19.

a step would require very little effort or expense, yet would ensure that victims are given the relevant information and accorded some respect in the diversion decision-making process. This would also be in line with the requirements under the revised Victim's Charter, the revised Mental Health Act Code of Practice, and official policy, to ensure 'greater involvement and improved rights for victims in the criminal justice system.

1.5.2.2. The Lack of Accountability and Unfettered Discretion

Many critics of diversion policy argue that it places too much discretion in the hands of the professionals without any legal safeguards or controls.[309] The decision whether or not to divert a particular offender is largely a matter for individual discretion. There is therefore much scope for personal influences and prejudices to affect the decision to divert. As Ashworth has identified, it is important to preserve principles of fairness, equality, and accountability within the criminal justice system and an important question, therefore, is precisely how much is known about the variations in practice nationally about decisions to prosecute and diversion? Are there regional variations? If so, there is a danger that the practice of diversion is abrogating such principles. Both Herschel Prins and Adrian Grounds regard this issue as essential: 'There are few mechanisms for ensuring that the discretion to exercise diversion is operated fairly and that requirements of justice are met.'[310]

Doubts have also been expressed about diversion in this respect from a clinical perspective. One article[311] raises many arguments against diversion from a medical viewpoint. Particularly, the concern is reiterated that no standard legal criteria or specific clinical guidelines exist as to whom to divert and under what circumstances, the decision is often based entirely upon individual discretion. Further, it is argued that there may be a degree of bias in the process, and the role of clinicians in assessments may be distorted due to their involvement in the process. That is, individual clinicians' views as to diversion are likely to prejudice their diversion decision-making.

Whilst it is accepted that this is a potential danger, one could argue that this factor applies equally to any other area involving such ethical medical decisions. For example, the outrage in the mid-1990s over the decisions by doctors not to operate on people who smoke may be completely based upon personal prejudices. Furthermore, it is a decision with potentially fatal consequences yet it is one to which no strict guidelines or controls are applied. It could also be argued that it is perhaps not so much the individual clinician's view but the availability of the appropriate resources which determines the fate of a mentally disordered offender. As Adrian Grounds has identified, 'Similar cases may be given wholly

---

[309] See e. g. D. Carson, 'Holding the Patient to Account at the Gatekeeping Stage' (1992) 2 *Criminal Behaviour and Mental Health* 224–33.

[310] Grounds, *Mental Health Problems*, 297.

[311] Rogers and Bagby, 'Diversion: Role for Clinicians?' 407–18.

different outcomes depending on the availability and efficiency of local services.'[312]

It will be seen in following chapters how courts have been forced to send mentally ill people to prison on several occasions due to the lack of suitable facilities. The same limitations clearly apply to the formal diversion of the mentally ill. Despite the intentions of the individual clinician, a mentally disordered offender will not be diverted unless the court is satisfied that appropriate arrangements for that person's care and treatment are securely in place. Obviously the clinician will influence the decision, however, ultimately, it falls upon the shoulders of the service into which the mentally disordered offender is being diverted. If it refuses to offer treatment or cannot accept him/her, then diversion will not be achieved, despite the wishes of the clinician to the contrary.

This notion of discretion and lack of formalization and accountability is an important one, however, and indeed one about which many commentators have expressed doubts within the context of the criminal justice system as a whole. As noted by Ashworth, just as one can argue that diversion decisions lack any form of standardization and are open to manipulation, the same can also be said about most other decisions taken within the criminal justice system. In particular, those 'gatekeeping decisions' taken by the various prosecuting authorities and the police: 'Decisions taken by law enforcement agents have a considerable influence on the selection of cases that go forward into the criminal process. . . . The offenders who find themselves in court are not a random group of the totality of offenders . . . they are chosen.'[313]

He states that, although guidelines are issued to the police, for example in terms of cautioning practice and procedure,[314] it is ultimately an issue for their individual discretion whether or not to proceed with a particular prosecution, as Home Office guidelines relate to an 'extra-legal' set of practices and therefore have no binding legal force. And one officer faced with a particular offender may choose to issue a caution, whereas another officer would decide to proceed with the charges. The same applies with respect to Crown Prosecutors, it is their responsibility to assess evidence and decide whether or not to proceed with a prosecution. They too are issued with guidelines in their Code for Crown Prosecutors, it is not legally binding,[315] thus, ultimately it will be a subjective and value-laden decision made by individual prosecutors who all have differing values and notions of justice. Plea bargaining at court may also result in variations in practice. The same charge may be reduced to a lesser one in a particular court as the defendant expresses that s/he is willing to plead guilty to that lesser charge and therefore receive a more lenient penalty than s/he would have had if

---

[312] Grounds, *Mental Health Problems*.
[313] Ashworth,*Criminal Process*, 126 (1st edn 1984).
[314] *The Cautioning of Offenders,* Home Office Circular 18/1994 .
[315] Note however that decisions based upon it can be subject to judicial review.

s/he had been found guilty of the more serious charge by the court. So, undoubtedly, regional variations and variations in practice will exist there too. The same process of selectivity and discretion applies with respect to the various regulatory agencies, such as the Pollution Inspectorate and the Consumer Protection Departments. Each individual agency adopts its own approach towards initiating prosecutions, and very little exists in the way of formal mechanisms to ensure meaningful review or accountability for decisions.[316] Such decisions therefore potentially obscure many of the principles of criminal justice, such as respect for victims' rights and equality before the law.

This is a danger that is also inherent within diversion decisions concerning mentally disordered offenders. However, one could argue that to a lesser extent respect for the victims can be maintained as prosecutions invariably proceed. And with regard to equality of treatment, as noted above, juvenile and mentally ill defendants are particularly vulnerable and deserve some form of special consideration and treatment. Despite such optimistic arguments, however, it is accepted that the discretion element is an unsatisfactory feature of the notion of diversion. As Ashworth has identified, some element of discretion is inevitable in relation to such gatekeeping decisions, but it must not be absolute and should be subject to certain limitations, monitoring, and guidelines. And it is argued by many that whilst mentally disordered offenders deserve access to the health and social services, it must be provided formally and fairly.

One final criticism of diversion in this respect has been posed by Jill Peay who casts doubts that the mentally ill should be singled out for special treatment in this way. Peay believes that given the problems surrounding the definition of mental disorder, diversion decisions will be very difficult to agree upon and achieve. Failure to agree on a definition is likely to result in their being a mismatch of expectations among the various agencies dealing with these people, which will undoubtedly have an impact upon diversion: 'If the mentally disordered cannot be effectively identified . . . diversion and transfer can never be the solution'.[317]

The problematic definition has been discussed at length earlier in this chapter, and is central to the successful treatment of mentally disordered offenders, as it can militate against successful inter-agency co-operation. The solution would perhaps be to reach an agreed strategy at the outset, which not only spells out the roles and responsibilities of each agency and clearly identifies the services available, but one that also specifies precisely with whom the diversion scheme is dealing by reference to standard referral criteria. This issue will be

---

[316] Ashworth, *Criminal Process*, 162–6. See e.g. *R. v IRC ex p. Mead* [1992] STC 482 where Stuart-Smith LJ held that 'A decision to prosecute by the prosecuting authorities is in theory susceptible to judicial review, albeit *the circumstances in which such jurisdiction could be successfully invoked will be rare in the extreme*' (emphasis supplied).

[317] Peay, 'Mentally Disordered Offenders' in Maguire, Morgan, and Reiner (eds.), *Oxford Handbook of Criminology*, 1154; see also Peay, J., 'A Criminological Perspective: The Influence of Fashion and Theory on Practice and Disposal: Life Chances in the Criminological Tombola' in Watson and Grounds, *Mentally Disordered Offender: New Perspectives*.

vital when considering the actual practice of diversion schemes in West Yorkshire in Part II.

1.6. CONCLUSION

> The mentally ill, far from being guilty persons who merit punishment, are sick people whose miserable state deserves all the consideration due to suffering humanity.[318]

This chapter has shown that it is preferable to regard this group of people primarily as mentally disordered persons who have committed offences, rather than as offenders who are mentally disordered.[319] The main focus should be upon treating the mental disorder and not punishing the crime. Adopting the medical model and discretional approach, the view that the medical profession has a valuable role to play is affirmed. It is acknowledged, however, that this is far from uncontested and many of the difficulties encountered in this complex sphere where both medical and legal concepts overlap have been discussed.[320]

It has also been shown how mentally disordered offenders should, wherever possible, be received into the health and social services, to be cared for by medical and social work personnel. This can take place in addition to the offender being processed by the criminal justice system and so in many cases, duality of action occurs whereby prosecution and treatment are ensured at the same time. What is important, however, is that the treatment is provided within a therapeutic environment and so it is maintained that prison and the detrimental effects of the prison environment must be avoided wherever possible. It is further suggested that this therapeutic intervention depends upon the co-operation and collaboration of the professions involved. A fundamental requirement is therefore a level of inter-agency co-operation. This can be extremely problematic, given the differing traditions, viewpoints, and approaches. Diversion policy and schemes aim to reduce this conflict by encouraging inter-agency collaboration. So the issue to be addressed in the research study in Part II is an evaluation of how far a group of existing diversion schemes further these aims through the operation of inter-agency working.

Chapter 2 will now explore the historical perspective and the origins of this diversionary approach; this will be taken further in Chs. 3 and 4, as the existing provisions to divert mentally disordered offenders will be considered and the inadequacies which led the 1979–97 Conservative Government to introduce an explicit diversion policy will be outlined.

---

[318] Philippe Pinel (1745–1826) quoted in P. Bean (ed), *Mental Illness: Changes and Trends* (John Wiley 1983), 15.

[319] A. de Reuck and A. Porter (eds.), *The Mentally Abnormal Offender* (Churchill 1968), 251.

[320] See also J. Arboleda-Florez, 'Two Solitudes: Mental Health and Law' (1990) 1 *J For Psych* 143–65.

2

The Historical Context

The problem of managing effectively the mentally abnormal who offend against the law seems to be one of those chronic problems that our society and many others cannot solve. For as long as history has noticed such people, they have drifted from prisons to hospitals, [and from] . . . asylums to hostels.[1]

2.1. INTRODUCTION

This chapter will briefly outline the reports, reforms, and major developments that have taken place throughout the latter half of the twentieth century and that influence the present-day provisions and approaches towards mentally disordered offenders.[2] Many of these developments have heightened the plight of such an offender, and so this chapter also strives to underline that the current emphasis upon diversion and therapeutic care has its origins firmly rooted in the past. It has been customary for decades to protect the mentally ill from punitive sanctions and the normal operation of the criminal law by affording them the care and treatment they deserve.[3] The legislative and policy developments that have facilitated and perpetuated these humane principles will be briefly considered. In this respect it will be more pertinent to consider the major reports and the philosophies which underpin them, rather than a detailed consideration of the legislative provisions themselves. Emphasis will be placed upon the emergence and dominance of the medical profession and psychiatry which has taken place in the latter half of the past century, which strongly influences the treatment of the mentally ill today. And a brief look into the history of the mental health service is also necessary, as it enables a better understanding of the nature of the system into which mentally disordered offenders are diverted.

It will also be shown how history has reflected the tensions that exist between

---

[1] R. Smith, *Prison Health Care* (BMA 1984), 43.

[2] For detailed accounts of these and earlier developments relating to mentally disordered offenders see N. Walker, *Crime and Insanity in England* i. *The Historical Perspective* (Edinburgh University Press 1968); K. Jones, *A History of the Mental Health Services* (Routledge & Kegan Paul 1972); see also the official reports of the Royal Commission on the Care and Control of the Feeble-Minded (1908) Cd. 4202, and the Royal Commission on Lunacy and Mental Disorder (1926) Cmd. 2700, which illustrate the early twentieth-century attitudes towards the mentally ill.

[3] See E. Parker, 'Mentally Disordered Offenders and their Protection From Punitive Sanctions: The English Experience' (1980) 3 *Int J Law & Psych* 461–9.

differing schools of professional opinion as outlined in the preceding chapter. Disciplines of law, medicine, and social work agencies have all struggled to find a solution to the care and treatment of the mentally disordered offender.

2.2.1. The Growth of Psychiatry and Community Mental Health Services

The origins of the existing provisions and the emphasis upon diversion and therapeutic intervention[4] are to be found in the 1950s, with the advent of revolutionary treatments for the mentally ill and the growth of the psychiatric profession.[5] Kathleen Jones has chronicled the 'three revolutions' which took place during the 1950s, which heralded the reforms and which will be outlined here as they are highly instructive and were major catalysts for change.[6]

The first was the 'pharmacological revolution' whereby psychotropic drugs such as tranquillizers were developed and were a vital breakthrough in the treatment of the insane. They were widely prescribed, with the result that in-patients were discharged much sooner than had been the case and some now had no need to come into hospital at all. She charts how new physical methods of treatment were also being introduced, and allied to this was the 'administrative revolution', which involved therapeutic experimental developments within the psychiatric system. This modern approach involved flexible and pioneering methods such as open-door policies, group therapy, out-patient clinics, therapeutic social clubs, day hospitals, hostels, psychiatric units in general hospitals, and growing social work involvement.[7] The health and social work professions were therefore given increased recognition and the psychiatric profession had also gained prominence since the Second World War as a result of its work with war-torn soldiers returning home after battle.

The final impetus for change was the 'legislative revolution'. A Parliamentary debate at the beginning of 1954[8] was initiated by a Private Member's Bill which paved the way for reform. During the debate, the 'advances made in recent years in the treatment and care of the mental patients' were firmly acknowledged, but

---

[4] For a full and detailed account of the developments in this area see K. Jones, *History; Asylums and After: A Revised History of the Mental Health Service* (Athlone 1993); Walker, *Crime and Insanity*, i; N. Walker & S. McCabe, *Crime and Insanity in England* ii: *New Solutions and New Problems* (Edinburgh University Press 1973); C. Unsworth, *The Politics of Mental Health Legislation* (Oxford University Press 1985).

[5] See G. L. Klerman, *The Psychiatric Revolution of the Past 25 Years* in W. R. Gove (ed), *Deviance and Mental Illness* (Sage 1982).
[6] K. Jones, *History*, 289.

[7] As a result of the 1959 Younghusband Report (Ministry of Health Report of the Working Party on Social Workers in the Local Authority Health and Welfare Services) the restructure of the social work services to cater for the needs of the mentally ill began. See further K. Jones, *History*, 293–303.

[8] Session 1953–4 HC Debs Vol. 523 cols 2293–379 (19 Feb. 1954).

concern was expressed at the serious overcrowding, the 'obsolete and unstable buildings' and the staff shortages in the mental health services. Consequently, the Government of the day and hospital authorities were called upon 'to make adequate provision for the modernization and development of this essential service'.[9] The House acknowledged that this was a 'really difficult human problem',[10] and sympathies clearly lay with the mentally ill: 'These people are a small minority with no voice with which to speak . . . all the more reason why we in this House should see to it that they are getting the best that we can give.'[11]

Furthermore, it was recognized that mental illness was now being regarded in a different light. At last, people were 'slowly but inevitably coming to appreciate that mental sickness is not fundamentally different from physical illness . . . and that it is something which can be treated in a mental hospital.'[12] Consequently, it was announced that 'The House of Commons wants to examine thoroughly and sympathetically, and at the same time with a great deal of knowledge, this whole field in the interests of suffering humanity'.[13] This debate resulted in the appointment of a Royal Commission under the Chairmanship of Lord Percy in February 1954.

2.2.2. The Royal Commission on the Law Relating to Mental Illness and Mental Deficiency

The Commission published its final recommendations in May 1957.[14] The basic premise of the Report was that people suffering from mental disorder should as far as possible be treated in the same way as those suffering from physical illness. After all, '[d]isorders of the mind are illnesses which need medical treatment'.[15] Allied to this was the underlying humanitarian principle that people suffering from mental disorder should be cared for 'with no more restriction of liberty or legal formality than is applied to people who need care because of other types of illness'.[16] The Commission clearly advocated the medical model of mental illness and stated that compulsory hospitalization powers were to be used only when 'positively necessary'.[17]

The observations and recommendations will not be considered here in detail, as, in the main, they governed the civil status of the mentally ill and thus fall beyond the scope of this book. Overall, however, the Commission recommended sweeping changes in the definition of mental disorder, the hospital admission procedures, supervision in the community, and the control, care, and treatment of the mentally disordered. The report was 'well-received',[18] and in December 1959 Mr Derek Walker Smith, then the Minister of Health, introduced a new Mental Health Bill 'to make fresh provision with respect to the

    [9] HC Debs Vol. 523. col. 2293.   [10] Ibid. col. 2329.   [11] Ibid. col. 2296.
    [12] Ibid. col. 2295.   [13] Ibid. col. 2363.   [14] Cmd. 169 (HMSO 1957).
    [15] Ibid. Paras. 5, 132–5.   [16] Ibid. Para. 7.   [17] Ibid.
    [18] Session 1956–7 HC Debs Vol. 573 cols 35–103, 36.

treatment and care of mentally disordered persons with respect to their property and affairs'.[19]

The differences of approach between the opposing proponents of liberalism and medical discretion were evident in the discussion of the detailed provisions of the proposed Mental Health Bill.[20] In particular, Baroness Wootton in the House of Lords[21] adopted a legalistic approach and expressed her fear that too great a discretion lay with the medical profession and that safeguards were insufficient.[22] However, as observed by Jones, given the general determination to enact the legislation in order to relieve the suffering of the mentally ill, such opposition was successfully resisted and the Bill was eventually passed largely in its original form.

This shift towards the reorientation of mental and physical health services was also demonstrated by the Royal Commission's endorsement of the concept of 'community care' and the establishment of less formal treatment facilities. The Government of the day actively supported this principle, as Derek Walker Smith stated, 'One of the main principles we are seeking to pursue is the re-orientation of the mental health service away from institutional care towards care in the community.'[23] Here was the first official recognition and support for the principle of community care. This was taken further in 1962 when that Government introduced its Hospital Closure plan,[24] which was complemented in 1963 by its plans for developing community care.[25] The Government proposed a reduction in the provision of hospital services and a corresponding increase in the provision of community accommodation, training centres, and social work support for the mentally ill. The overall aim was to 'provide care at home and in the community for all who do not require the specialised types of diagnosis and treatment which only a hospital can provide'.[26]

Both documents were welcomed at the time. In terms of the principles they expounded, community care was seen as desirable, and it is from this particular point in history that community care policy stems. It is therefore vital in the consideration of the historical developments that form the basis of the law today. In particular, as will be discovered in Ch. 4, community care policies have had an impact upon diversion policy, as diversion from the criminal justice system invariably means diversion to hospital or community care, thus the effectiveness and adequacy of such arrangements and facilities must be considered.

Consideration of community care at this stage is also vital as it exemplifies the

---

[19] Session 1958–9 HC Debs Vol. 597 col. 1131.

[20] See further Session 1958–9 HC Debs, Standing Committee E Vol. IV cols 1–816 (10 Feb.–21 Apr. 1959).   [21] Session 1958–9 HL Debs Vol. 217 col. 394.

[22] See also C. Unsworth, *The Politics of Mental Health Legislation* (Clarendon 1985) ch. 9; C. Greenland, *Mental Illness and Civil Liberty* (Bell 1970).

[23] Session 1958–9 HC Debs Vol. 598 col. 704.

[24] Ministry of Health, *A Hospital Plan for England and Wales* (1962) Cmnd. 1604.

[25] Ministry of Health, *Health and Welfare: The Development of Community Care* (1963) Cmnd. 1973.   [26] Cmnd. 1604 Para. 31.

level of optimism, reliance, and faith now being placed in the powers of medicine and the health and social service professionals to help the mentally ill, and enable them to live as normal a life as possible receiving care in the community. Clearly, the emphasis upon the ability of psychiatry to assist the mentally ill and effect a cure 'reinforces the medical model of insanity',[27] thereby promoting humane and beneficent principles. Furthermore, this policy received some support in academic circles from the critics of the asylum system. Erving Goffman[28] and Andrew Scull[29] have specifically described the destructive and 'baneful effects' of institutional life upon its mentally ill inmates; the move away from institutional care was therefore an extremely favourable one from that perspective.

And so, at this stage, the medical view of mental illness was firmly endorsed in principle and mentally ill people were given access to medical care, which they need and to which they are entitled. Due to the pharmacological and administrative revolutions, the faith and confidence in the abilities of psychiatry and the medical profession were evident, as it had by now come to be regarded as a highly respected specialism of its own.[30] Again, from the perspective adopted throughout this book, this was a pivotal development, and many of the philosophies endorsed then still underpin the legislation in force today.

2.2.3. The Mental Health Act 1959

The Government accepted the majority of the Percy Report's recommendations and the new Mental Health Act received the Royal Assent in July 1959. It has been heralded as a major example of 'enlightened social welfare legislation', which has been widely influential: '[T]he Act reflects the new and enlightened approach to the treatment of mental disorder and has placed us in the forefront of those countries with progressive legislation on the subject.'[31]

Particularly with regard to mentally disordered offenders, based on the Commission's recommendations, the Mental Health Act made several new and sweeping changes.[32] Primarily, it introduced wide powers which enabled the courts, on the basis of medical evidence, to order an offender's admission to hospital or guardianship.[33] The order could include restrictions on the discharge of the patient if required.[34] Prior to this the courts' powers to order treatment

---

[27] A. Scull, *Decarceration: Community Treatment and the Deviant: A Radical View* (Polity 1984), 81.   [28] E. Goffman, *Asylums* (Penguin 1961).
[29] Scull, *Decarceration*, 95.
[30] M. M. Belli, 'Did McNaghten Need a Psychiatrist, a Lawyer or a Definition?' (1971) 11 *Med, Sci & Law* 25–30, 29: 'In the past century, psychiatry has evolved from tentative, hesitant gropings in the dark of human ignorance to a recognised important branch of modern medicine.'
[31] J. D. J. Havard, 'The Mental Health Act and the Criminal Offender' [1961] *Crim LR* 296–308, 298.
[32] Ibid. See further Walker and McCabe, *Crime and Insanity*, ii. chs. 3, 4, 5, for a detailed account of the origins of the Act and its application with regard to mentally disordered offenders.
[33] Mental Health Act 1959 ss. 60, 62.   [34] Ibid. s. 65.

instead of a prison sentence were limited and they could only order detention in an institution if the defendant was 'certifiable' under the old Lunacy or Mental Deficiency legislation.[35] The Home Secretary was also granted a power to transfer prisoners in need of psychiatric care from prison to hospital.[36] Moreover, the new definition of mental disorder covered a far wider range of conditions than had been included under the previous legislation, thereby allowing far more mentally disordered offenders to be given access to therapeutic care and treatment. Furthermore, these developments reinforced the Criminal Justice Act 1948, which had introduced the probation order with a condition of psychiatric treatment for offenders willing to undergo such treatment voluntarily.[37] This was also a welcome development which increased access to therapeutic care, and this power forms the basis of the present-day psychiatric probation order.

Notably, the new Mental Health Act received wholehearted support from the Prison Authorities who 'firmly endorse[d] the Mental Health Act general purpose to make the treatment of mental disorder more readily accessible and acceptable'.[38] It was hoped that the new disposal powers would enable more mentally disordered offenders to be cared for and treated in hospital settings and diverted out of the prison system. And so, the diversion of mentally ill offenders to the health care service was further facilitated.

2.2.4. Mentally Disordered Offenders and the Mental Health Act 1959 in Practice

Throughout the first half of the 1960s, the 1959 Mental Health Act was increasingly implemented. In relation to mentally disordered offenders, the hospital orders provided by the Act were very popular, and as noted by Nigel Walker, they now accounted for the overwhelming majority of cases where courts officially recognised that an offender was mentally disordered. He noted that the number of hospital orders doubled during the Act's first year of operation and that psychiatric probation orders under the Criminal Justice Act 1948 were also frequently invoked.[39]

D. A. Thomas, writing in 1965, considered the operation and application of the new hospital order powers and also the use of probation orders with psychiatric treatment. He concluded that

A survey of the decisions of the court since the passing of the Mental Health Act, 1959, suggests that the powers given by the Act are being used whenever possible. The court is quite prepared to abandon concepts of retribution and deterrence when dealing with a mentally disordered offender who has committed a serious offence . . . and sentences of

---

[35] See further Havard, 'Mental Health Act', 299–303.
[36] Mental Health Act 1959 ss. 72, 73.
[37] See further Walker and McCabe, *Crime and Insanity*, i. 64–7.
[38] *Report of the Commissioner of Prisons 1960* (1960–1) Cmd. 1467 Para. 24.
[39] Walker and McCabe, *Crime and Insanity*, i. 73–8.

imprisonment are used only where a hospital order or probation order with a condition for treatment are unsuitable.[40]

But the dawn of the 1970s witnessed a dramatic decline in the number of hospital orders being made, and it was felt that the intentions of Part V of the Act in relation to mentally disordered offenders were not being fulfilled. Notably the Prison Service, which had so wholeheartedly welcomed these new powers, once again repeated its concerns over the number of mentally ill people still in its custody. Throughout the 1970s, the Prison Service Annual Reports continually noted the decline in therapeutic disposals and drew attention to the difficulties faced in securing hospital places. This was a problem faced both by the prisons by way of transfers and by the courts at the sentencing stage.[41] The pressures on the prison accommodation and staff were constantly emphasised.[42] Not only did the prisons suffer, but this also had 'distressing and disturbing' consequences for the mentally disordered offenders themselves, as noted in the Prison Service Reports: 'Apart from the inhumane aspects of committing mentally disturbed offenders to prisons, . . . *it is not possible to provide many of these unfortunates with the medical and nursing care their condition requires whilst they are in custody.*'[43]

What brought about this dramatic decline in numbers? The evidence would seem to suggest that the difficulties did not lie with the actual provisions themselves nor in the courts' reluctance to use them, but in their actual implementation—in finding appropriate and sufficiently secure hospital beds for many mentally disordered offenders. By now, three Special Hospitals were in existence—Broadmoor, Rampton, and Moss Side—which offered high-security accommodation.[44] However, the number of available beds was limited, indeed the Hospitals were severely overcrowded, so the only alternative was prison, as the majority of wards in NHS psychiatric hospitals were not sufficiently secure.[45] This was a problem that had already been identified by a Ministry of Health White Paper on Special Hospitals in 1961.[46]

The lack of appropriate facilities and resources and the resulting burden placed upon the Prison Medical Service is one to which many commentators have alluded:

---

[40] D. A. Thomas, 'Sentencing the Mentally Disturbed Offender' [1965] *Crim LR* 685–99, 698.

[41] *Report on the Work of the Prison Department 1979* (1979–80) Cmnd. 7965 paras. 159, 161, 162. See also the 1971 Report (1970–1) Cmnd. 4724 para. 158; the 1973 Report (1974–5) Cmnd. 5767 para. 217; and the 1975 Report (1975–6) Cmnd. 6523 para. 218.

[42] *Report on the Work of the Prison Department 1978* (1979–80) Cmnd. 7619 para. 206.

[43] *Report on the Work of the Prison Department 1976* (1976–7) Cmnd. 6877 para. 258 (emphasis supplied).

[44] See Walker and McCabe, *Crime and Insanity*, i. ch. 1, for an account of the development of these institutions.

[45] P. Noble, 'Mental Health Services and Legislation: An Historical Review' (1981) 21 *Med, Sci & Law* 16–24, 22: 'The special hospitals are appallingly overcrowded.'

[46] HMSO 1961.

[The] figures illustrate the increasing difficulty being experienced by medical officers in finding hospitals willing to receive and treat their mentally disordered patients, particularly in those cases where courts considered an order restricting discharge from hospital to be necessary. Where a suitable hospital place cannot be found, courts often feel that there is no alternative to a custodial sentence, and the burden of caring for the persons concerned falls on the Prison Medical Officer and his/her staff.[47]

A study conducted by Parker and Tennent into the operation of Part V of the Act clearly showed that the intention built into the Act of vesting the care of such offenders in the psychiatric services was not being met.[48] This 'demonstrated the reluctance of the NHS to take mentally disordered offenders, the increasing pressures on the Special Hospitals and the mounting numbers of mentally disordered in the prisons'.[49] These findings were reinforced by Walker and McCabe's research.[50] They conducted a national study investigating 1,160 offender-patients subjected to s. 60 hospital/restriction orders during a twelve-month period (April 1963–March 1964). They identified many practical problems with the new powers. They found that summary courts misused the hospital order and recommended that they should be given an express power to find a defendant unfit to plead;[51] there was a need for a power to remand the accused to a psychiatric hospital so as not to rely on remand on bail;[52] hospital orders should not be confined to imprisonable offences; and with regard to restriction orders, they felt it was irrational for courts to specify a time limit for them.[53] Indeed, as the title of their book suggests, the 'new solutions' provided by the 1959 Act had, in turn, produced 'new problems', which had to be resolved.

In particular, Henry Rollin highlighted the Act's failings with regard to mentally abnormal offenders: 'no matter how successful the Mental Health Act has been in elevating the social and legal status of the mentally ill, there can be little doubt . . . that the same Act, in relation to the mentally abnormal offender, has been a failure'.[54]

Rollin regards the 'lack of communication between the psychiatric and legal professions' as a major stumbling-block. Many of the therapeutic disposal powers rely on the co-operation and exchange of information between the health and criminal justice professionals, which was not always taking place. The need for such agencies to work together was outlined in the previous chapter, and these observations further reinforce the need to do so. Rollin further argues that, in addition to the shortage of secure beds, too much faith was placed in the concept of 'community care': 'but before venturing on this great social expedition, no one

---

[47] H. Prins, *Offenders, Deviants or Patients? An Introduction to the Study of Socio-Forensic Problems* (Tavistock 1980), 335.

[48] E. Parker and G. Tennent, 'The 1959 Mental Health Act and Mentally Abnormal Offenders: A Comparative Study' (1979) 19 *Med, Sci & Law* 29–38. [49] Ibid. 37.

[50] Walker and McCabe, *Crime and Insanity*, i. [51] Ibid. 107.

[52] Ibid. 103. [53] Ibid. 91.

[54] H. Rollin, *The Mentally Abnormal Offender and the Law* (Pergamon 1969), 116.

took the elementary precaution of finding out in advance if . . . the community cared'.[55] As time passed it became clear that communities were 'sadly lacking in their willingness to care for their mentally ill brethren'.[56] Accordingly, the gates of the institutions were flung open and the mentally ill were discharged only to find that no adequate support existed for them in the community, and thus the process of the 'open door' became the 'revolving door'—'the ping pong sequence begins'.[57] Frequently such offenders break into houses for shelter and steal food to survive, only to be arrested and fed back into the system again. Under the provisions of the Mental Health Act they would be transferred from prison to hospital, only to be discharged, to be allowed to discharge themselves, or to abscond back out into society, alone again. This argument is further reinforced by the fact that the 1963 policy document for the development of community care was subsequently regarded by many as a major failure as it did not go far enough. In the words of Kathleen Jones, 'It consisted of 48 pages of general text on the desirability of community care, some glossy photographs, and 321 pages of detailed local authority returns on their future plans. Those who looked for . . . a positive lead from central Government were disappointed.'[58]

The Government acknowledged the truth of this in 1975 when it reappraised and reviewed mental health and community care policy. The Department of Health produced its progress report in 1975.[59] It acknowledged that the projections announced in 1962 had not been fulfilled and the asylum population had not been halved, and although overcrowding had been reduced, no single hospital had closed. The Secretary of State expressed concern at these unfulfilled hopes, stating that there were many problems, particularly in terms of shifting resources,[60] consequently, some hospitals would remain in use for many years. Nevertheless, it stated that the 'concept of community care still remains valid' and 'the philosophy of integration rather than isolation which has been the underlying theme of development still holds good . . . the main aims must continue to be the development of more locally-based services and a shift in the balance between hospital and social services [community] care'.[61]

The policy of community care was thus further reinforced and would continue to be implemented. However, in terms of its practical application its development was severely hampered by resource problems, and this fact will be vital in the consideration of the existing framework in the following chapters. Just as the implementation of the 1959 Act was failing due to the lack of facilities, the policy of community care was also suffering the same fate. As Brenda Hoggett has noted

---

[55] H. Rollin, *The Mentally Abnormal Offender and the La* (Pergamon 1969), 116.*w*.
[56] Ibid. See e.g. *Sunday Times*, 20 May 1973: 'NHS diagnosis for a cure: An injection of political will'—'The Act announced the concept of community care without adequately planning for it.'
[57] Rollin, *Mentally Abnormal Offender*, 119.   [58] K. Jones, *Asylums and After*, 183.
[59] DHSS, *Better Services for the Mentally Ill* (1975) Cmnd. 6233. The Department had also issued a similar document in 1971, containing similar proposals with regard to the services for the mentally handicapped: DHSS, *Better Services for the Mentally Handicapped* (1971) Cmnd. 4683.
[60] Cmnd. 6233, Foreword, para. 5.   [61] Ibid. Para. 2.17.

'[t]he problem of community care is practical and financial rather than legal',[62] and this is one of the main thrusts of Andrew Scull's criticisms of the implementation of community care policy.[63]

The Mental Health Act was therefore 'ailing' and in order to restore it to vitality, Rollin made several suggestions for reform.[64] Secure community care had to be provided—an increase in hostel provision and greater probation and aftercare services established. It had to be more readily accepted that a person can be both mad and bad, and a greater attempt to combine the two systems of care was both necessary and desirable. To achieve such changes, far more commitment and communication between jurists, psychiatrists, and lawyers was required so that the 'strong arm of the law knows what the weak hand of psychiatry is doing'. If possible, special multidisciplinary panels should be set up to collaborate and consider the disposal of the mentally abnormal offender.

Clearly, therefore, many problems existed in the operation of the 1959 Act. At the root of the difficulties lay the lack of communication between the agencies and the inadequate facilities and resources which frustrated attempts to implement the therapeutic disposal powers: 'Perhaps the principal reason for dissatisfaction with the Mental Health Act 1959 has been, not its philosophy or its formulation, but the dearth of resources allocated for its implementation.'[65] Such criticism and dissatisfaction paved the way for the vast array of official reports which were produced throughout the 1970s and spurred the wheels of change into motion once again.

2.3. THE 1970S REFORM MOVEMENT

2.3.1. The Report of the Committee on Mentally Abnormal Offenders

The increasing emphasis upon the plight of the mentally ill in prison coupled with the concerns about the discharge of dangerous mental patients and public safety[66] dictated that the time was now also ripe for a complete review of the law relating to mentally disordered offenders. This came in the form of the Report of the Committee on Mentally Abnormal Offenders[67] which was appointed by the

---

[62] B. Hoggett, 'What is Wrong with the Mental Health Act?' [1975] *Crim LR* 677–83.
[63] Scull, *Decarceration*.   [64] Rollin, *Mentally Abnormal Offender*, 121–3.
[65] Editorial Note, 'The Butler Report' [1975] *Crim LR* 661.
[66] See the *Report on the Review of Procedures for the Discharge and Supervision of Psychiatric Patients Subject to Special Restrictions* (The Aarvold Committee Report) (1973) Cmnd. 5191, appointed as a result of the case of discharged hospital patient Graham Young who was convicted of murder and several poisoning offences committed following his release. See further Session 1971–2 HC Debs Vol. 839 cols 1673–85.
[67] DHSS/Home Office, *Report of the Committee on Mentally Abnormal Offenders* (HMSO 1975) Cmnd. 6244.

Government in 1972 under the chairmanship of Lord Butler.[68] The terms of reference were extremely wide and essentially covered all aspects of a mentally disordered offender's passage through the criminal justice system, from his/her entrance to aftercare upon departure.

As noted by other commentators, the Committee conducted a detailed review of the law in this area and received a wealth of evidence. In April 1974, it submitted an Interim Report[69] which recommended, 'as a matter of urgency'[70] the establishment of Regional Medium Secure Units to relieve the pressure of overcrowding in the high-security Special Hospitals.[71] The Committee were both 'astonished and shocked'[72] at the level of overcrowding they found, particularly in Broadmoor where patients were literally 'living out of suitcases' with beds only '18 inches apart'! To remedy this 'yawning gap'[73] between NHS and Special Hospital provision, the Committee recommended the establishment of such units in each Regional Health Authority area. It estimated that the total number of beds required would be 2,000, catering for 'those mentally disordered persons, offenders and non-offenders alike, who do not require the degree of security offered by the special hospitals, which in any event are overcrowded, but who, nonetheless, are not suitable for treatment under the open conditions obtaining in local psychiatric hospitals'.[74] There was a clear need for such facilities as identified earlier, the courts were increasingly faced with having to impose sentences of imprisonment on mentally disordered offenders who were in need of hospital treatment, as no bed was available in a sufficiently secure facility.[75]

A 1961 Working Party had already recommended the establishment of such secure units,[76] but not one materialized due to the lack of financial provision. A later Working Party on security in NHS Psychiatric Hospitals set up by the DHSS to address the needs of those already in hospital also echoed these sentiments, calling for secure provision of at least 1,000 beds.[77] Consequently, the Interim Report recommended that the provision of secure units should be 'financed by a direct allocation of central government funds to the Regional Health Authorities for this purpose'.[78] When the Interim Report was presented to Parliament in July of that year, the Government supported its recommendations and 'shared the Committee's concern'.[79] Accordingly, it would begin to make adequate provision and Dr David Owen, then the Minister of State for

---

[68] The terms of reference were outlined in ch. 1.   [69] (1974) Cmnd. 5698.

[70] Ibid. Para. 8.   [71] Ibid. Para. 3.   [72] Ibid. Para. 4.

[73] Ibid. Para. 5.   [74] Cmnd. 6244 para. 1.4.

[75] See e.g. *R.* v. *Parker, Griffiths and Rainbird* unreported, Judgment given 21 March 1975, quoted in Cmnd. 6244 para. 1.4.

[76] Ministry of Health, *Working Party on Special Hospitals* (HMSO 1961) paras. 23–9.

[77] DHSS, *Revised Report of the Working Party on Security in NHS Psychiatric Hospitals* (DHSS 1974)—the Glancy Report.   [78] Cmnd. 5698 para. 21.

[79] Session 1974–5 HC Debs Vol. 877 cols 220–1, Written Answer by the Rt. Hon. Roy Jenkins MP, Secretary of State for the Home Department.

Social Services, immediately announced that the Government 'accept[s] the recommendation of both reports that urgent action should be taken to establish in each health region, secure psychiatric units . . . [and would] begin by providing a total of 1,000 places'.[80]

A Circular was issued to all Regional Health Authorities with guidance as to the action to be taken and a financial allocation was to be made by the Government to the regions to help translate the recommendation into practice. In the words of the then Minister of State for the Home Office, 'I think that we can state this problem very simply so far as secure units are concerned. If we do not get them, a large number of mentally ill people are going to remain in prison.'[81] The Government had therefore firmly acknowledged the need to divert and transfer mentally disordered offenders from prison and to provide alternative and additional therapeutic facilities for them.

The final report of the Committee was presented to Parliament in October 1975. As a basis, the Committee had adopted several guiding principles setting the direction which the report would take. Foremost, they believed that mentally disordered offenders should receive treatment, at the earliest possible stage and in the most appropriate setting.[82] Thus, the medical model and the diversion of the mentally ill into appropriate health care was strongly endorsed: treatment should be made available *as soon as possible . . .* [and] there should be the *greatest possible flexibility in disposal'*.[83] The Committee's recommendations followed in this vein. It agreed in principle with the system introduced by Part V of the 1959 Act with regard to mentally disordered offenders, and fully supported the humane principle that the courts should opt for care and treatment rather than (or at least as well as) punishment: 'The overriding need is to provide the best possible treatment for the patient's mental disorder and he should have full access to treatment in the best location to suit his needs. Ultimately in individual cases this must depend on clinical judgement, but *in general policy we hope humane counsels will prevail.*'[84] Clear recognition had been made of the need for increased and specialized facilities for this group of offenders in the Interim Report. The Committee expressed their disappointment that, despite the Government's commitment, so little progress had been made thus far. Clearly there were many practical difficulties to be overcome, but the Committee urged the Government of the time to make increased funding available to encourage Regional Health Authorities to make such provision.[85]

In order to resolve the problem of the increasing numbers of mentally disordered offenders in prison, much more needed to be done, however. The

[80] Session 1974–5 HC Debs Vol. 882 cols 373–4, Written Answer by Dr David Owen; see also Session 1974 HC Debs Vol. 877 cols 225–7, Written Answer by Barbara Castle.
[81] Session 1977–8 HL Debs Vol. 389 col. 1886 *per* Minister of State for Home Office. For an account of the development of regional secure units see L. Gostin, (Ed), *Secure Provision* (Tavistock 1985) and P. Bowden, 'Forensic Psychiatric Services and Regional Secure Units in England and Wales: An Overview' [1986] *Crim LR* 790–9.
[82] Cmnd. 6244 para. 1.21 (emphasis supplied).   [83] Ibid. (emphasis supplied).
[84] Ibid. para. 1.10 (emphasis supplied).   [85] Ibid. para. 1.9.

Committee urged that far greater use should be made of Social Inquiry (Pre-
Sentence) and Medical Reports, to enable the court to be in full possession of all
the relevant information about mentally disordered defendants to enable it to
make appropriate disposals. This increased co-operation and communication
would clearly better serve the interests of the mentally disordered defendants. As
already noted in Ch. 1, and identified earlier by Rollin, the 'lack of satisfactory
co-ordination of the various services involved in the treatment of the mentally
disordered offender'[86] was also perceived to be a major obstacle to the development of the 1959 Act. The Committee stressed 'the need to develop closer relationships among the various services responsible for treating the mentally
disordered offender and to improve mutual understanding'.[87]

In line with the guiding principles, throughout the report reference is continually made to the desirability of treating mentally disordered offenders in a health-
care setting: 'the treatment of mental disorder is most appropriately provided by
the health service . . . [as] . . . conditions in prisons are not favourable for the
identification and treatment of mental disorder'.[88] Accordingly, the Committee
fully endorsed the existing therapeutic disposals, but urged that far greater use
should be made of them.[89] In further recognition of the need for treatment and the
problems faced by the prison service, the Committee proposed the introduction
of several new therapeutic remand and disposal powers to enable far more
mentally disordered defendants to be given access to treatment, care, and assessment in therapeutic settings.[90] This was regarded as imperative, as

The guiding principle . . . is that [mentally disordered offenders] should be sent wherever
they can best be given the treatment they need; generally treatment by health services is
appropriate. If it is necessary to impose a prison sentence on a mentally disordered
offender *the court should not hold out to him the prospect that he will receive medical
treatment in prison*.[91]

In relation to the criminal law provisions affecting the mentally ill, the recommendations followed this treatment-based approach. With regard to the insanity
defence[92] and the unfitness plea, the need for the judge to have discretion in
disposal was paramount—'an overtly penal disposal should be excluded'[93]—
thereby allowing the mentally disordered defendant increased access to therapeutic treatment and supervision.

Such philosophy echoes the thoughts of the earlier Percy Commission by placing the main emphasis upon care and treatment, not custody and punishment. The
Committee stated that 'we have no criticism of the underlying principles [in the
1959 Act]. The provisions of the Act have enabled many such offenders to be
treated in hospital or in the community, in accordance with their medical needs,

---

86 Cmnd. 6244. para. 3.2.   87 Ibid. para. 20.1.   88 Ibid. para. 13.10.
89 Ibid. ch. 15, 16.   90 Ibid. ch. 12.
91 Ibid. para. 13.10–12 (emphasis supplied).   92 Ibid. para. 18.42–5.
93 Ibid. para. 10.27–9.

like any other patients, without undue risk to other people'.[94] The Report contained a host of recommendations in relation to every aspect of the law relating to mentally abnormal offenders, which were primarily aimed at securing treatment and access to therapeutic care.[95] From the perspective of the philosophy which underpins this book therefore, the Butler Report clearly represents a landmark development seeking to ensure that mentally disordered offenders receive the appropriate mental health care and treatment at the earliest possible opportunity.

2.3.2. General Reaction to the Butler Report

In general, the Butler Report was well received: 'There are 330 pages of solid stuff here; 140 paragraphs alone in just the summary of the recommendations. Lord Butler and his colleagues are to be congratulated,'[96] and, '[It] ... is a remarkable document, characterised by humanity ... and a pragmatic approach to the task of adopting the machinery of the law to contemporary liberal views as to the treatment of the mentally disturbed.'[97]

'Let's Implement Butler on Mental Disorder and Crime' was Edward Griew's favourable reaction.[98] Other commentators however, were not so enthusiastic. Not surprisingly, those who adopted a civil-libertarian and legalistic stance were highly sceptical of the proposals, which relied heavily upon 'the rise to power of the medical profession', so it was claimed that 'the rationalization of the State's agencies of repression continues'.[99] The Committee's approach was perceived as problematic to lawyers, who, as outlined in the previous chapter, are traditionally concerned with establishing guilt and imposing punishment upon offenders.[100]

Others, who supported the principles expounded by the Report, nevertheless acknowledged other difficulties with the proposals, in particular the massive resource implications of adopting such measures. Just as community care was hampered and the 1959 Act had foundered due to the lack of resources, fears abounded that these proposals would also suffer the same fate. An article in *The Times*[101] considered this 'humane' report, stating that the main problems would be in terms of funding as it required a 'massive injection of money' on the part of the Government in order to implement many of the recommendations. Indeed, this had been acknowledged at the time by the Government itself.[102] Brenda

---

[94] Ibid. para. 3.1.
[95] A summary of the principal recommendations can be found in [1975] *Crim LR* 673–6, and they will also be considered further in ch. 3.
[96] R. Fox, 'Butler on Sickness and Crime' [1975] *Crim LR* 683–7, 683.
[97] A. W. B. Simpson, 'The Butler Committee Report: The Legal Aspects' (1976) 16 *Brit J Criminol* 175–8, 175.   [98] [1984] 37 *CLP* 47–62.
[99] D. Ewins, 'The Butler Report' (1976) 3 *Brit J Law & Soc* 101–9, 101, 109.
[100] Simpson 'Butler: Legal Aspects', 176.
[101] 'Broadmoor and Beyond', The Times, 3 October 1975 p. 15; 'The Total Banishment of Bedlam', *The Times* 3 November 1975, p. 13.
[102] Session 1974 HC Debs Vol. 877 cols 225–7.

Hoggett, whilst welcoming the proposals to enable courts to make increased therapeutic disposals and remands, regarded them as 'costly [and] likely to founder for lack of resources'.[103] Many other commentators echoed such concerns at the time.[104] Although the Government had allocated specific funding for the Regional Secure Units, it was far from adequate and progress had been extremely slow. The implementation of these proposals, encouraging mentally disordered offenders to be diverted into health-care settings to receive treatment and proposing new powers to enable it to take place, would involve further financial commitment from the Government. Yet again, the issue of resources was evident; it is an extremely important issue which has major implications for any developments in this field. The danger of underfunding has already been identified in this and the previous chapter.

Despite such concerns, it is essential to note the significance of this Report as it represented the first major review of the law exclusively governing mentally disordered offenders. Many of its recommendations were to form the basis of the legislation which emerged eight years later, and which is still in force today.

2.3.3. Government Reaction: The 1976 Consultative Document

In 1976, the Government announced its intention to review this area of the law in the light of the Butler Committee recommendations.[105] It responded by setting up an Interdepartmental Committee in 1975 representing the DHSS, the Home Office, the Welsh Office, and the Lord Chancellor's Department to undertake the review. The Committee had before it the numerous reports that had been conducted in the preceding years, with suggestions for amendment. A year later, the Committee published a Green Paper in the form of a Consultative Document with its initial observations.[106] The Review started from the general premiss that the 1959 Act 'is generally accepted as having been enlightened and forward looking',[107] but 'there may now be room for improvement in certain respects'.[108]

The Document welcomed Butler's proposals for new therapeutic remand powers.[109] Furthermore, the police powers to remove mentally disordered offenders to a place of safety, as the Butler Committee had recommended, were 'a useful and important service in diverting mentally disordered individuals from the

---

[103] Hoggett, 'What is Wrong?' 678.

[104] See e.g. P. D. Scott, 'The Butler Committee Report: Psychiatric Aspects' (1976) 16 *Brit J Criminol* 178–81, 179; P. Bowden, 'The Review of the Mental Health Act 1959: A Medical Comment' (1979) 19 *Brit J Criminol* 263–9; J. Gunn, The Law and the Mentally Abnormal Offender in England and Wales' (1979) 2 *Int J Law & Psych* 199–214.

[105] Session 1974–5 HC Debs Vol. 884 cols 2172–3 *per* Dr D. Owen, Minister of State for the DHSS: '[we] do need to look critically at the detailed working of the Act'.

[106] DHSS Consultative Document, *A Review of the Mental Health Act 1959* (HMSO 1976).

[107] Ibid. Intro. para. 1.   [108] Ibid. Intro. para. 4.

[109] Ibid. paras. 10.7, 10.14–15, 11.17.

criminal justice system, where this seemed appropriate . . . and in securing rapid medical attention for them'.[110] The Document also clearly acknowledged the need to provide secure accommodation and better provision for the mentally disordered offender.[111]

Following its publication, a National Conference was held and comments were invited from all interested parties. And on that basis the Consultative Committee made its recommendations to Ministers, which resulted in the publication of a White Paper presented to Parliament in 1978 announcing the Government's proposals for change.

2.3.4. MIND: Further Calls for Reform[112]

In the meantime however, the voluntary mental health group MIND had become increasingly concerned with these issues, and it produced a review of the existing provisions in the mid-1970s which was extremely influential and provided further impetus for reform.

In 1975, MIND published a critical analysis of the existing legislation regarding the civil powers for mental patients, which was written by Larry Gostin.[113] It contained a comprehensive review and criticism of the existing powers in relation to the care and treatment of the mentally ill. The main aims for reform were the introduction of stricter criteria for compulsory admission to mental hospitals and the introduction of formal machinery to protect patients' rights. MIND adopted a civil-libertarian stance and such proposals clearly represented a liberalist approach.

Shortly after, in 1977, and largely in response to the Butler Committee report, MIND published the second volume of *A Human Condition*[114] which was this time concerned with the provisions in the Mental Health Act relating to mentally abnormal offenders (essentially Part V of the Act). MIND was sympathetic to the plight of the mentally abnormal in prison and, for the most part, endorsed the recommendations of the Butler Report. It is interesting to note here that liberalists such as MIND found these recommendations acceptable, even though they represented an expansion of medicalization and the intervention of the medical profession. In contrast, the first volume of Larry Gostin's analysis had campaigned vigorously for increased controls upon the intervention of the medical profession and tightened procedural safeguards for patients detained under the civil sections of the Act.[115] Perhaps this difference of approach is attributable to the fact that

[110] Ibid. para. 2.23.　　　　　　　　　　　　　　　　[111] Ibid. para. 10.15.

[112] See further Unsworth, *Politics of Legislation*, 334–43.

[113] L. Gostin, *A Human Condition*, i. *The Mental Health Act from 1959 to 1975: Observations, Analysis and Proposals for Reform* (MIND 1975); for further criticism see P. Fennell, 'The Mental Health Review Tribunal (1977) *Brit J Law & Soc* 186–219.

[114] L. Gostin, *A Human Condition*, ii. *The Law Relating to Mentally Abnormal Offenders: Observations, Analysis and Proposals for Reform* (MIND 1977).

[115] Gostin, *A Human Condition*, i.

patients detained under the criminal sections are already being processed within the criminal justice system, subject to the primary goals of arrest and conviction, which is not present in the civil cases. MIND was highly concerned for the welfare of mentally disordered prisoners, however, and may also have felt that there is no greater infringement of a mentally disordered person's civil liberties than to languish in prison without access to appropriate medical care and treatment.

MIND was clearly sympathetic to the plight of mentally ill prisoners and recognised the urgent need for increased access to health care and greater provision of resources. Accordingly, it supported the need for new disposal powers and the revision of the existing ones.[116] It had received substantial evidence of the difficulties and an alarming number of examples were provided of cases where mentally disordered offenders suffered in prison and were denied treatment because hospital beds could not be found.[117] MIND therefore lent its full support to the proposals for establishing Regional Secure Units, in the hope that they would achieve the high expectations set for them.[118]

Reinforcing its demands for reform, MIND produced a further call for action in 1978.[119] Particular attention was again drawn to the fact that the use of hospital orders under the Act was declining. This was attributed to the fact that specified hospitals often refused to accept patients, as sufficiently secure facilities were not available: 'Local hospitals may fear that they cannot provide sufficient security. . . . Alternatively, the special hospitals may feel that the problems posed by the offender are not sufficiently grave to warrant a bed in their already over-crowded institutions.'[120] Massive improvements in the services and provision for this category of offenders were therefore required.

2.4. GOVERNMENT ACTION

2.4.1. The 1978 White Paper

The resulting White Paper[121] complemented the Percy Commission and the 1959 Act in its enlightened approach to the treatment of mental illness. However, the changes that had taken place in the supervening years dictated the need for reform. Generally, the philosophy behind these proposals was the need to strengthen the rights and safeguard the liberties of the mentally disordered (in line with MIND's proposals), whilst at the same time respecting the rights of the staff and general public.

With regard to mentally disordered offenders, the White Paper firmly endorsed

[116] Gostin, ibid ii. chs. 2, 3, 4, 5.   [117] Ibid. ii. 45–56.   [118] Ibid. ii. ch. 9.
[119] L. Gostin, *Is it Fair? The Mental Health Act 1959* (MIND 1978, 3.
[120] Ibid. 32.
[121] *Review of the Mental Health Act 1959* (1978) Cmnd. 7320; see further J. Gunn, 'The Law and the Mentally Abnormal Offender', and Bowden, 'Review of Mental Health Act'.

the majority of the Butler Committee's proposals, emphasizing the need for care and treatment and that 'humane counsels' prevail. It devoted an entire chapter to a consideration of offender-patients and many of its proposals advocated increased access to health care and treatment. As Butler and MIND had both previously noted, the paper also commented upon the regrettable decline in the numbers of offenders committed to hospital; from a total of 1,440 hospital orders in 1966 to 924 in 1976: 'The Government is concerned about the difficulties this creates for the courts and prisons and for offenders whose mentally disordered condition warrants detention in hospital for treatment, but who may have to be sent to or kept in prison rather than in hospital for want of a suitable hospital place.'[122] Accordingly, it strongly supported the proposals for Regional Secure Units in line with the Butler proposals.[123] Greater use of the existing therapeutic disposal powers was also urged, hospital orders in particular,[124] and improved co-operation between the courts and hospitals was also encouraged to enable fuller use to be made of such powers.

Finally, in support of the Butler Report recommendations and further promoting diversion, the introduction of new powers to remand mentally disordered offenders to hospital and to impose interim hospital orders were proposed. They were regarded as being 'in principle, a useful addition to the criminal courts and their ability to dispose of each case in the most appropriate way'.[125]

2.4.2. The 1979 Parliamentary Debate

The proposals were considered by Parliament in 1979, in a debate in which, it has been noted, several MPs were highly sympathetic to the plight of the mentally ill. The Motion to take note of these proposals was introduced by the then Secretary of State for Social Services, Mr David Ennals. He praised the welcome changes that had taken place in public attitudes in recent years and the advances and developments in the treatment of the mentally ill: 'Gone are the whips, chains and fetters of previous centuries. Gone are the ignorance, superstition and inhumanity which could leave a patient in Bethlem chained to a wall for years. Gone too, are some of the fears and ridicule which produced labels such as "imbecile" and "lunatic".'[126] This was felt to be largely due to the introduction of the 1959 Mental Health Act and the humane principles that it expounded: 'The bed-rock upon which this Act rested was the principle that people suffering from mental disorder should, as far as possible, be treated in the same way as those suffering from physical sickness.'[127] The mentally ill were now increasingly being treated in the community, compulsion was used as little as possible, and the emphasis was on care rather than custody.[128] These principles were greatly valued, and would in no way be overturned by any proposed new legislation.

---

[122] Cmnd. 7320 para. 5.2.   [123] Ibid. para. 5.3.   [124] Ibid. para. 5.7.
[125] Ibid. para. 5.61.   [126] Session 1978–9 HC Debs Vol. 963 cols 642–755.
[127] Ibid. col. 642.   [128] Ibid. col. 643.

The debate also focused upon the plight of mentally abnormal offenders, who received the sympathy of the House. The members clearly recognized the need for the provision of secure units and improved services and provisions for mentally disordered offenders: 'It is a national scandal that we should allow ourselves to put sick people into prison rather than into hospital or secure units as we should'.[129]

Thus, the White Paper was welcomed and accepted by the House, and as soon as parliamentary time permitted, the Government intended to translate the White Paper into an amending bill. Many of the general proposals relating to the civil powers attracted criticism from civil libertarians who strongly advocated increasing and safeguarding the rights of the mentally ill. In particular, Philip Bean, in his analysis of the White Paper from a legalistic stance, stated that 'the White Paper offers no hope for those expecting radical change'.[130] As noted earlier, there is a clear difference of approach towards patients detained under the civil and criminal provisions of the Act, which has been recognized with respect to MIND's earlier calls for reform.

Temporary relief came to those who were critical of the proposals, as the Labour Government failed to translate them into an amending bill, being defeated at the General Election the following year.

2.4.3. The 1981 White Paper

Fortunately, the new Conservative Government was equally eager to enact legislation in this area and presented its proposals for legislative reform in the form of the Mental Health (Amendment) Bill and an accompanying explanatory White Paper in November 1981.[131] This White Paper stated that, in the main, the previous Government's proposals had been generally welcomed by the health and social service professionals and other bodies involved in the care of mentally disordered people.[132] This Government would therefore proceed on the same basis, giving high priority to developing services for the mentally ill and mentally handicapped. The main objectives of the legislation were to improve the safeguards for detained patients, to clarify the position of staff, and to remove any uncertainties existing in the law. With regard to mentally disordered offenders, some of the Butler Committee's proposals were to be given statutory blessing as there would be increased opportunity for and improved access to psychiatric assessment and treatment for those appearing before the courts, with the introduction of remands to hospital and interim hospital orders.[133]

Generally, the definition of mental disorder would remain unaltered and

[129] HC Debs Vol. 963. col. 693 *per* R. Kilroy-Silk MP.
[130] P. Bean, 'The Mental Health Act 1959: Rethinking an Old Problem' (1979) 6 *Brit J Law & Soc* 99–108, 100.
[131] *Reform of the Mental Health Legislation* (HMSO 1981) Cmnd. 8405.
[132] Ibid. Intro. para. 3.   [133] Ibid. paras. 49–51.

'psychopathic disorder' would be retained, as there were some psychopaths who would benefit from treatment and the new Government did not wish to deny them this opportunity.[134] The inclusion of this category is highly controversial, however, and, as outlined in the previous chapter, the role which the medical profession can play in the treatment of psychopathic disorder has been the subject of much debate. The Government acknowledged that '(t)he weight of current medical opinion is that *most* psychopaths are not likely to benefit from treatment in hospital and are for the penal system to deal with when they do commit offences'.[135] Accordingly, a 'treatability' test, in line with the 1978 White Paper proposal, was introduced,[136] so that patients suffering from psychopathic disorder or mental handicap cannot be detained in hospital 'unless there is medical evidence that medical treatment in hospital is likely to alleviate or prevent a deterioration in the offender's condition'.[137] The Government was to an extent motivated by humanitarian concerns in recommending the term's inclusion as it clearly felt that the small proportion of those who might benefit from treatment should not be denied access to it under the Act. From the perspective of the medical model, the continued inclusion of psychopathic disorder is a welcome development, ensuring that at least those in need of and who may benefit from care and treatment are given access to it. Finally, the criteria for hospital orders and transfers by the Home Secretary would be tightened[138] and the restriction order would be reworded as the Butler Committee proposed.[139]

Again, the humane philosophies expounded by the 1959 Act would be preserved, as the Bill was 'not a new statement or philosophy of the law, but a set of proposals to update and improve the existing Act which had stood the test of time'.[140]

The White Paper also announced that the Government of the day intended to introduce a further bill to consolidate the law once this Bill had received the Royal Assent.[141]

2.5. THE MENTAL HEALTH (AMENDMENT) ACT 1982

The Bill was introduced in the House of Lords in November 1981,[142] but did not receive the Royal Assent until almost a year later. The debates in both Houses were lengthy: 'the year long passage of the new Bill through Parliament was a

---

[134] Ibid. para. 12: 'there are some persons suffering from psychopathic disorder who can be helped by detention in hospital'. [135] Ibid. (emphasis supplied).

[136] Cmnd. 8405 paras. 12–20. [137] Ibid. para. 47.

[138] Ibid. Including shorter periods of detention, greater access to the Mental Health Review Tribunal and the presence of the Mental Health Act Commission watchdog body.

[139] So that it could now only be ordered when the judge felt it necessary to 'protect the public from serious harm'.

[140] R. Bluglass, *A Guide to the Mental Health Act 1983* (Churchill Livingstone 1983), 7.

[141] Cmnd. 8405 para. 54. [142] Session 1981–2 HL Debs Vol. 425 col. 106.

fascinating and at times exciting spectacle. In the debates, battle was joined between those who wished to dispense with constraints wholesale and those whose pragmatic sense gave voice to the dangers of doing so.'[143] Again, it was stated during the Bill's passage through the House of Lords that it sought to promote the humane principles which had been expounded in the 1959 Act: 'The Mental Health Act 1959 was a landmark in the development of care for the mentally disordered. It established many important principles. ... I doubt whether anyone would challenge those principles today, the Bill seeks to amend the 1959 Act but it does not challenge those principles. On the contrary, it seeks to ensure that they are more perfectly implemented.'[144]

The Bill moved to the House of Commons where it was introduced by the Secretary of State for Social Services, who echoed the sentiments which had been expressed earlier in the House of Lords:

'The government are deeply committed to the Bill. It is important that we should give as much consideration to mental health as to physical health. It is also important that we should continue to push forward with the work that was at the heart of the 1959 Act—that those suffering from mental disorder of whatever kind should not be seen as isolated and different, but should have their disability accepted as on a par with the other disabilities of life.'[145]

The humane philosophies and principles of the 1959 Act were therefore still supported, but it was now necessary to modify some of the detailed provisions. Given the importance and complexity of the issues and the 'many difficult and technical aspects to explore',[146] the Bill was dealt with by a Special Standing Committee procedure which enabled a small number of members to investigate each new clause in detail and assess the overall need for the Bill at the Committee stage of its passage. In terms of its detailed provisions, many of the amendments were based upon the recommendations of MIND and the Butler Committee. In particular, great importance was placed upon the interim hospital orders and remands to hospital as mechanisms for ensuring that mentally disordered offenders received appropriate medical care. During the Parliamentary debates they were described as being 'two of the most important and beneficial provisions in this Bill':[147] 'The objective . . . for the courts is to increase the opportunities for mentally disordered persons to be dealt with in hospital rather than in prison whenever appropriate and to facilitate the process in finding hospital places for them'.[148] Thus, the need to ensure that mentally disordered offenders receive appropriate medical care was affirmed and their 'diversion' from the criminal justice system was further ensured and facilitated.

---

[143] K. Rawnsley, Foreword in Bluglass, *Guide*.
[144] Session 1981–2 HL Debs Vol. 425 col. 933.
[145] Session 1981–2 HC Debs Vol. 20 cols 688–768, 694 *per* Mr Norman Fowler.
[146] Ibid. col. 707; see also Session 1981–2 HC Debs Vol. 20 col. 726.
[147] Session 1981–2 HL Debs Vol. 425 col. 935.
[148] Session 1981–2 Vol. XI col. 8 Special Standing Committee Mental Health (Amendment) Bill (22 Apr. 1982).

The Committee took evidence from experts and interested organisations which included MIND, MENCAP, the Royal College of Psychiatrists, the Royal College of Nursing, the British Association of Social Workers, and the National Association of Probation Officers.[149] At this stage also, the Committee had to consider adding an important amendment to the powers of the Mental Health Review Tribunals. This was a direct result of a decision by the European Court of Human Rights that Britain was in contravention of Article 5 of the European Convention on Human Rights. The decision in the case of *X* v. *UK*[150] in 1981 had prompted the Government to bring the mental health legislation into conformity with the convention. Article 5(4) of the Convention (to which the United Kingdom is a signatory) provides that 'Everyone who is deprived of his liberty by arrest or detention shall be entitled to take proceedings by which the lawfulness of his detention shall be decided speedily by a court and his release ordered if the detention is not lawful.'

The case involved a conditionally discharged Broadmoor patient who was recalled. He challenged the grounds for his recall and one of his objections was that in England there was no procedure that would allow the lawfulness of his detention in hospital to be reviewed by a court. Although the Mental Health Review Tribunal existed to review other compulsorily detained patients, it had no powers to review the continued detention of restricted patients. The European Court held that although X was legally detained, a restricted patient should be entitled to a periodic review of his case by a court and should be released if his continued detention was not justified because he no longer suffered from mental disorder as defined in the Act. Accordingly, the Bill was amended to make provision for offenders detained under restriction orders to have their case reviewed and apply for discharge once every twelve months to the Mental Health Review Tribunal, and for those tribunals to have the power to order discharge if necessary.[151] This was a welcome addition to those who had supported MIND's campaign for improved rights for detained patients.

The Committee's recommendations were mainly responsible for the final Bill, which represented a 'compromise package'[152] and received the Royal Assent in October 1982, to take effect from the end of September 1983.[153] Thus, the Mental Health (Amendment) Act took its place on the statute books 'touch[ing] upon principles of profound importance affecting the liberties and rights of those of our fellow citizens who are, least able to look after themselves'.[154] The final step

---

[149] Ibid. cols 63–140, 143–207 (27, 29 Apr. 1982).   [150] (1982) 4 EHRR 188.

[151] For further commentary see L. Gostin, 'Human Rights, Judicial Review and the Mentally Disordered Offender' [1982] *Crim LR* 779–93; N. Walker, N. 'X v. The UK' (1982) 22 *Brit J Criminol* 315–17.   [152] Rawnsley, Foreword in Bluglass, *Guide*.

[153] See M. J. Gunn, 'The Mental Health (Amendment) Act 1982' (1983) 46 *MLR* 318–29 and L. Gostin, 'Review of the Mental Health (Amendment) Act' (1982) 132 *NLJ* 1127–32, 1151–55, 1199–203 for a review of the Act.

[154] Session 1981–2 HL Debs Vol. 425 col. 934 *per* Lord Elton, Under-Secretary of State introducing the Bill.

forward was taken when the Mental Health Act was enacted to consolidate the law in 1983.[155]

2.6. THE MENTAL HEALTH ACT 1983

The Act received the Royal Assent in May 1983. Generally, it narrowed the definition of mental disorder. Section 1(2) of the Act replaced the division of mental handicap into subnormality and severe subnormality, and new concepts of mental impairment and severe mental impairment were introduced. Behavioural and treatability tests were introduced to certain subcategories which placed further restrictions on the use of compulsory powers.[156]

The requirements regarding compulsory admission and discharge are now 'procedurally weighted in favour of the patient's liberty'.[157] There are specific personnel, such as the 'approved social worker' to deal exclusively with the mentally ill and the opportunities for tribunal review are increased. The duration of the periods of detention for admission for treatment is reduced. The final major development 'which substantially bolsters legal safeguards'[158] was the introduction of the new statutory body to monitor, report on, and participate in the procedures designed to protect and strengthen patients' rights—the Mental Health Act Commission. In general, therefore, the Act can be said to reflect a 'reassertion of legalism', providing 'a clear legal framework which gives detained patients more rights than they have ever had before in this country'.[159]

Whilst reaffirming legalism by tightening admission criteria, however, the Act does also, to a certain extent, recognise the importance of the medical profession and a humane approach. This has been shown in Ch. 1 in the application of the definition of mental disorder as being, in practice, largely a matter for clinical judgement. The Act also reinforced the humane philosophy advocated by the Butler Committee and increased the opportunities for access to medical care, wherever possible, for the majority of mentally disordered offenders. These remand and disposal powers will be considered in depth in the following chapter.

This is essentially the legislative framework as it stands today which 'leaves the essential structures of mental health provision very much intact'.[160] At the time of its inception, it was regarded by some as 'an event in the history of mental health care of the greatest importance' which was hoped to 'have far-reaching effects on the standards of care and treatment in the decade ahead'.[161]

---

[155] Session 1982–3 HL Debs Vol. 437 col. 1533.
[156] See further L. Gostin, *Mental Health Services: Law and Practice* (Shaw & Sons 1986) para. 1.11.1–1.11.3.   [157] Unsworth, *Politics of Legislation*, 319.   [158] Ibid. 322.
[159] Session 1981–2 HL Debs Vol. 427 col. 1434 *per* Lord Elton.
[160] Unsworth, *Politics of Legislation*, 332.   [161] Bluglass, *Guide*, Preface.

2.7. REACTION TO THE NEW ACT

Not surprisingly, the Prison Service was wholehearted in its support for the new legislation. In 1983, the Chief Inspector of Prisons had expressed concern about the continued detention of the mentally ill in prison, 'when what they need is treatment in an appropriate psychiatric institution. Prison Medical Officers have frequently told us that managing the mentally ill offenders was the hardest part of their duties and it was hoped that the new Act would do something to remedy the situation.'[162]

Such were the hopes entertained for the new powers and Part III of the Act in general. However, this would succeed only if the requisite resources were made available, in order fully to implement these provisions. 'It is essential that the Government face the question of resources,' asserted one MP in Parliament during the passage of the amending 1982 Act.[163] As shown earlier, many of the failures of the 1959 Act were attributed to the lack of resources, and facilities. Although the Conservative Government allocated specific funding to finance the Regional Secure Unit programme, it had initially offered only half the resources recommended by Butler. In the following chapter it will be seen whether the 1983 Act has succeeded in remedying the situation and justified the high hopes entertained for it, or whether once again the wheel has come full circle and mentally disordered offenders are still in the same position—incarcerated in prison and being denied access to appropriate health care.

2.8. CONCLUSION

This chapter has shown how the services and provisions relating to mentally disordered offenders have developed during the last fifty years. Clearly evident is the growth of a humane and enlightened approach, the emergence of psychiatry as a respected discipline, and a comprehensive mental health service. Although it has not been considered here in detail, it must be noted that the criminal law has also expanded in this area further to accommodate mentally ill defendants who may be legally insane, or unfit to plead, or whose responsibility is diminished, to ensure access to health care.[164] As the century has progressed, far more emphasis has been placed upon the existence and effects of mental disorder and the need to ensure and increase access to therapeutic care and treatment for the mentally disordered offender. Nigel Walker has described this process as the 'utilitarian revolution' motivated by practical and humanitarian considerations, which

---

[162] *Report of HM Chief Inspector of Prisons*, Session 1983–4 HC 618 para. 2.19.
[163] Session 1981–2 HC Debs Vol. 20 col. 699.
[164] See further Walker, *Crime and Insanity*, i.

dictated the need for change.[165] The observations of the Butler Committee and the Prison Commissioners have clearly served to emphasize that the notion of diverting mentally disordered offenders out of the criminal justice and penal system is not a new and revolutionary idea, but has been a necessary and desirable goal for many decades.

Overall, however, a number of themes have emerged which have influenced the shape and success of the developments and which will also undoubtedly influence the future direction and, in particular, the implementation of an explicit diversion policy. Firstly, the fluctuating patterns in the care and management of the mentally ill generally over the years can be seen. As noted by Gostin: 'there is perhaps no other body of law which has undergone as many fundamental changes in approach and philosophy as mental health law'.[166] This is particularly so with regard to the treatment of the mentally ill and mental health law in general where the tension between those who campaign for increased legal rights and those who campaign for increased medical intervention has been felt, and the conflict between law and psychiatry has been evident, particularly as psychiatry gained increasing prominence and credibility in the late twentieth century with the advent of the 1950s drugs revolution, an open-door policy, and the trend towards community care. Increasing confidence has been placed in the ability of the medical profession to alleviate the symptoms of, and provide support for, the mentally ill. The tension can be seen particularly in the debates which preceded the 1959 and 1982 Acts, where those campaigning for increased patients' rights strongly opposed those in support of medical discretion and unfettered access to therapeutic care. A strong lobby from the Royal College of Psychiatrists during the 1982 debates and at the Special Standing Committee stage ensured that the 1983 Act did not become too legalistic, thus the conflict between opposing professions and differing attitudes and approaches towards mental illness has influenced the developments greatly.

Despite such flux, which has taken place generally in the sphere of mental health, a general theme is evident with regard to the treatment of mentally disordered offenders. The need to ensure and secure access to appropriate medical care and to guard against imprisonment has been restated on innumerable occasions throughout the past century. And the developments that have taken place which relate to mentally disordered offenders have all emphasised the importance of diverting them out of prison and into therapeutic care. Several aspects of the present legislation support this approach, particularly the new powers to remand to hospital and the interim hospital orders recommended by the Butler Committee

---

[165] Walker and McCabe, *Crime and Insanity*, ii. 243

[166] L. Gostin, 'The Ideology of Entitlement' in P. Bean (ed) *Mental Illness Changes and Trends* (John Wiley 1983) p. 28; see also P. Alldridge, 'Hospitals, Madhouses and Asylums: Cycles in the Care of the Insane' (1979) 134 *Brit J Psych* 321–34 and H. Prins, 'The Diversion of the Mentally Disordered: Some Problems for Criminal Justice, Penology and Health Care' (1992) 3 *J For Psych* 431–43.

which increase the opportunities of access to medical care. With regard to mentally abnormal offenders, the Act has at least succeeded in principle to perpetuate the medical model by introducing flexible powers to enable the courts to make therapeutic disposals. Some other elements of the 1983 Act, however, have injected a degree of legalism into the system,[167] largely due to the concerns expressed by the anti-psychiatry and civil-libertarian camps. But this is not necessarily the approach which is in the best interests of the offender-patient.[168]

Finally, it is crucial to note that many of the failures of the past in relation to mentally disordered offenders are attributed to the lack of communication and co-operation amongst the agencies concerned and the clear lack of resources and facilities for this group of offenders. These are problems which have constantly dogged the treatment of such offenders. And this is particularly evident in the implementation of the 1959 therapeutic powers and the development of community and hospital facilities, as outlined earlier and noted by several commentators and specifically the Butler Committee report. As Lord Mustill has stated, what is urgently required is to 'make available more human, physical and financial resources'.[169]

The difficulties in achieving inter-agency collaboration and the lack of resources and facilities are fundamental issues that significantly affect the developments in this area. The lessons that have been learnt in the past enable more to be understood about making a success of the future. Accordingly, these problems must be addressed so that future developments do not suffer the same fate. These issues will therefore form an important element in the consideration of the existing provisions and the introduction and evaluation of the explicit diversion policy in Part II. The remainder of Part I will outline the existing provisions in this area which enable mentally ill offenders to be given access to appropriate care and assess whether the Mental Health Act 1983 has been successful in providing such access, or whether it has suffered the same fate as some of its predecessors.

---

[167] F. M. Martin, *Between the Acts: Community Mental Health Services 1959–1983* (Nuffield Provincial Hospitals Trust 1984), 61.

[168] See e.g. Prins, 'Diversion'.

[169] Lord Mustill, 'The Mentally Disordered Offender: A Call for Thought' (1992) 3 *KCLJ* 1–28, 10–11.

3

Diversion under the Mental Health Act 1983 and Related Provisions

3.1. INTRODUCTION

This chapter will consider the various ways with which a mentally disordered offender comes into contact with the criminal justice system and the legal powers that are in existence at its various stages to divert him/her into therapeutic care. These are principally contained in the Mental Health Act 1983 and a few related provisions[1] and the operation and implementation of these powers throughout the 1980s will be outlined. Consideration will also be given here to the relevant legal powers under under the Crime (Sentences) Act 1997. The Act was introduced subsequently to the introduction of an explicit diversion policy in 1990; however, it does introduce a new disposal power—the hospital direction—in relation to some mentally disordered offenders, and it is therefore significant as it facilitates access to hospital care.

It will be shown that the 1983 Act 'embodies the principle of *treatment* of mentally disordered offenders *instead of punishment*',[2] and so the intention was to ensure that those in need of care and treatment should receive it from the health and social services. However, as the 1980s progressed, it became clear that the powers were not being effectively nor adequately implemented—too few mentally disordered offenders were being routed to psychiatric care and too many were finding their way into prison. This prompted the 1979–97 Conservative Government to take action by introducing an explicit diversion policy at the beginning of the 1990s. The problems that exist with these provisions will therefore be fully explored, thereby allowing consideration in succeeding chapters of whether the introduction of this formal diversion policy and assessment and diversion schemes, particularly in West Yorkshire, has provided a solution to the deficiencies and succeeded in ensuring access to therapeutic care, where, in the past, these powers have sadly failed.

---

[1] See Appendix A for an outline of the main provisions. For further details on the operation and application of these powers see B. Hoggett, *Mental Health Law* (Sweet & Maxwell 1996) ch. 5 and L. Gostin, *Mental Health Services: Law and Practice* (Shaw & Sons 1986), both of which have formed a basis for the outline of the legal provisions in this chapter.

[2] *Review of Health and Social Services for Mentally Disordered Offenders and Others Requiring Similar Services* (Reed Report) (1992) Cm. 2088, Report of the Hospital Advisory Group para. 6.1 (emphasis supplied).

3.2. ARREST

The first point of contact between the criminal justice system and a mentally disordered person is often the police, who may be called to intervene in incidents involving him/her or come into direct contact with him/her themselves. Historically, managing the mentally ill in the community has been a large part of police work.[3] So, the first stage at which a mentally disordered offender may be diverted into therapeutic care is at the point of arrest, and the powers of the police at this initial stage will be considered.

3.2.1. Police Powers

The police have been given a number of specific powers under legislation, principally under the Mental Health Act 1983 and its supplemental revised Code of Practice.[4] In addition, the Police and Criminal Evidence Act (PACE) 1984 and its accompanying Code of Practice also provide certain guidelines and safeguards for the mentally disordered offender when being dealt with by the police and particularly whilst being detained in police custody. These provisions are important to consider, as they provide the police with powers to take mentally ill people to hospital, or, should they be taken into custody, the police can decide whether or not to initiate a prosecution. Accordingly, these powers and the opportunities for diversion created by them will be discussed below.

3.2.1.1. Section 136

3.2.1.1.1. The Provisions

Section 136 of the Mental Health Act 1983 gives the police power to remove a mentally disordered person found in a public place to a place of safety: 'if a constable finds, in a place to which the public have access, a person who appears to him to be suffering from mental disorder and to be in immediate need of care/control; the constable may remove that person to a place of safety'.[5] The constable must think it necessary to do so in the interests of the person concerned or for the protection of the public. A person removed to a place of safety may be detained there for a period no longer than 72 hours for the purpose of enabling

---

[3] L. A. Teplin and N. S. Pruett, 'Police as Streetcorner Psychiatrist: Managing the Mentally Ill' (1992) 15 *Int J Law & Psych* 139–56.

[4] Published by the DoH and the Welsh Office pursuant to s. 118 of the Mental Health Act 1983 (HMSO 1999).

[5] Mental Health Act 1983 s. 136(1); note however the powers of the police to arrest without warrant for offences to protect 'vulnerable' persons under s. 25(3)(e) of PACE 1984 which is an additional power to the arrest powers presented under mental health legislation, Schedule 2 PACE 1984; see further V. Bevan & K. Lidstone, *The Investigation of Crime: A Guide to Police Powers* (Butterworths 1991) para. 5.30.

him/her to be examined by a registered medical practitioner and to be interviewed by an 'approved social worker',[6] and of making any necessary arrangements for that person's treatment and care.[7]

The person need not actually *be* mentally disordered, but must *appear* to the police constable to be disordered. The police are effectively given a wide discretionary power under this section. Evidence submitted to the Butler Committee indicated that people dealt with under this section tend to come to the attention of the police due to their 'threatening or bizarre behaviour',[8] which is often potentially indicative of some form of mental disorder/disturbance. This would include behaviour such as 'wandering; self-neglect; suicidal threats or attempts; verbal and physical aggression; expressions of gross delusions; sexual misbehaviour and traffic disturbances'.[9] So, the section is usually invoked 'where the police have to deal with a person who is causing some disturbance or concern'.[10] It is also vital to note here that the police need not suspect that any offence has been committed. However, in practice, it has been suggested that it is possible that the behaviour in question could amount to some form of public order offence, such as 'disorderly conduct' under s. 5 of the Public Order Act 1986,[11] or even a 'breach of the peace' for which the police may invoke their common-law power of arrest.[12] The essential requirement for the application of this power is that a person must be found in 'a place to which the public have access'[13]. Much discussion has arisen over the precise meaning and application of these terms, suffice it to say that it includes public highways and places where the public normally come and go, and extends also to places where members of the public are admitted upon payment.[14]

Having been found in a public place, the mentally disordered person may be removed to a 'place of safety'. This is defined in s. 135(6) and includes both a hospital and a police station, as well as local authority residential accommodation of all types, residential/nursing homes for the mentally disordered, and any other suitable place the occupier of which is willing temporarily to receive the patient.

---

[6] As defined in s. 145(1) of the Mental Health Act 1983. See also s. 114.
[7] s. 136(2). [8] Butler Committee Report Cmnd. 6244 para. 9.11.
[9] Ibid. [10] Ibid. para. 9.1.
[11] This power is capable of applying to a wide variety of conduct, such as public nuisance or behaviour likely to cause harassment, alarm, or distress. Thus it is conceivable that it could apply to a mentally disordered person displaying bizarre or eccentric behaviour in the street. See further R. Card, *Public Order: The New Law* (Butterworths 1987), 49.
[12] 'A constable has power at common law to arrest without warrant any person whom he sees breaking the peace or who so conducts himself that he causes a breach of the peace to be reasonably apprehended' (L. H. Leigh, *Police Powers in England and Wales* (Butterworths 1985), 184; see also Cmnd. 6244 para. 9.3.
[13] A concept which has long been used under public order legislation; see *R.* v *Wellard* (1884) 14 QB 63 *per* Grove J, 'a public place is one where the public go, no matter whether they have a right to go or not'. See also *Cawley v Foot* [1976] 3 All ER 743 for a definition under the Public Order Act 1936 s. 9(1) and the Criminal Justice Act 1972 s. 33, and see now ss. 4 and 16(b) of the Public Order Act 1986. See further P. Thornton, *Public Order Law* (Financial Training Publication 1987), 136.
[14] See further Hoggett, *Mental Health Law*, 97–103.

The revised Code of Practice accompanying the Mental Health Act advises that the 'identification of preferred places of safety is a matter for local agreement', but that regard should be had to the impact of different types of places of safety upon the person held.[15] Moreover, the Code of Practice accompanying PACE expressly states that if s. 136 is used, it is imperative that the person concerned be assessed as soon as possible.[16]

Once at the place of safety, no medical treatment can be imposed without the patient's consent.[17] When the patient has been seen and the necessary arrangements have been made, the authority for detention under s. 136 expires,[18] even if the 72-hour period has not yet expired. Thus, if a person has been examined and interviewed, but no immediate arrangements are being made for his/her treatment and care, the person cannot be detained further, and must simply be let out onto the streets once more. It is therefore vital that all concerned co-operate and act promptly. In particular, the social worker and doctor should consider the range of alternatives to ensure that the most appropriate treatment is given as soon as possible. Should compulsory admission to a mental institution or hospital be necessary for the welfare of the patient, they may apply to do so under Part II of the Act, in order that the desired care and treatment is provided.[19]

3.2.1.1.2. Commentary

The use of s. 136 has been criticized by some commentators.[20] Statistics show that it is rarely used outside London, its greatest use being in the four London Metropolitan regions.[21] There are therefore substantial regional variations in its application.[22] The Butler Committee received evidence of such inconsistency[23] and the earlier Percy Commission had already identified this anomaly and had recommended that a safeguard should be introduced—the police should only use the power where they had a power of arrest[24]—to insure against inconsistent use and undoubtedly to introduce an element of proportionality and due process into the procedure.

These regional variations, however, could be accounted for by the fact that there are more homeless and obviously disordered people wandering the streets and public places in the Metropolis. Other provincial cities and less-populated areas of the country do not encounter such large numbers of homeless people, therefore the problem is not as acute. Consequently, there is a greater demand for

---

[15] Para. 10.5.   [16] See PACE 1984 Code C para. 3.10.
[17] Mental Health Act 1983 s. 56(1)(b).
[18] DoH/Welsh Office *Mental Health Act 1983 Revised Code of Practice* (HMSO 1999), para. 10.8.   [19] Ibid. para. 10.17–18.
[20] See e.g. P. Bean, *Mental Disorder and Legal Control* (Cambridge University Press 1986) ch. 4.   [21] See *Revolving Doors* (NACRO 1992), 12.
[22] Recent Mental Health Act Commission Reports have also expressed similar concerns about the regional variations. See e.g. MHAC, *Sixth Biennial Report 1993–1995* (HMSO 1996), 77; MHAC, *Seventh Biennial Report 1995–1997* (HMSO, 1997) para. 3.3.
[23] Cmnd. 6244 para. 9.8.   [24] Cmd. 169 para. 412.

this provision in London, in order to deal appropriately with these people. Much research has been conducted which seems to support this proposition, in particular the link between homelessness, crime, and mental disorder has been widely documented.[25] Research on behalf of the Home Office found that there is a 'large visible homeless population based in the City of Westminster', of which 'at least one third suffer from mental illness'.[26] And a study conducted during 1985–8 concluded that 'many psychiatrically very ill people are living like feral children in the forest of the city, scavenging for garbage and subsisting on charitable handouts'.[27]

In addition to this expanding homeless population, another possible explanation for the regional variation is that London may have the advantage of a greater range of facilities—emergency assessment units, hospitals, and police stations—from which to make psychiatric referrals. Thus the use of s. 136 can be facilitated.

There have also been strong representations that the period of detention should be reduced from 72 to 24 hours, thus emphasising the fact that it is only intended to be used in cases of crisis and emergency. This was submitted to the Butler Committee by the National Council for Civil Liberties, but they did not agree and felt that there was no evidence that abuse of the section took place in terms of unnecessarily long periods of detention at police stations. Furthermore, 'the law must make some allowance for exceptional difficulties, such as might arise, for example, in remote areas or at holiday periods'.[28]

Evidence suggests that many of the criticisms and fears are largely unfounded. Research conducted in 1987 indicates that there is, in practice, no obvious abuse of the section by the police.[29] Walker and McCabe observed that 'almost any behaviour of a markedly abnormal kind in a public place can be made the basis of some sort of charge'.[30] Thus, the police could almost always arrest for a crime instead. In addition, they found that almost all the patients admitted in this way had been in hospital before. So it would seem that s. 136 provides the police with the opportunity to divert offenders with mental health problems into appropriate care. This is reinforced by the fact that another concern often expressed about the lack of training given to police officers to make such mental health judgements has also been challenged by research findings. In addition to what Walker and McCabe found indicating previous hospitalisation of s. 136 cases, most such

[25] NACRO, *Revolving Doors*, esp. p. 9.

[26] P. Joseph, *Psychiatric Assessment at the Magistrates' Court* (Home Office 1992), 4.

[27] M. Weller *et al.,* 'Psychosis and Destitution at Christmas: 1985–88' (1989) 2 *The Lancet* 1509–11, 1511. See also NACRO, *The Imprisonment of Mentally Disturbed Offenders* (NACRO Briefing Dec. 1990), 6, and A. M. C. A. Ford, 'Homelessness and Persistent Petty Offenders: The Impact of Intervention and its Implications for Punishment in the Community' (unpublished Ph.D. Thesis, Leeds University 1992), p. 38: 'for some people, the path to homelessness is paved with psychiatric ills'.   [28] Cmnd. 6244 para. 9.13.

[29] A. Rogers and A. Faulkner, *A Place of Safety* (MIND 1987).

[30] Walker and McCabe, *Crime and Insanity,* ii. 258; Appendix A. The research was conducted into the operation of this power under the 1959 Act.

offenders were also considered to be mentally ill by psychiatrists, thereby confirming police suspicions.[31] Research conducted in 1972 states that the police were in fact efficient at recognizing people in need of psychiatric care and there was no evidence to suggest that they misused such powers.[32] The most recent extensive research in this area conducted by MIND simply echoes this fact: 'The findings show that according to the psychiatrists' diagnoses the police were generally referring people considered to be mentally disturbed.'[33] Nearly 80 per cent of the referrals had a previous psychiatric history.[34] So, despite the criticism, 'research and experience have proved the need for these powers',[35] and in general, the research suggests that the police are making accurate decisions as to when to implement the section. At the end of the day, it is often the best way of ensuring that a disordered person receives medical attention at the earliest stage possible. In many instances it also avoids prosecution, as a s. 136 case will rarely be prosecuted.[36] This clearly enables diversion to take place and facilitates access to psychiatric care, and evidence indicates that the police themselves value this power greatly in terms of dealing with the mentally ill.[37] In the light of the type of people identified by the police as s. 136 cases, it 'acts as a valuable "back-up" for those patients who would otherwise fail to benefit from the Mental Health Act'.[38]

The Butler Committee were in wholehearted support of this particular power; receiving a wealth of evidence to that effect they recommended that 'These arrangements should continue to be used to the maximum to ensure that as many as possible of the mentally disordered offenders within the scope of the provision are *referred at the outset to the treatment agencies, without the need to bring them*

---

[31] See further Cmnd. 6244 para. 9.10.

[32] M. J. Kelleher and J. R. M. Copeland, 'Compulsory Psychiatric Admissions by the Police: A Study of the Use of Section 136' (1972) 12 *Med, Sci & Law* 220–4.

[33] Rogers and Faulkner, *Place of Safety*, 41. See also T. Fahy, 'The Police as a Referral Agency for Psychiatric Emergencies: A Review' (1989) 29 *Med, Sci & Law* 315–22.

[34] Rogers and Faulkner, *Place of Safety*, 21; this is confirmed by the second stage of this research—P. Bean *et al.*, *Out of Harm's Way* (MIND 1991), 102: 'The police tend to make common sense, behaviourally based diagnoses of mental disorder.' Philip Bean has further reinforced this view in his other research—Bean, *Mental Disorder*, 60; see also K. Cherrett, 'The Last Resort' (1994) *Police Review*, 14 October pp. 16–17: 'The very nature of police work requires patrolling officers to be ready for almost anything. They become adept at recognizing the bizarre behaviour often symptomatic of mental illness.'

[35] B. Andoh, 'The Job that Nobody Wants' (1994) *Police Review*, 4 March, pp. 23–4.

[36] N. Walker, *Sentencing: Theory, Law and Practice* (Butterworths 1985) para. 21.66–7; Cmnd. 6244 para. 9.15.

[37] Comments of Insp. Ian Blair presenting a paper at a conference on Implementing Inter-Agency Initiatives held at the LSE in Sept. 1992; see further D. Tonak, 'Mentally Disordered Offenders' (1993) 157 *JP* 332–3; see also A. C. P. Sims and R. C. Symonds, 'Psychiatric Referrals from the Police' (1975) 127 *Brit J Psych* 171–8, who found that there had been an increase in emergency referrals over a 10-year period in Birmingham due to a greater willingness of the police to be involved; see also evidence to the Butler Committee, Cmnd. 6244 para. 9.7.

[38] A. S. E. Mokhtar and P. Hogbin, 'Police May Underuse Section 136' (1993) 33 *Med, Sci & Law* 188–96, 195.

before the courts.'[39] Clearly, therefore, this general satisfaction with the police reinforces the view that identification and diversion can operate successfully at this early stage in the criminal justice process.

In order to achieve this, however, much more efficient use must be made of the powers. Official statistics reveal that throughout the 1980s there was a significant decline in the number of s. 136 admissions to NHS facilities. In 1984, a total of 1,959 admissions took place under s. 136, and by 1989/90, this figure had almost halved to 1,032 admissions.[40] This was extremely worrying because, as the evidence above has indicated, the section provides a valuable route into psychiatric care for disordered individuals. A number of practical problems have been identified which may have hampered the use of the section.

It has been found that, in some cases, hospitals are reluctant to admit patients under this procedure, as the people may appear very disturbed, sometimes violent, and the incident often occurs in the middle of the night. Also, difficulty may lie in the police negotiation with the hospital owing to unfamiliarity with hospital boundaries and catchment areas.[41] These practical problems associated with s. 136 were also identified by the second stage of MIND's research. Notably, the study showed the extremely poor relations which often exist between the police and the social and psychiatric services;[42] the crux of the difficulties in obtaining appropriate assessments and in arranging conveyance to hospital as a place of safety appears to be the lack of communication and co-operation between the police and local health and social services. If such obstacles were overcome, even more effective use could be made of this section. This has recently been recognized by the Mental Health Act Commission, which noted that improvements have been made in recent years, but that there is much more to be done in terms of improving liaison, standardizing documentation, and ensuring that police cells are not the designated place of safety.[43]

An increase in training for the police in this area could also help, so that they become more familiar and conversant with the power. It would undoubtedly go some way to allaying the fears and scepticism of the other agencies, causing them to be more willing to co-operate with the police when making referrals. Indeed, this is seen as necessary by the police themselves.[44] Positive action has been taken recently by the police in recognition of their important role as a contact agency with the mentally ill. A new training video has been devised and circulated to every police force in England and Wales. The video is designed to promote a better understanding of mental illness and the issues involved, and has

[39] Cmnd. 6244 para. 9.12 (emphasis supplied).

[40] *In-patients Formally Detained in Hospitals under the Mental Health Act 1983 and Other Legislation, England: 1984–1989/90,* DoH Statistical Bulletin 2(7)92 p. 13.

[41] Fahy, 'Police as Referral Agency'; See also Cmnd. 6244 para. 9.8.

[42] Bean, *et al.* Out of Harm's Way, 154–5.

[43] MHAC, *Report 1993–5,* 77–8; MHAC, *Report 1995–7,* para. 3.3.

[44] See NACRO, *Revolving Doors,* 10; see also R. Berry, 'Police Contact with Mentally Disordered Persons in the Northumbria Force Area' (1996) 69 *Police Journal* 221–6, 226.

been incorporated into probationer training. The training package has been produced by the National Schizophrenia Fellowship in conjunction with West Midlands Police.[45] This development indicates that the police are taking their powers seriously and tackling the problem of increasing numbers of mentally ill offenders head on.[46]

The key to the future is perceived to be to encourage co-operation amongst all the relevant agencies:

there is a case to consider a wider co-operation between the social and health care facilities and the police with an aim to provide more support to the police in dealing with individuals who come to their attention and are showing evidence of mental disturbance. This is likely to provide a minimum 'safety net' for this . . . group which otherwise remains largely silent and deprived of care and treatment.[47]

Research conducted as long ago as 1972[48] concluded by suggesting that delivery of care to these difficult cases might be improved by increased 'co-operation of both the medical profession and the police' and that mentally ill offenders could be best served if they were conveyed directly to the nearest hospital where psychiatric consultation should be available on an emergency basis. This is supported by the results of a recent survey of police officers within the Gwent Constabulary, which found that the custody staff regarded the facilities within the police station as unsuitable for the detention of mentally disordered persons.[49] Research conducted by NACRO has also drawn attention to these practical difficulties. It recommended that joint training of the police with other professionals from the key mental health services would be the best way of ensuring that the police, and indeed the other health professionals too, have sufficient understanding of and access to the mental health resources and options available to them.[50] This was confirmed by research conducted by the police into the use of s. 136 in the West Midlands.[51] And it has been demonstrated, for example, in London, where police have also produced a training handbook and

---

[45] NSF/West Midlands Police, 'The Police and NSF Training Video: A Meeting of Minds' in J. Braggins and C. Martin (eds.), *Managing Risk: Achieving the Possible: ISTD's Annual Conference 1995* (ISTD 1996), 48–49; MHAC, *Report 1993–5*, 78.

[46] See C. Casey 'Forces to get Mental Illness Video' (1994) *Police Review*, 21 October, p. 8, 'New Training will Help Cope with Mentally Ill' (1994) *Police Review*, 23 December, p. 10; K. Potter 'Cries for Help' (1995) *Police Review*, 10 February, pp. 24–5.

[47] Mokhtar and Hogbin, 'Police may Underuse', 196.

[48] Kelleher and Copeland, 'Compulsory Psychiatric Admissions'.

[49] K. Cherrett, 'Policing the Mentally Ill: An Attitudinal Study of Police Contact with Mentally Disordered Persons within the Gwent Constabulary' (1995) 68 *Police Journal* 22–8; id., 'The Last Resort'; see also F. L. Lowe Ponsford and A. Begg, 'Place of Safety and S 136 at Gatwick Airport' (1996) 36 *Med, Sci & Law* 306–12.

[50] NACRO Mental Health Advisory Committee, *Diverting Mentally Disturbed Offenders from Prosecution*, Policy Paper 2 (NACRO 1993), 6–7.

[51] A. Roughton, *An Investigation into the Operation of Section 136 of the Mental Health Act 1983 in the West Midlands* (West Midlands Police 1994), 24.

video, with the assistance of local mental health professionals, designed to assist the police and others in dealing with mentally disordered offenders.[52]

To ensure that this vital provision is actively pursued, part of the answer is the establishment of clear and coherent collaborative policies. The Butler Committee noted this almost two decades ago, stressing the need for 'greater local consultation and mutual understanding'.[53] The revised Code of Practice accompanying the 1983 Act already stresses the need for the health and social services and the police to have a 'clear' local policy in order to ensure quick and competent assessment by a doctor and social worker.[54] There is, however, an urgent need to go further and provide more efficient back-up and access to supporting services.[55] This is particularly so in view of the increasing numbers of long-term mentally ill patients who have been discharged into the community under the 1979–97 Conservative Government's care in the community policy,[56] as a consequence of which police contact with such people, who typically have poor social support and unsettled accommodation, has inevitably increased,[57] as the police themselves confirm.[58] MIND's research clearly indicated that the police are a major source of referral to the psychiatric services.

The power is therefore an essential mechanism for diverting mentally disordered offenders at the outset, and its continued use, in collaboration with other agencies, to secure appropriate places of safety and care is paramount. Further, its use reinforces the need for diversion and supports the view that what mentally disordered offenders need is medical and therapeutic care and support at the earliest possible stage. As has been argued in Ch. 1, the unnecessary incarceration and imprisonment of the mentally ill can have an extremely damaging and detrimental effect upon their mental state. And so the continued and more effective use of this power by the police is vital as it is an important means of ensuring that diversion to health-care settings can take place at the earliest possible stage.[59] This can only happen however, if the police and health service professionals actively co-operate

---

[52]   Potter, 'Cries for Help', 24–5.

[53]   Cmnd. 6244 para. 9.8, 13, 14, p. 141; see also MHAC, *Report 1993–5*, para. 3.12.

[54]   *Mental Health Act 1983 Revised Code of Practice*, para. 10.1—6.

[55]   Fahy, 'Police as Referral Agency', 320; see also J. Dunn and T. Fahy 'Section 136 and the Police' (1987) 11 *Bull RC Psych* 224–5.

[56]   This is a vital aspect in relation to the treatment of mentally disordered offenders and will be considered at length in the following chapters. See esp. Ch. 4.

[57]   See the recent report of the Royal Commission on Criminal Justice—the 'Runciman Commission' (HMSO 1993) Cm. 2263 para. 84; T. Fahy, D. Berningham and J. Dunn 'Police Admissions to Psychiatric Hospitals: A Challenge to Community Psychiatry' (1987) 27 *Med, Sci & Law* 263–7; NACRO MH Adv. Com. *Community Care and Mentally Disturbed Offenders*, Policy Paper 1 (NACRO 1993), 15: 'There is widespread recognition that mentally disordered people are increasingly coming into contact with the criminal justice system.'

[58]   See 'Instant Victims' (1993) *Police Review*, 26 November, pp. 26–8; *The Guardian*, 1 June 1994, 'Picking up the Pieces'. Indeed, police contact is likely to increase even more in future if new mental health laws to ensure that the mentally ill in the community take their medication are introduced. See further Ch. 4.

[59]   See further Cherrett, 'The Last Resort', for the views of a serving police officer.

to secure appropriate care. And this, in turn, can only materialize if the relevant facilities are in place to receive and support mentally ill people, and this is a crucial issue which will be further discussed in subsequent chapters.

3.2.1.2. Section 135

3.2.1.2.1. The Provisions

Section 136 applies to cases where the patient is found in 'a place to which the public have access', but where it is necessary to gain access to a mentally disordered person in a private place the police are given powers of entry under s. 135 of the Act. This power is not concerned with diversion from prosecution, as an offence has not necessarily been committed, but it is noted here as it is another example of how the police may come into direct contact with a mentally disordered person, and also shows how they are further entrusted with his/her welfare in trying to secure some form of social or psychiatric support.

This section empowers a Justice of the Peace, on information on oath laid down by an approved social worker, to issue a warrant authorizing any constable to enter specified premises to remove (for a period of up to 72 hours) to a place of safety—which should normally be a hospital—a person who is believed to be suffering from mental disorder who has been or is being ill-treated, neglected, or not kept under proper control; or who is living alone and unable to care for him/herself. The social worker and doctor concerned will advise whether the patient should be removed to a 'place of safety' pending an application for compulsory admission in order to receive care and treatment under Part II of the Act. The section also provides for the issue of a warrant to take/retake a patient who has escaped from hospital, or is absent without leave.[60]

3.2.1.2.2. Commentary

This provision has been criticized as being too complicated. Perhaps as a result, in practice it is rarely used in comparison to the s. 136 power, and accounts for between 50 and 150 cases per year.[61] It is hardly ever used in circumstances which could lead to the prosecution of the offender and so it is essentially regarded as an interventionist measure which is a fundamental fall-back to protect the individual from hurting him/herself[62] and a means of providing the appropriate psychiatric assessment and care for a mentally disordered individual. Despite its drawbacks, it is vital in this sense and should be advocated as and when the

---

[60] See further *D'Souza v DPP* (1992) 1 WLR 1073 HL.

[61] DoH, Statistical Bulletin 2(7)92 p. 13 table 1; DoH, Stat. Bull. 1996/10 table 1. During the year 1989/90, the total number of s. 135 warrants resulting in formal admissions to NHS facilities was 82. The remaining annual figures have fluctuated between 58 in 1987/88 and 145 in 1994/95.

[62] Walker, Sentencing: Theory, Law and Practice (Butterworth 1985) para. 21.68.

need arises; the revised Code of Practice accompanying the Act stresses the consideration that must be given to it.[63]

3.2.1.3. Summary

The police have wide, express powers at this initial stage to divert mentally disordered offenders to psychiatric care. As has already been noted, they may employ their power of removal under s. 136 if an offender is found in a public place; alternatively the police may make use of their general powers of arrest which exist for particular offences,[64] or of their wider powers in the prevention of crime or a breach of the peace.[65]

These extensive powers accorded to the police serve to highlight that they are both trusted and effective agents in picking up the mentally ill and that there is considerable scope at this early stage to divert mentally disordered offenders into health-care settings, provided the police have the relevant and sufficient psychiatric assistance, co-operation, and facilities available to them at the earliest possible opportunity.

3.2.1.4. In Police Custody: Interviewing, Questioning, and Charging

3.2.1.4.1. The Provisions

Having used any one of the wide-ranging powers at the initial stage, the police must then make the important decision as to whether the matter will proceed any further by detention, questioning, or charging. This stage may play an extremely important part as it may be that during questioning a person's disordered mental condition may come to light, particularly if the mental illness is sporadic or the suspect is not obviously mentally ill.

Discussion of the powers at this stage will also highlight how vulnerable mentally disordered people are whilst in police custody,[66] which again reinforces the need to ensure that they are not unnecessarily subjected to it. The revised Code of Practice accompanying the Mental Health Act stresses the need for all professionals involved to note 'that mentally disordered people in police or prison custody may be very vulnerable. The risk of suicide or other self destructive behaviour should be of special concern'.[67] It has already been noted that police

---

[63] *Mental Health Act 1983 Revised Code of Practice*, para. 10.19.

[64] Of particular relevance here is the police power to arrest under section 25(3)(e) PACE 1984— where a child or vulnerable person is threatened with physical injury. It would seem that this is also wide enough to cover psychological damage. See further Bevan and Lidstone, *Investigation of Crime*, para. 5.30.

[65] See further D. Lanham, 'Arresting the Insane' [1974] *Crim LR* 515–28.

[66] See G. H. Gudjonsson, *The Psychology of Interrogations, Confessions and Testimony* (John Wiley 1992); and also G. H. Gudjonsson *et al.*, *Persons at Risk during Interviews in Police Custody: The Identification of Vulnerabilities*, Royal Commission on Criminal Justice (Cm. 2263) Research Study 12 (HMSO 1993), 2, 3, 9.

[67] *Mental Health Act 1983 Revised Code of Practice*, para. 3.2(a).

cells should be used only as a last resort as a 'place of safety', as research has shown that even the smallest amount of time spent in custody can have a highly damaging and detrimental effect upon a person's mental condition. Indeed, recent Home Office research has highlighted the continuing concerns about the number of deaths which occur in custody.[68] Thus, custody should be avoided at all costs thereby strengthening the need for diversion and early access to the health-care services.

This conclusion is reinforced by the fact that mentally disordered persons in custody are entitled to the same rights of psychiatric assessment and treatment as other mentally disordered citizens.[69] It is expressly provided that the overriding objective is to ensure that everyone in police custody/prison in need of mental health treatment is admitted to a suitable mental hospital.

The initial decision to prosecute lies with the police, but, in practice, they may seek the guidance of the Crown Prosecution Service. Overall, however, the police have complete discretion to initiate a prosecution.[70] Part of this decision-making process will be to interview the suspect at the police station. Indeed, it may play a vital role as the defendant's possible disordered mental state may not yet have manifested itself. Special procedures are present for the detention and questioning of people with mental disorders.[71] Under the Police and Criminal Evidence Act 1984[72] special guidelines are included in relation to the questioning of persons 'at risk', namely arrested juveniles and mentally ill and mentally handicapped people. These safeguards are vital; as research has shown that a mentally disordered person, particularly if mentally handicapped, may be vulnerable and highly suggestible, and may even incriminate him/herself where s/he is in fact not guilty of the offence s/he is charged with.[73] This is a particularly important consideration in view of the fact that the police may use persuasive and oppressive interview techniques. Furthermore, this may be exacerbated by the procedures which take place prior to the interview, such as incarceration in a police cell.

In England and Wales, the detention, treatment, and questioning of persons by police officers is governed by a Code of Practice (Code C) which lays down the guidelines for the police when detaining and questioning a suspect. Foremost it is stipulated that if an officer suspects that a person in custody is mentally disordered

[68] A. Leigh, *et al., Deaths in Police Custody: Learning the Lessons*, Police Research Series Paper 26 (Home Office 1998); see also Home Office Press Release 405/98, 'Government Calls for Action on Deaths in Police Custody', 16 October 1998.

[69] *Mental Health Act 1983 Revised Code of Practice*, para. 3.1.

[70] See Prosecution of Offences Act 1985.

[71] Laid down in the Code of Practice for the Detention, Treatment and Questioning of Persons by Police Officers issued under the Police and Criminal Evidence Act 1984 (Code C). They were essentially brought into force as a result of the recommendations of the Royal Commission on Criminal Procedure (1980) Cm. 8092, and recently revised following the recommendations of the Royal Commission on Criminal Justice Cm. 2263.   [72] Ss. 66, 67.

[73] Gudjonsson, *Psychology of Interrogations*.

or handicapped then that person shall be treated as such and this applies to persons in custody whether or not they have been arrested or if they have been brought to the police station under ss. 135 or 136 of the Mental Health Act 1983.[74] The provisions will not be considered here in great detail; however, it is important to note that these special procedures do exist as they reinforce the need to ensure that vulnerable mentally disordered offenders are protected and afforded special treatment. The most important protection at this stage is that, if the police believe a detainee to be mentally ill or handicapped, an 'appropriate adult' must be informed and asked to come to the police station to assist the suspect.[75] The presence of this independent and responsible adult is desirable in order to provide advice and assistance thereby guarding against abuse and exploitation. This category of detainee is particularly suggestible and his/her propensity for suicide and self-harm because of his/her mental state exacerbates vulnerability whilst in police custody. Accordingly, the appropriate adult is not simply required to act as an observer, but is expected to 'advise the person being questioned', which will normally require him/her to outline and explain the procedures to the detainee. Secondly, s/he is expected 'to observe whether or not the interview is being conducted properly and fairly'. And finally, s/he will be expected to 'facilitate communication with the detainee'.[76] The appropriate adult may be a relative or guardian of the suspect, a person who is experienced in dealing with the mentally disordered or handicapped, or some other responsible adult.[77] Should the police interview such a person without the presence of an 'appropriate adult', then it is regarded as a serious breach of the Code of Practice. The result may be that the police officer(s) concerned may be subject to disciplinary action. Furthermore, breaches of the Code and the defendant's mental condition are factors to be taken into account by the court in deciding whether to exclude confessions under various other sections of PACE.[78]

3.2.1.4.2. Commentary

The report of the Royal Commission on Criminal Justice (the Runciman Commission)[79] in the early 1990s paid great attention to this area of the law in its consideration of, and proposals regarding, the safeguards for suspects in police

---

[74]   Code of Practice C, para. 1.4, 10.

[75]   For further discussion and criticism of the role of the appropriate adult see T. Nemitz and P. Bean, The Use of the Appropriate Adult Scheme (A Preliminary Report)' (1994) 34 *Med, Sci & Law* 161–6; P. Fennell, 'Mentally Disordered Suspects in the Criminal Justice System' (1994) 21 *J Law & Soc* 57–71; B. Littlechild, 'Reassessing the Role of the Appropriate Adult' [1995] *Crim LR* 540–5; T. Thomas, 'The Continuing Story of the Appropriate Adult?' (1995) 34 *How J of Crim Just* 151–7; C. Palmer, 'Still Vulnerable after All These Years' [1996] *Crim LR* 633–44; J. Hodgson, 'Vulnerable Suspects and the Appropriate Adult' [1997] *Crim LR* 785–96; J. Pearse and G. Gudjonsson, 'How Appropriate are Appropriate Adults?' (1996) 7(3) *J For Psych* 570–80.

[76]   Code of Practice C, para. 11.16, Notes for Guidance, para. 9.

[77]   Ibid. para. 1.7(b).

[78]   See further Bevan and Lidstone, *Investigation of Crime*, para. 7.127; Fennell, 'Mentally Disordered Suspects'; R. v. Aspinal (1999) *The Times* 4 February.

[79]   Cm. 2263.

custody. The Commission was dissatisfied with the current arrangements and rules regarding the advice and protection afforded to mentally disordered suspects.[80] This was largely based on a research study conducted by Gisli Gudjonsson and colleagues on persons at risk during police interviews.[81] It identified more than 20 per cent of its sample group as needing an appropriate adult to be present during the police interview, while the police only made such an arrangement in 4 per cent of cases. Thus, it seems that, despite the positive findings in relation to the use of s. 136, the police called in appropriate adults in exceptional circumstances only. Consequently, the Commission felt that there should be clearer guidelines and increased training for the police concerning the need for, and suitability of, an appropriate adult. This has been reinforced by the findings of other studies into the use of appropriate adults[82] and the effectiveness of the safeguards under PACE.[83] Accordingly, the Commission recommended that there should be a comprehensive review of the role, functions, qualifications, training, and availability of appropriate adults.[84] A Working Party on Appropriate Adults was indeed established in the wake of the Royal Commission's concerns.[85] It made a host of recommendations, in particular calling for specialist and trained advisers to fulfil the role, preferably by virtue of a specialist local panel or team to be available on an on-call basis, thereby ensuring prompt and effective assistance. It also recommended that a clear definition of the role should be provided in the Code and more detailed guidance should be made routinely available. The Working Party published its report in 1995, but, unfortunately, very little action has been taken since then to implement its recommendations. However, there have been a few positive developments in this respect in recent years.

For example, a number of volunteer pilot appropriate-adult projects have been established in particular geographical areas, which have proved to be successful and effective.[86] On a national scale, the National Schizophrenia Fellowship, in conjunction with National Police Training, has produced some guidance and published a leaflet explaining the role of the appropriate adult and the rights available to vulnerable suspects.[87] The leaflet has been distributed to police stations throughout England and Wales, and was welcomed by the Government at the time.[88] This represents a small step in the right direction; however, it is

---

[80] Ibid. paras. 81–7.
[81] Gudjonsson, *et al. Persons at Risk*.
[82] Nemitz and Bean, 'Appropriate Adult Scheme'.
[83] T. Bucke and D. Brown, *In Police Custody: Police Powers and Suspects' Rights under the Revised PACE Code of Practice*, Home Office Research Study, 174 (Home Office 1997) ch. 2.
[84] Cm. 2263 Recommendations 72, 73.
[85] See further Palmer, 'Still Vulnerable'.
[86] T. Nemitz and P. Bean, 'The Effectiveness of a Volunteer Appropriate Adult Scheme, (1998) 38(3) *Med, Sci & Law* 251–7.
[87] NSF/National Police Training, *The Appropriate Adult and the Mentally Vulnerable Suspect* (NSF 1996).
[88] Home Office Press Release 165/96, 'Help for Vulnerable in Custody'.

possible that an even greater step may be taken in the foreseeable future as there is formal provision for the establishment of appropriate-adult schemes in the Crime and Disorder Act 1998.[89] The majority of the Act's provisions are targeted at young offenders and the schemes will be directed at the provision of appropriate adults in that context, as previous research has also indicated failure in that area.[90] It is intended that provision of an appropriate adult will form one of the functions and duties of the newly created inter-agency Youth Offending Teams.[91] However, it is likely that the existence of the panels will also assist mentally vulnerable suspects, provided that they are adequately resourced and the members receive sufficient and specialist training.[92] It is envisaged that their composition will be primarily of social work personnel, and there will be a statutory obligation imposed upon Local Authorities to ensure that such appropriate adult provision is in place. However, it has been identified previously that social workers are not always best placed to act as appropriate adults. Social workers are not required to receive any training about the role of the appropriate adult and there may be a conflict of interest, especially in relation to childcare and abuse cases, where there may be a tendency to side with the police.[93] The 1998 Act has only just taken its place on the statute books and it is, therefore, too early to predict to what extent this proposal will impact upon mentally vulnerable suspects. However, some commentators are optimistic about this, and about the effect on vulnerable suspects in custody.[94]

Nevertheless, the overall shortcomings in the treatment of the mentally ill whilst in police custody serve to strengthen further the argument for greater medical involvement and diversion into a health-care setting. The mentally disordered suspect is obviously at a clear disadvantage and not being accorded the full care and protection which s/he requires and deserves whilst in custody. This failure may be partly due to the fact that the police themselves may not recognize that a particular person is disordered and in need of appropriate adult assistance. This bolsters the view that qualified psychiatric personnel should be present at police stations to afford the suspects with this protection, or at least to ensure that they receive it.[95] Indeed, as will be seen in the following chapter, part of the official diversion policy statement is that psychiatric services and assessments should be made routinely available to the criminal justice system at this earliest possible stage.

[89] Home Office, *No More Excuses: A New Approach to Tackling Youth Crime in England and Wales*, Session 1997–8 Cm. 3809 para. 8.10. s. 39 of the Crime and Disorder Act 1998 makes provision for Youth Offending Teams. One of their functions will be the provision of an appropriate adult service. The likely impact and implications of the new provisions will be discussed at length in the following chapters.

[90] See e.g. R. Evans, *The Conduct of Police Interviews with Juveniles* (HMSO 1993); Palmer, 'Still Vulnerable'.

[91] Cm. 3809 ch. 8; Session 1996–7 HC Debs Vol. 299 cols 341–57.

[92] B. Littlechild, 'An End to Inappropriate Adults?' (1998) 144 *Childright* 8–9.

[93] See further Hodgson, 'Vulnerable Suspects', 790–1.   [94] Littlechild, 'An End'.

[95] J. M. Laing, 'The Mentally Disordered Suspect at the Police Station' [1995] *Crim LR* 371–81.

Linked to this is the role that the police surgeon (Forensic Medical Examiner (FME)) has to play at this stage of the process. This was also considered by the Royal Commission and was the subject of another Research Study.[96] The study found that FMEs now play an important role in identifying and assessing mentally ill and mentally handicapped people. If the police suspect that a person in police custody is mentally disordered, they must seek a medical opinion to assess if s/he is fit to be interviewed or requires the assistance of an appropriate adult. The police will inevitably call out the FME,[97] who is available to them to provide medical assistance, who will be required to diagnose a disordered mental state. The role of the FME has, however, attracted much criticism in this respect, notably by the Royal Commission, but the Mental Health Act Commission,[98] the Police Complaints Authority,[99] NACRO,[100] MIND,[101] and the BMA[102] have also expressed similar concerns.

As has been more fully explained elsewhere,[103] there are many difficulties to be overcome. In particular, the concern is voiced that FMEs are not required to receive any formal training at all, let alone have knowledge in the field of psychiatry, and so they are not sufficiently qualified or skilled in dealing with the mentally ill. Indeed, most are busy GPs who receive little or no training in mental health.[104] This is all linked to the notion of diversion of the mentally disordered into health-care settings and the provision of psychiatric assessments at courts and police stations to enable this to take place. These studies clearly call into question the ability of FMEs to identify mental disorder, thereby strengthening the need for psychiatric assessments by qualified medical professionals to be made available at this stage. The Royal Commission itself emphasised that psychiatric assistance should always be available to the police whenever it is required and proposed that a Working Party should be set up to consider in particular the role of psychiatry and the availability and use of psychiatric nursing staff.[105] Furthermore, it recommended that experiments should be set up to determine whether diversionary schemes would be appropriate at busy police stations.[106] This is a core issue, as many of the powers are not as effective or as

---

[96]   G. Robertson, *The Role of Police Surgeons*, Research Study 6 (HMSO 1993).
[97]   PACE 1984 Code of Practice C para. 9.2.   [98]   MHAC, *Report 1993–5*, 78.
[99]   *The 1996/1997 Annual Report of the Police Complaints Authority*, Session 1997–8 HC 95 p. 34.   [100]   MH Adv. Com. Policy Paper 2, 15–16.
[101]   P. Bean *et al.*, *Out of Harm's Way*, 155: 'Assessments by divisional surgeons were generally very brief and from the officers' accounts provided little more information than they already had.'
[102]   *Health Care of Detainees in Police Custody* (BMA 1994); see also *Independent*, 'Doctors warn on police cell care', 21 June 1994.
[103]   J. M. Laing, 'The Mentally Disordered Suspect' 371–81; id., 'The Police Surgeon and Mentally Disordered Suspects: An Adequate Safeguard?' [1996] 1 *Web JCLI*.
[104]   See S. P. Savage *et al.*, 'Divided Loyalties? The Police Surgeon and Criminal Justice' (1997) 7(2) *Policing & Society* 79–98, where it was found that only 51% of the FMEs in the sample had undertaken a psychiatric element in their GP training and only 9% were approved under s. 12 MHA 1983.   [105]   Cm. 2263 paras. 88–92, Recommendation 74.
[106]   Ibid. para. 92, Rec. 75.

appropriate in achieving diversion to health care as was initially anticipated. The discussion above has emphasized that increased training for police and appropriate adults would enable greater numbers of cases to be picked up at this early stage, thereby averting the need for detention and perhaps subsequent prosecution and imprisonment, and ensuring access to health care for more mentally disordered people. In the following chapters it will be considered how diversion policy and inter-agency diversion schemes have been introduced to try to combat previous ineffectiveness, and evaluate whether they have succeeded in doing so, particularly in the West Yorkshire area.

3.3. PROSECUTION

The next stage in the criminal justice process is the decision of whether or not to initiate a prosecution. Here also there may be an avenue into psychiatric care as it may be decided not to take any further action and the offender referred to the relevant health services; so diversion can also be achieved at this stage in the process. The initial decision lies with the police, who will then pass the case on to the Crown Prosecution Service who will consider, on the basis of the evidence, whether or not to proceed with the prosecution. Both agencies have discretionary powers at this stage and they will be considered in turn below.

3.3.1. The Police

3.3.1.1. The Provisions

The police do not have specific criteria which they consider to decide whether or not to prosecute a mentally disordered person,[107] however the Attorney General issued Criteria for Prosecution in 1984[108] to guide police discretion in initiating prosecutions which continue to be applied by the police.[109] The criteria provide that there are two general factors governing decisions to prosecute—the evidential criteria and the public interest criteria. The first consideration is the 'evidential sufficiency', or the so-called '51% Rule'. A prosecution should not be started unless there is a 'reasonable prospect of a conviction'.[110] Assuming that there is sufficient evidence, the police should then consider the 'public interest' criteria. This means considering such factors as the likely penalty, old age and infirmity, the complainant's attitude, and, in particular, the defendant's mental state. Again, this

---

[107] The Runciman Commission, however, recommended that police cautioning should be governed by statute, under which guidelines should be laid down in regulations, Cm. 2263 para. 109. If implemented, it would at least impart a degree of uniformity into the prosecution and the cautioning of suspects.

[108] Following the recommendation of the Royal Commission on Criminal Procedure, the 'Philips Commission' (1981) Cm. 8092 para. 9.10.

[109] *Blackstone's Criminal Procedure* (1992) D1.54–1.63.   [110] Ibid. D1.61.

is a vital stage as diversion is possible if the police believe it not to be in the public interest to effect a prosecution, as it would have such a detrimental effect on the defendant's mental state.

The questioning stage is vital in achieving possible diversion as the police have a wide range of options available to them, and the interviewing of the suspect enables the police fully to assess the situation and decide whether to continue with the proceedings or to take no further action and perhaps issue a caution. The police may decide to drop any charges against the defendant so that s/he will not have a criminal record. However, this course of action does not automatically offer the opportunity of health care to a mentally disordered person: 'the police have no duty to look at the community care needs of such an individual, and little time or expertise to do anything on an informal basis'.[111] Alternatively, the police can issue a caution rather than charge the offender. However, certain conditions must be met before a formal caution can be administered, one of which is that there must be 'informed consent' to being cautioned and also that there must be an admission of guilt. It is generally suggested that if there are any doubts as to an individual's mental state or ability to make a reliable admission of guilt or to give proper and full consent, then cautioning is inappropriate. Further, should this course of action be taken, then again, it provides no access to health care or accommodation, which is of particular relevance if the suspect is homeless, as it simply puts him/her back on the streets, with the possibility that s/he may end up in court again. Moreover, the 1979–97 Conservative Government introduced guidelines and standards which were aimed at restricting the use of cautions, particularly repeat cautions with regard to juvenile offenders.[112] So, the use of the caution has been further discouraged in certain contexts at this stage.

The third alternative to prosecution at this stage is the possibility of police bail. Section 38 of PACE requires that a custody officer should release a person from police detention, with or without bail, when certain conditions are met. Furthermore, the police have been given extended powers to impose conditional bail under the Criminal Justice and Public Order Act 1994.[113] It has been observed that police bail decisions have been influential upon subsequent decisions by magistrates in relation to remands in custody.[114] NACRO's Mental Health Advisory Committee felt that the Home Office should encourage police to

---

[111] NACRO, *Revolving Doors*, p. 12; see also G. Robertson *et al.*, *The Mentally Disordered and the Police*, Home Office Research Findings, 21 (Home Office 1995).

[112] *The Cautioning of Offenders*, Home Office Circular 18/1994; see further C. Ball, 'Cautioning: A Radical Shift in Policy?' (1994) 144 *NLJ* 495–6; indeed, official statistics reveal that Circular 18/94 has had the desired effect and that the overall number of cautions has reduced since its publication (Home Office, *Criminal Statistics England and Wales 1996*, Session 1996–7 Cm. 3764 para. 5.22).

[113] Criminal Justice and Public Order Act 1994 s. 27. See further M. Wasik and R. Taylor, *Blackstone's Guide to the Criminal Justice and Public Order Act 1994* (Blackstone 1995), 29–36.

[114] NACRO, MH Adv. Com., Policy Paper No 2, 23.

make a presumption in favour of bail for a mentally disturbed offender, given the probable detrimental effect of custody on the defendant's mental condition.[115] Again, however, this option does not automatically provide any form of health care, and is therefore inadequate where the mental disorder is serious and the individual concerned is homeless.

Should the police finally decide to charge the defendant having considered and assessed the evidential and public interest criteria, then the file will be taken out of their hands for the CPS to consider, who are required to make a similar assessment.

3.3.1.2. Commentary

The Runciman Commission felt that the caution was an important power for the police in ensuring that mentally disordered offenders are not unnecessarily charged and kept in custody. The Commission noted that a simple caution is unsatisfactory, but combined with a requirement that the offender must co-operate with other agencies, particularly where the offender is suffering from mental disorder, it would be extremely beneficial. The offender could be required to co-operate with social work agencies or the probation service and to attend a clinic or be seen by a consultant directly, perhaps under the overall responsibility of the probation service.[116] Indeed, the NACRO Mental Health Advisory Committee felt that 'the police would have greater confidence in exercising their powers to administer a caution if they were reassured that they could make informal referrals to health or social services for an appropriate assessment to be made'.[117] It recommended, therefore, that increased co-operation should take place between the police and health and social services so that adequate arrangements could be made should the police decide to issue a caution or take no further action. The new cautioning guidelines restrict the use of cautions, and this may have an impact upon cautioning practice with regard to mentally disordered offenders. However, the Criminal Justice and Public Order Act 1994 gave new powers to the police to grant conditional bail.[118] This has extended the police's discretion at this stage, and they may now attach a wide variety of conditions, such as curfews and residence at a particular place, to police bail. These powers have previously been reserved only for the courts but their introduction may counteract the restrictions on the use of cautions. The police, following consultation and co-operation with other agencies, may, in future, be more confident and willing to grant conditional bail to mentally disordered

---

[115] Policy Paper No 2.

[116] Cm. 2263 para. 60 Rec. 111; see further Editorial, 'Royal Commission on Criminal Justice' (1993) 143 *NLJ* 993–6 for a summary of the recommendations regarding police investigations, safeguards for suspects, the right of silence, and confession evidence.

[117] NACRO, MH Adv. Com., Policy Paper No 2, 22.

[118] For further details see J. W. Raine and M. J. Willson, 'Just Bail at the Police Station?' (1995) 22 *J Law & Soc* 571–85; C. Williams, 'New Bail Powers for Custody Officers' (1995) 145 *NLJ* 685–6; Wasik and Taylor, *Blackstone's Guide to CJPO Act*.

suspects to enable them to be referred to appropriate health care. Indeed, research conducted by the Home Office suggests that the police are beginning to use their new conditional bail powers imaginatively and this is extremely encouraging.[119]

3.3.2. The Crown Prosecution Service

3.3.2.1. The Provisions

The CPS[120] will consider the case in accordance with the Code for Crown Prosecutors which is issued by the Director of Public Prosecutions as guidance in this decision-making process.[121] They now have complete discretion as to whether to continue with the prosecution or to drop all the charges against the offender. Similarly here, the two overriding factors to be considered by the CPS are the 'evidential sufficiency' and the 'public interest' elements. As regards the former, in order to proceed, the prosecutor must be certain that there is a 'realistic prospect of a conviction' having regard to all the relevant evidence. When the prosecutor is satisfied that the evidence itself can justify proceedings s/he must then consider whether the public interest requires a prosecution. This is not an easy decision however, as 'defining where the public interest lies is frequently a complex and difficult process'.[122]

Nevertheless, the same considerations apply as with the Attorney-General's criteria. The Code was revised in 1994 and expressly lists some common public interest factors both for and against prosecution.[123] Important factors in favour of prosecution are the seriousness of the offence, whether it was motivated by any form of discrimination, or whether there are grounds for believing that the offence is likely to be continued or repeated. Furthermore, the Code expressly states that 'Crown Prosecutors must always think carefully about the interests of the victim, which are an important factor, when deciding where the public interest lies.'[124] However, there is also particular concern shown for the probable effect of a prosecution upon the mentally ill, as a prosecution is less likely to proceed if the defendant 'is, or was at the time of the offence, suffering from significant mental or physical health'.[125]

In considering whether a discontinuance is preferable in the case of a mentally

---

[119] D. Brown, *Offending on Bail and Police Use of Conditional Bail*, Home Office Research Findings, 72 (Home Office 1998).

[120] As a result of the Philips Commission Cm. 8092 recommendations, the CPS was set up in the mid-1980s as an independent prosecuting body.

[121] See Prosecution of Offences Act 1985 ss. 3, 10; see also the Annual Reports of the Crown Prosecution Service.

[122] R. K. Daw, 'The "Public Interest" Criterion in the Decision to Prosecute' (1989) 53 *J Crim Law* 485–501, 500; A. Ashworth, 'The Public Interest Element in Prosecutions' [1987] *Crim LR* 595–607; see also the Butler Committee Report Cmnd. 6244 para. 9.19.

[123] *CPS Annual Report 1996–7*, Session 1997–8 HC 68 Code for Crown Prosecutors.

[124] Ibid. Code for Crown Prosecutors, para 6.7.   [125] Ibid. para. 6.5.

disordered defendant, therefore, the Prosecution must evaluate all the factors in co-operation with other relevant agencies (police, doctors, and social workers) and should obtain independent evidence both of the illness and the probable effects (adverse or otherwise) of prosecution.[126] Where the continuation of proceedings is likely to have an adverse effect upon an individual's mental ill health, then consideration should be given to discontinuance.

Section 23 of the Prosecution of Offences Act 1985 permits discontinuance of a case, irrespective of the 'evidential sufficiency', on 'public interest' grounds. However, it is available only during the preliminary stages of the case in the magistrates' court and must be effected before the court has begun to hear evidence at any summary trial or before the magistrates have committed the accused for trial in the Crown Court. Alternatively, the CPS can terminate the proceedings by applying to the court to withdraw the proceedings, or by offering no evidence and inviting the court to acquit or discharge the defendant.

The Butler Committee urged extreme caution before deciding to prosecute a mentally disordered person—s/he should not be prosecuted if this would 'serve no useful purpose'.[127] It noted that, where any person is clearly in need of urgent psychiatric treatment and there is no question of risk to members of the public, the question should always be asked if any 'useful purpose' or any 'public interest' would be served by a prosecution. Indeed, the presumption against prosecution should have particular force with regard to patients already in hospital. Wherever possible such patients should not be prosecuted, thereby removing the stigma of conviction. The Committee received much evidence expressing such concerns. Thus, it strongly supported discontinuance and diversion, as prosecution should only be seen as a last resort, and should not be embarked upon where it is clearly not in the interests of the patient or the community.[128]

3.3.2.2. Commentary

The first Code for Crown Prosecutors was issued in 1986, and a second edition was published in January 1992. It emphasised the importance of the accused's mental state upon the decision to prosecute: 'Where there is evidence to establish that an accused or a person under investigation was suffering from a mental disorder at the time the offence was committed, the Crown Prosecutor will observe the principle that prosecution will not be appropriate in the circumstances unless it is overridden by the wider public interest, including the gravity of the offence'.[129] So the Code initially included a rebuttable presumption that a person suffering from a mental disorder should not be prosecuted unless there is a wider public interest in requiring such action.[130] At that time, therefore, the CPS firmly

---

[126] See further DPP, *Criteria for Prosecution* (HMSO 1982).
[127] Cm. 6244 Recommendations 6, 7 para. 9.16 'Such appearances may impede treatment and delay recovery'.   [128] Ibid. para. 9.16–25.
[129] See *CPS Annual Report 1992–3* (HMSO 1993), 50.
[130] Ibid. 47, Code for Crown Prosecutors, para. 8(v)(a).

endorsed diversion and the emphasis upon the mental health of the accused, and this was welcomed by the Royal Commission on Criminal Justice.[131]

There are major implications for diversion in the fact that a further revision took place in 1994 which, some argue, has watered down the commitment towards diverting mentally disordered offenders. Ashworth and Fionda argue that although the Code still acknowledges Home Office guidance and the importance of diversion, this is now expressly qualified and must be carefully balanced against the need to safeguard the general public.[132] So it is acknowledged that there are limitations to diversion and that other factors, in particular the safety of the public and the interests of the victim, must also be fully considered.

R. K. Daw, in a response to Ashworth and Fionda, has reaffirmed the commitment and support of the CPS to the diversion of mentally disordered offenders.[133] And in its 1993–4 Annual Report, the CPS expressly stated that Home Office guidance on mentally disordered offenders will always be considered in assessing the public interest.[134] However, it is acknowledged that 'helping the defendant must be balanced against the needs of society' and if the offence is serious or there is a danger of repetition then 'it remains likely that a prosecution will be needed in the public interest'.[135] So some of the dangers in relation to public safety and the interests of victims which were outlined in Ch. 1 have been recognized by the CPS and will be considered carefully as part of the diversion decision-making process.

Diversion attempts are further hampered at this stage due to the friction which often exists between the police and the CPS, which has been noted most recently by the Runciman Commission[136] and numerous commentators.[137] The main bone of contention is that the police are given too much discretion and the CPS too little.[138] The CPS do indeed have the final word, but only for those cases of which they become aware, thus there is perhaps too much emphasis on the police and too much scope for personal influence in initiating a prosecution. The Philips Commission on Criminal Procedure also noted this possible tendency on the part of the police: 'A police officer who carries out an investigation, inevitably and properly, forms a view as to the guilt of the suspect. Having done so, without any kind of improper motive, he may be inclined to shut his mind to other evidence telling against the guilt of the suspect, or to overestimate the strength of the evidence he has assembled'.[139]

---

[131] Cm. 2263 para. 41.

[132] A. Ashworth and J. Fionda, 'The New Code for Crown Prosecutors: Prosecution, Accountability and the Public Interest' [1994] *Crim LR* 894–903, 900; see also A. Sanders, 'The Silent Code' (1994) 144 *NLJ* 946.

[133] R. K. Daw, 'The New Code for Crown Prosecutors: A Response' [1994] *Crim LR* 904–9, 908.

[134] *CPS Annual Report 1993–1994* (HMSO 1994), 8.   [135] Daw, 'Response', 908–9.

[136] Cm. 2263 para. 3.

[137] See A. Samuels, 'Prosecution and the Public Interest' (1987) 151 *JP* 362–3; N. Addison, 'Them and Us' (1995) *Police Review*, 11 August, pp. 15–17.

[138] A. Sanders, 'The Limits to Diversion from Prosecution' (1988) 28 *Brit J Criminology* 513–32.

[139] Cm. 8092 para. 6.24.

Other research further identifies the fact that the police manage to take the decisions they want by controlling which cases enter the system and by managing the procedure and the information that enters the system.[140] Given that the CPS depends upon the police for the information upon which it makes its decisions, it therefore cannot prosecute or divert unless the correct evidence is presented. In the words of one Chief Crown Prosecutor, 'I feel we suffer from a lack of information . . . There's still the possibility that police can construct files; there is certainly a need for more background information [especially] . . . Public Interest information.'[141] This is a major flaw, as the Home Office has subsequently highlighted how vital the powers of the CPS are with respect to mentally disordered offenders.[142] Their discretion, provided they are given sufficient information, could result in discontinuance and diversion, thus reducing the likelihood of incarceration and removing the stigma of prosecution from mentally disordered offenders. But, sadly, it seems that 'the police have the interest, but not the powers; and the CPS, which does have both the power and interest, lacks information'.[143] Criticism that the CPS is not taking a strong stance[144] is therefore misplaced, as it can only act upon the information it receives and has no express power to demand additional and further information. This lack of co-operation and information, and constant friction, clearly hampers the diversion of mentally disordered offenders and this is a serious downfall which must be remedied.

The Runciman Commission recommended that there should be more consultation and co-operation to resolve disputes with the police.[145] This was indeed suggested by the CPS itself in its Submissions of Evidence to the Commission,[146] and has been supported by NACRO.[147] This would further facilitate diversion attempts by providing full and accurate information, as the CPS will only discontinue when they are in possession of all the relevant information and the implications for the safety of the public have been fully considered.

In this respect, some measures have been taken in recent years which are encouraging and are likely to increase the scope for co-operation and collaboration. First, the CPS has acknowledged that 'effective partnership' is vital, particularly with the police. Consequently, pilot schemes have been established in twelve sites enabling representatives from the CPS to be based in police stations to provide early prosecution advice on complex cases.[148] Research suggests that

---

[140] M. McConville, A. Sanders and R. Leng, *The Case for the Prosecution* (Routledge 1991), 56, 122, 124, 141, 153.

[141] S. Elliman, 'Independent Information for the CPS' (1990) 140 *NLJ* 812–14, 812.

[142] *Provision for Mentally Disordered Offenders*, Home Office Circular 66/90; see further Ch. 4.

[143] Sanders, 'Limits to Diversion', 513.

[144] See e.g. Liberty's submissions of evidence to the Runciman Commission, ch. 4, where dissatisfaction with the CPS was expressed.   [145] CM. 2263, pp. 69–81.

[146] Para. 5.5.1, 'some police officers . . . are unable or unwilling to comply with requests for further investigation to be made post-charge'.

[147] NACRO, MH Adv. Com., Policy Paper 2, 23.

[148] *CPS Annual Report 1996–7*, 11–13; CPS Press Release, 26 January 1996.

the schemes are being effective in promoting good working relationships,[149] and it is anticipated that such schemes will continue to be extended and adopted in other areas across the country. The CPS is also developing joint training with the police to try to improve understanding and liaison.[150]

Secondly, as a result of the concerns outlined above, the Labour Government has conducted a comprehensive review of the CPS which has recommended a new structure and complete reorganization.[151] It is intended that the CPS will be reorganized into forty-two areas, which will be coterminous with police force boundaries. The report also recommended the establishment of a single integrated unit—a Criminal Justice Unit—to assemble and manage case files, which would combine the roles of the police and CPS. The report recognized that there are often tensions between the CPS and other agencies such as the police, and the new proposals are therefore intended to counteract this and 'to bridge the gulf between the police and the CPS'.[152] The Government has announced that it will be implementing some of these proposals during the course of the next few years; in particular, the CPS reorganization process will begin as soon as possible.[153] Clearly, this is an extremely welcome and far-reaching development, which will go some way towards improving the liaison and communication between the two organisations and will therefore be valuable in enabling the full exchange of information and promoting inter-agency working and diversion.

Finally, and linked to this, is the fact that it is stressed that the CPS will always consider information concerning the mental health of an offender, whatever its source, and as it is not allowed to approach the police, it is reliant on other agencies—the Probation Service and social services—to provide them with this. However, prosecutors need speedy and accurate information about the defendant which it may not be possible to collect from such varied sources. To counteract this problem and to ensure that other professionals pass on all the relevant information to the CPS, an effort has been made in many areas in recent years to overcome this information gap which the CPS face. First, Bail Information Schemes which are operated around the country by the Probation Service have been introduced. They are invaluable as they ensure that the relevant information about offenders and their circumstances is provided after being collected by the probation officer, and this is then submitted to the prosecution. The provision of this information can often avoid the making of unnecessary custodial remands. Suspects detained overnight are interviewed by a probation officer and, often, indications that the suspect is mentally disturbed may come to light during this

---

[149] J. Baldwin and A. Hunt, 'Prosecutors Advising in Police Stations' [1998] *Crim LR* 521–36.
[150] *CPS Annual Report 1996–7*, 13.
[151] *Report of the Review of the CPS: 1998*, Session 1997–8 Cm. 3972; *The Review of the CPS: A Report*, Session 1997–8 Cm. 3960; see also J. N. Spencer, 'Reviewing the CPS' (1998) 162 *JP* 22–4; A. Ashworth, 'Reviewing the CPS' [1998] *Crim LR* 517–20.
[152] Cm. 3972 p. 28.   [153] CPS Press Release 118/98, 20 May 1998.

interview, thus enabling appropriate arrangements to be made.[154] The Tumim Report on suicide and self-harm in prison firmly believed that the accelerated expansion of Bail Information Schemes is highly desirable, as they 'aim to provide the court with more information about the background and circumstances of the defendant in order to allow a more balanced view to be made regarding the granting of bail . . . hopefully mak[ing] a major impact on the numbers of defendants currently being remanded in custody'.[155] These schemes therefore have a central role to play in ensuring co-operation, providing information, and facilitating therapeutic disposal options and diversion.

Secondly, the probation service has been operating several Public Interest Case Assessment (PICA) projects. The first of these was established by the Inner London Probation Service in 1990,[156] and subsequently three similar pilot schemes were established in 1991 in other parts of the country.[157] The scheme involves probation officers obtaining verified information, with the defendant's consent, about his/her circumstances, in particular any previous involvement with psychiatric services. If necessary, an appropriate assessment of the defendant's mental health is obtained and this information is all made available to the CPS before a first or second court appearance. No recommendations are made—it is essentially a source of valued information to assist the CPS in making their decisions. The CPS in its Submissions of Evidence to Runciman supports these schemes and will always pay regard to the information received from them, as it is extremely helpful.[158] The evaluation of the pilot scheme showed that the discontinuance rate rose from 1 per cent to 7 per cent as a result.[159] Given that the national discontinuance rates are very low—in 1988 only 1.5 per cent of summary offences and 3 per cent of indictable offences—the nation-wide establishment of these schemes could only further benefit the mentally disordered offender. They clearly have a valuable role to play in promoting diversion by assisting the CPS to make more informed decisions regarding discontinuance. Not only is this recommended by NACRO,[160] but the Runciman Commission,[161] the Woolf Report on Prison Disturbances,[162] and the Tumim Report on Suicides in Prison[163] have all recommended their continued and expanded development.

---

[154] NACRO, MH Adv. Com., Policy Paper 2 pp. 10–11.

[155] *Report of a Review by HM Chief Inspector of Prisons for England and Wales of Suicide and Self-Harm in Prison Service Establishments in England and Wales* (HMSO 1990) Cm. 1383 para. 3.77.

[156] See A. J. Brown and D. Crisp, *Diverting Cases from Prosecution in the Public Interest*, Home Office Research and Statistics Department Research Bulletin, 32 (Home Office 1992), 7–12.

[157] See further D. Crisp *et al., Public Interest Case Assessment Schemes*, Home Office Research Study, 138 (HMSO 1995).   [158] Paras. 4.1.3(iii), 4.3.9.

[159] NACRO, *Revolving Doors*, 13–14.

[160] NACRO, MH Adv. Com., Policy Paper 2, 23.

[161] Cm. 2263 para. 61: the expansion of such schemes nationally can only lead to significant benefits.

[162] *Prison Disturbances April 1990: Report of an Inquiry by the Right Hon L J Woolf and His Honour Judge S Tumim* (HMSO 1991) Cm. 1456 para. 10.88, 104–6.

[163] Cm. 1383 para. 3.77–8, Rec. 7.98.

There is, therefore, an urgent need for greater co-operation between the agencies involved. In particular, defence solicitors should become aware that they are well placed to be the most helpful source of any medical evidence, and thus the CPS will always take this type of information into account, whatever the source.[164]

The difficulties at this stage are further exacerbated by the fact that the response of the CPS may be influenced and constrained by the availability of local and regional resources. It has been noted that if regional mental health facilities have no available beds or adequate support, the CPS may be forced to prosecute the mentally disordered offender in the hope that a custodial sentence will be given by the court in an effort to ensure the safety of the general public.[165] This again highlights the need for greater collaboration and commitment, and increased comprehensive mental health service provision to achieve diversion.

3.4. REMAND

The next stage in the criminal justice system (assuming that the prosecution is to proceed) is the actual court appearance, and so all the differing powers and provisions which enable diversion to take place at this stage will be considered. Initially, the procedures with respect to mentally disordered defendants which may occur in court before the actual trial itself takes place will be outlined. Relevant routes to psychiatric care here are, specifically, the power of the Home Secretary to transfer unsentenced prisoners to hospital (s. 48 of the Mental Health Act 1983) and any hospital care which may be required whilst the defendant is awaiting trial in the form of remands to hospital or hospital attendance as a condition of bail.

3.4.1. The Right to Bail

3.4.1.1. The Provisions

Mentally disordered persons are entitled to the same rights as other persons, which at this stage include the right to bail, so the courts should always bear this in mind.[166] The Butler Committee stressed the importance of the right to bail with

---

[164] A. Edwards, 'Criminal Law Update: Mentally Disordered Suspects' (1991) 88 *Law Soc Gaz* 29; see also NACRO MH Adv. Com., Policy Paper 2, 16; M. Kennedy, Commissioning Services for Mentally Vulnerable Defendants' (1997) *Legal Action* October pp. 27–9.

[165] M. Pinder and H. Laming, 'Time to Re-think', in K. Herbst and J. Gunn (eds.), *The Mentally Disordered Offender* (Butterworth-Heinemann 1991) 190.

[166] It must be noted here that the Criminal Justice and Public Order Act 1994 has restricted the use of bail in two particular cases. First, the presumption in favour of it is removed if the offence was committed whilst the defendant was on bail for a previous offence (s. 26), and secondly, where the offence is murder, manslaughter, or rape and the defendant has similar previous convictions, then bail will not be granted (s. 25). See further Wasik and Taylor, *Blackstone's Guide to CJPO Act*.

respect to the mentally disordered defendant: 'Bail should always be the first choice of the courts, and remand to hospital should be considered only if remand on bail is not feasible'.[167] This is still the primary consideration today, as the Home Office expressly advises that where the CPS decides to proceed with such a case, the court will be required to consider the question of bail in the normal way, and both the Crown Court and the magistrates' court have powers to grant bail to a mentally disordered defendant.[168] It has been suggested that, where medical treatment is desirable or medical reports on the accused's mental condition are required by the court, this may be achieved as a condition of bail, such as the requirements of residence at a hospital or attendance at an out-patient clinic. The Crown Court may grant bail with a condition that the defendant attends a hospital where appropriate psychiatric care and supervision can be made. The magistrates' court has a similar power under s. 30 of the Magistrates' Court Act 1980. It enables a magistrates' court to remand an accused person (in custody) for a medical report without convicting him/her where it is satisfied that s/he did the act or made the omission charged.[169] The medical report can be obtained whilst in custody, or the court can impose conditions under s. 3(6)(d) of the Bail Act 1976 including the requirement that s/he undergoes an examination of his/her mental condition by two registered doctors and, for that purpose, s/he attends such institution or place as the court directs. It is advised that the court should always bear in mind the desirability of arranging for a medical report on the defendant's mental condition. Obtaining a medical report is vital at this stage, essentially because a court cannot make any order that will result in compulsory hospital admission without the necessary medical reports. It is also advisable at this stage as medical evidence will be required should the accused be unfit to plead or where the defences of insanity/diminished responsibility may arise, thus it is desirable for the sake of expediency.[170]

3.4.1.2. *Commentary*

The Butler Committee expressed its concern in this area that many defendants in need of psychiatric treatment could 'slip through the net'. After all, 'busy magistrates' courts, dealing with armies of offenders, are unlikely, unless prompted by strange behaviour in the dock, . . . to know of any previous psychiatric treatment, unless the defendant volunteers it'.[171] The courts are clearly 'hampered by their inexperience in dealing with mentally disordered offenders'.[172] As noted by one

---

[167] Cm. 6244 p. 174, para. 12.10.   [168] See Bail Act 1976 s. 4.

[169] Note also that s. 10(3) of the Magistrates' Court Act 1980 gives the court a general power to adjourn a case after conviction for the purpose of enabling inquiries to be made or of determining the most suitable method of dealing with the case.

[170] See Hoggett, *Mental Health Law*, 108–15.

[171] D. P. Allam, 'Sentencing of the Mentally Disordered' (1990) 46 *The Mag* 176–7; see also W. M. Donovan and K. P. O' Brien, 'Psychiatric Court Reports: Too Many or Too Few?' (1981) 21 *Med, Sci & Law* 153–8.

[172] NACRO Briefing, *The Imprisonment of Mentally Disturbed Offenders* (December 1990), 3.

magistrate, 'Magistrates are laymen and have no legal qualifications. Further, in common with most people, the majority of magistrates come to the Bench with little or no knowledge of mental illness.'[173]

The Butler Committee advocated the greater use of obtaining medical and social inquiry (now pre-sentence) reports as a 'screening process for mental disorder'[174] and as a safeguard to ensure that 'in every case the court . . . should, so far as possible, be in possession of all relevant information about the present mental state of the accused and any previous psychiatric history'.[175]

Although bail is seen as the most preferable option, ensuring that mentally disordered defendants are not unnecessarily remanded in custody for medical reports, it has been identified that the main problem with the bail provisions with respect to mentally disordered offenders is that in practice, the presumption in favour of it[176] is 'weakened for the mentally disordered defendant due to the clause allowing remand in custody for his own protection'.[177] Further, if a mentally disordered defendant is homeless, the court may decide on a remand to custody to ensure future attendance, as 'lack of community ties' is specified in the Bail Act 1976 as a reason for the magistrates to believe that the defendant will not return to court. This has recently been noted by both NACRO[178] and the Tumim Report.[179] Given that the court can refuse bail on this ground, and also for the purpose of securing the preparation of medical reports, it can result in an excessive number of defendants being remanded in custody for medical reports: 'mentally disordered homeless defendants charged with minor offences are more likely to be remanded in custody than others charged with similar offences'.[180]

Compounding these difficulties is the fact that although the court may stipulate hospital residence or attendance as a condition of bail, unless the defendant is formally 'sectioned' under the civil admission sections of the Mental Health Act, s/he cannot be detained against his/her will. One answer which Tumim advocated was the greater provision of bail hostels, thereby ensuring that some form of 'community tie' is present.[181] However, it has been noted that these hostels can still refuse admission to mentally disordered defendants.[182]

Furthermore, an offender's disability may not have been recognized or diagnosed until s/he appears in court. As Nigel Walker has observed,[183] many disorders are not obvious and some may be episodic or sporadic. Furthermore, the mentally disordered offender may refuse to discuss his/her behaviour with

---

[173] J. Major, 'What Can a Magistrate Do?' in Herbst and Gunn (eds.) *Mentally Disordered Offender*, 50.   [174] Cm. 6244 p. 166.   [175] Ibid. para. 11.1.
[176] Bail Act 1976 s. 4(4).
[177] P. Joseph, *Psychiatric Assessment at the Magistrates' Court* (Home Office 1992), 2.
[178] *Revolving Doors*, 14.
[179] Cm. 1383, para. 3.72.
[180] Joseph, *Psychiatric Assessment*; see also J. J. Hylton, 'Care or Control?' Health or Criminal Justice Options for the Long Term Seriously Mentally Ill in a Canadian Province' (1995) 18(1) *Int J Law & Psych* 45–59, 47.   [181] Cm. 1383 paras. 3.77, 7.96, 7.97.
[182] Ibid. para. 3.72.   [183] Walker, *Sentencing*, para. 21.6.

anyone. And even if the offender has a psychiatric history, s/he may evade diagnosis by having changed his/her name for example. In addition, psychiatric hospital records are confidential. So unless the patient's history is known to the relevant agencies—police, probation court, or prison staff (if remanded in custody), or unless s/he displays strange behaviour, then the disordered mental condition may go undiagnosed until it is too late: 'From the moment of summons, the court is dependent upon manifestly unusual behaviour or being tipped off by another agency, advocate, policeman, social worker or probation officer.'[184] This is an ever-present danger which must be minimized as much as possible at this stage. Undoubtedly, the best way forward is greater co-operation and exchange of information between all the agencies involved, and a greater effort in trying to identify mental disorder in the first place: 'In order for the system to work, or the reports to be understood and for communication between the court and the NHS to be effective, it requires the police, probation service and medical professions to talk to one another.'[185] This has been reiterated by Ian Bynoe, the Legal Director of MIND. He believes that the quality of the decision-making must be improved if it is to be ensured that mentally disordered offenders are not unnecessarily sent to prison 'courts need to be reined in from making bad decisions, or given powers to obtain information, or require co-operation from others'.[186]

Courts can only act upon the information they receive, in the words of one magistrate:

once they realise that a medical element is involved, magistrates will lean over backwards to obtain a medical report and to co-operate with the recommendations in it. . . . [They] may only act on the information they receive . . . If the mentally disordered offender . . . behaves normally in court, the magistrates will not realize there is a psychiatric problem and will take the case as a straight criminal charge.[187]

This problem further reinforces the argument for psychiatric assessments to be made routinely available at the court so that mental health problems can be identified by skilled psychiatric professionals screening defendants at court. Thus, mentally disordered offenders can be accorded medical assessment, care, and treatment and not simply pass through the system unidentified and languish without care, in prison, or incurring other punitive sanctions.

Although bail is a highly desirable option, as noted by many commentators presently it has many drawbacks as the hospital has no power to detain the person should s/he break this bail condition by discharging him/herself. Further, a remand on bail is regarded as inappropriate where the person poses a serious danger to the public. Consequently, it is often inappropriate or impractical and the alternatives will now be considered.

---

[184] Allam, 'Sentencing the Mentally Disordered'.   [185] Ibid. 176.
[186] Cited in Lord Longford, *Prisoner or Patient* (Chapmans 1992), 62.
[187] J. Major, 'What Can a Magistrate Do?' 47.

3.4.2. Remands to Hospital for Report or Treatment (ss. 35, 36)

3.4.2.1. The Provisions

Should bail be considered undesirable, the courts, by virtue of the Mental Health Act 1983 now have general powers to remand directly to hospital.[188] But these powers should not be exercised where a custodial remand is not necessary. The detailed evidential and procedural requirements of both these sections are set out in Table 3.1.

First, with regard to s. 35 which is a remand for report, it is vital to note that during the period of detention in hospital under this section, the defendant is not to be subjected to any treatment against his/her will. Treatment may only be given when s/he consents (s. 56(1)(b)). Indeed, it was made clear at the time of the conception of the Act that Parliament did not intend to force people on remand for report to be treated without consent: 'this power is intended to be used only for diagnostic purposes . . . There need be no concern that a remand for a medical report would otherwise expose a person to the risk of receiving unnecessary treatment without his consent because . . . there is no intention that a person remanded under this [section] should be regarded as "detained for treatment" '.[189]

In order to supplement this s. 35 power where treatment is required, s. 36 provides for a remand for treatment to be made by the Crown Court, and the Home Secretary has an additional power under s. 48 to transfer unsentenced prisoners to hospital to receive care and treatment. Prior to the 1983 Act where a mentally disordered person had to be kept in custody on remand, s/he would have had to remain in a prison until the case was heard in court. A mentally ill person's condition could deteriorate in prison because of the regime, and the lack of adequate facilities and staff. Thus, s. 36 was introduced to ensure that this did not occur.

3.4.2.2. Commentary

These new powers were warmly welcomed[190] as they provided the court with greater flexibility at this stage, and, as outlined in the previous chapter, were largely the result of the Butler Committee's recommendations.[191] Their introduction, as was outlined by the preceding ministerial statement, was that, wherever possible, sick people should be treated in hospital.[192] At that time, the

---

[188] Ss. 35, 36, 40(3); for further guidance as to the use of these sections see DoH/Welsh Office, *Mental Health Act 1983 Memorandum on Parts I to VI, VIII, X* (HMSO 1998) paras. 142–51, and *Mental Health Act 1983 Revised Code of Practice* paras. 17.1–4.

[189] Session 1981–2 HL Debs Vol. 426 cols 769–70 *per* Lord Belstead speaking for the Government in the House of Lords debate at the Committee stage of the 1982 Mental Health (Amendment) Bill (emphasis supplied).

[190] B. Hoggett, 'What is Wrong with the Mental Health Act?' [1975] *Crim LR* 677–83.

[191] Cm. 6244 ch. 12.

[192] Session 1983–4 HC Debs Vol. 65 col. 544 *per* K. Clarke Minister for Health: 'The mentally ill should be treated in hospital wherever possible, and we do not wish the courts to have to send sick people to prison.'

TABLE 3.1. *Pre-trial therapeutic powers*

MHA power	Authorizing body	Medical evidence	Other requirements	Duration and effect	Discharge and appeal
s. 35. Remand for assessment and report on accused's mental condition	Crown Court: Any person awaiting trial for an imprisonable offence Mag. court: After convicting the accused/ finding s/he did the act charged/with the consent of the accused s. 35(2)	Written/oral evidence of one Registered Medical Practitioner (RMP) that accused is suffering from one of the four forms of mental disorder. It must also be impracticable for the report to be made on bail. s. 35(3)	Written/oral evidence of RMP that a bed is available within 7 days. Accused may be conveyed to a place of safety pending admission s. 35(4)	Up to a period of 28 days, renewable for further periods of 28 days to a maximum of 12 weeks s. 35(7)	Appeal to the magistrates' court or Crown Court
s. 36. Remand for medical treatment	Crown Court only: Any person awaiting trial for an imprisonable offence/ in custody at any stage of such a trial prior to sentence s. 36(2)	Written/oral evidence of two RMPs that accused is suffering from mental illness/severe mental impairment of a nature/degree which makes it appropriate to be detained for treatment s. 36(1)	Written/oral evidence that a bed is available within 7 days. Accused may be conveyed to a place of safety pending admission s. 36(3)	Same as s. 35 s. 36(6)	Appeal to the Court of Appeal
s. 48. Transfer to hospital for medical treatment before sentence	Home Secretary: Any person in prison on remand from the Mag. Court /any other person detained in prison but not serving a custodial sentence s. 48(2)	Written/oral evidence of two RMPs that accused is suffering from mental illness/severe mental impairment and is in 'urgent need of treatment' s. 48(1)	Must be transferred within 14 days of the order being made. s. 48(3)	Duration is of no fixed time limit. The transfer has the same effect as a hospital order. (s. 49) Expiry is governed by the detailed provisions in ss. 51, 52	Appeal to Mental Health Review Tribunal

Note: A 'place of safety' is defined by s. 55(1) and includes a police station, prison/remand centre, or hospital. When the evidence of two RMPs is required, at least one must be 'approved' under s. 54(1) as having special experience in the diagnosis and treatment of mental disorder.

Government's hopes were high that this would indeed occur, and the prison medical service had similar hopes that the introduction of these more flexible powers would achieve a significant reduction in the numbers of mentally disordered people held in prison on remand. This hope, however, has not been fully realized.

During their first few years of operation, the total number of such orders fell dramatically short of expectations. Statistics reveal that in 1984, s. 35 was used on only 27 occasions and s. 36 on 6 occasions to formally admit patients to NHS facilities.[193] Throughout the early 1980s this underuse and the plight of the mentally ill continually being remanded and sentenced to periods of imprisonment was highlighted.[194] Particularly in Leeds, one study found that during the four years from the inception of the Mental Health Act, there had been very little change, and the only improvement had been in the rate of use of the civil s. 4 powers for emergency assessment.[195] As Adrian Grounds observed,

Clearly, no conclusions can be drawn about the likely future use of these provisions on the basis of the first year's figures, and it is expected that the number of orders made under the new sections will increase as hospitals and courts become more familiar with them. However, there remains the question of whether the underlying intention of the new powers, namely to divert substantial numbers of remanded mentally disordered defendants from prison to hospital, is likely to be realised. . . . The new provisions are to be welcomed for the flexibility they allow in assessing and treating mentally disordered defendants, but whether they can provide an alternative to prison for the majority of psychiatric custodial remands is less certain.[196]

The figures have improved over the supervening years, however, and in 1989/90 the total number of s. 35 orders used to admit patients to NHS facilities was 283. The corresponding figure for s. 36 was 38.[197] The initial underuse is perhaps attributable to unfamiliarity and unawareness of the new powers during the early stages. Despite the increase, however, it has generally been accepted that these figures are still alarmingly low and that the powers are being consistently underused. This has been noted by several prominent bodies and committees.

The Mental Health Act watchdog body—the Mental Health Act Commission— in its second biennial report in 1987 commented upon the persistent underuse of

---

[193] DoH Statistical Bulletin 2(7)92 p. 13.

[194] M. Benn, 'Jail or Hospital?—Nobody Wants Them', *New Statesman*, 25 October 1985, pp. 15–16.

[195] A. M. Mortimer, 'Changes in the Use of the Mental Health Act 1983 Four Years from its Inception in Leeds' Eastern Health Authority' (1990) 30 *Med, Sci & Law* 309.

[196] A. Grounds, 'The Mentally Disordered Offender in the Criminal Process', in Herbst and Gunn (eds.), *Mentally Disordered Offender*, 41. See also 'The Use of the Remand Provisions in the 1983' Mental Health Act 1983 (1988) 12 *Bull R Coll Psych* 125–6.

[197] Throughout the 1990s the figures have remained fairly constant, although there have been overall increases in the number of admissions under these sections. See *In-Patients Formally Detained in Hospitals under the Mental Health Act and Other Legislation, England: 1991–92 to 1996–97*, DoH Statistical Bulletin 1998/01 Table 1. These figures will be discussed in more depth in the next chapter, when assessing the impact of the introduction of diversion policy in 1990.

the disposal powers, particularly the s. 35 remand power. The Commission had conducted a study of the use of remands for psychiatric reports and concluded that 'The relatively high proportion of remands into custody for psychiatric reports . . . calls into question whether this section is proving as useful as had been intended.'[198] It concluded this part of its report on a rather sombre note, stating firmly that diversion to medical care under the Act was nowhere near reaching its full potential

Whatever the true magnitude of the problem, as a result of our preliminary survey, we are left with the strong impression that there is certainly more work to be done before it can be said that Part III of the 1983 Act has come near to achieving its aims of ensuring that offenders who are mentally disordered within the meaning of the . . . Act and who require care in hospital are not imprisoned instead.[199]

This prompted parliament to consider this area of the law. In 1986, the House of Commons Social Services Select Committee on the Prison Medical Service reached similar conclusions stating what little use had been made of s. 35 remands under the new legislation: 'too many people are being remanded to custody for medical assessment. . . . Without doubt prisons are not the best place to assess the psychiatric state of a person: there must be a risk that diagnosis will in some way be distorted by the fact of imprisonment.'[200] The Committee had received a wealth of evidence to this effect echoing the sentiments of an earlier Home Affairs Select Committee Report on Remands in Custody.[201]

Another study also highlighted the weaknesses of s. 35. The authors conducted a case study in a South-East London Court of the use of this section. They noted its importance and stated that it should be increasingly advocated and realize its full potential.[202] The Woolf Report on Prison Disturbances also received evidence of this underuse which 'regularly results in mentally disordered offenders being remanded in custody for the purpose of medical reports, when they might more suitably be remanded to a hospital'.[203] It is therefore imperative that this section be implemented as fully and as frequently as possible, as research conducted on behalf of the Home Office has shown that 'remands in custody are an *inefficient, ineffective* and *inhumane* way of securing psychiatric assessment and treatment'.[204]

Often it appears that the courts are reluctant to use this provision. But one magistrate has presented the court's perspective, stating that

---

[198] MHAC, *Report 1985–7* (HMSO 1987), 46.   [199] Ibid. 47.
[200] Social Services Select Committee, *Third Report on the Prison Medical Service*, Session 1985–6 HC 72 para. 56.   [201] *First Report*, Session 1983–4 HC 252 para. 51.
[202] T. Exworthy and C. Glenn, 'A Case for Change: Section 35, Mental Health Act 1983' (1992) 156 *JP* 663–4.   [203] Cm. 1456 para. 10.128.
[204] A. Grounds, *et al.,* 'Mentally Disordered Remanded Prisoners', Unpublished Report to the Home Office (July 1991), 423 para. 5 (emphasis supplied); see also G. Robertson *et al., Mentally Disordered Remand Prisoners,* Home Office Research and Statistics Department Bulletin, 32 (Home Office 1992), 1–6.

Rather unfairly, courts have come in for a lot of criticism for not making more use of these measures. There are regular press reports of frustrated judges and magistrates compelled to remand in custody, or to give custodial sentences, because of the non-availability of hospital beds. The tragic suicide of Mr Michael Flynn . . . is a striking example of such failure to provide a hospital bed. Flynn was moved 16 times while on custodial remand from a London court, and had to be accommodated not even in prison, but in police cells as far afield as the Midlands, under conditions which made it impossible to prepare a psychiatric report.[205]

It seems that the blame does not lie squarely upon the shoulders of the legal system, but also falls upon those within the health and social services. In many areas, this section has been underused due to the lack of suitable provision within the health service. As noted by Hoggett, hospitals often reject such defendants[206] as they may be disruptive, readily abscond, or create problems when staffing is low, many defendants may not be seriously ill, or it may be simply that there are no suitable beds available.[207] Part of the problem lies with the fact that hospitals are not obliged to accept the patients from the court, so there is a real problem in finding a suitable hospital bed. Although s. 39 of the Act provides a fall-back provision as it enables the court to require information from Regional Health Authorities as to the availability of beds,[208] unfortunately it does not apply to the remand powers and can only be used with regard to hospital orders under ss. 37 and 38. This limitation has been criticized.[209]

To remedy this, perhaps one solution would be the provision of psychiatric bail hostels.[210] As outlined earlier, providing a health as opposed to a penal environment would be better for the patients and would greatly relieve prisons, and also be more suitable and convenient for assessment.[211] A group co-ordinated by the Law Society (including the Criminal Bar Association, the Justices' Clerks

---

[205] Major, 'What Can a Magistrate Do?', 48.

[206] Evidence shows that this is very often the case, particularly with violent and seriously disturbed offenders with little prospect of recovery. See J. Gunn *et al.*, *How Many Prisoners should be in Hospital?* Home Office Research and Statistics Department Research Bulletin, 31 (Home Office 1991), 13.

[207] See e.g. J. W. Coid, 'Mentally Abnormal Prisoners on Remand: I. Rejected or Accepted by the NHS' (1988) 296 *BMJ* 1779–84; see further Hoggett, *Mental Health Law*.

[208] Para. 3.4 of the Revised Code of Practice reminds regional health authorities of their responsibility to comply with the court's request under this section and of any other proper request. It also states that the authorities should appoint a named person to respond to those requests. See also *Mental Health Act 1983: Memorandum* (HMSO 1998), para. 173.

[209] Major, 'What Can a Magistrate Do?', 52.

[210] Bail hostels are under the direction of the probation service. The Tumim Report called for an increase in the number of bail hostel placements so that the number of defendants currently being remanded in custody decreases (Cm. 1383 paras. 3.77, 7.97). Many believe, however, that psychiatric bail hostels should be provided (presently there is only one in this country, Elliott House in Birmingham—see J. Kennedy-Herbert and S. D. Geelan, 'Bail and Probation Hostel for Mentally Disordered Offenders in Birmingham' (1998) 37(1) *How J of Crim Just* 112). They would ensure that the defendant receives the psychiatric assessment and support s/he requires whilst on bail in the community (Major, 'What Can a Magistrate Do?', 52–3).

[211] Major, 'What Can a Magistrate Do?', 52–3.

Society, the CPS, and the Association of Chief Police Officers) called for increased funding for existing and new psychiatric bail hospitals, and for special accommodation, preferably in hospitals for those requiring medical or mental treatment.[212] This was prompted as a result of an Interdepartmental Report of Home Office and DHSS officials on mentally disturbed offenders in the prison system.[213] The Group was appointed by the 1979–97 Conservative Government to 'consider the problems posed by mentally disordered offenders in the Prison System . . . with a view to . . . minimising the numbers . . . [and] facilitating their management and treatment'. The report noted that there had been a significant rise in the number of mentally ill people inappropriately placed in prison, and attributed this increase, in particular, to the persistent underuse of the remand and therapeutic disposal powers.[214] Unfortunately, however, to date, there is only one such specialist bail hostel in existence, Elliott House in Birmingham which has a total number of 20 beds. This hostel can potentially accept referrals from any court throughout the country, however, given the extremely limited number of beds, it is highly unlikely to accept such wide-ranging referrals. Demand therefore greatly outweighs provision and this is completely unsatisfactory. There is a clear need for such nation-wide provision of specialist bail hostels for mentally disordered offenders, which has been identified by several researchers in this area.[215]

Added to this are the particular concerns which have been continually expressed by the Prison Service[216] about the high numbers of mentally disordered remand prisoners in their custody: 'imprisonment may adversely affect their condition; they create undue pressure on already stretched resources, and they could well be dealt with in better ways'.[217]

Section 36 has also attracted specific criticism. Its implementation is regarded as both 'time consuming and administratively difficult'.[218] This section has also been criticized as not having gone far enough, as it is a power to remand for treatment, but provides no power to commit to hospital—this is still at the discretion of the hospital. So the powers of the court are not as wide as they may seem and

---

[212] F. Gibb, 'Legal groups in call for action on remand crisis', *The Times*, 12 December 1988, p. 6.

[213] HO/DHSS, *Report of an Interdepartmental Working Group on Mentally Disturbed Offenders in the Prison System* (HMSO 1987).   [214] Ibid. 6–9.

[215] See T. Kennedy, *et al.*, 'Supported Bail for Mentally Vulnerable Defendants' (1997) 36(2) *How J of Crim Just* 158–69; J. Evans and A. Tomison, 'Assessment of the Perceived Need for a Psychiatric Service to a Magistrates' Court' (1997) 37(2) *Med, Sci & Law* 161–4, where the need for specialist bail provision was stressed.

[216] See e.g. *Report on the Work of the Prison Service 1986–87* Cm. 246 paras. 34–6; *Report on the Work of the Prison Service 1987–88* Cm. 516 paras. 51–3.

[217] Cm. 246 para. 34.

[218] Walker, 'Sentencing', para. 14.14.4; see also A. Akinkunmi, *et al.*, 'Inadequacies in the Mental Health Act 1983 in Relation to Mentally Disordered Remand Prisoners' (1997) 37(1) *Med, Sci & Law* 55–7: the authors identify the problems with these provisions in the Act which, they argue, are too restrictive and time-consuming, thereby frustrating the policy of ensuring access to hospital for mentally disordered offenders at the earliest possible stage.

consequently this power 'is not used with any great frequency by the courts'.[219] The hospital managers can refuse to supply a bed—the prisons, on the other hand, have no such choice to refuse, so as a result mentally disordered offenders on remand invariably end up there.[220] This should not be the case, as outlined in Ch. 1, mentally disordered offenders should not be unnecessarily subjected to the prison regime, and may suffer as a result. Much of the evidence seems to support this, as a remand in custody 'exposes mentally disordered people to conditions and regimes which are cruelly harsh and inappropriate'.[221]

3.4.3. The Transfer of Unsentenced Prisoners (s. 48)

3.4.3.1. The Provisions

If a mentally disordered person awaiting trial or sentence is actually remanded into custody by the court, then the Home Secretary has a discretionary power to direct his/her transfer to hospital for 'urgent treatment' under s. 48. It is strongly emphasized that this power is only to be used as a 'last resort' in cases where 'urgent treatment' is needed.[222] The basis for this power was set out in the Report of the Royal Commission on Capital Punishment: 'the power of the Home Secretary should be exercised only when there is likely to be a scandal if the prisoner is brought up for trial'.[223] The detailed requirements of this section are also set out in Table 3.1.

3.4.3.2. Commentary

The number of s. 48 orders has increased throughout the 1980s. In 1985, only 41 such transfers were made, but there was almost a fivefold increase to a total of 181 transfers in 1990,[224] as Table 3.2 illustrates.

TABLE 3.2. *Section 48 transfers*

	1985	1986	1987	1988	1989	1990
s. 48	41	53	77	85	100	181

[219] P. Fennell, 'Diversion of Mentally Disordered Offenders from Custody' [1991] *Crim LR* 333–48, 338.

[220] Research seems to bear this out. See Grounds *et al.,* 'Mentally Disordered Remanded Prisoners'. [221] Robertson *et al., Remand Prisoners,* 6.

[222] See Gostin, *Mental Health Services,* para. 14.15. The concept of 'urgent need' was introduced by the Mental Health (Amendment) Act 1982 (s 23(2)) to indicate that this section is intended to be an emergency procedure to be invoked only where there is an urgent need for hospital treatment which the prison cannot provide.

[223] Cmd. 893 (HMSO 1953) para. 219.

[224] *Statistics of Mentally Disordered Offenders: England and Wales 1993,* Home Office Statistical Bulletin, 01/95 Table 11. See also *Statistics of Mentally Disordered Offenders in England and Wales 1996,* Home Office Statistical Bulletin 20/97 para. 5. The number of transfers has continued to rise dramatically throughout the 1990s and increased almost fivefold between 1989 and 1994. This will also be considered in more depth in the context of the impact of diversion policy in Ch. 4.

This massive increase in use of s. 48 transfers was undoubtedly as a result of the concerns expressed throughout the 1980s about the growing numbers of mentally ill people being remanded and sentenced to periods of imprisonment. This was especially noted by the Social Services Committee[225] and the 1987 Interdepartmental Group[226] reports. The latter concluded that even greater use should be made of this power 'to enable appropriate mentally disturbed persons to be taken into the health system rather than the penal system'.[227] This was echoed by the Tumim Report on Prison Suicides which recommended that the Prison Service should be actively encouraged to make greater use of this section.[228]

It would seem that, in the past, this power had tended to be used 'as a last resort'[229] only in those cases where 'health was very seriously deteriorating or there was a danger of suicide or of violence'.[230] This was due to a variety of reasons, amongst which was the familiar 'chronic difficulty of finding a bed in the NHS' which invariably 'dissuaded prison doctors from even bothering'.[231] Other criticisms which have been aimed at the section focus on the restrictive criteria, which exclude offenders suffering from psychopathic disorder and limit transfers for the purposes of treatment only.[232] It is argued that the ambit should be extended to include transfers for the purposes of assessment as well as treatment, which would increase the opportunities for transfer, and this may also be a factor which has contributed to the underuse.

Despite the increase in numbers, it seems that the Prison Service has as much difficulty as the courts in trying to find an appropriate hospital bed for the mentally disordered offender and 'many of the applications for transfer to special hospitals [have been] turned down'.[233] Research conducted by the Home Office clearly evinced this.[234] The report concluded that far greater use should be made of s. 48 of the Act as it would enable those in urgent need of treatment to be rapidly transferred to hospitals, thereby 'avoid[ing] delays attendant on court procedure and enabl[ing] ill people to be rapidly moved'.[235] The Chief Inspector of Prisons Annual Reports[236] and the Mental Health Act Commission's Biennial Reports[237] have also constantly alluded to the delays in securing prompt transfers. Despite the welcome increase in the number of transfers, the average waiting times for hospital placements is still perceived to be far too long.

---

[225]　HO Statistical Bulletin 20/97 para. 5.1–7.　　　　[226]　HO/DHSS, Report (1987), para. 62.
[227]　Ibid. 1.　　　　　　　[228]　Cm. 1383 paras. 3.64, 7.94.　　　　　　　[229]　Ibid. para. 3.64.
[230]　Ibid. para. 3.58.　　　　　　　　　　　　　　　　　　　　　　　　　　　　[231]　Ibid.
[232]　DoH/HO, *Report of the Department of Health and Home Office Working Group on Psychopathic Disorder* (Home Office 1994) para. 10.35, 44.
[233]　R. Smith, *Prison Health Care* (BMA 1984), 49.
[234]　Robertson *et al.*, *Remand Prisoners*, 2; see also Grounds *et al.*, 'Mentally Disordered Remanded Prisoners'; see also R. D. Mackay and D. Machin, Transfers from Prison to Hospital: The Operation of Section 48 of the Mental Health Act 1983 (Home Office 1998).
[235]　Ibid.　　　　　　　　　　　　　　[236]　*HMCIP Annual Report 1993–1994* para. 5.08.
[237]　See e.g. MHAC, *Report 1993–5*, 75.

Throughout the 1980s, too many mentally disordered defendants were being remanded in custody, not because of the nature of the offence but due to their need for care and treatment.[238] This was clearly wholly unsatisfactory for the reasons which have been outlined above. It has been noted that, as a method for obtaining psychiatric help 'the custodial remand has nothing to commend it. . . . It brings into prison thousands of defendants who do not need to be there and for whom penal disposals are never contemplated'.[239] This again reinforces the need for specialized psychiatric units to be set up to which these disturbed people can be sent at this stage, as they will provide the necessary care and treatment.[240] It also emphasizes the need for greater resourcing to provide adequate levels of psychiatric facilities. The study conducted by Grounds *et al.* showed that the section was previously rarely employed as many prison doctors mistakenly believed that it covers only those whose physical health is at risk from their mental illness.[241] There is, however, no reason for this, therefore s. 48 should be increasingly advocated to ensure that mentally disordered offenders are not remanded in custody.

The statistics show that the numbers of transfers, both before and after sentence, have increased in recent years. However, whilst its increased use must surely be welcome in the sense that it is clear recognition that mentally disordered offenders are inappropriately placed in prison and it provides a means of getting them out, in another sense it is worrying as it is also a clear indication of the high levels of mentally ill people who have been inappropriately imprisoned in the first place. They will have already spent damaging amounts of time in custody, and even the shortest time can have an extremely detrimental effect upon a person's mental state. The increasing number of prison suicides that took place during the 1980s bears this out. An analysis of prison suicides between 1972 and 1987 by Dr Edna Dooley found that mental disorder was among the reasons for suicide in 20 per cent of cases.[242] Furthermore, over one-third of inmates committing suicide had a previous history of psychiatric contact, whilst over a quarter had previous in-patient admissions. In a Written Answer in the House of Commons, Mr Douglas Hogg stated that in 1987, 30 per cent of inmates committing suicide had undergone psychiatric assessment or treatment before they had gone into custody.[243] So, whilst attempts were being made during the 1980s to get these offenders out of prison, attempts to stop them getting there in the first place were failing, and it was necessary to remedy this situation.

---

[238] This has been echoed by Dr J. Coid who conducted a retrospective survey of mentally abnormal men remanded to Winchester Prison 1979–83: Coid, 'Prisoners on Remand: I'.

[239] Robertson *et al., Remand Prisoners*, 6. [240] Ibid.

[241] Grounds *et al.*, 'Mentally Disordered Remanded Prisoners'.

[242] E. Dooley, 'Prison Suicide in England and Wales: 1972–87' (1990) 156 *Brit J Psych* 40–5; see also J. Gunn, A. Maden and M. Swinton, 'Treatment Needs of Prisoners with Psychiatric Disorders' (1991) 303 *BMJ* 338–41: 'Surveys of remand prisons show high levels of psychiatric illness and prison suicides are more common in this group. These prisoners add to the demands on psychiatric services in prisons.'

[243] Session 1988–9 HC Debs Vol. 149 col. 232.

A report by Professor John Gunn, *Mentally Disordered Prisoners*,[244] published a study of the sentenced prison population. It found that there were many difficulties in this area. These included a lack of co-operation between prisons and hospitals, lack of appropriate beds, and a poor visiting psychiatrist service. During the 1980s it would seem that this was an extremely problematic area, and there was much scope for reform because, generally, the use of such powers at this stage was not as widespread as it should be.[245] It seems that there existed a difficult choice for the courts of which is the lesser of two evils as Brenda Hoggett has noted: is it worse to 'languish in prison without treatment or to languish in hospital without trial'?[246]

3.4.4. Additional Criminal Law Provisions

Before considering the powers and provisions at the sentencing stage, it is important to note that there are several criminal law provisions which can apply at the trial stages which may also provide a mentally disordered offender with routes into psychiatric care. It is not proposed to conduct a detailed evaluation of these provisions as they are primarily concerned with the offender's liability and degree of responsibility rather than achieving treatment, and clearly it is far more desirable to achieve diversion at earlier stages in the process. Furthermore, these provisions account for very few hospital admissions every year, and so essentially fall beyond the scope of this book.[247] A brief note of them will be made at this stage, however, as, assuming the offender proceeds thus far, these provisions do provide routes into psychiatric care and so are relevant to the general theme of diversion from punishment and towards humane and therapeutic treatment.

3.4.4.1. Unfitness to Plead

The first provision is unfitness to plead[248] which can apply at the defendant's first court appearance and essentially allows the court to make certain therapeutic orders, similar to those found under the Mental Health Act 1983. Where a defendant is mentally ill and unable to understand the court proceedings for example, s/he can be made subject to a hospital order, a guardianship order, or a supervision and treatment order.[249] Studies into the number of unfitness pleadings have

---

[244] (Home Office 1991).

[245] J. R. Hamilton, 'Mental Health Act 1983' (1983) 286 *BMJ* 1720–25.

[246] Hoggett, *Mental Health Law*, 108.

[247] For a fuller and more detailed account of these provisions see R. D. Mackay, *Mental Condition Defences in the Criminal Law* (Clarendon 1995).

[248] See further D. H. Grubin, 'What Constitutes Unfitness to Plead?' [1993] *Crim LR* 748–58.

[249] Criminal Procedure (Insanity and Unfitness to Plead) Act 1991 ss. 3, 5; see further S. White, 'The CP(I and UP) Act 1991' [1992] *Crim LR* 4–14; P. Fennell, 'The CP(I and UP) Act 1991' (1992) 55 *MLR* 547–55. This does not apply to the offence of murder, however, as its penalty is fixed by law.

shown that its use had declined dramatically during the 1970s and 1980s.[250] This was largely due to the harsh consequences, as under the Criminal Procedure (Insanity) Act 1964 a finding of unfitness could only result in an order for detention during Her/His Majesty's Pleasure. New flexible disposal powers were therefore introduced by a new Act in 1991 and provide another avenue to psychiatric care enabling 'psychiatrists [to] be approached more frequently by their legal colleagues to assist the court in making specific recommendations for psychiatric disposal within the context of the new Act'.[251]

A study by Mackay and Kearns into the first year of operation of the new Act revealed that in the eleven cases where unfitness was pleaded, the courts took full advantage of the new powers and the majority of such defendants were given hospital/guardianship or supervision/treatment orders.[252] So it would seem that the new provisions in the Act are playing a part to 'help in the implementation of the policy—agreed by all parties—of diverting mentally disordered people from the criminal justice system'[253] as the 1979–9 Conservative Government intended.

3.4.4.2. *Insanity, Infanticide, and Diminished Responsibility*

The remaining criminal provisions are the 'psychiatric defences'[254] which can operate to diminish the defendant's liability and guilt at the trial stage if s/he is pleading not guilty to the offence. The annual number of such defences is small, but if successful can result in an order for admission to a psychiatric hospital or community psychiatric supervision. This is now possible for an insanity verdict along the same lines as unfitness to plead under the 1991 Act,[255] and a successful diminished responsibility (which reduces a murder charge to manslaughter) or infanticide (which applies to mothers who kill their babies) defence has always allowed the judge discretion in sentencing. The criminal statistics reveal that although the annual numbers are small, the majority of those found guilty by reason of diminished responsibility do receive hospital or probation/supervision orders and the same applies for those who plead successful infanticide defences.[256]

---

[250] R. D. Mackay, 'The Decline of Disability in Relation to the Trial' [1991] *Crim LR* 87–97; D. H. Grubin, 'Unfit to Plead in England and Wales, 1976–1988: A Survey' (1991) 158 *Brit J Psych* 540–8.

[251] M. C. Dolan and A. A. Campbell, 'The CP (I & UP) Act 1991' (1994) 34 *Med, Sci & Law* 155–60, 159.

[252] R. D. Mackay and G. Kearns, 'The Continued Underuse of Unfitness to Plead and the Insanity Defence' [1994] *Crim LR* 576–9.

[253] Session 1990–1 HC Debs Vol. 186 cols 1269–81, 1271.

[254] See further J. C. Smith and B. Hogan, *Criminal Law* (Butterworths 1996) for a detailed account of these provisions.

[255] See A. Tomison, 'McNaughton Today' (1993) 4 *J For Psych* 371, for a case report of the first successful defence under the 1991 Act and also Mackay and Kearns, 'Continued Underuse'.

[256] *Criminal Statistics England and Wales 1995* (HMSO 1996) Cm. 3421 Table 4. 9.

Having been found guilty of the offence, or assuming that one of the psychiatric defences applies, the mentally disordered defendant reaches the final stage in the criminal justice process, that of sentencing. The courts have a wide range of powers, essentially under the Mental Health Act 1983, to ensure that a therapeutic as opposed to a penal disposal is given where it is appropriate.[257] Where such a course of action is contemplated the court must first obtain medical reports. Not only does the Mental Health Act expressly state this, but the Criminal Justice Act 1991 also makes specific mandatory provision for obtaining medical reports in relation to mentally disordered offenders.

3.5.1. Obtaining Medical Reports

3.5.1.1. The Provisions[258]

The Mental Health Act sets out the procedural requirements for obtaining the medical report and provides that the written/oral evidence of two doctors is required for a s. 36 remand for treatment, any type of hospital order (either an interim order or an ordinary order with/without restrictions), or a guardianship order. A s. 35 remand for report or a probation order with a condition of psychiatric treatment requires the evidence of only one doctor. Where the evidence of two doctors is necessary, at least one of them must be an approved medical practitioner (under s. 12), thereby possessing special skill in the treatment and diagnosis of mental disorder. Where the evidence of only one doctor is required, s/he must also be an approved practitioner.[259]

The Criminal Justice Act 1991 introduced some radical changes in a number of areas in relation to sentencing, but of particular relevance here is s. 3, as it sets out various procedural matters that the court must consider before passing a custodial sentence.[260] This consideration includes obtaining a pre-sentence report—which replaces the social inquiry report—where this is necessary,[261] and it will contain detailed information about how the offender could be punished in the community, with a view to assisting the court in determining the most suitable method of dealing with the offender. This report will be prepared by a probation officer and may refer to any concerns about the offender's mental health. In addition, the court is required to consider any other information available to it about the circumstances of the offence, including any aggravating or mitigating

---

[257] For a detailed review of these powers see Walker, *Sentencing*, ch. 21; Hoggett, *Mental Health Law*, ch. 5; Gostin, *Mental Health Services*; A. Ashworth, and L. Gostin, 'Mentally Disordered Offenders and the Sentencing Process' [1984] *Crim LR* 195–212.
[258] See Tables 3.1 and 3.4.   [259] Mental Health Act s. 54(1).
[260] M. Wasik and R. Taylor, *Blackstone's Guide to the Criminal Justice Act 1991* (Blackstone 1994), ch. 1.   [261] As amended by the Criminal Justice and Public Order Act 1994.

factors. However, especially in the case of an 'offender [who] is or appears to be mentally disordered', the court must, in addition to obtaining a pre-sentence report, obtain a medical report (in accordance with the Mental Health Act), unless it is of the opinion that it is unnecessary.[262] Before passing a custodial sentence on such an offender, the court must consider any information before it relating to the offender's mental condition, whether given in a medical report, pre-sentence report or otherwise; and the likely effect of a custodial sentence on that condition and on any treatment which may be available for it.[263]

The aim of s. 4, therefore, is to supplement the mental health legislation, by ensuring that the courts have all the necessary information at their disposal when sentencing an offender who is mentally disordered, so that, whenever possible, s/he receives treatment under the Mental Health Act, rather than being at risk of a custodial sentence. This is reinforced by the provision in s. 28(4) of the 1991 Act which provides that nothing in the Act is to be taken as requiring a court to pass a custodial sentence on a mentally disordered person, or as restricting any power of the court to deal with such an offender in the manner it considers most appropriate.[264]

3.5.1.2. Commentary

These provisions under the 1991 Act are extremely welcome,[265] as research conducted in the past had pointed to the decline in the use of psychiatric reports by the courts.[266] Watson's research concluded that there has been a dramatic decline in the use of such reports, partly as a the result of a general disaffection with psychiatry on the part of the courts. This is perhaps due to the lack of understanding which has arisen between the agencies involved, which has been widely documented here and in Ch. 1. What is required is improved communication and understanding between the courts, the lawyers, and the health and social services so that the information required by the courts to enable them to consider making therapeutic disposals is readily available.[267]

These provisions make it mandatory to obtain the requisite medical opinion, thereby reducing the conflict, assisting the court in making a therapeutic disposal when necessary and also ensuring that many people suffering from mental disorder

---

[262] Criminal Justice Act 1991 s. 4(1)(2); see also *Mental Health Act 1983 Revised Code of Practice*, para. 3.12.

[263] Ibid. s. 4(3); see further Wasik and Taylor, *Blackstone's Guide to CJA*, 32–3.

[264] See further D. Tonak, 'Mentally Disordered Offenders and CJA 1991' (1992) 39 *Probat J* 99–102.

[265] A. James, 'The Criminal Justice Act 1991: Principal Provisions and their Effects on Psychiatric Provisions' (1993) 4 *J For Psych* 286–94.

[266] See e.g. S. Watson, 'Changes in the Use of Psychiatric Reports in Magistrates' Courts' (unpublished M.Phil. thesis, York University 1986): 'The use of psychiatric opinion is an infrequent event in the business of the courts', p. 1; W. M. Donovan and K. P. O' Brien, 'Psychiatric Court Reports: Too Many or Too Few?' (1981) 21 *Med, Sci & Law* 153; R. D. Mackay, 'Psychiatric Reports in the Crown Court' [1986] *Crim LR* 217–25: 'The role of the psychiatric report is often of great significance in the criminal process.'

[267] See further P. Lewis, Shall We Ask for a Psychiatric Report?' (1979) 143 *JP* 518.

in court whose condition may not be obviously apparent do not slip through the net. The increased use of such information was strongly recommended by the Butler Committee over twenty years ago, 'In order that the courts should be in possession of all relevant information about the mental state of defendants we propose that greater use should be made of social inquiry reports as a screening process for mental disorder and to indicate the need for a full psychiatric report.'[268] Thus the emphasis upon medical opinion and the provision of information for the courts and upon care for the mentally disordered offender is now, at last, firmly stated. These provisions of the 1991 Act clearly represent a humanitarian approach as they are concerned with 'the welfare of those who are mentally ill and who come before the courts'.[269] During the Parliamentary debates which preceded the Act in 1991, this was constantly repeated: '[These] new provisions in the Criminal Justice Bill make it possible for the courts to specify at an early stage that they have psychiatric reports before them to avoid the unfortunate event of someone being committed to prison if he/she should not be so committed.'[270]

This clearly enables the welfare of mentally disordered offenders to be considered fully, is extremely positive, and in line with the underlying assumption that treatment is preferable to punitive sanctions in the majority of cases. Although this chapter is essentially concerned with the provisions that were in existence prior to the implementation of an explicit diversion policy in 1990, the Criminal Justice Act 1991 has also been considered because its introduction, whilst clearly reinforcing diversion policy, was initially independent of it. Moreover, it does allow the court to consider medical evidence more readily to enable them to make appropriate therapeutic disposals.

3.5.2. The Therapeutic Disposals

Having obtained the requisite medical evidence, upon its basis the court must decide which is the most appropriate method of disposal: 'While the law has so far stuck to a very strict view on criminal responsibility, it has now been provided with a *wide range of non-penal methods of disposal after conviction*.'[271] Five psychiatric orders are present at this stage, and this is supplemented by the fact that an offender who is sent to prison may later be transferred to hospital by the Home Secretary under s. 47 of the Act.[272]

3.5.2.1. The Psychiatric Probation Order

3.5.2.1.1. The Provisions

If the medical reports do not advise hospital treatment but indicate that some form of medical supervision is required, the court can consider imposing a psychiatric

---

[268] Cmnd. 6244 p. 166.   [269] Session 1990–1 HC Debs Vol. 186 col. 1277.
[270] Ibid.   [271] Hoggett, *Mental Health Law*, 115 (emphasis supplied).
[272] For further details see ibid. 115–32; Gostin, *Mental Health Services*, ch.s 15, 16; R. Jones, *Mental Health Act Manual* (Sweet & Maxwell 1996), 90–135.

probation order. Once the defendant has been convicted, a probation order can be imposed by the court (magistrates' or Crown) for any offence other than murder (which has a fixed penalty). An offender subject to a probation order will be under the supervision of a probation officer for a specified period of between 6 months and 3 years. When an order is made, it may also require the offender to comply with such requirements as the court considers necessary for securing his/her good conduct or for preventing him/her from offending again.[273]

With respect to mentally disordered defendants, the court may place the offender on probation with a condition that s/he submit to treatment by or under the direction of a qualified medical practitioner with a view to the improvement of the offender's mental condition.[274] The Criminal Justice and Public Order Act 1994 has inserted an additional condition so that treatment for the mental illness may now alternatively be provided by a psychologist.[275] This is known as a 'psychiatric probation order', and to effect one, the evidence of a qualified and approved medical practitioner must be produced, stating that the mental condition of the offender requires and will be susceptible to treatment, but does not warrant his/her detention in hospital.[276]

Such an order is normally used only where there is no danger that the offender will commit further serious offences, because s/he will not be in custody for the duration of the order. Consequently the court must assess the extent to which the public will be at risk.[277]

The court is empowered under the legislation to specify a variety of treatments for the offender. These are: treatment as a resident in a hospital or mental nursing home (not a special hospital); treatment as a non-resident patient at a specified institution, or treatment by/under the direction of a specified qualified medical practitioner/chartered psychologist. However, alternative arrangements can be made where the doctor responsible for the probationer believes the medical treatment could be better or more conveniently given at another place. The doctor must provide written notice of this to the probation officer.[278] The law states that the doctor may also report to the officer if s/he believes that the treatment should continue beyond the specified period, or a different kind of treatment which the court can specify is needed, or if the probationer is not susceptible to treatment, if no further treatment is required, or if the doctor is unwilling to continue to treat

---

[273] Powers of Criminal Courts Act 1973 Schedule 1A.
[274] Powers of Criminal Courts Act 1973 Act as amended by the Criminal Justice Act 1991 Schedule 1(A), Part II, para. 5—the requirement for 'treatment for mental condition' as a condition of probation; see further Hoggett, *Mental Health Law*, 115–17.
[275] Criminal Justice and Public Order Act 1994 Schedule 9 para. 10. See further Wasik and Taylor *Blackstone's Guide to CJPO*, para. 1.12.
[276] Powers of Criminal Courts Act 1973 Schedule 1A para. 5.
[277] D. A. Thomas, *Current Sentencing Practice* (Sweet & Maxwell) Part F1–2B. See *R.* v. *Nicholls* (1981) *The Times* 14 February.
[278] Powers of Criminal Courts Act 1973 ss. 3(5), (6); see further Gostin, *Mental Health Services*, para 15.24–5.

the probationer. To make such a variation or cancellation, the probation officer in receipt of the information will apply to the court and the probationer must be in agreement with the amendments.[279]

3.5.2.1.2. Commentary

Psychiatric probation orders have frequently been invoked, and to some are regarded as useful alternatives to hospital orders. They are described as being 'tailor-made' for in/out patient treatment,[280] providing a 'healthy balance of care and control'.[281] Indeed, the Morrison Report on the Probation Service as long ago as 1962 recognized that 'mental treatment requirements are a valuable part of the probation service and should be retained'.[282]

The Annual Probation statistics reveal that the number of probation orders with additional requirements for mental treatment have remained high over the last decade, averaging 1,000 per year,[283] as shown in Table 3.3.

Very little research has been conducted in this area, however,[284] and consequently doubts do exist as to the efficacy of these orders. Many believe that they have their shortcomings from a legal point of view; in particular, some magistrates often feel that making such an order or giving an absolute discharge is 'mistaken kindness', as in some cases it is not long before the offender is in court again as s/he returns to the situation which led to the arrest.[285] This is perhaps due to the inadequate supervision and facilities within the community which hamper the effectiveness of this power. The orders seem a viable alternative in principle, but an increase in community support and care provision is required, as their successful implementation requires appropriate and adequate mental health services support. Furthermore, research has concluded that these orders can be extremely useful, but only if adequate support does in fact exist.[286] Without the proper community support and specialized measures, once the offender is

TABLE 3.3. *Psychiatric probation orders*

	1985	1986	1987	1988	1989	1990
PPOs	1,190	1,060	1,030	990	1,020	1,012

[279] Powers of Criminal Courts Act 1973. Schedule 1 para. 4; see further Gostin, *Mental Health Services*, para. 15.25.
[280] N. Walker, 'Fourteen Years on', in Herbst and Gunn, J. (eds.) *Mentally Disordered Offender,* 10.
[281] J. Peay, 'Mentally Disordered Offenders', in M. Maguire, R. Morgan and R. Reiner (eds.), *The Oxford Handbook of Criminology* (Oxford University Press 1994), 1135.
[282] *Report of the Departmental Committee on the Probation Service* (Home Office 1962) Cmnd. 1650 para. 83.
[283] *Probation Statistics England and Wales 1993* (Home Office 1994) Table 2.8 p. 30. This includes probation orders with requirements for non-residential and residential mental treatment.
[284] P. Lewis, *Psychiatric Probation Orders* (Institute of Criminology, Cambridge University 1980); M. Grunhut, *Probation and Mental Treatment* (Tavistock 1963).
[285] Major, 'What Can a Magistrate Do?', 53.
[286] Lewis, *Psychiatric Probation Orders*, 36.

discharged or released into the community: '[he] will simply . . . [be] condemned to a life of aimlessness, isolation and social nuisance in which he will be constantly recycled through the courts, until ultimately the magistrate or judge is driven to conclude that enough is enough. . . . There is nothing humane about this, nothing to promote the interests of either the offender or the public.'[287]

Research has further suggested that although such orders are frequently invoked by the courts, there is still substantial underuse of the provision. This is often attributed to the lack of understanding and co-operation between the agencies involved—probation, mental health, and social services. A survey into the effectiveness of probation orders in North Wales also identified this lack of communication problem.[288] A recent Thematic Inspection was conducted by HM Inspectorate of Probation on Probation Orders with requirements of psychiatric treatment which also noted these shortcomings.[289] The Inspectorate conducted a thorough review of this power and concluded that the value of these orders should not be underestimated. They should be increasingly advocated and in order to achieve this, greater levels of co-operation should take place amongst the agencies involved in their implementation.

The Butler Committee also gave detailed consideration to such orders, and noted that they are an extremely 'valuable form of disposal', which 'can be made to work well', provided there is sufficient resourcing and co-operation amongst the agencies involved.[290] Accordingly, it recommended their continued and increased use. Psychiatric probation orders represent a humanitarian approach to the mentally disordered offender, as, 'The order is a recognition by the court that the offender needs treatment, and gives him the opportunity of receiving it.'[291]

3.5.2.2. The Hospital Order (s. 37)

3.5.2.2.1. The Provisions

Should hospital care be required, then the court may make a hospital order[292] with respect to the mentally disordered offender. Table 3.4 outlines the judicial

---

[287] M. Mustill, 'Some Concluding Reflections' in Herbst and Gunn (eds.), *Mentally Disordered Offender*, 244.

[288] G. Jones, 'The Use and Effectiveness of the Probation Order with a Condition of Psychiatric Treatment in North Wales' (1989) 20 *Camb L Rev* 63–82; see also T. C. N. Gibbens, K. Soothill and P. Way, 'Psychiatric Treatment on Probation' (1981) 21 *Brit J Criminology* 324–34; M. Woodside, 'Probation and Psychiatric Treatment in Edinburgh' (1976) 118 *Brit J Psych* 561–70; A. Roberts *et al.*, 'The Supervision of Mentally Disordered Offenders: Work of Probation Officers and their Relationship with Psychiatrists in England and Wales' (1995) 5 *Crim Beh & Ment Health* 75–84.

[289] *Probation Orders with Requirements for Psychiatric Treatment: Report of a Thematic Inspection* (HMSO 1993); see also N. Stone, 'The Decline and Fall of the Psychiatric Probation Order' (1994) 158 *JP* 380–1, 402–4. [290] Cmnd. 6244 para. 16.18.

[291] Ibid. para. 16.4.

[292] Further guidance as to the use and effect of this power is found in *Mental Health Act 1983: Memorandum* (1998), paras. 157–61, 171–187; see also Gostin, *Mental Health Services*, para. 15.02–10; Hoggett, *Mental Health Law*, 117–21.

TABLE 3.4. *Therapeutic sentencing powers*

MHA power	Authorizing body	Medical evidence	Other requirements	Duration and effect	Discharge and appeal
s. 37. Hospital or guardianship order	Crown Court: Any person convicted of an imprisonable offence Mag. Court: As with the Crown Court but also without conviction where satisfied the accused did the act and is suffering from mental illness/severe mental impairment s. 37(1), s. 37(3)	Written/oral evidence of two RMPs that accused is suffering from one of the four forms of disorder. If it is psychopathic disorder/ mental impairment and a hospital order is being made then it must be 'treatable', i.e. treatment is likely to alleviate or prevent a deterioration of the condition. This must also be the most suitable method of dealing with the case. s. 37(2)	Written/oral evidence from the RMP in charge that a bed will be made available within 28 days. Defendant may be conveyed to a place of safety pending admission s. 37(4) If guardianship, the court must be satisfied that the Local Authority is willing to receive the offender. s. 37(6)	For a period of 6 months which is renewable for a further 6 months, then for periods of 12 months at a time. The effect is the same as a civil hospital admission under s. 3 or guardianship under s. 7. s. 40	Discharge by the doctor in charge of treatment (Responsible Medical Officer RMO), the hospital managers, or an appeal to the Mental Health Review Tribunal (MHRT)
s. 38. Interim hospital order	Crown Court: Any person convicted of an imprisonable offence Mag. Court: Any person convicted of an offence punishable on summary conviction with imprisonment s. 38(1)	Written/oral evidence of two RMPs that the accused is suffering from one of the four forms of mental disorder. A hospital order must be contemplated by the court as appropriate s. 38(1)	Written/oral evidence of the RMP in charge that a bed will be available within 28 days. Defendant may be conveyed to a place of safety pending admission s. 38(4)	For a period of up to 12 weeks and renewed for further periods of up to 28 days, up to a maximum total period of 12 months in all. Same effect as a civil admission s. 38(5)	Appeal to the magistrates' court, Crown Court, or the Court of Appeal

TABLE 3.4 (cont.):

MHA power	Authorizing body	Medical evidence	Other requirements	Duration and effect	Discharge and appeal
s. 41. Restriction order	Crown Court only: Any peson convicted of an imprisonable offence s. 37(1)	Same as under a hospital order, but at least one of the doctors must give evidence orally s. 41(2)	Same as under an ordinary hospital order but in addition the court must feel that it is necessary to protect the public from serious harm s. 41(1)	The duration may be specified by the court, or the order may be made without limit of time s. 41(1)	Discharge by the Home Secretary or by appeal to the MHRT to recommend discharge to the Home Secretary
s. 47. Transfer to hospital for medical treatment	Home Secretary s. 47(1)	Written/oral evidence of two Registered Medical Practitioners that the accused is suffering from any one of the four forms of disorder of a nature/degree which warrants hospital admission. If the condition is psychopathic disorder/mental impairment then it must me treatable, as required under a hospital order s. 47(1)	Must be transferred within 14 days of the order being made s. 47(2)	The transfer direction may be made with/ without restrictions, and will therefore have the same effect as a hospital/ restriction order s. 47(3)	Discharge by the RMO, the hospital managers, or by appeal to the MHRT to recommend discharge to the Home Secretary

Note: A place of safety is defined in s. 55(1), and where the evidence of two RMPs is required, at least one must be approved under s. 54(1).

criteria and the basic procedural and evidential requirements for making such an order.

Once the requisite medical evidence and procedural requirements have been fulfilled, the court must decide whether the order is the most suitable way of disposing of the case, having regard to all the circumstances including the nature of the offence, the character and antecedents of the offender, and the available methods of dealing with him/her.[293] It is stated that, in principle, the court should consider whether punishment or treatment is appropriate and make its decision accordingly.[294] As a general rule, where sufficient medical evidence is given to satisfy the criteria of the Act and there is no risk to public safety,[295] the court should make a hospital order. As outlined by Gostin,[296] the only exceptions to this are where it is necessary to mark the gravity of the offence with punishment,[297] the offender presents a danger to the public and a bed cannot be found for him/her in a secure hospital,[298] or the offender is suffering from mental disorder for which there is no reasonable prospect of treatment.[299] Furthermore, it has been held that there is no need for a causal connection between the offence and the mental disorder.[300]

The principle for making a hospital order was outlined in the case of *Birch*: 'In effect—the [mentally disordered person] passes out of the penal system and into the hospital regime.'[301] Thus, as noted by Hoggett, the legal effect of a hospital order is almost identical to that of an admission for treatment under the civil powers (P. II of the Act), and the rules relating to duration and renewal are essentially the same.[302]

3.5.2.2.2. Commentary

'In principle, the task of dealing with mentally disordered offenders should be approached on the basis that the law should facilitate treatment where it is possible and available.'[303] Clearly, hospital orders facilitate the possibility of treatment and have indeed been found to be useful and effective.[304] But the main

---

[293]   Mental Health Act 1983 s. 37(2)(b).

[294]   *R.* v. *Gunnell* (1966) 50 Cr App R 242.

[295]   *R.* v. *Higginbotham* [1961] 1 WLR 1277.

[296]   *Mental Health Services*, para. 15.03.

[297]   *R.* v. *Gunnell*, (1966) 50 Cr App R 242.

[298]   *R.* v. *Morris* (1961) 45 Cr App R 185; [1961] 2 QB 237.

[299]   *R.* v. *Gills* [1967] *Crim LR* 247.

[300]   D. A. Thomas, *Current Sentencing*, Part F2–2A, *McBride*, unreported 13 January 1972.

[301]   (1989) 11 Cr App R (S) 202, 210; see further D. A. Thomas, *Current Sentencing*, Part F2–2; see also R. Bluglass, *A Guide to the Mental Health Act 1983* (Churchill Livingstone 1983), 51: 'A Hospital Order or Guardianship Order is not a sentence, it is an alternative disposal and the person becomes a patient not a prisoner.'

[302]   Mental Health Act 1983 s. 40(4) and Schedule 1, P. 1. There are two differences however. First, the patient's nearest relative cannot discharge him/her, but can instead apply to the tribunal for the case to be reviewed, s. 69(1)(a). Secondly, the offender has the same right as any other to appeal to a higher court against the order. However, s/he does not have the same right as a civil patient to apply to a tribunal within the first 6 months of admission. See further Hoggett, *Mental Health Law*, 117–21.

[303]   Ashworth and Gostin, 'Sentencing Process', 225.

[304]   G. Robertson, *et al.*, 'A Follow-up of Remanded Mentally Ill Offenders Given Court Hospital Orders' (1994) 34 *Med, Sci & Law* 61–6.

problem here is the availability of that treatment; it seems that the difficulty in this area, as experienced by the courts and prisons at earlier stages, is that of finding a hospital bed.[305] The courts are constantly faced with this problem, and increasing numbers of cases have been reported where the admission of a mentally disordered offender has been barred because of the refusal of nursing staff to accept difficult or potentially dangerous patients under a hospital order,[306] or indeed, simply due to the lack of suitable hospital accommodation. It has been widely noted that, if the court considers the offender to be a serious danger to the public and no bed is made available in a secure hospital, it may have no option but to pass a sentence of imprisonment. The tragic suicide of Lionel Clarke which was debated in Parliament in the mid-1980s clearly highlights the problem.[307] He was a severely mentally ill person in need of psychiatric care, but due to the lack of adequate resources and facilities he was unable to be placed in a psychiatric facility. Consequently, he spent damaging amounts of time in police custody and while on remand he committed suicide.

Judges have expressed frustration at the difficulties of finding a hospital bed for mentally disordered offenders on several occasions. In the case of *Officer*,[308] the medical report clearly recommended hospital admission, but no sufficiently secure bed was made available, so the judge had no alternative but to imprison the mentally disordered offender. Likewise, in the case of *Gordon*, McCullough J condemned the lack of adequate facilities, stressing that imprisonment would 'positively cause harm' and lead to a deterioration of the mentally disordered defendant's condition: 'In the view of every member of this Court it is nothing short of a public scandal that a woman such as this should have been sent to prison. It is not fair to her, it is not fair to the prison service, and it is not fair to the other prisoners. She should have a bed in a Special Hospital.'[309]

The House of Commons initially debated the issue of whether courts should have the power to force hospitals to admit offenders under a hospital order. Much evidence was received, particularly from MIND,[310] by the Special Standing Committee of the difficulties faced by courts in finding appropriate facilities. This unsatisfactory situation had led to far too many mentally ill defendants being 'driven backwards and forwards, 100 miles up and down the motorway, for innumerable court hearings while judges and barristers try to find beds in hospitals that

---

[305] L. Gostin, *Mental Health Services*, para. 15.08.

[306] See further L. Gostin, *A Human Condition* (MIND 1977), ii. 45–57; see also J. Mulvany, 'Professional Conflict and the Sentencing Process: The Case of the Hospital Order' (1995) 18(1) *Int J Law & Psych* 101–15, where similar concerns have been voiced about the use of the hospital order in Australia.   [307] Session 1984–5 HC Debs Vol. 81 cols 412–18.

[308] *The Times*, 20 February 1976, *per* Lawton LJ; see also *R.* v. *McFarlane* (1975) 60 Cr App R 320, where the judge was forced to impose a sentence of imprisonment on a mentally ill defendant as no sufficiently secure bed was made available.

[309] (1981) 3 Cr App R(S) 352, 358; [1982] *Crim LR* 240.

[310] See Gostin *A Human Condition*, ii.

do not exist'.[311] Unfortunately, however, the proposal was defeated,[312] but the outcome was s. 39, whereby courts can now more readily obtain information as to the availability of hospital beds. The Memorandum to the Mental Health Act which was published in 1987 stated that this 'implies the need to ensure that the facilities of the Region offer in total a comprehensive service for the Region's patients, both offenders and non-offenders'.[313] There is nothing in the section, however, that obliges regions to provide such services and placements. So although this was a tentative step in the right direction it was by no means a leap forward, and this perhaps explains the reluctance of the courts to make such orders. There is a clear lack of co-operation between the hospitals and the courts, and what is needed, in addition to increased facilities, is increased collaboration to ensure that hospital orders are executed more effectively. This was highlighted by MIND[314] almost twenty years ago, and some believe that this section should be completely reworded to compel hospitals to accept mentally disordered offenders.[315]

However, this will only achieve the desired result if adequate hospital provision is in existence. And here lies the heart of the problem, as several judges have expressed their concerns about the inadequate levels of secure hospital beds available.[316] Indeed, on a couple of occasions the presiding judges have threatened to order the Health Secretary to appear in court before them to explain why hospital beds could not be found for the defendants who are suffering from mental illness![317] And the Lord Chief Justice has criticized this unavailability of sufficiently secure hospital beds: 'In my view, it is no more acceptable for the government to deny the courts the ability to order the detention of disturbed and dangerous offenders in secure hospitals than it would be to deny them the ability to send ruthless criminals to prison'.[318] Clearly the courts do not always have a free hand and the making of hospital orders is constrained by the lack of appropriate resources and facilities.[319]

---

[311]   *Per* T. Davis MP, Session 1981–2 HC Debs Special Standing Committee, 13th Sitting col. 511 (15 June 1982).

[312]   Ibid.; also Session 1981–2 Special Standing Committee 12th Sitting cols 474–508 (10 June 1982).

[313]   DoH/Welsh Office, *Memorandum on Parts I to VI, VIII and X of the Mental Health Act 1983* (HMSO 1987), para. 150.

[314]   Gostin, *A Human Condition*, ii. 46, 57.

[315]   J. MacKeith, 'A Critical Examination of the Current Legal Arrangements for the Treatment or Punishment of Mentally Disordered Offenders', The Robert Maxwell Memorial Lecture delivered at a joint Law Society/Institute of Psychiatry/Mental Health Act Commission conference, 'The Mental Health Act 1983: Time for Change?', held 12 November 1993 (pp. 6, 8).

[316]   *The Times*, 23 November 1994, 'Welsh Office finds secure bed for man'; *The Times*, 17 December 1994, 'Dangerous patient denied NHS bed'.

[317]   *The Times*, 8 November 1994, 'Second judge calls on Bottomley to explain the lack of hospital beds'.

[318]   'Lord Chief Justice criticizes shortfall in secure beds', *The Times*, 1 April 1995.

[319]   See e.g. *Guardian*, 11 December 1993, p. 4, 'Mentally ill face care beds crisis in cities'; *The Times*, 28 September 1994, p. 4, 'Mental care crisis "puts public and patients at risk" '; see also S. N. Verdun-Jones, 'Sentencing the Partly Mad and the Partly Bad: The Case of the Hospital Order in England and Wales' (1989) 12 *Int J Law & Psych* 1–27, 16–17.

Despite these drawbacks, 'there is little doubt that the hospital order provides a humane alternative'.[320] The Butler Committee emphatically stated that the hospital order is the humane option, enabling the patient to receive medical treatment and care:

It should be more clearly understood and accepted that the court, in making such an order . . . is deciding henceforward the offender is to be dealt with on the basis of the same medical considerations as would govern the treatment and discharge of any other patient. He is being *removed from the penal process*; it is being decided *not to punish* him. . . . In making a hospital order, the court is *placing the patient in the hands of the doctors, foregoing any question of punishment.*[321]

This therapeutic disposal option must be regarded as essential and this argument is further reinforced by a study conducted in London of mentally ill offenders given hospital orders. It noted on the positive side that hospital orders were appropriately made in 93 per cent of cases, as the majority were responding to treatment. On the other hand, the study also highlighted the severe shortage of suitable treatment facilities, the presence of which would facilitate the making of these orders.[322] The research concluded with an urgent plea for the provision of more facilities to enable more mentally ill offenders to be given appropriate hospital care.

All such obstacles hinder the successful implementation of the hospital order, and this is reflected in the annual figures throughout the 1980s, which have remained low. As shown in Table 3.5, during the period 1984–9/90, the number of hospital orders made to formally admit patients to NHS facilities fell by 6 per cent, from a total of 839 in 1984 to 605 in 1989/90.[323]

Throughout the 1980s, this route to psychiatric care was little used, a situation which clearly had to be remedied, and it will be considered in the following chapters whether the introduction of diversion policy in 1990 has remedied any of these difficulties and the impact it has made in this respect.

TABLE 3.5. *Hospital orders*

	1984	1985	1986	1987	1988	1989
Hospital orders	839	745	744	497	462	605

---

[320] Verdun-Jones, ibid. 10. [321] Cmnd. 6244 para. 14.12, 18 (emphasis supplied).
[322] Robertson *et al.*, *Remand Prisoners.*
[323] DoH Statistical Bulletin 2(7)92 p. 13. The annual number of hospital orders used has remained fairly constant throughout the early 1990s and this will be considered in more depth in Ch. 4 when the impact of diversion will be considered—DoH Statistical Bulletin 1996/10 p. 13.

3.5.2.3. *The Interim Hospital Order (s. 38)*

3.5.2.3.1. The Provisions

The option of an interim hospital order[324] is now available to the courts under the 1983 Act largely as the result of the Butler Committee recommendations. As noted by Hoggett, it is an important power as it provides the opportunity of returning the defendant to court for a more suitable disposal should s/he refuse to co-operate, if there has been a mistake in diagnosis, or if there is no appropriate treatment.[325]

The detailed requirements for this order are set out in Table 3.4. Similar conditions apply as with the making of hospital orders, and the s. 39 power to require information from the health authority also applies here. Once the conditions have been fulfilled and the order is at an end, the court has complete freedom of choice among the disposals available for the offence in question. It may make a full hospital order or any other therapeutic disposal if there is sufficient medical evidence. Alternatively, the court may choose to impose a penal sanction if it turns out that the offender is not mentally disordered or responding to treatment. As Brenda Hoggett has observed, it is important to note here that although a further custodial sentence may be undesirable, the court would not have the option to do so had a full hospital order been made in the first place.[326]

3.5.2.3.2. Commentary

Interim hospital orders were warmly welcomed, but despite the fact that they are invaluable in that they enable the court to have a 'second bite at the cherry',[327] they have not been popular in practice and remands to hospital are invariably the most frequent method advocated by the court.[328] Again, very little research has been conducted to account for this underuse, but it is disturbing, as this order is potentially of great value in ensuring and securing appropriate therapeutic disposals. This was recognized by the recent Working Group on Psychopathic Disorder which was established in the wake of the Reed Committee Report.[329] It suggests that, the underuse could be due to the courts' unfamiliarity with this section or the doctors' reluctance to admit in case they make a mistake. What little research there is, however, indicates that it is a useful option where there is clinical uncertainty with regard to assessing the treatability of offenders suffering from psychopathic disorder. A study was conducted at a Regional Secure Unit which stressed

---

[324] Fur further guidance see the *Mental Health Act 1983: Memorandum* paras. 152–6; *Mental Health Act 1983 Revised Code of Practice*, para. 3.10.

[325] Hoggett, *Mental Health Law*, 121.   [326] Ibid. 122.   [327] Ibid. 121.

[328] DoH Statistical Bulletin 2(7)92 p. 13 reveals that over 300 remands to hospital to NHS facilities were made in 1989/90 compared with only 69 interim hospital orders. This great variation has been present throughout the 1980s.

[329] DoH/HO, *Report of the Department of Health and Home Office Working Group on Psychopathic Disorder* (Home Office 1994) para. 9.7–8, 29.

this order's utility in this respect. Of their sample of eleven s. 38 admissions in 1988, half were ultimately given hospital orders and over a quarter were given probation orders.[330] Accordingly, this section was regarded as particularly 'beneficial in assessing the treatability of psychopathic disordered offenders', and this is encouraging in view of the controversy which surrounds this particular category of disorder. At the very least the opportunities for assessment are being increased and the section should therefore be further promoted in other areas of the country where research has indicated that its use has not been as prominent.[331] It can only be hoped that this may now be facilitated in view of the extended time limit for an interim hospital order, from 6 to 12 months, which was introduced by s. 49 of the Crime (Sentences) Act 1997, following the recommendations of the Working Group on Psychopathic Disorder.[332] This period will be subject to review by the courts, and the court may terminate the order by disposing of the case at any stage before the expiry of the 12-month period.[333] It is envisaged that this time limit extension will provide the opportunity for a much more thorough and detailed assessment,[334] which will in turn, it is hoped, increase clinicians' confidence in using the section for assessment purposes. As noted by some commentators, this will allow the suitability of treatment to be fully assessed before making the final disposal decision: 'Twelve months is arguably sufficient to ascertain whether an offender suffering from psychopathic disorder is likely genuinely to be treatable or not ... If the offender proves untreatable, the courts can then sentence (solely) to prison.'[335]

3.5.2.4. The Restriction Order (s. 41)

3.5.2.4.1. The Provisions

Should a degree of security be required, another option available to the Crown Court is the hospital order with restrictions.[336] The basic requirements are the same as with the hospital order (see Table 3.4). But, in addition, the court must consider this type of order necessary to protect 'the public from serious harm', having regard to the nature of the offence, the antecedents of the offender, and the risk of committing further offences.[337] This requirement was introduced into the

---

[330] A. Kaul, 'Interim Hospital Orders: A Regional Secure Unit Experience' (1994) 34 *Med, Sci & Law* 233.

[331] See e.g. M. A. Munro and K. A. Fraser, 'New Provisions for Mentally Disordered Offenders: The Use of Sections 35, 36 & 38 in Two Regional Secure Units' (1988) 28 *Med, Sci & Law* 227–32.

[332] DoH/HO, *Report on Psychopathic Disorder*, (1994), para. 10.41.

[333] Home Office Circular 52/1997, *Crime Sentences Act 1997: Provisions Amending the Mental Health Act 1983* (Home Office 1997) para. 16.

[334] Ibid. para. 15.

[335] N. Eastman and J. Peay, 'Sentencing Psychopaths: Is the Hospital and Limitation Direction an Ill-Considered Hybrid?' [1998] *Crim LR* 93–108, 105.

[336] For further guidance see *Mental Health Act 1983: Memorandum* (1998), paras. 162–7, 171–8; see also Gostin, *Mental Health Services*, paras. 15.11–21; Hoggett, *Mental Health Law*, 122–6.

[337] Mental Health Act 1983 s. 41(1); *Royse* (1981) 3 Cr App R (S) 58; see further D. A. Thomas, *Current Sentencing*, Part F2–4A.

legislation as a result of the Butler Committee recommendation that such orders should only be made in severe cases. Thus, there are now much-tightened criteria in the making of restriction orders.[338] Again, in the case of *Birch*[339] the court considered the grounds for the application of such orders and laid down guidelines for judges to follow in future. In making such an order the courts must consider the medical evidence in addition to other factors to conclude the risk of the defendants' offending causing serious harm. Particular consideration should be given to the nature of the offence, previous offending history, and the risk of him/her committing further offences if set at large. Overall, the decision is to be made by the sentencer[340] and the court must be completely satisfied that the restriction order is necessary to protect the public from serious harm.[341]

The order may be imposed for a fixed period or without limit of time. As noted by Gostin, its purpose is to ensure that the patient is not discharged until s/he is ready, and not primarily to reflect the seriousness of the offence. Given that it will be extremely difficult to know when the likely date of recovery will be, the court has stated that unlimited orders should be made unless the doctors can confidently predict recovery.[342] Throughout the duration of the order, the patient cannot be discharged, transferred to another hospital, or given leave of absence without the Home Secretary's consent.[343] However, the Home Secretary can lift the restrictions at any time, provided s/he is satisfied that they are no longer necessary to protect the public from serious harm.[344] But, unless and until this occurs, the restriction will continue.

Finally, an important change was introduced to this order as a result of the *X v UK*[345] decision. This case was outlined in the previous chapter and formed a hasty addition to the Act during the passage of the Bill. It resulted in restricted patients being given the right to apply to and be reviewed by Mental Health Review Tribunals, which was clearly welcomed by those who campaign for increased legal safeguards and patients' rights.

3.5.2.4.2. Commentary

As their name implies, restriction orders are the most prohibitive therapeutic option available to the court at this stage. Throughout the 1980s the number of people formally admitted to NHS facilities under s. 41 has fluctuated, averaging

---

[338] See e.g. *R.* v. *Courtney* [1988] *Crim LR* 130; *R.* v. *Khan* (1987) 9 Cr App R(S) 455.
[339] (1989) 11 Cr App R (S) 202; see also M. Gunn, 'Case Note on *Birch*' (1990) 1 *J For Psych* 88–92; B. Andoh, 'The Hospital Order with Restrictions' (1994) 58 *J Crim Law* 97–108.
[340] *R.* v. *Royse* (1981) 3 Cr App R(S) 58.
[341] *R.* v. *Courtney* (1987) 9 Cr App R(S) 404, [1988] *Crim LR* 130; *Khan* (1987) 9 Cr App R(S) 455; see further D. A. Thomas, *Current Sentencing*, Part F2–4.
[342] *R.* v. *Gardiner* [1967] 1 WLR 464; and approved in *R.* v. *Birch* (1989) 11 Cr App R (s) 202; the Butler Committee also preferred the use of restriction orders without limit of time, Cmnd. 6244 para. 14.25.; see also *R.* v. *Nwolia* [1995] *Crim LR* 668–9.
[343] Mental Health Act 1983 s. 41(3).   [344] Ibid. s. 42(1).
[345] (1982) 4 EHRR 188.

200 per year.[346] Despite the changes introduced by the 1983 Act as a result of the *X v UK* decision, these orders remain the 'most controversial form of psychiatric disposal'.[347] Unlimited restriction orders have been criticized, particularly in their application to psychopathic disorder, as they can result in disproportionately long periods of detention.[348] Furthermore, it is argued that the legislation imposes upon the judge the ultimate responsibility of deciding whether the offender is too dangerous to impose an ordinary hospital order, and that 'the judge has no qualifications for making such a prognosis, beyond his experience as advocate and judge in seeing dangerous people sentenced by the courts'.[349]

Many believe that given such difficulties in principle, perhaps a better alternative is for the court to impose a prison sentence with a possibility of a later transfer to hospital under s. 47, which is perhaps a better alternative to ensure the protection of the public.[350] But this does nothing to compensate for the damaging amounts of time which the defendant has already spent in custody which may adversely affect his/her mental condition. And it is argued that if the defendant needs psychiatric care and treatment it should be provided at the earliest possible opportunity, if the mechanisms exist to ensure this.

Recent research has indicated that restriction orders do have a valuable role to play in terms of sharing responsibility for the disposal and management of dangerous offenders between the different agencies. Furthermore, it has also been demonstrated how the order can be effective in the long term by ensuring that appropriate care and support and continuing supervision is provided upon discharge, which ultimately lowers the reconviction rates for such offenders.[351] Indeed, restriction orders are perceived to be a 'clinically useful tool' in many cases.[352] Unfortunately, however, the difficulties in finding a sufficiently secure hospital bed are also present here. The three Secure Hospitals have only a limited number of beds, and the available places in Regional Secure Units still fall short of the number recommended by the Butler Committee over twenty years ago. The Government at the time accepted Butler's plea for interim secure provision and resources were made available for Regional Health Authorities to develop 1,000 places. By January 1992, only 600 places, less than two-thirds of the initial

---

[346] DoH Statistical Bulletin 2(7)92 p. 13.

[347] Hoggett, *Mental Health Law*, 122; see also the comments of MHAC, *Report 1995–7* para. 10.8.3.

[348] See R. Henham, 'Dangerous Trends in the Sentencing of Mentally Abnormal Offenders' (1995) 34 *How J of Crim Just* 10–18; L. Gostin, 'Towards the Development of Principles for Sentencing and Detaining Mentally Abnormal Offenders', in M. Craft and A. Craft (eds.) *Mentally Abnormal Offenders* (Balliere 1984), 229–35.

[349] Walker, 'Fourteen Years On', 244.

[350] Hoggett, *Mental Health Law*, 126–8.

[351] R. Street, *The Restricted Hospital Order: From Court to Community*, Home Office Research Study, 186 (Home Office 1998) ch. 12.

[352] See M. Humphreys *et al.*, 'Restricted Hospital Orders: A Survey of Forensic Psychiatrists' Practice and Attitudes to their Use (1998) 9(1) *J For Psych* 173–80.

Glancy recommendation, were in existence.[353] As Professor Bluglass has noted, 'Perhaps the greatest danger is financial. Other medical specialities will always be strong competitors for limited resources and it requires a firm commitment on the part of Regional Health Authorities and central government to ensure the continued support that the units require.'[354]

It is encouraging to note that more recent figures suggest that the Butler target is now much more likely to be achieved. In a parliamentary Written Answer in January 1998, Paul Boateng, Junior Minister for Health, stated that there are now thirty-three medium secure units, with a total number of 1,504 beds, all of which are running at capacity.[355] The recent reports of the Mental Health Act Commission have also commented upon such positive developments. In its Sixth Biennial Report it noted that the Glancy target had now been met and a substantial amount of funds had been allocated by the 1979–97 Conservative Government to achieve the Butler target.[356] This optimism was echoed in its Seventh Biennial Report, where it welcomed the expansion and significant increase in medium secure provision.[357] However, on a more sombre note, it stressed that despite the increase in the number of beds, 'demand still greatly outstrips provision in many places'. There was still high pressure on the service and whilst a number of new units had been established, the Commission was extremely concerned. There has been a massive expansion in the number of buildings, but this has not been accompanied by a corresponding increase in other resources, especially staffing levels and discharge facilities. This inevitably affects the overall delivery, standard, and quality of care which is provided. Accordingly, whilst the expansion is welcomed, there is still no room for complacency and much more needs to be done to ensure that the Butler target is met and that patients are provided with high quality care and treatment.[358]

This inadequate provision has, however, meant that in many cases courts have again been forced to impose a sentence of imprisonment as no sufficiently secure hospital bed was available,[359] and the age-old problem of the lack of appropriate facilities to accommodate the mentally ill has been, and still is, present. This will be major consideration in the following chapters, when the introduction and implementation of diversion policy will be considered. This funding and facilities

---

[353] *Report of a Review of Services for Mentally Disordered Offenders and Others Requiring Similar Services* (HMSO 1992) Cm. 2088 para. 2.7; *Guardian*, 23 October 1993, 'Minister accused over secure units'. See further ch. 4.

[354] R. Bluglass, 'The Development of Regional Secure Units' in Gostin (ed.), *Secure Provision*, 173.   [355] Session 1997–98 HC Debs Vol. 306 col. 262.

[356] Cmnd. 6244 p. 70.   [357] MHAC, *Report 1995–7*, para. 10.8.1.

[358] It must be noted here that, on a more positive note, the Government has recently acknowledged the need to provide more secure beds in its proposals for a modern mental health service which were announced in December 1998 (see DoH, *Modernising Mental Health Services: Safe, Sound and Supportive* (DoH 1998)). It remains to be seen, however, to what extent the proposals will fully remedy the exisiting shortfall in provision. This will be discussed at greater length in chs. 4 and 7.

[359] *R.* v. *Clarke* (1975) 61 Cr App R 320 *per* Lawton LJ; see also Bridge LJ in *R.* v. *Tolley* (1978) 68 Cr App R 323 and Shaw LJ in *R.* v. *Slater* (1979) 1 Cr App R(S) 349.

issue is extremely important and will clearly have a significant impact upon the success of diversion policy. New changes may well be introduced, but they will simply fall on fallow ground without the resources to implement them adequately and accommodate the mentally ill, and the use of these powers will not increase without the facilities to accommodate the corresponding increase in admissions.

3.5.2.5. The Guardianship Order (s. 37)

3.5.2.5.1. The Provisions

The detailed requirements for the guardianship order[360] are outlined in Table 3.4. and it is made largely on the same basis as an ordinary hospital order, except that the 'treatability test' does not apply here in relation to psychopaths or people suffering from mental impairment. The duration and procedure with respect to these orders is basically the same as with hospital orders, but rather than being admitted to hospital the offender will be placed in the guardianship either of the local social services or of some other individual approved by them, and their consent must be given.[361] The Criminal Justice Act 1991 s. 27(1) inserted a new s. 39A into the Mental Health Act 1983 which enables the court to request information from the appropriate local social services authority as to whether it is willing to receive the offender into guardianship.[362] So this section facilitates the provision of information and operates on a similar basis to the s. 39 power to request information from hospital managers as to the availability of beds.

It is provided that the guardian has three basic powers in relation to the patient. S/he may decide where the patient should live; when and where the patient should receive treatment, occupation, education, or training; and may insist that any named doctor or social worker sees the patient.[363] As noted by other commentators, although this order may appear to be very similar to the psychiatric probation order, in practice it differs greatly from it. First, it involves local authority social services personnel rather than probation officers and doctors. And secondly, there are no formal sanctions against a patient who refuses to co-operate with a guardianship order, nor can the guardian insist that the patient accepts any medical or other treatment on offer.

3.5.2.5.2. Commentary

Guardianship orders were regarded as a major breakthrough in 1959 and reinforced in the 1983 Mental Health Act as a useful 'alternative to hospital orders'.[364] But these powers have also been continually underused; as one

---

[360] See further DoH/Welsh Office, *Memorandum*, paras. 157–61,179–87; Hoggett, *Mental Health Law*, 128; Gostin, *Mental Health Services*, para. 15.22.
[361] Mental Health Act 1983 ss 40(2), 37(2); Hoggett, *Mental Health Law*, 128.
[362] *Mental Health Act 1983 Revised Code of Practice*, para. 3.5.
[363] Mental Health Act 1983 s. 8(1).
[364] *Mental Health Act 1983 Revised Code of Practice*, para. 13.10.

observer has noted, the use of guardianship is 'rarer than snow in summer'.[365] So, it would seem that 'The attractiveness of guardianship as a means of legal control of the mentally disordered has often been endorsed e.g. by the Butler Committee ... but it has nevertheless failed to mature into a viable routine alternative to hospitalization.'[366] Not only are such orders infrequent in a criminal context (under s. 37), but their use is also minimal as a civil power under s. 7 of the Act. Indeed, the majority of cases are made under the civil section,[367] but even then are not frequently invoked.[368]

The Butler Committee gave careful consideration to the guardianship powers. It had received evidence testifying to their usefulness and the fact that the behaviour of those under such supervision generally improved greatly. They are therefore potentially extremely beneficial, but regrettably, have 'not [been] used in many cases where they should be'.[369] The Butler Committee regarded improved liaison between courts and local authorities as essential, as it could 'lead to improved understanding of the nature and value of the order and result in its increased use'.[370] So, once again, the need is for increased collaboration and communication amongst the agencies concerned to improve the use and effectiveness of the guardianship power.

The underuse is, therefore, unfortunate, as it has been widely noted that guardianship orders can be effective in appropriate cases and that 'they provide a useful alternative to detention in hospital by providing a means by which the offender can be made subject to some control, supervision and support in the community'.[371]

The Law Commission considered the concept of guardianship in its Consultation Paper on *Mentally Incapacitated Adults and Decision Making.*[372] Although it was largely concerned with guardianship as a civil power, it noted the persistent underuse of this concept generally. This was attributed to the restrictive criteria as to who can be subject to guardianship (people suffering from mental impairment must be displaying abnormally aggressive or seriously irresponsible

---

[365]　NACRO, *Revolving Doors*, 16.

[366]　C. Unsworth, *The Politics of Mental Health Legislation* (Oxford University Press 1985), 321.

[367]　In a review of the use of guardianship under the 1983 Act, 114 out of 123 cases between April 1986 and March 1987 were under s. 7; W. Grant, Guardianship Orders: A Review of their Use under the 1983 Mental Health Act' (1992) 32 *Med, Sci & Law* 319–24.

[368]　Ibid.; see also J. P. Wattis, W. Grant, J. Traynor and S. Harris, 'Use of Guardianship under the 1983 Mental Health Act' (1990) 30 *Med, Sci & Law* 313; M. Fisher, 'Guardianship under the Mental Health Legislation: A Review' [1988] *JSWL* 316–27; G. Hughes, 'Trends in Guardianship Usage Following the Mental Health Act 1983' (1990/91) 22 *Health Trends* 145–7. Recent statistics would seem to suggest that their overall use has been increasing throughout the 1990s and this will be discussed further in the following chapter: DoH Press Release 96/101, 'Statistics on Guardianship under the Mental Health Act 1983'.　　　　　　　　　　　　　[369]　Cmnd. 6244 para. 15.8.

[370]　Ibid. para. 15.5.

[371]　Gostin, *Mental Health Services*, para. 15.22; see also C. Gordon, 'Guardianship in Oxfordshire: Hits and Misses' (1998) 22 *Psych Bulletin* 223–35.

[372]　*Mentally Incapacitated Adults and Decision Making: An Overview*, Consultation Paper 119 (HMSO 1991).

conduct) and the restrictive powers of the guardian coupled with the absence of any sanctions should the patient refuse to co-operate. The Paper recommended that there was an urgent need to review guardianship, to widen the criteria and extend the powers of the guardian to include a power to impose certain kinds of treatment, which would undoubtedly make guardianship a much more attractive option. Similar observations have also been made by several legal commentators.[373]

Another obstacle to guardianship, similarly with probation orders, is the fact that community services have been slow to develop. The successful implementation of this order requires the close liaison of the courts, the guardian, doctors, and social services. As already found, such active co-operation is not always easy to achieve and sustain. But, if greater use is to be made of this convenient power, then services must be developed and collaboration must be improved, and so this also has implications for diversion policy which also has significant implications for the treatment of mentally disordered offenders. The arguments in favour of therapeutic treatment and disposal have been abundantly stated and described, however, this can only be achieved if the relevant facilities and services exist in which these offenders can be treated.

3.5.2.6. The Hospital Direction

3.5.2.6.1. Introduction

Following the introduction of the Crime (Sentences) Act 1997, another disposal option, which is also now available to the Crown Court at the sentencing stage, is the hospital direction.[374] It was introduced in response to the spate of attacks and killings by former psychiatric patients, and it is regarded as a mechanism to allow the courts more flexibility 'in responding to serious offending by people suffering from a mental disorder'.[375]

The main thrust of the Crime (Sentences) Act 1997 was to increase the protection afforded to the public from serious, dangerous, and persistent offenders.[376]

---

[373] Fisher, 'Guardianship'; Hughes, 'Trends in Guardianship'.

[374] Mental Health Act 1983 s. 45(A). See further *Mental Health Act 1983: Memorandum*, (1998), paras. 168–70, 188–90; *Mental Health Act 1983 Revised Code of Practice*, para. 3.15–18; Home Office Circular 52/1997, *Crime Sentences Act 1997: Provisions Amending the Mental Health Act 1983* (Home Office 1997); J. M. Laing, 'The Likely Impact of Mandatory and Minimum Sentences on the Disposal of Mentally Disordered Offenders' (1997) 8(3) *J For Psych* 504–5; id. 'Mentally Disordered Offenders: Sentencing Policy under the Crime (Sentences) Act 1997' (1998) 9(2) *J For Psych* 424–34; id. 'A Change of Direction in the Disposal of Mentally Disordered Offenders: The Impact of the Crime (Sentences) Act 1997' (1998) 38(3) *Med, Sci & Law* 1–9; N. Walker, 'Hybrid Orders' (1996) 7(3) *J For Psych* 469–72; Eastman and Peay, 'Sentencing Psychopaths' 93–108; D. A. Thomas, 'The Crime (Sentences) Act 1997' [1998] *Crim LR* 83–92.

[375] Home Office/DoH, *Mentally Disordered Offenders—Sentencing and Discharge Arrangements: A Discussion Paper on a Proposed New Power for the Courts* (HO/DoH 1996) para. 1.4.

[376] Home Office, *Protecting the Public: The Government's Strategy on Crime in England and Wales* (HMSO 1996) Cm. 2190.

The main provisions of the Act are aimed at repeat offenders and introduce mandatory and minimum sentences, as well as giving the courts a new power to dispose of mentally disordered offenders. Section 2 requires the court to impose an automatic life sentence for a second serious violent or sexual offence unless there are exceptional circumstances. And s. 3 requires the court to impose a minimum sentence for certain repeat drug-trafficking offenders unless it would 'be unjust in all the circumstances'. These powers will be considered in more depth in Ch. 4, when the impact of such retributive sentencing measures upon diversion policy will be assessed more fully.

Specifically, however, in relation to mentally disordered offenders, the legislation introduces the new hospital direction which allows the court to sentence a mentally disordered offender but, at the same time, order his/her direct admission to hospital. The provision is contained in s. 46 and applies principally to offenders suffering from psychopathic disorder under the Mental Health Act 1983. It can, however, also be extended to cover offenders suffering from any of the other types of mental disorder under the Act (i.e. those suffering from mental illness or mental/severe mental impairment). It is also available as an alternative to the mandatory and minimum sentences in s. 2 and 3. This 'hybrid order' is based on the proposals articulated in a Discussion Document, which was issued subsequent to the White Paper which preceded the 1997 Act in June 1996.[377]

This approach towards the disposal of mentally disordered offenders has its origins in a joint DHSS/Home Office Consultation Document which was produced by a Working Group on Psychopathic Disorder a decade ago.[378] The Group was appointed as a result of the concern about the release of dangerous psychopaths coupled with the long-term anxiety over the treatment of 'dangerous' offenders in general.[379] The Group recommended the introduction of this type of order, but the proposals were rejected largely due to the negative response received from the professionals involved with these particular offenders at that time. Nevertheless, the proposal was subsequently resurrected by the Reed Committee Working Group on Psychopathic Disorder which has already been discussed and produced its report in 1994.[380] The Group was appointed to consider exclusively the needs of offenders suffering from psychopathic disorder, who are a particularly problematic group, as is obvious from the need to review their treatment for the second time in a decade. Amongst the proposals was the possibility of a hybrid order similar to the one advocated by the 1986 Working Party. The Group felt that this new order would more accurately reflect the

---

[377] HO/DoH *Discussion Papers.*

[378] DHSS/HO, *Offenders Suffering from Psychopathic Disorder Joint DHSS/HO Consultation Document* (DHSS/HO 1986).

[379] J. Peay, 'Offenders Suffering from Psychopathic Disorder: The Rise and Demise of a Consultation Document' (1988) 28 *Brit J Criminology* 67–81.

[380] HO/DoH, *Report of the Department of Health and Home Office Working Group on Psychopathic Disorder* (DoH/HO, 1994).

current state of psychiatric knowledge and treatability of psychopathy. It was also perceived to be helpful in overcoming the concerns of the medical profession, in so far as they may be left with potentially dangerous offenders who are untreatable, but whose discharge from hospital would pose risks to public safety.[381] The Group concluded that there was 'considerable merit in the idea of a hybrid order'.[382] Accordingly it was recommended that the 1979–97 Conservative Government should give firm consideration to this particular proposal. To a certain extent, this aspiration has been fulfilled, as the hospital direction was included in the Crime (Sentences) Act 1997. It was introduced by that Government and has, in the main, been accepted by the new Labour Government.[383]

3.5.2.6.2. The Provisions: The Scope of the Hospital Direction

Section 46 of the 1997 Act has inserted new ss. 45A and 45B into the Mental Health Act 1983 to introduce the new power, which is effective from 1 October 1997. In practice, the hospital direction enables the Crown Court to direct the offender's immediate admission to hospital when imposing a prison sentence (s. 46). The court must have received sufficient and appropriate medical evidence and must have felt minded to make an ordinary hospital order under s. 37 of the 1983 Act.[384]

As with the hospital order under the 1983 Act, the hospital direction can be made either with (a 'limitation direction') or without restrictions on discharge and is primarily aimed at offenders suffering from psychopathic disorder.[385] This is largely due to the controversy that surrounds this category of mental disorder and the uncertainty surrounding its treatment. However, the 1983 Act, by virtue of s. 45A(10), does enable the Secretary of State to extend its availability to other categories of mental disorder.[386]

The offender will remain in hospital for as long as s/he requires treatment for the mental disorder. But, should treatment be unsuccessful, or should the offender recover from the illness before the end of the sentence and no longer require treatment, then s/he will be remitted to prison to serve the remainder of the sentence. Alternatively, the offender will continue to receive treatment in hospital throughout the period of the sentence should his/her mental disorder warrant it.[387]

The hospital direction is available in the Crown Court only, thereby limiting its application to the most severe cases where the offender clearly poses a serious threat to the safety of the public and the nature of the offending is grave. It is

---

[381] Ibid. para. 10.24.   [382] Ibid. para. 10.26.

[383] Home Office, *Annual Report 1998: Government's Expenditure Plans 1998–1999,* Session 1997–8 Cm. 3908 para. 4.16, 26.

[384] Home Office Circular 54/1997 para. 62; see also *Mental Health Act 1983: Memorandum* (1998), para. 169.   [385] Ibid.

[386] Home Office Circular 54/1997 para. 62.

[387] HO/DoH, *Discussion Paper* (1996) para. 2.8.

therefore reserved only for the most serious, controversial, and uncertain cases appearing before the Crown Court: 'The hybrid order would be *reserved for those cases where there was substantial doubt* over whether the offender would benefit from hospital treatment.' [388]

As previously noted, it is provided that the power should be available for offenders suffering from any of the four types of mental disorder specified in s. 1 of the Mental Health Act 1983, i.e. psychopathic disorder, mental illness, mental impairment, and severe mental impairment.[389] Whilst initially the order is primarily directed at offenders suffering from psychopathic disorder, it has been stipulated that it can also be extended, where appropriate, to offenders suffering from any of the other types of mental disorder.

The detailed procedures and safeguards for the review of detention, and the supervision and discharge arrangements which will be put in place for an offender subject to such a direction were contained in the Discussion Document. In the main, release and discharge arrangements operate on the same basis as for other sentenced prisoners.[390] But the procedures for review and detention while subject to the new hospital direction (i.e. throughout the period of hospitalization) are identical to those for prisoners transferred to hospital under ss. 47 and 48 of the Mental Health Act 1983.[391] Accordingly, patients are given access to the Mental Health Review Tribunal to review the grounds for their continued detention in hospital. The Tribunal will decide whether it should recommend to the Home Secretary that the patient no longer requires treatment and should therefore be remitted back to prison to serve the remainder of the sentence.[392] Access to the Tribunal to review the grounds for continued detention in a therapeutic environment is highly significant and crucial from a legal standpoint, as it would ensure compatibility with the European Convention on Human Rights, in particular, Article 5(4). This requires that in cases where a person is deprived of his/her liberty on the grounds of mental disorder, s/he must be given access to a judicial body to review the lawfulness of his/her detention, and is highly significant in view of the controversy which has surrounded this area in the past[393] and the recent developments to incorporate the Convention directly into UK law, by virtue of the Human Rights Act, 1998.[394]

Section 46 is supplemented by s. 47 which enables the Crown Court, when making a restricted hospital order or such a hospital direction, to specify the precise hospital unit to which the direction/order is made. As outlined in the

---

[388] HO/DoH, *Review of Health and Social Services for Mentally Disordered Offenders and Others Requiring Similar Services* (HMSO 1992) Cm. 2088 para. 10.22 (emphasis supplied).

[389] Ibid. para. 1.7. [390] Ibid. para. 3.1.

[391] *Mental Health Act 1983 Memorandum* (1998), para. 189.

[392] Cm. 2088 para. 2.9.

[393] e.g. the decision in *X v UK* which was discussed earlier in this and the previous chapter in relation to the detention of restricted patients.

[394] See Human Rights Act 1998, s. 3; see further J. Wadham and H. Mountfield, *Blackstone's Guide to the Human Rights Act 1998* (Blackstone 1999).

Circular which accompanied the 1997 Act, given that many of the offenders subject to such provisions will have committed serious offences and require restrictions/limitations on discharge, this section allows the court to specify the particular level of security that is required, thereby ensuring adequate protection of the public.[395] The hospital direction will therefore enable the court to reflect the gravity of the offence and emphasize the retributive and punitive element, but at the same time ensure that the offender receives appropriate treatment for his/her mental disorder.

A Home Office Circular[396] has been published in the wake of the Act which contains additional guidance on these specific powers relating to mentally disordered offenders. It is expressly stipulated in the Circular that the hospital direction does not affect the existing arrangements whereby the court is bound to consider any information relating to the defendant's mental condition prior to sentencing him/her under s. 4 Criminal Justice Act 1991.[397] Section 45A(1)(b) of the 1983 Act requires the court to consider making a hospital order in all cases before attaching a direction to the prison sentence. It is envisaged that there will be no changes to the existing procedures relating to the provision of medical evidence, as the requirements for the direction are the same as those for a restricted hospital order. The court will simply additionally be given the option of directing to hospital when it concludes that a custodial sentence is appropriate.[398] Although the reason why a hospital direction as opposed to a restricted hospital order should be made in such cases has not been stipulated. The medical evidence may therefore become increasingly significant in this respect. Given the absence of specific guidance, the court may exert far greater pressure upon the medical profession to provide advice and give reasons for making the hospital direction. Consequently, increasing reliance may be placed upon the medical profession to assist the court in determining appropriate cases when a hospital direction should be made.

It is provided that this hospital direction will be available, where appropriate, as an alternative to the mandatory prison life sentence in s. 2 of the 1997 Act. However, it is expressly provided that an ordinary hospital order under s. 37 of the Mental Health Act 1983 will not be an option in such circumstances.[399] In relation to mentally disordered offenders convicted of a second serious offence, therefore, the court has the option of attaching a hospital direction to the automatic life sentence, to ensure that the offender is punished but, at the same time, that s/he receives appropriate treatment for the mental disorder. Essentially, it allows the court to impose a sentence of imprisonment upon an offender but, at the same time, order his/her immediate admission to hospital, should medical

---

[395] Home Office Circular 54/1997, para. 64; see also *Mental Health Act 1983 Memorandum* (1998), para.170.   [396] 52/1997.   [397] Ibid. para. 4.
[398] Ibid. para. 5.
[399] Home Office Circular 54/1997, para. 11.

evidence indicate that it is both necessary and desirable. However, where the court is required to impose a mandatory minimum sentence under s. 3, then it is stipulated that the court may, alternatively, impose a hospital direction *or* an ordinary hospital, as opposed to a sentence of imprisonment.[400] So the court is given greater flexibility in sentencing disordered offenders who have committed repeated burglary offences, and has the option of directing the offender to hospital, either under a hospital order or a hospital direction. There is no guidance provided as to precisely when the court should consider making a hospital direction in conjunction with or as an alternative to the s. 2 or s. 3 mandatory sentence. Presumably it will be when there is sufficient evidence of a mental disorder and, given the rationale behind the new power, it will be the preferable course of action in relation to serious and repeat offenders suffering from psychopathic disorder, where there is much uncertainty about their suitability for treatment.

The practical effects of the direction will be the same as under a transfer direction (s. 47 of the 1983 Act). The offender may serve the entire sentence in hospital if s/he is benefiting from treatment, alternatively, the Home Secretary may transfer him/her back to prison at any time on the recommendation of the Responsible Medical Office/Mental Health Review Tribunal. Although this will not completely eliminate any future transfer back to hospital, which would still fall to be considered in the normal way under s. 47 of the 1983 Act.[401]

Furthermore, the making of a hospital direction will be subject to the requirements in s. 45A(5) of the 1983 Act, which are identical to the requirements under s. 37(4) of the same Act in relation to the imposition of restricted hospital orders. This ensures uniformity and consistency and Responsible Medical Officers and hospital managers will therefore be well aware of the need to provide written/oral evidence that arrangements have been made for the offender's admission to the hospital within 28 days. Additionally, s. 47 of the 1997 Act stipulates that admission must be to a *named* hospital. This section amends the 1983 Act and empowers the courts or the Home Secretary to specify the particular unit of the hospital in which the offender subject to the direction should be detained. This applies only in respect of offenders subject to restrictions/limitations thereby ensuring that the public will be sufficiently protected from serious offenders requiring a particular level of security. Circular 52/1997 specifies that this should be considered when 'the risk of serious harm to others if the offender were to abscond is assessed is high'.[402] Again here, however, the court may rely upon the medical evidence to assist it in determining this issue.

It is interesting to note, however, that this section is not confined to the making of the new hospital direction. It is far more extensive in its application and also applies to offenders subject to a restricted hospital order under s. 37 of the 1983 Act; to prisoners transferred to hospital by the Home Secretary under ss. 47/48 of the 1983 Act; and also to offenders found unfit to plead/not guilty by reason of

---

[401] Home Office Circular 54/1997, para. 8.   [402] HO Circular 52/1997, para. 11.

insanity, and who require hospital admission under the Criminal Procedure (Insanity and Unfitness to Plead) Act 1991.[403] Similarly here the 1979–97 Conservative Government obviously felt that these disordered offenders also require a particular level of security and have given the courts the power to ensure that it is achieved.

The ability to specify a particular unit of detention under s. 47 will mean that there is a greater responsibility upon health-care professionals to comply with the requirement. This section represents an extension to the powers of the court and is undoubtedly a step in the right direction, as it provides the court with the power to direct an offender to a particular secure unit. As noted earlier in the chapter in relation to other sections of the 1983 Act, the court does not have the power to order an offender's admission to a particular unit, it has simply been able to require information as to the availability of hospital beds (s. 39 of the 1983 Act). The court had no authority to direct precisely where an offender should be detained, but this new power under s. 47 of the 1997 Act clearly enables the court to ensure that disordered offenders will be accepted by, and detained in, a suitably secure facility. This may go some way towards remedying some of the difficulties that have been experienced in finding a sufficiently secure bed in previous years. However, whilst the section gives the court the power to direct the level of security which is required in a particular unit, it is unclear to what extent it will be able to compel that facility to accept the offender. Consequently, there may still be difficulties in actually securing admission.

3.5.2.6.3. Commentary

Whilst the new power is to be welcomed in some respects, its introduction has also caused much concern and there is some dissatisfaction with the hospital direction. The 1979–97 Conservative Government acknowledged that the origins of the new power stem from the 1986 and 1994 Working Groups' proposals. However, their proposals were aimed solely at one particular category of offender—those suffering from psychopathic disorder. The new power will be far more extensive and could apply to offenders suffering from any of the other categories of mental disorder under s. 1 of the Mental Health Act 1983. This aspect of the power, however, is open to serious objection. Whilst the difficulties in diagnosis are acknowledged,[404] it is maintained that those offenders suffering from a serious mental illness (other than psychopathic disorder) who successfully recover in hospital should not then simply be remitted to prison for the remainder of their sentence. There is a need for continuity of care in order to prevent relapse. Such offenders will be especially vulnerable at this stage and thus should not be unnecessarily subjected to the damaging and detrimental effects of the prison regime. The prison system as currently constituted is not able to offer such

---

[403] HO Circular 54/1997, para. 64.
[404] HO/DoH, *Discussion Paper*, (1996), para. 1.8.

offenders the support and continuity of care which they need and to which they are entitled. In light of this, it is therefore questionable whether the hybrid order does in fact ensure 'access to effective treatment . . . and the *effective management of throughcare*'[405] in all cases, as the 1979–97 Conservative Government would claim.

This aspect of the power occupied much of the discussion during the Parliamentary Debates which preceded the legislation and has been opposed by the pressure group MIND in particular.[406] The former Government, however, clearly preferred that it should be available for all categories of mental disorder, in view of the possible overlap between the various categories, the potential for dual diagnosis and the apparent difficulties in making a firm diagnosis.[407] But, its application to other categories raises serious problems, as an offender suffering from a serious mental illness who successfully recovers in hospital may still be extremely vulnerable and should not then simply be remitted into the prison system. Indeed, remission to prison may well negate the benefits of any treatment which has already been received in hospital in a therapeutic environment. This will greatly disadvantage the mentally ill offender, and it also potentially runs counter to diversion policy, which seeks to obviate the detrimental and damaging effects of the prison regime. This issue will be explored in greater depth in the following chapter.

Whilst the introduction of the new power in relation to all types of mental disorder is welcome from the point of view that it would not have the effect of treating offenders with psychopathic disorder any differently from those suffering from other forms of mental disorder, it must be accepted that offenders suffering from psychopathic disorder are particularly problematic and given the difficulties surrounding their treatment and management (which are not present to the same extent with offenders suffering from other types of mental disorder) it is surely correct that they should be singled out and treated differently in this way. They are clearly a distinct category for whom a different approach is required and the available evidence indicates that offenders suffering from psychopathic disorder can respond positively in a variety of settings.[408] The hybrid order should therefore be available exclusively for them, in order to facilitate this. This is supported by the fact that there is currently much 'dissatisfaction among many psychiatrists over the efficacy of disposals under section 37 and 41 of the 1983 Act' in relation to this particular group of offenders, therefore, it is surely correct that an alternative approach which 'reflects the current state of knowledge of psychopathy'[409] is introduced in relation to them.

In a similar vein, doubts have been expressed about the new power by the

---

[405] *Discussion Paper*, para. 2.1 (emphasis supplied).

[406] MIND, *Diversion from Custody and Secure Provision: A MIND Policy Consultation Document on Mentally Disordered Offenders* (MIND 1996).

[407] HO/DoH, *Discussion Paper* (1996), para. 1.8.

[408] HO/DoH, *Report on Psychopathic Disorder* (1994).   [409] Ibid.

Mental Health Act Commission.[410] It has opined that 'the continuing threat of a transfer to prison could be anti-therapeutic, could sour relations between patients and staff; or it might enable patients to avoid confronting their problems by engineering a retreat to prison'. The Commission felt that greater use of s. 37 and 41 restriction orders of limited duration would be a preferable solution. But, it is doubtful whether this would have been a realistic solution, however, as it is highly debatable to what extent the judiciary would be willing to impose limited restriction orders. As outlined earlier in this chapter, the current climate clearly favours unlimited restriction orders, given the uncertainty surrounding treatment and the inability confidently to predict recovery in such cases.

It is evident, therefore, that in general this new power has not been well received and was greeted with scepticism by several prominent bodies and Committees. Legal commentators such as Ashworth were highly sceptical of the new power and asserted that it fails to tackle the 'key practical problem of securing the admission to hospital of mentally disordered offenders'.[411] It has already been considered at length that this has been a problem which has faced the courts for years, as they do not have the power to compel hospitals to accept such patients; the prisons on the other hand have no choice but to accept them. This is perhaps the crux of the issue. Despite the need to direct such offenders to hospital, the introduction of the new power does nothing to remedy the lack of suitable hospital facilities. And such offenders in need of hospital care who are subject to a hospital direction may still end up in prison, despite the well-meaning contrary intention if the appropriate hospital facilities are simply not available.

The Discussion Paper, rather naïvely and optimistically, stated that 'release or discharge arrangements would be on the same basis as for other sentenced prisoners, with provision for *medical after-care where necessary*'.[412] This statement presupposes that comprehensive aftercare arrangements are already in existence at this stage. However, it is highly questionable whether adequate support and medical aftercare arrangements are ever put in place upon a mentally ill offender's discharge from prison. The aftercare facilities and support systems are generally perceived to be inadequate, but it is only when a fully comprehensive aftercare service is put in place that 'the effective management of throughcare overall'[413] will fully materialize.

A final general issue which has also been raised by the introduction of the new hybrid order which is also cause for concern is to what extent it departs from the philosophy of the existing mental health legislation whereby the emphasis is placed upon timely therapeutic intervention[414] and whether the recent policy of

---

[410] MHAC, *Report 1993–5*, 72.
[411] A. Ashworth, 'Sentencing Mentally Disordered Offenders' [1996] *Crim LR* 457–8, 457.
[412] HO/DoH, Discussion Paper (1996), para 3.1.   [413] Ibid. para. 2.1.
[414] It is also questionable to what extent the introduction of this new disposal power affects and runs counter to the implementation of diversion policy, and this will be considered in more depth in the following chapters.

diverting mentally disordered offenders (articulated in Home Office Circulars 66/90 and 12/95) will be overshadowed. This issue will be explored in greater depth in the following chapters; however, it must be noted that, inevitably, such approaches are inherently offender-oriented, as they focus exclusively upon the needs of the offender. None the less, the new power would appear, in principle, to shift the balance and place more emphasis upon the rights of society to punish the offender, and the need for retribution, incapacitation, and public protection. The therapeutic remand/disposal powers and diversion policy are aimed at directing offenders away from the damaging and detrimental effects of the prison regime and punitive sanctions, but the new proposal, at least, in part, embraces a different approach. It is therefore difficult to reconcile the two; it is arguable that this is achieved by reserving the new power for only the most serious cases in the Crown Court, many of whom would not necessarily be appropriate candidates for diversion schemes which operate mainly at the magistrates' court level.[415] But limiting the application of the new power only to a limited group of offenders— those suffering from psychopathic disorder—would have gone some way further towards allaying such fears.

Additionally, it must be noted that it has been expressly announced that the introduction of this new hospital direction is not intended to represent a fundamental shift in policy direction, nor a shift away from the philosophy of the Mental Health Act 1983.[416] The Reed Committee Working Group Report on Psychopathic Disorder commented that its introduction would be in line with diversion policy,[417] although it did not provide any explanation as to why this was felt to be the case. Presumably the hospital direction is consistent with such goals as it maximizes the treatment opportunities for mentally disordered offenders, particularly for those who are suffering from psychopathic disorder, who may previously have been sentenced to a term of imprisonment. This is further evinced by the fact that the hospital direction, which facilitates therapeutic intervention, is available as an *alternative* to the mandatory and minimum sentences under the 1997 Act. The emphasis is therefore upon ensuring that mentally disordered offenders who have committed serious offences, but are in need of care and treatment, actually receive it, and are not unnecessarily subjected to the prison regime. The introduction of the hospital direction will ensure that this takes place, whilst at the same time safeguarding the public.

Nevertheless, there are still many problems with the scope and application of the new order that may hinder its practical implementation.[418] It is suggested that

---

[415] See further ch. 4.

[416] HO Circular 52/1997, para. 2: 'It is the Government's policy that an offender needing specialist care and treatment for mental disorder should where possible receive it in hospital rather than in custodial care ... The hospital direction does not represent a departure from that policy ... The advice given on inter-agency provision for dealing with mentally disordered offenders in Home Office Circulars 66/1990 and 12/1995 remains in force.'

[417] HO/DoH, *Report on Psychopathic Disorder* (1994), para. 10.24.

[418] See further J. M. Laing, 'Mentally Disordered Offenders'.

the current scope is far too wide and should have been confined to those suffering from psychopathic disorder for whom this type of disposal could be particularly beneficial. The reaction to the new Act has generally been unfavourable, particularly from a health service perspective. To many it would seem that the new power will simply be solving the prison service problems, but will increase those facing the medical professionals and impose an increasing burden upon an already stretched health service budget. The new order does not address the real issue of resources and the lack of appropriate health service facilities and, despite some of the other difficulties identified with the new power, this is undoubtedly the most glaring practical obstacle to stand in its way.

Furthermore, the introduction of the hospital direction may mean that greater emphasis will be placed upon the medical evidence and mental health professionals may find that they are being increasingly asked by the court to recommend and comment upon the suitability of the particular disposal. Indeed, the revised Mental Health Act Code of Practice expressly recognizes the significance of the medical evidence, stating that 'A medical report will be of crucial importance in determining whether or not sentence of life imprisonment should be imposed where this is not mandatory.'[419] The new powers are complex and varied and will undoubtedly involve a significant amount of resources—both human and physical. In light of the opposition and criticism which the main provisions of the 1997 Act have faced (from all quarters, including the judiciary),[420] it will therefore be interesting to see to what extent the powers, such as the hospital direction, are fully embraced and implemented by the courts.

3.5.2.7. The Transfer of Sentenced Prisoners (s. 47)

3.5.2.7.1. The Provisions

Section 47 enables an offender serving a sentence of imprisonment, but identified in prison as suffering from mental disorder, to be transferred to hospital. The need to transfer may be for a variety of reasons. As noted by Larry Gostin, the prisoner may have been suffering from a minor form of disorder which was exacerbated by the prison regime, or the disorder may develop or be first detected in prison, or simply, given the difficulties already highlighted experienced by the courts, a bed may not have been found at the time of sentencing.[421] The prison hospital wing does not have sufficient facilities or staffing adequately to care for and treat those with a serious mental disorder. Thus, if a sentenced prisoner is diagnosed as suffering from one of the four forms of mental disorder specified under s. 1 of the Act and the relevant medical evidence is provided, the Home Secretary can direct his/her transfer to hospital.[422] As with a hospital order, the transfer may be

---

[419] Para. 3.13.   [420] D. A. Thomas, *Current Sentencing.*
[421] Gostin, *Mental Health Services*, para. 16.01; see also Hoggett, *Mental Health Law*, 127.
[422] Mental Health Act 1983 s. 47; see Gostin, *Mental Health Services*, paras. 16.01–3.

made with or without restrictions, and its legal effect is the same.[423] The detailed procedural and evidential requirements are set out in Table 3.4.

It has been observed that it is normal practice for the Home Secretary to impose a transfer direction with restrictions, unless a prisoner is transferred very close to the earliest date of his/her release from prison. As highlighted by Gostin,[424] perhaps one of the most important reasons for this is to enable arrangements for the supervision of a patient to be made conditional upon his/her discharge, thereby ensuring that s/he is cared for adequately in the community and preventing any possibility of reoffending.

3.5.2.7.2. Commentary

The total number of s. 47 transfers rose from 108 in 1984 to 156 in 1990,[425] as Table 3.6 illustrates.

It seems that successive Governments are committed to getting mentally disordered prisoners into hospital, as they will not receive the same standard of care and treatment in prison. The Tumim Report on Prison Suicides noted the value of s. 47 and recommended its continued and increased use,[426] and its merit has recently been confirmed by other researchers in this area. [427] Despite the gradual increase in it use throughout the 1980s, however, concerns have been continually expressed by the Prison Service about the high numbers of mentally disordered offenders still in their custody, and, particularly, about the inadequate medical facilities available to these prisoners: 'Imprisonment may adversely affect their condition; they create undue pressure on already stretched resources, and they could well be dealt with in better ways.'[428]

Particular emphasis was placed in the Annual Reports upon the length of time spent in prison for those still awaiting transfer. A survey was conducted requiring prison officers to note the number of mentally ill offenders in their care which they considered to meet the criteria for transfer under the Mental Health Act. In 1985 the total number was 268,[429] in 1986 it totalled 306,[430] and in 1987 it was 298.[431] Many mentally disordered offenders clearly met the criteria for transfer but were still inappropriately detained in prison. Moreover the Chief Inspector of

TABLE 3.6. *Section 47 transfers*

	1984	1985	1986	1987	1988	1989	1990
s. 47	108	100	107	127	121	131	156

[423] Mental Health Act 1983 s. 47(3).   [424] *Mental Health Services*, para. 16.03.
[425] HO, Statistical Bulletin 01/95 Table 7.   [426] Cm. 1383 para. 7.94.
[427] P. L. Huckle, 'A Survey of Sentenced Prisoners Transferred to Hospital for Urgent Psychiatric Treatment over a Three Year Period in One Region' (1996) 36(4) *Med, Sci & Law* 37–40.
[428] Cm. 246 para. 34; see also Cm. 516 para. 52; Cm. 1302 para. 47.
[429] Cmnd. 11.   [430] Cm. 246.   [431] Cm. 516.

Prisons in his 1990/1 annual report noted, for example, the 'considerable delays faced in transferring offenders with severe mental illness from Brixton to the NHS'.[432] Several years earlier, in his 1985 report, he had already commented upon the delays in facilitating such transfers.[433] Indeed, whilst there has been a marked increase in the number of s. 47 transfers since the introduction of an explicit diversion policy in recent years (which will be considered in greater depth in the following chapter), there is still much concern expressed about the unacceptable delays in securing the transfers.[434]

An article written by Adrian Grounds has highlighted the difficulties that exist in achieving hospital care for mentally disordered people in the penal system.[435] He emphasizes how difficult it can be to find a hospital bed within the 14-day time limit provided by the section—if at all—'no allowance is made for the possibility that finding a hospital bed may take longer'.[436] Clearly there are strong arguments in favour of relaxing the requirements and criteria of this section. As Brenda Hoggett has noted, Special Hospitals will only admit 'the most dangerous patients', Regional Secure Units tend to admit only short-term patients, and local hospitals are overcrowded and not sufficiently secure.[437]

Concerns have also been expressed about the inadequacy of safeguards for individuals transferred under this section at a late stage in their sentence which results in detention beyond the length of their sentence. The Mental Health Act Code of Practice specifies that transfers should 'take place as soon as possible after the need has been identified',[438] but Adrian Grounds' research considered this issue and concluded that new safeguards are required to ensure that delay does not occur.[439] However, it must be noted that one particular study has investigated this issue and concluded that, to a large extent, fears are unfounded. The authors conducted a comprehensive review of the total number of s. 47 transfers since the introdcution of the 1983 Act and found that they have not been used in such a way that would result in disproportionate sentencing.[440]

Given the shortage of facilities, reluctance to admit such patients, the concerns expressed about late transfers, and the completely inadequate facilities in prison, as Hoggett argues 'Better still . . . to avoid their being sent to prison at all.'[441] Which is clearly why the emphasis should be upon earlier identification, assessment, and diversion, increasing s. 48 transfers, therapeutic remands, and disposals.

---

[432] Session 1991–2 HC 54 para. 4.26.   [433] Session 1986–7 HC 123 para. 2.20.
[434] See e.g. MHAC, *Report 1993–5*, 77; D. Hargreaves, 'The Transfer of Severely Mentally Ill Prisoners from HMP Wakefield: A Descriptive Study' (1997) 8(1) *J For Psych* 62–73.
[435] 'Transfers of Sentenced Prisoners to Hospital' [1990] *Crim LR* 544–51.
[436] Ibid. 550.   [437] Hoggett, *Mental Health Law*, 127.   [438] Para. 3.21.
[439] A. Grounds, 'Transfers of Sentenced Prisoners to Hospital' [1990] *Crim LR* 544–51; id. The Transfer of Sentenced Prisoners to Hospital 1960–1983: A Study in One Special Hospital' (1991) 31 *Brit J Criminology* 54–71.
[440] R. Huws, *et al.*, 'Prison Transfers to Special Hospitals since the Introduction of the Mental Health Act' (1997) 8(1) *J For Psych* 74–84.   [441] *Mental Health Law*, 194.

3.6. CONCLUSION

It has been shown that, initially, the courts welcomed these flexible powers of disposal under the Mental Health Act 1983, and were constantly reminded of the range of options available to them when dealing with a mentally disordered offender.[442] The courts have been advised that, where appropriate, the emphasis should always be on treatment, and not punishment. Despite this initial encouragement, however, the evidence indicates that, as the 1980s progressed, the powers were still sparingly used and '[t]he plight of mentally ill people imprisoned when they should be receiving other treatment has still not been resolved'.[443] In 1988, for instance, magistrates remanded only 2 per cent of the total court turnover for report, and even then there were wide regional variations in doing so.[444] Consequently, therapeutic disposals through the courts under the Mental Health Act were, as already indicated, generally very limited in number. The number of hospital orders declined and the number of restriction orders made by the Crown Court remained relatively low. Interim hospital orders, although regarded as a major innovation, were also limited in number. The psychiatric probation order has many advantages; most importantly, it enables the offender to be returned to court should treatment be unsuccessful. Yet their use was still regarded by commentators as meagre and inconsistent. This chapter has shown that there is very little to support a belief that courts and psychiatrists were making more use of these provisions as they gained experience in dealing with them throughout the 1980s.[445]

This chapter has also outlined a number of positive developments that took place, however, in an attempt to combat the problem, such as the introduction of bail information and public interests case assessment schemes, for example. But, despite such initiatives, there was still much room for improvement in this area of the law and practice. There was substantial underuse of the wide range of powers available to the court and this was compounded by the deficiencies present in many of the actual provisions themselves.[446] Indeed, many of the criticisms were aimed at relaxing the provisions to enable more mentally disordered offenders to fall within their ambit and their diversion to take place at a much quicker pace without the periods of delay which they presently entailed.

The opportunities for psychiatric care for mentally disordered offenders were not as widespread as they could and should have been. This underuse, and in many cases non-use, is attributed to the lack of familiarity, lack of information,

---

[442] D. Aires, 'Mentally Disordered Offenders and Magistrates' Courts' (1986) 42 *The Mag* 156–7; M. Dodds, 'Mentally Disordered Offenders and Magistrates' (1987) 43 *The Mag* 45–6; A. Barker, 'Mentally Disordered Offenders and the Courts: Some Aspects of the Problems as seen by a Beak and a Quack' (1988) 152 *JP* 55–7, 71–4, 100–4.

[443] Major, 'What Can a Magistrate Do?', 46.   [444] A. Barker, 'Beak and Quack'.

[445] See Munro and Fraser, 'New Provisions'.

[446] See D. Carson, 'Mental Processes: The Mental Health Act 1983' [1983] *JSWL* 195–211, 210.

and lack of communication amongst the criminal justice, health, and social services agencies involved in their implementation. It has been outlined that the lack of use of the powers, in particular the community-based guardianship and probation orders, has been due to the failures of the relevant agencies to co-operate and collaborate in many cases. So, it would seem that the 1983 Act has suffered the same fate as many of its predecessors, and the failures which have plagued past attempts, which were outlined in the previous chapter, had still not been resolved. These deficiencies have been observed by many:[447] 'A great deal of legislation currently exists to allow the diversion of mentally ill offenders from the criminal justice system. Unfortunately, the provisions which do exist to divert the mentally ill are under-used, primarily because *there is a fundamental lack of communication between the mental health and criminal justice systems*'.[448] Gillian Shephard MP echoed these sentiments in Parliament when initiating a debate on the ineffective powers in the Mental Health Act 1983:

Despite the legal framework that exists to prevent it, there is still an imperfect understanding on the part of the courts of the alternatives available to them, and an imperfect relationship at local level between the judiciary, the penal system and the health service, which, if it were used properly, could ensure a better use of facilities and a better disposal for the individual.[449]

The lack of communication and collaboration has clearly been a major contributing factor, but, at the heart of the problem, has been the lack of resourcing and insufficient facilities within the psychiatric and social services to enable the full application of these powers to take place. This was a major failing to which the outcries of a disgruntled judiciary have plainly borne testimony. And this will be an extremely important consideration in the evaluation of diversion policy to be conducted in the following chapters.

The tragic consequences of this situation, however, were the increasing numbers of mentally disordered offenders still being inappropriately remanded and sentenced to periods of imprisonment. Despite the intention to the contrary, and the powers which existed to prevent it, far too many mentally ill people were ending up in prison—not receiving the psychiatric care and treatment which they needed and to which they were entitled. This chapter has already alluded to the concerns of the 1986 Select Committee report and the 1987 Interdepartmental Working Group in this area. Such was the unease that a study by Professor John Gunn and his colleagues at the Institute of Psychiatry was commissioned by the 1979–97 Conservative Government to investigate the true

[447] See e.g. G. Richardson, *Law, Process and Custody: Prisoners and Patients* (Weidenfeld & Nicolson 1993), 230, 233; Peay, 'Mentally Disordered Offenders', in Maguire, Morgan, and Reiner (eds.), *Oxford Handbook of Criminology*, 1132.

[448] P. Joseph, 'Mentally Disordered Offenders: Diversion from the Criminal Justice System' (1990) 1 *J For Psych* 133–8 (emphasis supplied).

[449] Session 1987–8 HC Debs Vol. 137 cols 530–6, 532.

extent of the problem.[450] The only information previously known was a study conducted by Gunn *et al.* in 1972 which estimated that 30 per cent of the prison population were in need of psychiatric treatment.[451] The 1990 study, which focused on the prevalence of mental illness in the sentenced prison population, found that approximately 20 per cent of all sentenced prisoners required some form of psychiatric help or assessment.[452] It has already been substantiated that those suffering from mental illness are highly susceptible and at an increased risk when in custody, and should not be unnecessarily subjected to it. There is indeed a wealth of evidence to this effect, particularly that received by the 1986 House of Commons Social Services Select Committee on the Prison Medical Service[453] from professional bodies as wide-ranging as the BMA, MIND, the Prison Officers' Association, and the Prison Reform Trust. As outlined in Ch. 1, no matter how hard the prison hospital staff work, the conditions in the prison medical wing are in no way comparable to those in an NHS hospital[454] and 'a man in prison is first and foremost a prisoner'.[455]

Many voluntary organisations and charities took an extremely active role in the fight to better the lot of the mentally ill and reduce the numbers of the mentally disordered in prison at this time. NACRO, for example, published numerous reports which continuously highlighted the plight of the mentally ill.[456] In July 1990 a joint letter on behalf of the National Schizophrenia Fellowship, the Howard League, the Prison Reform Trust, and NACRO was sent to the Home Secretary expressing concern about the great numbers of mentally vulnerable people in prison. These organisations urged the 1979–97 Conservative Government to take action to ensure that these people were actually diverted from the criminal justice system.[457] The climate was therefore one which dictated that far more positive steps had to be taken by the Government at the time.

The problem was particularly acute given the general crisis which was taking place in the prisons at that time. As the Government of that day acknowledged in its response to the Social Services Committee Report, the climate was unquestionably one of 'gaunt, ill-equipped and overcrowded prisons'.[458] The 1987 Working Group had also noted the immense pressures already being placed upon the prison system and their grave effect upon the health of the prisoners themselves: 'the

---

[450] DHSS/HO, *Report on an Interdepartmental Working Group of Home Office and DHSS Officials on Mentally Disturbed Offenders in the Prison System in England and Wales* (DHSS/HO 1987) para. 5.6.

[451] J. Gunn, *et al., Psychiatric Aspects of Imprisonment* (Academic Press 1978).

[452] J. Gunn, *et al., Mentally Disordered Prisoners* (HMSO 1991).

[453] *Third Report on the Prison Medical Service*, Session 1985–6 HC 72.

[454] Ibid. para. 55.   [455] Major, 'What Can a Magistrate Do?', 54.

[456] See e.g. the policy papers produced by the NACRO MH Adv. Com. on the Diversion of Mentally Disordered Offenders; NACRO's Briefings on the Imprisonment and Diversion of Mentally Disordered Offenders (Dec. 1990 and Feb. 1992); NACRO *Revolving Doors*; *The Resettlement Needs of Mentally Disordered Offenders* (NACRO 1991).

[457] See the Woolf Report, Cm. 1456 para. 10.116.

[458] Session 1985–6 Cm. 115 para. 2 (Mar. 1987).

degree of overcrowding and pressure of facilities in the local prisons and remand centres is at a level which militates against the promotion of health-care, both physical and mental'.[459] The penal crisis which took place during the 1980s has been widely documented,[460] and the prison conditions became so unbearable that they led to a series of highly publicized prison riots, culminating in the Strangeways Prison riot in April 1990. These disturbances led to the Woolf Report on Prison Disturbances, which also commented upon the high proportion of mentally disturbed offenders improperly placed in the prison system.[461]

It is against this background of crisis and concern that the 1979–97 Conservative Government responded and a new approach to the problem of the mentally disordered in prison was introduced: 'By the end of the 1980s, and partly in recognition of the under-use, non-use and delay these provisions entailed, a movement developed towards even earlier assessment and diversion'.[462] In 1990, the Conservative Government introduced an explicit policy of diverting mentally disordered offenders into the health and social services and away from the damaging effects of custody and imprisonment. Guidance was issued to all the agencies involved alerting them to the value of the therapeutic powers and provisions and encouraging their increased implementation. This was complemented by the promotion of multi-agency psychiatric assessment and diversion schemes, which were introduced to enable even earlier and greater assessment and diversion to take place. A number of other initiatives to promote diversion and inter-agency working were also introduced to complement the objectives of this policy.

The introduction of diversion policy, its practical implications and effects, particularly upon the use of the therapeutic powers, and the range of new initiatives will be considered fully in the following chapters. The impact of other legislative and policy developments, such as the Crime (Sentences) Act 1997 will also be considered in greater depth, as they may influence the future direction of diversion policy. However, emphasis will be placed upon the impact of the explicit diversion policy in the West Yorkshire area and, especially, it will be considered whether it does in fact enable more mentally ill people to be given access to and actually receive the appropriate health care and treatment in the appropriate facilities. And, also, whether the required level of inter-agency co-operation and exchange of information has taken place to enable this to be achieved.

---

[459] DHSS/HO, para. 5.1.
[460] See e.g. Lord Longford, *Punishment and the Punished* (Chapmans 1991).
[461] Cm. 1456 para. 10.118.
[462] Peay, 'Mentally Disordered Offenders', in Maguire, Morgan, and Reiner (eds.), *Oxford Handbook of Criminology*, 1133.

4

The Development of Diversion Policy for Mentally Disordered Offenders

The urgent need to divert mentally disordered offenders from custody has been echoed from sentencing bench and parliamentary committee, from prison gate and academic lectern.[1]

4.1. INTRODUCTION

Previous chapters have shown that mentally disordered offenders merit special care and treatment and should therefore, wherever possible, receive it from the health and social services. Diversion policy aims to secure adequate and appropriate medical care for mentally disordered offenders by diverting them out of the criminal justice system. This chapter documents the introduction and development of diversion policy in this country describing its general implementation nationally. The problems and practicalities which have been encountered will also be highlighted as they will be relevant to the consideration of the implementation of diversion policy specifically in West Yorkshire in Ch. 5.

4.2. SETTING THE STAGE FOR REFORM: THE FAILURES OF THE 1980S

It has already been identified in the preceding chapter how the Mental Health Act 1983 principally provided the courts with a range of flexible therapeutic powers of disposal. So mechanisms already existed within the legislation to divert the mentally disordered out of the criminal justice system and away from traditional penal disposals. But, as the 1980s progressed, it became evident that diversion was not being achieved in many cases as the powers were not being used to their full potential.[2] This failing had been observed by several prominent bodies and committees who expressed their concerns that far too many mentally disordered offenders were being remanded and sentenced to periods of imprisonment when what they really needed was care, supervision, and treatment. These were the

---

[1] S. Shaw and A. Sampson, 'Thro' Cells of Madness: The Imprisonment of Mentally Ill People', in K. Herbst and J. Gunn, *The Mentally Disordered Offender* (Butterworth Heinemann 1991), 105.

[2] See further P. Joseph, 'Mentally Disordered Offenders: Diversion from the Criminal Justice System' (1990) 1 *J For Psych* 133–7, 137.

catalysts that led the 1979–97 Conservative Government to take measures to try to combat the problem.[3]

4.3. THE SOLUTION: THE DIVERSION OF MENTALLY DISORDERED OFFENDERS

Having accepted that steps had to be taken, the Conservative Government announced various changes and introduced new policies and provisions which would enable even greater consideration and diversion of the mentally disordered offender.[4]

4.3.1. 'The Sentence of the Court'

One of the first steps it took to translate them into practice was to revise the handbook on sentencing for the courts.[5] The aim was to draw the attention of the sentencers to 'the basic principle applicable in all cases, that custody must be used only as a last resort, applies with particular force in respect of the mentally disturbed. It will seldom be appropriate—or effective—to give a mentally disturbed offender a custodial sentence'.[6] The handbook contained an entire chapter devoted to mentally disordered offenders drawing the courts' attention to the broad range of therapeutic disposal powers available and providing clear guidance as to their implementation. Above all, it was vital to note that the medical facilities in prison were in no way comparable to those provided in psychiatric hospitals in the community. Consequently, 'It would be unsafe to reach judgements on the assumption that an offender is ensured of treatment while serving a prison sentence [and] . . . it would be wrong to indicate to an offender that he or she would receive psychiatric treatment in prison.'[7] The handbook stressed that whilst every effort was being made to improve the medical facilities in prisons, 'in general terms the fact of imprisonment and *the overcrowding and conditions in prisons are not conducive to a healing environment*'.[8] This is highly significant, as the courts have been expressly advised to adhere to the principle that prison is wholly inappropriate for those mentally disordered offenders who require medical care, treatment, and support.

---

[3] Session 1988–9 HC Debs Vol. 153 col. 758 *per* Mr Douglas Hurd Secretary of State for Home Department; Session 1989–90 HL Debs Vol. 516 cols 1168–70: 'at a time when there is increasing evidence of inappropriate placing of people with psychiatric illness in the criminal justice system, where so few treatment facilities exist . . . Our common aim is to ensure that where possible such offenders are dealt with without resort to the courts or, failing that, without resort to the penal system. We recognize that there is scope to increase the level of diversion.'

[4] Session 1989–90 HC Debs Vol. 177 cols 133–4, Written Answer by Peter Lloyd, Parliamentary Under-Secretary of State for the Home Department.

[5] *The Sentence of the Court: Handbook for the Courts on the Treatment of Offenders* (HMSO 1991). [6] Ibid. para. 12.1. [7] Ibid. para. 12.21.

[8] Ibid. para. 12.20 (emphasis supplied).

4.3.2. Home Office Circular 66/90

Later in 1990, the 1979–97 Conservative Government took these principles further forward by introducing an explicit policy of diverting mentally disordered offenders from the criminal justice system. On 3 September, the Home Office issued a Circular[9] to all the criminal justice agencies expressly stating: 'It is government policy that, wherever possible, mentally disordered persons should receive care and treatment from the health and social services.'[10] This Circular was accompanied and supported by a statement issued by the Department of Health, which reaffirmed the Government's commitment and alerted the health and social services to the need for diversion, assessment, and effective facilities.[11]

The Home Office Circular drew attention to the range of powers available to all the different agencies, and provided guidance to ensure they would now be used *effectively* and to their *fullest extent*. The police were urged to make better use of ss. 135 and 136 of the Mental Health Act and of their power to drop charges. In particular, Chief Officers of Police were asked to ensure that 'consideration is always given to alternatives to prosecuting mentally disordered offenders, including taking no further action where appropriate, and that effective arrangements are established with local health and social services authorities to ensure their speedy involvement when mentally disordered persons are taken into police custody'.[12] This has subsequently been taken a step further in the Revised Code of Practice accompanying the Mental Health Act. It specifically provides that agreed procedures for implementing s. 136 must be formulated in all areas between the police, local health service, and criminal justice agencies,[13] thereby ensuring effective co-operation, early identification, and treatment of offenders suspected of suffering from a mental illness.

The Crown Prosecution Service was urged to use its power to discontinue prosecution if it did not serve the public interest to pursue it: 'Any information provided by the police with the papers regarding that person's mental condition, or discussions held with other agencies to consider the advisability of *diverting* him from court, *will be taken into account*.'[14] The courts were also reminded of their duties and powers under the Mental Health Act and other legislative provisions to ensure that the mentally disordered receive therapeutic care and treatment wherever possible: 'It is desirable that alternatives to prosecution, such as cautioning by the police, and/or admission to hospital, if the person's mental

---

[9] Circular 66/90, *Provision for Mentally Disordered Offenders* (Home Office 1990); see also E. Petch, 'Mentally Disordered Offenders and Inter-Agency Working' (1996) 7(2) *J For Psych* 376–82. [10] HO Circular 66/90 para. 2.

[11] NHS Management Executive Letter, EL(90)168 para. 1.

[12] HO Circular 66/90 para. 26.

[13] DoH/Welsh Office, *Mental Health Act 1983 Revised Code of Practice* (HMSO 1999) para. 10.1–5. [14] HO Circular 66/90 para. 6 (emphasis supplied).

condition requires hospital treatment, or support in the community, should be considered first before deciding that prosecution is necessary.'[15]

In particular, the Probation Service has a valuable and 'special' role to play in diverting the mentally disordered offender, by providing information to the CPS and courts and by providing accommodation, supervision, and throughcare for the diverted offender: 'The probation service should act as part of a network of agencies (social services, health services, voluntary organisations) providing accommodation, care and treatment in the community for mentally disordered offenders.'[16]

In order to achieve all this, a high level of co-operation and collaboration would need to take place between all the agencies involved to ensure that all the information required to make such decisions would be available: 'The government recognizes that this policy can be effective only if the courts and criminal justice agencies have access to health and social services. This requires consultation and co-operation, and this circular aims to provide guidance on the establishment of a *satisfactory working relationship between courts, criminal justice agencies and health and social services.*'[17]

Such laudable principles are not new and revolutionary, but have their origins firmly rooted in the past and were emphasized by the Butler Committee in particular.[18] Now, over two decades later, it has at last been officially recognized and formally accepted that, as a matter of policy, 'the mentally ill should be treated in hospital, wherever possible, and we do not wish the courts to have to send sick people to prison'.[19]

The mechanisms that already exist which do enable diversion to take place have already been outlined in the previous chapter. However, as identified, these powers have not been used adequately, therefore the 1979–97 Conservative Government introduced this explicit diversion policy so that more efficient and frequent use will be made of them. The Home Office Circular not only urged more effective and increased use of these powers, but also described how this could best be achieved.

The solution was perceived to be the introduction of inter-agency 'diversion schemes' operating at various stages in the criminal justice system. Such schemes could be accessed at the police station at the point of arrest, at the magistrates' court, or, alternatively, within the prisons to secure appropriate mental health assessments, transfers, and treatment.

4.3.3. Experiences in Other Jurisdictions

Analogous arrangements with respect to mentally ill offenders have been in successful operation in several other jurisdictions, but it is not clear to what extent

---

[15] Ibid. para. 2.   [16] Ibid. para. 17.   [17] Ibid. para. 2 (emphasis supplied).
[18] *Butler Report* (1975), Cmnd. 6244, para. 20.3.
[19] Session 1983–4 HC Debs Vol. 65 col. 544 *per* K. Clarke Minister for Health; see also Session 1997–8 HL Debs Vol. 586 col. 412 WA—where the Labour Government reaffirmed its commitment to diversion policy, announcing that it shares the view that mentally disordered offenders require ready access to treatment and care and should not be imprisoned unnecessarily.

they have been influential in the United Kingdom. The Home Office was clearly aware of such arrangements, as Philip Joseph's research identified that Australia and the United States, for example, have had such diversion arrangements in place at courts for several years. Similar difficulties with increasing numbers of mentally ill offenders have been identified widely in the United States' jails; consequently, it boasts over 250 diversion schemes operating at courts throughout the country.[20] In Milwaukee for example, an assessment and diversion scheme has been operating at the County Jail whereby mentally ill offenders, through a co-operative screening system at booking, are promptly identified and referred for psychiatric care to the Milwaukee County Mental Health Complex.[21] And in Montgomery County, Pennsylvania, an emergency intervention and assessment service (Montgomery County Emergency Service) has been available to the police, courts, and jails via the local Psychiatric/Drug/Alcohol Crisis Intervention Center since 1982. The services provide 'legitimate opportunities for diversion from criminal justice processing before, during and after adjudication. . . . [And] ensure that criminal justice staff at all stages of criminal processing are aware of the treatment alternatives, that the client's chances for continuity of care are maximized, and that referring agents are satisfied that the emergency victim has received or is receiving treatment.'[22] The benefits to the individual are immediate access to much needed services, as well as long term follow-up. For the police, courts, and prisons, there are savings in both time and money, whereby unnecessary court appearances and lengthy periods of incarceration can be avoided: 'MCES provides an alternative to incarceration—and provides criminal justice liaison personnel who interact daily with the police and the local Montgomery County Prison to help accomplish pre- and post-arrest diversion. Any community, any city, any town can do the same.'[23]

It is not surprising to hear therefore that a little closer to home, in Scotland, a similar diversionary practice is well established. The Scottish legal system differs from that in England and Wales as the Procurator-fiscal (state prosecutor) has the sole responsibility of evaluating the evidence against the accused and on that basis decides whether or not to prosecute. S/he can therefore divert certain offenders from the court process into treatment. Consequently, since the mid-1980s, diversion schemes have been set up in Scotland whereby offenders who are suspected of having psychological or psychiatric difficulties are referred for treatment to medical centres by the Procurator-fiscal before, and generally in lieu

---

[20] P. Joseph, *Psychiatric Assessment at the Magistrates' Court* (HO 1992), 3; see also R. Roesch *et al.*, 'Mental Health Research in the Criminal Justice System' (1995) 18(1) *Int J Law & Psych* 1–14, which considers the origins and development of diversion in this context in the USA.

[21] G. B. Palermo, M. B. Smith and F. J. Liska, 'Jail Versus Mental Hospitals: The Milwaukee Approach to a Social Dilemma (1991) 35 *International Journal of Offender Therapy & Comparative Criminology* 205; see also id. 'Jail Versus Mental Hospitals: A Social Dilemma' (1991) 35 *International Journal of Offender Therapy and Comparative Criminology* 97–104.

[22] N. Dank and M. Kulishoff, 'An Alternative to Incarceration of the Mentally Ill' (1983) 3 *J Prison & Jail Health* 95–100, 97.   [23] Ibid. 100.

of, prosecution.[24] A study of such a system operating in Glasgow found that such schemes, which have been set up 'both [for] financial and humanitarian reasons' are very 'flexible' and an extremely 'valuable development'.[25] And it was sincerely hoped that the Scottish schemes would 'act as a stimulus for other diversion schemes within the UK'.[26]

4.4. THE INTRODUCTION OF DIVERSION SCHEMES

This aspiration has indeed been fulfilled, as, annexed to the 1990 Home Office Circular were examples of good practice. These included an account of a multi-disciplinary panel court diversion scheme already in existence in North-West Hertfordshire, and a court duty-psychiatrist diversion scheme operating at two London magistrates' courts. Such a scheme was regarded as an essential element in translating the diversion policy into practice, ensuring a better deal for the mentally disordered, and achieving the desired level of co-operation and 'satisfactory working relationships between the courts, criminal justice agencies and health and social services'.

4.4.1. The Hertfordshire Panel Assessment Scheme[27]

This multidisciplinary diversion scheme evolved from a pilot project set up in 1985. The pilot scheme was funded by the Mental Health Foundation and involved a community psychiatric nurse working part-time as a link between all the other services. Whenever the court has any doubts as to a defendant's mental health, a referral is made to an assessment panel, co-ordinated by a probation officer, and including psychiatrists, psychologists, GPs, social workers, and other interested agencies, to consider the case during the period of adjournment for psychiatric, psychological, and/or social inquiry reports. It provides an improved service and more detailed information to the courts, and the collaboration between agencies helps to ensure the best support for mentally disordered persons

---

[24] See D. J. Cooke, 'Treatment as an Alternative to Prosecution: Offenders Diverted for Treatment' (1991) 158 *Brit J Psych* 785–91; id. 'Psychological Treatment as an Alternative to Prosecution: A Form of Primary Diversion' (1991) 30 *How J of Crim Just* 53–65; id., Primary Diversion for Psychological Treatment: The Decision-Making of Procurators Fiscal' (1994) 17 *Int J Law & Psych* 211–23; see also P. Duff and M. Burman, *Diversion from Prosecution to Psychiatric Care* (Scottish Office Central Research Unit 1994); id. 'Diversion from Prosecution to Psychiatric Care' (1995) 18 *SLT* 159–63; P. Duff, 'Diversion from Prosecution into Psychiatric Care: Who Controls the Gates?' (1997) 37(1) *Brit J Criminology* 15–34.

[25] Cooke, 'Treatment as Alternative', 789.   [26] Ibid. 790.

[27] See further A. Osler, 'Mentally Disordered Offenders' (1991) 47 *The Mag* 161–2; C. Hedderman, *Panel Assessment Schemes for Mentally Disordered Offenders*, HO Research and Planning Unit Paper, 76 (HMSO 1993); D. Gordon and C. Hedderman, *Panel Assessment Schemes and Other Responses to Mentally Disordered Offenders: A Survey of Probation Areas*, HO Research and Statistics Department Research Bulletin, 34 (HMSO 1994), 9–12.

diverted from prison.[28] The panel may also be convened at the request of the police or CPS when cautioning or discontinuance is considered and also when a person is being discharged from hospital, Regional Secure Unit, or prison. Funding has subsequently been provided by the Hertfordshire Care Trust.

This scheme is aimed at achieving diversion in its broadest sense, not simply diversion from prison custody, but diversion from prosecution, criminal proceedings, and criminal justice agencies enabling transfer to the health and social services. The benefits of such a scheme are manifest: from the offender's perspective it results in diversion from prosecution and prison, and reoffending and relapse rates have been found to be much lower. From the point of view of the agencies concerned, responsibility is shared and consequently resources are fully mobilized.

The Home Office Research and Planning Unit conducted an evaluation of the scheme in 1993, and found that, in terms of the diversion rates of mentally disordered offenders, the scheme had made an extremely positive impact. Moreover, all the agencies at court were co-operating well, in particular the magistrates, who made good use of the assessment referral service to provide them with the relevant information and invariably acted upon the recommendations provided.[29] The study also included an evaluation of two other such panel schemes which were by then also in operation. Taken as a whole the results were extremely encouraging. Referrals were made to the panels from a variety of agencies, notably the magistrates, probation staff, and police. Of the total sample of referrals during the period of study (April 1991–April 1992) the majority of defendants referred were given an absolute discharge, probation order, or some form of medical disposal, and so diversion was clearly taking place.[30]

4.4.2. The Bow Street and Marlborough Street Magistrates' Courts' Psychiatrist Assessment Scheme

Another example of psychiatric assessment and liaison which was also attached to the Circular was the scheme operating at Bow Street and Marlborough Street Magistrates' Courts in Central London. Discussions began in 1989 to set up a psychiatric assessment service at these courts. The main aim was to provide greater and better information for the court to enable the magistrates to make better-informed decisions and therapeutic disposals, by identifying mental disorder at the earliest possible stage.[31] It is stated that the overall objective is therefore

---

[28] See further HO Circular 66/90 Annexe C; D. Tonak and G. Cawdron, 'Mentally Disordered Offenders and the Courts: Co-operation and Collaboration of Disciplines Involved' (1988) 152 *JP* 504–7; A. Barker, 'Mentally Disordered Offenders and the Courts: Some Aspects of the Problems as Seen by a Beak and a Quack' (1988) 152 *JP* 55–7, 71–4, 100–4.

[29] Hedderman, *Panel Assessment.*   [30] Ibid. 20–1.

[31] See further HO Circular 66/90 Annexe B; Joseph, *Psychiatric Assessment*; id., 'Mentally Disordered Homeless Offenders: Diversion from Custody' (1990) 22 *Health Trends* 51–3; id. and M. Potter, 'Diversion from Custody, 1: Psychiatric Assessment at the Magistrates' Court' (1993) 162 *Brit J Psych* 325–30.

to achieve diversion from custody in the narrowest sense as outlined in Ch. 1, i.e. to avoid remands in custody solely for the preparation of medical reports. Achieving diversion in its broadest sense however is also a possible and desired objective of the scheme, wherever necessary and appropriate. A psychiatric on-call service is available at court for two sessions per week and referrals are accepted from any other agency at the court. The defendant is assessed by the duty-psychiatrist in the gaoler's area at the court. Following assessment, recommendations are made to the court, and if a hospital bed is required then the appropriate arrangements are made. The scheme relies upon co-operation between all the agencies to ensure that the appropriate defendants are identified and diverted from the prison system.

Dr Philip Joseph from the Institute of Psychiatry at the University of London conducted a study of this scheme on behalf of the Home Office.[32] He found that it had been welcomed by all the agencies at court—all had been extremely willing to make referrals to the scheme and there has been a 'strong spirit of co-operation'. Indeed, a total of 201 referrals were made to the duty-psychiatrist during the period of study (February 1989–September 1990). The assessments proved extremely valuable as the outcomes illustrate. Both diversion in its broadest and its narrowest sense has been achieved as a result of the psychiatrists' intervention. The majority of the offences committed were relatively minor in nature—only 4 per cent of offenders were committed to the Crown Court.[33] Consequently, almost a third of the cases were discontinued; given the nature of the charges and the degree of mental illness, prosecution would serve no useful purpose and would waste court time and money. A further 23 per cent were conditionally discharged, 39 per cent were given some form of therapeutic disposal (hospital order, probation order, or other non-custodial disposal), and only 6 per cent were given a penal sentence.[34] The scheme was also highly successful in significantly reducing the average time spent on remand between arrest and admission to hospital. Joseph's conclusion was that such duty-psychiatrist schemes 'can operate successfully to divert appropriately referred defendants', and '[t]he psychiatrist at court can provide a more efficient, cost-effective service for mentally disordered offenders'.[35]

Both schemes outlined above are operating at a magistrates' court. However, it will be shown below that since the policy has been introduced, different types of schemes have evolved throughout the country, involving different agencies and operating at different stages in the criminal justice process. The type of scheme implemented is entirely dependent upon local needs and resources, and the models outlined above have been adapted and tailored to suit these differing needs and localities.

[32] Joseph, *Psychiatric Assessment*.   [33] Ibid. 13–14.   [34] Ibid. 16.
[35] Ibid. 32.

4.5. NATIONAL RECOGNITION AND IMPLEMENTATION OF DIVERSION POLICY

A series of Government-inspired investigations and commissions throughout the 1990s have subsequently demonstrated the commitment to and interest in this area; and wide support has been generated from all perspectives, as will be seen.

4.5.1. Official Recognition

4.5.1.1. *The Department of Health Perspective*

In 1991 the Conservative Government appointed a Steering Committee[36] to consider further the plight of mentally disordered offenders; it produced its final summary report in November 1992 and contained a wealth of evidence and information, making a total of nearly 300 recommendations.[37] The Committee was asked to review the entire range of health and social services for mentally disordered offenders and to recommend detailed improved service provision and resource allocation. Consequently it devoted a section of its report to a consideration of the need for assessment and diversion of the mentally disordered. The Committee was fully in favour of the diversion schemes being established and recommended that:

There should be nationwide provision of properly resourced court assessment and diversion schemes. . . . There is a growing diversity among schemes which we welcome. Some schemes rely on a court psychiatrist; some others (for example) use a community psychiatric nurse or a multi-disciplinary 'panel'. In every case the chosen model must be adapted to local circumstances and effective planning and operational links made with other services and disciplines, including social work. The longer-term future of many schemes is not yet assured, but experience increasingly suggests that, where diversion schemes become established, these come to provide a broader multi-agency focus which, of itself, can make effective disposals easier.[38]

In line with this, the Final Summary Report further recommended that increased use should be made of bail information and public-interest case assessment schemes, which would complement the development of diversion and assessment schemes and ensure that the court was in full possession of all the information required to enable it to make the appropriate disposal.[39] The need to achieve this has already been noted in the previous chapter. The Committee also recommended that the ambit of many of the therapeutic disposal powers should be extended to ensure that as many mentally disordered offenders as possible are

---

[36] Session 1990–1 HC Debs Vol. 183 cols 241–2 Written Answer.
[37] DoH/HO, *Review of Health and Social Services for Mentally Disordered Offenders and Others Requiring Similar Services* (Reed Committee Report) (1992) Cm. 2088.
[38] Ibid. para. 5.3, 6.　　　　　　　　　　　　　　　　　　[39] Ibid. para. 5.3.

able to receive appropriate medical care and supervision. In particular, it felt that s. 36 should be extended to magistrates' courts, ss. 36 and 48 should include all categories of mental disorder, and that prisoners should be admitted/transferred for assessment as well as treatment under ss. 36/48.[40]

The work of the review was carried out by several advisory groups which looked at particular aspects of service provision. In particular, Community, Prison, and Hospital Advisory Groups were appointed, and considered the issues in great depth.[41] The Community and Hospital Advisory Groups were whole-hearted in their support for this policy, recommending that such diversion schemes should come to be regarded as the norm.[42] The Prison Advisory Group Report noted that the conditions in prison are not favourable for the assessment and custody of the mentally ill: 'there is little specific provision made in regimes, facilities or staffing for people with mental health care needs'.[43] Accordingly, prison staff should be fully aware of the need to divert and transfer at the earliest possible stage. Greater use should therefore be made of the transfer provisions.[44]

The Community Advisory Group Report devoted an entire chapter to the opportunities for diversion and discontinuance at various stages within the criminal justice process and clearly echoed the sentiments expressed in Circular 66/90. Each agency should take full account of its responsibilities and the opportunities for assessment and diversion at each stage of the process and ensure that access to a wide range of services is available, in line with official guidelines: 'The Home Office Circular 66/90 has provided a valuable stimulus ... [but] Further progress is crucially important if many mentally disordered offenders are not to be drawn too far into the criminal justice system or deprived of the opportunity to receive the care, treatment and support that they may need in hospital or in the community.'[45]

In a Parliamentary written answer in November 1992, Mr Tim Yeo, then the Under-Secretary of State for Health, confirmed the Government's general welcome of the report and reaffirmed that 'mentally disordered offenders who need care and treatment should receive it from health and personal social services rather than in the criminal justice system'.[46] This diversionary goal was further expounded by the Department of Health with the publication of the *Health of the Nation* White Paper in 1992: 'The essential task here is to ensure that mentally disordered offenders who need specialist health and social care are diverted from the criminal justice system as early as possible. This requires close co-operation between all the local agencies concerned.'[47] It identified five key areas where

---

[40] Ibid. ch. 9.   [41] Cm. 2088 Vol. 2, *Service Needs* (HMSO 1993).
[42] Ibid. Community Advisory Group Report, para. 2.29, Hospital Advisory Group Report, para. 4.11.   [43] Ibid. Prison Advisory Group Report, para. 4.1.
[44] Ibid. para. 3.4.   [45] Ibid. Community Advisory Group Report, para. 2.36.
[46] Session 1992–3 HC Debs Vol. 214 cols 877–8; see also Session 1991–2 HC Debs Vol. 198 cols 583–4 *per* Stephen Dorrell.
[47] *Health of the Nation (A Strategy for Health in England)* Session 1992–3 Cm. 1986 para. C19.

significant improvements could be made to enhance the health of the nation. One of these key areas was mental illness, and the former Government emphasized that steps must be taken to combat it, as those who suffer from mental illness are such a vulnerable group.[48] A series of mental illness initiatives and regional conferences were organised to increase awareness of this policy. This *Health of the Nation* strategy tied in closely with diversion policy—the emphasis clearly being placed upon inter-agency co-operation as the way forward to improve the treatment of and services for this group. The White Paper focused specifically upon mentally disordered offenders, 'a particularly vulnerable group. There is a risk that if their health and social care needs are not recognized and met, they may slip into a vicious circle of imprisonment, re-offending and deteriorating mental health.'[49] Accordingly, the document recommended the continued and sustained development of inter-agency diversion schemes, and pledged the 1979–97 Conservative Government's commitment and support by announcing that additional pump-priming funding would be made available to promote psychiatric assessment schemes linked to the courts. Thus, the commitment to this policy has, to a degree, been supported by the allocation of specific funding to develop such diversion schemes, which is being continued and further supported by the Labour Government.[50]

Indeed, this strategy has been reinforced and taken a step further by the current Labour Government, with the publication in 1997 of a Green Paper entitled *Our Healthier Nation*.[51] It underlines the importance of the mental health of the nation and takes forward the *Health of the Nation* philosophy and, in particular, adopts the targets to reduce the rates of suicide amongst the adult population even further. Mental illness has also been identified as one of four key areas for development and strategy, and the Government has reaffirmed its commitment to prioritizing mental health[52] and developing comprehensive mental health services.[53] It has also subsequently published a White Paper on the future of the NHS,[54] which proposes far-reaching reforms, but the emphasis is firmly placed upon partnership, closer co-operation, and collaboration between the health and social

---

[48]   *Health of the Nation.* para. C1, 'Mental illness is a leading cause of illness and disability. . . . The cost in human misery and suffering to individuals and their families is incalculable.' See further K. Jones, *Asylums and After: A Revised History of the Mental Health Services* (Athlone 1993), 234–6.

[49]   Cm. 1986, para. C5; see also para. C20.

[50]   HO, *Annual Report 1998: Government's Expenditure Plans 1998–1999*, Session 1997–8 Cm. 3908 para. 4.24; Session 1997–8 HL Debs Vol. 586 col. 412; Session 1997–8 HC Debs Vol. 309 col. 168.   [51]   See Session 1997–8 HL Debs Vol. 585 cols 1225–56 at 1233, 1254.

[52]   DoH, NHS Management Executive Letter, EL(97)39; Session 1997–8 HL Debs Vol. 586 col. 1255; DoH, *Modernising Mental Health Services: Safe, Sound and Supportive* (DoH 1998) para. 2.3.

[53]   Session 1997–8 HL Debs Vol. 585 col. 1254; see also *Departmental Report: Government's Expenditure Plans 1998–1999*, Session 1997–8 Cm. 3912 Paras. 4.101, 5.21; DoH, *Safe, Sound and Supportive*.

[54]   *The New NHS*—see Session 1997–8 HL Debs Vol. 584 cols 119–20; Session 1997–8 HL Debs Vol. 585 col. 1252; DoH Cm. 3912 para. 4.45.

services, in order to pursue strategy further.[55] It is clear that the Labour Government intends to proceed on a similar basis and take forward some of the previous Conservative Government's targets. It has pledged its commitment to diversion policy and that it will continue to allocate specific funding to develop such inter-agency initiatives. In principle, therefore, the Government has clearly accorded priority towards bettering the lot of this disadvantaged group.

4.5.1.2. *The Criminal Justice Perspective*

Diversion policy and the collaborative diversionary schemes have also been supported in the criminal justice arena. The 1990 Woolf Report into Prison Disturbances concluded that the 'range of initiatives being undertaken to minimise the number of mentally disordered people within the penal system should be continued and further developed'.[56] Circular 66/90 was greeted with much enthusiasm by the Woolf Committee[57], and it proposed the continued expansion of diversionary schemes as they made an extremely 'valuable contribution' to reducing the numbers of mentally vulnerable people in prison.[58]

The 1979–97 Conservative Government responded to the Woolf report by producing a White Paper with its plans for the future of the prison service.[59] It firmly endorsed these conclusions reached by the Woolf report and expressly stated that

Prison is not a suitable place for people suffering from serious mental disturbance. Whenever possible, such offenders should be diverted to the health or social services when they first come into contact with the criminal justice system. Where it is unavoidable that those requiring in-patient treatment are committed to prison, then they should be transferred to suitable health service facilities as soon as possible.[60]

The Tumim Report on Prison Suicides also devoted its report to a consideration of diversion policy. It commended the scheme operating at the Marlborough and Bow Street Magistrates' Courts: 'The advantages of this scheme are clear'.[61] Diversion from custody was regarded as an essential objective: 'the commitment to avoid remanding in custody for medical reports *must* continue . . . [and] We would like to see these schemes developed on a nationwide basis. They illustrate how pragmatic and flexible the courts can be when dealing with mentally ill petty offenders, if psychiatric assessment and liaison can be provided at an early stage

---

[55] The emphasis upon closer partnership and co-operation has also been stressed in several other DoH publications. See e.g. *The Health of the Nation, Building Bridges: A Guide to Arrangements for Inter-agency Working for the Care and Protection of Severely Mentally Ill People* (DoH, 1995): inter-agency working is regarded as essential for the delivery of appropriate and co-ordinated care to mentally ill people in the community; and DoH Social Care Group, *Services for Mentally Disordered Offenders in the Community: An Inspection Report* (DoH, 1997) para. 1.3.

[56] Cm. 1456 para. 10.118 Recommendation 89.   [57] Ibid. para. 10.119.

[58] Ibid. para. 10.106.

[59] *Custody, Care and Justice: The Way Ahead for the Prison Service in England and Wales* (1991) Cm. 1647.   [60] Ibid. para. 9.9.   [61] Cm. 1383, para. 3.75.

of the court proceedings.'[62] This was echoed by another official report—the Runciman Royal Commission on Criminal Justice.[63] It received a wealth of evidence from bodies as wide-ranging as the Crown Prosecution Service,[64] the Law Society,[65] and NACRO[66] who all testified to the great advantages achieved by diversion policy.

Such sentiments have also been expressed by the Prison Service. Since the introduction of the policy in 1990, several of the annual reports of the Prison Service have been wholehearted in their support of diversion, and urged its increased implementation as the only way to reduce the mentally disordered prison population and prevent their inappropriate admission into the penal system.[67] This is not surprising in view of their earlier concerns, outlined in previous chapters. The Chief Inspector of Prisons in his annual reports was also highly critical of the wholly inadequate facilities and the poor levels of care provided for the mentally ill in prison. Accordingly, the new initiatives to identify and divert the psychiatrically ill were an extremely welcome development which it was hoped would significantly ease such problems.[68] This was echoed by the Lord Chancellor's Department which also welcomed the policy and, in its wake, issued practical guidance to the courts on setting up the proposed diversion schemes.[69]

4.5.1.3. *Home Office Circular 12/95*

The Home Office further announced its commitment to diversion policy by way of a supplementary Circular issued in May 1995.[70] The Circular outlined the various central and local initiatives which have taken place, many as a result of central Government funding, and the relevant agencies were once again reminded of the options and the range of powers that exist to divert mentally disordered offenders. The importance of inter-agency working and developing shared agendas and an agreed framework has been firmly underlined as this is regarded as the key to achieving diversion and appropriate disposals.

The publication of this Circular did not amount to a momentous new statement of policy, but essentially served as a timely reminder of the need to establish diversion schemes to work together to divert mentally disordered offenders. At the time, it also represented, at least on paper, further affirmation of the 1979–97 Conservative Government's commitment to diversion policy.

---

[62] Cm. 1383. para. 3.77, 78 Recommendation 7.99 (emphasis supplied).
[63] Cm. 2263, paras. 56–63 Recommendation 75.
[64] Evidence of the CPS to the Runciman Commission, para. 2.1.5.
[65] Evidence to the Royal Commission, p. 29.
[66] NACRO MH Adv. Com., Policy Papers 2, 3 (NACRO 1993).
[67] See e.g. *Report on the Work of the Prison Service 1989–90*, Session 1989–90 Cm. 1302 paras. 47–9; *1990–1 Report*, Session 1991–2 Cm. 1724 para. 51; *1991–2, Report*, Session 1992–3 Cm. 2087 para. 49; *1992–3 Report*, Session 1992–3 Cm. 2385 para. 101.
[68] *Report of HM Chief Inspector of Prisons 1991*, Session 1992–3 HC 203 para. 4.18; *Report of HM Chief Inspector of Prisons 1992*, Session 1992–3 HC 904 para. 6.02–07.
[69] Lord Chancellor's Department Best Practice Advisory Group, *Mentally Disordered Offenders* (HO 1992).   [70] *Mentally Disordered Offenders: Inter-Agency Working* (HO 1995).

4.5.1.4. Home Office Circular 52/97

It is evident that the vast majority of the recent diversionary and inter-agency initiatives have been the product of the 1979–97 Conservative Government's term in office, and they must be strongly congratulated for their efforts. However, it is also encouraging to note that, since its election into Government in May 1997, the new Labour Government has adopted a similar stance and subsequently declared and further underlined its continued support for this policy. After all, as noted in Ch. 2, it has been widely accepted and there has always been cross-party agreement that mentally ill people should, wherever possible, be treated with humanity and compassion. Paul Boateng, the Junior Minister for Health, recently clarified the Labour Government's intentions in Parliament and pledged its continued financial support,[71] and rhetorical commitment to the policy has also been reiterated by virtue of Circular 52/1997.[72] The Circular emphasizes that the advice given in Circulars 66/90 and 12/95 remains in force and that the introduction of the hospital direction, as outlined in the previous chapter, is not intended to represent a departure from that policy. However, it is interesting to note that the policy has now been expressly qualified by the need to protect the safety of the public,[73] and the implications of this will be discussed in later chapters.

4.5.1.5. The General Reaction

In the light of its earlier concern for this category of offenders, the Mental Health Act Commission was extremely complimentary about these initiatives introduced by the Government. It warmly welcomed both the Home Office Circular 66/90 and the establishment of the Reed Committee review in its Fourth[74] and Fifth[75] Biennial Reports. Subsequent reports have also further applauded the developments and the Commission has welcomed the range of Home Office initiatives.[76]

Other interested bodies, such as MIND and NACRO[77] have praised the introduction of this policy, which again, is not surprising in view of their previous campaigns and comments. And the Home Office Research and Planning Unit has conducted extensive research into this area:

---

[71] Session 1997–8 HL Debs Vol. 586 col. 412; HO, *Annual Report 1998: The Government's Expenditure Plans 1998–99*, Session 1997–8 Cm. 3908 para. 4.24.

[72] Para. 2.   [73] Ibid.

[74] 1989–91 (HMSO 1991) para. 9.2: 'The Commission welcomes the support given to efforts at diversion in the Home Office Circular (66/90), which draws attention to Sections 135, 38, 35, 36 of the 1983 Act and to the availability of probation orders with treatment requirements.'

[75] 1991–3 (HMSO 1993) para. 10.1, 2: 'The Commission has welcomed the majority of the . . . recommendations made in the [Reed] report . . . [it] makes 276 recommendations, a reflection perhaps of the serious inadequacies in the current service which have been identified repeatedly in previous Biennial reports.'   [76] MHAC, *Reports 1993–5, 1995–7*.

[77] MH Adv. Com., Policy Papers 2, 3; Penal Affairs Consortium, *An Unsuitable Place for Treatment: Diverting Mentally Disordered Offenders from Custody* (NACRO 1998).

There has been long-standing concern that the criminal justice system deals inappropriately with the mentally disordered when they break the law. This inspired the recent 'Reed Committee' review of services for mentally disordered offenders. It also caused the Home Office Research and Planning Unit to set up a programme of research projects to investigate the numbers of mentally disordered who are brought into the criminal justice system and the scope for diverting them at different stages of the process.[78]

Indeed, this published study has shown that diversion schemes have a valuable role to play and are welcomed by all involved.[79]

Finally, from an academic perspective, diversion policy and the varying schemes have been embraced by numerous disciplines, both medical[80] and legal: 'There can be little doubt that it is right to seek to divert mentally disordered offenders from the penal system.'[81]

4.5.2. Increasing Awareness and Implementing Diversion

Local interest across the country has undoubtedly been raised. Numerous conferences and seminars have been arranged both at regional and national levels, and not only on a Governmental level; voluntary organisations such as NACRO, the National Schizophrenia Fellowship, and the Mental Health Foundation have also played an active role in developing promotional seminars throughout the country. For example, an international two-day conference was held in London in 1992 which drew attention to the scope for diversion and implementing inter-agency initiatives.[82] The Law Society and Institute of Psychiatry have also demonstrated their willingness to try to work together by organizing a multi-agency conference to increase awareness in this area.[83] Finally, the Mental Health Foundation was commissioned by the Home Office and the Department of Health to organize a

---

[78] Hedderman, *Panel Assessment*, 1.   [79] Ibid. 47.

[80] J. Gunn *et al.*, *Psychiatric Aspects of Imprisonment* (Academic Press 1978), 258; see also Cooke, 'Treatment as Alternative'; R. Rogers and M. R. Bagby, 'Diversion of Mentally Disordered Offenders: A Legitimate Role for Clinicians?' (1992) 10 *Behavioural Sciences and the Law* 407–18.

[81] P. Fennell, 'Diversion of Mentally Disordered Offenders from Custody' [1991] *Crim LR* 333–48, 346; see also Osler, 'Mentally Disordered Offenders', 161–2; J. M. Laing, 'The Mentally Disordered Suspect at the Police Station' [1995] *Crim LR* 371–81; E. Burney and G. Pearson, 'Mentally Disordered Offenders: Finding a Focus for Diversion' (1995) 34(4) *How J of Crim Just* 291–313.

[82] Implementing Inter-Agency Initiatives for Mentally Disordered Offenders, held at the Mannheim Centre for Criminology and Criminal Justice at the LSE, London, 28–30 September 1992. See further D. Tonak, 'Mentally Disordered Offenders' (1993) 157 *JP* 332–3; see also Mental Disorder and the Courts: The Interface, conference held at Gray's Inn on October 14 1993: Editorial, 'Mental Disorder and the Courts: Report of a Joint BAFS/CBA/LCCSA 1993 Seminar' (1994) 34 *Med, Sci & Law* 250–1; R. D. Atkins, 'Diversion of Mentally Ill Defendants in the Magistrates' Courts' (1994) 47 *Crim Law* 1–3 for an account of a joint Criminal Bar Association, London Solicitors Association, and Academy of Forensic Sciences seminar.

[83] The Mental Health Act 1983: Time for Change? A joint conference of the Law Society, Institute of Psychiatry, and Mental Health Act Commission, London, 11–12 November 1993.

series of regional conferences in the wake of the Reed Committee Report.[84] The Home Office Research and Planning Unit conducted an assessment of the conferences by way of postal and telephone surveys which revealed that they were perceived to have 'facilitated joint working, by improving inter-agency contact [and] . . . contributed to the development of arrangements for dealing with mentally disordered offenders by raising the profile of mentally disordered offenders and drawing attention to the importance of providing appropriate services for them'.[85]

Thus, Government, criminal justice, voluntary and health agencies, and professionals have all made a conscious effort to try to implement the new initiatives, to raise awareness, and to stimulate joint working in achieving diversion. And so, it would seem, in the light of the high level of concern expressed throughout the 1980s, that the aim to divert mentally disordered offenders has been universally accepted.

4.5.3. National Diversion Schemes

Awareness has been raised to such an extent that almost 200 diversion schemes of various forms have now been established across England and Wales.[86] By February 1997, the 1979–97 Conservative Government had provided £1 million to fund the establishment of such initiatives.[87] A survey of diversion schemes conducted in 1992 indicated that over forty solely duty-psychiatrist schemes (similar to that operating at Bow Street and Marlborough Street Courts) are in operation nationally.[88] The Reed Committee also conducted a survey and found that half of all district health authorities were currently planning to make provision for diverting mentally disordered offenders.[89] Moreover, Carol Hedderman's research into panel assessment schemes also involved conducting a telephone survey of all probation areas in England and Wales in order to obtain an overview of such provision for mentally disordered offenders. The results of this particular exercise were encouraging. Most areas had specific arrangements or policies in place to deal with such offenders. Eight areas were already operating such a panel scheme, and a further forty-seven probation areas were in the process of establishing some form of diversion scheme for future implementation.[90] So it would appear that diversion arrangements are now fairly widespread and that various agencies are taking responsibility to establish them.

[84] C. Newman (ed.), *Promoting Care and Justice: Report of the Mental Health Foundation Regional Conferences on Improving Services for Mentally Disordered Offenders* (Mental Health Foundation 1994); see also C. Truman and S. Keyes, *Commissioning Services for Offenders with Mental Health Problems: Measuring the Performance of Court-Based Psychiatrist Schemes* (Mental Health Foundation 1997). [85] Ibid. app. 2 p. 54.
[86] Session 1996–7 HL Debs Vol. 578 col. 1368. [87] Ibid.
[88] S. Blummenthal and S. Wessely, 'National Survey of Current Arrangements for Diversion from Custody in England and Wales' (1992) 305 *BMJ* 1322–5.
[89] Cm. 2088, para. 5.5, figs. 2, 3. [90] Hedderman, *Panel Assessment*, ch. 4.

It has already been noted that diversion can take place at various stages and levels in the criminal justice process, and diversion schemes can operate at each of these stages.[91] Consideration will now be given to the differing schemes which are in operation at each stage, across the country.

4.5.3.1. At the Police Station: The Police Station Assessment Model (PSA)[92]

At Bournville Lane Police Station in South Birmingham, a diversion scheme was set up involving the attachment of a forensic community psychiatric nurse (CPN) to the police station to ensure that, where appropriate, mentally disturbed offenders are diverted out of the criminal justice system at this earliest possible stage.[93] The impetus for the scheme came from NACRO and the initial funding from the Mental Health Foundation. A multi-agency Steering Committee was formed to discuss the possibilities and to develop a model for diversion. The aims of the project were to provide better and more comprehensive assessments at police stations, to provide a more consistent service, better liaison and networking amongst the different agencies, and to provide follow-up care and support. The scheme was launched in November 1992, and an experienced CPN provides a 24-hour, 7-day week service to the police station to make mental health assessments and any consequent care and treatment arrangements. The CPN is present at the police station for part of the day, and on call for the remainder. Much time was spent during the initial stages on building good working practices between the police and the CPN—getting to know each other, gaining a better understanding of police procedures, and devising complimentary working practices: 'The early induction process proved to be a crucial element in ensuring a successful partnership between the FCPNs and the police, and helped to establish complementary working practices.'[94]

The scheme has been successful in terms of making assessments and diverting offenders into appropriate care. During the period November 1992 to April 1993, a total of 336 people were screened, which represents 19.16 per cent of all cases passing through the custody suite at the police station. Twenty-five people were identified as having a mental health problem, which was 7.44 per cent of the total screened. In fourteen of these cases medical care was arranged and the police took no further action. The majority of those referred and assessed subsequently received some form of medical care or supervision. Thus it can be concluded that 'the model is one which could be established almost anywhere and that it will prove to be an important and cost-effective contributor to the various efforts to divert the mentally disturbed offender from the criminal justice system'.[95]

---

[91]   MHAC, *Report 1991–3*, para. 10.5: 'There is an advantage in a diversity of schemes'.

[92]   See Appendix B for a diagrammatic outline of the basic operation of this type of scheme.

[93]   S. Wix, 'Keeping on the Straight and Narrow: Diversion of Mentally Disordered Offenders at the Point of Arrest' (1994) 1 *Psychiatric Care* 102–4; see also M. Cheung Chang, 'A Description of a Forensic Service in One City in the UK' (1998) 38(3) *Med, Sci & Law* 242–50.

[94]   Ibid. 103.

[95]   West Midlands Police, *Diversion at the Point of Arrest Interim Report* (July 1993), 18.

The scheme has been adopted by the mental health unit of South Birmingham Health Authority and is seen as so successful that it has now been extended to other police stations in the area, thereby providing a comprehensive assessment and diversion service in South Birmingham police stations. This model is particularly attractive given the early point of intervention, which saves time and money and reduces the amount of time spent by an offender in police custody. It is also extremely valuable given the doubts expressed in Ch. 3 about the ability of police surgeons (FMES) accurately to identify and assess mental disorder among police detainees: 'Police surgeons believe the project to be highly successful and estimate it has reduced the number of mental health referrals by as much as 95 per cent.'[96]

Three of London's busiest police stations have also taken the initiative and set up a similar scheme whereby a CPN is available to make assessments and divert mentally ill suspects at the earliest possible stage to psychiatric teams and hospitals.[97]

4.5.3.2. At the Court

A natural variation upon the PSA Model is to provide psychiatric assessment and diversion at the magistrates' court, for those defendants in need of psychiatric assistance who have been kept overnight in custody to appear before the magistrates the following morning. Those mentally ill defendants who may not have been identified as such earlier in the process can be provided with direct access to much-needed help at this stage. Several such court-based assessment and liaison schemes are now in operation in different parts of the country. There are three principal models which will be outlined below. However, given the differing requirements and resources in different parts of the country, each model adopted is normally tailored to suit the local needs.

4.5.3.2.1. Community Psychiatric Nurse Assessment Schemes: The Nurse Assessment Court Model (NAC)[98]

After several months of discussion and liaison between a number of agencies, a CPN-led Court Diversion Scheme at Sheffield Magistrates' Court was brought into operation in March 1993.[99] The stated aims of the scheme are two fold. First, the scheme aims to identify mental illness at the earliest possible stage, to offer advice to the other agencies, and to arrange referrals for assessment, treatment, and admission. Secondly, the broader aims of the scheme are to build lasting links

---

[96] Wix, 'Straight and Narrow', 104.

[97] 'Psychiatric Nurse helps police to distinguish the mentally ill', *The Times*, 17 January 1995, p. 5; see also M. MacFadyean, 'LAW: Locking away our problems—a fledgling scheme is struggling against the odds to keep the mentally ill out of jail', *Guardian*, 30 November 1993, p. 18.

[98] See Appendix C for a diagrammatic outline of the basic operation of this type of scheme.

[99] L. Marshall, *Review of the Development of the Court Diversion Scheme* (Community Health Sheffield 1993).

between the health and social services and the criminal justice system, thereby promoting inter-agency collaboration, and to increase awareness by providing education and support for other professionals and services who find themselves dealing with those suffering from mental health problems. Clear recognition of the need to work together has therefore been given by the agencies involved.

The CPN attends the custody area below the court every weekday morning, reading through the prosecution files to see if any detainees require screening. Should this be the case, then an assessment is carried out, usually in the interview room in the custody area. Any resulting action is dependent upon the outcome of the assessment. Should there be severe doubts as to the mental state of a particular individual, an attempt is made to have a medical assessment carried out by a psychiatrist. Once this has been received, then a decision regarding discontinuance and diversion can be made, involving collaboration between all the other agencies involved. If a serious mental disorder within the meaning of the Mental Health Act 1983 is diagnosed, then formal hospital admission may be required. Once that decision has been made, the CPN has the responsibility of making any necessary arrangements. Should there be evidence of a lesser mental disorder, not necessarily within the meaning of the Act, but perhaps involvement with drugs, alcohol, or mild depression which is not directly relevant to the proceedings, the CPN will offer advice and a local community referral is often made. Should there be no evidence of mental ill health following assessment, then no further action is taken by the CPN and the appropriate persons are informed. The CPN therefore has many responsibilities and is central to the operation of the scheme, acting as a link between all the other agencies: 'the Community Psychiatric Nurse is striving to encourage communication and co-operation from all services involved, encouraging agencies to work together and to gain support from one another'.[100]

During its first six months of operation, the total number of people assessed who appeared to have a significant degree of mental health problems was fifty-one, and positive recommendations and referrals were made in 80 per cent of these cases, with some (10 per cent) being referred to secure facilities, 12 per cent being admitted to local psychiatric facilities and 52 per cent being referred to out-patient/community mental health services.

The scheme has clearly shown that there are a significant number of people within the Criminal Justice system who are suffering from mental health problems and are in need of some level of care, support and treatment. . . . It has also demonstrated that a CPN can play a pivotal role in the diversion and future care of the mentally disordered offender, as well as acting as a resource for other services providing education and support.[101]

In North Humberside, in response to the Circular 66/90 policy statement and the problems experienced by the police, courts, and Hull Prison, MIND acted as a link to bring together a wide range of agencies to form a working party to

---

[100]   Marshall, *Review of the Court Diversion Scheme*. 5.   [101]   Ibid. 12.

develop a diversion scheme in the area.[102] The aims of the project were 'to prevent mentally disordered offenders from being prosecuted, remanded, and sentenced to custody; and from reoffending'.[103]

A diversion scheme based at Hull Magistrates'Court was devised, based on the NAC Model, whereby CPNs take the lead role in making assessments and care arrangements. This scheme is a variation on the Sheffield NAC Model, as the CPN is also assisted by an Approved Social Worker and a Probation Officer, thereby providing a truly multi-agency response and access to a wide range of manpower, resources, and facilities. The team visit the three main Hull police stations and then the magistrates' court every weekday morning to make assessments and recommendations to the court. An independent evaluation of the scheme was commissioned by the Centre for Systems Studies at Hull University.[104] Again, the scheme was evaluated in terms of its diversionary effect, as opposed to its effect upon reoffending, and the study found that 85 per cent of interventions by the diversion team resulted in diversions to appropriate health-care settings. Furthermore, 'it is reasonably safe to conclude that many of these diversions would not have happened without the Team's interventions: the Team acted in an assessing and co-ordinating capacity, bringing services on line to make non-custodial outcomes possible for mentally disordered offenders'.[105] The results have therefore been extremely encouraging and in the words of some of the professionals involved with the scheme, 'The plight of mentally ill people in our prisons has become one of the major scandals of our time, but in North Humberside and where other diversion schemes operate, magistrates need not feel that there is "nothing else we can do".'[106]

Finally, Birmingham has developed another scheme under the auspices of the local regional secure unit—the Raeside Clinic. This particular scheme operates at the court as an NAC Model whereby a Forensic Community Psychiatric Nurse (FCPN) attends the court every weekday morning to accept referrals and to make assessments and recommendations to the court.[107] During its first two years of operation (1991–3) it succeeded in assessing a total of 998 defendants which resulted in 504 psychiatric recommendations being made to the court, the majority of which were accepted and resulted in 262 out-patient treatment/assessment referrals being made. Again, in terms of diversion rates, the initial evaluation of the scheme was positive: 'The aims of the service are to pro-actively divert

---

[102] C. Staite and N. Martin, 'What Else Can We Do? New Initiatives in Diversion from Custody' (1993) 157 *JP* 280–1; C. Staite, N. Martin, M. Bingham and R. Daly, *Diversion from Custody for Mentally Disordered Offenders* (Longmans 1994) ch. 2.

[103] Staite and Martin, 'New Initiatives', 280.

[104] C. Cohen and G. Midgley, *The North Humberside Diversion from Custody Project for Mentally Disordered Offenders* (MIND 1994).   [105] Ibid. 5.

[106] Ibid. 281.

[107] See N. M. J. Kennedy, 'Training Aspects of the Birmingham Court Diversion Scheme' (1992) 16 *Psychiatric Bulletin* 630–1; G. Hillis, 'Diverting Tactics' (1993) 89 *Nursing Times* 24–7; Cheung Chang, 'A Description'.

mentally disordered offenders from the courts into health care settings thus avoiding damaging lengthy periods of remand in custody. The first six month evaluation showed remarkable success and has continued to develop and grow for the
past two and a half years'.[108]

4.5.3.2.2. Duty-Psychiatrist Assessment Schemes: The Psychiatrist Assessment Court Model (PAC)[109]

This model is a variation on the NAC Model, adopting a similar structure at court,
but utilizing the direct assessment services of a qualified psychiatrist as opposed
to a psychiatric nurse.

In Manchester a diversion scheme of this type has been set up at its busy inner-
city magistrates' court.[110] This scheme involves duty psychiatrists making evaluations at the Central Detention Centre, accepting referrals from a wide range of
agencies. Following assessment, psychiatric reports are given to the magistrates
to help them make their decision. Initially, the scheme was successful in identifying many defendants who were suffering from some form of psychiatric illness.
In a follow-up study, it was found that of the twenty-two patients for whom
psychiatric or social care was arranged, most were still being seen by district
psychiatric services or other agencies involved 18 months later. Thus

Our study suggests that a significant number of people who appear before the court require
psychiatric intervention. A court-based psychiatric service . . . will provide earlier psychiatric care to some mentally abnormal offenders, may uncover patients otherwise lost to the
Health Service and sometimes simply delay remand for a group of difficult, disorganised
and mentally disordered individuals. Such a service will lead to financial savings for the
penal system as well as better speedier service for the patients.[111]

And the follow-up study indicates that 'mentally ill patients diverted from the
criminal justice system into the health service *are maintained there*.[112]

Several PAC Model diversion schemes are now fully operational in London.
At inner-city Clerkenwell Magistrates' Court, for example, a duty-psychiatrist
scheme, similar to that in Manchester, has been operational since 1990.[113] This
scheme was also monitored and the results show that the scheme greatly
reduced the length of time (by 80 per cent) spent in custody by those remanded

---

[108]   G. Hillis, *Birmingham Diversion Services*, Report to the Forensic Services Management Team
(1993), 3.
[109]   See Appendix C for a diagrammatic outline of the basic operation of this type of scheme.
[110]   J. Holloway and J. Shaw, 'Providing a Forensic Psychiatry Service to a Magistrates' Court
(1992) 3 *J For Psych* 153–9; id., 'A Follow-up Study' (1993) 4 *J For Psych* 575–81.
[111]   Ibid. (1992), 159.   [112]   Ibid. (1993), 579 (emphasis supplied).
[113]   D. V. James and L. W. Hamilton, The Clerkenwell Scheme: Assessing Efficacy and Cost of a
Psychiatric Liaison Service to a Magistrates' Court (1991) 303 *BMJ* 282–5; id., 'Setting Up
Psychiatric Liaison Schemes to Magistrates' Courts: Problems and Practicalities' (1992) 32 *Med, Sci
& Law* 167–76; D. V. James, *et al.*, 'A Court-Focused Model of Forensic Psychiatry: Abolishing
Remands to Prison?' (1997) 8 *J For Psych* 390–405. See also N. D. Purchase, *et al.*, 'Evaluation of a
Psychiatric Court Liaison Scheme in North London' (1996) 313 *BMJ* 531–2.

for psychiatric reports.[114] Further, almost half of those assessed by the duty psychiatrist were given some form of hospital/therapeutic disposal.[115]

Another PAC scheme has been established in East London[116] at the four magistrates' courts within the catchment area of the forensic mental health service based at Bracton Clinic: 'The principal aim was to decrease the frequency and length of custodial remands for psychiatric reports by diverting, where appropriate, mentally disordered offenders from custody. . . . Evaluation of the scheme shows that a psychiatric assessment service can be satisfactorily provided to a number of courts within a defined catchment area.'[117] The evaluation of the scheme also revealed that 64 per cent of those assessed were diverted—given bail, received a non-custodial disposal, or admitted to hospital. And many more defendants received psychiatric treatment and supervision on a voluntary basis in the community which was often combined with a conditional discharge from the court.

4.5.3.2.3. Multi-Agency Assessment Panel Schemes: The Multi-Agency Assessment Panel Model (MAAP)[118]

As its name implies, this final MAAP Model, of which the Hertfordshire project was the pioneer, is yet another variation upon the NAC and PAC models. This approach however is a completely multi-agency response as the scheme involves an inter-disciplinary panel available at court to provide assessments and make recommendations to the court.

MAAP diversion schemes have been established in Dorset and Luton.[119] The MenDos Scheme was set up in February 1992 to ensure that co-ordinated care is an alternative to custodial sentences for mentally disordered offenders in West Dorset. It involves a full-time CPN convening a panel to which mentally disordered offenders are referred. The panel will always consist of the CPN, a probation officer, and a consultant psychiatrist, but may also include a psychologist, a senior police officer, a social worker, and GPs or relatives and carers. The panel is normally convened at the request of the court. However, should the police, CPS, probation or social work staff require assistance, then they may also refer mentally disordered offenders to the panel. The advantages of the scheme are manifold. Primarily it enables alternatives to remands or prison sentences to be made at the earliest possible stage and those involved claim that it ensures that 'each individual offender has his/her own personal care plan worked out with all the agencies concerned'. Thus, it is claimed that the agencies concerned share

---

[114] James and Hamilton, 'Clerkenwell Scheme', 284.

[115] id., 'Problems and Practicalities', 168.

[116] T. Exworthy and J. Parrott, 'Evaluation of a Diversion from Custody Scheme at Magistrates' Courts (1993) 4 *J For Psych* 497–505; id., 'Comparative Evaluation of a Diversion from Custody Scheme' (1997) 8 *J For Psych* 406–16. [117] Ibid. (1993), 497.

[118] See Appendix D for a diagrammatic outline of the basic operation of this type of scheme.

[119] See further D. Tonak, 'Mentally disordered offenders'.

responsibility for this category of offender, thereby fully mobilizing the existing resources.

A similar MAAP scheme has been operating in Luton, in which a Probation Officer, acting as a link, forwards requests for psychiatric assessment from the courts to a consultant psychiatrist, psychologist, and CPN. They, along with the Probation Officer, will prepare individual assessments prior to the next panel meeting when the case will be jointly discussed. On that basis, a report will be prepared and submitted to the court containing a co-ordinated management plan. The panel ordinarily meets during the fourth week of every month. However, it can be convened at other times if necessary. The primary objective of the scheme is 'to divert as many mentally disordered offenders as possible from custody by offering appropriate and well worked out treatment plans'. Secondary aims are to improve the quality of assessment by sharing information gained from individual work; to maintain and promote the notion of shared responsibility by all the agencies concerned for these offenders; and to prevent recidivism and relapse by extending this responsibility beyond the point of assessment to subsequent management or appropriate treatment of individuals in this client group.

Finally, a MAAP diversion scheme—DIVERT—has also been operating at the magistrates' courts in Reading. The Hertfordshire diversion team presented a seminar about panel assessments to an inter-disciplinary audience at Reading in September 1989, the result being the formation of a Steering Group which established the DIVERT Scheme. The scheme involves a Probation Officer acting as a co-ordinator between the court and the other professionals. A team comprising the co-ordinator, a CPN, a forensic psychiatrist, and an Approved Social Worker attend court to offer guidance on dealing with mentally disordered defendants. An independent evaluation of the scheme was conducted between March 1992 and February 1993. It found that ninety-two referrals were made to the team during that period, the majority of whom were 'those who have committed relatively minor offences . . . rather than violent offenders who may prove a serious risk to the public if they are not contained in a secure setting'.[120] Of those referred to the scheme over 90 per cent received some form of psychiatric diagnosis and the majority received some form of psychiatric disposal or referral.[121] The scheme therefore operates on a similar basis to the Hertfordshire model, and both have been evaluated by the Home Office.[122] The results of the study showed that 'panel assessment arrangements are making a significant contribution to ensuring that mentally disordered offenders are being dealt with appropriately'.[123]

The study found that a high number of cases were referred to the panels and the majority of panel recommendations were acted upon by the courts (only 15 per cent were rejected). Thus it was obvious that the courts welcomed and made

---

[120] T. Wickham, *A Psychiatric Liaison Service for the Criminal Courts* (Norwich Social Work Monographs 1994), 33.   [121] Ibid. 36–8, 41.   [122] Hedderman, *Panel Assessment.*
[123] Ibid. 47.

good use of the scheme. A clear indicator of this was the fact that the number of cases remanded for psychiatric reports increased at the court in Reading immediately after panel assessment schemes were introduced. This was 'the clearest sign that the courts there welcomed and made use of formal arrangements for assessing mentally disordered offenders'.[124] The views of many of the practitioners who were involved with or affected by the schemes were sought. All those interviewed welcomed the introduction of such arrangements and expressed their willingness to become involved in their implementation.[125]

4.5.3.3. Prison Assessment and Transfer: The Prison Psychiatric Assessment Model (PPA)

The final stage whereby diversion and transfer may be achieved is at the prison, where remand or sentenced prisoners can be assessed and transferred by psychiatric personnel. This type of prison-based model is now being developed at several prisons across the country to catch those mentally disordered offenders who, because of the current strains on psychiatric services, may have slipped through the nets provided at earlier stages in the process or who may develop mental illness once in prison.

A PPA scheme has been set up at Brixton prison to provide a filter for diversion at this latest stage for those who might otherwise still end up in prison despite an earlier intention to divert.[126] The diversion team consists of two psychiatrists and a psychologist, who make assessments on the basis of referrals from prison officers of those thought to be at risk. The team will also routinely assess those remanded into custody for a medical report and also those who require psychiatric assessment by nature of the charge against them. If such prisoners require transfer under the Mental Health Act following assessment, this will be organized by the team, and is facilitated by the links which have been established with the agencies and services outside the prison in the community. The scheme is particularly important in terms of ensuring appropriate aftercare once the prisoner has been released.[127]

The value of such procedure has been further recognized at Belmarsh, Winchester, and Wormwood Scrubs prisons, where similar PPA services are now routinely provided to identify those remand or sentenced prisoners who may find their way into prison due to the lack of sufficiently secure health facilities or who may develop mental illness whilst in prison.[128] Belmarsh and Wormwood Scrubs

---

[124] Ibid. 30. [125] Ibid. ch. 3.

[126] Ibid. 51; R. Savournin et al., 'The Brixton Diversion Project: Evaluating a New Service for Mentally Disordered Offenders' (1993) 91 *Prison Service Journal* 20–4.

[127] Ibid. 24.

[128] Papers presented at the High Sheriff of Merseyside Conference, Diversion from Custody—A Practical Approach, held at Liverpool University, 31 March 1995; see also T. Weaver et al., 'Impact of a Dedicated Service for Mentally Disordered Remand Prisoners in North West London: Retrospective Study' (1997) 314 *BMJ* 1244–5; T. Hardie et al. 'Unmet Needs of Remand Prisoners' (1988) 38(1) *Med, Sci & Law* 233–6.

provide a psychiatric assessment service on a weekly basis to provide assessments and arrange transfers where necessary. The scheme at Winchester, however, consists of a multi-agency team including a Probation Officer, social worker, and CPN, and is not only concerned with arranging appropriate assessments and transfers, but also committed to ensuring that those identified as having a mental disorder are given access to the appropriate community resources upon release.[129] This aspect is particularly significant and clearly ensures that those who are mentally ill but have been unable to be transferred are provided with adequate care once they are returned into the community, thereby preventing their relapse, ensuring continuity of care and going some way towards slowing down the 'revolving door'.

4.6. A COLLABORATIVE STRATEGIC APPROACH

All such diversion schemes are firmly characterized by inter-agency co-operation. As Circular 66/90 acknowledged, 'The Government recognizes that this policy can be effective only if the courts and criminal justice agencies have access to Health and Social Services. This requires consultation and co-operation.'[130]

Circulars 12/95 and 52/97 further emphasized the importance of inter-agency arrangements.[131] Multi-agency working is a key component in ensuring appropriate disposals for mentally disordered offenders, and this is, at last, being increasingly recognized. The Crown Prosecution Service has expressly recognized the importance of establishing links and building relationships with other agencies.[132] Local authorities have been expressly advised upon 'the need for close co-operation between local social services and probation services' in providing community care assessments and support for mentally disordered offenders.[133] This is mirrored in the guidance provided to health and local authorities for the supervision and care of discharged mentally ill patients in the community.[134] Moreover, the Reed Committee's underlying philosophy concerned the need to work together to provide a comprehensive and continuing service for the mentally disordered offender. And the recent White Paper on the future of the NHS firmly endorsed the philosophy and principles of inter-agency co-operation.[135] This has been further underlined in the Green Paper on the future

[129] See further R. Lart, 'The Wessex Project: Meeting the Needs of Mentally Disordered Prisoners' (1998) 115 *Prison Serv J* 20–1, M. Barker and B. Swyer, 'Communication and Collaboration in Community Care for Mentally Disordered Offenders' (1994) 41 *Probat J* 130–4; R. Lart, *Crossing Boundaries: Accessing Community Mental Health Services for Prisoners on Release* (Policy Press University of Bristol 1997).   [130] Para. 2.

[131] Circular 12/95, paras. 10, 11; Circular 52/97 para. 2.

[132] *CPS Annual Report 1988–9* (HMSO 1989) para. 2.1.

[133] HO Circular 29/93, Local Authority Social Services Letter (LASSL) (93) 11 '*Community Care Reforms and the Criminal Justice System*'.

[134] *The Health of the Nation, Building Bridges* (DoH 1995).

[135] Session 1997–8 HL Debs Vol. 584 cols 119–20; HL Debs Vol. 585 col. 1252.

of mental health services which was published in December 1998 and will be discussed in more detail later in this chapter. The Labour Government has highlighted that co-operation and the exchange of information between health and local authorities is a fundamental requirement.[136] Partnership is clearly regarded as a key element for future development.[137]

A plethora of multi-disciplinary conferences have been organized, some of which have been outlined above, which all serve to highlight the need to promote good inter-disciplinary working practices. Furthermore, the diversion scheme accounts above illustrate that the agencies are concerned with establishing sound links, sharing information and the securing of resourcing, and joint planning and training. Thus, most of the professionals involved are committed to sharing responsibility for this category of offender which is in line with the Reed Committee recommendations—'Effective multi-agency working is indispensable for services with so many diverse components.'[138] The need for agencies to work together is imperative and diversion schemes seek to ensure that this takes place.

4.7. THE IMPACT OF DIVERSION POLICY

It is difficult to ascertain and evaluate the overall national impact of diversion policy. Undoubtedly it has served to raise awareness, and the host of diversion schemes now in operation bear testimony to this. One of the main aims of the policy, however, has been to increase the number of therapeutic remands, disposals, and transfers, and so it is pertinent to consider whether an impact has been felt in this respect. The national statistics do indeed reveal that this has materialized in many cases. There has been a gradual increase in the number of remands to hospital for report, and the number of interim hospital and ordinary hospital orders since the introduction of diversion policy. Official figures reveal that, since the late 1980s and through to the mid-1990s, there has been a 17 per cent increase in s. 35 remands and a 35 per cent increase in the number of interim hospital orders. The number of ordinary hospital orders has also increased and remained high. We have also witnessed a steady increase in the number of occasions when a mentally disordered person has been taken to a place of safety under s. 136.[139] The most dramatic increase has been felt in the number of prison transfers under s. 47 and 48 of the Mental Health Act 1983. As Table 4.1 illustrates, since 1989 there has been a fivefold increase in the number of s. 48 transfers and the use of

---

[136] DoH, *Safe, Sound and Supportive*, paras. 1.10–6, 4.56–62; see also DoH, *Partnership in Action: New Opportunities for Joint Working between Health and Social Services* (DoH, 1998).

[137] See further DoH, *Departmental Report: Government's Expenditure Plans 1998–1999*, Session 1997–8 Cm. 3912 paras. 4.45, 5.21; DoH, *Partnership in Action*.

[138] Cm. 2088 para. 4.8.

[139] *In-Patients Formally Detained in Hospitals under the Mental Health Act 1983 and Other Legislation, England: 1991–92 to 1996–97*, DoH Statistical Bulletin 1998/01 para. 4.10.

s. 47 has almost trebled during that period.[140] This is extremely encouraging as it exemplifies that efforts are clearly being made to remove those in need of hospital care from the prison system and that some of the problems which were present throughout the 1980s are being addressed. Indeed, Mackay and Machin have conducted research into the use of s. 48 on behalf of the Home Office and noted how the use of the section has changed over the past decade. The number of transfers has increased greatly and this can be attributed, in part, to greater awareness and better identification of the needs of mentally disordered offenders as a result of official guidance and policy.[141]

Even though the use of other diversionary powers, such as s. 36, has not increased, it has remained fairly constant during that period.[142] The use of probation orders with conditions of mental treatment in particular has remained at an average annual figure of 900,[143] but it is difficult to make a comparison with the figures prior to 1992, as new requirements were added to probation orders by the Criminal Justice Act 1991. In particular, treatment for drug/alcohol abuse was included, so the figures may cover some mentally ill offenders who also have such problems.[144]

It would seem that, on the whole, the available evidence indicates that diversion policy has had a positive effect in terms of promoting the use of therapeutic

TABLE 4.1. *Therapeutic disposals 1988–1995*

MHA Power	1988	1989	1990	1991	1993	1995
s. 35	234	297	299	364	320	350
s. 37	762	952	957	970	943	937
s. 38	54	62	86	85	93	116
s. 47	94	120	145	182	284	250
s. 48	82	98	180	264	483	473

Statistics taken from DoH *In-patients Formally Detained in Hospitals under the Mental Health Act 1983 and Other Legislation, England: 1987–88 to 1992–93*, Statistical Bulletin, 1995/4 (DoH 1995), Table 1; DoH, *In-patients Formally Detained in Hospitals under the Mental Health Act 1983 and Other Legislation, England: 1989–90 to 1994–95*, Statistical Bulletin 1996/10 (DoH 1996), Table 1; DoH *In-patients Formally Detained in Hospitals under the Mental Health Act 1983 and Other Legislation, England: 1991–92 to 1996–97*, Statistical Bulletin, 1998/01 (DoH 1998), Table 1; and HO, *Statistics of Mentally Disordered Offenders in England and Wales 1996*, Statistical Bulletin, 20/97 (HO 1997), Table 3.

[140] *Statistics of Mentally Disordered Offenders in England and Wales 1996*, HO Statistical Bulletin 20/97, para. 5; *Statistics of Mentally Disordered Offenders in England and Wales 1997*, Home Office Statistical Bulletin 19/98, para. 8, Table 3.

[141] R. D. Mackay and D. Machin, Transfers from Prison to Hospital: The Operation of Section 48 of the Mental Health Act 1983 (Home Office 1998).

[142] HO Statistical Bulletin 1995/4, Table 1.

[143] *Probation Statistics England and Wales 1993* (HO 1994) Table 2.8.

[144] See M. Wasik and R. Taylor, *Blackstone's Guide to the Criminal Justice Act 1991*, 2nd edn. (Blackstone 1994) ch. 1.

powers. Furthermore, HM Inspectorate of Probation conducted a thematic review of psychiatric probation orders in 1993, and commended the role which diversion schemes play in promoting psychiatric probation orders. The Inspectorate observed that

the two areas showing the best work with requirements for treatment were those where inter-agency court diversion schemes had been well developed. Such schemes, operated with the knowledge and co-operation of the magistrates, provide an excellent basis for later co-operation if a probation order with a requirement is made. Perhaps, even more importantly, they ensure that courts are properly advised and credible proposals made if the offender continues to the point of sentence.[145]

So the value of diversion schemes in facilitating the use of psychiatric probation orders has been firmly acknowledged, and similar observations have been made with regard to hospital orders.[146]

Moreover, particular research studies have indicated that court-based assessment schemes are highly effective in identifying mental illness in prisoners and their introduction has led to a reduction in the number of remands to custody and facilitated therapeutic transfers and disposals.[147] And research conducted by the Revolving Doors agency has highlighted how effective police station assessment schemes can be in identifying mental illness and facilitating therapeutic responses.[148] This has also been observed by the Mental Health Act Commission in its most recent biennial report.[149]

There is also some additional positive evidence of the impact of diversion when considering the post-release reconviction rates for restricted patients. Official statistics reveal that between 1987 and 1993, the two-year reconviction rates for restricted patients who had been conditionally discharged were lower than for earlier years.[150] It has been suggested that this could be due to a number of factors, such as 'more effective supervision', however, the increased diversion of mentally disordered offenders has also been regarded as a contributing factor,[151] which is further positive evidence of the value of diversion.

---

[145] *Probation Orders with Requirements for Psychiatric Treatment: Report of a Thematic Inspection* (HO 1993) para. 7.21.

[146] G. Robertson *et al.,* 'A Follow-up of Remanded Mentally Ill Offenders Given Court Hospital Orders' (1994) 34 *Med, Sci & Law* 61–6.

[147] See Burney and Pearson, 'Finding a Focus'; P. L. Joseph and M. Potter, 'Diversion from Custody, 1. Psychiatric Assessment at the Magistrates' Court'; '2. Effect on Hospital and Prison Resources' (1993) 162 *Brit J Psych* 325–4; P. Pierzchniak *et al.,* 'Liaison between Prison, Court and Psychiatric Services' (1997) 29 *Health Trends* 26–9; L. Birmingham *et al.,* 'Prevalence of Mental Disorder in Remand Prisoners' (1996) 313 *BMJ* 1521–4.

[148] Revolving Doors, *The Management of People with Mental Health Problems by the Paddington Police* (Revolving Doors 1994); see also D. Etherington, 'The Police Liaison Community Psychiatric Nurse Report' (1996) 1(2) *Mental Health Review* 21–4.

[149] MHAC, *Report 1995–7* (HMSO 1997) para. 10.8.2.

[150] *Restricted Patients—Reconvictions and Recalls by the end of 1995: England and Wales,* HO Statistical Bulletin 1/97, Table 2.

[151] Ibid. para. 6.

Whilst such comments and the figures above are encouraging, it must be noted that this is not conclusive evidence of the success of diversion policy. It is not known how many offenders are still passing through the criminal justice system or remain in prison unidentified. HM Chief Inspector of Prisons has recently commented that several prisons have reported a reduction in the number of seriously mentally ill prisoners admitted on remand, which could be attributed to the introduction of court diversion schemes and a greater awareness of the problem.[152] But this was purely anecdotal evidence, and even though increases and positive developments have been observed, there is still no room for complacency, particularly in the light of the evidence in earlier chapters, which indicated that previous attempts to divert under the legislation have also resulted in immediate diversion increases in the short term, but this has not always been sustained. It must also be borne in mind that the figures outlined above must be balanced against the total prison population during that period so that a more accurate overall picture can be formed. The prison statistics reveal that the general level of the prison population has increased dramatically between 1989 and 1996[153] so that must also be taken into account when considering the massive increase in s. 47 and s. 48 transfers. There may have been proportionately more mentally ill people in prison who needed to be transferred during that period in relation to the rising total prison population.

4.8. THE DIFFICULTIES WITH DIVERSION

Having outlined the development and implementation of diversion policy, some of the difficulties with the diversion process will now be considered from both a principled and a practical perspective.

4.8.1. Practical Limitations

One of the most glaring and difficult obstacles to overcome is that of obtaining the initial and subsequent funding to establish a diversion scheme.[154] As already noted, the Mental Health Foundation and central Government have allocated some pump-priming funding for the purposes of developing local diversion initiatives,[155] which is still currently available, but its long-term and permanent availability is not assured. And as the Mental Health Act Commission has recognized, 'More than "pump priming" will be needed if

---

[152] HM Chief Inspector of Prisons, *Annual Report 1994–5*, Session 1994–5 HC 760 para. 5.37.

[153] *The Prison Population in 1996*, HO Statistical Bulletin 18/97, paras. 2, 3.

[154] Staite *et al.*, *Diversion from Custody*, ch. 7; James and Hamilton, 'Problems and Practicalities'.

[155] Session 1992–3 HC Debs Vol. 230 cols 603–4 *per* John Bowis the Parliamentary Under-Secretary of State for Health.

diversion schemes are to be preserved, to develop and to *become an established feature* nationally.'[156]

A national survey of duty-psychiatrist diversion schemes identified this as a major impediment: 'Even when a need for diversion schemes was recognized, regular and formal contact with the criminal justice system [by mental health services] was often seen as impractical because of resource implications.'[157] This problem has been repeatedly identified elsewhere. In an article applauding the introduction of this policy, it was also stated that its implementation can easily be frustrated by the lack of adequate resourcing: 'one pilot scheme . . . will not be continued (for the time being) because health service resources could not provide a psychiatrist to attend panel meetings and the community psychiatric nurse was only permitted to pursue cases already known to the local health service'.[158]

Indeed, the pioneering Hertfordshire scheme has not always been in continuous operation since its inception due to many of the practical difficulties experienced, most notably in obtaining secure long-term funding. Many of the schemes outlined above relied on the central Government or the Mental Health Foundation for the initial funding, but once the scheme had been established, local health and social services were willing to continue providing the resources. Some schemes, duty-psychiatrist models in particular, were able to finance the scheme within existing service provision. However, this is clearly dependent upon local health and social services, and whilst central Government has encouraged such authorities to prioritize services for the mentally ill and make such provision for mentally disordered offenders,[159] it is guidance only, and cannot prescribe the precise form that provision should take. Thus funding is an extremely difficult issue, and the success of such diversion schemes is often entirely dependent upon local health and social services policies, priorities, and levels of commitment.

Such funding difficulties tie in very closely with many of the other practical problems identified which often hamper the development of the schemes:

lack of adequate transport arrangements, difficulties in hospital admissions, and overdependence on key people. . . . The difficulty concerning arrangements to transport mentally disordered offenders to hospital highlights the issue of who takes responsibility for the patient or offender. In many cases ambulance staff refuse to take the defendant to hospital because of their security risk, the police refusing because transport to hospital is the responsibility of the health service. One psychiatrist arranged taxis to convey mentally disordered offenders to hospital.[160]

---

156 MHAC, *Report 1991–3*, para. 10.5 (emphasis supplied); see also MHAC, *Reports 1993–5* and *1995–7*, where similar concerns have been expressed about the insecure nature of the funding.
157 Blummenthal and Wessely, 'National Survey', 1325.
158 Osler, 'Mentally Disordered Offenders', 161–2.
159 *The Health of the Nation* White Paper, Cm. 1986, required health authorities to include mentally disordered offenders in their strategic and purchasing plans; see also Session 1997–8 HL Debs Vol. 585 cols 1225–56, where the government has made it clear that mental health services remain very high on its agenda and is one of six medium term priorities in 1999. See also DoH, NHS Executive EL(97)39.   160 Blummenthal and Wessely, 'National Survey', 1322.

Again, linking in with such problems are the difficulties often experienced in finding both beds and appropriate facilities to which to divert the mentally ill: 'co-operation with hospitals is impeded by fear of violence, reluctance to accept unpopular patients, and increasingly, a shortage of hospital based resources'.[161] There appears to be a clear lack of facilities—both in hospital and in the community—for this category of patient, 'bedevilled as they have been (and still are) by under-funding, lack of co-ordination and co-operation'.[162]

This was a major problem which was identified by the Reed Committee report. In its comprehensive review of services for this category of offender, it concluded that dramatic improvements were required. The majority of its recommendations concerned the provision of increased resourcing and provision of services. As the Finance Advisory Group report highlighted, to translate such improvements into practice would require a substantial allocation of resources and commitment by the central Government and regional health and social services: 'The resource implications of this review are considerable. Much could be achieved through better co-ordination and more effective use of resources, but we are recommending substantial service development which, taken as a whole, *cannot be met within existing resources.*'[163] These are important limitations which will now be fully explored below.

4.8.2. Resource Difficulties

4.8.2.1. Compounded by Community Care

Provision of appropriate resources is hindered by the 1979–97 Conservative Government's inadequate implementation of its community care policy. This failing is potentially a major obstacle to diversion, as diversion from the criminal justice system inevitably involves hospital or community care. It was shown in Ch. 2 how community care has been inadequately resourced since its introduction in 1962, and there is evidence to suggest that these failings have also accounted for the increasing numbers of mentally ill people who have been coming into contact with the criminal justice system in the past decade.

The concept of community care has been an important aspect of policy for more than three decades, and in 1980 the Conservative Government reaffirmed this approach by publishing *Care in Action,*[164] a document which illustrated its continued rhetorical commitment to community care. This policy, whilst laudable in theory, has, however, been severely criticized in terms of its practical implementation. The Social Services Select Committee was highly critical of the inadequate

---

[161] Blummenthal and Wessely, 'National Survey'.

[162] H. Prins, 'Is Diversion just a Diversion?' (1994) 34 *Med, Sci & Law* 137–47, 137.

[163] Cm. 2088 para. 8.1 (emphasis supplied).

[164] *A Handbook of Policies and Priorities for the Health and Social Services in England and Wales* (DHSS 1980). See further K. Jones, *Asylums and After.*

implementation in 1985.[165] It stated that community care policies would only be achieved if there was a real increase in expenditure.[166] Community care at that time had simply meant that patients had been let out of the hospitals but no adequate provision had been made for them in the community: 'There are hundreds if not thousands of mentally ill people living unsupported in the community, many of them former hospital patients. Large numbers are sleeping rough in archways and under railway bridges.'[167] The Committee were highly condemnatory of the implementation of the policy, and a further report was commissioned in 1986 which simply echoed the sentiments of the earlier Select Committee report.[168] There was clearly a 'wide gap between political rhetoric and the realities of the situation'.[169] Resources and finance allocation were totally inadequate and responsibility was fragmented.[170]

The Conservative Government responded by publishing a White Paper in 1989, setting out its plans and proposals for community care for the next decade,[171] which acknowledged that community care resources were inadequate 'The Government recognizes that progress has not been uniformly satisfactory and there are legitimate concerns that in some places hospital beds have been closed before better, alternative facilities were fully in place'[172]—but was hopeful about the future; and again the previous Conservative Government pledged its long-standing commitment to community care.[173] It provided an assurance that dramatic improvements would be taking place in community care provision as a wide range of services in a variety of settings would be developed.[174] This was followed by the National Health Service and Community Care Act 1990 which placed the proposals on the statute book and, transferred the responsibilities for community care from health to local authorities.

The Parliamentary Social Services Select Committee considered these proposals in 1990,[175] but sadly concluded that the problems in community care provision were still present; the services and facilities had simply not been adequately provided. Indeed, the policy was perhaps more aptly named 'carnage in the community',[176] and, to many, mentally abnormal offenders are regarded as the biggest casualties of this inadequate implementation.[177] Bean and Mounser, in

[165] *Second Report*, Session 1984–5 HC 13.   [166] Ibid. para. 8.
[167] Ibid. para. 162.   [168] *Community Care: Agenda for Action* (DHSS 1988).
[169] K. Jones, *Asylums and After*, 230.
[170] See further A. Scull, *Decarceration: Community Treatment and the Deviant—A Radical View* (Polity 1984), 162. He is highly critical of the 'decarceration' movement, or rather, what it has come to mean in practice as 'there is a profound disjuncture between the myth and the reality of "community care" '; see also K. Jones, *Asylums and After* for a detailed account of community care
[171] *Caring for People: Community Care in the Next Decade and Beyond* (HMSO 1989) Cm. 849.
[172] Ibid. para. 7.5.   [173] Ibid. para. 1.1–3.   [174] Ibid. para. 2.2.
[175] *Eleventh Report Community Care: Services for People with Mental Illness and Mental Handicap*, Session 1989–90 HC 664.
[176] A. Palmer, 'Carnage in the Community' (1994) *Spectator*, 7 May, pp. 9–11.
[177] P. Bean and P. Mounser, *Discharged from Mental Hospitals* (Macmillan & MIND 1993), esp. ch. 7; see also NACRO MH Adv. Com., *Community Care and Mentally Disordered Offenders*, Policy Paper 1 (NACRO 1993).

their account of the effects of this 'decarceration' process, devoted an entire chapter to mentally abnormal offenders, stating that they are 'one of the key casualties of the decarceration movement . . . once able to find sanctuary in mental hospitals, they are now ending up in the penal system'.[178] So the failures of community care policy have also contributed to the plight of the mentally disordered in prison.[179] Indeed, as noted somewhat sardonically by some researchers, the position has been so bad in relation to mentally disordered offenders, that 'for many, a court appearance may be the only way that their needs become apparent'.[180]

A House of Commons Health Select Committee reported in 1994,[181] and whilst declaring its support for the continuing closure of the psychiatric hospitals, it sadly concluded that urgent action and injections of cash were needed to make it work. It observed that between 25 and 45 per cent of homeless people were mentally ill, rising to 60 per cent of the young homeless. Many of these people were being discharged and left to fend for themselves without adequate support and with little prospect of being housed: 'It is wrong that vulnerable and, in some cases potentially violent individuals may be discharged abruptly, inappropriately and without adequate support into the community.'[182] The problems were particularly acute in inner-city areas where extra money was urgently required.[183]

The tragic murder of Jonathan Zito at the hands of the mentally ill Christopher Clunis, is one amongst a long line of glaring examples of the failure of adequate case.[184] Clunis' care was described as a 'catalogue of failure and missed opportunity'[185] whereby the blame fell not only upon the professionals involved, but also upon the Conservative Government for not granting sufficient funding to provide the facilities and supervision required.[186] This is mirrored by the murder of 11-year-old Emma Brodie by a discharged mental patient in a Doncaster shopping centre,[187] the case of Michael Buchanan who was convicted of manslaughter following his discharge from a psychiatric hospital,[188] and the murder of care

---

[178]   Bean and Mounser, *Discharged*, 134. This is in complete contrast to the views of Foucault and Goffman as seen in the earlier discussion of the 'baneful effects' (Scull, *Decarceration*, 56) of institutional life in mental hospitals in Ch. 1.

[179]   D. Brahams and D. Weller, 'Crime and Homelessness among the Mentally Ill' (1985) 135 *NLJ* 626–7, which noted the inverse relationship between the number of psychiatric beds and the prison population, and how the process of transfer from one to the other can easily occur due to inadequate community care. See also A. J. Fowles, 'The Mentally Abnormal Offender in an Era of Community Care in A. Grounds and W. Watson (eds.), *The Mentally Disordered Offender in an Era of Community Care* (Cambridge University Press 1993).

[180]   Burney and Pearson, 'Finding a Focus', 309.

[181]   *First Report: Better off in the Community?* Session 1993–4 HC 102; see also K. Jones, *Asylums and After.*   [182]   Ibid. para. 45.

[183]   See e.g. DoH, *Mental Health in London: Priorities for Action* (1994).

[184]   See *The Report of the Inquiry into the Care and Treatment of Christopher Clunis* (HMSO 1994); 'Catalogue of failure left sick man free to kill', *Daily Telegraph*, 25 February 1994; 'Schizophrenic killer who was failed by professionals', *The Times*, 25 February 1994, and *Police Review* (1994) 4 March, p. 9.   [185]   The Christopher Clunis Report, para. 42.1.1.

[186]   Ibid. para. 42.2.1.–3.   [187]   Session 1993–4 HC Debs Vol. 239 cols 371–8.

[188]   Ibid. col. 727 Written Answer; see also 'Mentally ill people kill 32 in a year, study finds' *Independent*, 14 August 1993.

worker Georgina Robinson.[189] The tragic case of Ben Silcock is yet another horrifying example, but this time illustrates the effects of inadequate community care provision upon the mentally ill victims themselves. A severely ill schizophrenic, Ben climbed into the lions' den at London Zoo in an attempt to feed them. He was attacked by one of the lions and spent several hours in the operating theatre. Ben's parents stated that they had been left alone to cope with him and had been given very little help by the professionals.[190]

This tragedy repeated itself a year later when another severely mentally ill individual followed in Ben's footsteps.[191] Indeed, the daily newspapers are constantly filled with reports of such tragic cases where both the mentally ill and innocent members of the public suffer due to the inadequate mental health facilities and the lack of appropriate supervision and treatment within the community.[192] Such tragedies have recently been the subject of some lengthy and sympathetic debate in the House of Commons.[193]

The inexorable link between inadequate community care and the high numbers of mentally disordered prisoners is clear to many.[194] It was identified by the Tumim Report on prison suicides,[195] and also by the 1987 Interdepartmental Working Group Report: 'the recent increase especially in the number of unsentenced inmates considered by medical officers to be detainable under the MHA, may lend further encouragement to the view that the rise in the prison population may be due in part to the discharge from hospital of patients who subsequently prove unable to cope in the community'.[196] As already noted, the majority of offences committed by the mentally disordered are typically 'nuisance' offences, a plea for help, food, warmth, and shelter, possibly as a result of inadequate care in the community. So '[a]n absence of adequate community care and support can increase vulnerability to contact with the criminal justice system'.[197]

---

[189] L. Blom-Cooper *et al.*, *The Falling Shadow: One Patient's Mental Health Care 1978–93* (Duckworth 1995); see also D. Sheppard, *Learning the Lessons* (Zito Trust 1998), for a fuller account of the recent tragedies and the long line of inquiries.

[190] K. Jones, *Asylums and After*, 238.

[191] 'Bible man mauled in zoo lions' den', *Daily Telegraph*, 13 September 1994.

[192] See e.g. 'Mentally ill being failed by flaws in community care', *Daily Telegraph*, 20 April 1994; 'Mental care crisis "puts public and patients at risk" ', *The Times*, 28 September 1994; 'Mentally ill face care beds crisis in cities', *Guardian*, 11 December 1993; 'System Failure', *Guardian*, 14 July 1998, pp. 2–3; 'Community care blamed for killings', *Guardian*, 13 October 1997, p. 10. See also the debates in Parliament, Session 1993–4 Vol. 234 cols 1441–7 and Session 1997–8 HC Debs Vol. 302 cols 1263–330, which highlighted the inadequacies.

[193] See e.g. the debate on mental illness on 10 May 1995, Session 1994–5 HC Debs Vol. 259 cols 661–82: 'This debate is in the interest of thousands of mentally ill individuals who are inadequately treated under the present system' *per* John Marshall MP, col. 661.

[194] Social Services Select Committee, *Second Report: Community Care with Special Reference to Adult Mentally Ill and Mentally Handicapped People*, Session 1984–5 HC 13 para. 161: '*It is a mockery of community care that mentally ill or mentally handicapped offenders should be dumped on the prisons.*' There is also evidence from the USA: see M. L. Durham, 'The Impact of Deinstitutionalization on the Current Treatment of the Mentally Ill (1989) 12 *Int J Law & Psych* 117–31.   [195] Cm. 1838 para. 1.07.   [196] Para. 5.2.

[197] NACRO MH Adv. Com., Policy Paper 1, 15.

There has consequently been much discussion about the inadequate supervision in the community of the mentally ill, particularly those at risk to themselves and others, and the possible introduction of community treatment or supervision orders.[198] The independent inquiry which was set up after the murder of Emma Brodie concluded that community care and supervision was wholly inadequate, and recommended that there were grounds to consider introducing legislation to bring in powers of supervised discharge.[199] This issue has been widely debated and the 1979–97 Conservative Government set up a review team, which resulted in the introduction of new supervised discharge powers,[200] regarded as essential to the care in the community policies, as the reason so many mentally ill people are seen in court is that on leaving hospital they discontinue medication and their condition inevitably deteriorates.[201] A variety of other measures were also introduced which were designed to enable the closer supervision of severely mentally ill people in the community, thereby preventing them from slipping through the net or passing through the revolving door: 'It is envisaged that supervised discharge will enable problems to be picked up early before a crisis occurs, and then hopefully, along with the impact that court diversion schemes are having, that our courts in the future will see fewer mentally ill defendants coming before them'.[202]

These plans were perceived to be crucial, as, sadly, the low level of care and supervision provided has resulted in those suffering from mental illness being unable to care for themselves, perhaps resorting to committing minor offences in search of food and shelter as a means of attracting help. The new supervised discharge power was introduced in the Mental Health (Patients in the Community) Act 1995[203] and came into force in April 1996. It was envisaged that, together with the introduction of supervision registers for those at risk in the

---

[198]   Health Select Committee, *Fifth Report: Community Supervision Orders*, Session 1992–3 HC 667; *Government Response to the Health Committee*, Session 1992–3 Cm. 2333; see also comments of the Health Select Committee, *Sixth Report: Community Care: The Way Forward*, Session 1992–3 HC 482, and *Government Response*, Session 1993–4 Cm. 2334; 'New rules on release of mental patients', *The Times*, 5 August 1993; 'Mentally Ill face tighter controls' *The Times*, 13 August 1993; see further T. Exworthy, 'Compulsory Care in the Community: A Review of the Proposals for Compulsory Supervision and Treatment of the Mentally Ill in the Community' (1995) 5 *Crim Beh & Ment Health* 218–41.

[199]   *Confidential Inquiry into Homicides and Suicides by Mentally Ill People*, chaired by Dr William Boyd of the Royal College of Psychiatrists (HMSO 1994). See also *The Times* and *Guardian*, 17 August 1994.

[200]   Session 1992–3 HC Debs Vol. 216 col. 371 Written Answer by the Secretary of State for Health. See also 'Controls promised to protect public from mentally ill', *The Times*, 17 November 1995; 'New powers to curb dangerous mental patients', *Daily Telegraph*, 17 November 1995.

[201]   R. Macrowan, 'The Supervised Discharge of Mentally Ill People from Hospital' (1994) 50 *The Mag* 71. This formed part of the Secretary of State for Health's infamous 10-point plan which was announced in August 1993. See further *Daily Telegraph*, 5 August 1993, 10 August 1993, 13 August 1993, and *The Times*, 13 August 1993.   [202]   Macrowan, 'Supervised Discharge', 71.

[203]   Session 1994–5 HL Debs Vol. 561 col. 699 First Reading.

community,[204] and the mandatory Care Programme Approach[205] which must be put in place upon an individual's discharge from hospital, greater and better supervision for those mentally ill patients at risk in the community would take place.[206]

Unfortunately, however, these new provisions have not gone far enough,[207] and the controversies and tragedies have continued. Consequently, the new Labour Government has been forced to reconsider this entire area and has recently announced what it perceives to be 'a third way' for mental health.[208] In recognition that the poorly resourced community care policies have failed, it has announced its proposals for a new system—a 'new vision'—for mental health services, which will provide security and support to the patients and the public alike. Included amongst the proposals are 24-hour crisis helplines and emergency outreach teams, more acute beds and support accommodation, specialist secure units, and improved training and guidance. This clearly represents a compromise between a return to the Victorian lunatic asylum system of control and the open-door policies of the 1980s. The Labour Government appointed an External Reference Group to consider and formulate the reforms and it produced a Green Paper for wider consultation in December 1998.[209] It has been recognized that community care has suffered due to inadequate resourcing and lack of support, and the Government intends to remedy such deficiencies with the introduction of the new framework. The new proposals have indeed been warmly welcomed, and there is no doubt that the provision of such comprehensive support systems will represent a significant improvement. The presence of these systems in a wide range of settings could, undoubtedly, have a positive impact upon the treatment of mentally disordered offenders, as it would ensure that they do actually receive appropriate care and support, and are not simply abandoned, left to deteriorate in the community, and become stuck in the ever-revolving door. However, there are

[204] Health Service Guidelines (94) 5.

[205] Session 1994–5 HC Debs Vol. 251 cols 683–4; HC (90) 23 LASSL (90) 11. The Care Programme Approach is aimed at improving collaboration between professionals and developing care in the community to meet individual needs. All patients referred to the psychiatric services will be assessed, involved in the development of a care plan, regularly reviewed, and have a nominated key-worker responsible for co-ordinating and managing their care. See J. Jameson, The Care Programme Approach: A Descriptive Study of its Use among Discharges from the Southsea Acute Psychiatric Services' (1996) 20(9) *Psych Bulletin* 550–2.

[206] It must be noted here that some commentators are critical of these new measures and regard them primarily as a means of policing the mentally ill rather than enabling therapeutic supervision to take place. See e.g. T. Thomas, 'Supervision Registers for Mentally Disordered People' (1995) 145 *NLJ* 565–6; K. Harrison, 'Patients in the Community' (1995) 145 *NLJ* 276–7.

[207] See e.g. A. Parkin, 'Caring for Patients in the Community' (1996) 59 *MLR* 414–26; P. Bean, 'Supervision Registers for the Mentally Disordered' (1997) 161 *JP* 477–8; D. Mohan *et al.*, 'Preliminary Evaluation of Supervised Discharge Order in the South and West Region' (1998) 22 *Psych Bull* 421–3; N. Eastman, 'The Mental Health (Patients in the Community) Act 1995: A Clinical Analysis' (1997) 170 *Brit J Psych* 492–6.

[208] DoH Press Releases 98/311, 29 July 1998, and 98/580, 8 December 1998; see also Session 1997–8 HC Debs, 29 July 1998.   [209] DoH, *Safe, Sound and Supportive*.

already concerns that the changes must be accompanied by a corresponding and sufficient increase in resources and financial commitment from the Government in order to succeed. A certain amount of funding has been promised, but some argue that sufficient financial support has not been pledged.[210] The new measures must be accompanied by ample funding, or else they will suffer the same fate as their predecessor, the well-intentioned community care policy, and this will clearly impact upon the treatment of mentally disordered offenders and the future of diversion policy.

In order to achieve the successful diversion of mentally disordered offenders from the criminal justice system, adequate packages of care must be arranged and appropriate support must exist within the community. The new Government proposals are long overdue and must therefore be welcomed in this respect, as they represent an attempt to ensure a comprehensive mental health service. However, they will only succeed if they are accompanied by adequate funding. The provision of adequate facilities and support will therefore also be vital considerations in the evaluation of diversion schemes operating in West Yorkshire in Part II. Given such incriminating evidence of previous failure, it is essential that the new measures are not simply platitudes and that ample facilities and funding are provided so that attempts at diversion are not frustrated.

4.8.2.2. Diversion to Where?

Another aspect of the inadequate resourcing and facilities argument is the question, which Phil Fennell has raised, 'Where are we diverting mentally disordered offenders to? . . . If a policy of diversion of mentally disordered people from the penal system is to succeed, it is clearly essential that the psychiatric system is geared up to meet the increased demand which will be placed upon it.'[211] As the Community Advisory Group of the Reed Committee found,

the identification of mentally disordered offenders requiring diversion . . . is only one half of an equation. It is not in itself a panacea. There must also be a *range of services* which is *capable of addressing and providing for the care and treatment needs of individual offenders* . . . whether *in hospital or in the community*. It is here that the major investment of resources will be needed. Unless both elements of the equation are available and properly co-ordinated, diversion may well flounder, with unacceptable consequences for the offender and anxiety for his family and friends.[212]

And this is indeed the crux of the issue. No matter how well and carefully constructed the formal diversion and assessment arrangements are, diversion in itself will easily be frustrated if the relevant resources, facilities, and services are not in place. In order for diversion to succeed and make a positive impact, the

---

[210] 'Overdue reforms welcomed as long as the funding follows', *The Times*, 30 July 1998, p. 4; see *also* 'Civil liberty row on mental health law', *Guardian*, 9 December 1998: 'This is a package with glossy wrapping, but when you look inside it's half empty.'
[211] P. Fennell, 'Diversion of Mentally Disordered Offenders from Custody' [1991] *Crim LR* 346.
[212] Cm. 2088 paras. 3.1, 5.25 (emphasis supplied).

place to which the mentally disordered offender is being diverted must be an improvement upon where s/he comes from. If the only alternative to imprisonment is to be let out into the community with no treatment or support, then surely prison, which at least offers some degree of supervision and security, is the preferable alternative. The damaging effects of inadequate care in the community have already been outlined above, and until the proposed improvements are in place and increased funding provided in order to achieve it, diversion will not necessarily be the most viable and beneficial solution. This final issue is perhaps the most crucial of all, and is potentially the major obstacle to diversion as many of the schemes already in existence have emphasized.[213] If diversion to the health and social services is regarded as the preferable solution then those services must provide good and adequate care, treatment, and support. After all, '[Diversion] is not . . . an end in itself, but rather a component of a much wider service.'[214]

So what is the current state of the general psychiatric services, and in particular the secure hospital services often required by this category of offender? It was outlined earlier how Glancy and Butler, over twenty years ago, recommended that 1,000 and 2,000 secure beds respectively must be provided. Yet in 1992 only half the initial figure (635) had been provided—'This number clearly falls short of present known needs.'[215] The Reed Committee recommended that urgent action was required to remedy this: 'We recommend that the number of medium secure places should be increased . . . at least 1,500 places will be required nationally.'[216]

In this sense the 1979–97 Conservative Government took positive action and announced that it had allocated over £47 million of central funds to increase the number of secure NHS beds to a total of almost 1,200 by the end of 1996.[217] Indeed, by the end of 1997, there were thirty-three Regional Secure Units in existence with a total number of 1,504 beds, operating at capacity most of the time.[218] This still fell short of the Butler target, but it was clearly an improvement. There has been a clear increase in the number of available beds, but there is still much concern that demand greatly outstrips provision, and that the increase in beds and buildings has not been accompanied by a corresponding increase in staffing and support.[219] The need for more secure beds and the unacceptable delays in securing transfers and accepting patients has recently been recognized by the Labour Government, and there will be some provision for additional secure beds in the

---

[213] See e.g. Hedderman, *Panel Assessment*, 40.
[214] Community Advisory Group Report para. 5.29.
[215] Cm. 2088, Overview of the Community, Hospital and Prison Advisory Group Reports para. 22; see also K. Murray, 'The Use of Beds in NHS Medium Secure Units in England' (1996) 7(3) *J For Psych* 504–24; D. Mohan *et al.*, 'Developments in the Use of Regional Secure Unit Beds over a 12-year Period' (1997) 8(1) *J For Psych* 321–35.
[216] Hospital Advisory Group Report Para 5.36.
[217] Session 1994–5 HC Debs Vol. 251 col. 681 Written Answer by John Bowis Under-Secretary of State for Health; Session 1993–4 Vol. 239 col. 888 Written Answer; Session 1994–5 HC Debs Vol. 260 col. 244 Written Answer.
[218] Session 1997–8 HC Debs Vol. 306 col. 262 Written Answer.
[219] MHAC, *Report 1995–7*, para. 10.8.

new reform proposals for a comprehensive mental health service.[220] But there is still no room for complacency. And what of the general service provision? Again the Reed Committee Report in 1992 recommended that dramatic improvements were needed: 'There must ... be access to a range of supported and non-supported accommodation, as well as day care, social security, and other services, and a co-ordinated approach to care fostered by a multi-professional, multi-agency team responsible for services for mentally disordered offenders.'[221]

Given the current dismal state of community psychiatric facilities and service in general, ensuring that such services and support are in place would clearly require massive injections of money. However, the former Conservative Government effectively 'poured cold water'[222] on the majority of such recommendations. Whilst accepting them in principle, in practice, it passed the buck, announcing that their implementation was a matter for each individual health and local authority.[223]

Although the 1979–97 Conservative Government gradually increased expenditure upon mental health services generally,[224] no extra funding was provided centrally to implement the vast majority of Reed's recommendations. In the words of the then Under-Secretary for Health, 'Much progress can be achieved by better use of existing services and resources and improved co-ordination between the responsible agencies.'[225] And whilst that Government issued clear guidance to health authorities to ensure that 'adequate liaison arrangements' were in place[226] and that services for mentally disordered offenders were to be a 'first order' priority with future development following the course set by Reed,[227] it failed to provide additional funding to ensure that this took place. It made clear that it was a matter for each individual health authority to ensure that the relevant facilities were in place to meet the needs of this type of offender and, in particular, for diverted mentally disordered offenders, that they received the long-term care, treatment, and support which they required; but whilst endorsing the rhetoric of diversion, in reality, it failed to provide adequate support.

This is also evident in relation to the present Labour Government's mental health policy. As noted previously, services for the mentally ill have been prioritized and the policy of diversion is firmly endorsed, but there is still a lack of adequate long-term care and support. The new proposals for a third way for

---

[220] DoH, *Safe, Sound and Supportive*, para. 4.14–17.

[221] Cm. 2088 para. 25; see also 'Review highlights care confusion', *Independent*, 21 February 1996.

[222] 'Funding setback for disturbed offenders', *Guardian*, 28 November 1992.

[223] Session 1992–3 HC Debs Vol. 230 cols 603–4 *per* John Bowis: despite the 'considerable resource implications ... The implementation of these recommendations falls largely to the agencies concerned at the local level'.

[224] Ibid.; see also Session 1991–2 HL Debs Vol. 532 cols 701–3 and DoH/OCPS, *The Government's Expenditure Plans 1995–1996 to 1997–1998* (1994) Cm. 2812 para. 4.39–46.

[225] Session 1992–3 HC Debs Vol. 214 col. 878 *per* Tim Yeo.

[226] EL(92)6.   [227] EL(93)54.

mental health which were announced in December 1998 clearly represent a big step in the right direction and may go some way towards remedying such deficiencies, but only if they are accompanied by sufficient funds, and some argue that the Government has not gone far enough in this respect. Whilst it has pledged a certain amount of funding, it will not all be available immediately and anyway falls dramatically short of the £1.5 billion which has been estimated is required to implement the proposed changes.[228]

The present level of social services support and provision must also be considered. The previous discussion has clearly highlighted the perceived general inadequate level of community care provision, and the new proposals will clearly remedy some of the deficiencies. But what facilities and services *must* be provided? Local authorities are obliged by statute to provide certain services and facilities for mentally ill people. The Mental Health Act 1983 and its accompanying Code of Practice require the appointment of Approved Social Workers to carry out certain duties with regard to s. 136 assessments, hospital admission, and guardianship applications. S. 117 of the 1983 Act places a statutory duty on health and local authorities to provide after care and support for patients upon discharge from hospital,[229] and there are obligations to provide after-care supervision under the Mental Health (Patients in the Community) Act 1995. Furthermore, the NHS and Community Care Act 1990 requires local authorities to prepare plans for the provision of community services in their area. In this respect, a Local Authority Social Services Letter issued guidance to local authorities stating that this provision must also include mentally disordered offenders who may require community care services.[230] This was in line with the recommendations of the Reed Committee.[231] Social services therefore have an important role to play and are obliged to provide a certain range of services and facilities. Since 1991, central Government has allocated specific funding—the Mental Illness Specific Grant (which has now been replaced by the Mental Health Grant)—to local authorities, which is to be spent solely upon services for the mentally ill. The Mental Health Challenge Fund and the Homeless Mentally Ill Initiative have also been introduced, to provide further financial support to health authorities to develop services for the mentally ill.[232] And a specific allocation of funding—the Special Transitional Grant—has been provided for community care expenditure. In theory, therefore, it would seem that there exists a wide range of services and support and the funding with which it can be achieved. However, in so far as the 1979–97 Conservative and new Labour Government's policy and actual allocation of funding is concerned, yet again problems arise. The rhetoric is always far from the reality, and local government expenditure faces increasing constraints

---

[228] See further, 'Civil liberty row on mental health law', *Guardian*, 9 December 1998.
[229] See *R. v Ealing DHA ex p F* (1992) *The Times* 24 June QBD.
[230] LASSL (93) 11 '*Community Care and the Criminal Justice System*'.
[231] Cm. 2088 para. 10.10.
[232] See DoH Press Releases 95/310, 96/135, 96/253.

but these expanding obligations still have to be met. Furthermore, given that local authorities, unlike criminal justice and health authorities, form a much more direct part of the democratic process, prioritizing the needs of this often unpopular group can be difficult, particularly if local politicians are not willing to recognize the benefits. As noted recently by one Member of Parliament, 'there are no votes in mental health'.[233]

On this basis, in the consideration of the effectiveness of diversion in the following chapters, the level of psychiatric hospital and community services provided by the relevant authorities in West Yorkshire will be carefully analysed in order to assess whether they are adequate and meet the demands placed upon them by diversion schemes. As the Staffing and Training Group Report of the Reed Review concluded 'the greatest resource implication of diversion schemes is consequent provision of health and social services'.[234]

4.8.3. Inter-Agency Collaboration: 'Cold War or *Entente Cordiale?*'

Many of the practical difficulties outlined above in arranging transport, finding beds, providing facilities, and assuming responsibility also tie in closely with the practical difficulties in successfully achieving inter-agency co-operation: 'Working together is not easy. Old rivalries, old misconceptions—even old personal animosities—can act as a barrier to creative multi-agency working.'[235]

Indeed, one of the main shortcomings in the care of Christopher Clunis was the persistent catalogue of failure on the part of all the agencies concerned to share their information and knowledge about him and to work together.[236] Thus, by encouraging inter-agency co-operation, repetition of these kinds of tragedies can be minimized, if not altogether averted. The official report into the Christopher Clunis case stated that there were important failures 'to communicate, pass information and liaise between all those who were or should have been concerned with Christopher Clunis' care'.[237] Accordingly, it recommended that increased collaboration must now take place.[238] This has been a recurrent theme throughout the long list of similar inquiries which have been published in the wake of the Clunis Report.[239]

Although inter-agency collaboration is highly commendable in theory, it is questioned whether it can ever be successfully translated into practice. It has already been identified in the context of diversion schemes that 'it would be naïve to suggest that inter-agency co-operation in the field of mental health has been

[233] Session 1997–8 HC Debs Vol. 302 col. 1269.
[234] Cm. 2088 para. 5.25; see also comments of MHAC, *Report 1993–5*, p. 74.
[235] Staite and Martin 'New Initiatives', 280.
[236] H. Prins, 'All Tragedy is the Failure of Communication: The Sad Saga of Christopher Clunis' (1994) 34 *Med, Sci & Law* 277–8.
[237] *Report . . . Christopher Clunis*, para. 42.2.1.
[238] See also (1994) *Police Review* 4 March, p. 9.
[239] See further, Blom-Cooper, *Falling Shadow*; Sheppard, *Learning the Lessons*.

universally successful or, indeed, that local health authorities have always shared in the enthusiasm. Some schemes have started and failed, others have identified fresh problems beyond the compass of co-operation which would require fundamental reforms and policy change.'[240]

Many of the reports of the diversion schemes have testified to the difficulties in achieving satisfactory inter-agency co-operation, working practices, and sharing of information. The success of some has relied purely upon the goodwill and determination of one committed individual. Clearly, this is far from adequate if an inter-agency assessment and diversion scheme is to succeed in the long term. Whilst clearly acknowledging the need to work together, it is extremely difficult to achieve in practice and requires careful planning and constant sharing of information to ensure that mentally disordered offenders actually receive the appropriate attention. This was noted by the Reed Committee throughout its report.

There are a vast array of hurdles to overcome—boundary difficulties, professional rivalries, and conflicting interests and policies. Such barriers are present with any form of multi-agency approach and there is a wealth of evidence to this effect. For example, the 1979–97 Conservative Government also placed increasing emphasis upon the adoption of multi-agency initiatives to tackle crime in general, but the implementation of such approaches has often faltered due to the same problems.[241]

The situation has been compounded by the changes which were introduced by the NHS and Community Care Act 1990.[242] The health service is now a much more complex and fragmented structure—not simply run by central Government via Regional Health Authorities. The 1990 Act created a clear division—an internal market within the NHS for the provision of services. Now, the entire system is governed by the NHS Management Executive which has regional offices and is accountable to the Department of Health and ultimately to the Secretary of State for Health. At the local level, a clear split was created between health service purchasers and providers. The former consist of District Health Authorities and fundholding GPs who buy the relevant and required services for the district and their patients from the service providers, which are the newly created NHS Trusts and GPs. Given this new complex structure, it is extremely difficult, particularly for criminal justice professionals such as the police and the probation service, to know with precisely whom they must co-operate to provide the necessary services for mentally disordered offenders. It is also increasingly difficult to co-ordinate the appropriate services. In recognition of this, the Association of Chief Officers of Probation (ACOP) has produced a practical guide to assist Chief Probation Officers, as recommended in Circulars 66/90 and

---

[240] D. P. Allam, 'Inter-Agency Co-operation: A Geological Fault-line' (1994) 158 *JP* 147–8.

[241] H. Blagg *et al., Inter-Agency Co-operation: Rhetoric and Reality*, in T. Hope and M. Shaw (eds.), *Communities and Crime Reduction* (HMSO 1988).

[242] See also T. R. Hadley and H. Goldman, 'Effect of Recent Health and Social Services Policy Reforms on Britain's Mental Health System' (1995) 311 *BMJ* 1556–8.

12/95, to establish working links with the health and social services.[243] The guide acknowledges that achieving the desired levels of co-operation requires much detailed work and careful planning, involving compromise on all sides. It is clearly a difficult and lengthy process, but once it is achieved, the benefits are manifold not just to the mentally disordered offenders in terms of enhanced service provision, but, great savings and improvements can be made to the agencies themselves. It must be noted here, however, that the situation is likely to be exacerbated even further by the fact that the Labour Government has announced that it intends to abolish this internal market with the creation of the new NHS whereby there will be improved scope for pooling health and social care budgets and for commissioning services jointly.[244] This new framework will undoubtedly improve the opportunities for communication and enhance collaboration, but could also, in turn, create further confusion and complexity.

Formulating an agreed strategy and operational policy in advance is a necessary pre-condition if disharmony and dissension is to be avoided: '[Diversion schemes] should be based on a clear local understanding as to the contribution of each agency and where the lead responsibility lies'.[245] This is a pivotal prerequisite to inter-agency working.[246] Adopting a clear, well-devised strategy, agreed objectives, and joint policy and planning is crucial. The court diversion team from Hull have produced guidance along these lines,[247] as has NACRO,[248] and the importance of devising a clear plan and allocation of responsibility has been firmly underlined. The Reed Committee report was particularly concerned with this aspect of diversion and proposed models and processes to overcome many of the difficulties.[249] Overall, 'we believe that, with imagination and a willingness to break out of what some may perceive to be a strait-jacket, potential difficulties can be overcome'.[250]

Clearly, therefore there is no set formula to achieve inter-agency co-operation—it is entirely dependent upon individual commitment, compromise, and concerns. Many of the difficulties have already been identified,[251] and are particularly acute in the area of the mentally disordered offender as such diverse

---

[243] ACOP, *Probation Actively Working with Health and Social Services in the Management of Mentally Disordered Offenders: A Report Produced by the Committee on Work with Mentally Disordered Offenders* (ACOP Wakefield 1994); DoH, *Probation and Health: A Guidance Document Aimed at Promoting Effective Inter-Agency Working between Health and Probation Services* (DoH 1996). [244] DoH, *Safe, Sound and Supportive*, para. 2.16–19.

[245] Cm 2088, Community Advisory Group Report para. 2.37.

[246] T. Locke, *New Approaches to Crime in the 1990s: Planning Responses to Crime* (Longmans 1990). [247] Staite *et al.*, *Diversion from Custody*.

[248] NACRO, *Working with Mentally Disordered Offenders: A Training Pack for Social Services and Others Dealing with Mentally Disordered Offenders* (DoH/NACRO 1994) Module 8.

[249] Community Advisory Group Report para. 3.24–32; Cm. 2088 para. 10.16—the way forward is to agree a local framework for inter-agency working and multi-agency plans for services for mentally disordered offenders. [250] Community Advisory Group Report para. 3.24.

[251] See also A. Crawford and M. Jones, 'Inter-Agency Co-operation and Community-based Crime Prevention' (1995) 35 *Brit J Criminology* 17–35.

disciplines as medicine and the law are involved. Each has its own conflicting ideologies, principles, objectives, and approaches, which poses an even greater hurdle to overcome. None the less, it has been outlined throughout this book that inter-agency working is a key component of diversion and service provision. Previous attempts at diversion have failed due to the lack of communication and collaboration and these issues will therefore be considered carefully in the following chapters when assessing the efficacy of diversion arrangements, particularly in West Yorkshire.

4.8.4. Improving Prison Mental Health Care

A final major consideration, as Herschel Prins argues, is that no matter how successful the diversion schemes are, some offenders will still slip through the net, so should the emphasis not be placed upon improving the medical facilities within the prison system for those who will still end up there? This is also an extremely important factor, and clearly there is tremendous room for improvement in this respect within the prison health service. It has already been noted how the courts have been expressly advised not to send sick people to prison, it is 'not conducive to a healing environment', and the deficiencies and damaging effects of the prison system, as currently constituted, have been documented. However, there will undoubtedly always be offenders who cannot be transferred to hospital, despite the firm intention to the contrary, given the minimal levels of, and strains placed upon, the secure hospital facilities. And those who are not ill enough to be classified as mentally disordered within the meaning of the mental health legislation may suffer as they cannot be transferred, thus there will be a need for adequate and better treatment facilities within the prisons. These imprisoned mentally ill offenders should be entitled to the same level of care in the prison hospital as is provided by the NHS and psychiatric hospitals.[252] Clearly, arrangements should be in place to ensure that mental disorder is identified in prison, particularly for those offenders who may develop an illness once they have been admitted. And obviously, as the 1979–97 Conservative and new Labour Governments have encouraged, transfers to NHS facilities should be arranged as soon as possible in such cases. However, where this is not possible for the reasons outlined above, then appropriate care should be provided to ensure that the condition does not deteriorate. The Prison Advisory Group report devoted an entire chapter to such health-care needs: 'in general there is little specific provision for offenders with mental health care needs beyond that provided by visiting psychiatrists in order to provide assessments and reports for court etc.— a task which is shared with full time prison medical officers who do not always

---

[252] HMIP for England and Wales, *Patient or Prisoner? A New Strategy for Health Care in Prisons* (HO 1996) p. 1: 'Prisoners are entitled to the same level of health care as that provided in society at large. Those who are sick, addicted, mentally ill or disabled should be treated, counselled, and nursed to the same standards demanded within the National Health Service.'

have recognized psychiatric qualifications,'[253] and on that note concluded that dramatic improvements were required to accommodate those mentally disordered prisoners awaiting transfer.[254]

The Director of Health Care for Prisoners 1992–3 Annual Report acknowledged that the number of transfers has increased in recent years, and in line with official policy the Prison Service aims 'to do everything possible to arrange for such prisoners to be removed to hospital care'.[255] However, the report also indicated that there are still many prisoners suffering from mental illness who would benefit from hospital care but are not being transferred,[256] and this problem has been identified more recently in HM Chief Inspector of Prisons reports[257] and a specific Discussion Document which directly addressed the issue and emphasized the need to bring the standard and quality of care in prisons up to that provided by/in the NHS.[258] So there is still much room for improvement generally.

Assessment and diversion schemes are being developed at this latest stage, and clearly go some way towards more accurately identifying, assessing, and facilitating transfers for those in need. The Prison Advisory Group, however, also recommended that prisons should contract-in such specialist mental health care from the NHS to further improve the situation. A joint Home Office and Department of Health Efficiency Scrutiny report on the prison health service proposed that such contracting-in arrangements should be introduced, particularly for remand prisoners, to ensure that accurate and appropriate mental health assessments are prepared. The Reed Committee strongly supported such proposals, which would not only benefit the mentally ill prisoners, but also reinforce links between the prisons and local services. And more recently, a Discussion Document by HM Chief Inspector of Prisons strongly recommended and urged that the NHS should assume responsibility for the delivery of all health care within the Prison Service, as it is 'fundamentally unsound' for the two systems to continue to operate independently.[259]

Such a service would require consultants with access to services and beds and other professionals to act as a team in prison to provide a wide range of services—psychiatric assessments, treatments, court reports, and arrangement of transfers to hospitals.[260] Indeed, this particular nettle has already been grasped to a certain extent by three prisons in the North East. As part of a pilot project, all three prisons contracted the appropriate services from the Newcastle Mental Health NHS Trust to ensure that the mentally ill are adequately served. The Prison Service Director-General welcomed the move, saying, 'Nobody wants to

---

[253] Cm. 2088, Prison Advisory Group Report para. 5.25.   [254] Ibid. ch. 5.

[255] *Report of the Director of Health Care for Prisoners April 1992–March 1993* (HM Prison Service 1994) para. 3.8; see also *Annual Report of the Director of Health Care 1996–97* (HMSO 1998), ch. 1.   [256] *Report of DHCP 1992–3*, para. 3.9.

[257] *Annual Report of HM Chief Inspector of Prisons for England and Wales 1995–96*, Session 1996–7 HC 44 pp. 22–4.   [258] HMIP, *Patient or Prisoner*, 4.

[259] HMIP *Patient or Prisoner*, ch. 2; see also 'NHS should cover prisons', *The Times*, 22 October 1996.   [260] Cm. 2088, Prison Advisory Group Report para. 5.25–31.

see mentally disordered offenders being cared for in custody and I hope, with this new contract, we will see more movement out of prison into psychiatric units where they belong.'[261]

Such developments are also a priority and clearly complement diversion, forming part of the comprehensive range of services which must be provided and improved upon for the mentally disordered offender. Despite the need and intention to divert and transfer, due to the financial constraints and lack of secure facilities, it will not always be possible to achieve at present, and until it can be, mentally ill prisoners are entitled to equal care and treatment and should not be left to suffer in prison. This is why it is highly significant to note the recommendations of the Discussion Document in relation to the new direction for health care and the response of the Director of Health Care for Prisons. The Discussion Document was published in 1996 in an attempt to start the ball rolling and promote discussion in this area. Unfortunately, however, by early 1999, almost three years later, no further action has been taken and the Health Care Service is still operating independently of the NHS. Despite some recent encouraging developments and improvements, such as the introduction of the Prison Service strategy for the care of the suicidal in custody, and pilot projects such as those outlined above,[262] no further action has been taken to enable wholesale reform. This is extremely unfortunate. It can only be hoped that the nettle will soon be grasped and that, as noted by the Director of Health Care in his most recent report, meaningful and long overdue discussions between the relevant ministerial departments will begin to take place.[263] It is extremely encouraging to note that the Directorate has convened a Working Group in order to take forward such proposals and ensure that the treatment of mentally disordered prisoners is significantly improved. As noted in Chapter 1, it produced its report in March 1999 and recommended a joint approach to the organization and delivery of prison health care between the Prison Service and the NHS.

4.8.5. Addressing the Theoretical Concerns

The final issue to consider here is the actual operation of diversion policy within the wider context of the criminal justice system as a whole, as it raises many difficult and complex issues.[264] It is therefore necessary to address some of the basic questions about the diversion of mentally disordered offenders which were briefly raised in Ch. 1, to assess how far they are addressed and overcome in the

---

[261] H. Tyrrell, 'Jails sign mental health care deal with NHS', *Press Association Newsfile*, 21 June 1993; D. Barnes and F. Robinson. 'Purchasing Prison Health Care Services' (1998) 115 *Prison Serv J* 40–3.
[262] Prison Service, *Annual Report 1995–96*, Session 1997–8 HC 247 pp. 22–3.
[263] *Report of DHCP 1996–7*, ch. 1.
[264] See e.g. N. McKittrick and S. Eysenck, 'Diversion: A Big Fix?' (1984) 148 *JP* 377–9, 393–4; see also M. Davies, H. Croall and J. Tyrer, *Criminal Justice: An Introduction to the Criminal Justice System in England and Wales* (Longmans 1998) ch. 5.

actual practice of diversion. In particular, concerns for the victims of crime, public safety, accountability, and discretion issues were highlighted, which will be considered here in terms of their practical implications. The destiny of diversion policy within the context of the Labour Government's overall criminal justice policy will also be considered.

The policy of diversion raises concerns about the victims of crimes and public safety. It is an inherently offender-oriented process, and so there is a danger that these parallel issues may be forgotten. This is indeed a legitimate concern; however, as has been seen, in practice the majority of prosecutions still proceed and justice is seen to be done, and so the concern for victims is not totally ignored and possible claims for compensation are not thwarted. It is therefore clear that diversion is rightly concerned with achieving treatment and appropriate disposals but that it does not forbid prosecution. Accordingly, the interests of offender and victim are not necessarily mutually exclusive in the diversion process. All these relevant factors will be carefully considered in assessing what is appropriate for each particular offender in view of the seriousness and circumstances of the offence and the nature of the mental disorder. Furthermore, the CPS has recently revised its Code,[265] the police have been issued with stricter cautioning guidelines,[266] the Victim's Charter has been revised and Circular 55/98 has been published, all of which now expressly state that the victim's views should be accorded more primacy in the decision-making process.[267] In addition, the Code expressly advises that the seriousness of the offence and the public safety are also important factors that must be considered. So the CPS and police now routinely take these issues into account as part of the decision whether or not to caution or prosecute an offender, and hence whether s/he should be diverted. This is clearly an important consideration which places limits upon the diversion decision-making process and ensures that, in practice, such issues are given weight.

Moreover, the current Government has affirmed its rhetorical commitment to diversion policy and Circular 52/97, which accompanied the Crime (Sentences) Act 1997, stressed that the advice given in Circulars 66/90 and 12/95 remains in force.[268] However, it must be noted that the policy statement has now been expressly qualified by the need to protect the safety of the public, thereby ensuring that the rights of victims and public safety are accorded sufficient consideration within the diversion decision-making process. As stated in Circular 52/97, 'It is the Government's policy that an offender needing specialist care and treatment for mental disorder should where possible receive it in hospital rather than in

---

[265] *CPS Annual Report 1993–1994* (HMSO 1994) Code for Crown Prosecutors, para. 6.7.

[266] HO Circular 18/1994, *The Cautioning of Offenders*, para. 7 'Efforts should be made to find out the victim's view about the offence, which may have a bearing on how serious the offence is.'

[267] See further J. Shapland and E. Bell, 'Victims in the Magistrates' Courts and Crown Court' [1998] *Crim LR* 537–46; A. Gillespie, 'Victims and Sentencing (1998) 148 *NLJ* 1263–5; HO Circular 55/1998, *Keeping victims informed of developments in their case* (Home Office 1998).

[268] HO Circular 52/97 para. 2 (emphasis supplied).

custodial care, wherever this is *consistent with the needs of protecting the public*.[269] Arguably, therefore, whilst the need to promote diversion and thera-peutic disposals has been firmly underlined, there is now much greater emphasis upon the needs of the victims and the public. This was not as explicit or evident in the previous official guidance contained in Circulars 66/90 and 12/95, which accorded primacy to the mental health care needs of the offender. The revised Code of Practice accompanying the Mental Health Act 1983 also now makes express reference to the need to provide information to and respect the rights of victims, when health care decisions are made.[270] This modified guidance will also ensure that due consideration is given to the need to protect the public and respect the rights of victims in the decision-making process.

Legitimate concerns have also been expressed about the unfettered discretion and lack of accountability that the operation of diversion schemes permits.[271] It is accepted that this discretion element is an unsatisfactory feature of the notion of diversion. As Andrew Ashworth has identified, some element of discretion is inevitable in relation to such gatekeeping decisions, but it must not be absolute and should be subject to certain limitations, monitoring, and guidelines.[272] In practice, the difficulty can be overcome to a limited extent by the adoption of formal practices, operational policies, procedures, and standardized referral crite-ria, which would clearly go some way towards minimizing variations and ensur-ing against prejudicial and discriminatory decision-making. As has been seen, many of the schemes do operate standard referral criteria and procedures. Accountability is perhaps best ensured by reference to constant overview by each scheme's Steering Committee to monitor the development of diversionary prac-tices. Moreover, publication of the reports and research studies about the diver-sion schemes also opens the decisions and practices to scrutiny and review. Finally, those schemes which are in receipt of funding from the Home Office are required to submit annual reports and statistics to central Government and this acts as a further control mechanism. Thus, provided such measures are adopted, at least some degree of consistency and uniformity can be achieved with regard to diversion decisions. Furthermore, the individuals involved are professionals who are overseen by their peers and constrained by time and resources, thus the potential for abuse is perhaps further marginalized.

Adopting an agreed strategy at the outset, outlining with whom and how the scheme is to operate, would also go some way towards alleviating the difficulties posed by the problematic definition of the 'mentally disordered offender', which has been discussed in previous chapters. It is a central issue, as it can militate against successful inter-agency co-operation, and will therefore be crucial when considering the actual operation of diversion schemes in West Yorkshire in the

---

[269] Ibid. [270] See *Mental Health Act Revised Code of Practice*, para. 1.9.
[271] Similar concerns have been expressed by a Social Services Inspectorate Report into services for this category of offender—DoH Social Care Group, *Services for Mentally Disordered Offenders in the Community: An Inspection Report* (DoH 1997) para. 5. [272] See Ch. 1.

following chapters. The solution would perhaps be to reach an agreed strategy at the outset, one that not only spells out the roles and responsibilities of each agency and clearly identifies the services available, but also specifies precisely with whom the scheme is dealing by reference to standard referral criteria.

Many of the theoretical concerns and dangers about diversion can be overcome, or at least minimized to a degree, by adopting formalized and agreed practices and procedures, and it will be considered in the following chapters to what extent these have been adopted and applied in the actual practice of diversion in one particular geographical area.

4.8.6. Criminal Justice Policy: 'Tough on Crime and the Causes of Crime'

A final difficulty here is to reconcile diversion policy with the Labour Government's recent crackdown on crime and its move towards introducing tougher penalties and retributive sentencing. Towards the end of the 1980s, the 1979–97 Conservative Government introduced several measures and guidelines plainly in favour of diversion for certain categories of offender. Home Office Circular 66/90 was introduced, which was accompanied by Circular 59/90, *The Cautioning of Offenders*, which strongly advocated the increased use of cautioning by the police as a diversion mechanism, particularly with regard to juvenile and young adult offenders. In terms of general criminal justice policy, however, the 1979–97 Conservative Government subsequently adopted a much more hardline approach which was particularly evident in the Green Paper, *Strengthening Punishment in the Community,* which was announced in March 1995 by the then Home Secretary.[273] It proposed the abolition of probation and wider powers for the courts to impose tough community sentences. The same Government also revised the cautioning guidelines and issued a further Circular which now restricts the use of cautions and marks a significant U-turn in policy direction.[274] This shift was also evident to a degree in some of the measures introduced by the Criminal Justice Act 1991, which indicated the primacy to be accorded to retribution and denunciation.[275] More recently, the emphasis has therefore been placed upon punishment, and protecting the public is to be regarded as paramount when making sentencing decisions. The introduction of the Crime (Sentences) Act 1997 shortly before the 1979–97 Conservative Government was defeated at the General Election, with its provisions for mandatory and minimum sentences, is a further indication of this hard-line approach.[276] And the provisions in the

---

[273] 'Howard moves to replace probation with tougher policy', *The Times,* 13 March 1995, p. 1.

[274] HO Circular 18/1994; see also C. Ball, 'Cautioning: A Radical Shift in Policy?' (1994) 144 *NLJ* 495–6.

[275] See M. Davies *et al., Criminal Justice: An Introduction to the Criminal Justice System in England and Wales* (Longmans 1998) ch. 9.

[276] See further D. A. Thomas, 'Crime (Sentences) Act 1997' [1998] *Crim LR* 83–92; R. Henham, 'Making Sense of the Crime (Sentences) Act 1997' (1998) 61 *MLR* 223–35.

Protection from Harassment Act 1997, which received the Royal Assent at the same time, also testify to the emphasis being placed upon public protection from, and penal sanctions for, people displaying harassing behaviour.[277]

Furthermore, it is clear that the current Labour Government intends to adopt a similar stance,[278] which is evident in its slogan 'tough on crime and the causes of crime'[279] and can also be seen in the recent comments of the Home Secretary in Parliament: 'my overriding priority is to secure the safety of the public'.[280] Some of the measures in the recent Crime and Disorder Act 1998 would also seem to reflect this philosophy. Whilst the main thrust of the Act is to introduce a radical overhaul of the youth justice system, it also contains certain provisions which emphasize retribution, denunciation, and punishment, for example, the anti-social behaviour order, which is designed to counteract anti-social/disorderly behaviour which may cause nuisance/alarm/distress in public places, but without the need for a direct victim. This clearly represents a massive expansion of police powers and the criminalization of bizarre/odd behaviour that previously may not have attracted criminal/penal sanctions.

If the new hard-line approach is to be the continued future direction for the Labour Government's policy on crime, then diversion, which focuses upon the needs of the offender, is clearly at odds with it and will inevitably be affected. As yet it is too early to predict the precise long-term effects of the new proposals, as many have only just taken their place on the statute books. However, it must be borne in mind that hard-line policy background may well adversely affect central Government's future commitment towards diversion, and consequently the long-term financing and implementation of diversion schemes may lie in the balance. As has been seen, the Labour Government has recently reaffirmed its rhetorical commitment to the continued implementation of diversion policy and indicated the funding which has been provided to assist in its implementation.[281] Whilst this is extremely encouraging, no promises about further long-term resourcing have been made and so there is still much uncertainty and instability about the future direction of inter-agency working and diversion policy.

4.9. CONCLUSION

This chapter has sought to trace the origins of diversion policy and outline its reception and implementation nationally. In general, the policy has been regarded

---

[277] See further L. Davies and M. Lawrenson, 'Protection from Harassment Act 1997' (1997) *Legal Action*, August, p. 23.

[278] See further I. Brownlee, 'New Labour, New Penology? Punitive Rhetoric and the Limits of Managerialism in Criminal Justice Policy' (1998) 25(3) *J Law & Soc* 313–25; I. Brownlee, *Community Punishment: A Critical Introduction* (Longmans 1998) ch. 8.

[279] Session 1996–7 HC Debs Vol. 294 col. 475.

[280] Session 1996–7 HC Debs Vol. 299 col. 341 *per* Jack Straw MP.

[281] Session 1997–8 HL Debs Vol. 586 col. 412 WA; HO, *Annual Report 1998: Government's Expenditure Plans 1998–99*, Session 1997–8 Cm. 3908 para. 4.24.

as making a valuable contribution to reducing the mentally ill prison population and increasing access to therapeutic care, as intended. The varied accounts and empirical data of the emerging diversion schemes have clearly revealed that they are making an impact in terms of identifying offenders suffering from mental illness, reducing inappropriate remands in custody, and providing access to mental health care and support. Furthermore, their development is contributing towards raising the profile of mentally disordered offenders and is recognition that their plight is multifaceted and requires a multi agency response. The process of achieving such desired goals, however, is not without difficulty, and turning the rhetoric into reality requires many obstacles to be overcome. Most notably the funding issue is crucial, as are the difficulties in achieving inter-agency co-operation to ensure that the mentally disordered offender is successfully diverted. These problems are not new, but in order to make inter-agency diversion schemes work, careful planning and multi-disciplinary co-operation must take place in advance to ensure that allocation of responsibility and resourcing is agreed. Only then can a diversion scheme be successfully translated into practice.

The principle of diversion raises many broader issues in the context of the criminal justice system as a whole. The rights of victims, public protection, and the inherent dangers within discretional decision-making must not be forgotten, and this chapter has also sought to address some of these limitations from a practical perspective. It is acknowledged that such issues are highly relevant and are important to the debate, yet the emphasis should be upon ensuring that mentally disordered offenders receive appropriate health care and treatment, and in the majority of cases, this can be achieved with the minimum disregard and abrogation of the principles noted above. So, in most cases, both objectives can be achieved. However, one of the most worrying broader aspects of diversion is its position within the context of the Labour Government's general criminal justice policy. The future development of diversion is clearly in jeopardy if the Government propose to 'get tougher on tackling crime and the causes of crime'.

In many cases diversion in its broadest sense is not always achieved, the majority of cases will not be discontinued. Nor is diversion simply concerned with reducing custodial remands, which has clearly been achieved. Although such aims are included within the diversion formula, the analyses above illustrate that given the nature of the offender and the offence, diversion schemes are primarily concerned with providing quicker and easier access to needed services. So some form of middle ground is achieved, and diversion in the true sense of the word is perhaps not an appropriate description, as most mentally disordered offenders will still be prosecuted, but given a lesser penalty or a therapeutic disposal, provided access to the relevant service is ensured. Thus, most diversion schemes would seem to provide a gateway to contact with health and social services rather than a 'get out of jail free' card.

The importance of diversion must not be understated, however. By avoiding inappropriate custodial penalties and giving access to appropriate support systems, an invaluable service is provided, as the Finance Advisory Group report noted:

Although superficially criminal justice system disposals may appear relatively inexpensive, in reality they cost more than proper intervention by health and social services. A mentally disordered offender who goes to prison and does not receive the treatment and care he or she needs will be released from prison and may well commit another offence upon release, resulting in a further penal disposal. Mentally disordered offenders, who are not imprisoned because of the relatively less serious nature of their offences, may pass repeatedly through the hands of the police and courts . . . inappropriate criminal justice system disposals almost certainly represent a less than efficient (and certainly) ineffective use of public money.[282]

But this saving in criminal justice terms can only be achieved if the mentally disordered offender is actually diverted to a better place with continued support and adequate care and supervision, and does not simply end up back in prison several months later. As the discussion above has highlighted, this is perhaps the most important aspect of all, and unless and until adequate alternative provision is made, mentally disordered offenders will still pass through the ever-revolving door. As the Reed Committee Staffing and Training Advisory Group Report highlighted, 'diversion schemes serve to point a mentally disordered offender in the right direction, but are . . . merely the end of the beginning'.[283]

It will be seen whether mentally disordered offenders have been pointed in the right direction in one particular geographical region—West Yorkshire, and the following chapters will demonstrate whether or not the obstacles have been overcome and whether the implementation of diversion schemes has been successful in securing the appropriate contact and care.

---

[282] Cm. 2088, Finance Advisory Group para. 2.4.
[283] Ibid. Staffing and Training Advisory Group para. 1.15.

PART II

5

Diversion in West Yorkshire: A Process Study

5.1 INTRODUCTION

Against the background of developments outlined in the previous chapter, the nettle of diversion was grasped in the West Yorkshire area, and there are six varying court-based projects operating within the five petty sessional divisions in the region. Taken as a whole, this represents comprehensive court diversion arrangements in West Yorkshire, and is clearly in line with official policy in terms of seeking to improve inter-agency working and increasing the opportunities for access to appropriate therapeutic care for mentally disordered offenders.

This chapter, which is based upon empirical research conducted in West Yorkshire, outlines the process of development of each of these diversion schemes, from the early stages of their conception to their implementation and subsequent operation. This is not a simple process, and is often thwarted by financial constraints, inadequate service provision, and, particularly, the difficulties in achieving inter-agency co-operation. In this respect, the *process* of diversion schemes will be considered and those in operation will be assessed in relation to the extent to which they have succeeded in overcoming these obstacles. Not only will the specific local initiatives be considered, but also the region-wide developments which have been taking place in the wake of Circular 66/90 and the Reed Committee report. A brief note on the research methodology is outlined below, followed by an empirical account of the process of the diversion schemes.

5.2. RESEARCH METHODOLOGY

Part II considers the local dimension and explores how diversion policy and practices are being implemented in the West Yorkshire region. Thus it includes an account of an empirical survey, investigation, and evaluation of diversion schemes in the area. In this chapter, the implementation and operation of diversion schemes in the courts in the region are discussed. This is a **Process Study** and includes a process evaluation based upon the data collected during an empirical study of the schemes, which attempts to assess how far the schemes are overcoming the practical obstacles and limitations outlined in Ch. 4. Chapter 6 is in two parts, the first of which is a quantitative evaluation of each diversion scheme and the second part is a qualitative evaluation which draws upon an analysis of the same data. It is an **Impact Study** and seeks to assess whether the diversion schemes are fulfilling the basic objective, that of ensuring that mentally disordered offenders have access to appropriate health and social services care.

5.3. IDENTIFYING THE RESEARCH SITE

The study was conducted at all magistrates' courts in the West Yorkshire area and took place over a period of 18 months between November 1993 and April 1995. This was the period during which each scheme was introduced and implemented. The courts included in the study are Leeds, Bradford, Bingley and Keighley, Wakefield and Pontefract, Calderdale, Huddersfield, and Dewsbury/Batley. Together they comprise all Petty Sessional Divisions in West Yorkshire. West Yorkshire was chosen because of ease of access and because it is a diverse region which is representative of all the different types of courts and districts, ranging from busy and dense inner-cities to quieter rural areas. The courts are of various sizes, ranging from the largest court in Leeds city centre (which is the busiest single court in the country with over twenty courts sitting daily) followed by Bradford, which is also among the top twenty busiest courts in the country, to smaller and quieter courts such as Calderdale and Dewsbury, which are based in the outlying and rural areas.

5.4. THE DATA COLLECTION PROCESS

The results used in the study were derived from three basic sources. The first was quantitative data obtained from the records of CPNs and other agencies. This was supplemented by qualitative data derived from a period of observation and informal discussions with CPNs and other professionals at the courts. And finally, further qualitative data was obtained from a series of semi-structured interviews with a sample of the service users—mentally disordered offenders who had been identified and assessed by the nurses at the courts.

5.5. THE QUANTITATIVE STUDY

5.5.1. Method

Initial contact was made with the relevant nurses who had been appointed as court diversion personnel. Several visits were made to CPNs for informal discussions and the author accompanied the CPNs to the courts to observe the operation of the diversion schemes and the interaction with the court personnel on numerous occasions. The quantitative data for this research was collected from the records of the CPNs at the court. Each CPN has a standardized assessment form which includes basic demographic and personal details. In addition, information is recorded as to the source of the referral, the index offence, any previous psychiatric/criminal history and the outcome of the assessment. Access to the records was therefore negotiated and the relevant details recorded and collated.

This quantitative data was supplemented by additional information and statistics provided by the West Yorkshire Probation Service (WYPS), the Prison Service, and the Health Service. Again, contact was made with the relevant personnel and additional information was collected. At the beginning of 1995, the WYPS Information Office began to collect general information in addition to their own data from the police, CPS, and prisons about their contact with mentally disordered offenders. This formed part of a WYPS monitoring exercise and was a useful primary source for the research.

The author's own observations and informal discussions with many of the court personnel also formed an important part of the data upon which this research is based. Visits were made to the local prison in Leeds, the local Regional Secure Unit (Newton Lodge) in Wakefield, Ashworth Special Hospital, and several local psychiatric units in the area, which provided valuable insights and anecdotal evidence.

5.5.2. Objectives

Overall, this empirical data was collected for the purpose of evaluating and assessing the impact and effectiveness of these schemes in terms of identifying and diverting mentally disordered offenders into appropriate care. Thus, this data sought to reveal whether mentally disordered offenders were actually being identified, referred, assessed, and diverted. Supplemented by additional information,[1] the quantitative data also sought to assess whether, in line with official policy, therapeutic disposals and transfers were being widely advocated in the region.

Many practical and process-based obstacles to the diversion process have been identified in the previous chapter, in particular inter-agency working, training and funding difficulties, and the 'diversion to where?' issue. This study also sought to assess whether the diversion schemes in West Yorkshire have managed to overcome these difficulties, based upon some of the statistical data and the author's observations and discussions with CPNs and other professionals at court.

5.6. THE QUALITATIVE STUDY

5.6.1. Method

Whilst the quantitative data collected clearly provides an indication as to the rates and outcomes of diversion, i.e. whether mentally disordered offenders are being

---

[1] See 5.6.

identified and assessed and thus an impact is being made, without more, the data does not present a truly accurate and complete picture of the long-term impact of the schemes. It has been demonstrated that mentally disordered offenders merit special care and treatment and should receive it from the health and social services wherever possible; it was, therefore, pertinent and appropriate to conduct a further evaluation in this respect, so an additional aspect of the fieldwork involved conducting interviews with a sample of mentally disordered offenders whom the CPNs had assessed which would enable an appraisal of the personal impact of diversion.

5.6.1.1. Identifying the Sample

It was necessary to use a self-selecting sample for the study, as there were many practical obstacles to using a random sample. First, there were difficulties in contacting and gaining access to many mentally disordered offenders who are often rootless and unco-operative individuals. Furthermore, it was necessary to contact interviewees who would be *willing*, *able*, and *capable* of responding and communicating during the interview. Time constraints were also present. In order to provide a useful and accurate evaluation it was clearly necessary to ensure that interviews took place with individuals who had been assessed by the nurses several months prior to the interview. An original sample of 20 was chosen, which included individuals who has been assessed by all nurses in all courts. However, given the limitations noted above, several individuals did not respond to repeated requests and others simply failed to turn up although they had agreed to an interview. The final sample included a total of 15 face-to-face interviews which took place between February and May 1995. This sample may seem small, accounting for 5 per cent of the total number in the study, but, given the practical limitations, it is not an insignificant number and will provide some insight into the ability of the schemes to assess and divert mentally disordered offenders.

The interviewees were contacted by letter[2] or alternatively, those who were receiving in-patient hospital care at the time were contacted directly via the CPNs. A mutually agreed venue was arranged to ensure that the interviews took place in relaxed and informal settings. Confidentiality was assured at the outset and the relaxed atmosphere was important given the vulnerability and potential suggestibility of these individuals. Most interviews lasted between 30 minutes and 2 hours.

5.6.1.2. The Interview Schedule

The interviews were semi-structured, based on an interview schedule[3] which was designed as an aid to discussions and also to ensure uniformity. The schedule was split into four sections. The first contained basic personal demographic details; the second was concerned with the offence details and previous offending details

---

[2] See Appendix E.   [3] Ibid.

and outcomes; the third concerned previous psychiatric history and treatment; and the final section was concerned with the actual assessment and the perceptions of the interviewees as to the impact and effect of the CPNs' involvement and a comparison, with previous sentencing outcomes and treatment, if any. Thus, the interviewees were encouraged to describe in their own words their personal experiences and impressions of the scheme, and were prompted only when it was absolutely necessary.

5.6.2. Objectives

This type of study was chosen to supplement the quantitative data as it was felt that it would provide the relevant information as to whether the schemes had been successful in diverting a sample of mentally disordered offenders into appropriate and lasting care. It would also enable the views of those whom the schemes were designed to benefit to be considered.

Moreover, it was decided to conduct a study of this type given the difficulties in achieving results in terms of presenting an accurate 'before and after' impact study. No systematic information on the processing of mentally disordered offenders prior to the introduction of the diversion schemes existed and thus the information available was extremely limited and insufficient to make a valid comparison. An evaluation based upon reconviction rates of diverted offenders was also considered; however, this was also out of the question given the time constraints of the study. The maximum total period for the study was 18 months,[4] which made it impossible to examine the extent to which levels of relapse and reconviction were affected by diversion arrangements. It would also require a comparison with a control sample of disordered offenders who had not been diverted, which would be extremely difficult to carry out in practice. These difficulties and limitations have been identified by other researchers in this area.[5] Furthermore, that type of study was also inappropriate as the object of the research was not to evaluate whether the schemes affected reconviction rates, but whether they succeeded in identifying and assessing mentally disordered offenders. And, more importantly, whether they succeeded in diverting them from penal

---

[4] This was the period from when initial contact was first made with the diversion personnel at Wakefield and Pontefract, which was the first scheme in operation, and so 18 months is the maximum timescale during which the observations, informal discussions, and quantitative data collection in all areas took place. However, in many respects, the timescale for collecting the qualitative data by way of interviews was considerably shorter, as the scheme in Dewsbury was in operation for only six months prior to the expiration of the period of the study and it was necessary to ensure that sufficient time had elapsed between the assessment and the interview; so time was even more limited in that respect.

[5] See e.g. C. Hedderman, *Panel Assessment Schemes for Mentally Disordered Offenders* (Home Office 1993) 5; P. Duff, and M. Burman, *Diversion from Prosecution to Psychiatric Care* (Scottish Office Central Research Unit 1994) para. 7.20; D. J. Cooke, 'Reconviction Following Referral to a Forensic Clinic: The Criminal Justice Outcome of Diversion' (1992) 32 *Med, Sci & Law* 325–30 where the total period of the study of reconviction rates was 31 months.

disposals and/or provided access to appropriate health and social services care and support. The qualitative study, combined with the quantitative data, would enable this to take place.

5.7. STIMULUS FOR REFORM: THE CONFERENCE ON MENTALLY
DISORDERED OFFENDERS

The seeds for the development of diversion in the region were planted at a West Yorkshire regional conference held at Harrogate in June 1992. The impetus came the from the Yorkshire Regional Health Authority in the light of official guidance and the various national initiatives. The conference targeted health, social services, and criminal justice personnel of all levels who were involved with mentally disordered offenders in West Yorkshire, and delegates attended from all disciplines in the region. The stated aims of the conference were threefold. Primarily, it was anticipated that full consideration of inter-agency diversion schemes would be given to raise the regional awareness of the difficulties in this area and the possible solutions to them. Secondly, it would give opportunity for the local issues and problems in this area to be aired and addressed. And ultimately it was hoped that the conference would stimulate joint working and enable the establishment of Steering Committees within each petty sessional division to deal with local arrangements and take the relevant action to ensure such diversion arrangements would be put in place.

In order to achieve the first objective Dorothy Tonak, the force behind the pioneering Hertfordshire diversion scheme, was invited to give a presentation on the mechanics of putting the policy into practice. She was by now seconded to the Home Office, acting in a consultancy capacity based on her experiences in Hertfordshire, and the Lord Chancellor's Best Practice Advisory Group on Mentally Disordered Offenders had encouraged agencies to make use of her services in this way.[6] She outlined the mechanics of the Hertfordshire Panel Scheme and how the model could be adapted to suit the differing needs and demographies of each petty sessional division. Various models were outlined which would form a suitable base for action. For example, Leeds, the busiest inner-city magistrates' court, would be suited to some form of permanent Multi-Agency Assessment Panel (MAAP)[7] scheme to ensure effective assessment. Bradford Magistrates' Court, which is also a busy inner-city court, would require a similar full-time service. The other courts in the area are considerably smaller and would be suited to the services of a CPN/psychiatrist on a more flexible basis, thus some form of Nurse (NAC) or Psychiatrist Assessment Court (PAC) Model[8]

---

[6] Lord Chancellor's Department Best Practice Advisory Group, *Mentally Disordered Offenders* (London 1992) para. 4.2.   [7] For further details see ch. 4 and App. D.
[8] Ibid. and App. C.

was proposed. For the larger urban courts such as Huddersfield, Wakefield, and Pontefract, a full-time CPN could provide an assessment service, and at the courts in the more outlying areas, such as Dewsbury/Batley and Calderdale, where the demand is perhaps not so great, a part-time CPN could be accessible to provide a similar service. The model adopted would therefore be wholly dependent upon local needs and resources.

The afternoon session was entirely devoted to petty sessional division discussions, in which the individual agency members within each division were brought together to discuss local issues and establish Steering Groups to form a baseline for action.

A feedback report was prepared shortly after the conference to highlight the outcomes and subsequent developments. Undoubtedly, the conference had succeeded in raising awareness across the agencies of the problems posed by the mentally disordered offender. More importantly, however, it had highlighted some of the solutions to them. The report emphasized how the representatives from each division were committed to try to provide these solutions. Each division would begin by forming a multi-agency Steering Group to try to devise the appropriate solution in that particular division.

Following this initial conference interest was generated, and relevant groups were formed at varying stages within each division to try to formulate appropriate diversion schemes. The development and operation of the schemes during the period of this study will be considered in turn on a divisional basis.

5.8. THE DEVELOPMENT OF LOCAL DIVERSION INITIATIVES

5.8.1. Leeds Magistrates' Court: A Pilot Duty Psychiatrist Scheme

Diversion arrangements in Leeds will be considered initially in isolation, as the original diversion project which was established at the court was simply a 3-month pilot exercise in 1992. The subsequent diversion arrangements which were in existence at the time of this research study formed part of a separate evaluation study funded by the Mental Health Foundation, which considered and compared the outcomes of NAC and PAC Models, and a period of non-intervention at the court over a 12-month period.[9] It was hoped that the results of that study would act as a stimulus to enable funding to be obtained on a permanent basis. And, indeed, this would seem to have been the case, as there is now a permanent NAC/PAC assessment scheme based at the court, funded by the local

---

[9] See C. Chambers, and K. J. B. Rix, 'A Controlled Evaluation of Assessments by Doctors and Nurses in a Magistrates' Court Mental Health Assessment and Diversion Scheme' (1999) 39(1) *Med, Sci & Law* 38–48.

NHS Trust, as part of the comprehensive forensic mental health service within the city.

That study clearly made an extremely valuable contribution; however, it will not be considered within this research. It was conducted from a medical perspective and the information was collected in different ways. There were also difficulties of access to relevant information and so no adequate or appropriate comparisons can be made between it and the arrangements throughout the rest of West Yorkshire. The initial pilot diversion project at Leeds Magistrates'Court will be considered here, however, as it made an important contribution to the regional developments and, at the time, it was a clear example of the effect of one of the major barriers encountered in the diversion process—the inability to obtain secure funding.

5.8.1.1. Background to the Project

Leeds Magistrates' Court is the busiest and biggest court within the Leeds Petty Sessional Division, with over twenty courts available six days a week serving a highly populated metropolitan area.[10] The impetus for the diversion project came from Dr Keith Rix, a consultant psychiatrist based at St James's University Hospital in Leeds, who has a particular interest in mentally disordered offenders.[11] Given the national guidance and local conference, it was decided to establish an experimental project to ascertain the need for an ongoing assessment service to the court. The running costs for the initial 3-month period came from within existing service provision, but the court agreed to meet the additional cost of the assessments to be carried out by the psychiatrists.

5.8.1.2. The Operation of the Project

The scheme essentially operated on a PAC Model basis. All defendants remanded overnight in police custody in the Leeds area were brought to the Bridewell (Central Charge Office) below Leeds City Court to appear before the magistrates the next morning. Throughout September to November 1992, prisoners in custody in the Bridewell were assessed prior to their court appearance by one of four duty psychiatrists who attended the court on a rota basis three mornings a week. The defendants who required assessment were identified by inspecting the custody records and liaison with the Bail Information Officer, the custody sergeant, and defence solicitors.

The referral criteria were deliberately wide, encompassing those displaying

---

[10] Figures from the Lord Chancellor's Department reveal that outside London, Leeds is the busiest Petty Sessional Division in the country with an annual throughput in 1993 of over 200,000 cases.

[11] N. M. Greenhalgh *et al.*, 'Pilot Mental Health Assessment and Diversion Scheme for an English Metropolitan Petty Sessional Division' (1996) 36 *Med, Sci & Law* 52–8; 'Court checks move to curb jailing of the mentally ill', *Yorkshire Evening Post*, 27 March 1993, p. 8.

any evidence suggestive of past or present psychiatric history or drug/alcohol misuse. When a referral was made, the defendant's permission would be sought and on that basis a psychiatric assessment would be carried out in the police surgeon's room in the custody area. Any additional information required regarding current/previous psychiatric contact could be obtained from GPs or local facilities by telephone or fax, as full access to such police and probation facilities was provided. Following the assessment, a psychiatric report was prepared, on a standardized form, indicating immediate medical needs, legal issues, and recommendations for treatment. Copies would be forwarded to the magistrates, CPS, Bail Information, defence solicitor, and also to the prisoner to forward to his/her GP, the hospital, or the prison medical officer, depending upon the outcome of the recommendation.

An operational procedure form was devised to outline and formalize the entire process, and a multidisciplinary Steering Group was involved with the early planning, implementation, and oversight of the project, which met at regular intervals to discuss its operation. It was truly multidisciplinary, comprising representatives from the court—magistrates and clerks, the police, probation, CPS, Leeds Law Society, social services, health service, the local prison—Armley Gaol, police surgeons, and the consultant psychiatrists involved.

5.8.1.3. Outcomes of the Project

Throughout the 3-month period, 57 prisoners were assessed, the majority of whom were single, young, male, unemployed adults. A total of 44 (77 per cent) of those assessed were described as suffering from a recognizable psychiatric disorder, and half the sample were suffering from alcohol/drug dependence. Psychiatric recommendations were made in 37 cases (61 per cent), ranging from in-patient admission in 3 cases to out-patient appointments and community treatment and support in 25. Five were identified as requiring a full psychiatric assessment, but given the serious nature of their offences and the pressures upon the local medium secure services, this had to be arranged in custody.

It could be argued that the level of in-patient admissions is extremely low, accounting for just under 2 per cent of the total referrals. However, this must be considered in the light of the existing arrangements between the police and the psychiatrists to provide assessments at an earlier stage in the police station. In line with official policy,[12] a s. 136 policy has been devised between the local police and health and social services, and there is an established practice in Leeds where the psychiatrists have been willing to co-operate and provide prompt examinations at the police station. During the period of study, 17 seriously mentally disordered offenders were diverted directly from police stations to psychiatric in-patient care. Thus, the scheme at court was catching those who had slipped

---

[12] Home Office Circular 12/95, *Mentally Disordered Offenders: Inter-Agency Working* para. 19(1); see further chs. 3, 4.

through the net and was providing a much broader service to those in need of out-patient and community support.

5.8.1.4. Problems and Practicalities

The vast majority of the recommendations were accepted by the court. In one case the recommended course of action was refused due to the concerns of one magistrate, based on personal experiences, about the levels of security within the secure unit for that particular offender. In other cases where the psychiatric recommendations were not followed the main reason was the unavailability of a sufficiently secure bed in a local facility. This inadequate level of regional secure beds has already been identified.[13] In terms of general psychiatric facilities however, the levels were, in the main, perceived to be sufficient—there are psychiatric units at the Leeds General Infirmary, St James's, and Highroyds Hospital in Ilkley boasts a special-care low-security unit. There were no difficulties identified in securing out-patient appointments or referrals to community health teams. Whilst the scheme faced no problems in terms of accessing facilities, it has been identified elsewhere that, despite the comprehensive provision, many patients in the community have unmet needs for access to staffed community psychiatric accommodation.[14]

In addition to the funding, the main obstacle faced by the Leeds project was the lack of medium secure provision, as was identified nationally by the Reed Committee report.[15] The Regional Secure Unit in the Yorkshire region is Newton Lodge at Wakefield. It has a capacity of 67 beds, but it is always faced with long waiting lists. So the Leeds scheme echoed Reed and identified a clear need for increased service provision in this area.

Given the pressure on secure beds, the study also identified the need for specialized bail hostels for this category of offender, to ensure that remands in custody are not the only other available option. This issue has already been addressed in Birmingham,[16] and there is a clear need for such provision nationally, as identified by the Reed Committee: 'Specialised bail hostels should be developed for some mentally disordered offenders who might otherwise have to be remanded unnecessarily in custody.'[17]

Another problem encountered by the project, which has also been identified by other schemes was the difficulty in arranging transport from court to hospital for those for whom in-patient care was arranged. In one extreme case, the indi-

---

[13] J. O'Grady, 'The Provision of Secure Psychiatric Services in Leeds: Paper 1. A Point Prevalence Study' (1992) 24 *Health Trends* 49–50; id., 'The Provision of Secure Psychiatric Services in Leeds: Paper 2. A Survey of Unmet Need' (1992) 24 *Health Trends* 51–3.

[14] Ibid. 51.

[15] Cm. 2088 para. 11.56, 59, 274; Hospital Advisory Group Report, para. 5.25.

[16] Insp. A. Roughton, 'Diversion at Point of Arrest', Paper presented at the High Sheriff of Merseyside Conference, Diversion from Custody—A Practical Approach' held at Liverpool University, 31 March 1995.

[17] Cm. 2088 para 11.6, Community Advisory Group Report Para. 2.21.

vidual concerned was told to make his own way to hospital and was found wandering aimlessly without a clue as to his destination. Clearly, this was a problem which had not been overcome at the outset and consequently became a major deficiency. It was subsequently addressed by the Steering Committee during the operation of the Mental Health Foundation Project.

5.8.1.5. Inter-Agency Co-operation

The Steering Group meetings provided an opportunity for formal inter-agency collaboration to take place, and it would appear that a degree of informal co-operation was also taking place at the court. Referrals were being made by other agencies and in the majority of cases the recommendations were accepted and effected. The obstacles were due to the lack of available facilities rather than unwillingness to collaborate. This is supported by the anecdotal evidence submitted to Dr Rix by the other professionals. The views of all agencies involved with the project at the court were sought, revealing that the scheme was extremely well received. The Leeds Law Society, CPS, and court personnel were all greatly assisted by the presence of the psychiatric personnel enabling them to act in the best interests of mentally disordered defendants in line with official policy. All such agencies came to rely heavily upon the advice afforded to them by the scheme, in order to make the appropriate applications and decisions.

5.8.1.6. Future Developments

The pilot project concluded at the end of November 1992 having fully demonstrated a need for the service and having sought to provide it. In December 1992, in the wake of Circular 66/90, the Home Office wrote to all health authorities and social services departments notifying them of the availability of centrally funded pump-priming resources to fund court diversion schemes. Bids were invited for funding from bodies proposing to establish such a scheme. Accordingly, the Leeds Steering Group submitted a bid early in 1993 based on the pilot project findings, for a full-time psychiatrist and CPN to provide a psychiatric assessment and diversion service to the courts. The bid was fully supported by all the agencies involved.

The Home Office response was disappointing, however, and the bid was unsuccessful. Not to be deterred, in August 1993 an alternative bid was submitted to the Mental Health Foundation which had also indicated that funding would be available on a similar basis. This second bid was successful and provided the costs of funding a full-time consultant psychiatrist to conduct a comparative study into the use of CPNs and psychiatrists at the court. The project was developed by the Steering Committee and began in May 1994.[18]

In 1995, at the time of the study upon which this research is based, the future of diversion arrangements in Leeds was bleak. The MHF project was extremely

---

[18] See Chambers and Rix, 'Controlled Evaluation'.

worthwhile, but the funding was short-term only, and it would seem that permanent arrangements in Leeds had been frustrated in the past due to the lack of resourcing. So, despite the goodwill and intentions of the professionals involved, diversion arrangements in Leeds, which had proved worthwhile and fulfilled a need in the past, have suffered due to the lack of secure funding. Despite the rhetoric, no support was forthcoming from central Government, but it would seem now that the relevant local authorities have recognized the need for this service and provided increased resources to fund a court-based NAC/PAC Model scheme. This is extremely encouraging and the value of providing a court-based forensic service as part of the comprehensive mental health services in the region has, at last, been recognized. Much of this has been due to the efforts of committed individuals, such as Dr Keith Rix and his colleagues, who have clearly demonstrated the benefits which can be gained. The initial inability to obtain secure funding was, however, the most glaring obstacle to establishing permanent diversion arrangements in Leeds. Fortunately, it has now been overcome, and the s. 136 arrangements which exist, coupled with the arrangements now at court, at least ensure that the process of diversion has not been completely frustrated.

5.8.2. Bradford, Keighley, and Bingley Magistrates' Courts: Court Liaison and Assessment Service

5.8.2.1. Background to the Service

Very little immediate action took place in Bradford in the wake of the Harrogate conference. However, the local NHS Trust was keen to take advantage of the 1979–97 Conservative Government's invitations for bids for funding, and so an application was made early in 1993 by the Bradford Community Health NHS Trust to fund a full-time court diversion nurse to provide an assessment service at Bradford, Keighley, and Bingley Magistrates' Courts, which are all within the Bradford Metropolitan Petty Sessional Division. This bid was successful, and funding was initially granted for one year, but was renewable subject to satisfactory progress. The Trust utilized the funding initially to conduct an assessment of need in the area, and on that basis a full-time NAC Model was set up at the courts in January 1994. The funding also included a consultant psychiatrist available to the scheme for two days a week on a sessional basis to make fuller assessments when required. This duty-psychiatrist system was subsequently modified, however, and it was agreed that a more effective service would be provided by the psychiatrist on an on-call basis, so the psychiatrist is now available to make medical reports as and when required. Both team members are based at the local psychiatric facility—Lynfield Mount Hospital in Bradford. The scheme operates at inner-city Bradford Magistrates' Court, which is among the top twenty busiest courts in the country,[19]

---

[19] Figures from the Lord Chancellor's Department indicate that the 1993 annual caseload for Bradford Magistrates' Court was 104,900.

and also at Keighley and Bingley Magistrates' Courts which are smaller, quieter,[20] and based in less-populated areas.

5.8.2.2. *The Operation of the Service*

The Court Diversion Nurse was in post from January 1994, but the scheme did not begin operating on a formal basis until April 1994. During the first few months the nurse attended each court to familiarize himself with the structure, procedure, and personnel, raise awareness, and provide information about the introduction of the scheme. This lead-in period was regarded as an important exercise in forming relationships and establishing the agreed procedure at all three courts. In particular, a Bail Information Service operates at Bradford Magistrates' Court and it was important to link in and liaise with the officers and liaise to ensure access to facilities.

When the scheme began in April 1994, it operated on the basis that the nurse would routinely attend the cells in the Bridewell below Bradford Magistrates' Court early every weekday morning to screen the custody records and accept referrals. The nurse was also available on call by mobile phone to accept referrals from the smaller courts in Keighley and Bingley. As with most NAC Models, the nurse accepts referrals from any agency at the court. No referral criteria are formally specified, but during the lead-in period the nurse informed the police and probation of the aims of the service and stated that he was willing to assess anyone who had a previous psychiatric history or one of self-harm, or anyone who was believed to be suffering from a mental illness. Drug and alcohol abuse problems were excluded, unless this was linked to an underlying mental illness, in which case the nurse would be willing to intervene. In addition to accepting referrals in this way, the nurse initially proactively screened all the custody records, as the circumstances of the offence and other indicators could show up a mental health element which the nurse might recognize where the police might not.

All referrals are accepted and an assessment is conducted by the nurse who will use his clinical judgement to assess whether intervention is necessary. A standard assessment form is used for the interview, which proceeds only with the interviewee's consent, and normally takes place in the interview room at the Bridewell. The outcome of the assessment would determine the nurse's course of action.

The nurse will write a brief report following the assessment indicating the mental health issues and the recommended course of action. Copies will be forwarded to the CPS, court, probation, and defence solicitors with whom the

---

[20] Lord Chancellor Department figures indicate that the 1993 combined annual caseload for both courts was 34,673, which is a comparatively low annual figure nationally. It must be noted here that Keighley Magistrates' Court has now been combined with Bingley and is, therefore, no longer a separate court, although it was at the time of the study and is therefore regarded as such for the purposes of this study.

nurse will liaise to determine the appropriate course of action. Should a psychiatric report be required, this will be arranged and the psychiatrist will be contacted. The nurse is given full access to probation administrative facilities, and is required to liaise with all the other agencies to try to secure the appropriate and desired care. The recommendations vary considerably, depending upon the degree and nature of the mental illness. In some instances an out-patient appointment or referral to the community mental health or drug/alcohol services may be required. This will be arranged by the nurse and the court will be informed as it may have an impact upon its decision to grant bail. Should an in-patient admission be required, the nurse will make the necessary arrangements and convey the person to the appropriate facility. The precise outcomes will be discussed in greater depth in the following chapter.

The scheme operated on this basis for a period of 6 months. However, in October 1994 Bradford Magistrates' Court underwent a massive refurbishment programme, and all the agencies based in offices at the court were required temporarily to vacate the building. Consequently, the diversion nurse was now only able to accept referrals from the three courts on an on-call basis. This modified system continued once the refurbishment was complete, however, as the nurse felt that proactively screening police records was time-consuming, particularly at such a busy court as Bradford, and did not necessarily highlight any more cases than those already being referred by the other agencies. Firm relations had by this time developed with the police and the probation staff at the court, and it was generally felt that the police and other agencies were good at identifying those in need. The nurse is now available every weekday morning to accept referrals over the phone from these agencies and will immediately attend the Bridewell to make a mental health assessment. The procedure once the nurse arrives at the court is the same and he is still on call to Keighley and Bingley Magistrates' Courts.

This revised procedure ensures that unnecessary amounts of time are not wasted at the court and enables a truly ongoing service to be provided by the scheme. The nurse is full-time and is now available to ensure a thorough follow-through of cases and to maintain contact with the diverted offenders. As the Reed Committee noted, diversion is only one half of the equation and the nurse now seeks to provide the other half by ensuring that the service into which the offender is diverted is ongoing and fully provided. So this service aims to ensure access to appropriate care and treatment, follow-through to final disposal, and continued support.

5.8.2.3. Inter-Agency Co-operation

The modified on-call system now also enables the nurse to spend more time working directly with the police and the probation service generally, providing training and advice where necessary on mental health issues, which is an important contribution to improving inter-agency collaboration and joint working. A pamphlet containing information about the aims of the scheme and the services offered has been produced by the Trust and circulated to other professionals. This informs the magistrates, police, probation, solicitors, and other agencies working with mentally disordered offenders that the service is available to provide psychiatric assessment and access to appropriate health services at any point in the criminal justice system—first appearance, pre-sentence, probation, and imprisonment. Advice, information, and education about mental health issues are also offered, thereby providing a comprehensive service to the mentally disordered offender and the criminal justice system. The nurse regularly attends the probation office for risk assessment meetings for mentally ill or dangerous offenders who are on probation or in prison, thereby providing a multidisciplinary response. The value of such an exercise was strongly affirmed by the Staffing and Training Advisory Group Report of the Reed Committee.[21] The nurse is also regularly called upon by probation staff to assist with pre-sentence reports and provide assessments should concerns arise about a person's mental health. This will enable a clear, agreed treatment plan to be presented to the court. Training on mental health issues is also provided at Lynfield Mount Hospital to the local police, as encouraged by Reed.[22] This revised system therefore allows for a more effective and efficient use of time, and enables the nurse to build upon the links with the other agencies.

A multi-agency Steering Group was appointed to consider the overall running and development of the service. Its members are drawn from the disciplines involved with the operation of the scheme—health, police, probation, and court personnel—many of whom are at a managerial level and are therefore in a position to ensure that the service is maintained and guide its future direction. The Group meets on a quarterly basis and so provides a multi-agency forum to resolve any difficulties which may arise as the scheme progresses.

The modified operational procedure is particularly suitable given that an agreed s. 136 policy operates in the area which allows the police, where appropriate, to convey mentally disordered offenders directly to Lynfield Mount Hospital. This policy was devised by the local Police, Lynfield Mount Hospital, and Bradford Social Services in accordance with the Mental Health Act Code of Practice. The agreed procedure states that police officers may convey a mentally ill person found in a public place to Lynfield Mount Hospital for a psychiatric assessment, provided that s/he is not violent or aggressive. Alternatively, the police station is regarded as the place of safety, and the police will contact the duty consultant at the hospital and the social services to arrange for an assessment to be made. As noted in Ch. 3, it is, unfortunately, rare for a hospital to be regarded as a place of safety for the purposes of s. 136 as they are generally reluctant to become directly

---

[21] Cm. 2088, STA Group Report, para. 5.36–.40: 'It is important that, wherever possible, assessments of risk . . . are undertaken on a multi-disciplinary basis.'
[22] Cm. 2088 para. 11.197; STA Group Report para. 4.62.

involved. Lynfield Mount, however, has expressed its willingness to act in this way and this is therefore further evidence of the good relations which exist between the criminal justice and health services in Bradford and is in accordance with the guidance in the Mental Health Act Code of Practice. Despite the fact that the decision is at the discretion of the duty psychiatrist, it would appear that this procedure is used effectively and accounts for numerous admissions to Lynfield Mount. This further reinforces the commitment to improve inter-agency co-operation and services for mentally ill offenders in the Bradford region and is in line with the official guidance contained in Circulars 66/90 and 12/95.[23]

5.8.3. Wakefield and Pontefract Magistrates' Courts: Diversion from Custody Scheme

5.8.3.1. Background to the Scheme

Although very little immediate action took place in the district, awareness had been raised by the conference and when central Government invited applications for funding in December 1992 the local NHS Trust were keen to take advantage. Both magistrates' courts fall within the jurisdiction of the Wakefield and Pontefract Community NHS Trust, so a bid was submitted by the Trust to the Home Office for a full-time CPN to provide an assessment and diversion service to the courts. The bid was successful, and funding was granted to provide this service, on the same basis as the Bradford bid. A Steering Committee was appointed to oversee the implementation and the scheme began in July 1993. Following Steering Group discussions, an Approved Social Worker (ASW) was also appointed to the scheme in March 1994 to provide an improved response and liaison with social services. The local Wakefield Metropolitan District Council is particularly committed to this category of patient, and so the Social Worker post is full-time, permanent, and funded by the Mental Illness Specific Grant[24] as recommended by Reed.[25] In recognition of the need for a truly multi-agency response, the local probation service has also taken an active role and provided a dedicated Probation Officer (PO) who joined the team in August 1995. The three members work together in shared offices in Wakefield. They attend Pontefract and Wakefield Magistrates' Courts which are both relatively busy courts[26] based in urban environments.

5.8.3.2. The Operation of the Scheme

The scheme operates on a variation of the NAC and MAAP Models. The CPN, ASW, and PO will routinely attend each court on alternate days of the week. They

---

[23] Circular 66/90 para. 4(i): 'It is desirable that, wherever possible, the place of safety in which the person might be detained should be a hospital and not a police station'.

[24] The MISG was introduced in April 1991 and encouraged applications from Local Authorities in order to develop services to bring about significant improvements in social care for mentally ill people. See Ch. 4.   [25] Cm. 2088 para. 11.263.

[26] Figures form the Lord Chancellor's Department indicate that the Wakefield Petty Sessional Division's 1993 annual caseload was 64,739.

will first make contact with the custody area below the court and are available to accept referrals from any agency at the court. The team has a mobile phone and is therefore available on an on-call basis to the other court should an assessment be required. Should its services be required at both courts, the members of the team will attend each to make the necessary assessment. The team have been given full access to police and probation facilities and, using a standard assessment form (which has been agreed by health and social services) will conduct the assessment in the interview room. No formal referral criteria have been established, but the team is willing to assess any individual who is believed to be suffering from mental illness and who consents to the assessment. Again, drug/alcohol abuse problems (exclusively) are not within the ambit of the scheme. However, such abuse may be indicative of an underlying mental illness, and there may be potential for dual diagnosis, and the team is willing to assess the individual to ascertain the appropriate course of action. It must be noted here that the absence of formal referral criteria does raise serious gatekeeping issues, which will be addressed further in the general process evaluation section later in the chapter. Intervention and diversion will take place only where, in the opinion of the team, there is a definite mental health element involved. Should a fuller psychiatric assessment be required with a view to arranging in-patient care, the team is required to access on-call psychiatrists from the mainstream psychiatric services, as no designated psychiatrist is appointed to the scheme. The absence of the direct input of a psychiatrist is potentially a major shortcoming of this diversion scheme, and this will also be discussed further later in the chapter.

Following the assessment, a brief report is made which contains recommendations for care and support. Copies are given to the CPS, the solicitor, and probation, and on that basis the court will make a decision. As with the Bradford service, it is the responsibility of the team to liaise with the agencies and make the appropriate arrangements for that person's care and treatment.

As the team is devoted to the scheme on a full-time basis it also has the opportunity to attend the court to follow the cases through to their final disposal and ensure that access and support is maintained. In addition, the ASW has a minimal caseload of convicted offenders who have been in contact with the scheme. This also enables a broader service to be provided, as the ASW may supervise individuals who have been placed on a guardianship order as a result of the team's intervention or alternatively may provide community support to other diverted offenders. The ASW is also willing, when she is in the custody area, to act as an 'appropriate adult'[27] if required. These additional support activities therefore seek to ensure that the other half of the Reed Committee equation is in place in Wakefield and Pontefract.

Additionally, the CPN regularly attends the local police training unit at Wakefield to provide instruction and advice to the police on mental health and

---

[27] See Ch. 3.

related issues, the application of Mental Health Act powers, and the scope for liaison and diversion. The CPN and ASW also work closely with other members of the probation service in general to provide health and social work input and advice in conducting risk assessments for potentially dangerous offenders. The team is also useful in providing advice and input in relation to the compilation of Pre-Sentence Reports for disordered offenders, particularly in the light of the PO's permanent presence on the team.

5.8.3.3. Inter-Agency Co-operation

A Steering Group oversees the operation and development of the scheme and consists of senior representatives from all the disciplines involved—health, social services, the police, probation, CPS, and the magistrates at the courts. The group meets on a quarterly basis, and the team members attend to provide regular reports on progress and submit scheme data for review. An additional forum is provided by an Operational Group, which consists of the CPN, ASW, PO, the police, and other probation staff who are all in contact with the scheme on a daily basis. Similarly, they meet regularly to iron out any minor procedural problems which may arise.

A most encouraging development was the formal appointment of the designated Probation Officer who has joined the team and provides probation input on a full-time basis. The scheme therefore works along similar lines to that in Hull, outlined in Ch. 4. A database has been installed which contains all client details, providing handy reference and automatic reminders when cases are due to reappear in court. This enables even greater follow-through to take place.

5.8.4. Huddersfield Magistrates' Court: Court Diversion Scheme

5.8.4.1. Background to the Scheme

Additional developments have taken place in Huddersfield, Dewsbury, and Calderdale which are considered below as they also form an important part in the diversion process and have further prioritized the needs of mentally disordered offenders in the area.

5.8.4.1.1. The NACRO Kirklees Diversion Project[28]

The impetus for developments in the Kirklees Metropolitan region (which covers Huddersfield and Dewsbury) also came from a NACRO diversion project which operated in the region in 1992. In 1990, NACRO approached the Home Office and the Mental Health Foundation for grants to encourage and facilitate diversion arrangements in three chosen areas across the country. One of these was Kirklees, as NACRO were keen to promote developments in rural areas as well as inner cities, and the other chosen project sites were Liverpool and Birmingham.

---

[28] NACRO, *Diverting Mentally Disordered Offenders from the Criminal Justice System in Kirklees* (NACRO 1993).

The project was essentially a recording and monitoring exercise about mentally disordered offenders who came into contact with the criminal justice system in Kirklees. The research involved a study of the use of s. 136 in the Kirklees division and so was concerned with police involvement with the mentally ill and diversion at the point of arrest. The study found that s. 136 was used on 42 occasions between April 1992 and March 1993, the vast majority of which resulted in successful referrals to social and psychiatric services. As a result of these research findings, NACRO's involvement stimulated the formulation of an agreed inter-agency local policy on the use of s. 136 as stipulated by the Revised Mental Health Act Code of Practice.[29] NACRO acted as a co-ordinator to form a local Steering Group which developed the policy to ensure competent and speedy assessment by a doctor and an ASW, so that detainees taken to the police station would be ensured easy access to services. The Steering Group consisted of senior representatives from all the agencies involved.

The Home Office Research and Planning Unit conducted an evaluation of NACRO's involvement in Kirklees, and also evaluated similar projects in Liverpool and Birmingham.[30] The author conducted a series of interviews with the professionals who had been involved with the Steering Committees. The interviews were designed to assess the impact of the projects and the role which NACRO played in each area in stimulating change and promoting inter-agency working.

NACRO's main aim had been to act as an 'honest broker'—a catalyst for change. The majority of respondents felt that NACRO had indeed 'facilitated' change and its involvement had significantly raised the profile of mentally disordered offenders in the region. Respondents from Kirklees felt that NACRO's involvement was positive in establishing a locally agreed s. 136 policy, and that relationships with other agencies had improved as a result of the Steering Committee meetings.[31] Even though it was felt that the Kirklees Steering Group would probably wind up as NACRO's involvement drew to a close, the process of change would continue in the region with other initiatives to develop a wide range of services and diversion arrangements.[32] The results of the Home Office research suggested that NACRO's presence had set the stage for further reform and the development of a formal court diversion service.

5.8.4.1.2. The West Yorkshire District Health Authority Partnership Strategy[33]

Following the recommendations of the Reed Committee report and the changes to the NHS following the NHS and Community Care Act 1990, in April 1993

---

[29] DoH/Welsh Office, *Mental Health Act 1983 Revised Code of Practice* (HMSO 1999) paras. 10.1–5.

[30] Home Office/NACRO/Mental Health Foundation, *The NACRO Diversion Initiative for Mentally Disturbed Offenders: An Account and an Evaluation* (Home Office 1994).

[31] Ibid. 54–6, 58–60.   [32] Ibid. 59.

[33] Partnership Strategy for agencies in the West Yorkshire Health Authority area—Calderdale and Kirklees, *Meeting the Needs of People with Mental Health Problems who Commit Criminal Offences and/or Present Challenging Behaviour* (WYDHA, 1993).

senior managers in the West Yorkshire District Health Authority (which covers Calderdale and Kirklees) decided to develop a joint strategy on promoting services for mentally disordered offenders. As outlined in the previous chapter, the Reed Report had identified the need to ensure multi-agency working in this area, and all agencies concerned had been instructed to prioritize the needs of the group. So, the NHS Trusts in Dewsbury, Huddersfield, and Calderdale, the local authorities in Calderdale and Kirklees, and the local probation offices all joined forces to develop a plan for co-ordinated services for mentally disordered offenders. A Senior Probation Officer was seconded to the health service to work together to devise this shared agenda.

The strategy was launched in March 1994 and included a variety of measures to be implemented within the region by probation, health, and social services to ensure that the needs of mentally disordered offenders are met 'effectively, equitably and efficiently'.[34] The problems of definition were acknowledged,[35] but an agreed definition of the mentally disordered offender under the strategy was outlined. It covers people with mental health problems who offend, which is extremely wide and includes those with acute mental health problems as defined under the Mental Health Act 1983, and also people with mental health problems linked to alcohol/substance misuse, or with significant behavioural/psychological problems. The aim of the strategy was to develop co-operative working arrangements, pool resources, and share responsibility to further develop services for mentally disordered offenders. Certain targets were set and these include the development of local secure services (including extra beds, staffing and outreach teams), the development of joint risk-assessment and management teams for potentially dangerous offenders, and joint training for all agencies on mental disorder. The essential factor is therefore to ensure that sufficient facilities and multidisciplinary support are available in hospital and the community. In Huddersfield and Dewsbury, therefore, it was decided to begin to develop a coherent service before establishing formal diversion mechanisms, as the Reed Committee noted, diversion schemes are not an end in themselves but form part of a much wider service available to mentally disordered offenders.

It is for this reason that the bid for funding for diversion schemes at Huddersfield and Dewsbury Magistrates' Courts was not submitted until the 1994/5 financial year. A joint bid was submitted to the Home Office early in 1994 on behalf of Huddersfield and Dewsbury NHS Trusts, which was successful. The operation of the Huddersfield Scheme will be considered initially, followed by a consideration of the Dewsbury Scheme (below). The funding included the costs of a part-time CPN to provide a diversion service to Huddersfield Magistrates' Court which began in August 1994. The CPN is based at St Luke's Hospital in

---

[34] Calderdale and Kirklees, *Meeting the Needs of People with Mental Health Problems.* 16.
[35] As noted in Ch. 1.

Huddersfield, which houses psychiatric facilities, and attends the local magistrates' court which is a busy court in Huddersfield town.[36]

5.8.4.2. The Operation of the Scheme

The scheme essentially operates on the NAC Model, whereby the nurse attends the magistrates' court every weekday morning to accept referrals and make assessments. The CPN operates on a part-time basis, and the initial bid did not include funding for designated psychiatrist input, so the CPN would contact the on-call sector psychiatrists when full psychiatric assessments were required. The basic process is broadly similar to the other schemes outlined above and the CPN will first contact the custody area to see whether an assessment is required but will also accept referrals from any other agency at the court. No formal referral criteria have been specified, but a Strategy definition has been adopted (see 5.8.4.1.2) which encompasses a broad range of disordered behaviour. Despite this, however, the absence of formal referral criteria raises serious questions about the CPN's level of discretion and the lack of accountability for the diversion decisions, and this issue will be further analysed in the process evaluation section later in the chapter. Should an assessment be required, it will be conducted in the interview room in the custody area. The CPN will proceed only with the defendant's consent, and a standard assessment form is used. Should a fuller psychiatric assessment be required, then the CPN will attempt to contact local psychiatrists based at the hospital. Again, the CPN will present a written report to the agencies concerned to assist the court, and is also expected to liaise with the other agencies to make the necessary arrangements.

5.8.4.3. Inter-Agency Co-operation

A multi-agency Steering Committee monitors the development of the scheme, and is again composed of representatives from all the relevant agencies meeting on a regular basis to monitor developments and guide future direction.

As with other schemes in the region, the CPN has also been requested to provide advice to probation staff and attend the probation office regularly to collaborate on joint risk assessments. Joint training with the police on mental health issues is also a desired objective. However, such developments are time-constrained as the CPN is assigned to the scheme for mornings only, and is required to perform other duties in the afternoon, so there is no opportunity fully to develop the service in this way. However, it is important to note that the Partnership Strategy is in place and by promoting joint training and risk-assessment groups between health, social service, and probation staff, some of the other diversion nurses are enabled to fill these gaps. Part of the Strategy has also been

---

[36] The 1993 annual caseload for the Kirklees Metropolitan Division (Huddersfield and Dewsbury) was 92,051, which is high number in comparison with the other national magistrates' courts' annual statistics.

the development of a forensic service at St Luke's Hospital. This comprises a multidisciplinary team which seeks to provide advice, support, and assessment services to criminal justice professionals and disordered offenders at all stages in the criminal justice system. This operates on a similar basis to the Bradford Forensic Service and aims to provide advice and ongoing support.

5.8.5. Dewsbury and Batley Magistrates' Court: Court Diversion Scheme

5.8.5.1. Background to the Scheme

The establishment of a formal court diversion arrangement in Dewsbury was deferred to ensure that comprehensive services were first in place into which mentally disordered offenders could be diverted. The Dewsbury NHS Trust submitted a bid for funding, and so a CPN was appointed to Dewsbury and Batley Magistrates' Court to provide a part-time diversion service to the court from October 1994. The CPN is based at a local Community Mental Health Unit nearby, which is a similar situation to that at Keighley and Bingley, being relatively small and sited in a less-populated area outside Leeds.

5.8.5.2. The Operation of the Scheme

The scheme operates on the NAC Model basis, with a part-time CPN providing an advice and assessment service to the court every weekday morning. The funding for Dewsbury included duty-psychiatrist involvement, and he is available to conduct fuller psychiatric assessments every Wednesday morning. The scheme operates on the same basis as the Huddersfield scheme, so the CPN attends the custody area and is willing to accept referrals from any agency at court. The assessment normally takes place in the cell area below the court and will proceed only with the defendant's consent. A standard assessment form is used and a report including recommendations for mental health care will be forwarded to all agencies concerned. The CPN in Dewsbury will routinely contact each defendant's GP following an assessment and will notify him/her of the recommendations made. This provides a degree of follow-up after the court appearance which is clearly valuable, as the CPN in Dewsbury is only part-time and so is not in a position to ensure thorough follow-through of cases and on-going support. Similarly, training and advice to local police and probation would be a desirable development, but again, the CPN is constrained by time and does not have the opportunity to provide these wider services. The Partnership Strategy is in place in Dewsbury too, however, and so joint training and mental health advice for risk assessments are provided as part of that.

5.8.5.3. Inter-Agency Co-operation

A Steering Group oversees the overall operation of the scheme, and is again composed of senior representatives from the main agencies involved in the area and meets regularly. The Group has undertaken a variety of local initiatives: for example, in 1995 it established a road show in conjunction with the Huddersfield and Calderdale Groups which was aimed at enhancing the profile of the schemes and further informing other professionals and agencies of the services offered at the court.

5.8.6. Calderdale Magistrates' Court: Diversion of Mentally Disordered Offenders Scheme

5.8.6.1. Background to the Scheme

Following the Conservative Government's invitation for bids for funding, Calderdale Healthcare NHS Trust, which covers the Calderdale Petty Sessional Division, submitted a bid early in 1993. The bid was successful, and so a CPN was appointed to work as the court diversion nurse on a part-time basis. The bid also initially included sessional costs for a duty psychiatrist to attend court to conduct psychiatric assessments one afternoon a week. The scheme operates at Calderdale Magistrates' Court in Halifax town which is in a relatively rural and less densely populated area in the region.[37] The West Yorkshire Partnership Strategy outlined above also includes the Calderdale area, but unlike Huddersfield and Dewsbury, Calderdale Trust were keen to proceed with the bid at the early stage to establish diversion arrangements as soon as possible, and so the CPN was appointed to the scheme in August 1993.

5.8.6.2. The Operation of the Scheme

Again, this scheme operates on the NAC Model on a very similar basis to the Huddersfield and Dewsbury schemes. There are no prescribed referral criteria,[38] but the CPN has issued an information pamphlet which informs the agencies that he is willing to assess any offender whom it is believed is suffering from a mental illness and this is in line with the broad definition within the Partnership Strategy. Assessments are usually conducted in the interview room, or in the cells if the interview room is occupied by duty solicitors. Again, the interview proceeds only with the defendant's consent and a standard assessment form is used. Should the mental disorder be of such a degree as to warrant a fuller psychiatric assessment with a view to arranging in-patient care, the duty psychiatrist will be contacted to conduct an assessment on a Wednesday afternoon. The CPN has full use of the probation office facilities to make the relevant enquiries and again is expected to liaise to make the necessary arrangements.

5.8.6.3. Inter-Agency Co-operation

A multi-agency Steering Group also oversees the operation of the scheme and regularly meets to discuss developments and services for this category of

---

[37] Figures from the Lord Chancellor's Department indicate that the 1993 annual caseload for Calderdale was 36,558.

[38] As noted previously this does raise serious gatekeeping problems, which will be explored fully later in this chapter.

offender. Its members include senior police, probation, CPS, court, and health service representation.

As with other areas, working with police and probation to provide advice and assistance are all desired objectives, but this is difficult as the CPN is part-time only and is required to perform other duties in the afternoons. Latterly, however, the CPN has successfully negotiated one afternoon session per week to provide advice to the local probation service on client mental health issues and provide mental health assessments as part of the pre-sentence report proposals where necessary. This is clearly a welcome development which is in line with the Reed Committee report and enables greater joint working to take place.

With regard to joint training, a component of the Partnership Strategy involves multidisciplinary training sessions, and so a Mentally Disordered Offenders Training Subgroup has been developed in the region as part of the strategy. Consequently, a series of seminars was arranged for all professionals working with mentally disordered offenders in Calderdale and Kirklees, and this included all diversion personnel (i.e. court CPNs) in those regions.

5.9. REGION-WIDE DEVELOPMENTS

The health service, social services, and the criminal justice sector have all been encouraged to prioritize the needs of the mentally disordered offender within their respective service provision. This includes securing that diversion arrangements are in place, but there are also many other supplementary developments which have taken place on a region-wide basis which have further prioritized the needs of mentally disordered offenders. As identified by a recent Social Care Group Inspectorate Report, the needs of mentally disordered offenders should be included within comprehensive community care and mental health service plans, which should focus upon the development of services as well as arrangements for the diversion from the criminal justice system.[39] This chapter will now consider some of the regional initiatives which have been put in place to ensure that mentally disordered offenders are recognized and diverted to therapeutic care wherever possible.

5.9.1. The West Yorkshire Probation Service

The West Yorkshire Probation Service, which covers all Petty Sessional Divisions in the area, has taken an active role in raising awareness and prioritizing the needs of this particular group. This is clearly in line with official policy, as Circular

---

[39] DoH Social Care Group, *Services for Mentally Disordered Offenders in the Community: An Inspection Report* (DoH, 1997).

66/90 emphasized the 'special role' which the probation service has to play,[40] and this was reaffirmed by the Reed Committee report.[41] Indeed, WYPS has been pioneering in this respect, as Circular 66/90 expressly referred to an inter-agency seminar organised by the WYPS in 1989 as an example of good working practice in promoting inter-agency co-operation.[42] There is also direct involvement of probation staff in diversion arrangements, for example, in Wakefield and Pontefract, which also underlines their commitment.

5.9.1.1. Partnership Strategy for Mentally Disordered Offenders

This approach has subsequently been further promoted. A Senior Probation Officer was seconded to the West Yorkshire District Health Authority (which covers Calderdale and Kirklees) to devise a multidisciplinary strategy on developing services for mentally disordered offenders in the region. In line with this strategy, the WYPS has devised a partnership strategy and stated key objectives in dealing with mentally disordered offenders.[43] This is again in line with official recommendations, in particular, Circular 12/95 has expressly asked Chief Probation Officers to consider the needs of mentally disordered offenders when partnership plans are drawn;[44] accordingly, those needs have been explicitly acknowledged. The WYPS strategy outlines several objectives for the service to achieve in dealing with mentally disordered offenders. Among these are the development of Bail Information Schemes at each court and the appointment of five divisionally based, specialist, mentally disordered offender, partnership officers. The strategy also aims to ensure greater inter-agency working between the health and probation service in terms of risk assessment and substance misuse. In its 1994 Annual Report, the WYPS noted that the targets to appoint specialist Probation Officers to deal with mentally disordered offenders in each area and the establishment of further Bail Information Schemes had been achieved, thereby providing a comprehensive service at each court.[45] This is clearly in line with the Reed Report[46] and affirms many of the Woolf and Tumim

---

[40] Para. 26: the Circular urges the probation service to ensure that courts are provided with information and advice to enable them to make use of alternatives to imprisonment and emphasizes the need to co-operate with other agencies to achieve this.

[41] Cm. 2088 para. 11.7, 17, 66; Community Advisory Group Report Paras. 2.22, 3.19: The Reed Committee strongly recommended that probation officers should become involved before a mentally disordered offender has been charged with an offence and that increased use should be made of psychiatric probation orders and bail information schemes.

[42] Circular 66/90, Annexe E.

[43] WYPS, *Partnership Strategy for Mentally Disordered Offenders: Protecting the Public and Developing Provision of Services to Meet the Needs of People with Mental Health Problems who Commit Criminal Offences* (March 1994).

[44] *Mentally Disordered Offenders: Inter-Agency Working*, para. 19(2); see also Circular 66/90, para. 26; Cm. 2088 para. 11.19.

[45] WYPS, *Probation Works and Everyone Benefits Annual Report 1993–94* (WYPS 1995), 22.

[46] Cm. 2088 para. 11.6, 66, Community Advisory Group Report, para. 2.22.

Report recommendations. These Bail Information Schemes and specialist officers provide a valuable contact and referral point for all the CPNs involved at the courts, promoting increased liaison. Indeed, in Wakefield and Pontefract, the Probation representative is an active member of the diversion scheme. Consequently, greater information and advice is provided to the courts across the region by the officers and the CPNs to assist them in making appropriate therapeutic decisions and disposals. This is an extremely valuable development.

5.9.1.2. The WYPS Monitoring Exercise

As a result of NACRO's involvement in the Kirklees diversion project, the WYPS Information and Research Office has developed a data collection system about the treatment and disposal of mentally disordered offenders in the region. This is also a component of the WYPS Strategy which encourages the sharing of information and provides a monitoring system as recommended by Reed. The WYPS routinely collect data from the police, CPS, the courts, and prison about the use of s. 136, rates of discontinuance, and the incidence of therapeutic disposals and transfers. This supplements the WYPS data about the incidence of mental illness noted in pre-sentence reports. Those involved with the diversion schemes have also been requested to provide data about the outcomes of their intervention at court. This information has been requested on a quarterly basis and will enable an accurate picture to be drawn about the treatment of mentally disordered offenders in West Yorkshire and inform future developments.

5.9.1.3. The WYPS Research Project

The WYPS has also conducted research into the mental health of offenders serving community sentences. Much research has been conducted into the mental health of the prison population, but the WYPS felt that very little attention had been paid to that of those under community supervision. Consequently, a study was conducted in conjunction with West Yorkshire Health Authority and the Association of Chief Officers of Probation revealing the extent to which incidents of self-harm occur amongst those with whom the Probation Service is regularly in contact.[47] The study was conducted within West Yorkshire and found that a very high incidence of deliberate self-harm occurs among offenders supervised by the Probation Service. Mental illness was a contributing factor in many cases, consequently the research confirmed that probation staff need to be able to harness health resources to much better effect in work with individual offenders. One of its main aims was to identify this group of people at risk 'to ensure targeted and accessible community care provision'.[48] This again reinforces both the recognition being accorded to the needs of the mentally ill but also the need

---

[47] M. Akhurst, I. Brown and S.Wessely, *Dying for Help: Offenders at Risk of Suicide* (WYPS, WYHA, ACOP 1995). [48] Ibid. 2.

to improve access to services for those with mental health problems in the region. So, despite the developments, the study identified that there is still room for improvement in the provision of appropriate community services for this group of offenders.

5.9.2. The Yorkshire Regional Health Authority

5.9.2.1. The Needs Assessment Exercises

In 1992 Regional Health Authorities were requested by the Department of Health to conduct 'needs assessment' exercises of services for mentally disordered offenders, focusing particularly upon the levels of secure provision which they provided for this category of patient.[49] The Reed Committee recommended that priority should be given to such local joint assessments of need by the agencies concerned for this group, which should be repeated in future years. The assessments would be required to estimate the proportion of individuals who would be required to receive hospital or community care, and in particular the level of secure provision necessary. This would enable the needs of this category to be considered and would determine the required level of services to ensure that their health and social services care needs were fully addressed.[50] It would also ensure that the services were regularly reviewed and developed.

Yorkshire Regional Health Authority (which covers all the West Yorkshire county area and also extends to North Yorkshire) embarked upon this exercise in line with official guidance and the Reed Committee report. The initial assessment was conducted in June 1992,[51] and it confirmed that, given the emphasis upon diversion and transfer, formal diversion arrangements would be developed in the region. As a result, it anticipated that increased pressure would be placed upon the local secure and general psychiatric services. The exercise identified urgent needs and requirements in local secure provision. Accordingly, it proposed major developments and expansion in low-secure facilities and a small-scale increase in the Regional Secure Unit beds in the region which would take place over the next few years.

Again, in 1993 a similar exercise was conducted which confirmed the proposals of the 1992 Action Plan.[52] The 1993 report noted that 'all of the regional action in the plan has been completed or is in train. In particular, an additional 36 beds are being added to the region's collective provision between Jan 94 and November 1995 with developments in Leeds, Bradford and Humberside.'[53] The assessment also focused upon the extent of the diversion arrangements in the

---

[49] NHS Management EL(92)24; see Reed Report Cm. 2088 Annexe G.
[50] Ibid. para. 4.5–7; Community Advisory Group Report para. 4.2–10; Hospital Advisory Group Report para. 5.10.
[51] Yorkshire Regional Health Authority, *Assessment of Need for Services for Mentally Disordered Offenders and Patients with Similar Needs* (YRHA 1992), as per EL(92)24.
[52] Ibid. (YRHA 1993), as per EL(93)68.   [53] Ibid. para. 3.

region. Three Petty Sessional Divisions had by this time established court-based schemes, and plans were underway in the remaining divisions. It was found, however, that the greatest need of diverted offenders was access to general hospital- and community-based treatment and support. Fewer than 10 per cent required some form of low/medium-secure provision. Consequently, the assessment noted the importance of ensuring that sufficient support is provided and that the agencies work together to maintain and develop a range of appropriate facilities.

5.9.2.2. The Section 39 Handbook

The Regional Health Authority has also taken an active role in ensuring that the Reed Committee recommendations are further implemented, in terms of providing guidance and information to the courts about the level and availability of services for mentally disordered offenders. The importance of providing the courts with full and appropriate information to enable them to make therapeutic disposals is imperative. Section 39 of the Mental Health Act 1983 requires Regional Health Authorities to furnish the courts with information as to the availability of psychiatric services. The Reed Committee report recommended that each health authority should take an active role in ensuring that patients who are diverted at courts are admitted for assessment and/or treatment as soon as is clinically required.[54] To this end, Yorkshire Regional Health Authority produced a Section 39 Guidance Handbook for the courts, which ensures that they and other criminal justice professionals are provided with sufficient information as to the levels and availability of local psychiatric facilities to enable them to effect therapeutic disposals. The document was introduced in February 1995 at an inter-agency seminar which sought to increase awareness of the developments in this area.[55] The value of such regional inter-agency seminars was noted by the Reed Committee, who felt that every opportunity should be taken to establish joint initiatives and that locally organized multi-agency conferences provided an important forum 'to stimulate awareness and co-ordinated action'.[56]

The handbook contains detailed information about the services available to the courts and includes details of important contact points to arrange assessment, admission, and treatment. This includes details of all court diversion personnel in the region. It is a valuable source of referral available to criminal justice professionals and further enhances the advice and information provided to the courts, as official policy and the revised Code of Practice accompanying the Mental Health Act 1983[57] prescribes. This is also a welcome development which seeks

---

[54] Cm. 2088 para. 11.41.

[55] Nuffield Institute for Health, *Managing Mentally Disordered Offenders: Meeting the Challenge* (Priority and Community Services Group, Nuffield Institute for Health University of Leeds 1995).   [56] Cm. 2088 para. 10.13.

[57] Para. 3.4, 'Regional Health Authorities . . . should be able to provide in response to a request from a court under section 39 of the Act . . . up-to-date and full information on the range of facilities that would be available for a potential patient including secure facilities . . . [and] appoint a named person to respond to requests for information.'

to improve access to health and social services facilities for mentally disordered offenders in need.

5.9.3. The Area Criminal Justice Consultative Committee

The 1990 Woolf Report on Prison Disturbances highlighted a number of deficiencies within the criminal justice system, amongst which lack of co-operation and consultation were regarded as major flaws. Accordingly, the report recommended that a national forum, the Criminal Justice Consultative Council, should be established, comprising senior members from each agency, to 'ensure that there [is] a proper exchange of information within the criminal justice system and a careful consideration of developments within that system. It would identify and encourage useful initiatives.'[58] In addition to this national inter-agency forum, Local Committees would be required to address the issues and ensure co-ordination at a local level. These Committees would follow the proposals set by the Consultative Council, as well as facilitating local initiatives of their own.[59] In particular, with regard to mentally disordered offenders, the Woolf Report suggested that representatives from the health service could be co-opted to the Committee to address those particular issues.[60] These recommendations were accepted by the former 1979–97 Conservative Government in its resulting White Paper on the future of the Prison Service: 'The Government has decided to establish a Criminal Justice Consultative Council to promote better understanding, co-operation and co-ordination in the criminal justice system'.[61]

5.9.3.1. The Mentally Disordered Offenders Subgroup

The important role which the local multidisciplinary Committees have to play in achieving objectives with regard to mentally disordered offenders was stressed by the Reed Committee report, which recommended that advantage should be taken of this forum to consider the plight of mentally disordered offenders on a regional basis.[62] It is, after all, necessary to co-ordinate action at regional and national levels, as well as locally.

Accordingly, an Area Consultative Committee has been established in the West Yorkshire region, and in 1993 it appointed a Mentally Disordered Offenders Subgroup to consider exclusively the area-wide needs and policy developments for this particular category of offender.[63] The Probation Service was nominated to take the lead role in developing partnership arrangements with the health and

---

[58] Cm. 1456 para. 10.180.   [59] Ibid. para. 10.181–8.   [60] Ibid. para. 10.165–6.
[61] Cm. 1647 (1991) ch. 1.
[62] Cm. 2088 paras. 10.7; 11.19, 125; Community Advisory Group Report, para. 3.31–3; see also the Tumim Report on Prison Suicides, Cm. 1383 paras. 3.30–3, 4.20.
[63] Mentally disordered offenders are also regarded as a national priority for the Criminal Justice Consultative Committee and a number of national conferences have been organized to promote the development of inter-agency arrangements.

social services. Accordingly, the WYPS partnership strategy outlined earlier has played an important part in this process, and this is firmly in line with recent official policy.[64] The group consists of senior representatives from the Probation Service, the CPS, the Magistrates' Courts, Leeds Prison, West Yorkshire Police, and the Regional Health Authority. One of the main objectives is to ensure that services available for mentally disordered offenders are consistent throughout the county area. In furtherance of this objective, the Subgroup organized a Partnership Seminar on Mentally Disordered Offenders in April 1994 to share progress between the four District Health Authority Areas within the county boundary. Senior health service, social services, and criminal justice professionals from across the region attended the seminar to highlight the service developments to date and outline key action points for the future. In line with the Reed Committee report, this provided another valuable opportunity for exchanging information and ensuring co-ordinated action.

The Subgroup meet quarterly to highlight areas for concern, share information, and guide future developments. In particular, the group's concern to ensure consistency resulted in the appointment of a Probation Officer to devise an area Statement of Principles and Practice with regard to court diversion in West Yorkshire. A seminar was arranged in November 1994 to bring together all the professionals involved with the operation of the court diversion schemes. The recommendations of the Reed Committee were endorsed, and an agreed regional policy on diversion was formulated. In particular, based on the CPN's experiences, an agreed definition of 'mentally disordered offenders' for the purposes of diversion was stated and the general referral, assessment, and diversion procedure outlined. This represents an attempt to achieve uniformity in the region so that mentally disordered offenders, no matter where they live or at which court in the region they appear, will receive a broadly similar assessment service. The agreed statement was discussed by the Subgroup and forwarded to all diversion personnel and their respective Steering Groups for their consideration and adoption.

5.9.4. The Local Prisons

Experience has already shown that despite an intention to divert earlier in the process, many mentally disordered offenders may still slip through the net, or develop mental illness once in prison. Furthermore, Circulars 66/90 and 12/95 reminded prison medical officers of the need to sustain and develop the identification and transfer of mentally ill prisoners.[65] It is therefore important to consider the residual role of the prison in relation to mentally disordered offenders in West Yorkshire. First, it must be considered in terms of the facilities and conditions available for the treatment and transfer of those mentally disordered offenders

---

[64]   Home Office Circular 12/95, para. 17.
[65]   Circular 66/90 paras. 23–4; Circular 12/95 para. 19(5).

who are not diverted, or who may become ill once in prison. And secondly, the prison perspective must also be considered in terms of the impact the diversion schemes are making upon the level of admissions and liaison with other professionals in the process. The main local remand prison is Leeds Prison (Armley Gaol), which houses a wide range of prisoners, over half of whom are unconvicted inmates on remand. It serves the Crown Courts at Leeds and Bradford and a large number of the magistrates' and county courts throughout North and West Yorkshire. Full consideration will therefore be given to Leeds Prison, but there is a male remand prison at Doncaster (HMP Moorland) and a female remand prison at Wakefield (HMP Newhall) which will also be considered below.

5.9.4.1. HM Prison Leeds

5.9.4.1.1. The Positive Developments

With regard to the conditions for psychiatrically ill inmates, the report of HM Chief Inspector of Prisons following an inspection of Leeds Prison in June 1994 must be considered.[66] The report was highly condemnatory of the 'deeply unsatisfactory and well below standard' conditions generally in the prison. However, it also focused specifically upon the conditions in the Prison Health Care Centre and the psychiatric facilities provided for mentally ill prisoners.

The report recognised that the new Health Care Centre 'has improved substantially' since the last inspection.[67] In particular, attention was paid to the mentally ill who form 75 per cent of the Health Centre population[68] and on the positive side, the Inspector was pleased to find that visiting psychiatrists 'had seen a dramatic improvement in the care of the seriously mentally ill in the prison in recent years'.[69]

In line with the Reed Committee recommendations,[70] evidence showed that all psychiatric reports were conducted by doctors with psychiatric qualifications and that s. 48 of the Mental Health Act 'was often used'. Indeed, some 37 inmates are transferred to a psychiatric hospital each year under sections of the Mental Health Act, which was possible due to the 'good co-operation with local psychiatrists . . . and regional secure units'.[71] Furthermore, in the light of the recommendations of the Tumim Report[72] and the Reed Committee report,[73] improvements have been made with regard to suicide awareness and related services. Services have been developed to provide further assistance and support to vulnerable and disturbed prisoners, and in the opinion of the Samaritans, the care of the suicidal in the prison is 'very good'.[74]

Such developments are an improvement and are clearly in line with official

---

[66] *Report of an Inspection by HM Chief Inspector of Prisons: HM Prison Leeds* (Home Office 1994).   [67] Ibid. ch. 6.   [68] Ibid. para. 6.37.
[69] Ibid. para. 6.66.   [70] Cm.2088 para. 11.67–9.
[71] *HM Prison Leeds*, para. 6.67.   [72] Cm. 1383.
[73] Cm. 2088 para. 11.82, 105–6, 160.   [74] *HM Prison Leeds*, para. 6.109.

policy, further ensuring that wherever possible mentally disordered offenders in the region are given access to appropriate care and support. The Governor of the Prison Health Care Centre acknowledges that conditions and facilities for those suffering from mental illness do not match those provided by the NHS; however, improvements have been made in recent years and every attempt is being made to identify and transfer those in need of psychiatric treatment. Psychiatrists from local psychiatric hospitals visit the Centre on a regular basis to make assessments and reports and the health care staff reported that a good degree of co-operation is felt to exist between them and the psychiatrists.

Anecdotal evidence from many of the Health Care Officers reported favourable contact with the local diversion personnel, many of whom had been to visit the prison. They felt that this was extremely important as it was essential for the court diversion nurses to be aware of the alternative to diversion—the implications of a remand in custody and the limited psychiatric facilities available in the prison—when considering their recommendations to the court.

Whilst the Officers could not confirm a definite marked decrease in the numbers of mentally disordered offenders entering the prison since the advent of the diversion schemes, they felt that the schemes were making a valuable contribution towards raising awareness and expediting the process of identification and assessment of mentally disordered offenders in the prison.[75] The nurses will routinely contact the prison medical staff when magistrates make a remand in custody (perhaps due to the seriousness of the offence or the danger presented by the offender), but the nurse still feels that psychiatric care is required. This will alert the officers to enable them to secure admission to the Health Care Centre and arrange necessary psychiatric assessment. The Officers were therefore willing to co-operate and provide psychiatric assistance wherever possible to try to ensure that the mental health care needs of these offenders are addressed. It is interesting to note the positive attitudes of the officers, in marked contrast to Joe Sim's account and perceptions of the prison medical service which were noted in Ch. 1.

Diversion schemes have therefore been welcomed by the Health Care Officers as they have improved relations with many health care professionals in the region[76] and hastened the diversion process at this later stage in the criminal justice system. Improvements in this direction have clearly been taking place and it would seem that the diversion schemes are making a positive impact, mirroring some of the constructive developments which have been taking place in the prison in recent years.

---

[75] This has been confirmed by anecdotal evidence from other prisons received by HMCIP. See *Annual Report 1994– 5*, Session 1994–5 HC 760 para. 5.37.

[76] Which is clearly in line with the Reed Report, Prison Advisory Group Report para. 5.33–8, and has also been recommended by the HMCIP, *Annual Report 1993–4*, Session 1993–4 HC 688 para. 5.08.

5.9.4.1.2. The Main Deficiencies

Despite the many encouraging responses and developments, however, HM Chief Inspector's report was also disparaging of many aspects of the service for the mentally ill in prison. Whilst a small minority of the s. 48 patients were transferred to hospital within a desirable time, the majority were left in prison for several months, and the report was highly critical of this delay: 'This is far too long to leave seriously ill people in prison. Pressure should continue to be applied on the relevant NHS authorities to provide a better system'.[77]

Indeed, the report recorded one particular case of a sentenced inmate who was obviously psychotic and in need of treatment but was placed on ordinary location. He was well-known to the services but the NHS were not prepared to offer him a bed: 'He is perhaps another example of the failure of the NHS to provide for this group of patients'.[78]

The Governor of the Health Care Centre has noted that subsequent attempts to transfer are often frustrated by the lack of secure beds available to receive such prisoners. And a study by Rix *et al.* of psychiatric morbidity at Leeds Prison found a high proportion of psychiatrically disordered inmates in the hospital wing (33 out of a total of 36 residents), of whom 10 were awaiting transfer, but the 'transfers were not taking place as soon as was clinically desirable'.[79] Unless adequate funding and facilities are provided, attempts to transfer and divert will be frustrated and this crucial issue will also be addressed later in the process evaluation.

Clearly this is highly unsatisfactory and indicates that there is still much more room for improvement in many of the facilities for and transfer of the mentally ill. In particular, there will always be mentally ill people who will remain in prison, overlooked by the diversion system, and not ill enough to be transferred, and the services provided for them must be comparable to the psychiatric services in the NHS. The Reed Report recommended that prisons should be encouraged to contract-in prison health care from the NHS,[80] and similar recommendations have subsequently been made by HMCIP[81] and the Director of Prison Health Care.[82] In line with this, the 1993 Needs Assessment conducted by Yorkshire RHA incorporated a regional initiative for contracting NHS care into the local prisons to provide better health care, particularly for mentally disordered offenders awaiting transfer. The initiative outlined the need to develop a comprehensive service specification for each prison to be negotiated in partnership with local

---

[77] *HM Prison Leeds*, para. 6.67. [78] Ibid. para. 6.68.
[79] K. J. B. Rix, S. Mitchison, E. B. Renvoize and M. Schweiger, 'Recorded Psychiatric Morbidity in a Large Prison for Male Remanded and Sentenced Prisoners' (1994) 34 *Med, Sci & Law* 324–30, 329.
[80] Cm. 2088 para. 11.16, .84, 211–13; Prison Advisory Group Report, para. 5.25–31.
[81] HMIP England and Wales, *Patient or Prisoner? A New Strategy for Health Care in Prisons: A Discussion Paper* (HO 1996).
[82] Home Office, *Annual Report of the Director of Health Care 1996–97* (HMSO 1998); see also Home Office, *Report of HM Chief Inspector of Prisons 1996–1997* (HO 1998) HC 763.

District Health Authorities. However, despite these well-laid plans and good intentions, this initiative failed to mature into a viable practical solution, and so many aspects of the service provision are still wholly unsatisfactory.

The Reed Committee report also recommended that the Care Programme Approach should be extended to mentally disordered offenders leaving prison,[83] thereby ensuring that a multidisciplinary team have put a package of care in place for a mentally ill person upon his/her discharge from prison. This is also an area where there is a need for further development at Leeds Prison, as the governor of the Health Care Centre maintains that only minimal health care arrangements are made upon release. Normally some form of contact with the discharged prisoner's GP is made which falls dramatically short of the comprehensive care plan envisaged by Reed. The research conducted by Rix *et al.* also identified the need for a more effective system to arrange care plans and aftercare which will not lose their continuity upon release,[84] so this is also an area where reform is required in Leeds Prison.

5.9.4.2. HMP Newhall, HMP Moorland

Although Armley houses the vast majority of remand prisoners from the local courts, there are prisons at Moorland and Newhall which may hold prisoners in the region, and HMCIP has conducted inspections of both establishments in recent years.

With regard to Moorland Prison which was regarded by the Inspector as being 'in most respects impressive',[85] suicide awareness arrangements were particularly commended by the Chief Inspector: 'Given . . . the vulnerable and disturbed nature of many of the young men held at Moorland we felt the suicide awareness procedures and prevention measures were thorough and appropriate. . . . More impressive still was the caring attitude shown by the large majority of staff at all levels.'[86] However, 'not everything was worthy of praise', and the health care facilities were not perceived to be adequate, particularly with regard to psychiatrically ill inmates. As noted in Leeds Prison, the report was highly critical of the time taken to transfer patients to NHS facilities and also strongly recommended the need to provide full-time and permanent psychiatric and psychological input and improved facilities for these inmates.[87]

Similarly, in Newhall Prison, which houses young, female offenders, comparable comments were made by HMCIP in his report. In general, the prison regime was regarded as 'positive, open and stimulating',[88] but the prison regularly held

---

[83]   Cm. 2088 para. 11.16,87,93, 211–13, 11.272; Community Advisory Group Report, para. 3.15; see also NACRO MHA dv. Com., *The Resettlement of Mentally Disturbed Prisoners*, Policy Paper 5 (NACRO 1995).   [84]   K. J. B. Rix *et al.*, 'Psychiatric Morbidity', 330.

[85]   Home Office, *HM Prison and Young Offender Institution Moorland: Report by HM Chief Inspector of Prisons* (Home Office 1994) para. 7.01.

[86]   Ibid. para. 6.62.   [87]   Ibid. para. 6.16, 6.31–6.38.

[88]   Home Office, *HM Prison and Young Offender Institution New Hall: Report by HM Chief Inspector of Prisons* (HO 1992) para. 7.01.

psychiatrically disturbed women and the psychiatric facilities were inadequate. There was an urgent need to improve the accommodation and facilities for this group of prisoners, and the report recommended that additional psychological and psychiatric resources and input were required.[89] The inspection was conducted in 1992, and an extension to the hospital was due to start in 1993, which it was hoped would remedy some of these deficiencies.

On the whole, it would appear that there is still room for improvement in the prisons in the region in terms of the facilities for and transfer of mentally ill prisoners. And whilst some positive developments have taken place, there is still much more work to be done, and this has been acknowledged and recommended by the Chief Inspector in his reports.

5.10. A PROCESS EVALUATION: OVERVIEW

5.10.1. Practical Problems

5.10.1.1. Funding

The two main practical problems which were identified by Blummenthal and Wessely in the national survey of diversion schemes were funding and transport arrangements.[90] In Leeds, without a doubt, the initial inability to obtain secure funding was especially problematic, but all other areas have placed successful bids to the Home Office, and the funding has been renewed in all cases. Indeed, several years later, it would seem that all other schemes in the region are still in receipt of Home Office funding to assist in their operation and development. It is unclear, however, whether the development of the schemes would have been as rapid and as comprehensive had the central Government not made pump-priming funding available.

Looking to the future it would appear that the outlook for most, if not all schemes, is reasonably secure. In Bradford, based upon an initial progress report, the Trust has received funding for the past five successive years and the local NHS Trust is now committed to providing this service as part of its general forensic service provision in the region. Major developments have taken place in Bradford in this area in recent years, the development of the special care low-security unit has formed an integral part of that, and the diversion nurse links in closely with the senior Community Psychiatric Nurse in charge of forensic services to provide liaison and arrange community support and treatment. Together, these services form part of the comprehensive forensic service in the region. This is therefore extremely encouraging and it would

---

[89] Ibid. para. 6.09–10.
[90] S. Blummenthal and S. Wessely, National Survey of Current Arrangements for Diversion from Custody in England and Wales (1992) 305 *BMJ* 1322–5; see also P. Joseph, *Psychiatric Assessment at the Magistrates' Court* (HO 1992) 8.

seem that the future of the court liaison and assessment service is now reasonably secure.

In Wakefield and Pontefract, the scheme has also been partly funded for the past five years by the Home Office and the Mental Illness Specific Grant (MISG), and a further bid will be submitted for 1999. The ASW funding is secure for the foreseeable future by virtue of the MISG to which the Labour Government is still committed.[91] Similarly here, however, should future bids be unsuccessful, it is highly likely that the Trust will continue with the funding as the CPN post is now permanent and the diversion service is clearly regarded as an integral part of the general health and social services in the region. A guide to local mental health services and agencies has been published by the Trust which prominently featured the diversion service as an important element in the mainstream community mental health provision, as the Reed Committee recommended.[92] Discussions with the professionals involved reveal that the Trust is committed to providing this service, irrespective of Home Office funding, and this is extremely encouraging.

The outlook in Calderdale and Kirklees is equally bright for the foreseeable future. The Trusts in Huddersfield and Dewsbury have also been in receipt of Home Office funding since the schemes' inception. Given the earlier difficulties experienced by the Huddersfield scheme, the funding now also includes the costs of a designated duty psychiatrist as part of the scheme, which enables prompter psychiatric assessments to be provided.

It is now highly likely that the local Trusts in Calderdale and Kirklees will continue with the funding should future Home Office bids be unsuccessful, given the commitment to the Partnership Strategy of which the diversion and liaison service forms an important part. In addition, the Government issued express guidance to health service purchasers and providers in its recent NHS Planning and Priorities Guidance for 1998–9 that services for the mentally ill are still a high priority[93] and that they will continue to give priority to developing comprehensive services for this category.[94] This further reinforces the need for health authorities to provide and fund a permanent full-time diversion service as part of a comprehensive mental health service in the region.

However, there is still general uncertainty, which is particularly acute in view of the internal market which now operates within the NHS, which has created further doubt. Indeed, one particular commentator, David Allam, is highly sceptical of the long-term future of diversion schemes.[95] He argues that there is a danger that this subject is suffering from 'compassion fatigue' and that the Government will believe that the problem is being adequately addressed and so

---

[91]   Session 1997–8 HC Debs Vol. 305 cols 505–6 WA.

[92]   Community Advisory Group Report, para. 4.25.

[93]   NHS Management EL(97)39.

[94]   DoH, *Departmental Report: Government's Expenditure Plans 1998–99*, Session 1997–8 Cm. 3912 para. 4.5, 101.

[95]   D. P. Allam, 'Diversion Schemes for Mentally Disordered Offenders: A Service under Threat' (1995) 51 *The Magistrate* 90–1.

pump-priming funding will cease. However, this comes at a time when there is still much more work to be done, as the Mental Health Act Commission has noted in some of its recent biennial reports.[96]

Consequently, David Allam argues that funding arrangements should be formalized by central Government so that the future of such schemes is fully secured. Furthermore, statutory responsibility for diversion schemes should be given to agencies 'thereby leaving schemes less dependent on the motivation of individuals and less subject to the uncertainties of local inter-agency co-operation'.[97] This is an extremely valid argument because the difficulties in achieving inter-agency co-operation are manifold and in many cases the success of diversion schemes relies upon the services of a few committed individuals.[98] Given the 'climate of budget restrictions and competing agendas' where the battle for scarce resources is greater than ever, it is almost certain that 'such individuals would struggle to maintain the enthusiasm of their colleagues to support the schemes no longer pump primed by Central Government'.[99]

The need for a statutory basis is compelling as it would ensure that there is firm commitment to the establishment of such initiatives and assure their future development and success. It would also counteract some of the concerns about the diversion process, such as the lack of accountability, unfettered discretion, lack of confidentiality, and national inconsistency. This will be explored in more detail in subsequent chapters. However, unless and until there is some action taken in this respect, this general uncertainty is a major issue which is likely to impact upon the overall development of the schemes. Where the long-term future is not assured, there is no great incentive to further develop and enhance the service and the performance of certain tasks may be undermined or frustrated as there is no guarantee of resources to support them. This has been identified by other researchers in this area[100] and is an issue which must be addressed if diversion arrangements are to succeed in the long term as part of a much broader comprehensive mental health service.

5.10.1.2. Transport Arrangements

Difficulties are often encountered by diversion personnel in organizing transport for diverted offenders for whom in-patient care is arranged.[101] This was also

---

[96] See e.g. MHAC, *Fifth Biennial Report 1991–9* (HMSO 1993) para. 10.5: 'More than pump-priming money will be needed if diversion schemes are to be preserved, to develop and to become an established feature nationally.' [97] Allam, 'Service under Threat', 91.

[98] See Blummenthal and Wessely, 'National Survey', 1324.

[99] Allam,'Service under Threat', 91.

[100] B. Bowling and W. Saulsbury, *A Multi-Agency Approach to Racial Harassment*, Home Office Research and Statistics Department Research Bulletin, 32 (HO 1992) 37.

[101] See also comments of MHAC, *Report 1995–7* (HMSO 1997) para. 10.8.1. Although it must be noted here that the Mental Health Act Code of Practice places the responsibility on the court to oganize transport to hospital for patients detained under s. 35, 36, 37, and 38 (para. 7.3). Despite this, however, transport difficulties are often felt by diversion personnel.

experienced by the initial Leeds pilot project, as the issue had not originally been addressed by the Steering Group. During the negotiations prior to the commencement of the second project, however, the Steering Group arranged that the police would convey patients where necessary. Thus, transport problems in Leeds were resolved and formed part of the formal operational policy.

Suitable arrangements have also been made in all other areas. All nurses involved are willing to transport the diverted offender as part of the diversion service, and where the offender presents violent or aggressive behaviour, then the local police have been willing to co-operate by providing an escort or secure transport. The diversion personnel stated that no difficulties had been experienced in making such arrangements. In most cases the agreement is informal, having been negotiated by the Steering Groups or between the police and the nurses at court. In Wakefield and Pontefract, however, it is a formal arrangement: an agreed local policy exists between the police, health, and social services in accordance with the Mental Health Act Code of Practice regarding s. 136 and conveying patients to hospital. And in compliance with this, where necessary, an ambulance will be provided and the police are also willing to provide transport for disruptive or dangerous individuals. The Reed Committee recommended that transport arrangements should be formalized in this way;[102] nevertheless, the informal arrangements in all other areas are felt to be working well and the police have been willing to co-operate in all cases where necessary.

5.10.1.3. *Securing Prompt Psychiatric Assessments*

A major difficulty, experienced in Wakefield and Pontefract and also in Huddersfield, is securing prompt psychiatrist assessment and involvement when there is no designated psychiatrist attached to the scheme. This has been problematic on several occasions in Wakefield, when psychiatrists based at the Regional Secure Unit who are on call have been unable to attend, thereby resulting in major delays and defendants being remanded into custody. In Huddersfield, during the first nine months of operation, it was also a major problem as there was no designated psychiatrist, so the CPN has had to rely upon contacting on-call psychiatrists who form part of the mainstream services. This was not satisfactory as many were not able to attend immediately and so mentally disordered offenders who, in the opinion of the nurse, were in need of medical care but were not suitable for bail, would be remanded in custody to Armley. Every attempt would be made to contact the Health Care Officers at the prison to ensure that the defendant's health care needs would be addressed. In Huddersfield this difficulty has been remedied by a revised Home Office bid which now includes funding for a duty psychiatrist, but it has still not been resolved in Wakefield and Pontefract.

This is a major failing which impedes the diversion of mentally disordered offenders to in-patient care. It also serves to emphasize the need to provide a

---

[102]   Cm. 2088 para. 11.218, 11.273.

designated psychiatrist as part of the scheme to provide full psychiatric reports to the court when in-patient assessments and care are required.[103] Clearly, on-call cover is far preferable and should be a requirement, as the other schemes in Calderdale and Dewsbury where duty-psychiatrist involvement is provided have also experienced difficulties in this respect. Defendants not suitable for bail but requiring a psychiatric assessment in court on a Thursday may be remanded in custody until the following Wednesday until the psychiatrist is on duty and a full medical report can be prepared. Again, every attempt is made to notify the prison health care staff, but it would clearly be more effective and efficient if the funding could be redirected to provide psychiatrist input on an on-call basis to avoid unnecessary remands in custody. In Bradford an on-call psychiatrist is provided and the nurse has not expressed any great difficulties in securing prompt assessments and admissions; this approach ensures that mentally disordered offenders in need of in-patient care are given immediate access to appropriate services.

5.10.1.4. Other Difficulties

Apart from these specific problems, discussions with the diversion personnel reveal a general level of satisfaction with arrangements and no other specific difficulties were identified. Full access has been negotiated and given to the police and probation facilities at court to enable the necessary enquiries and arrangements to divert offenders. It would seem that any other minor practical difficulties which have been encountered as the schemes have progressed have been addressed by the Steering Groups. In particular, the provision of holiday cover was an issue which had not originally been considered and so during the first few months of operation many schemes did not have arrangements in place when the diversion nurse was ill or on holiday. This was addressed by the Groups, however, and there are now on-call locum arrangements in place.

5.10.2. Diversion to Where?

This issue is central to the notion of diversion. Thus, it is necessary to ask, in relation to the schemes in West Yorkshire, whether adequate facilities and support exist into which mentally disordered offenders can be diverted. This chapter considers the general level of facilities available in the region at the time of the study, and the perceptions and experiences of the scheme personnel with regard to securing appropriate care. This issue, however, will be further addressed in the following chapter as it will consider in detail the outcomes of the diversion process and, in particular, consider the qualitative data collected by way of interviews with diverted offenders to assess the degree to which they have been given

---

[103] This has also been emphasized by other studies. See Joseph, *Psychiatric Assessment*, and C. Cohen, and G. Midgley, *The North Humberside Diversion from Custody Project for Mentally Disordered Offenders* (Centre for Systems Studies, Hull University 1994) ch. 14.

access to appropriate care and support. The 1992 Needs Assessment exercise conducted by the Yorkshire Regional Health Authority has already been outlined above, which identified the need to increase low- and medium-secure provision within the region. Accordingly, developments have been taking place in this respect during recent years and these will be outlined below.

5.10.2.1. Medium-Secure Provision

Medium-secure provision is available at Newton Lodge in Wakefield which was developed in 1984 as the Secure Unit within the Yorkshire Regional Health Authority following the Butler Committee recommendations. Despite its 67-bed capacity, it is subject to long waiting lists, and demand always greatly exceeds supply. This was one of the problems encountered by the Leeds pilot scheme, and the shortage resulted in remands in custody to Armley on a couple of occasions. Other schemes in the region have occasionally experienced such problems, but, on the whole, admission to the district low-secure provision has been achieved in most cases. The Unit's capacity was increased from 52 to 67 beds in October 1995, in the light of the Reed Committee recommendations. It was anticipated that this would make at least a small contribution towards alleviating some of the problems in this area, although it is doubtful that this will be sufficient, as a study of secure psychiatric services in Leeds has identified significant unmet need in terms of medium long-stay Secure Unit beds in the region.[104] So it is likely that the additional numbers provide only the minimum level of beds required. There are additional beds available at Stockton Hall in York which is a private medium-secure facility. The cost varies considerably however, so admission is dependent upon the willingness of the District Health Authority to make such extra-contractual referrals.

5.10.2.2. Local Secure Provision

In Bradford, the local Trust has developed a 12-bedded Special Care Unit at Lynfield Mount Hospital to accommodate people who require low-security provision in the region. This has been complemented by the development of a 12-bedded forensic unit at the hospital to accommodate the mentally ill who have come into contact with the criminal justice system and are in need of care and supervision. Referrals to the unit can be made by any criminal justice agency. These developments have been mirrored in Huddersfield where the Castle Hill Unit has been developed on a similar basis. It is a low-security intensive care unit based at St Luke's Hospital and also serves Dewsbury and Calderdale. So there is low-security provision which was developed as part of the district strategy in line with the Reed Committee recommendations.[105] Indeed, the Hospital

---

[104] J. O'Grady *et al.*, 'The Provision of Secure Psychiatric Services in Leeds, Paper 2. A Survey of Unmet Need' (1992) 24 *Health Trends* 51–3.

[105] Cm. 2088 para. 5.16: 'Many patients needing in-patient care can be accommodated in ordinary psychiatric provision. But, although many offenders can be managed satisfactorily in "open" wards, there must also be better access to local intensive care and locked wards.'

Advisory Group emphasized the need for every district health authority to 'ensure the availability of secure provision for patients with mental illness or learning disability. This should include provision for intensive care.'[106] And a forensic service has been developed at St Luke's which operates along lines similar to the Bradford service. There is potential access in Leeds to locked wards at Highroyds Psychiatric Hospital; and in Wakefield and Pontefract, Fieldhead Hospital has a special care locked ward with a limited number of beds, which houses those requiring low-secure provision in the region. A research study of secure psychiatric services in the Leeds area identified that the Yorkshire Regional Health Authority has a comprehensive policy on the provision of secure services, and this network of local Secure Units provide useful and beneficial support for mentally abnormal offenders in particular.[107]

5.10.2.3. General Psychiatric Services

Within each region there are general psychiatric in-patient facilities provided at all hospitals—Lynfield Mount in Bradford, St Luke's in Huddersfield, Northowram Hospital and Halifax General in Calderdale, Dewsbury District Hospital, Fieldhead Hospital and Pontefract General Infirmary all have open wards and a range of out-patient services.

Within each district there is also a range of community facilities and support systems available. Community mental health, outreach, and crisis intervention teams and a range of statutory and voluntary drug/alcohol abuse services are in existence to which the court diversion personnel also regularly make referrals. The voluntary services in particular are readily available and team members are aware of these services and will make referrals, in line with the Reed Committee recommendations.[108]

Generally, therefore, it would appear that there is varying provision made within each district at all levels and the s. 39 handbook has outlined the entire range of facilities available to the courts and other criminal justice agencies. It was identified in Ch. 3 and by the Leeds project that there is a great need for specialized psychiatric bail hostels. The author's discussions with other court diversion nurses reveal that finding bail hostel placements for disordered and often disruptive individuals can be a difficult task. Bail hostel staff may be unwilling to accept responsibility for such individuals and, similarly, hospital staff may be wary of accepting an offender where treatment is a condition of bail. Some mentally disordered offenders may not require in-patient care, but without alternative secure

---

[106] Hospital Advisory Group Report, para. 5.37; Reed Committee Final Summary Report, Annexe J.

[107] J. O'Grady, 'The Complementary Role of Regional and Local Secure Provision for Psychiatric Patients' (1990) 22 *Health Trends* 14–16; The value of such units has been echoed by J. Cripps *et al.*, 'Bridging the Gap in Secure Provision: Evaluation of a New Local Combined Locked Forensic/Intensive Care Unit' (1995) 6 *J For Psych* 77–91.

[108] Cm. 2088 para. 4.20.

arrangements the court will remand them into custody. Specialized bail hostels would play an important part in accommodating these individuals and this was firmly acknowledged by the Reed Committee report.[109] Whilst this is an extremely desirable development, no such plans are in the pipeline in the region for the foreseeable future. In the meantime, however, certain court diversion nurses are working with bail hostel staff offering advice and support in dealing with mentally ill residents. The Bradford nurse has developed such relations and other nurses are seeking to promote such support. Fostering relations in this way clearly goes some way towards improving access to bail hostel accommodation for mentally disordered offenders in the region. But only the provision of specialized bail hostels would ensure that the problem is fully addressed.

5.10.2.4. Accessing Facilities

In terms of actually getting patients accepted at these facilities, the nurses have all stated that the receiving facilities have, in general, been willing to accept referrals. This is especially true in Bradford, Wakefield and Pontefract, and Huddersfield where the diversion personnel are all based within the relevant local psychiatric facilities and so have easier access to and improved links with the hospital and ward staff. The only difficulty and delay in the process has been securing prompt psychiatric assessments by consultants for formal admissions. Admission has also been facilitated where necessary in Calderdale and Dewsbury, however, as the duty psychiatrists involved are based at the local facilities and have direct links to arrange admission, and as soon as they become involved, admission can normally be arranged. A range of facilities exist and others have been developed into which mentally disordered offenders can be diverted, and the effectiveness of these facilities will be considered in further detail in the following chapter. The experiences of the diversion personnel, however, would suggest that, on the whole, no major difficulties have been encountered in securing access to local and low-secure care and support. Access to medium-secure provision in the region, however, was not as satisfactory, and this was experienced particularly by the Leeds diversion pilot project.

Where in-patient admission or a package of care is arranged, however, the full-time status of the personnel in Bradford and Wakefield and Pontefract allows them the advantage of being able to provide ongoing support and follow-through of cases to their final disposal. This is an extremely important factor as their full-time position allows them the opportunity to monitor the diverted individuals, report on progress to the court at each appearance, and ensure that support consequent upon diversion is maintained. The nurses at Kirklees and Calderdale are not

---

[109] Ibid. para. 11.6; the need has also been identified by other diversion schemes; see T. Wickham, *A Psychiatric Liaison Service for the Criminal Courts* (Social Work Monographs, Norwich 1994), 29, 42; see also P. Joseph, and J. Ford, 'A Psychiatric Bail Bed in a Residential Sick Bay: A One Year Pilot Study' (1995) 6 *J For Psych* 207–17, whose findings testify to the value of such specialized bail hostels and support their establishment in London.

in the same position and thus are not able to provide such a thorough and ongoing service, although they do try to maintain some contact and monitor progress. This is lamentable, as the Reed Committee repeatedly emphasized the need to ensure that support is sustained.[110] As Philip Joseph has noted, without this continued support and an increase in locked wards and specialized bail hostels, 'there will be nowhere to divert [mentally disordered offenders] to, and there is a danger that court psychiatrists . . . will do little for their patients, simply leading them out of the 'revolving door' and up a blind alley'.[111]

The nurses in Wakefield and Pontefract and Bradford are clearly in a better position to ensure that this does not take place. However, it could be argued that the presence of the Partnership Strategy in Calderdale and Kirklees seeks to ensure that the needs of this category of offender are being prioritized amongst the other agencies and so, even though the diversion personnel are not able to provide follow-through and support, the other services in the district are at least aware of their responsibilities towards mentally disordered offenders.

A final point must be made here, however, which will become clearer in the following chapter when the outcomes of the diversion process and the comments of the diverted offenders will be considered in more detail. As the 1992 Needs Assessment identified, in the majority of cases in-patient/secure care is not required. Where the offender is not suffering from a mental illness of a degree that warrants in-patient care or compulsory admission, all that the nurse can do is simply refer the offender to the appropriate community services. Offenders cannot be compelled to accept community treatment and support, and whilst the CPN is clearly required to have knowledge of the range of local services available and liaise with them to provide care, ultimately, participation is dependent upon the co-operation of the individual concerned. So in most cases the ASW/CPN can only point him/her in the right direction and put the appropriate arrangements in place, possibly as a condition of bail. And whilst a range of facilities exist and staff have been willing to accept referrals, attendance and compliance is ultimately dependent upon the mentally disordered person him/herself. This is an important issue, which clearly raises many questions about the effectiveness of diversion and the need for compulsory treatment powers in the community. The arguments in favour of such a power have already been considered and the obstacles to diversion posed by inadequate community care outlined. Detailed consideration of the need for compulsory community supervision is beyond the scope of this book; however, its absence is clearly an important limitation to diversion. In many cases, the success of diversion schemes in ensuring lasting support and treatment will be dependent upon the diverted individual him/herself. And whilst community services and supervision do exist, these individuals cannot be compelled to comply as there are no powers to treat them in the community. The Labour Government has recently

---

[110] Cm. 2088 para. 5.13, 'Merely finding a placement is unlikely to be sufficient.'
[111] P. Joseph, 'Diversion Revisited' (1992) 3 *J For Psych,* Editorial.

announced major reforms in this area and appointed an expert scoping group to consider the need for and scope of new legislation. This was considered in Ch. 4 and it is probable that the case for introducing some form of community treatment order will be made. The reform process is likely to take some time and until the new Act takes its place on the statute books, all that can be hoped is that the intervention of the diversion personnel at court serves to point these offenders in the right direction and stimulate personal motivation to comply. This issue will be discussed further in the next chapter, when the personal views of diverted mentally disordered offenders will be considered, as the qualitative study revealed that many such diverted offenders felt that ultimately, success depended on personal motivation and willingness to co-operate and comply.

5.10.3. Discretion and Accountability

It is clear that there is a strong element of discretion involved in the diversion process. There are no substantive referral criteria and very few of the schemes operate any formalized procedure or structure. Indeed, research conducted in Canada, where similar developments have been taking place, indicates that the diversion decision is very much dependent upon the perceptions and discretion of individual clinicians.[112] Whilst acknowledging the need to 'provide for the unique aspects and demands of particular cases'[113] the study also recognized the dangers posed by unfettered discretion. Consequently, 'more consistent policies and protocols should be developed concerning a decision that may constitute a significant event in the life of a patient'.[114]

5.10.3.1. The Statement of Principles and Practice

In this sense, the Criminal Justice Consultative Committee Subgroup has sought to inject a degree of consistency and uniformity into the operation of diversion schemes in West Yorkshire. All the nurses involved have formulated, agreed to, and accepted the Statement of Principles and Practice which has been devised. The Statement included an agreed definition of the mentally disordered offender in this context, which is extremely wide, encompassing a broad range of behaviour so as not to exclude any individual who may benefit from treatment or support. This wide definition, however, means that, ultimately, it is still largely a matter of clinical judgement based on experience in each case.

---

[112]   S. Davis, 'Factors Associated with the Diversion of Mentally Disordered Offenders' (1994) 22 *Bull Am Acad Psych.& Law* 389–97. The Canadian study also acknowledged that clinicians are not 'lone actors' in the use of discretion—decisions by the police, prosecutors and judges will also affect the ultimate disposal of the mentally ill offender. See further ch. 4.

[113]   Ibid. 396.

[114]   Ibid.; see also the comments in the House of Lords echoing such concerns: Session 1992–3 HL Debs Vol. 542 col. 725 'the system should be formally legitimized and . . . standards and mechanisms should be formally established even if informally administered, otherwise we shall get inconsistencies'.

An agreed statement on the referral and assessment procedure itself was also formulated. This was the result of mutual discussion with each scheme representative, and so the statement is a broad account of the procedure adopted by all schemes. As can be seen from the accounts above, most schemes do operate on a similar basis. Even so, each scheme employs a different assessment form and report for the court, and so varying levels of information will be collected and distributed. The three schemes operating within the Partnership Strategy area—Huddersfield, Dewsbury, and Calderdale—have sought to develop a common assessment form and thereby achieve consistency within the district. But, whilst all areas do collect the same basic details, they all adopt differing documentation, and some nurses will perhaps conduct a fuller and more detailed assessment.

5.10.3.2. Other Safeguards

Certain other limited safeguards are present in the diversion procedure to guard against abuse. One of the conditions of the Home Office funding was that basic data about the scheme's operation would be collected and submitted at the end of each year, which includes details of the number of recommendations for hospital treatment (out-patient, informal, or formal admissions), the percentage of recommendations followed by the court, and the other decisions by the court. This provides a degree of oversight and monitoring. Many of the Steering Committees act in a supervisory capacity and require the nurses involved regularly to submit details about the assessments and referrals. And finally, the court diversion personnel are required to report progress and account to their respective health, probation, and social services managers, most of whom are also Steering Group members.

As described in the previous chapter, part of this research study included a period of observation at the court. Based upon the author's own observations, anecdotal evidence, and informal discussions with the nurses and other staff at court, it was clear that the ASW/CPNs will not deliberately exclude any person who is obviously in need of help. There is no evidence to suggest that the diversion personnel are acting discriminately or improperly. Indeed, in the majority of cases, referrals are made by the other agencies and the nurse will always consider the individual referred who is giving cause for concern, provided s/he consents to the assessment. Thus, there is a limited degree of scrutiny by the other agencies taking place at the court. In addition the WYPS regularly requests information about the outcomes and disposals from all professionals involved in the process, thereby providing another source of scrutiny and indirect monitoring.[115]

Moreover, most of the schemes, despite the absence of a formal document, have outlined their operational procedure on an information pamphlet which is distributed throughout the courts, the local legal profession, and health, probation, and

---

[115] See Reed Committee Final Summary Report, para. 11.205.

social services. This also aims to achieve a degree of formality and ensure a consistent approach.

Whilst there are some limited monitoring mechanisms and reporting procedures in place, it is argued that unless and until these diversionary practices are placed on a more formal statutory footing, thereby making the decisions more accountable and open to scrutiny, these inherent dangers and discretions will persist. The schemes in West Yorkshire have certain limited safeguards in place, but ultimately it is still an informal process which is dependent upon individual discretion in most cases. However, as the accounts above have shown, each scheme operates on a comparable basis and has dealt with a similar group of offenders, and so there do not appear to be any wide variations in practice across the region.[116] Whilst no evidence of discriminatory practices and wilful abuse was observed or found, there is a clear need to place these decisions on a more formal footing nationally, and one solution would be to give certain agencies statutory responsibility for diversion schemes, thereby opening their decisions to greater scrutiny. This would also provide a firmer foundation for the development of such initiatives and ensure continuity and consistency. The issue will be explored in more detail in the following chapters, where a recent unsuccessful attempt to introduce such a degree of formality into the diversion process will be considered. Suffice it to say at this stage, however, central Government are unlikely to take a lead role in this respect, at least for the foreseeable future, and this is extremely unfortunate.

A final point to note here is that the diversion schemes are concerned only with adult offenders, and young offenders are not included within the referral criteria. Diversion policy is directed only at adult offenders and this is an interesting issue, as the criminal statistics reveal that a great proportion of offenders are in fact juveniles and so it must be asked why they are excluded. It could be explained by the fact that the medical profession is unwilling to become involved with young offenders and label them as 'mentally ill' at such an early age. It can be a controversial label which attracts much stigma. So perhaps psychiatric professionals are more willing to attribute certain behaviour or conditions to the normal growing-up process, and to the changes that occur during adolescence, whereas in adults, where development and growth has reached its maturity, such conditions or behaviour are more likely to be attributable to an underlying mental illness. The exclusion of juveniles could also be explained by the fact that, as Nigel Walker has noted, many of the principal disorders, such as schizophrenia, mania, and depression 'seldom manifest themselves—at least in a clinical degree—until adulthood'.[117] Indeed, his research into hospital orders identified only a very small percentage of juveniles (persons under 17) in the psychiatric population sample.

---

[116] See further the quantitative data discussed in Ch. 6.

[117] N. Walker and S. McCabe, *Crime and Insanity in England* ii. (Edinburgh University Press 1973) 119.

5.10.3.3. *Public Safety and the Role of the Victim*

A final important question related to the issue of discretion is the safety of the public and, within that, the role of the victim in the diversion process. The difficulties in balancing the conflicting interests in this area have already been identified in Chs. 1 and 4. The question is particularly acute in view of the revised Victim's Charter and increasing emphasis upon victim's rights,[118] and the public concerns in the wake of the Christopher Clunis and similar tragedies. Indeed, a Mori poll in the mid-1990s indicated that most people regard the mentally ill as 'axe-wielding maniacs' and that public fear of the mentally ill has increased greatly in recent years.[119] It is therefore important to ensure that these competing rights and interests are balanced in the diversion decision, and that the division personnel are alive to these legitimate and important concerns. Informal discussions with the diversion personnel reveal that whilst there are no explicit/formal guidelines, these factors will be considered and taken into account in assessing the appropriate course of action. This is in line with the guidance contained in the revised Mental Health Act Code of Practice. Part of the mental health assessment process includes an assessment of dangerousness and the offender's risk to him/herself as well as to others. And the nature and seriousness of the alleged offence are also important considerations. It could be argued that the diversion personnel are not qualified to make such difficult decisions; however, it is important to note the limitations placed upon them. They can only make recommendations and offer advice and guidance; the ultimate decision lies with the police, CPS, or in most cases the court. The final determination will be made by these agencies in accordance with their respective codes and criteria, which now place increasing emphasis upon the role of the victims and public safety.

Furthermore, as will be seen in the next chapter, in the vast majority of cases the prosecution will still proceed but at the same time the mentally ill offender is given access to needed services. 'Diversion' is not necessarily synonymous with 'discontinuance', and so it is the exception rather than the rule for the charges to be dropped completely. Even so, should complete diversion be recommended in the form of a discontinuance, once again it is the CPS or the police who will ultimately make the decision, and so the nurse can only guide their decision-making. The rights of the victims are being respected to a degree as the offender is invariably still subjected to the normal operation of the law and justice/due process can be achieved. Moreover, as will be revealed in the following chapter, in some instances the nurses will recommend that an offender should be remanded in custody, due to

---

[118] B. Mills, 'Victims' Influence on the Criminal Justice System' (1995) 51 *The Magistrate* 83, 99; see also J. Shapland and E. Bell, 'Victims in the Magistrates' Courts and Crown Court' [1998] *Crim LR* 537–46; Mental Health Act 1983 Revised Code of Practice para. 1.9.

[119] 'Majority see mentally ill as axe-wielding maniacs' *The Times*, 18 April 1995, p. 4; see also S. Levey and K. Howells, 'Dangerousness, Unpredictability and the Fear of People with Schizophrenia' (1995) 6 *J For Psych* 19–39; id. 'Accounting for the Fear of Schizophrenia' (1994) 4 *J Com & App Soc Psych* 313–28.

the seriousness of his/her offence, the minor nature of the mental disorder, and the danger posed by the offender. So, in this sense, the safety of the victim and the public at large are important considerations in the diversion decision; the nurses are aware of the dangers and will endeavour to ensure that justice is done. This will ensure that there is a minimum of respect for the victims, but a further practical safeguard would be for the police to inform the victims of the diversion decision and seek their views as to the proposed course of action, which would ensure that they are kept informed of the outcome in line with the Victim's Charter and the guiding principles contained in the revised Mental Health Act Code of Practice.

5.10.4. Inter-Agency Co-operation

5.10.4.1. General Issues

With regard to the diversion of mentally disordered offenders, the need to work together and collaborate is regarded as a fundamental requirement and was repeatedly stressed by the Reed Committee during the course of its review.[120] The main thrust of Circular 66/90 was 'the desirability of ensuring effective co-operation between agencies to ensure that the best use is made of resources and that mentally disordered persons are not prosecuted where this is not required in the public interest', which was reaffirmed in Circular 12/95.[121] Hence it is particularly important here to consider the effectiveness of the inter-agency relationships in implementing diversion arrangements in West Yorkshire. Indeed, it is a key factor in ensuring appropriate therapeutic disposals, and so it is important to assess how far this has been achieved.

Achieving inter-agency co-operation is an extremely difficult and delicate task, and much research has been conducted into the difficulties in successfully achieving collaboration and communication.[122] 'Any number of difficulties lie in the path of effective inter-agency co-operation'[123] which must be addressed and overcome if it is to succeed. These difficulties are particularly acute with regard to mentally disordered offenders however. The differing approaches and perspectives of the medical/social work and legal professions and the tensions which exist in this area have already been identified. These disciplines are required to work together to divert the mentally ill, and so their differing traditions, philosophies, and ultimate objectives are additional barriers which must be overcome.[124]

---

[120] Cm. 2088. para. 10.2.

[121] Circular 12/95, para. 10–11: 'active co-operation between all agencies . . . is . . . essential'.

[122] See e.g. G. Pearson, *et al.*, 'Crime, Community and Conflict: The Multi-Agency Approach', in D. Downes (ed.), *Unravelling Criminal Justice* (Macmillan 1992); H. Blagg *et al.*, 'Inter-Agency Co-operation: Rhetoric and Reality' in T. Hope and M. Shaw (eds.), *Communities and Crime Reduction* (HMSO 1988); A. Crawford and M. Jones, 'Inter-Agency Co-operation and Community-Based Crime Prevention' (1995) 35 *Brit J Criminol* 17–33.

[123] Pearson, 'Crime, Community and Conflict' 55.

[124] D. P. Allam, 'Inter-Agency Co-operation: A Geological Fault-Line' (1994) 158 *JP & Loc Gov Law* 147–8.

A study into the multi-agency approach generally has identified a number of common obstacles and areas of potential conflict between agencies.[125] In particular, this research identified the 'formidable difficulties in establishing effective performance indicators'[126] in assessing the effectiveness of inter-agency initiatives. This limitation must be borne in mind here when considering the effectiveness of the diversion schemes. However, the factors raised by Pearson *et al.*'s study will be considered in the context of inter-agency working here.

With regard to the implementation of diversion schemes, there are two distinct levels of inter-agency working taking place. On a formal level there are the Steering Groups, which are composed of multidisciplinary, largely managerial-level representatives who meet regularly to discuss the development of the schemes. The second level of inter-agency working takes place more informally between the nurses and other professionals in and outside court. They operate on the front line, liaising to provide information and make the necessary practical diversion arrangements. The findings of Pearson *et al.*'s research will be considered in relation to both levels of co-operation in turn.

5.10.4.2. Formal Inter-Agency Working: The Steering Groups

The formal Steering Groups are potentially a valuable forum for inter-agency collaboration. The precise composition of each group varies slightly; however, all Groups have representatives from the 'core' agencies—police, probation, and health services—who are all directly involved with mentally disordered offenders and the diversion schemes. The representatives are largely drawn from a senior level—all police representatives are of the rank of Inspector and above, Senior Probation Officers from local offices attend to represent the probation service, and the health service representation is drawn from managers. In addition to the diversion personnel and the Bail Information Officers at the court, this essentially forms the composition of the Steering Groups in Bradford and Huddersfield. The Steering Groups in Dewsbury, Calderdale, and Wakefield and Pontefract are of a broader composition also including social services and housing department representation. In addition, the Calderdale and Wakefield Groups have involved CPS, magistrates' clerk, and court clerk members.

Trevor Locke argues that the choice of 'constituent agencies' is an important factor in the success of inter-agency initiatives. Groups of this nature must 'not be too big to work effectively', accordingly the key agencies should be directly involved and other representatives should be called in when required.[127] In this sense the groups in Bradford and Huddersfield are potentially more effective as they are smaller and involve only the main agencies concerned with the practical implementation of the diversion schemes. Other agencies such as magistrates and solicitors can be consulted when necessary to address issues which may arise. On

---

[125] Pearson, 'Crime, Community and Conflict'.   [126] Ibid. 69.
[127] T. Locke, *New Approaches to Crime in the 1990s* (Longmans 1990) 59.

the other hand, it could be argued that it is important that the membership is drawn from other court personnel and social services representation, because they too play an important part in the diversion process and their views should also be considered in this formal arena. So whilst the Bradford and Huddersfield Groups are smaller and thus have the advantage that issues may be resolved more expeditiously, the other groups represent broader interests and this is also important. After all, the Home Office guidance has been issued to social services departments and court personnel as well, so it is important that they are directly involved in the diversion process. A wider forum also raises awareness of the diversion scheme amongst the other agencies, and groups with a broader representation are perhaps more likely to receive a wider range of referrals.[128]

The need for multi-agency groups to be representatives of the agencies involved was also identified by the research conducted by Pearson and colleagues.[129] In this sense, the presence of managers and senior representatives on the Steering Groups is effective as they are clearly in a better position to truly represent their agencies' policies and approaches.[130] As senior individuals in their own agencies, they are in a position to make the decisions and guide the future policy direction. They are also able to motivate colleagues and subordinates working on the front line and have the authority to deal with the problems which may arise.[131] Clearly this would not be possible if the Groups simply consisted of those who operate at ground level and are not in a position to make decisions on behalf of the agencies without first consulting their managers and senior officers.

Whilst this principle of representation has clear advantages, Pearson et al.'s study also identified a number of difficulties which can be encountered by groups of this nature. A frequent complaint made to Pearson and his colleagues during the course of the study was that 'multi-agency panels were too often located at management level, and hence removed from the actualities of "day to day" work'.[132] The 'unintended consequences' of this are that 'Policy agreements conceived at chief officer level between agencies can therefore sometimes be difficult for "front-line" personnel to negotiate and implement with their colleagues.' Pearson et al. regarded this as a key issue and in the light of the composition of these Steering Groups it is potentially a major barrier to successful inter-agency co-operation. This has not been problematic in West Yorkshire, however, as in many cases the diversion personnel are also members of the Steering Groups and are therefore in a position to ensure that the Group as a

---

[128] See Figs. 5.1–5 which outline the referral sources.
[129] Blagg, 'Inter-Agency Co-operation', 215.
[130] Other research has also identified the need to ensure and preserve management support for diversion schemes. Without it, arrangements can often falter. See C. Hedderman, *Panel Assessment Schemes for Mentally Disordered Offenders,* Research and Planning Unit Paper, 76 (HO 1993) 12.
[131] See also Cohen and Midgley, *North Humberside Project,* 76.
[132] Pearson et al., 'Crime, Community and Conflict', 63.

whole is not divorced from 'the realities' and that the decisions made are capable of implementation. Where diversion personnel are not permanent members, they are still required to attend meetings periodically to provide progress reports, and so this also provides the opportunity to keep the group in touch with the experiences of those who operate the scheme on a day-to-day basis. This also ensures that information and communication has the opportunity to pass freely between both levels.[133]

The nature of the work of each Steering Group has varied and some have adopted a more active role than others. But the range of activities undertaken clearly indicates that the Groups are more than just 'talking shops' or 'rhetorical devices'.[134] Some of them have been responsible for resubmitting bids for funding to the Home Office, developing information pamphlets, and organizing promotional roadshows. This formal arena 'enables agency members to articulate their own specific identities, tasks and responsibilities'.[135] Such activities are in addition to the general problem-solving that also takes place in this forum. The Steering Group in Wakefield and Pontefract, for example, addressed the issue of assessment facilities and negotiated access to the police surgeon's examination room in the custody area at Pontefract. And a wide range of other practical issues must also have been addressed in this way by the Steering Groups.

The Steering Groups are locally based, with representatives from local agencies, and an agreed agenda is formulated each time a meeting takes place. This ensures a formal and 'localized focus' and, as Pearson *et al.*'s research identified, 'Multi-agency initiatives stand more chance of being effective where they are closely focused on specific issues and attuned to local needs and circumstances.'[136] On the positive side, therefore, it would seem that the groups are achieving a certain degree of success. They provide a formal opportunity to discuss the development of the schemes. Their decisions seem to be well-informed and to promote the aims of diversion, and all members are permanent, so that consistency and continuity is achieved.[137]

5.10.4.3. *Informal Inter-Agency Working*

Consideration will now be given to the degree of inter-agency collaboration that takes place on a more informal basis at the ground level, where any difficulties tend to be of a more practical nature. Differing geographical boundaries have been identified as a major obstacle by other researchers;[138] however, there have been no real problems experienced in this respect as all health service Trust,

---

[133] This is also a potential difficulty which has been encountered by other schemes. See Cohen and Midgley, *North Humberside Project*, 76.

[134] Blagg *et al.*, 'Inter-Agency Co-operation', 204.

[135] Pearson *et al.*, 'Crime, Community and Conflict', 57.   [136] Ibid.

[137] Allam, 'Geological Fault Line', 147: 'The worst, and most common, compromise is to send a different representative to each meeting so that continuity of debate and understanding is quite lost.'

[138] Locke, *New Approaches*, 57.

local authority, and petty sessional division boundaries within West Yorkshire are relatively coterminous. Thus, the precise ambit of each scheme's operation has been defined from the outset. The proposed reorganization of the CPS will also ensure that there is greater consistency in future, as the boundaries will be coterminous with police force areas, thereby promoting continuity and closer collaboration.

The diversion scheme accounts indicate that there is a great deal of practical assistance being given to the diversion personnel at the courts. In terms of providing access to administrative facilities and transport, the other agencies have been co-operative and a good rapport was observed between the diversion personnel and the other agencies at the courts. It would appear that the ASW/CPN's are now, in general, well respected at the courts and form an important part of the court structure. This is demonstrated by the referrals which have been made to the diversion personnel by the other agencies at court outlined below.

Statistics were collected from the period of commencement of each scheme until April 1995, when the study drew to a close. The development of the schemes in the region has been somewhat staggered, and some schemes have been in existence for much longer periods. This must be borne in mind when considering the statistics below, as the number of referrals and range of sources will vary according to the length of operation of the scheme.

5.10.4.3.1. Bradford, Bingley, and Keighley

The nurse works closely with the probation service and police to ensure that access to necessary and required services is obtained. The Bail Information Officers at the court conducted a brief review of the diversion service which concluded that 'close links' have been established with the nurse and that the service is valued greatly by all agencies concerned.

The agencies at the courts have welcomed the scheme and have been eager to make referrals and utilize the assessment service. The number of referrals made to the scheme during its first twelve months of operation (April 1994 to April 1995) was 112.[139] Many of these 'referrals' during the first six months came via the nurse's own inspection of the custody records at Bradford. However, as time progressed and the professionals became more aware of the nurse's presence and the services available, increasing numbers of referrals have been made by other agencies at the courts. The chart at Fig. 5.1 indicates the sources of referrals during the period of the study—April 1994 to April 1995—in which the scheme was in operation. The police and probation became increasingly eager to make referrals as were many solicitors, and this is an indication of the increasing awareness of mental illness and the level of inter-agency working taking place at the courts.

---

[139]   The vast majority of referrals (108) were at Bradford where the demand is clearly greatest. The other referrals were made at Keighley (3) and Bingley (1) by the probation service and police.

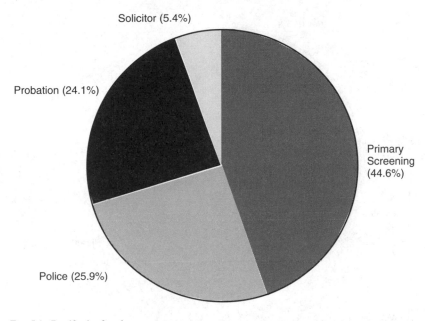

Solicitor (5.4%)

Probation (24.1%)

Primary
Screening
(44.6%)

Police (25.9%)

FIG. 5.1. Bradford referrals

The range of referral sources indicate that those not identified by the police are later picked up by other agencies at court and that referrals were also being made for defendants who are not necessarily in custody, illustrating that the scheme is flexible enough to compensate for problems experienced in picking up referrals at the earliest stage. The same can be seen below with many of the other schemes.

5.10.4.3.2. Wakefield and Pontefract

The inter-agency nature of the scheme at the ground level is perhaps best evidenced by the formal presence of the ASW and the Probation Officer on the diversion team. Together they accepted many referrals from a wide range of agencies, all of whom are willing to co-operate as the chart at Fig. 5.2 illustrates.

A total of 126 referrals were made to the team between July 1993 and April 1995, the period of the study during which the scheme was in operation, by a wide range of agencies both in and out of the courts.[140] The police (custody sergeant) were clearly the main referral source, but as the chart illustrates, the magistrates, solicitors, and other probation/bail information staff were also

[140] The referrals are equally distributed with 66 referrals from Wakefield and 60 referrals from Pontefract.

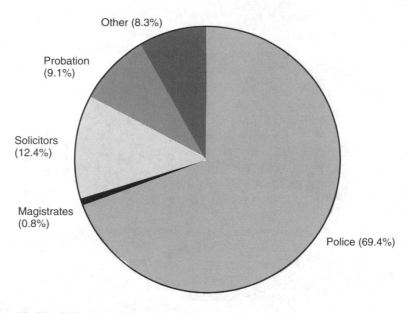

FIG. 5.2. Wakefield and Pontefract referrals

willing to make referrals to the team. In addition, the final 8.3 per cent includes referrals made to the team by other agencies outside the court (social workers and health professionals) who may have had concerns about a client or patient who was due to appear in court.

So referrals are not only made at the courts, but the team are often contacted outside court to accept referrals and provide information. Solicitors, social workers, or other probation officers may have concerns about a client or patient who is under their supervision or due to appear in court, and they will contact the team to notify them of the court appearance. This allows the team an opportunity to obtain any information about that individual's past history in advance of the court appearance, enabling a fuller assessment and more informed decision to be made. And finally, some of the health professionals working on the hospital wards may have a mentally ill patient who has come into contact with the police for whom they require the team's services. Several assessments have been conducted on the wards as a result of a patient's contact with the police. One particular example emphasizes the importance of the team's role in terms of providing information and acting as a link between agencies. Staff on the psychiatric ward at Stanley Royd Hospital (the former psychiatric hospital in Wakefield which has now been closed) were suspicious of a particular in-patient who had been admitted voluntarily. He was an individual who was known to the local services and was potentially violent and disruptive. The ward staff contacted the diversion team as they were extremely concerned, particularly for the safety of female patients on the ward. The team contacted the local police who informed them that this particular individual was currently on police bail and was under suspicion of having committed several attempted rapes in the area. The team then took appropriate action to ensure the safety of the other patients and that the needs of the individual concerned were addressed.

Thus, the team has a pivotal role in providing an interface and link between the criminal justice and health/social services professionals, and they regard the liaison service that they perform to be an integral part of the scheme, a view shared by all other diversion personnel in the region.

5.10.4.3.3. Huddersfield

The level of co-operation taking place at court is again evinced by the willingness on the part of the other agencies to make referrals. A total of 30 referrals were made to the CPN throughout the period of the study—August 1994 to April 1995— during which the scheme was in operation. As Fig. 5.3 illustrates, the police and probation/bail information staff were eager to make referrals, and together they account for 85 per cent of the total number of referrals which were made at court during the period of the study. This is not surprising considering they are far more likely to come into initial and direct contact with defendants in custody.

Other court personnel—CPS, court clerks, and magistrates—also made referrals to the scheme and solicitors became increasingly aware of the assessment

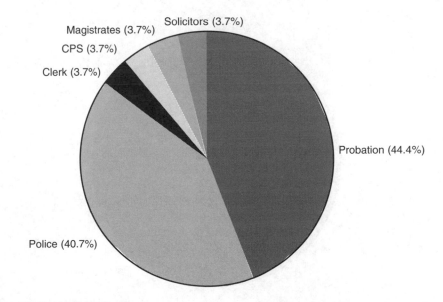

FIG. 5.3. Huddersfield referrals

service. As the chart illustrates, all made referrals, demonstrating that every attempt is being made to work together and identify those in need of mental health care.

5.10.4.3.4. Dewsbury and Batley

The Dewsbury scheme began operation in October 1994 and so was still in its early stages of development at the time of the study (up to April 1995), consequently the referrals at the court are not as widespread as many of the other schemes. The chart at Fig. 5.4 indicates that a total of 27 referrals were made during the scheme's first 6 months of operation, the great majority of which were made by the custody sergeant at the court. Informal discussions revealed that the police greatly value the service offered by the nurse at court and were willing to allow the nurse access to their facilities where necessary.

The figures could indicate that the police are actually identifying *all* those in need of the nurse's services, which would explain the absence of referrals from other agencies in comparison with the other schemes. There is no evidence to suggest that the police in Dewsbury are more effective at identifying mental illness than the other custody officers, however. The most likely explanation is that the scheme was still in its early stages and so was not as well publicized as the other schemes which were in existence over a longer period. Indeed, as awareness of the scheme was generated, several solicitors also made referrals, which is evinced on the chart. At the time of the study, therefore, there was still

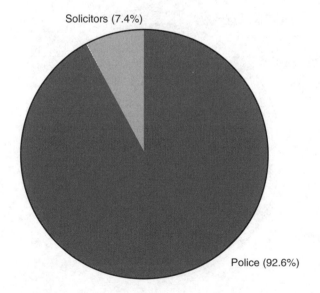

FIG. 5.4. Dewsbury referrals

much more work to be done with regard to raising awareness of the scheme generally at the court. The CPN was attempting to distribute information sheets and develop relations to further publicize the scheme amongst other agencies at court and to promote a wider range of referrals. There was also a change in the diversion scheme personnel in Dewsbury which undoubtedly had significant implications for the implementation of the scheme. It takes time to become a recognized and established feature at the court and to nurture relationships with other professionals, and so the change in personnel may also have accounted for the absence of referrals from other professionals in the early stages, in contrast to the other schemes where there have been no such changes and the referral sources are more wide-ranging.

5.10.4.3.5. Calderdale

During the period of the study, a number of referrals were made from a wide variety of agencies, both at court and also, on a similar basis to the Bradford and Wakefield schemes, the CPN was often contacted in advance by solicitors, social workers or probation staff. The chart at Fig. 5.5 outlines the sources of referrals which were made throughout the period of the study, from August 1993 to April 1995, during which the scheme was in actual operation. A total of 100 referrals were made during that time from a wide variety of agencies.

The majority of referrals came from the probation/bail information services and police, as they are obviously the initial point of contact with the defendants. However, all other agencies at court—the CPS, court clerks, solicitors, and

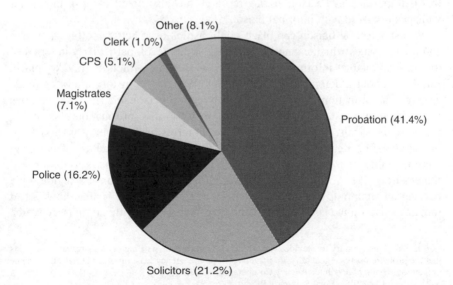

FIG. 5.5. Calderdale referrals

magistrates in particular were increasingly willing to make referrals and this is extremely encouraging. In addition, the 'Other' 8.1 per cent accounts for referrals made to the CPN outside court by social services, hospital staff, and, on a couple of occasions, the police surgeon (FME) at the local police station. This is an indication that the diversion scheme is being well utilized and that mentally disordered offenders are being identified and referred.

As with several other schemes, the magistrates were also willing to make referrals and request the nurses' opinion, and this further reinforces the presence of the nurses at court. In fact, a Calderdale court open day was held in April 1995, and the CPN assisted the probation service with a joint presentation to promote their services at the court, which emphasizes the degree of partnership which has evolved.

Figs. 5.1–5 indicate that the police and the probation staff in particular have taken an active role in terms of making referrals to the schemes.[141] This willingness is perhaps attributed to the fact that inter-agency working is mutually beneficial, and the nurses in turn have been willing to offer advice and assistance to these other agencies whenever necessary. The range of activities which have taken place as a result of the diversion personnel involvement indicate that 'where diversion schemes become established, these come to provide a broader multi-agency focus which, of itself, can make effective disposals easier'.[142]

The front-line relationships are reinforced in Wakefield, as the Operational Group meets regularly to discuss any practical issues which may arise. It consists of team members and the main agencies at the court who come into daily contact with the scheme. This group injects a degree of formality into this process, and this is important, as Pearson *et al.*'s research has also noted some of the disadvantages involved with informal liaison processes.[143]

Whilst informal liaison can place relationships on a better footing, there are significant issues which cannot be resolved at this level, particularly in terms of the unaccountable informal information exchanges which may take place. Enquiries about a defendant's offending and psychiatric history are often made amongst the probation, police, CPS, and diversion personnel. The firm relations which have been established at the courts result in this information often being given freely. Whilst this is to be welcomed in terms of the level of trust and co-operation being demonstrated, it does not resolve the difficulties of ensuring confidentiality of information. Reference has already been made to the agreed Statement of Principles and Practice which has been devised on a region-wide basis in an attempt to ensure consistency and continuity in this area; however, it remains silent on the issue of confidentiality. Consequently this is an issue which

---

[141]   This runs contrary to previous research findings however, as Blagg *et al.*'s research suggests that the probation service generally are perceived to be the agency least involved in liaison on crime prevention: Blagg *et al.*, 'Inter-Agency Co-operation', 209.

[142]   Reed Committee Final Summary Report, para. 5.6.

[143]   Ibid. 205 and see Pearson *et al.*, 'Crime, Community and Conflict', 64.

must be addressed by the diversion personnel and Steering Groups on an individual basis.[144] In particular, the guidance contained in the revised Code of Practice accompanying the Mental Health Act 1983 must be considered, and information should only be passed on in accordance with the guidelines.[145]

It is indeed a complex issue, as it is necessary to achieve a balance between ensuring that the needs of the offender are fully addressed, which can only be achieved if the nurses are in full possession of all the relevant information. But at the same time, the rights of the individuals concerned must be protected and access to certain confidential information must be carefully controlled or denied in order that civil liberties are not infringed. This is therefore a danger which must be recognized and it is argued that central Government should take a lead role in establishing national agreed standards and accountable systems of information exchange between agencies. Limited measures have been introduced with the publication of the revised Code of Practice and Department of Health Guidance on the use of patient information. But these are purely advisory measures, and there should be more direct and formal intervention and safeguards.This again reinforces the need for a statutory basis for such decision-making.

Certain difficulties have been identified in some cases with regard to securing prompt psychiatric assessments by psychiatrists. It is interesting to note the attitude of the Wakefield CPN, who firmly believes that 'it's more to do with personalities than protocol', and despite the presence of agreed protocols, certain individuals will always be more co-operative and committed towards inter-agency working than others.

The effectiveness of inter-agency working has therefore been considered and the evaluation suggests that a degree of communication and collaboration is taking place at all levels. It must be noted however that Pearson and his colleagues have identified a number of other important issues which militate against successful inter-agency co-operation, in particular they noted the significance of gender relations and the 'uneven traffic of power' which often runs between agencies which affects inter-agency relations. The police in particular are a male-dominated profession, and are often regarded as the most powerful agency in inter-agency working, who greatly influence the agenda for action. The author did not observe any significant differences in the relationships or attitudes of the police towards the different diversion personnel, two of whom were female and the others male. A good rapport was observed between the police, other professionals at court, and

---

[144] Evaluations of other schemes have also identified the need to establish formal policies regarding access to files and the exchange of information between agencies. See Cohen and Midgley, *North Humberside Project*, 110–111.

[145] Para. 1.8. The Code reaffirms the patient's right to confidentiality and urges all health care and social services professionals to bear in mind DoH Guidance on the Protection and Use of Patient Information contained in HSG(96)18. The Guidance outlines the circumstances in which information may be passed on, especially where offenders with mental health problems are concerned. See also DoH, *Comprehensive Guidance issued to NHS on Protection and use of Patient Information Press Release 96/68* (DoH 1996).

all diversion personnel, irrespective of their gender. And so on the ground level, it would not appear that gender was a major factor; however, the extent of its influence at Steering Group meetings is not known. The extent of the study did not provide the opportunity to investigate these issues in any great depth, as it was primarily concerned with the effectiveness of diversion rather than an investigation into inter-agency working. Multi-agency co-operation, however, is an important component of the diversion process and so it must be acknowledged that these additional issues identified by Pearson and his colleagues are also important factors which may have affected inter-agency working in West Yorkshire.

5.11. CONCLUSION

This chapter has sought to outline and assess the process of development and operation of the court diversion schemes in West Yorkshire. It has been shown that, in line with official policy, comprehensive and formal arrangements are in place at each court in West Yorkshire. In addition, this research has also identified that all areas now have an agreed s. 136 policy which operates to divert at an early stage in the process.

It has also sought to compare and contrast the different approaches adopted at each court. It was difficult to make appropriate comparisons and generalizations as, during the period of the study, each scheme was at a different stage of development and some were clearly more advanced than others. Generally, they operate on a broadly similar basis and the variations in practice and composition are dependent upon local needs, resources, and demands. However, all schemes provide a basic psychiatric assessment service and advice to criminal justice and other professionals at the court. Those that had been in operation for more than 12 months at the time of the study—Bradford, Wakefield, and Calderdale—had clearly had the opportunity to develop the service further and foster improved relations with the other agencies. The West Yorkshire Strategy, however, clearly aims to fill in some of the gaps in Kirklees and Calderdale by providing a forensic advice and assessment service to the criminal justice system at all levels. Joint training was also developed as part of the Strategy, so that the developments achieved by the other diversion personnel are being accommodated by the Strategy in the West Yorkshire Health Authority District. It would seem that many of the diversion schemes are not simply about assessing mentally disordered offenders at court, but are also aimed at providing advice and assistance at all stages of the criminal justice system. Furthermore, this chapter has revealed that a degree of inter-agency working is taking place at varying levels which has played an important role in facilitating diversion (by ensuring that referrals are made and accepted), accessing appropriate facilities, and improving awareness of the problems faced by mentally disordered offenders.

The process evaluation has revealed that implementing formal diversion arrangements has proved problematic at times and many obstacles lie in the path of diversion, not all of which have been successfully overcome. The major concern is that the future of some of the schemes may still hang in the balance as long-term funding is not completely assured. This raises serious issues about the allocation of funding by the relevant authorities and Trusts and the provision of resources by the central Government. The creation of the internal market within the NHS has exacerbated the difficulties in this area, as services are driven according to market forces, and not according to need. The diversion process is working well in achieving its aims, but much more could be achieved with sufficient political will to fund the service according to need and not supply. It is a political matter how society allocates its resources in assisting its deprived groups, and diversion schemes, which are dependent upon such funding, are also political matters. The mentally ill are a disadvantaged group, but in the battle for scarce resources they will not triumph. It is, after all, far more politically attractive to open a new children's ward than it is to build a secure ward for the mentally ill. And this is the central issue and the most glaring obstacle and limitation to diversion. The policies and the good intentions are simply platitudes without the provision of adequate hard cash to fund the initiatives and provide the appropriate services and facilities on a permanent basis.

Many difficulties and dangers are therefore still present; however, the level of commitment towards mentally disordered offenders in the region must not be underestimated. There is clear evidence of progress, and the range of developments which have taken place both at local and regional levels is highly commendable.[146] Health and probation agencies in particular have acknowledged their responsibilities and taken an active role in promoting diversion arrangements. Direct social services involvement has not been as widespread, however; the scheme in Wakefield and Pontefract is the only initiative with direct social work input. The difficulties faced by local authorities in allocating scarce resources to assist in providing a diversion service have already been recognized in the previous chapter,[147] but this is clearly an area where social services also have a responsibility and should therefore accept it, provided of course, that the Government is prepared to provide local authorities with sufficient funding to achieve this.

These schemes represent an attempt to identify, assess, and divert mentally disordered offenders into therapeutic care, and it will be seen in the next chapter how far they have actually succeeded in doing so and whether the other half of the Reed equation has been put in place.

---

[146] Reed Committee Final Summary Report para. 10.3.
[147] See further ch. 4 and also Session 1992–3 HL Debs Vol. 524 col. 731 'mentally disordered offenders will have to compete with others in need for scarce Local Authority money'.

6

Diversion in West Yorkshire: An Impact Study

6.1 INTRODUCTION

This chapter is concerned with assessing the *impact* of diversion in West Yorkshire, and it will essentially be considering whether the diversion schemes are actually providing mentally disordered offenders with access to appropriate health and social services care. It has already been shown that therapeutic disposals are preferable to custodial measures wherever possible and appropriate, and so this chapter examines to what extent the diversion schemes in West Yorkshire, which share this aim, are actually achieving it.

This impact assessment exercise is divided into two parts.[1] The first involves a consideration of the quantitative data collected from the court diversion personnel throughout the period of the study. This data outlines the basic demographic details of the diverted offenders assessed at court. In particular it indicates the index offences and any previous psychiatric and/or offending history. This will enable a profile to be constructed of the types of mentally disordered offenders who are being referred to and assessed as part of the schemes. This is significant, as the decision of suitable and appropriate candidates for diversion is an important one to ensure that resources are properly utilized and not wasted. This data also reveals the outcomes of the diversion process—the number of discontinuances, therapeutic remands, and disposals and precisely what was achieved in each case as a result of the CPN's involvement—and was supplemented by quantitative data from the West Yorkshire Probation Service on the incidence of therapeutic disposals. This also indicates the impact that the diversion schemes are making upon the levels of therapeutic disposals being made in the magistrates' courts in West Yorkshire. Considered as a whole, this data will enable an assessment to be made as to whether mentally disordered offenders are being given access to appropriate care and treatment.

The second part of the assessment exercise involves a consideration of the qualitative data obtained through a series of semi-structured interviews with a sample of mentally disordered offenders who have been assessed and diverted by the schemes. Their views were sought as to the impact that the diversion personnel's

---

[1] The methodology of this research was outlined in Ch. 5.

involvement had made, to what extent they had maintained contact with the services, and a comparison with previous sentencing outcomes where applicable. This evaluation will further inform the analysis of the effectiveness of diversion in West Yorkshire.

This evaluation will not be concerned with the diversion project operating at Leeds Magistrates' Court, as that formed part of a separate study and no appropriate comparisons can be made. This chapter will therefore focus upon the impact of the diversion schemes operating at all other courts in the region— Bradford (Bingley/Keighley), Calderdale, Dewsbury/Batley, Huddersfield, and Wakefield and Pontefract Magistrates' Courts.

6.2 PART ONE: THE QUANTITATIVE ANALYSIS

6.2.1. Distribution of Demographic Characteristics

Initial consideration will be given to the basic demographic characteristics of the offenders assessed by the diversion personnel. This will enable a general profile of the types of offender being diverted by the schemes in West Yorkshire to be constructed and comparison to be made with the offenders being diverted by other schemes in operation throughout the country. Tables 6.1–4 illustrate the gender and age distribution, marital and employment status of all the offenders diverted by each of the diversion schemes throughout the period of the study.[2]

TABLE 6.1. *Gender*

	Male		Female		TOTAL
	%	N	%	N	N
Bradford	87	41	13	6	47
Calderdale	90	90	10	10	100
Dewsbury	93	25	7	2	27
Huddersfield	90	27	10	3	30
Wakefield	85	107	15	19	126
Average	89	—	11	—	—

[2] This data was compiled from the records of the diversion personnel who all collected this basic information on the standard assessment form. In all but one area, the details for all offenders assessed were collected, irrespective of whether diversion arrangements were made. However, in Bradford the data was only recorded by the nurse for those offenders for whom arrangements were made. Where there was only a referral, a brief assessment, or a refusal to co-operate, and no other arrangements made, the information was not recorded by the CPN. These individuals were primarily those whom the nurse had identified in the primary screening process. So, the Bradford data applies only for those for whom some form of arrangements were made and is therefore incomplete to this extent, in comparison with the data from all the other schemes.

TABLE 6.2. *Marital status*

	Single		Married	
	%	N	%	N
Bradford	89	42	11	5
Calderdale	86	86	14	14
Dewsbury	85	23	15	4
Huddersfield	87	26	13	4
Wakefield	92	116	8	10
Average	88	—	12	

Note: Figures in the 'Single' column include a small minority who were divorced/separated.

TABLE 6.3. *Employment status*

	Unemployed		Employed	
	%	N	%	N
Bradford	94	44	6	3
Calderdale	88	88	12	12
Dewsbury	89	24	11	3
Huddersfield	93	28	7	2
Wakefield	94	119	6	7
Average	92	—	8	—

TABLE 6.4. *Age distribution*

	18+		20–9		30–9		40–9		50+	
	%	N	%	N	%	N	%	N	%	N
Bradford	9	4	45	21	23	11	21	10	2	1
Calderdale	8	8	51	51	20	20	11	11	10	10
Dewsbury	18	5	38	10	18	5	18	5	8	2
Huddersfield	23	7	33	10	23	7	17	5	4	1
Wakefield	9	11	48	60	17	22	17	22	9	11
Average	13	—	43	—	20	—	17	—	7	—

6.2.2. The Client Profile

Tables 6.1–4 above reveal that the vast majority of offenders referred to and assessed by the diversion personnel were single, young, male, unemployed adults. Single, unemployed males account for 90 per cent of the total client population on average, and in all areas, 56 per cent of the total population is under 30 years of age. Table 6.3 indicates a high level of unemployment (approximately 90 per cent in all areas) amongst the client population. A recent study into suicides in Bristol found that socio-economic deprivation is strongly associated with psychiatric morbidity.[3] So, there is a possible link between unemployment and mental illness and this may be reflected in the data.

The fact that there is such a small percentage of females is, in one sense, to be welcomed, as it is generally accepted that female offenders are over-represented in the psychiatric population. Women are far more likely to be to be referred for psychiatric treatment and a higher proportion are admitted to Special Hospitals.[4] It is clear that this is not the case in this sample. The low proportion of females in the client group is comparable with the general crime statistics, however, as women form a small proportion of the total number of offenders in comparison with the total female population.[5]

The pattern in the Tables is not analogous with the general population of West Yorkshire, however. The figures in the 1991 Census disclose that the resident population comprises a far greater percentage of female and employed residents. Of a total of 1,991,540 residents, 51.7 per cent were women,[6] and over 60 per cent of the total general population were in full- or part-time employment.[7] So the diversion population does not accurately reflect the local population, but, in comparison with the data available from other diversion schemes, it would seem that it is indeed the normal pattern.

For example, Philip Joseph's study of a psychiatric assessment service at magistrates' courts in London found that 84 per cent of those assessed were single males and a further 57 per cent were aged 30 and under.[8] This is mirrored in Hull, Reading, Hertfordshire, Bolton, and Manchester where similar studies into diversion schemes identified the majority of clients from predominantly the same groups.[9] So it would seem that the distribution found in West Yorkshire[10] is the general pattern, and as other researchers have identified, although it does not

---

[3] D. J. Gunnell *et al.*, 'Relation between Parasuicide, Suicide, Psychiatric Admissions, and Socio-economic Deprivation' (1995) 311 *BMJ* 226–30; see also R. M. Kammerling and S. O'Connor, 'Unemployment Rate as Predictor of Rate of Psychiatric Admission' (1993) 307 *BMJ* 1536–39.

[4] See further H. Allen, *Justice Unbalanced: Gender, Psychiatry and Judicial Decisions* (Open University Press 1988); A. Morris, *Women, Crime and Criminal Justice* (Blackwell 1987).

[5] Home Office, *Criminal Statistics England and Wales 1996* (HMSO 1997) Cm. 3764, Table 5.8.

[6] Office of Population Censuses and Surveys, *County Report 45: West Yorkshire* (HMSO 1993) Table B.   [7] Ibid. Table F.

[8] P. Joseph, *Psychiatric Assessment at the Magistrates' Court* (HO 1992) 10. The total sample was 185.

[9] C. Cohen and G. Midgley, *The North Humberside Diversion from Custody Project for Mentally Disordered Offenders* (Hull University 1994) 58; T. Wickham, *A Psychiatric Liaison Service for the Criminal Courts* (Social Work Monographs, Norwich 1994) 25; C. Hedderman, *Panel Assessment Schemes for Mentally Disordered Offenders* , Research and Planning Unit, Paper 76 (HO 1993) 15; J. Holloway and J. Shaw, 'Providing a Forensic Psychiatry Service to a Magistrates' Court' (1992) 3 *J For Psych* 153–9; N. Purchase *et al.*, 'Evaluation of a Psychiatric Court Liaison Scheme in North London' (1996) 313 *BMJ* 531–2.

[10] This was also the pattern found in the Leeds project as outlined in the previous chapter.

reflect the general resident population, it is indeed a more accurate reflection of the *general population of people in police custody*, and is therefore to be anticipated.[11] Whilst there is no conclusive data available, Home Office statistics reveal that the offending population is predominantly young males[12] and so it is also generally accepted that the majority of defendants in police custody are young males.

6.2.3. Ethnicity

Much concern has arisen about the over-representation of Afro-Caribbeans among the mentally ill and sentenced population.[13] As well as being over-represented in the prison system, certain studies have identified that non-white mental patients are over-represented among those diagnosed as mentally ill,[14] and are far more likely to be admitted to locked wards, secure units, and special hospitals.[15] Indeed, the Reed Committee produced a special report which considered the care and treatment provided for mentally disordered offenders from ethnic minorities and identified the concerns in this area. Accordingly, it recommended that professionals working in the criminal justice and health systems should be fully aware of these dangers.[16] In particular, it concluded that

The emphasis on multi-disciplinary assessment and diversion from custody is of particular importance to Afro-Caribbeans who statistically are more likely than the general population to be remanded into custody or receive prison sentences. It is important that diversion schemes provide a service which is appropriate and acceptable. This will require the involvement of members of the Afro-Caribbean community in developing the service, as well as the development of staff who are sensitive to the issues of race and culture.[17]

This has to a limited extent been considered in West Yorkshire, as, at the time of the study, the court diversion nurse in Huddersfield, which has the highest resident Afro-Caribbean population, was a native Black African and was, perhaps, more alive to these difficulties.

---

[11] Cohen and Midgley, *North Humberside Project*, 59.

[12] *Criminal Statistics England and Wales 1996*, ch. 5.

[13] D. Browne, *Black Patients, Mental Health and the Courts* (NACRO 1990), id. *Black People and Sectioning* (Little Rock 1997); see also 'Race bias found in diagnosis of mental patients', *Independent*, 8 September 1997.

[14] G. Harrison *et al.*, 'A Prospective Study of Severe Mental Disorder in Afro-Caribbean Patients (1988) 18 *Psychol Medicine* 643–57.

[15] See e.g. R. Cope and D. Ndegwa, 'Ethnic Differences in Admission to a Regional Secure Unit' (1990) 1 *J For Psych* 365–78; D. McGovern and R. Cope, 'The Compulsory Detention of Males of Different Ethnic Groups with Special Reference to Offender Patients (1987) 150 *Brit J Psych* 505–12; S. Davies *et al.*, 'Ethnic Differences in Risk of Compulsory Psychiatric Admission among Representative Cases of Psychosis in London (1996) 312 *BMJ* 533–7; K. Bhui *et al.*, 'African-Caribbean Men Remanded to Brixton Prison: Psychiatric and Forensic Characteristics and Outcome of Final Court Appearance' (1998) 172 *Brit J Psych* 337–44.

[16] DoH/HO, *Race, Gender and Equal Opportunities,* Reed Committee Report, Volume 6 (HMSO 1994) ch. 2, 3, 4.   [17] Ibid. para. 6.8.

Given the controversy in this area, however, consideration will be given to the ethnic composition and distribution of the client population. The offenders were asked to describe their ethnic origin during the assessment and so ethnic details were recorded by all the diversion personnel. Table 6.5 illustrates the outcomes. The figures indicate that the vast majority of those assessed were Caucasian. In comparison with the general population figures, this is indeed an accurate reflection of the local population, as Caucasians (White group) form 91.8 per cent of the resident population.[18] This ethnic pattern is also reflected generally in other schemes.[19] Thus it would appear that there is no significant over-representation. However, there are two points to be made relating to these figures. First, the Census figures show that the largest proportion of Asians (Indians, Pakistanis, and Bangladeshis) reside in Bradford, accounting for 13.3 per cent of the total population.[20] Surprisingly however, this is not reflected in the diversion scheme statistics, as Asians form only 6 per cent of the total client population. Thus, arguably, the Asian population is under-represented; however, it could be that a smaller proportion come into contact with the police. Indeed, national data indicates that the total proportion of Asian remand and sentenced prisoners is lower than that in the total resident population.[21] Several studies, one of which took place in West Yorkshire, have identified that Asians are indeed under-represented in the criminal justice system.[22] Secondly, in Huddersfield, Table 6.5 shows a greater percentage of Afro-Caribbeans and Asians being assessed by the nurse, accounting for 23 per cent and 7 per cent respectively of the total figure. In terms of the Asian population, this does in fact correlate to the Census figures of the local population, as 8 per cent of the population in Kirklees is Asian. Although the greatest percentage of Afro-Caribbeans does in fact reside

TABLE 6.5. *Ethnic origin*

	White		Afro-Caribbean		Asian		Other	
	%	N	%	N	%	N	%	N
Bradford	94	44	—	—	6	3	—	—
Calderdale	95	95	—	—	5	5	—	—
Dewsbury	100	27	—	—	—	—	—	—
Huddersfield	70	21	23	7	7	2	—	—
Wakefield	98.4	124	0.8	1	—	—	0.8	1
Average	91	—	5	—	4	—	—	—

[18] OPCS, *West Yorkshire*, Table J.
[19] See Hedderman, *Panel Assessment*, 15; Joseph, *Psychiatric Assessment*, 11.
[20] OPCS, *West Yorkshire*, Table J.
[21] '*The Ethnic Origins of Prisoners*' Home Office Statistical Bulletin, 21/94 (1994).
[22] T. Jefferson and M. Walker, 'Ethnic Minorities in the Criminal Justice System' [1992] *Crim LR* 83–95: '[Asians] tended to be less involved at every stage'.

in the Kirklees region, they form only 1.8 per cent of the total resident population, which does not correlate to the 23 per cent assessed by the CPN. Arguably, therefore, Afro-Caribbeans are over-represented in Kirklees and whilst no firm conclusions can be drawn from this data it could be interpreted by the fact that, during the course of the study, the CPN in Huddersfield was also Afro-Caribbean and perhaps more sympathetic towards, or more willing to offer assistance, to this group. In view of the disparity and general concerns about the over-representation of this group, however, it is imperative that the diversion personnel are aware of the dangers and seek to achieve a balance in terms of providing offenders from ethnic minorities with psychiatric care and processing them within the criminal justice system.[23]

6.2.4. Previous Psychiatric History

It is important to consider the previous psychiatric history of the offenders, as it indicates how far the schemes are helping those with recognized and enduring mental health problems. During the assessment, clients were asked whether they had received any previous assistance from the psychiatric services. Table 6.6 illustrates the nature of their responses. The figures demonstrate that more than half (64 per cent on average) the offenders had previously made contact with the psychiatric services and so they had identified mental health problems before they came into contact with the diversion schemes. Some responses were more comprehensive than others, so it is not possible to provide a further breakdown of the full nature of this previous contact. However, in general, it ranges from previous long-term hospitalization and in-patient treatment to out-patient appointments and community mental health support. The greater proportion of previous contact in Huddersfield and Wakefield (over 70 per cent) may be

TABLE 6.6. *Previous psychiatric history*

	Yes		No	
	%	N	%	N
Bradford	60	28	40	19
Calderdale	56	56	44	44
Dewsbury	59	16	41	11
Huddersfield	70	21	30	9
Wakefield	75	94	25	32
Average	64	—	36	—

[23] Similar concerns have been expressed by other researchers in this area. See E. Burney and G. Pearson, 'Mentally Disordered Offenders: Finding a Focus for Diversion' (1995) 34(4) *How J of Crim Just* 281–313.

explained by the fact that two large psychiatric hospitals in the region once housed a large mentally ill population. Stanley Royd Hospital in Wakefield has closed its doors within the last few years and Storthes Hall in Huddersfield closed several years ago as part of the 1979–97 Conservative Government's hospital closure and community care plan. Many of the former long-stay patients are now living in the community and, given their increased vulnerability, are perhaps more likely to come into contact with the criminal justice system.[24]

The data also suggests that the diversion personnel are assessing individuals with no previous psychiatric history, but who are also in need of psychiatric assistance. Thus, the diversion schemes are also making an impact in identifying those offenders who may have slipped through the net and not received any help in the past, but who are in need of future treatment and support, or those whose problems may have arisen since their last contact with the criminal justice system.

Again, no definitive conclusions can be drawn from this data, as the precise circumstances of each offence are not known and so the offending may not necessarily be related to the mental illness. It is clear, however, that the diversion personnel are, in the main, assessing individuals with enduring mental health problems who are coming into contact with the criminal justice system. This also correlates to the data available from other schemes where a large proportion of the offenders have a known psychiatric history.[25] And as other researchers have noted, this may suggest that aftercare and community support arrangements need to be more rigorous, particularly upon release from prison or hospital,[26] in order to prevent the mentally ill from coming into contact with the criminal justice system in this recurrent way.[27] Accordingly, despite the presence of wide-ranging mental health services and support systems, the evidence presented here would seem to suggest that there is still no room for complacency, and that there is a need for improved care plans and closer monitoring and supervision in the community in the region.

6.2.5. Previous Offending

A record was also made of any previous offending history and contact with the criminal justice system. Offenders were asked to indicate any previous convictions, and this data was also available from the custody records and prosecution files. Table 6.7. indicates the responses.

---

[24] See NACRO MHAC *Mentally Disordered Offenders and Community Care,* Policy Paper 1 (NACRO 1993).

[25] Hedderman, *Panel Assessment,* 18 (57% previous psychiatric history); Joseph, *Psychiatric Assessment,* 11–12 (70 per cent previous in-patient); D. V. James and L. W. Hamilton, 'The Clerkenwell Scheme: Assessing Efficacy and Cost of a Psychiatric Liaison Service to a Magistrates' Court' (1991) 303 *BMJ* 282–5 (73 per cent with known previous psychiatric admission).

[26] NACRO, *The Resettlement of Mentally Disordered Offenders* (NACRO 1991) 18–19.

[27] Wickham, *Liaison Service,* 35.

TABLE 6.7. Previous offending history

	Yes		No	
	%	N	%	N
Bradford	64	30	36	17
Calderdale	60	60	40	40
Dewsbury	81	22	19	5
Huddersfield	77	23	23	7
Wakefield	69	87	31	39
Average	70	—	30	—

The figures reflect that a much greater proportion of the offenders assessed by the diversion personnel during the period of the study had a previous offending history. There is variation within each district, but it amounts to an average of 70 per cent across the region. A homogeneous pattern is found with individuals assessed by other schemes across the country. Philip Joseph's study for example, found that 77 per cent of the assessed population possessed a criminal record: 'The population were predominantly petty criminals with numerous convictions and short periods of imprisonment.'[28] This is mirrored by the data from other similar diversion scheme research findings.[29]

The data also indicates that a small proportion of the offenders have not been in previous contact with the criminal justice system. This is also significant as it illustrates that the presence of the diversion personnel ensures that these first-time offenders requiring support and treatment will be given access to appropriate services, and not simply remain unidentified and get caught in a cycle of reoffending.

Overall, read in conjunction with Table 6.6, the data in Table 6.7 indicates that the schemes are identifying those with criminal records and psychiatric histories who appear to be passing through the 'revolving door'. This would seem to indicate, as other researchers have noted, that the schemes are targeting a group of individuals who have recognized problems with mental disorder and offending and are in need of help to try to break the cycle of crime: 'This not only indicates a real need for the project, but also that it is working with those with the most intractable problems. This is a crucial observation, because successes with clients with recurrent mental disorders who are trapped into cycles of offending should be regarded as important achievements'.[30]

---

[28] Joseph, Psychiatric Assessment, 12.
[29] Hedderman, Panel Assessment, 16 (76 per cent of those referred had previous convictions; the total sample was 187); James and Hamilton, 'Clerkenwell Scheme', 284 (82 per cent possessed a known criminal record; the total sample was 33).
[30] Ibid. Cohen and Midgley, North Humberside Project, 60.

6.2.6. Recidivism

It has already been noted in Ch. 5 that this study was primarily concerned with assessing the degree of access to therapeutic care as opposed to reconviction and relapse rates. However, rates of recidivism, where available, are clearly an important factor to be considered in assessing the efficacy of the diversion schemes. As a high recidivism rate would suggest that, despite diversion, individuals are not receiving the lasting health and social support they need to break the cycle of offending (assuming that there is a link between the offending and mental health). This may not necessarily reflect badly upon the schemes, but may indicate that there are insufficient support systems available to which offenders may be referred. It has been seen that diversion from the criminal justice system is preferable, but only where sufficient facilities exist into which offenders may be diverted. Given the limited timescale of the study and the fact that many of the schemes had been in operation for less than a year, it was not possible to show the full extent of recidivism. In the light of the information available and to the knowledge of the diversion personnel, however, approximately 10 per cent of the total sample reappeared in custody in the same court and were referred back to the same scheme within the period of operation. Many of these individuals were not sufficiently seriously ill to warrant in-patient care and so community support was arranged. The diversion personnel have observed that many such recidivists are typically non-compliant and have perhaps been unwilling to co-operate with the treatment arrangements, or the illness may be unrelated to their criminal behaviour. And so, despite the good intentions, perseverance, and intervention of the diversion personnel, some individuals will still reappear in court.[31]

Particular cases highlight these difficulties. For example, in Dewsbury, one individual was charged with theft, which was linked to his substance misuse. He reappeared in court and so was referred to the CPN on two separate occasions. On the first occasion, the CPN's intervention resulted in the offender's admission to a bail hostel and a referral to the local drug/alcohol services. This individual, however, was already awaiting admission to a rehabilitation unit in the South of England and was not willing to co-operate with the local drug/alcohol services. He was therefore in breach of the bail conditions and committed a further similar offence. Until he was in a suitable environment and receiving intensive support, he was not able to break the cycle of offending and substance misuse, so there was very little more which the CPN could arrange for him. Contact was made

---

[31] See also D. J. Cooke, 'Reconviction Following Referral to a Forensic Clinic: The Criminal Justice Outcome of Diversion' (1992) 32 *Med, Sci & Law* 325–30, where it was found that 25 per cent of those assessed by the diversion scheme reoffended up to 31 months after the assessment. But it was argued that psychological benefits may accrue, even in the absence of an effect on reconviction rates. See also R. Rowlands *et al.*, 'Diverted to Where? What Happens to the Diverted Mentally Disordered Offender (1996) 7(2) *J For Psych* 284–96 where the reconviction rate for a sample of diverted offenders within a 12-month period in Rotherham was 17 per cent.

with the relevant professionals to try to expedite his admission to the rehabilitation unit. Another case in Wakefield was of an elderly man who was charged with
a minor sexual offence and for whom community support was initially arranged.
He did not co-operate and consequently reoffended and was re-referred to the
scheme. His condition had deteriorated, and so the diversion team eventually
arranged compulsory in-patient admission to a psychiatric hospital, where he
would receive appropriate treatment and support.

Another example in Huddersfield highlights a further difficulty in this area. The
offender was a middle-aged man who was, in the opinion of the nurse, in need of
in-patient care. Consequently, admission to St Luke's Hospital in Huddersfield
was arranged. He was assessed by psychiatrists at the hospital, but they could not
agree upon a diagnosis and the individual concerned was eventually diagnosed as
suffering from a personality (psychopathic) disorder. This condition is generally
deemed to be untreatable under the Mental Health Act and so the individual
concerned was released. His condition deteriorated and he committed a further
offence and reappeared in court. However, this time he was remanded in custody,
but there are no special psychiatric management or treatment facilities available in
Leeds Prison. Liaison between the CPN and the Health Care Centre staff resulted
in a transfer from prison to the secure ward at the hospital, were he could receive
management and support. This clearly highlights another deficiency in this area,
namely the difficulties surrounding the concept of psychopathic disorder, which is
another obstacle to achieving successful diversion as outlined in Chs. 1 and 4.
Personality disorder is a complex and controversial 'illness', for which many
believe there is no treatment. These individuals do require management and
support, however, and their needs must be addressed, as the Reed Committee
Working Group Report on Psychopathic Disorder concluded, and which, it seems
the Labour Government has finally accepted.[32] The Report acknowledged that
there is a need for further research in this area but that there are major gaps in the
treatment of and services provided for this category of offender and that a range of
services and approaches must be developed. This has clearly been identified,
particularly in Huddersfield, and must be addressed if the diversion process is not
to be frustrated and such seriously ill individuals denied access to needed services.
The introduction of the new hospital direction in relation to this category of
offender may go some way towards allieviating the problem. However, this new
power is targeted at serious offenders and, consequently, there may still be difficulties with respect to the disposal and treatment of minor offenders who may be
suffering from psychopathic disorder. It can only be hoped that the Labour
Government's proposals will provide a better solution to these problems.

---

[32] *Report of the Department of Health and Home Office Working Group on Psychopathic
Disorder* (DoH/HO 1994) 41; see also Ch. 1 where the Government's new proposals in this area were
considered. Similar concerns have been expressed by the recent Fallon Inquiry Report of Ashworth
Special Hospital; see *The Report of the Committee of Inquiry into the Personality Disorder Unit,
Ashworth Special Hospital* (HMSO 1999) Cm 4194 ch. 6.

In the light of the limited information available, the vast majority of diverted offenders did not subsequently reappear in the same court during the period of the study, and this is extremely encouraging as it indicates that the diversion schemes are, to a certain extent, putting people into contact with relevant and needed services which are proving useful. It must be borne in mind, however, that the timescale was short, and that the individuals may have reappeared at other courts in the region or outside West Yorkshire, or may have been arrested but not taken into custody, so this data is not conclusive.

6.2.7. Drug and Alcohol Abuse

Drug and alcohol problems alone are not included within the diversion scheme referral criteria. However, they may often be linked to or consequent upon an underlying mental illness, and this will always be considered by the diversion personnel.

A study into the diversion of mentally disordered offenders by Procurators fiscal in Scotland identified drug abuse and alcoholism as major components. Alcoholism was diagnosed in 47 per cent of the total number of diverted cases and drug abuse was a factor in 17 per cent of cases.[33] A study into the incidence of mental illness amongst defendants appearing at a Liverpool magistrates' court also noted the high incidence of drug/alcohol abuse.[34] And this has also been recognized by the diversion personnel in West Yorkshire; drug and alcohol abuse was identified as a major component and contributing factor in the vast majority of cases, as offenders may present dual diagnosis difficulties. The abusive/addictive behaviour may have caused the mental illness or be consequent upon it and is often linked to the offending behaviour. Consequently, multiple referrals to drug alcohol services in addition to psychiatric services were often made. The diversion personnel clearly felt that a good range of voluntary and statutory services exist in the region and that referrals to these services are made and accepted. This is dependent upon the co-operation of the individual concerned however. There is therefore a clear link between drug/alcohol abuse, mental illness, and offending and this must be recognized, and the appropriate services maintained and further developed which are peculiar to the diverse needs of such disordered offenders. This was recently stressed by a Department of Health Inspection Report into services for mentally disordered offenders in the community.[35]

[33] D. J. Cooke, 'Treatment as an Alternative to Prosecution: Offenders Diverted for Treatment' (1991) 158 *Brit J Psych* 785–91, 787.

[34] C. J. Brabbins and R. F. Travers, 'Mental Disorder amongst Defendants in a Liverpool Magistrates' Court' (1994) 34 *Med, Sci & Law* 279–83; see also P. R. Menzes *et al.*, 'Drug and Alcohol Problems among Individuals with Serious Mental Illness in London' (1996) 168 *Brit J Psych* 612–19.

[35] DoH Social Care Group, *Services for Mentally Disordered Offenders in the Community: An Inspection Report* (DoH 1997).

6.2.8. Homelessness

The link between homelessness, mental illness, and offending has been widely noted.[36] Chapter 3 has already identified the difficulties posed by the homeless mentally ill, and the Reed Committee report commented that almost a third of homeless offenders have a mental illness and that special action must be taken to meet the needs of this group.[37] Philip Joseph's study of a diversion scheme in London also found that a large proportion of mentally disordered offenders appear to be homeless. Of the total number of those assessed by the psychiatric assessment schemes, only 28 per cent were living in settled accommodation. The remainder lived on the streets (49 per cent), in squats (8 per cents), or in hostel accommodation (15 per cent).[38]

Given such evidence, therefore, it was anticipated that homelessness would also be a significant factor among the sample in West Yorkshire, but this was not found. Of those for whom data was available, an overwhelming majority (90 per cent) lived in rented accommodation or with parents, family, and friends in the area. None of the diversion personnel expressed any major difficulties in securing accommodation and addressing housing needs and very few of the offenders lived outside West Yorkshire.

This is clearly contrary to Joseph's findings,[39] but it is supported by the data from other schemes in provincial and less deprived areas. In Reading for example, a similar pattern was found, and only a small minority of offenders assessed by the scheme were of no fixed abode.[40] Clearly therefore, the diverted individuals do not require housing support but may have a variety of other health, social, and financial needs. In particular, as has been seen, drug and alcohol abuse is a major problem. Thus it is conceded that there is a much greater visibly homeless population in London. Elsewhere in the country, even in other cities such as Bradford, this is not as evident and housing needs for diverted offenders are not as great.[41]

6.2.9. The Recorded Offence Categories

The alleged offence data is particularly important as it indicates the level of seriousness of the offences committed, which is a significant consideration in the

---

[36] H. Jones, *Revolving Doors* (NACRO 1992); J. Scott, 'Homelessness and Mental Illness' (1993) 162 *Brit J Psych* 314–24; W. Abdul-Hamid and C. Cooney, 'Homelessness, Mental Illness and the Law' (1997) 37(4) *Med, Sci & Law* 341–4; P. A. Zapf *et al.*, 'An Examination of the Relationship of Homelessness to Mental Disorder, Criminal Behaviour and Health Care in a Pretrial Jail Population' (1996) 41 *Can J Psych* 435–40. [37] Cm. 2088, Annexe F para. 8.

[38] P. Joseph and M. Potter, 'Mentally Disordered Homeless Offenders: Diversion from Custody' (1990) 22 *Health Trends* 51–3, 51; see also Purchase *et al.*, 'Evaluation of Liaison Scheme'.

[39] Joseph and Potter, 'Homeless Offenders'.

[40] Wickham, *Liaison Service*, 26 (during 1992–3 of the total sample of 92, only 16 (17.4%) were of no fixed abode).

[41] Indeed, as the Reed Committee, Cm. 2088, Annexe F para. 7, reported, of the 2,073 people identified by the 1991 Census as sleeping rough, almost 50% were in Greater London.

assessment process, because the nature and circumstances of the offence will indicate the level of danger posed by the offender and influence the psychiatric recommendation made to the court. Table 6.8 shows the distribution of offences committed by the defendants assessed by the diversion personnel in West Yorkshire during the period of the study. Some offenders were facing multiple charges; in these cases it is only the most serious charge which has been noted and included.

Table 6.8 illustrates that the distribution of offence categories varies within each region. In Bradford, offences against the person were the most common, accounting for 34 per cent of the total number. In Huddersfield and Calderdale acquisitive property offences form the greatest proportion and account for 56 per cent and 31 per cent respectively of the total number of offences. Finally, the Dewsbury and Wakefield and Pontefract figures clearly indicate that the majority of offenders referred to the schemes committed public order offences, accounting for approximately 30 per cent of the total in each area. There is no obvious explanation for these differences;[42] however, they clearly illustrate that the diversion schemes are not targeting particular categories of offences, but will assess individuals who have committed any type of offence, and each area has a substantial percentage of each category within it.

These statistics are not comparable with the general crime statistics, where motoring offences account for by far the greatest proportion of offences;[43] that situation is not reflected in Table 6.8, where motoring offences on average account for only 3 per cent of the total number in each area. This could be explained by the fact that motoring offences are 'mechanical', in the sense that no mental element is involved, and so mental illness is not such an important

TABLE 6.8. *The present charge*

	DPO%	APO%	OAP%	PO%	MOT%	Other%
Bradford	19	24	34	15	4	4
Calderdale	12	31	16	20	5	16
Dewsbury	7	15	11	33	4	30
Huddersfield	11	56	15	11	—	7
Wakefield	14	21	21	32	2	10
Average	13	30	19	22	3	13

Note: DPO = destructive property offences (include criminal damage and arson); APO = acquisitive property offences (include theft, deception, and related offences); OAP = offences against the person (include grievous/actual bodily harm, indecent assault, and common assault); PO = public order offences (include affray, breach of the peace, drunk and disorderly, and threatening behaviour); MOT = motoring offences; Other includes breach of bail, possession of drugs, and several other specific offences which will be discussed further below.

[42] Although the range of offences could reflect the differing arrest/charging policies of local police forces.   [43] *Criminal Statistics England and Wales 1996*, Table 5.8.

factor with this type of offence. The mentally ill are perhaps also less likely to commit motoring offences as the majority are unemployed persistent offenders and are less likely to own or have access to cars than ordinary offenders.

In terms of the type of offence committed in relation to the gender of the offenders, the data was not available in all cases. However, for those cases for which this information was available, it does not reveal that women commit less serious or violent offences in comparison with their male counterparts. The range of offences committed by the female client group varied greatly, ranging from breach of the peace and minor shoplifting charges to threatening behaviour, arson, and grievous bodily harm. So there is no pattern or direct correlation between the type of offence committed and the sex of the offender.

In comparison with the data available from other schemes, it would seem to indicate that the distribution in Huddersfield and Calderdale is typical. The data from the Reading DIVERT scheme,[44] Philip Joseph's study,[45] and Carol Hedderman's research[46] indicates that acquisitive property offences are the most common.[47] However, these are closely followed by public order, offences against the person, and destructive property offences. The distribution of each category varies greatly in each area, however, and so it is impossible to assert any general pattern of offences.

A further analysis of each offence category in Table 6.8 reveals that it is the less serious offences within each category that apply. Within each area, well over 50 per cent of the acquisitive property offences are theft (mainly by shoplifting), followed by burglary and then robbery. Criminal damage accounts for the greatest number of destructive property offences. The majority of offences against the person are common assaults and minor sexual offences, and charges of malicious wounding and grievous bodily harm form a smaller portion of the total. An overwhelming majority of the public order offences are breaches of the peace and drunk and disorderly charges. Indeed, the West Yorkshire Police data indicates that violent crime accounted for only 4.8 per cent of the total number of recorded offences in the region during the period of the study.[48] The final 'other' category consists largely of breaches of bail and possession of drugs. Indeed, in Dewsbury, 75 per cent of the 'other' charges are breaches of bail. It also includes two instances in Wakefield and Pontefract where the ASW on the diversion team was requested by the police to attend the police station for the purposes of s. 136 to make appropriate care arrangements. So the sample consists of petty offenders in the main.

---

[44] Wickham, *Liaison Service*, 32.   [45] Joseph, *Psychiatric Assessment*, 13.
[46] Hedderman, *Panel Assessment*, 16.
[47] The annual criminal statistics data reveals that the vast majority of notifiable offences recorded by the police are offences against property, and that violence against the person accounts for a very small percentage of all recorded crime: *Criminal Statistics England and Wales 1996*, para. 2.22. And the 1994 crime profile recorded by the West Yorkshire Police indicates that 95.2% of recorded offences in the region were indeed property offences: West Yorkshire Police Authority, *Policing Plan for West Yorkshire 1995–96* (WYPA 1995) 6–7.   [48] WYPA, *Policing Plan*.

However, this 'other' category also includes several more serious charges, amongst which are one each of rape, attempted murder and false imprisonment, kidnapping, and manslaughter. So, the diversion schemes are not exclusively assessing and diverting petty criminals facing minor charges but also those who have committed serious and often violent offences, who are likely to receive a custodial penalty.

Nevertheless, the majority of offences are relatively minor in nature, and according to the principles expounded in the Criminal Justice Act 1991, would not warrant a custodial remand or sentence.[49] However, the fact that many of these offenders do have a mental illness means they may be regarded as unpredictable and unreliable by the court. They may also have loose family ties, previous convictions, and multiple charges against them, and so the court may not be willing to grant bail. These offenders are more likely to be remanded into custody and so the intervention of the diversion schemes is important to ensure against this and to try to make alternative arrangements. As will be seen, this diversion from custody has been achieved in many cases.

Furthermore, although it is highly probable, given the nature of their offences, that many of these offenders would ultimately receive a community penalty, as other researchers have noted, what is important is that 'the community sentences should be linked to help and treatment'.[50]

6.2.10. The Outcomes

The outcomes of the assessment process and psychiatric recommendations to the court will now be considered. The intervention of the diversion personnel takes place at varying stages in the criminal justice process. The diversion personnel in Calderdale, Huddersfield, and Dewsbury do not have the opportunity to follow through the cases to their final disposal and so their intervention normally takes place at the beginning of the formal court process, either at the first bail application hearing or at the disposal hearing if the charge is minor and the defendant is pleading guilty. The diversion personnel in Wakefield and Pontefract and in Bradford adopt a much more proactive and ongoing role and will try to follow cases through to the final disposal, even after several adjournments and intermediary hearings. For this reason the outcomes of each scheme will be considered separately as it is difficult to make appropriate comparisons, given the different levels of intervention and the fact that the information regarding final disposals is not available in all cases. Tables 6.9–14 therefore indicate the psychiatric outcome of the diversion process and also the legal outcome where available. The

---

[49] One of the key principles expounded in the Criminal Justice Act 1991 is that custody should be reserved only for the most serious and violent cases. See M. Wasik and R. D. Taylor, *Blackstone's Guide to the Criminal Justice Act 1991* (Blackstone 1991).

[50] Wickham, *Liaison Service*, 40.

discussion below will also include an overview of the entire range of outcomes across the region to assess the degree to which they have enabled offenders to be given access to appropriate health and social services care and support.

6.2.10.1. Bradford/Bingley and Keighley Outcomes

In Bradford there were a total of 112 primary contacts, 65 of which did not result in any form of intervention taking place. Of those 65, 5 declined the assessment and the remainder did not, in the CPN's view, require therapeutic intervention. So a total of 47 diversions took place in the Bradford area, the precise outcomes of which are outlined below.

The figures in Table 6.9 indicate that a total of 20 in-patient admissions took place during the period of the study, so 42.5 per cent of the total number diverted were given access to in-patient care and treatment. This admission took place at varying stages of the criminal justice process and under various different procedures. In some cases it was effected during the course of the proceedings as a condition of bail or under s. 35 of the Mental Health Act 1983, and the final outcome was not yet known. Additionally, the number of in-patient admissions included several individuals admitted to Lynfield Mount Hospital in Bradford under sections of the Mental Health Act 1983, who were followed through to their final disposal. In 9 cases this was the final outcome of the proceedings and resulted in five psychiatric probation orders and one s. 37 hospital order. In 3 cases patients originally remanded or sentenced into custody by the court were subsequently transferred to Lynfield Mount Hospital under the Mental Health Act. In all these cases the offenders were still prosecuted, but were given a therapeutic disposal or access to psychiatric services at the same time.

However, included in the psychiatric outcomes below are 4 cases where the case was discontinued by the CPS following the nurse's intervention and so the offenders were completely removed from the criminal justice system and diversion in its broadest possible sense took place. The cases which were discontinued resulted in two informal admissions and two formal admissions under civil

TABLE 6.9. *In-patient care—Bradford*

As a condition of bail	5
Under s. 35 MHA 1983	2
As a condition of probation	5
Under s. 48 MHA 1983	3
Under s. 37 MHA 1983	1
Under s. 3 MHA 1983	2
Informal admission	2
TOTAL	20

sections of the Mental Health Act 1983 and account for less than 15 per cent of the total number diverted. The offences committed by these individuals included threatening behaviour, assault, robbery, and criminal damage, so the level of seriousness varied greatly. But they were all cases where the mental condition of the offenders was deteriorating rapidly and discontinuance only took place when the CPS had given full consideration to the case in accordance with Code for Crown Prosecutors[51] and were satisfied that alternative arrangements were firmly in place. So, the case was not necessarily discontinued at the defendant's first appearance.

The remaining 57.5 per cent resulted in referrals to psychiatric services in the community, which are outlined in Table 6.10. These referrals also took place at varying stages, and were always arranged *in addition to the criminal penalty*. In some cases a referral to community services took place as a condition of bail. In cases where the offender was facing multiple charges and had an offending history, the magistrates would be willing to consider granting bail as opposed to a remand in custody where the offender was willing to co-operate with the treatment arrangements. In other cases psychiatric support was arranged as an adjunct to the community penalty imposed by the court. Most of the offences were relatively minor in nature and did not warrant a custodial sentence. So what is important is that the offenders are still prosecuted and punished by way of a community sentence or nominal penalty,[52] while simultaneously being given access to care and treatment.

Overall, it would appear from the data that a substantial number of offenders have been referred to the local psychiatric services in the Bradford area as a direct result of the nurse's intervention, and that the courts were willing to consider the mental health of the offenders in their decision-making process.

TABLE 6.10. *Community support—Bradford*

Referral to drug/ alcohol services	18
Referral to community mental health team	8
Out-patient appointment arranged	1
TOTAL	27

6.2.10.2 Calderdale Outcomes

The 'assessment only' category in Table 6.11 indicates that the offender did not require therapeutic intervention, and so the figures reveal that some form of diversion was effected in 65 per cent of cases. Much of the CPN's final intervention took place at the bail application stage thereby enabling offenders to be

---

[51] See Ch. 3.
[52] The court may discharge the offender absolutely/conditionally, bind him/her over to keep the peace, or impose a fine or a community service order.

TABLE 6.11. *Calderdale outcomes*

Assessment only	35
Informal admission as a condition of bail	14
Community Mental Health support	14
Out-patient appointments arranged	16
Referral to drug/alcohol services	16
Remanded for psychiatric report	5
TOTAL	100

granted bail and given access to health care services so that they would not be remanded in custody. Alternatively, the psychiatric arrangements were organized in addition to the community penalty imposed. Although those remanded for a psychiatric report eventually received some form of therapeutic disposal, they were remanded in custody until the duty psychiatrist was available at the court to make an assessment. These final outcomes included one s. 37 hospital order and four psychiatric probation orders. Those requiring in-patient care were admitted to the local psychiatric wards.

This data also includes the outcome following the only case which resulted in a discontinuance by the CPS. The individual concerned was a first-time offender with no previous psychiatric history who was charged with a domestic assault. He was having severe personal difficulties and had suffered a major breakdown which prompted the assault. Following the CPN's intervention a home visit by the Community Mental Health Team was arranged. The offender was extremely distressed and willing to co-operate and on that basis the CPS agreed to discontinue the proceedings.[53]

Again, these figures illustrate that offenders are being given access to health and social support: of those referred, in almost 20 per cent of cases in-patient care was arranged and almost 50 per cent were put in contact with relevant community services.

6.2.10.3. Dewsbury and Batley Outcomes

Table 6.12 shows that some form of diversion took place in 25 cases (almost 93 per cent) as there were only two referrals where no further action was recommended. Of the five patients who were remanded for a psychiatric report, two were admitted informally to the Mental Health Unit at Dewsbury District Hospital by the duty psychiatrist. One person was remanded in custody by the

---

[53] It could be argued here that the CPS were willing to discontinue as it was a domestic violence charge and traditionally the police are reluctant to pursue such cases. However, this was the only situation where domestic violence was involved and in other areas several cases were discontinued where the offenders were facing a variety of other charges, so there is no such relationship between the type of offence and the decision to discontinue.

TABLE 6.12. *Dewsbury and Batley outcomes*

Assessment only	2
Remand in custody	1
In-patient admission as condition of bail	1
Remanded for psychiatric report	5
Out-patient appointment arranged	3
Referral to Community Mental Health Team	2
Referral to drug/alcohol services	10
Referral to GP and bail hostel arranged	1
Referral to RELATE counselling services	2
TOTAL	27

court despite the CPN's recommendations to the contrary, but the CPN immediately contacted the Health Care Centre at the prison to arrange admission as he was concerned about the offender's mental health. So, although diversion was not achieved here, the CPN was playing a useful role in trying to ensure that the offender's mental health needs were addressed in the Health Care Centre and that the damaging effects of the prison environment were minimized.

As noted in Calderdale and Bradford, the majority of psychiatric referrals were made in addition to the community penalty or bail imposed, so that the community outcomes above were not alternatives, but rather supplemented the penalty. In some cases they may have been imposed as a condition of bail or as part of the conditional discharge by the court. In other cases, the court advised the individual concerned to make use of the services and his/her willingness to co-operate may have been be a mitigating factor for the court to consider when imposing the sentence. During the period of the study, there were no cases discontinued in Dewsbury. However, a wide range of referrals have been made by the CPN to a broad range of services. Three (11 per cent) have been given access to in-patient care and 67 per cent were referred to appropriate community services to receive counselling, support, and treatment.

6.2.10.4. *Huddersfield Outcomes*

Table 6.13 indicates that 22 (73 per cent) of those assessed were given access to therapeutic treatment and services as a result of the CPN's intervention. Three individuals were remanded into custody despite recommendations to the contrary by the CPN, but one was subsequently transferred by the Home Secretary to St Luke's Hospital in Huddersfield, due to the intervention of the CPN, under s. 48 of the Mental Health Act 1983. A total of 7 offenders (26 per cent) therefore ultimately received in-patient care, 3 of whom were remanded under s. 35 and, following assessments by the psychiatrist, were admitted under s. 37 of the Mental Health Act 1983.

A total of 4 discontinuances took place following the nurse's intervention, the

TABLE 6.13. *Huddersfield outcomes*

Assessment only	7
Remand in custody	3
Formal in-patient admission (s. 35)	3
Informal in-patient admission	3
Out-patient appointment arranged	7
Referral to Community Mental Health services	5
Referral to drug/alcohol services	2
TOTAL	30

outcomes of which are included in the data above. One individual, whose case was discontinued, was referred to his GP and the community services to receive support. And in the other 3 cases the CPS discontinued the prosecution as informal admission to St Luke's Hospital in Huddersfield was arranged. The offences committed by these individuals were property offences, including burglary, criminal damage, and two cases of minor shoplifting, and discontinuance took place only when the police and CPS had given full consideration to the case and alternative arrangements had been secured.

Again, a wide range of referrals have been made to appropriate community services and in many cases, liaison with the probation service has resulted in 6 psychiatric probation orders being made by the court. This is corroborated by data from the West Yorkshire Probation Service which indicates that a total of 18 psychiatric probation orders have been made in the Kirklees region between April 1994 and March 1995. It must be borne in mind that this also includes Dewsbury and some of these orders will have been granted by the court prior to the establishment of the diversion schemes.

6.2.10.5 *Wakefield and Pontefract Outcomes*

A total of 94 (75 per cent) offenders were offered psychiatric assistance following the assessment by the diversion personnel. In four cases, the team recommended that the defendant was remanded in custody because of nature of the charges and the dangerousness of the offender. However, the team contacted the prison Health Care Centre to arrange admission as they were concerned about the offenders' mental health, which confirms that diversion personnel are aware of the dangers and will consider public safety in making their recommendations to the court. Again, Table 6.14 suggests that referrals have been made to a wide range of services, and similarly, in many cases where community support or informal admission was arranged this was a condition of bail or supplemented the community penalty. In-patient admission was arranged in 27 cases (21 per cent), and formal admission normally took place under the civil sections of the Mental Health Act 1983. Some form of community support was arranged in 67 cases (53 per cent), and this included 4 cases where the team conducted an assessment and

TABLE 6.14. *Wakefield and Pontefract outcomes*

Assessment only	28
Remand in custody	4
Formal in-patient admission	9
Informal in-patient admission	18
Out-patient appointment	21
Referral to drug/alcohol services	14
Community Mental Health services	23
Social Services support	5
Bail hostel placement found	4
TOTAL	126

liaised with the probation service to ensure a bail hostel placement was found. In 3 cases, the ultimate disposal was a probation order with psychiatric treatment which also took place following liaison with the probation service. Table 6.14 also indicates that social services support was provided in 5 cases. Two of these are instances where the team ASW attended the police station for the purposes of s. 136; however, this clearly shows that the presence of the ASW on this particular team enables easier access to social services support. So it would appear that the presence of the ASW on the diversion team has facilitated access to social services facilities, in contrast with the outcomes in all other areas.

This data includes cases which were discontinued by the police and CPS following the intervention of the diversion team. A total of 12 cases were discontinued by the CPS and in a further 9 cases the detainees were released without charge by the police following the diversion team assessment and advice. The team became involved with the police in this way in Pontefract, where the court cells and police cells are in the same building so the team are far more likely to come into contact with those defendants who have just been arrested and brought to the police station for questioning prior to being charged. (In all other courts in the region, the CPNs attend the cells below the magistrates' courts and will be assessing defendants who have already been charged by the police and so are not able to become involved earlier). This shows the willingness on the part of the police to involve the diversion team, and so Wakefield and Pontefract has the highest discontinuance rate in the region accounting for 16.6 per cent of the total number of diversions during the period of the study. Of these discontinued cases, 9 were admitted to local psychiatric facilities either informally or under civil sections of the Mental Health Act 1983. The remainder were referred to the community services. These offenders were facing a variety of charges, ranging from breaches of the peace and public order to assault, theft, and criminal damage. Most were comparatively minor in nature, but where a custodial penalty may have been imposed, the discontinuance was only effected where the police and the CPS had given full consideration to the case, and those admitted as in-patients were clearly in urgent need of treatment. This higher rate of discontinuances suggests that the team in Wakefield and Pontefract is more willing to participate in this way, and that the police and CPS are also more willing to discontinue cases. Even so, it is still a relatively low proportion of the total number of referrals in Wakefield and Pontefract, and the overwhelming majority of offenders were still prosecuted.

6.2.11. The Rates of Discontinuance

The data in Tables 6.9–14 show that the level of discontinuance is generally very low, less than 10 per cent of the total number assessed actually resulted in complete diversion from prosecution. This was only effected in exceptional circumstances, where the disorders have been severe, the condition deteriorating, and/or the offence was extremely minor in nature. Furthermore, the CPS were only willing to discontinue when the public interest had been fully considered, alternative arrangements were firmly in place, and the offender was willing to co-operate. This illustrates that diversion is not necessarily synonymous with discontinuance and that, in West Yorkshire, it is diversion in its narrowest possible sense that is normally achieved. So, here, in the majority of cases, offenders are diverted from custody and granted bail wherever possible to avoid a custodial remand. And they will be prosecuted and a community penalty imposed, but at the same time, the offender will be given access to needed services so that s/he can be supported and his/her mental illness treated. This is also reflected in the data of other diversion schemes, where discontinuance has clearly not been the primary goal.[54] The schemes are achieving diversion in its narrowest possible sense, which ensures that other values within the criminal justice system, such as fairness, due process, and the interests of justice and victims are accorded due respect.

The offender's mental health problem and willingness to co-operate with treatment or attend out-patient appointments are clearly regarded as 'mitigating factors' by the courts. So they are more inclined to grant bail or impose a community penalty to ensure that the offenders' needs are addressed and that s/he will be rehabilitated by being given access to therapeutic counselling, support, and treatment, in addition to being subjected to the normal operation of the law. The primary concern is to achieve appropriate care and treatment by virtue of diversion from custody or imprisonment and not from the criminal justice system, and the primary goal is to ensure that offenders are not remanded into custody or sentenced to periods of imprisonment, but are remanded to hospital, granted bail and given therapeutic or community penalties which ensure access to appropriate care and treatment. The outcomes listed above illustrate that this is taking place. That is not to say that where cases are discontinued it is inappropriate; on the

---

[54] See e.g. Cohen and Midgley, *North Humberside Project*, 71; Hedderman, *Panel Assessment*, 20; but compare Wickham, *Liaison Service*, 39 and Joseph, *Psychiatric Assessment*, 16, where a greater proportion of cases were discontinued by the CPS, accounting for 21.9 per cent and 29 per cent respectively of the total legal outcomes.

contrary, the nature of the disorder and the circumstances of the offence may indicate that it is the most appropriate course of action. And so diversion in its broadest sense is also achieved in a small minority of cases where it is perceived to be the most appropriate course of action in order to maximize care and treatment opportunities, provided of course that due consideration has been given to the other factors and that alternative arrangements are firmly in place.

So it is generally some form of 'therapeutic punishment' that is taking place, and this chapter has shown that this is what diversion really means in this context, which seeks to ensure that the principles of the criminal justice system are preserved but that mentally ill offenders and their need for treatment are equally respected in the process.

6.2.12. Discussion of the Quantitative Data

It can be argued that the quantitative data in the Tables show that mentally ill offenders are being protected from custodial sanctions and being given access to health and social services care and support as a result of the intervention of the court diversion schemes. This takes place at varying levels and at different stages in the criminal justice process. In most cases, those in need of in-patient care have been admitted to appropriate local psychiatric facilities and the courts have been willing to ensure that this takes place. A total of 71 offenders were admitted for in-patient treatment across the region and a further 177 have been referred to a variety of community psychiatric and social services throughout the period of the study. Only 10 offenders suffering from mental illness were recommended to be remanded in custody, and in all cases contact was made with the Health Care Centre in Leeds Prison. In some other cases offenders were initially remanded in custody, due to the unavailability of psychiatrists to conduct prompt assessments, but subsequent attempts to transfer and arrange bail were successful. Even though the total number of diversions in the region is small in comparison with the combined total number of cases at each court during that time,[55] it is likely that there are immense savings in terms of human misery and suffering. And, the primary consideration is to ensure that mentally disordered offenders are identified and given access to health and social services care and support to ensure that they do not suffer in that way. The important role which diversion schemes play in achieving this is to divert *all* mentally ill offenders in need of help to appropriate health care. Those suffering from mental disorder under the Mental Health Act 1983 are given therapeutic disposals and those offenders who are not acutely ill under the Act or who have drug/alcohol problems, but are suffering from other comparatively minor mental health problems, are also directed to appropriate care.

---

[55] Figures from the Lord Chancellors' Department reveal that the 1993 annual combined caseload for all these Petty Sessional Divisions was 332,921 cases. So the total number of diverted mentally disordered offenders account for approximately 0.01 per cent of the total number of cases.

It is extremely difficult to assess the cost implications and whether any financial savings are made to the criminal justice system as a result of diversion. Other researchers assert that there are immense savings in terms of the number of remands in custody that are avoided or reduced.[56] Clearly the cases which have been discontinued in this study have resulted in savings in court time and expenses, but, they have in turn resulted in increases to the health system. However, it can be argued that whilst there are no short-term benefits, if the offenders concerned are given the appropriate treatment and support and do break the cycle of offending, then there is reduced contact with the criminal justice system and there are clearly future savings to be made. This cannot be demonstrated by the study presented in this chapter however.

Whilst the ultimate disposal data is not complete, the Tables suggest that therapeutic disposals and transfers are being made in the region, and this is clearly in line with official policy. Furthermore, statistics from the WYPS reveal that since the introduction of the diversion schemes in 1993, there has been a slight increase in the total number of psychiatric probation and hospital orders in the region.[57] Whilst this cannot be definitively explained, it is perhaps attributable in part to the presence of the diversion schemes, the collaboration which has developed, and the increasing awareness of mental health issues in the area. Courts are now far more aware that a mental health element may be involved and are willing to call upon the services of the diversion personnel whenever necessary.

The data in Tables 6.9–14 also show the measure of the appropriateness of the referrals made to the scheme—on average, approximately 70 per cent of those referred were offered in-patient care or directed to other specialist services.[58] So the referrals made to the diversion schemes were appropriate and every effort was made by the diversion personnel to endeavour to arrange suitable care and treatment.

One question which needs to be addressed is whether those diverted would have had the same outcomes regardless of the intervention of the diversion personnel. This is a question which cannot be fully answered; what is clear, however, is that in many cases the outcome has been dependent upon the intervention of the diversion personnel, their liaison between professionals, and their knowledge of the appropriate facilities and the ability to access them. The community penalty for those prosecuted may well have been the same, but they

---

[56] Burney and Pearson, 'Finding a Focus', P. Pierzchniak *et al.*, 'Liaison between Prison, Court and Psychiatric Services' (1997) 29 *Health Trends* 26–9.

[57] In 1992/3 the combined total was 44, in 1993/4 it increased to 47, and in 1994/5, the total was 51.

[58] In Bradford the total percentage is 46 per cent, which is considerably lower than all other areas. This is calculated if 112 is considered as the total number of referrals, of which 47 actually received health and social care. It must be borne in mind however, that this is not a truly accurate reflection of the appropriateness of the referrals as many of the 112 'referrals' were the result of the nurse's primary screening process, the majority of which were not fully assessed. So the majority of the total diversions were the result of referrals from other professionals.

would not necessarily have received access to the services had the diversion personnel not become involved. Magistrates and other court staff receive very little, if any, training in mental health issues, and so would not be in a position to make such decisions and arrangements. Similarly, the police have traditionally received very little instruction in this area and so mentally ill offenders would undoubtedly slip through the net were it not for the intervention of the ASW/CPN.[59]

Furthermore, in many cases, based upon the author's own observations at court, were it not for the CPN's intervention certain offenders would undoubtedly have been remanded in custody by the court instead of being granted bail. This was evinced in Calderdale where a distressed defendant was facing a range of charges and the court was minded to remand him into custody. As a result of the CPN's involvement, however, the defendant was granted bail on condition that he attend an out-patient appointment with a local psychiatrist which had been organized by the CPN. Another example in Wakefield is a case in point: the defendant had been on remand in Armley for several months and was facing a custodial sentence. A psychiatric report had been prepared which recommended a psychiatric probation order. However, the defendant was unrepresented and the duty solicitor was unwilling to proceed with sentencing on that day. The case would therefore be adjourned and the defendant would be remanded in custody for a further period. The CPN contacted the psychiatrist to arrange for him to supervise the defendant and advised the solicitor to proceed on this basis as the defendant's mental state would further deteriorate in prison. Consequently, as a result of the nurse's intervention, a psychiatric probation order was granted by the court.

The diversion personnel are integral to the process and, as other researchers have identified, no other professionals at court are in that position nor do they receive the appropriate training, so it is extremely unlikely that, without them, many of the offenders would have received the same attention and access to care. Furthermore, it has been shown how the other professionals at court have been willing to make referrals and identify those in need of assessment. On the whole, the diversion personnel indicate that increasing numbers of referrals have been made as the schemes have progressed, and so it is unlikely that these professionals would have taken such an active role had the diversion personnel not been present, easily accessible, and in a position to help. Nobody else was filling this role in a systematic manner prior to the establishment of the schemes, and so the other professionals may not have known where to turn, and may not have taken any further action, and the defendant would have slipped through the net. The examples outlined above illustrate how the diversion personnel assess clients and co-ordinate agencies, and the previous chapter has already identified the level of collaboration which is now taking place in the region. As other researchers have

---

[59] See further J. M. Laing, 'The Mentally Disordered Suspect at the Police Station' [1995] *Crim LR* 371–81.

also found, it is the discussion, liaison, and co-ordination between agencies which is the key to successful diversion in most cases.[60]

The quantitative study has therefore shown that the diversion schemes are seeking to help those in need of health and social services care and support, which is in line with the treatment-based approach. The findings of the qualitative study will now be discussed in order to assess the degree to which those who have been provided with this care and support resound these findings.

6.3. PART TWO: THE QUALITATIVE ANALYSIS

6.3.1. Introduction

A sample of diverted offenders was interviewed about their experiences and perceptions of the diversion schemes several months after their initial contact with the diversion personnel. The importance of conducting such a follow-up study has been identified by other researchers;[61] however, given the time constraints and the difficulties in locating *all* diverted offenders, a self-selecting sample was chosen.[62]

A total of 15 interviews was conducted, which represents almost 5 per cent of the total number of offenders assessed by the diversion personnel in the region. Whilst it is a small sample, it does provide a valuable follow-up and additional insight into the effects and the personal impact of diversion schemes in the region.

6.3.2. The Interview Sample

6.3.2.1. Personal Details

The total sample comprised 15 offenders who had come into contact with each scheme, which included 4 from Bradford, 3 each from Wakefield, Huddersfield, and Dewsbury, and 2 from Calderdale. Thirteen men and 2 women were interviewed, all of whom were unemployed and 12 of whom were single. Their ages ranged from the youngest at 20 to the oldest at 57 and they all resided in the area either in rented accommodation, residential accommodation, or with parents, family, and friends.

6.3.2.2. Offence Details

The sample was facing a variety of charges ranging from breach of the peace, affray, and threatening behaviour to criminal damage, arson, theft, and burglary. Some offenders were facing multiple charges and this is an important consideration as the entire sample had previous convictions for similar offences and so there was

---

[60] Cohen and Midgley, *North Humberside Project*, 73.

[61] J. Holloway and J. Shaw, 'Providing a Forensic Psychiatry Service to a Magistrates' Court: A Follow-up Study' (1993) 4 *J For Psych* 575–81.

[62] See Ch. 5 for an account of the methodology of the study.

a real possibility of the court refusing to grant bail and imposing a remand in custody or custodial sentence in these cases. The majority had received community penalties in the past, however 4 had previous sentences of imprisonment and 6 had been remanded in custody to Leeds Prison on previous occasions.

6.3.3. The Interview Results

The interview schedule[63] was designed to elicit a range of information from the offenders. Primarily it was aimed at assessing the personal impact of the diversion schemes and the intervention of the diversion personnel. It also enabled a comparison to be made with previous sentencing outcomes where applicable. Finally, it permitted a degree of follow-up to take place as to whether the intervention had been of any value to the offenders, to what extent they had maintained contact with the services to which they had been referred, and whether they had subsequently been in contact with the criminal justice system.

6.3.3.1. Previous Psychiatric Contact

The respondents were asked whether they had any personal difficulties and had been in touch with the psychiatric services on previous occasions (Appendix E, Q. 9C). Of the total sample, 10 responded that they had previous contact with the psychiatric services. Half of these had previously received help from community and drug/alcohol services largely as a result of referrals by their GP, and the other half had received in-patient care for a period of time either voluntarily or under the civil commitment sections of the Mental Health Act 1983.

Of the 5 who had not received any previous psychiatric assistance, 2 acknowledged that they had felt in need of some kind of help, but did not know whether it existed nor how to go about getting it. The others were trying to cope on their own. So it would seem that the diversion personnel were playing an important role in putting these disordered individuals into contact with needed services.

It was also important to note whether any of the offenders were receiving psychiatric help at the time the offence was committed (Q. 10C). A total of 5 respondents indicated that they were currently receiving some form of treatment and support.[64] Three of these were between out-patient appointments, and so may possibly have been in need of medication or additional support. Indeed, one replied that his offence was committed over the Christmas holidays when he was feeling especially lonely and despondent, was unable to see his doctor, and had no access to appropriate facilities or support. The other 2 had recently been discharged from a psychiatric ward and stated that they were feeling particularly isolated and dejected. It is difficult to make generalizations about the levels of care provided in the region as a result of these few examples, however, it may

---

[63] See Appendix E.
[64] CALD 1, HUD 2, DEWS 1, DEWS 2, WAK 3.

suggest that there is a need to provide more rigorous aftercare arrangements and emergency support. This has been echoed by other researchers.[65]

The final question in Section C related to previous psychiatric contact as a result of previous contact with the criminal justice system (Q. 11C). None of the sample had received psychiatric assistance as a result of any previous court appearances. And only 2 individuals in Bradford had previously been taken to local psychiatric facilities as a result of contact with the police. This is highly significant, as it confirms the important role that the nurses are now playing in identifying those in need of help at court, where previously they may have slipped through the net. So, this reinforces the view that it is extremely doubtful that the same result would have been achieved had the diversion personnel not been present, and would also seem to reinforce the view of other researchers that 'as things stand at present, for many a court appearance may be the only way that their needs will become apparent'.[66]

6.3.3.2. The Assessment

With regard to the actual assessment itself, the respondents were asked certain questions to determine the impact that the nurse's involvement had made at the initial assessment stage. First, they were asked if they were aware of who had referred them to the CPN/ASW, which was important to determine how far they were involved in the diversion process (Q. D12). Only 3 respondents were unsure how the assessment came about, and so 75 per cent (12) of the sample were aware that the CPN/ASW became involved because the police or defence solicitor suggested that, although they did not have to, they might like to talk to them about their condition. The majority responded that, at the time, they felt indifferent about the nurse's involvement and were extremely ambivalent about the purpose of the interview. It was indeed a totally new and alien notion and so many were surprised when the nurse arrived and explained the purpose of the assessment and requested their consent to continue. This illustrates that initially, the majority did not simply perceive the nurse as a 'get out of jail free' card. Many were uncertain about what the nurse could do but feeling at such a low ebb and anxious in custody that they were willing to try anything, and saw the opportunity to talk to the nurse as a form of comfort and short-term relief, as the following quotations show: 'I was really frightened. I didn't know what would happen to me. I was so glad to talk to him, he was interested in me and wanted to help me'[67] and—'I just cracked up in the cell. I needed help and I hoped that [the nurse] could help me.'[68]

The respondents were then asked how they *now* felt about the nurse's involvement in view of the outcomes of the assessment. A marked change in attitudes was observed in almost all cases. Thirteen respondents remarked that they now

[65] See e.g. Purchase *et al.*, 'Evaluation of Liaison Scheme'.
[66] Burney and Pearson, 'Finding a Focus', 309.
[67] DEWS 3.
[68] HUD 1.

welcomed the advice given and the arrangements made. And the responses ranged from being 'happy', 'glad', 'thankful', and 'grateful' for having being given the opportunity to talk to the nurse. One particular individual was 'over the moon' at the positive arrangements that the nurse had made and was adamant that had it not been for the nurse's influence he would have received a custodial sentence.[69]

However, two particular individuals remained ambivalent and were not as receptive of the nurse's involvement. One case in particular involved a young, single male who had been arrested by the police for a property offence. He had a previous offending history and a major substance misuse problem linked to his mental illness. He had recently been released from hospital where he had been receiving treatment as an in-patient. He was therefore already in contact with health and social services and was awaiting admission to a special substance misuse rehabilitation clinic in the south of England. He was assessed by the CPN who arranged for him to be accepted at a bail hostel and referred him to the local drug/alcohol services. During the interview, he was particularly unresponsive and indifferent about the nurse's involvement and was not really aware of how much influence the CPN exerted in organizing his admission to the bail hostel. His only concern was his admission to the Special Unit and all he really wanted was for the nurse to organize his immediate admission. In view of the fact that this was not arranged (the CPN liaised with the offender's care worker who informed him that admission was subject to a long waiting list) the interviewee was not satisfied with the assessment. The other case involved a young female who lived in a residential home for people with acute mental health problems. She was violent and disruptive and was arrested by the police for a breach of the peace. The CPN liaised with local agencies and arranged for her to be readmitted to the residential home, however, she was dissatisfied with the arrangements, as she would have preferred to have been admitted to the local hospital. But, in the opinion of the nurse, she was not ill enough to warrant in-patient care and was receiving community support at the residential home instead. Both respondents felt that the diversion service did not meet their needs; however, they did express that they initially welcomed the opportunity to talk to the nurse in the cells. So, even though no long-term impact was felt, the nurse had succeeded in providing short-term relief from the distress of being detained in police custody.

Even so, 13 out of the 15 respondents, despite initial uncertainty and hesitance, subsequently appreciated the diversion personnel's intervention and were grateful for the assessment. And so favourable responses were received in 87 per cent of cases.

6.3.3.3. The Outcome

Questions D15 to D19 dealt with the outcome of the assessment and the respondents in the sample were asked about their degree of satisfaction with the arrangements which had been made for them by the diversion personnel.

---

[69] WAK 1.

All respondents were fully aware of what had been arranged for them by the diversion personnel. The outcomes varied greatly, as some interviewees had been admitted as in-patients, others had been referred to community services, and some had been admitted to bail hostels, as a result of the ASW/CPN's intervention. Twelve respondents were satisfied with the arrangements, and their responses ranged from feeling 'happy', 'good', 'secure', and 'satisfied' with the arrangements, irrespective of what level of intervention had taken place. Those who had been referred to community services and those who had received in-patient care were equally content. Two respondents who had been admitted as in-patients confessed that initially they had felt anxious about being admitted to the psychiatric ward. This was perhaps because of popular misconceptions about 'mental hospitals' and both acknowledged that they now realized that they are not 'nuthouses'. They said that, following their admission, they had been made to feel secure and supported by the staff. They felt much better as they had been given the support that they needed, and as one indicated, 'Looking back, I reckon I'd have killed myself if I hadn't come here, I felt so desperate.'[70]

Three respondents remained ambivalent and non-committal about the outcomes, however. As already noted, two respondents in particular felt that the nurse could have taken a different course, and the third respondent, whilst not expressing dissatisfaction with the outcome, simply replied 'It's all right. Better than being in prison I suppose.'[71]

In 9 cases the respondents felt that, had it not been for the diversion personnel's intervention, they would have been remanded in custody or sentenced to prison. Many stated that their solicitor or the police subsequently told them that this would indeed have been the case. These individuals were either remanded to hospital or bailed to hospital or community facilities and in many cases it ultimately resulted in a therapeutic disposal.[72] This is significant, as it reinforces the suggestion that the diversion schemes are successfully *diverting* mentally disordered offenders *from custody*.

Twelve respondents replied that they were still in contact with the services to which they had been referred and affirmed that they were receiving the help, treatment, and/or support that they needed. And only 3 out of the sample have subsequently reappeared in court, so, the recidivism rate in the sample is very low, amounting to only 13 per cent. Furthermore, two of the individuals who had reoffended were those who were the least responsive and complementary of the CPN's intervention, and who felt that more could have been arranged for them or were not willing to co-operate with the arrangements made.[73] The third reoffender was an individual who expressed grave remorse at his actions and stated that it was an isolated incident and a momentary lapse when he got drunk as a result of a row with his girlfriend. He was unable to contact his social worker at

---

[70] BRAD 4.
[72] BRAD 2, 3, 4; CALD 1, 2; HUD 3; WAK 1, 2, 3.

[71] CALD 1.
[73] DEWS 2, DEWS 3.

the time, and this led to his arrest by the police. He was, however, released without charge, following the subsequent intervention of the social worker, and so he reoffended but was not reconvicted.[74] It must be stressed here, however, that this recidivism rate is by no means conclusive as the total period was only 12 months and one would normally expect a period of at least 36 months to provide an accurate recidivism rate study.

Only a small minority (5) were aware of the particular service to which they had been referred, prior to the referral by the CPN/ASW. Of those, several felt that they needed help but did not know how or where to get it, and others were trying to cope on their own. In conjunction with the responses to question D14,[75] this indicates that the diversion personnel are putting the offenders in touch with needed services and are channelling people to appropriate care. As one respondent replied, 'He helped me to get the help that I really needed.'[76]

It could be argued, however, that these offenders may have ultimately come into contact with the services regardless of the diversion personnel's involvement. Whilst no guarantee can be made that this is not the case, in view of the nature of the diversion personnel's intervention in terms of co-ordinating services, it is doubtful that this would have occurred anyway at this stage. So the ASW/CPN's expedite access to care which helped to keep mentally ill people out of custody and this was clearly felt to be the case by many of the interview sample. One offender only wished he had been treated like this years ago and he had appeared in court on several previous occasions and never received this type of help. Other responses echoed this sentiment: 'I would never have gone to this service if it wasn't for him',[77] 'I'm so glad I saw him otherwise I'd still be stuck on my own,'[78] and 'I'd have ended up in prison without him, and I couldn't face that place again. They just don't care about how you feel.'[79]

The respondents were also asked if they had received any other help that they had found useful. None replied in the affirmative. Whilst they were happy with the referrals to the services, no other agencies or professionals were specifically singled out who had been of any great value. It was the efforts of the diversion personnel that had clearly made the greatest impact upon the lives of this sample in the majority of cases.

6.3.3.4. *Perceptions of the Diversion Personnel*

Some of the comments which have been recorded above illustrate the depth of gratitude which many offenders felt towards the diversion personnel. The general feeling is that the diversion schemes have been welcomed and this is encapsulated in the following quote.

'I've come further in the last six months than I have in the last five years with

---

[74] WAK 3.
[75] This question invited the respondents to comment upon how they now felt about the CPN's involvement.   [76] BRAD 2.   [77] DEWS 1.
[78] HUD 1.   [79] CALD 2.

the help of [the diversion personnel].'[80] Indeed, this particular individual had a long history of criminal offending and was facing multiple charges. He was a 27-year-old male who had been suffering from bulimia and had been abused as a child. He drank heavily and became extremely abusive and violent, which resulted in his arrest. The diversion team assessed him and concluded that psychological problems lay at the root of his offending. Consequently, a psychiatric probation order was arranged so that he would receive the counselling and support he needed. The interview took place 10 months after the assessment and he was full of praise for the diversion team's efforts. He now felt like 'a totally different bloke' and would 'never be able to thank them enough' for what they had done. The team had had a dramatic long-term influence upon his life. This enthusiastic response was also mirrored by another interviewee. He was a 46-year-old single man who was suffering from depression and alcoholism. He committed his offences during the Christmas period and was arrested by the police. He was assessed in the cells by the ASW who initially arranged for him to be bailed to the psychiatric ward at Pontefract General Infirmary. The case was followed through by the team and he was eventually given a psychiatric probation order on condition that he attend a rehabilitation unit which was arranged by the ASW. When asked how he now felt about the team's involvement, having had time to reflect, he replied: 'I can't say enough about how much [the ASW] has helped me. She's made me realize that people care and that I can get over this. I only wish she'd been here years ago.'[81]

In some cases, the diversion personnel have provided ongoing practical support which has been extremely welcome:'[The CPN's] helped me sort out my life, get a roof over my head and get my life sorted. She's been great. I only wish I could see her more often.'[82] In many cases the diversion personnel have had a dramatic impact upon the lives of the sample, and one respondent regarded the CPN as one of his 'best mates': '[The CPN] seems to care about me and that makes me feel so much better about myself. I'll really try to make a go of it now and show him I can do it.'[83]

When asked if there was anything further that the CPN/ASW could have arranged for them, the majority felt that they had received more than enough help and support already. However, the two dissatisfied respondents noted earlier clearly felt to the contrary and wished that preferable alternative arrangements could have been made for them.

The final question invited the respondents to comment generally and further about the involvement of the diversion personnel. Prompting only took place where necessary. A wide range of comments was received, the majority of which were highly favourable about all the diversion personnel and echoed earlier sentiments. Many felt that the diversion personnel's involvement had protected them

---

[80] WAK 3.   [81] WAK 3.   [82] WAK 2.   [83] HUD 3.

from punitive sanctions: 'If it weren't for [the CPN] I'd be in jail,'[84] and 'I'd have ended up in Armley without [the CPN].'[85] In comparison with previous sentencing outcomes, all respondents regarded this as a massive improvement: 'This is the best thing that's ever happened to me.'[86] And many felt that their condition had improved and that they now felt motivated to change as a result of the diversion personnel's intervention: 'I feel better now. I'm not brilliant, but I'm getting there and I will get there thanks to [the CPN].'[87]

6.3.4. Discussion of the Qualitative Data

Concerning the long-term impact that the diversion schemes were making upon the lives of this group of offenders, most stated that it had been a major turning-point and that the diversion personnel had influenced their lives greatly. However, actions speak louder than words, and, given the length of the study, it was still too early to confirm that this was definitely the case. In terms of reoffending, however, at the time of the study, only 3 offenders had reappeared in court, which may indicate that there was indeed an element of truth in their statements, particularly in view of the fact that the entire sample had previous convictions, and had therefore already established patterns of recidivism. It must be borne in mind, however, that the recidivism rate here is not wholly reliable, given the limited timescale.

To many, the diversion personnel had made a tremendous impact and they were very happy with the arrangements that were made. Favourable responses were received in 13 cases, the extent of which varied greatly, and 2 individuals in particular constantly praised the efforts of the diversion personnel. The responses would also seem to indicate that the offenders themselves preferred, and were willing, to be given access to in-patient care as opposed to being subjected to the penal system. This seems to run contrary to Nigel Walker's suggestion that 'Some mildly disordered offenders prefer a short term of imprisonment in the company of prisoners who they regard as normal and congenial to compulsory commitment to a hospital, with the resulting stigma, the uncertainty of the date of discharge and the enforced association with more severely disordered patients'.[88]

Only 2 respondents were not completely satisfied with the outcome. They did, however, appreciate the opportunity to talk to the nurse in the police cells, and so even where a long-term impact has not been felt, short-term relief has been provided by the diversion personnel.

In several cases, the diversion personnel have played an important part in identifying those in need of help who may have slipped through the net in the past. They are the offenders with no psychiatric history who have appeared in

---

[84] WAK 2. [85] CALD 2. [86] DEWS 1. [87] HUD 1.
[88] N. Walker and S. McCabe, *Crime and Insanity in England* (Edinburgh University Press 1973) ii 244.

court on numerous previous occasions but not received any psychiatric inter-vention. Some stated that they felt in need of help but didn't know how to go about getting it, so the nurses have played an integral role in ensuring that it is now provided.

In other cases, the ASW/CPNs have helped those with enduring mental health and offending problems who have been in need of care and treatment. One impor-tant question in relation to this category is, 'Why should this time be any differ-ent?' They have, after all received previous psychiatric treatment but have still ended up in court again, many facing a prison sentence. In view of their comments, however, it would seem that this time *is* different, and the determin-ing factor is that one specific individual has co-ordinated the arrangements. The diversion personnel have taken an active role and shown them that someone is concerned about them, whereas, in the past, these individuals have often felt as if they have been passed from pillar to post between different groups of profes-sionals, with no single agency taking responsibility, care, or control. But this time they feel that they have been shown that someone is concerned about them and their future, and is willing to help them, and it is this which motivates them to change. As one respondent noted, '[The CPN] put me in the right direction. I'm going to college now and I feel much better. It's down to [the CPN] and I want to show him I can do it 'cos he's got faith in me.'[89]

The ASWs/CPNs in many cases have persevered and become actively involved in the outcome and the defendants in turn have been far more willing and likely to co-operate, and this is the key to success. As one respondent said, 'At the end of the day, it's up to you. You've got to want to change and do some-thing about it. All they can do is put you in the right direction and the rest is up to you.'[90]

So what is important is that the presence of the diversion schemes and the work of the nurses involved shows these individuals that people are concerned and want to help, and it is that which motivates them to change.

6.4. CONCLUSION

Despite its limitations and the short timescale, the quantitative study has shown that mentally disordered offenders are being identified and directed into health and social services care. This diverted group is a homogenous group of socially disadvantaged individuals, the majority of whom are in need of psychiatric help to try to break the cycle of mental illness, crime, and reoffending.

The outcomes illustrate that the overwhelming majority are being given access to a wide range of treatment, care, and support. Furthermore, the low

---

[89] HUD 3.   [90] WAK 1.

rate of discontinuances indicates that the majority are not being completely removed from the criminal justice system. In most cases, offenders are diverted from imprisonment and being given therapeutic or community remands and sentences. They are still prosecuted and processed, but at the same time they are being given access to health and social services care and treatment, which has been provided in most cases. This is supported by the evidence from the qualitative study which has also been discussed. Eighty-seven per cent (13) of respondents felt that the diversion personnel had made a positive and welcome impact upon their lives. Many were adamant that without the intervention of the diversion personnel they would have been remanded or sentenced to custody, and would not have been given access to the services they felt they so badly needed.

There is, however, an important limitation to the research study, as the data does not show whether there are offenders who are not being identified and assessed. Perhaps one indicator is the level of mental illness that is still evident in the local prisons. Anecdotal evidence and the author's own discussions with Health Care Officers at Armley revealed that the true extent of psychiatric morbidity is not really known and it is difficult to confirm a general decline in the number of mentally ill inmates during the last few years. Furthermore, this data would be far from conclusive as the prison system is fluid and many such inmates may have originated from courts outside West Yorkshire. Moreover, the prison environment itself can cause or exacerbate mental illness, and so it is difficult to assert with any certainty the impact of the schemes on the prison psychiatric population, or to estimate the number who may still be slipping through the net. All that can be said is that, as a result of official diversion policy, prison officers are aware of the need to identify mental illness and the number of prison transfers is increasing. This would seem to be supported on a national scale by the evidence presented in Ch. 4, by the comments of the Mental Health Act Commission and HM Chief Inspector of Prisons, and the national statistics and research studies. So every effort is being made to ensure that those who do slip through the net are subsequently picked up and diverted.

Ultimately, however, the results of the research study do suggest that offenders are being diverted from prison and being given access to treatment and support in hospital and the community. This evidence is supported by other small-scale, short-term follow-up studies of court diversion schemes, such as the one conducted in Rotherham, which has a similarly low reconviction rate over a 12-month period, and which also found that the majority of the diverted sample had maintained contact with the services into which they had been diverted.[91]

[91]   R. Rowlands *et al.*, 'Diverted to Where? What Happens to the Diverted Mentally Disordered Offender' (1996) 7(2) *J For Psych* 284–96; see also M. Cheung Chang *et al.*, 'A Follow-up Study of Mentally Disordered Offenders after a Court Diversion Scheme: Six-Month and One-Year Comparison' (1999) 39(1) *Med, Sci & Law* 31–7.

This chapter has therefore shown that appropriate treatment and support is being provided by the diversion schemes, which are valued greatly by the mentally ill offenders concerned: 'There's no two ways about it. Without that help, I'd be in prison and I wouldn't be where I am today. I'll never, ever be able to thank [the CPN] enough.'[92]

[92] WAK 3.

7

Conclusion

As long as the mentally ill are being handled by the criminal justice system, they should be treated with empathy and understanding, not misunderstanding.[1]

7.1. CONCLUDING REMARKS

In a recent study of the mental health of the nation, it was estimated that 1 adult in every 7 suffers from depression, anxiety, or some other form of mental disorder. This suggests that approximately 6 million people in Britain have some kind of mental health problem, which requires care, treatment, or support.[2] Even more alarming is the fact that the latest Department of Health Statistics reveal that 1 adult in 4 will suffer from some form of mental illness at some stage in his or her life.[3] These figures clearly indicate the extent of the problem. Of course, not all these people are necessarily mentally disordered offenders, but there is a real danger for a few that if their conditions are left untreated and they do not receive the help they need, they may deteriorate and that could lead to tragic consequences for the individuals themselves, as Ben Silcock's parents would claim, or, in Jayne Zito's eyes, for their victims. It is therefore crucial that steps are taken to minimize this danger and ensure that appropriate treatment and support is provided. The main aim of this book has been to examine the process of diversion of mentally disordered offenders from the criminal justice system, which is one step that has been taken to seek to solve the problem and provide some of these people with the help that they need and to which they are entitled.

The problems posed by mentally disordered offenders are not exclusive to Britain however,[4] and throughout this book reference has been made to the host of literature testifying to similar difficulties and developments which have taken place in other jurisdictions. In particular, in countries such as Canada, Australia, and America it is now universally accepted that the plight of mentally disordered offenders can only be resolved by increased co-operation and collaboration, and

---

[1] P. Randall Kropp et al., 'The Perceptions of Correctional Officers towards Mentally Disordered Offenders' (1989) 12 Int J Law & Psych 181–8, 187.

[2] See The Times, 15 December 1994; The Guardian, 17 May 1995, p. 8.

[3] DoH Press Release 98/126, 2 April 1998; see also DoH, Modernising Mental Health Services: Safe, Sound and Supportive (DoH 1998), ch. 1.

[4] See e.g. P. Fennell and F. Koenraadt, 'Diversion, Europeanization and the Mentally Disordered Offender' in C. Harding et al., Criminal Justice in Europe: A Comparative Study (Clarendon 1995).

massive improvements in the provision of funding and facilities.[5] In America in particular, the American Bar Association has published *Standards for Criminal Justice* which includes a mental health section expressly aimed at lawyers and clinicians and covering all aspects of a mentally ill person's contact with the criminal justice system.[6] Foremost it is acknowledged that the need to work together is paramount as, in general, the standards recognize 'the need for co-operative, interprofessional programs designed . . . to generate understanding and co-operation and . . . to foster improved professional practice'.[7]

The need to ensure that mentally ill and retarded offenders receive appropriate psychiatric care has also been firmly recognized.[8] Furthermore, the United Nations has acknowledged the need to address the problems which are both faced, and posed by, such offenders on an international scale. The UN Interregional Crime and Justice Institute (UNICRI) has investigated the treatment of the mentally disordered within differing criminal justice systems and attempted to provide guidelines to improve treatment and ensure that the problems posed by mentally disordered offenders are universally acknowledged and addressed.[9]

An explicit diversion policy was introduced in England and Wales in 1990 in an attempt to combat some of the difficulties encountered by previous diversion attempts. As outlined in Part I, foremost the financial constraints were evident, and the need to promote inter-agency working was seen to be paramount. The author conducted a research study, which has been discussed in Part II of this book, which has shown how a group of diversion schemes in West Yorkshire has succeeded in establishing and improving inter-agency links, thereby facilitating the diversion of mentally disordered offenders from police stations and courts in the region. These attempts have been such a success that it is extremely encouraging to note that in 1999, several years after their conception, all are still operating effectively at the police stations and courts in West Yorkshire. In many cases the Home Office has continued to assist with the funding, but in several others, the relevant local trusts have clearly recognized the benefits and embraced the diversion schemes within their services. Indeed, Chs. 5 and 6 highlighted how, with a great amount of hard work and determination, many of the barriers traditionally operating between the law and psychiatry can be overcome, as nurses, doctors, social workers, the police, probation services, solicitors, and magistrates have all striven to work together. This has not been without difficulty, however, and in order to achieve such close collaboration, careful prior planning and negotiation is required. Furthermore, the

---

[5] See e.g. Special Issue, 'International Perspectives on Mental Health Issues in the Criminal Justice System' (1995) 18(1) *Int J Law & Psych.*

[6] ABA, *Standards for Criminal Justice*, 2nd edn. (Little, Brown & Co. 1980), ii. ch. 7.

[7] Ibid. p. xvi.

[8] Ibid. See e.g. Standards 7–2.2, 7–9.2, 7–9.3, 7–9.4, 7–10.2.

[9] UNICRI, *Pathways to the Management of Mentally Ill Offenders in the Criminal Justice System*, Publication 48 (UN Rome 1993); see also DoH Press Release 1998/0448, *International Mental Health Symposium Opens* (DoH 1998).

allocation of responsibility and sources of funding must be agreed at the outset. It is imperative that this is acknowledged and accepted by the agencies involved, so that diversion schemes are well-defined and carefully constructed to meet the needs of differing agencies, localities, and populations.

Indeed, one of the main advantages is the diversity of schemes which have evolved and which can be adopted and adapted to suit and reflect the differing needs and resources. Consequently, it is suggested that each particular inter-agency initiative should be developed in order to reflect the exclusive and special needs and resources of that particular locality. It is essential not to be too prescriptive about the nature of diversion arrangements, which should be designed and developed on an individual basis. Undoubtedly it is far preferable that diversion arrangements are established at the earliest possible stage in the process, with full psychiatric support (i.e. RMP/CPN and ASW), access to local facilities and ongoing support and follow up, as it ensures effective assessment and can avoid unnecessary and damaging amounts of time in custody. However, it has been recognized that the success of diversionary initiatives is dependent upon the firm commitment of the numerous agencies involved, and the recognition that, in order to succeed and become an established feature, they must simply form part of a much broader comprehensive mental health service which is available to this category of offender-patient. Inter-agency diversion arrangements will only succeed if they become a formal and permanent part of the range of acute psychiatric services which are provided within each health region. It has been stressed throughout this book that there must be sufficient services into which the offenders can be diverted, and this must be firmly recognized if such arrangements are to flourish in the long-term. This has also been noted on numerous occasions by several prominent bodies and committees, most recently by the Mental Health Act Commission[10] and a Social Services Inspectorate Report into services for Mentally Disordered Offenders.[11]

It has been shown in Part II that diversion schemes do enable the successful identification of mental illness and allow mentally disordered offenders to be given access to health and social services care and support, and that this has been facilitated by a successful degree of inter-agency working. Chapter 6 recognized that the offenders are identified by qualified professionals and are appropriate clients as they are predominantly petty offenders in need of care and support. It is evident that the process of diversion is not simply about diverting offenders from prosecution. In most cases, offenders are still prosecuted, but should be diverted from custody wherever possible and at the same time channelled to appropriate health care, so that the offenders' health care needs are addressed, but at the same time they are being held personally responsible for their crimes. It is

[10] MHAC, *Sixth Biennial Report 1993–95* (HMSO 1996), 73.
[11] DoH Social Care Group, *Services for Mentally Disordered Offenders in the Community: An Inspection Report* (HSMO 1997) ch. 5.

normally some form of middle ground which is achieved, between due process (liberalism), and humane treatment, whereby society's right to punish can also be recognized and respected.

It has also been shown that the diversion process is valued greatly by the mentally disordered offenders themselves. The comments from the study sample outlined in Ch. 6 indicate that the majority of offenders felt that they were, at last, being recognized and treated as human beings, and not simply shunted from one agency to another. Thirteen out of the total sample of fifteen expressed their gratitude and appreciation of the personnel's involvement. Many were feeling much improved as a result of the diversion personnel intervention and consequently regarded it as a welcome opportunity to change their lives for the better. A marked improvement in the offenders' attitudes was observed in many cases. So there is a clear consensus between the professionals and the offenders involved about the need to achieve diversion and the benefits to be gained from it, albeit on the small numbers involved in this current sample.

Diversion schemes can be effective in this way provided that they maximize the needs of the offenders and minimize the risk to the public, and it has been shown that this can be achieved. Many of the concerns of the sceptics of diversion can be kept at bay, as this study has shown how a balance can be struck and the rights of victims, public safety, and accountability of decision-making can be accorded a certain amount of respect and consideration in the diversion process. However, it has also been identified that there is a need for the central Government to take a much stronger lead and place such diversion decisions and the responsibility for them on a statutory basis so that consistency, responsibility, and accountability are secured and further ensured. To date, a vast array of different schemes has emerged across the country; however, they have been developed on a purely *ad hoc* and unco-ordinated basis. National provision of assessment and diversion schemes is therefore largely patchy and inconsistent, and there is a need for central co-ordination and monitoring. In this context, it is extremely unfortunate that recent attempts to provide a statutory framework have been thwarted.

A proposal to place such diversion decisions and the responsibility for them on a statutory basis was defeated in the parliamentary debates that preceded the Crime (Sentences) Act 1997. An amendment was tabled during the debates, which was designed to impose a duty on the Secretary of State to ensure that duty-psychiatrist assessment schemes are available at magistrates' courts throughout the country. It was envisaged that this would 'reinforce the trend towards their extension, promote consistency of provision throughout the country and safeguard such schemes in future against the risk that they might be sacrificed in expenditure cuts'.[12]

Whilst there was some clear support for the proposal in both Houses, for the

---

[12]   Session 1996–7 HC Debs Vol. 288 col. 54.

reasons outlined above and on the basis of the discussions earlier in this book, the 1979–97 Conservative Government did not agree and the proposal was defeated. In particular, it felt that the clause was much too restrictive and that it did not want to 'tie the hands of the local agencies' by being too prescriptive about the type of assessment scheme to be developed 'they are local initiatives and it would be unhelpful to tie the hands of the local agencies involved, which are best placed to devise the right response to local needs and to make the most effective use of the available resources'.[13]

The clause was also further limited to the establishment of solely *duty-psychiatrist court-based* assessment schemes. The presence of a specialist psychiatrist is clearly essential,[14] but, as has been outlined earlier in this book, a wide range of schemes have been developed at every stage of the criminal justice process involving a much broader range of personnel, which can be suited to reflect the needs and resources of each particular locality. Accordingly, the 1979–97 Conservative Government clearly felt that it would be wrong to restrict assessment to the pre-sentence stage by doctors alone

it would be a step back to restrict assessment to the pre-sentence stage, as that would limit examination to those who had been convicted and exclude those on remand. A major benefit of any assessment scheme would be the early identification of mental disorder and the availability of advice to the court at first hearings, to avoid unnecessary remands to prison.[15]

These are indeed legitimate criticisms, as noted above, the most attractive aspect of the schemes is their diverse nature and their ability to be adapted to reflect differing localities. In this respect, the 1979–97 Conservative Government was correct; however, rather than rejecting the clause outright, it would have been far preferable had it been subject to amendment and extended to reflect the fact that a number of agencies should be involved at different stages in the process. Indeed, the most favourable course of action would have been to impose a duty upon local agencies, such as the police, and probation and health services, to establish local multi-agency disordered offender teams in order to co-operate and collaborate to arrange suitable disposals. These could operate in a similar way to the new Youth Offending Teams that are being developed in the context of young offenders under the Crime and Disorder Act 1998.[16] It is also envisaged that a national Youth Justice Board will be established, which will consist of representatives of the main agencies at a national level, whose role will be to assist the Home Secretary to devise standards, identify good practice, and monitor the

---

[13] Session 1996–7 HC Debs Vol. 288 col. 62.

[14] See further C. Chambers and K. J. B. Rix, 'A Controlled Evaluation of Assessments by Doctors and Nurses in a Magistrates' Court Mental Health Assessment and Diversion Scheme' (1998) 39(1) *Med, Sci & Law* 38–48.   [15] Ibid.

[16] See further Home Office, *No More Excuses: A New Approach to Tackling Youth Crime in England and Wales*, Session 1997–8 Cm. 3809 esp. ch. 8.

operation of the youth justice system.[17] In order to promote partnership and effective disposals at a local level, a network of local inter-agency teams will be set up, who will have a variety of functions, including assessment and supervisory powers for young offenders as well as the provision of through-care and the preparation of reports. The Act places a duty on Local Authorities to ensure the provision of such teams; and other key agencies, such as the probation service, police, and health authorities, will be under a reciprocal duty to participate.[18] As stated in the White Paper which preceded the Act, 'It makes sense for the agencies . . . to come together locally to address [the range of] problems and so reduce the risk of further crime.'[19]

These developments are already taking place in relation to young offenders and it is argued that a similar structure in relation to disordered adult offenders could be established, whereby a national official body could be set up to monitor and guide future developments, thereby promoting consistency and accountability, and ensuring oversight and continuity. But at a local level, multi-agency teams could be required to collaborate to ensure effective and appropriate disposals for the disordered offenders. Given the nature of their problems, the relevant health authority, as opposed to the particular Local Authority, could take the lead role and be placed under a duty to ensure the provision of such teams, but the other agencies could be under a reciprocal duty to participate and collaborate. This structure and framework would ensure that there is a statutory obligation to establish such multi-agency assessments, ensure that co-operation and collaboration takes place, and provide a sufficient degree of national leadership, standard-setting, central scrutiny, and control. It would ensure that the future of such initiatives is relatively secure, and would also address many of the concerns with the diversion process, particularly in relation to unfettered discretion, lack of accountability and consistency, and absence of national agreed standards.

Until this is recognized, however, it leaves the future of such initiatives in an uncertain state. The current Labour Government has clearly pledged its continued rhetorical support to the policy, but it is doubtful whether it will take a much more proactive role. One can only hope that the provisions to adopt a lead role and provide a statutory framework in relation to young offenders under the Crime and Disorder Act 1998 will prove to be such a success that they will, in turn, filter through to other parts of the criminal justice system, and in particular to the diversion of mentally disordered offenders, of which the need for a statutory framework and central lead to steer and monitor local provision has been identified as an integral component.

Moreover, whilst the Labour Government has also pledged a certain degree of financial support to assist in the establishment of such initiatives, this is not

---

[17]   Home Office, *No More Excuses*. para. 8.2–6.
[18]   Ibid. para. 8.7–13; see Home Office, 'Twenty First Century Local Partnerships will Help to Cut Crime', Press Release 362/98, 18 September 1998.   [19]   Ibid. Para. 8.7.

assured in the longer term. It would seem that the Government does not perceive that central funding is to be the main way in which such schemes should be financed, despite the fact that the funding is available because they are extremely eager to encourage them.[20] Consequently, it is perceived that the funding should ultimately come from within existing and local resources in the long term. In one sense this is a sensible approach, as in order to succeed and become an established feature, such initiatives should simply be regarded as one component of a much broader service that is available to this category of offender-patient. And whilst the central Government funding is welcome and should continue to promote such schemes, it should also be recognized that it is available on a pump-priming basis only, and that the diversion arrangements must ultimately be provided and financed on a local level as part of the comprehensive and main-stream mental health services within each particular locality or region. It is only when this has been recognized that diversion arrangements will become a permanent, established, and adequately resourced fixture, and not entirely dependent upon central Government pump-priming funds and other external sources.

7.2. FUTURE DIRECTIONS FOR RESEARCH

Whilst identifying many positive aspects about the diversion process, the study which has been discussed in Part II has certain limitations, and there are several issues which have been left unaddressed.

In particular, it is not known precisely how many mentally disordered offenders are still not being identified and finding their way into the penal system, nor is it known what happens to those who are not diverted. These are areas where there is a clear need for further research to evaluate the overall effectiveness of diversion schemes in terms of appropriately identifying and diverting mentally disordered offenders in need of care and treatment. Further studies are therefore needed to ascertain the numbers who are still slipping through the net and precisely what happens to them which would involve focusing upon prison admissions and the prison population in addition to monitoring court records for persistent petty offenders.

There have been one or two encouraging developments in this respect in recent years, in particular, the Prison Service has taken an active role and promoted a comprehensive survey by the Office of National Statistics, into the levels of mental health in prison.[21] The results of this study were published in mid-1998 and, based on the responses of remand and sentenced prisoners, would

---

[20] See M. Farrar, 'Government Policy on Mentally Disordered Offenders and its Implementation' (1996) 5 *J Ment Health* 465–74 where the author argues that the policy of diversion has been clear and explicit, but that its implementation has been plagued by under-investment.

[21] Home Office, *Annual Report of the Director of Health Care 1996–97* (HMSO 1998), ch. 1.

seem to suggest that there are still high numbers of mentally ill offenders in prison.[22] Other recent, isolated, and small-scale studies would also seem to suggest that the level of mental illness in remand prisoners is still high.[23] The reasons for this are unknown, and it is unclear to what extent it is a reflection upon the 'failure' of diversionary initiatives introduced in the early 1990s to tackle the problem. As noted in Ch. 4, anecdotal evidence and health service statistics would suggest that this is not the case, as diversion arrangements have been effective in identifying the mentally ill and have promoted therapeutic disposals and reduced inappropriate remands in custody. So, the high levels of mental illness still in prison may be accounted for by the fact that there are significantly more people in prison in the late 1990s. The prison population has risen dramatically in recent years and is now standing at an all-time high, which could provide some explana- tion for the high numbers.[24] The reason could also be that these offenders may not be sufficiently ill to meet the criteria for transfer under the Mental Health Act 1983, which reinforces the urgent need dramatically to improve the health care facilities and support which is provided in the prison system.

However, there is also a need for large-scale follow-up studies to monitor *all diverted offenders* to ascertain the long-term impact of diversion on a national scale. The study in Part II was conducted within a short timescale and was able to show the short-term outcomes of a group of diversion schemes operating at courts in West Yorkshire. Furthermore, a limited follow-up study of a sample of offenders, for up to 12 months following their assessment, was also conducted and the results were extremely encouraging. The recidivism rate was low and most of the diverted offenders had maintained contact with the services into which they had been diverted.[25] The timescale and study sample were extremely limited, however, and the study was not able adequately to address the issue of whether diversion schemes in general are really slowing down the revolving door, keeping the mentally ill out of prison and providing all diverted mentally disordered offenders with lasting care and treatment and long-term support. There is some anecdotal evidence to date, which seems to suggest that the policy has had a positive impact in this respect,[26] but there is a need for much more concrete and reliable evidence. Moreover, some recent research studies, which were discussed in earlier chapters, have identified that diversion arrangements can

---

[22] ONS Press Release, *Mental Disorder among Prisoners*, 26 June 1998; ONS, *Psychiatric Morbidity among Prisoners in England and Wales* (ONS, 1998).

[23] L. Birmingham *et al.*, 'Prevalence of Mental Disorder Remand Prisoners' (1996) 313 *BMJ* 1521–4; D. Brooke *et al.*, 'Point Prevalence of Mental Disorder in Unconvicted Male Prisoners in England and Wales' (1996) 313 *BMJ* 1524–7.

[24] *The Prison Population in 1996*, Home Office Statistical Bulletin, 18/97 (Home Office 1997) Paras. 2, 3.

[25] See also R. Rowlands *et al.*, 'Diverted to Where? What Happens to the Diverted Mentally Disordered Offender' (1996) 7(2) *J For Psych* 284–96.

[26] See e.g. HMIP, *Annual Report 1994–95*, Session 1994–5 HC 760 Para. 5.37; MHAC, *Fifth, Sixth*, and *Seventh Biennial Reports* (HMSO 1993, 1996, 1997).

successfully identify mental illness and reduce unnecessary remands in custody, and that there is some health gain for diverted offenders. But these are isolated studies and there is a need for a much more comprehensive review. This is also an area where there is considerable scope for further research. NACRO has recently completed a comprehensive survey of the extent of national diversion arrangements.[27] It found that there are now almost 200 differing inter-agency assessment schemes operating at courts and police stations across the country. This is extremely encouraging. However, the study did not delve to any great depth into the efficacy of the arrangements, but even so found that monitoring and evaluation were wholly inadequate—generally poor and predominantly descriptive.[28] This clearly reinforces the need for larger-scale follow-up studies. A final area where further research is possible is in terms of testing the actual treatment that is provided for the diverted offenders. Persistent offending is only one emanation of the problems of this group of offenders and it is equally important to assess the long-term value and benefit of the treatment and support provided. It is only when all this information is available will the true value of diversion be known and it will be discovered whether diversion policy is completely, and on a long-term basis, solving the problems that the previous legislative and policy attempts have failed to address.

7.3 THE FUTURE OF DIVERSION POLICY

It is now nine years since the 1979–97 Conservative Government introduced an explicit diversion policy, so, finally, it is necessary to consider what the future now holds in store for this 'humane' approach. Attention has already been drawn to Home Office Circulars 12/95 and 52/97, which have served as timely reminders to all those agencies involved that the current Labour Government is still committed (at least in principle) to diversion policy, and that the continued development and implementation of diversion schemes is strongly encouraged and promoted.[29] Home Office Circular 52/97 has reinforced the new Labour Government's rhetorical commitment to the diversion policy, and it has been made clear that it intends to continue to promote such initiatives. The pump-priming funding is still in place and will continue for the foreseeable future,[30] and

[27] G. Sandell 'NACRO Survey of Existing Schemes in England and Wales', Paper presented at a National Conference on Psychiatric Court Liaison Schemes at Wadham College, Oxford, 22–3 September 1998.

[28] It is worth noting here that the Mental Health Foundation has recently produced some helpful guidance on measuring the performance of assessment schemes which would be useful for evaluation purposes: C. Truman, and S. Keyes, *Commissioning Services for Offenders with Mental Health Problems: Measuring the Performance of Court-Based Psychiatric Schemes* (Mental Health Foundation London 1997).

[29] See also M. Farrar, 'Government Policy on Mentally Disordered Offenders and its Implementation' (1996) 5 *J Ment Health* 465–74.

[30] Home Office, *Annual Report 1998: Government's Expenditure Plans 1998–1999, Session 1997–98*, Cm. 3908 para. 4.24, 30, 33.

recent figures suggest that the Home Office has now supported the establishment of almost 200 diversion arrangements across England and Wales.[31]

The Circulars do not represent dramatic new policy statements, but they are significant, as they reinforce the existing Government's rhetorical commitment to diversion, and this signifies that there is no present danger that the policy will be overtaken by the Government's 'tough on crime and tough on the causes of crime' approach. So it would seem that the implementation of diversion policy is relatively secure in this direction, at least for the foreseeable future: that is, unless the recent announcement to review the Mental Health Act 1983 will represent a marked departure from this philosophy. As part of the Government's recent review and proposals for a 'third way' for mental health which were outlined in Ch. 4, the Government has also announced its intention to review the existing mental health legislation and introduce proposals for reform and amending legislation.[32] This is in response to the pleas that have been made on numerous occasions in recent years that the mental health laws are obsolete and should be revised in order to reflect the move away from hospital- to community-based care, and to modern treatments and approaches.[33] Undoubtedly, the new pattern of services will result in the need for a new statutory framework and there is, therefore, likely to be much reform during the course of the next few years. The main thrust of the proposed new legislation is likely to be the need for compulsory treatment powers in the community, in order to bolster the other new measures.[34] The introduction of such powers would undoubtedly impact upon the process of diversion, as it would ensure that there are additional support structures into which offenders could be diverted.[35] Any new legislation will also be required to comply with the Human Rights Act 1998, which has incorporated international human rights law into the United Kingdom legal system. Future legislation will be required to emphasize and protect the rights of the disordered offenders in accordance with our obligations under the European Convention on Human Rights (ECHR), and this will obviously have a major impact on any future developments.[36]

---

[31] Session 1996–7 HL Debs Vol. 578 col. 1368.

[32] DoH, 'Frank Dobson Outlines Third Way for Mental Health', Press Release 98/311, 29 July 1998; DoH, 'Expert Advisor to Start Review of Mental Health Act', Press Release 98/391, 22 September 1998; DoH, *Modernising Mental Health Services: Safe, Sound and Supportive* (DoH 1998) para. 4.25–30.

[33] See e.g. 'Time to jettison the Mental Health Act 1983', *Independent*, 18 January 1995; 'Mental Health Law Obsolete' (1995) 310 *BMJ* 145–6; MHAC, *Sixth Biennial Report 1993–5* (HMSO 1996) p. 21; L. Blom-Cooper *et al., The Falling Shadow: One Patient's Mental Health Care 1978–1993* (Duckworth 1995).

[34] 'It will cover such possible measures as compliance orders and community treatment orders to provide a prompt and effective legal basis to ensure that patients get supervised care if they do not take their medication or if their condition deteriorates. The changes in practice we are seeking will be backed up by changes in the law', DoH Press Release 98/311.

[35] It is recognized, however, that the introduction of such intrusive powers would not be without difficulty and that there are many objections to compulsory treatment in the community. This issue is beyond the scope of this book, however, and will therefore not be considered here in any depth.

[36] See further K. Starmer, 'Mental Health and the Bill' (1998) *Legal Action* 8–9.

An expert scoping group has been appointed to review the existing mental health legislation. The final report has not yet been published, however, in April 1999, the group issued a basic draft outline of its proposals.[37] As anticipated, the focus of any new legislation is likely to be upon the protection and preservation of civil liberties. This would represent a move towards a much more liberal and legalistic stance. In view of our obligations under the ECHR, the general philosophy of the proposals is the principle of patient autonomy and non-discrimination, whereby the emphasis should be upon consensual care and that, as far as possible, people suffering from mental disorder should be treated in the same way as those suffering from physical disorder. The latter approach reinforces the medical model of mental illness, in accordance with the views of the Percy Commission and the Butler Committee. The need to move towards a framework for compulsory mental health care in the community has also been acknowledged.

The Group has not yet made any detailed proposals in relation to the structure and provisions of any new legislation, nor has it yet made any specific proposals in relation to offender-patients. Although, it has been accepted that there will be no need for a root and branch reform, as the Group is 'well aware of the value of retaining structures which are working well'.[38] Change will, therefore, only be recommended where it is necessary.

It is clearly too early to predict the precise scope and impact of any new legislation as the scoping group is not due to produce its final report until July 1999. That will be followed by a lengthy consultation, review, and reform process. It can only be hoped that the proposed reforms will continue in the same vein and strengthen and further promote the philosophy and principles of diversion and timely therapeutic intervention. Although, in view of the rhetoric in the draft report, and increasing emphasis being placed upon public protection in the Labour Government's Green Paper, *Modernising Mental Health Services*, it is unclear to what extent that will be the case, and there continues to be a threat to the long-term future of diversion.

Throughout the past decade, the plight of mentally disordered offenders has been heightened to its greatest level since the Butler Committee report over two decades ago, and this in itself is a notable achievement. Once again, the plight of mentally disordered offenders has been brought to the forefront of the minds of the agencies involved and the need to continue to work together to divert mentally disordered offenders has been emphasized. Moreover, national and local developments have been taking place which have sought to better the lot of mentally disordered offenders, and to an extent, the rhetoric has been turned into

---

[37] DoH, *Draft Outline Proposals Scoping Study Committee Review of Mental Health Act 1983 April 1999* (Doh 1999).

[38] Ibid. Introduction para. 5.

reality. The 1979–97 Conservative Government sought to provide a strong lead, which has now been adopted by the Labour Government, and the relevant Government departments now regularly meet to discuss developments.[39] The need now, however, is to maintain this concerted action so that the flurry of activity which has taken place develops into a long-term plan of sustained activity— a promise that can be kept.[40]

The study presented here, and other small-scale studies which have been outlined in previous chapters, have shown that a certain degree of inter-agency co-operation can be achieved which does facilitate the diversion of mentally disordered offenders. The levels of this achievement must be sustained and further developed, however, for otherwise the wheel will simply come full circle and at the turn of the new century, the prisons and courts will once again be pleading for central Government to take new measures to reduce the numbers of mentally ill people in prison.

The future of diversion policy also hangs in the balance amid public fear and scepticism and demands for greater protection and controls. Research indicates that in the wake of such highly publicized tragedies as Jonathan Zito, Michael Buchanan, Jonathan Newby, Georgina Robinson, and most recently the brutal murders of Lin and Megan Russell by Michael Stone, the public is increasingly fearful of the mentally ill in the community. This has indeed been borne out by research.[41] Diversion policy rests upon the principle of directing offenders into hospital and community care and cannot satisfy these public demands. There is therefore a need to educate society fully about the reality of mental illness and raise awareness that such tragic killings occur only in a tiny minority of cases. As noted earlier, mentally ill people pose a far greater threat to themselves than to others, and, as has been acknowledged, there are thousands of people suffering from mental illness who are living quiet and unobtrusive lives in the community.[42] But until or unless this is common and accepted knowledge, public pressure for stricter controls and harsher sentences is another potential danger which may hamper the future success of diversion policy.[43] It has been argued that the introduction of the mandatory and minimum sentences and the 'hospital direction' already represent one such threat.[44] Whilst the advice articulated in Circulars 66/90 and 12/95

---

[39] DoH/OPCS, *The Government's Expenditure Plans 1995–96 to 1997–98* (1995) Cm. 2182 Para. 4.43; Session 1997–8 HL Debs Vol. 586 col. 412 WA.

[40] See e.g. W. G. Matthews 'Pre-Trial Diversion: Promises We Can't Keep' (1988) 12 *Journal of Offender Counselling, Services and Rehabilitation* 191–202.

[41] See e.g. G. Wolff *et al.*, 'Community Attitudes to Mental Illness' (1996) 168 *British Journal of Psychiatry* 183–90.

[42] 'Community Care for the Mentally Ill', letter to the editor from John Bowis, Parliamentary Under-Secretary of State for Health, *The Times*, 2 August 1995, p. 13.

[43] See also G. Hughes *et al.*, 'Diversion in a Culture of Severity' (1998) 37(1) *How J of Crim Just* 16–33.

[44] J. M. Laing, 'Mentally Disordered Offenders: Sentencing Policy under the Crime (Sentences) Act 1997' (1998) 9(2) *J For Psych* 424–34.

remains in force, the policy has now been expressly qualified by the need to ensure that it is consistent with the requirements of public safety. Circular 66/90 referred to the fact that the offender's mental state should take precedence over the decision to prosecute.[45] There, the emphasis is firmly upon the needs of the offender, but Circular 52/97 has qualified this consideration. It is arguable that there has been a shift in focus, with greater emphasis now being placed upon the safety of the public. And the introduction of legislation such as the Crime and Disorder Act 1998, Crime (Sentences) Act 1997, and Protection from Harassment Act 1997 would seem to represent a move towards a much more retributive approach. The future is, therefore, still uncertain should the Labour Government continue to bow and eventually succumb to such increasing pressures and concerns.

Perhaps this danger is more apparent than real, however, as certain measures are already being taken to combat such fears in other respects. The Labour Government has launched a range of initiatives to improve education in an attempt to reduce the stigma and fear associated with mental ill health.[46] As noted by the Government, this is perhaps one of the greatest challenges that they face, and there is an urgent need to convince the public that they have nothing to fear.[47] Furthermore, the recently announced community care reforms, and particularly the introduction of round-the-clock and assertive outreach support, the possible introduction of special legislation, Secure Units and reviewable sentences for dangerous psychopaths,[48] and the future reform of the mental health legislation[49] may also counteract such fears and allay public concerns without the need for further harsh criminal justice and punitive legislative measures. Whilst the new proposals for reforming the mental health service are aimed at increasing the facilities and support systems, thereby facilitating access to therapeutic care, it could be argued that the reforms are perhaps, in reality, driven by the desire to protect the public and allay public fears and concerns. Indeed, one of the main thrusts of the new proposals is the need to protect the public and it is clearly regarded as the Government's primary concern.[50] Arguably, therefore, whilst the announcement of these measures is to be welcomed as it would seem that the Labour Government is, at last, willing and eager to tackle the root of the problem, in another sense there is, perhaps, some cause for concern, as it may signal a shift in philosophy and a move away from benevolent and therapeutic intervention towards a much more public protectionist and libertarian/legalistic approach. This could also pose a threat to the long-term future of diversion policy which

---

[45] Para. 2.

[46] Session 1997–8 HC Debs Vol. 306 col. 262 WA; see also DoH, *Safe, Sound and Supportive*, para. 1.11–15.

[47] Session 1997–8 HC Debs Vol. 309 col. 168; HL Debs Vol. 585 cols 1225–6.

[48] See further Ch. 1 and also 'Stone: danger men to be caged', *The Observer*, 25 October 1998; see also DoH, *Safe, Sound and Supportive*, Exec. Summ., para. 4.31–3.

[49] See further Ch. 4 and also DoH Press Release 98/311.

[50] DoH, *Safe, Sound and Supportive*, Para. 4.33.

places the emphasis firmly upon the needs of the offender-patient and represents a humane approach.

Ultimately, however, continued diversion will be achieved only if central Government and the relevant authorities are willing to provide adequate funding and facilities in order to maintain this action. Concern has been expressed about the long-term future of diversion policy and one commentator has expressed the view that this humanitarian approach towards some mentally disordered offenders may now be suffering from 'compassion fatigue', and the new Labour Government could believe that the problem is now being adequately addressed thereby withdraw its support.[51]

That the proposal in the Crime (Sentences) Act 1997, to provide a statutory framework for the provision of country-wide assessment schemes, was defeated is therefore extremely unfortunate, as the real threat to the future of diversion policy lies with the resource implications of diversion. As seen with some of the projects, the development of community facilities, the implementation of the 1959 Act and, to a large extent, the 1983 Act, the treatment of mentally disordered offenders has been and still is plagued by inadequate funding and insufficient facilities. The lack of adequate resources in this area has blighted the developments and diversion of mentally disordered offenders greatly, as the Reed Committee highlighted: 'Time and again in the course of this review the question has been asked, what about resources?'[52] It is feared that unless the Government places the diversion process on a firm statutory footing with permanent funding arrangements, it will simply suffer the same fate as the previous attempts to divert mentally disordered offenders.[53] As identified elsewhere, 'Each cycle of reform deplored existing conditions . . . each reform movement made dramatic treatment promises; . . . each suffered from grossly insufficient resources to accomplish its self-styled mandate.'[54]

This is the crux of the issue and the most worrying aspect of all the reforms. It has been identified here that the real question is one of resources and political will. As noted earlier, in the battle for scarce resources, mentally disordered offenders are an unpopular group and do not come high on the list.[55] But, with an estimated 1 in 4 of the adult population likely to suffer from some form of

---

[51] D. P. Allam, 'Diversion Schemes for Mentally Disordered Offenders: A Service Under Threat' (1995) 51(4) *The Mag* 90–1; P. Joseph, 'Diversion Revisited' (1992) 3(2) *J For Psych*, Editorial.

[52] Cm. 2088 Para. 8.5; Staffing and Training Advisory Group Report para. 1.14–17.

[53] See also Allam, 'Service Under Threat'; Joseph, 'Diversion Revisited'.

[54] M. L. Durham, 'The Impact of Deinstitutionalization on the Current Treatment of the Mentally Ill' (1989) 12 *Int J Law & Psych* 117–31, 131.

[55] For example, in North Wales, plans to build a local Secure Unit in Penmaenmawr have come up against a barrage of criticism and opposition from the local residents, see 'Mental unit battlers beaten', *North Wales Weekly News*, 10 November 1994; see also e.g. 'Rationing health care: who should come first? Public would give priority to people with families at the expense of mentally ill', *Daily Telegraph*, 12 September 1994, p. 5.

mental illness at some stage in their lives, it is clear that they deserve a more prominent position among the priorities. The future of diversion policy is therefore a political issue, the fate of which is left in the hands of central Government and MPs in Parliament. The Government must therefore take a much stronger lead and place such decisions and the responsibility for them on a statutory footing, provide funding on a permanent basis, further educate society about the reality of mental illness, ensure that disordered offenders continue to be a high priority and that there are sufficient facilities and services in place to accommodate diverted offenders. As previously noted, a variety of measures is already being taken in this respect, which is greatly welcomed. But as the quotation above indicates, there have been plenty of empty promises and reform proposals in the past which have failed to materialize into viable alternatives, largely due to inadequate funding and lack of continued financial support. The Government must therefore ensure that there is sufficient allocation of resources in the long-term to fund their proposed reforms. This is the primary concern of several mental health organizations who welcome the reform proposals, but acknowledge that in order to make them work there must be adequate—indeed ample—and sustained funding. The rhetoric must meet the reality. Unless and until this is firmly acknowledged and accepted, diversion policy will simply become a suitable device for 'diverting our attention away from the real issues of funding and facilities', and will almost certainly suffer the same fate as its predecessors.

The plight of mentally disordered offenders is one which our society and many others have been trying to solve for many years. As noted earlier, there are no quick or easy solutions as the treatment of mentally ill offenders raises serious financial, political, moral, and ethical issues. As one member of the House of Lords stated recently, 'I have a lurking suspicion that, if Jesus Christ were to return today, he would make a beeline for mental offenders.'[56]

It is sadly concluded that unless the Government is willing to learn from past experiences and make more financial and material resources available, then some form of divine intervention may be the only salvation for future improvements in the treatment of mentally disordered offenders.

---

[56] Session 1993–4 HL Debs Vol. 558 col. 904 *per* The Earl of Longford.

Appendix A.

Diversion under the Existing Provisions

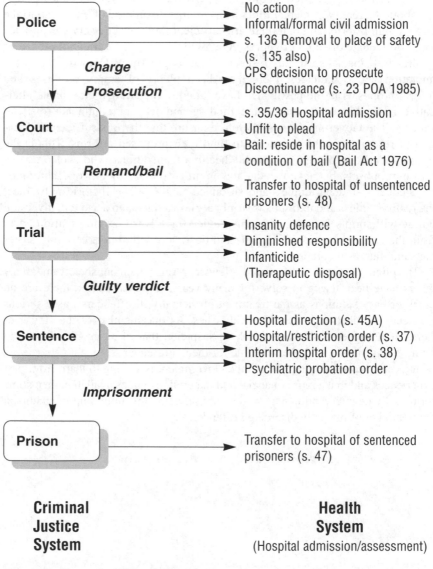

Police

→ No action
→ Informal/formal civil admission
→ s. 136 Removal to place of safety (s. 135 also)

Charge

Prosecution

→ CPS decision to prosecute
Discontinuance (s. 23 POA 1985)

Court

→ s. 35/36 Hospital admission
→ Unfit to plead
→ Bail: reside in hospital as a condition of bail (Bail Act 1976)

Remand/bail

→ Transfer to hospital of unsentenced prisoners (s. 48)

Trial

→ Insanity defence
→ Diminished responsibility
→ Infanticide
(Therapeutic disposal)

Guilty verdict

Sentence

→ Hospital direction (s. 45A)
→ Hospital/restriction order (s. 37)
→ Interim hospital order (s. 38)
→ Psychiatric probation order

Imprisonment

Prison

→ Transfer to hospital of sentenced prisoners (s. 47)

**Criminal
Justice
System**

**Health
System**
(Hospital admission/assessment)

Note: POA = Prosecution of Offences Act.

Appendix B.

Police Station Assessment (PSA Model)

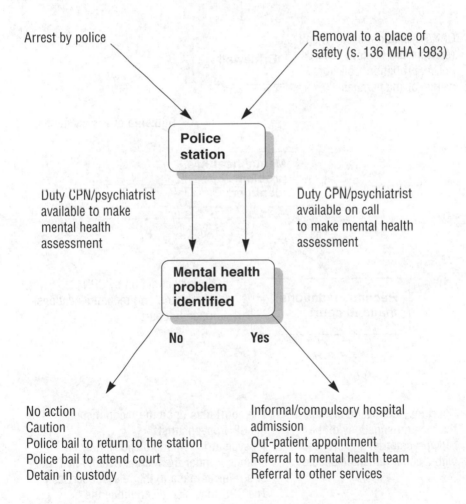

Arrest by police

Removal to a place of safety (s. 136 MHA 1983)

Police station

Duty CPN/psychiatrist available to make mental health assessment

Duty CPN/psychiatrist available on call to make mental health assessment

Mental health problem identified

No   **Yes**

No action
Caution
Police bail to return to the station
Police bail to attend court
Detain in custody

Informal/compulsory hospital admission
Out-patient appointment
Referral to mental health team
Referral to other services

Appendix C.
Court Psychiatric Assessment (NAC/PAC models)

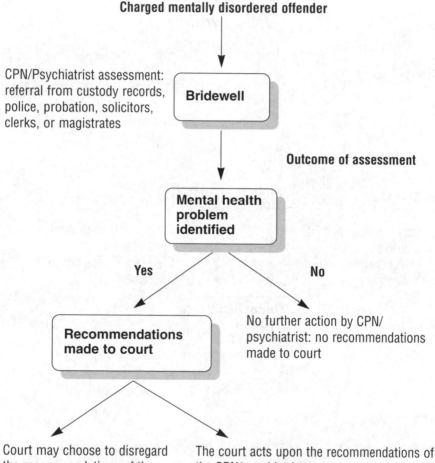

Charged mentally disordered offender

CPN/Psychiatrist assessment: referral from custody records, police, probation, solicitors, clerks, or magistrates

Bridewell

Outcome of assessment

Mental health problem identified

Yes

No

Recommendations made to court

No further action by CPN/ psychiatrist: no recommendations made to court

Court may choose to disregard the recommendations of the CPN/psychiatrist and proceed with a penal remand/disposal

The court acts upon the recommendations of the CPN/psychiatrist.
A psychiatric remand/disposal may be arranged under the Mental Health Act 1983, or a referral made to the relevant services. The CPS may also discontinue the prosecution if a psychiatric disposal/referral is secured

Appendix D.

Court Panel Assessment (MAAP model)

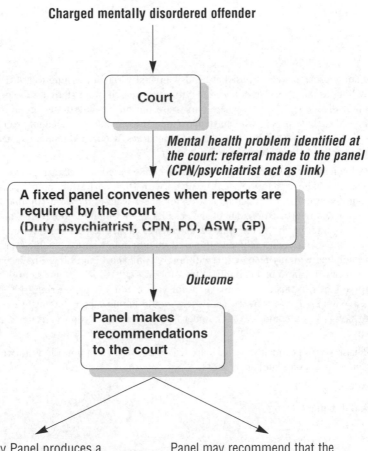

Charged mentally disordered offender

Court

Mental health problem identified at the court: referral made to the panel (CPN/psychiatrist act as link)

A fixed panel convenes when reports are required by the court (Duty psychiatrist, CPN, PO, ASW, GP)

Outcome

Panel makes recommendations to the court

Multi-Agency Panel produces a report and a package of care for the defendant to the court to enable a therapeutic remand/disposal to be made which will be followed through by the team. This may result in a discontinuance by the CPS, a remand for report, or a psychiatric disposal at the sentencing stage

Panel may recommend that the prosecution proceed as normal but that a mental element is involved and therefore refer the defendant to the relevant services

Appendix E. Covering Letter and Interview Schedule for Research Study

Covering Letter

23rd March 1995

Dear [Client name],

I am a research worker based at Leeds University and am writing to ask if you would be willing to talk to me in connection with my research. I am studying the development of court diversion schemes, where nurses are present at magistrates' courts to assess and provide help to people who may have a mental health, drug or alcohol problem. This type of scheme is operating at [Court name] Magistrates' Court and I am interested in the views of people who have seen the nurse at court.

[CPN name], the Community Psychiatric Nurse based at the court, put me in touch with you as I believe that you were involved with [him/her] at the court recently. I realise that appearing in court can be distressing and I want to reassure you that I do not want to ask detailed questions about the case itself, but mainly your views about the nurse and whether or not [his/her] involvement was of any help to you. Nothing will be written in my final report which will identify the people who have helped me. If you agree to help me with my research, it will involve one short interview. I have arranged for an interview room to be available at [venue] on [date] at [time] and would hope to speak to you then. If this is not convenient for you, could you please ring 0113 233 5033 and leave a message as to when and where would be more convenient for me to meet you, or perhaps you could leave a number for me to contact you to arrange a more suitable time.

Thank you very much for your help. If I do not hear from you I look forward to meeting you at [time] on [date] at [venue].

Yours sincerely,

Judith Laing

Interview Schedule

Interview No: _____
Interview date: ___/___/___

A. Personal Details

1. What is your name?:   2. Sex: M/F
3. In which town do you live?:
4. How old are you?:
5. How would you describe your ethnic origin?:

B. Offence Details

6. At which magistrates' court did you appear when you saw the CPN?:
7. Why were you in court at that time?:
8A. Have you ever been in trouble with the police or appeared in court before? [If No, go to Q.9]:
8B. How many times?:
8C. What were you supposed to have done?:
8D. What was the outcome?:

C. Psychiatric Details

9A. Have you ever had personal difficulties and been in touch with the psychiatric services before?: [If No, go to Q.12]:
9B. What sort of help did you receive from them?:
10. Were you receiving any psychiatric help/treatment/supervision when you committed the offence?:
11A. Have you received any psychiatric help as a result of any previous court appearances or police arrests? [If No, go to Q.12]:
11B. What sort of help was it (e.g. psychiatric probation order/remand for report/treatment in prison hospital wing)?:

D. Assessment Details

12. Who referred you to the CPN (Personal request/Police/Probation or Bail Information Officer/Solicitor/Magistrates/CPN)?:
13. How did you feel at first about having the CPN assessment and involvement (Good/Bad/Indifferent)?:
14. How do you feel now about the CPN's involvement?:
15. What did the CPN arrange for you—outcome of assessment (Appointment with Dr or CPN/ Hospital admission/ Referral to other agency/ Nothing)?:
16. How do you feel about what was arranged for you?:
17A. Are you still in contact with the services/agency to which you were referred? [If Yes, go to Q.18]:
17B. Why are you no longer in contact?:
18A. Were you aware of this service before your contact with the CPN? [If No, go to Q.19]:
18B. Why had you not already/previously made contact with it?:
19A. Are you receiving any other help that you have found useful? [If No, go to Q.20]:
19B. What sort of help?:
19C. How did you come about getting this help?:
20. Can you think of any way in which the CPN could have been of more benefit to you?:
21. Would you like to comment upon your involvement with the CPN and its effect upon you (perceived benefits—access to care/protection from punitive sanctions or custody/condition improved) or drawbacks (condition worsened/no real effect/comparison with how treated following previous sentencing outcomes) of the scheme? [Prompt only if necessary]:

Bibliography

BOOKS AND ARTICLES

ABBOTT, S., *Psychiatric Assessment and Diversion Panel for Mentally Disordered Offenders, Bolton: Report of a Needs Assessment Survey* (HACCRU, University of Liverpool, 1996).

ABDUL-HAMID, W. and COONEY, C., 'Homelessness, Mental Illness and the Law' (1997) 37(4) *Medicine, Science & Law* 341–4.

ADLER, F., 'From Hospital to Jail: New Challenges to the Law Enforcement Process' (1981) 17 *Criminal Law Bulletin* 319–33.

AIRES, D., 'Mentally Disordered Offenders and Magistrates' Courts' (1986) 42 *The Magistrate* 156–7.

AKHURST, M., BROWN, I., and WESSELY, S., *Dying for Help: Offenders at Risk of Suicide* (WYPS, WYHA, ACOP 1995).

AKINKUNMI, A. *et al.*, 'Inadequacies in the Mental Health Act 1983 in Relation to Mentally Disordered Remand Prisoners' (1997) 37(1) *Medicine, Science & Law* 55–7.

ALLAM, D. P., 'Sentencing of the Mentally Disordered' (1990) 46 *The Magistrate* 176–7.

—— 'Inter-Agency Co-operation: A Geological Fault Line' (1994) 158 *Justice of the Peace and Local Government Law* 147–8.

—— 'Diversion Schemes for Mentally Disordered Offenders: A Service Under Threat' (1995) 51 *The Magistrate* 90–1.

ALLDRIDGE, P., 'Hospitals, Madhouses and Asylums: Cycles in the Care of the Insane' (1979) 134 *British Journal of Psychiatry* 321–34.

ALLEN, H., *Justice Unbalanced: Gender, Psychiatry and Judicial Decisions* (Oxford University Press 1988).

ANDOH, B., 'The Job that Nobody Wants' (1994) *Police Review*, 4 March, 23–4.

—— 'The Hospital Order with Restrictions' (1994) 58 *Journal of Criminal Law* 97–108.

ANON., 'A Practising Psychiatrist: The Experience of Electro-Convulsive Therapy' (1965) 111 *British Journal of Psychiatry* 365–7.

APPELBAUM, P. S., *Almost a Revolution: Mental Health Law and the Limits of Change* (Oxford University Press 1994).

APPLEBY, L., SHAW, J., and AMOS, T., 'National Confidential Inquiry into Suicide and Homicide by People with Mental Illnes's (1997) 170 *British Journal of Psychiatry* 101–3.

ARBOLEDA-FLOREZ, J., 'Two Solitudes: Mental Health and Law' (1990) 1 *Journal of Forensic Psychiatry* 143–65.

ASHWORTH, A., 'The Butler Committee and Criminal Responsibility' [1975] *Criminal Law Review* 687–96.

—— 'Dealing with Mentally Disordered Offenders Classified as Psychopathic' [1986] *Criminal Law Review* 705–7.

—— 'The "Public Interest" Element in Prosecutions' [1987] *Criminal Law Review* 595–607.

—— 'Victim Impact Statements and Sentencing' [1993] *Criminal Law Review* 498.

—— 'Sentencing Mentally Disordered Offenders' [1996] *Criminal Law Review* 457–8, 457.

—— *The Criminal Process: An Evaluative Study* (Clarendon 1998).

—— 'Review of the Crown Prosecution Service' [1998] *Criminal Law Review* 517–20.

ASHWORTH, A., and FIONDA, J., 'The New Code for Crown Prosecutors: Prosecution, Accountability and the Public Interest' [1994] *Criminal Law Review* 894–903.

ASHWORTH, A., and GOSTIN, L., 'Mentally Disordered Offenders and the Sentencing Process' [1984] *Criminal Law Review* 195–212.

ASHWORTH, A., and SHAPLAND, J., 'Psychopaths in the Criminal Process' [1980] *Criminal Law Review* 628–40.

ASHWORTH, A. L., *Stanley Royd Hospital Wakefield: One Hundred and Fifty Years: A History* (Berrico Publicity London 1977).

Association of Chief Probation Officers, *Probation Actively Working with Health and Social Services in the Management of Mentally Disordered Offenders: A Report Produced by the Committee on Work with Mentally Disordered Offenders* (ACOP Wakefield 1994).

ATKINS, R. D., 'Diversion of Mentally Ill Defendants in the Magistrates' Courts' (1994) 47 *Criminal Lawyer* 1–3.

BALDWIN, J., and HUNT, A., 'Prosecutors Advising in Police Stations' [1998] *Criminal Law Review* 521–36.

BALL, C., 'Cautioning: A Radical Shift in Policy?' (1994) 144 *New Law Journal* 495–6.

BARKER, A., 'Mentally Disordered Offenders and the Courts: Some Aspects of the Problems as seen by a Beak and a Quack' (1988) 152 *Justice of the Peace* 55–7, 71–4, 100–4.

BARKER, M., and SWYER, B., 'Communication and Collaboration in Community Care for Mentally Disordered Offenders' (1994) 41 *Probation Journal* 130–4.

BEAN, P., 'The Mental Health Act 1959: Rethinking an Old Problem' (1979) 6 *British Journal of Law & Society* 99–108.

—— (ed.), *Mental Illness: Changes and Trends* (John Wiley 1983).

—— *Mental Disorder and Legal Control* (Cambridge University Press 1986).

—— 'Supervision Registers for the Mentally Disordered' (1997) 161 *Justice of the Peace* 477–8.

BEAN, P., and MOUNSER, P., *Discharged from Mental Hospitals* (Macmillan/MIND 1993).

BEAN, P.,and NEMITZ, T., 'The Use of the Appropriate Adult Scheme: A Preliminary Report' (1994) 34 *Medicine, Science & Law* 161.

BEAN, P., *et al.*, *Out of Harm's Way* (MIND 1991).

BELLI, M., 'Did McNaghten need a Psychiatrist, a Lawyer or a Definition?' (1971) 11 *Medicine, Science & Law* 25–30.

BENN, M., 'Jail or Hospital? Nobody Wants Them' (1985) *New Statesman*, 25 October 15–16.

BERRIOS, G., and FREEMAN, H. (eds.), *150 Years of British Psychiatry, 1841–1991* (Gaskell Books/Royal College of Psychiatrists 1991).

BERRY, R., 'Police Contact with Mentally Disordered Persons in the Northumbria Force Area' (1996) 69 *Police Journal* 221–6.

BEVAN, V,. and LIDSTONE, K., *The Investigation of Crime: A Guide to Police Powers* (Butterworths 1991).

BHUI, K., *et al.*, 'African-Caribbean Men Remanded to Brixton Prison: Psychiatric and Forensic Characteristics and Outcome of Final Court Appearance (1998) 172 *British Journal of Psychiatry* 337–44.

BIRMINGHAM, L., *et al.*, 'Prevalence of Mental Disorder in Remand Prisoners' (1996) 313 *British Medical Journal* 1521–4.

BLAGG, H., *et al.*, 'Inter-Agency Co-operation: Rhetoric and Reality' in T. Hope and M. Shaw (eds.), *Communities and Crime Reduction* (HMSO 1988).

BLOM-COOPER, L., *et al.*, *The Falling Shadow: One Patient's Mental Health Care 1978–1993* (Duckworth 1995).

BLUGLASS, R., 'Psychiatry, the Law and the Offender: Present Dilemmas and Future Prospects', The Seventh Denis Carroll Memorial Lecture (Institute for the Study and Treatment of Delinquency 1980).

—— *A Guide to the Mental Health Act 1983* (Churchill Livingstone 1983).

—— 'Mentally Disordered Prisoners: Reports but no Improvements' (1988) 296 *British Medical Journal* 1757.

BLUMMENTHAL, S., 'Diverting Mentally Disordered Offenders' (1993) 40 *Probation Journal* 98–100.

BLUMMENTHAL, S., and WESSELY, S., 'National Survey of Current Arrangements for Diversion from Custody in England and Wales' (1992) 305 *British Medical Journal* 1322–5.

BOWDEN, P., 'Men Remanded into Custody for Medical Reports: The Selection for Treatment' (1978) 132 *British Journal of Psychiatry* 320–31.

—— 'The Review of the Mental Health Act 1959: A Medical Comment' (1979) 19 *British Journal of Criminology* 267–9.

—— 'Madness or Badness?' (1983) 30 *British Journal of Hospital Medicine* 388–94.

—— 'Forensic Psychiatric Services and Regional Secure Units in England and Wales: An Overview' [1986] *Criminal Law Review* 790–9.

BRABBINS, C. J., and TRAVERS, R. F., 'Mental Disorder amongst Defendants in a Liverpool Magistrates' Court' (1994) 34 *Medicine, Science & Law* 279–83.

BRAGGINS, J., and MARTIN, C. (eds.), *Managing Risk: Achieving the Possible, Report of the ISTD Annual Conference 1995* (ISTD 1996).

BRAHAMS, D., and WELLER, M., 'Crime and Homelessness among the Mentally Ill' (1985) 135 *New Law Journal* 626–7.

BRIDGE, J., *et al.*, *Blackstone's Guide to the Children Act 1989* (Blackstone 1990).

British Medical Association, *Health Care of Detainees in Police Stations* (BMA 1994).

BROOKE, D., *et al.*, 'Point Prevalence of Mental Disorder in Unconvicted Male Prisoners in England and Wales' (1996) 313 *British Medical Journal* 1524–7.

BROWN, A. J., and CRISP, D., *Diverting Cases from Prosecution in the Public Interest*, Home Office Research and Statistics Department Research Bulletin, 32 (Home Office 1992), 7–12.

BROWN, D., *et al.*, *PACE 10 Years On: A Review of Research*, Research and Statistics Directorate, Research Findings, 49 (Home Office 1997).

BROWN, G. C., and GEELAN, S. D., 'Elliott House: Working with Mentally Disordered Offenders' (1998) 45(1) *Probation Journal* 10–14.

BROWNE, D., *Black Patients, Mental Health and the Courts* (NACRO 1990).

—— *Black People and Sectioning* (Little Rock 1997).

BROWNLEE, I., *Community Punishment: A Critical Introduction* (Longman 1998).

—— 'New Labour, New Penology? Punitive Rhetoric and the Limits of Managerialism in Criminal Justice Policy' (1998) 25(3) *Journal of Law & Society* 313–25.

BUCKE, T., and BROWN, D., *Suspects in Police Custody and the Revised PACE Code of Practice*, Research and Statistics Directorate Research Findings, (Home Office 1997).

—— *In Police Custody: Police Powers and Suspects' Rights under the Revised PACE Codes of Practice,* Home Office Research Study, 174 (Home Office 1997).

BULLIVANT, M., 'A Sense of Justice' (1996) 92(49) *Nursing Times* 44–5.

BURNEY, E., and PEARSON, G., 'Mentally Disordered Offenders: Finding a Focus for Diversion' (1995) 34(4) *Howard Journal of Criminal Justice* 281–313.

BUTTNER, E., 'Police Discretion in Emergency Apprehension of Mentally Ill Persons' (1967) 14 *Social Problems* 278.

BYNOE, I., 'The Prison Medical Wing: A "Place of Safety"?' (1990) 1 *Journal of Forensic Psychiatry* 251–7.

CAMERON, G. D. L., and McMANUS, J. J., *Consideration of the Mental State of Accused Persons at the Pre-Trial and Pre-Sentencing Stages* (Scottish Office Research Unit 1993).

CAPE, E., 'Mentally Disordered Suspects and the Right to Silence' (1996) 146 *New Law Journal* 80–3, 101.

CARD, R., *Public Order: The New Law* (Butterworths 1987).

CARSON, D., 'Detention of the Mentally Disordered' (1982) 146 *Local Government Review* 887–94.

—— 'Mental Processes: The Mental Health Act 1983' [1983] *Journal of Social Welfare Law* 195–211

—— 'Prosecuting People with Mental Handicaps' [1989] *Criminal Law Review* 87–94.

—— 'Holding the Patient to Account at the Gatekeeping Stage' (1992) 2 *Criminal Behaviour and Mental Health* 224–33.

CARSON, D., and WEXLER, D. B., 'New Approaches to Mental Health Law: Will the UK Follow the US Lead, Again?' (1994) 1 *Journal of Social Welfare and Family Law* 79–96.

CASEY, C., 'Forces to get Mental Illness Video' (1994) *Police Review*, 21 October, 8.

CAVADINO, M., *Mental Health Law in Context: Doctor's Orders?* (Gower 1988).

—— 'Mental Illness and Neo-Polonianism' (1991) 2 *Journal of Forensic Psychiatry* 295–304.

—— 'A Vindication of the Rights of Psychiatric Patients' (1997) 24 *Journal of Law and Society* 235–51.

CHAMBERS, C., and GILL, J., 'Psychiatric Assessment and Diversion Schemes: Problems Associated with Brief Court Reports' (1998) 22 (5) *Psychiatric Bulletin* 303–5.

CHAMBERS, C., and RIX, K. J. B., 'A Controlled Evaluation of Assessments by Doctors and Nurses in a Magistrates' Court Mental Health Assessment and Diversion Scheme' (1999) 39(1) *Medicine, Science & Law* 38–48.

CHERRETT, K., 'The Last Resort' (1994) *Police Review*, 14 October, 16–17.

—— 'Policing the Mentally Ill: An Attitudinal Study of Police Contact with Mentally Disordered Persons within the Gwent Constabulary' (1995) 68 *Police Journal* 22–8.

CHEUNG CHANG, M., 'A Description of a Forensic Diversion Service in One City in the UK' (1998) 38(3) *Medicine, Science & Law* 242–50.

CHEUNG CHANG, M., *et al.*, 'A Follow-up Study of Mentally Disordered Offenders after a Court Diversion Scheme: Six-Month and One-Year Comparison' (1999) 31(1) *Medicine, Science & Law* 31–7.

CHISWICK, D., 'Managing Psychopathic Offenders: A Problem That Will Not Go Away' (1987) 295 *British Medical Journal* 159–60.

COHEN, C., and MIDGLEY, G., *The North Humberside Diversion from Custody Project for Mentally Disordered Offenders* (Centre for Systems Studies, Hull University 1994).

COHEN, D., *Forgotten Millions: The Treatment of the Mentally Ill—A Global Perspective* (Paladin Grafton 1988).

COID, J., 'How Many Psychiatric Patients in Prison?' (1984) 145 *British Journal of Psychiatry* 78–86.

—— 'Mentally Abnormal Prisoners in Remand, I. Rejected or Accepted by the NHS'; 'II. Comparison of Services Provided by Oxford and Wessex Regions' (1988) 296 *British Medical Journal* 1779–82, 1783–4.

COLLINS, P., 'The Treatability of Psychopaths' (1991) 2 *Journal of Forensic Psychiatry* 103–10.

COLOMBO, A., *Understanding Mentally Disordered Offenders: A Multi-Agency Perspective* (Ashgate 1997).

COOKE, D. J., 'Treatment as an Alternative to Prosecution: Offenders Diverted for Treatment' (1991) 158 *British Journal of Psychiatry* 785–91.

—— 'Psychological Treatment as an Alternative to Prosecution: A Form of Primary Diversion' (1991) 30 *Howard Journal of Criminal Justice* 53–65.

—— 'Reconviction Following Referral to a Forensic Clinic: The Criminal Justice Outcome of Diversion' (1992) 32 *Medicine, Science & Law* 325–30.

—— 'Primary Diversion for Psychological Treatment: The Decision Making of Procurators Fiscal' (1994) 17 *International Journal of Law & Psychiatry* 211–23.

COOPER, D., *Psychiatry and Anti-Psychiatry* (Tavistock 1967).

COPE, R., 'A Survey of Forensic Psychiatrists' Views on Psychopathic Disorder' (1993) 4 *Journal of Forensic Psychiatry* 227–9.

COPE, R., and NDEGWA, D., 'Ethnic Differences in Admission to a Regional Secure Unit' (1990) 1 *Journal of Forensic Psychiatry* 365–78.

CRAFT, M., 'Should One Treat or Gaol Psychopaths?' in Craft, M. and Craft, A. (eds.), *Mentally Abnormal Offenders* (Balliere 1984).

CRAFT, M., and CRAFT, A. (eds.), *Mentally Abnormal Offenders* (Balliere 1984).

CRICHTON, J. H. M., 'Supervised Discharge' (1994) 34 *Medicine, Science & Law* 319–20.

CRIPPS, J., *et al.*, 'Bridging the Gap in Secure Provision: Evaluation of a New Local Combined Locked Forensic/Intensive Care Unit (1995) 6 *Journal of Forensic Psychiatry* 77–91.

CRISP, D., *et al., Public Interest Case Assessment Schemes*, Home Office Research Study, 138 (HMSO 1995).

CROWLEY-SMITH, L., 'Intellectual Disability and Mental Illness: A Call for Unambiguous and Uniform Statutory Definitions' (1995) 3 *Journal of Law & Medicine* 192–201.

DANK, N., and KULISHOFF, M., 'An Alternative to Incarceration of the Mentally Ill' (1983) 3 *Journal of Prison and Jail Health* 95–100.

DAVIES, L., and LAWRENSON, M., 'Protection from Harassment Act 1997' (1997) *Legal Action,* August, 23.

DAVIES, M., CROALL, H., and TYRER, J., *Criminal Justice: An Introduction to the Criminal Justice System in England and Wales* (Longman 1998).

DAVIES, S., *et al.*, 'Ethnic Differences in Risk of Compulsory Psychiatric Admission among Representative Cases of Psychosis in London' (1996) 312 *British Medical Journal* 533–7.

DAVIS, S., 'Factors Associated with the Diversion of Mentally Disordered Offenders' (1994) 22 *Bulletin of the American Academy of Psychiatry & Law* 389–97.

DAW, R. K., 'The Public Interest Criterion in the Decision to Prosecute' (1989) 53 *Journal of Criminal Law* 485–501.

—— 'The New Code for Crown Prosecutors: A Response' [1994] *Criminal Law Review* 904–9.

DE REUCK, A., and PORTER, A. (eds.), *The Mentally Abnormal Offender* (Churchill 1968).

DELL, S., *Murder into Manslaughter* (Oxford University Press 1980).

DELL, S., and ROBERTSON, G., *Sentenced to Hospital* (Oxford University Press 1988).

DIJK, P. VAN, and HOOF, F. VAN, *Theory and Practice of the ECHR* (Kluwer 1990).

DINGWALL, G., and HARDING, C., *Diversion in the Criminal Process* (Sweet & Maxwell 1998).

DODDS, M., 'Mentally Disordered Offenders and Magistrates' (1987) 43 *The Magistrate* 45–6.

DOLAN, M. C,. and CAMPBELL, A. A., 'The Criminal Procedure (Insanity and Unfitness to Plead) Act 1991' (1994) 34 *Medicine, Science & Law* 155–60.

DONOVAN, W. M., and O' BRIEN, K. P., 'Psychiatric Court Reports—Too Many or Too Few?' (1981) 21 *Medicine, Science & Law* 153–8.

DOOLEY, E., 'Prison Suicide in England and Wales, 1972–87' (1990) 156 *British Journal of Psychiatry* 40–5.

DRAKEFORD, M., 'The Appropriate Adult' (1994) 41 *Probation Journal* 135–9.

DUFF, P., 'Diversion from Prosecution to Psychiatric Care: Who Controls the Gates?' (1997) 37(1) *British Journal of Criminology* 15–34.

DUFF, P., and BURMAN, M., *Diversion from Prosecution to Psychiatric Care* (Scottish Office Central Research Unit 1994).

—— 'Diversion from Prosecution to Psychiatric Care' (1995) 18 *Scots Law Times* 159–63.

DUNN, J., and FAHY, T., 'Section 136 and the Police' (1987) 11 *Bulletin of the Royal College of Psychiatrists* 224–5.

DURHAM, M. L., 'The Impact of Deinstitutionalization on the Current Treatment of the Mentally Ill' (1989) 12 *International Journal of Law & Psychiatry* 117–31.

EASTMAN, N., 'Anti-Therapeutic Community Mental Health Law' (1995) 310 *British Medical Journal* 1081–2.

EASTMAN, N., and PEAY, J., 'Sentencing Psychopaths: Is the "Hospital and Limitation Direction" an Ill-Considered Hybrid?' [1998] *Criminal Law Review* 93–108.

Editorial, 'Royal Commission on Criminal Justice' (1993) 143 *New Law Journal* 993–6.

Editorial, 'Mental Disorder and the Courts: Report of a Joint BAFS/CBA/LCCSA 1993 Seminar' (1994) 34 *Medicine Science & Law* 520–1.

EDWARDS, A., 'Criminal Law Update: Mentally Disordered Suspects' (1991) 88 *Law Society Gazette* 29.

ELLIMAN, S., 'Independent Information for the CPS' (1990) 140 *New Law Journal* 812–14.

ETHERINGTON, D., 'The Police Liaison Community Psychiatric Nurse Project' (1996) 1(2) *Mental Health Review* 21–4.

EVANS, J., and TOMISON, A., 'Assessment of the Perceived Need for a Psychiatric Service to a Magistrates' Court, (1997) 37(2) *Medicine, Science & Law* 161–4.

EVANS, R. and ELLIS, R., *Police Cautioning in the 1990s,* Research and Statistics Directorate, Research Findings, 52 (Home Office 1997).

EWINS, D., 'The Butler Report' (1976) 3 *British Journal of Law & Society* 101–9.

EXWORTHY, T., 'Compulsory Care in the Community: A Review of the Proposals for Compulsory Supervision and Treatment of the Mentally Ill in the Community' (1995) 5 *Criminal Behaviour and Mental Health* 218–41.

EXWORTHY, T., and GLENN, C., 'A Case for Change: Section 35, Mental Health Act 1983' (1992) 156 *Justice of the Peace* 663–4.

EXWORTHY, T., and PARROTT, J., 'Evaluation of a Diversion from Custody Scheme at Magistrates' Courts' (1993) 4 *Journal of Forensic Psychiatry* 497–505.

—— 'Comparative Evaluation of a Diversion from Custody Scheme' (1997) 8 *Journal of Forensic Psychiatry* 406–16.

EYSENCK, H. J., and GUDJONSSON, G. H., *The Causes and Cures of Criminality* (Plenum 1989).

FAHY, T. *et al.*, 'Police Admissions to Psychiatric Hospitals: A Challenge to Community Psychiatry' (1987) 27 *Medicine, Science & Law* 263–7.

—— 'The Police as a Referral Agency for Psychiatric Emergencies: A Review' (1989) 29 *Medicine, Science & Law* 315–22.

FARRAR, M., 'Government Policy on Mentally Disordered Offenders and its Implementation' (1996) 5 *Journal of Mental Health* 465–74.

FAULK, M., and TRAFFORD, P. A., 'Efficacy of Medical Remands' (1975) 15 *Medicine, Science & Law* 276–9.

FENNELL, P., 'The Mental Health Review Tribunal' (1977) *British Journal of Law and Society* 186–219.

—— 'Law and Psychiatry: The Legal Constitution of the Psychiatric System' (1986) 13 *Journal of Law & Society* 35–65.

—— 'Diversion of Mentally Disordered Offenders from Custody' [1991] *Criminal Law Review* 333–48.

—— 'The Criminal Procedure (Insanity and Unfitness to Plead) Act 1991' (1992) 55 *Modern Law Review* 547–55.

—— 'Diversion from Custody: An Examination of the Provisions Made to Avoid Sending Mentally Disordered Offenders into Custody' (1993) 90 *Law Society Gazette* 18.

—— 'The Appropriate Adult: Criminal Justice Policy towards Mentally Disordered Suspects' (1993) 90 *Law Society Gazette* 19.

—— 'Mentally Disordered Suspects in the Criminal Justice System' (1994) 21 *Journal of Law & Society* 57–71.

FENNELL, P., and KOENRAADT, F., 'Diversion, Europeanization and the Mentally Disordered Offender' in C. Harding *et al., Criminal Justice in Europe: A Comparative Study* (Clarendon 1995).

FISHER, M., 'Guardianship under the Mental Health Legislation: A Review' [1988] *Journal of Social Welfare Law* 316–27.

FORD, A. M. C. A., 'Homelessness and Persistent Petty Offenders: The Impact of Intervention and its Implications for Punishment in the Community' (unpublished Ph.D. thesis, University of Leeds 1992).

FOUCAULT, M., *Madness and Civilisation: A History of Insanity in the Age of Reason* (Tavistock 1971).

FOX, R., 'Butler on Sickness and Crime' [1975] *Criminal Law Review* 683–7.

FREEMAN, R. J., and ROESCH, R., 'Mental Disorder and the Criminal Justice System' (1989) 12 *International Journal of Law and Psychiatry* 105–15.

GIBBENS, T. C. N., SOOTHILL, K., and WAY, C., 'Psychiatric Treatment on Probation' (1981) 21 *British Journal of Criminology* 324–34.

GILLESPIE, A., 'Victims and Sentencing' (1998) 148 *New Law Journal* 1263–5.

GOFFMAN, E., *Asylums: Essays on the Social Situation of Mental Patients and Other Inmates* (Penguin 1968).

GORDON, C., 'Guardianship in Oxfordshire: Hits and Misses' (1998) 22 *Psychiatric Bulletin* 223–35.

GORDON, D., and HEDDERMAN, C., *Panel Assessment Schemes and Other Responses to Mentally Disordered Offenders: A Survey of Probation Areas*, Home Office Research and Statistics Department Research Bulletin, 34 (HMSO 1994), 9–12.

GOSTIN, L., *A Human Condition*, i. *The Mental Health Act 1959–1975: Observations, Analysis and Proposals for Reform* (London MIND 1975).

—— *A Human Condition*, ii. *The Law Relating to Mentally Abnormal Offenders: Observations, Analysis and Proposals for Reform* (London MIND 1977).

—— *Is it Fair? The Mental Health Act 1959* (London MIND 1978).

—— 'Review of the Mental Health (Amendment) Act' (1982) 132 *New Law Journal* 1127–1132, 1151–1155, 1199–1203.

—— 'Human Rights, Judicial Review and the Mentally Disordered Offender' [1982] *Criminal Law Review* 779–93.

—— 'Contemporary Social Historical Perspectives on Mental Health Reform' (1983) 10 *Journal of Law and Society* 47–70.

—— (ed), *Secure Provision: A Review of Special Services for Mentally Ill and Mentally Handicapped People in England and Wales* (Tavistock 1985).

—— *Mental Health Services: Law and Practice* (Shaw & Sons 1986).

GOVE, W. R., *Deviance and Mental Illness* (Sage 1982).

GRANT, W., 'Guardianship Orders: A Review of their Use under the 1983 Mental Health Act' (1992) 32 *Medicine, Science & Law* 319–24.

GREEN, M., *et al.,* 'Criminal Responsibility and Mental Disorder in Britain and North America: A Comparative Study' (1991) 31 *Medicine, Science & Law* 45–53.

GREENHALGH, N. M., *et al.,* 'Pilot Mental Health Assessment and Diversion Scheme for an English Metropolitan Petty Sessional Division' (1996) 36 *Medicine, Science & Law* 52–8.

GREENLAND, C., *Mental Illness and Civil Liberty*, Occasional Papers on Social Administration, 38 (Social Administration Research Trust 1970) .

GRIEW, E., 'Let's Implement Butler on Mental Disorder and Crime' [1984] 37 *Current Legal Problems* 47–62.

GROUNDS, A., 'The Use of Remand Provisions in the 1983 Mental Health Act' (1988) 12 *Bulletin of the Royal College of Psychiatrists* 125–6.

—— 'Transfers of Sentenced Prisoners to Hospital' [1990] *Criminal Law Review* 544–51.

—— 'The Mentally Disordered in Prison' (1991) 81 *Prison Service Journal* 29–40.

—— 'The Transfer of Sentenced Prisoners to Hospital 1960–83: A Study in One Special Hospital' (1991) 31 *British Journal of Criminology* 54–71.

—— 'Mental Health Problems', in Stockdale, E. and Casale, S. (eds.), *Criminal Justice Under Stress* (Blackstones 1992).

GROUNDS, A., *et al.,* 'Mentally Disordered Remanded Prisoners' (unpublished Report to the Home Office 1991).

GRUBIN, D. H., 'Unfit to Plead in England and Wales, 1976–1988: A Survey' (1991) 158 *British Journal of Psychiatry* 540–8.
—— 'What Constitutes Fitness to Plead?' [1993] *Criminal Law Review* 748–58.
GRUNHUT, M., *Probation and Mental Treatment* (Tavistock 1963).
GUDJONSSON, G. H., *The Psychology of Interrogations, Confessions and Testimony* (John Wiley 1992).
GUDJONSSON, G. H., *et al.*, *Persons at Risk during Police Interviews: The Identification of Vulnerabilities*, Royal Commission on Criminal Justice Research Study, 12 (HMSO 1993).
GUNN, J., 'Disasters, Asylums and Plans: Forensic Psychiatry Today' (1974) 3 *British Medical Journal* 611–13.
—— 'The Law and the Mentally Abnormal Offender in England and Wales' (1979) 2 *International Journal of Law & Psychiatry* 199–214.
GUNN, J., and JOSEPH, P., 'Remands to Hospital for Psychiatric Reports: A Study of Psychiatrists' Attitudes to s. 35 of the Mental Health Act 1983' (1993) 17 *Psychiatric Bulletin* 197–199.
GUNN, J., *et al.*, *Psychiatric Aspects of Imprisonment* (Academic Press 1978).
—— *Mentally Disordered Prisoners* (HMSO 1991).
—— *How Many Prisoners Should be in Hospital?* Home Office Research and Statistics Department Research Bulletin, 31 (HMSO 1991).
—— 'Treatment Needs of Prisoners with Psychiatric Disorders' (1991) 303 *British Medical Journal* 338–41.
GUNN, M. J., 'The Mental Health (Amendment) Act 1982' (1983) 46 *Modern Law Review* 318–29.
—— 'Mental Health Act Guardianship: Where Now?' [1986] *Journal of Social Welfare Law* 144–52.
—— 'Case Note on *Birch*' (1990) 1 *Journal of Forensic Psychiatry* 88–92.
GUNNELL, D. J., *et al.*, 'Relation between Parasuicide, Suicide, Psychiatric Admissions, and Socio-economic Deprivation' (1995) 311 *British Medical Journal* 226–30.
HADLEY, T. R., and GOLDMAN, H., 'Effect of Recent Health and Social Service Policy Reforms on Britain's Mental Health System' (1995) 311 *British Medical Journal* 1556–8.
HALL WILLIAMS, J. E., 'Legal Views of Psychiatric Evidence' (1980) 20 *Medicine, Science & Law* 276–82.
HAMILTON, J. R., 'Diminished Responsibility' (1982) 138 *British Journal of Psychiatry* 434–6.
—— 'Mental Health Act 1983' (1983) 286 *British Medical Journal* 1720–5.
—— 'Insanity Legislation' (1986) 12 *Journal of Medical Ethics* 13–17.
HARDIE, T. *et al.*, 'Unmet Needs of Remand Prisoners' (1988) 38(3) *Medicine, Science and Law* 233–6.
HARGREAVES, D., 'The Transfer of Severely Mentally Ill Prisoners from HMP Wakefield: A Descriptive Study' (1997) 8(1) *Journal of Forensic Psychiatry* 62–73.
HARRISON, G., *et al.*, 'A Prospective Study of Severe Mental Disorder in Afro-Caribbean Patients' (1988) 18 *Psychological Medicine* 643–57.
HARRISON, K., 'Patients in the Community' (1995) 145 *New Law Journal* 276–7.
—— 'Supervision in the Community' (1994) 144 *New Law Journal* 1017.
HART, H. L. A., *Punishment and Responsibility: Essays on the Philosophy of Law* (Oxford University Press 1968).

HAVARD, J. D. J., 'The Mental Health Act and the Criminal Offender' [1961] *Criminal Law Review* 296–308.

HEDDERMAN, C., *Panel Assessment Schemes for Mentally Disordered Offenders*, Home Office Research and Planning Unit Paper, 76 (Home Office 1993).

—— *The Supervision of Restricted Patients in the Community*, Research and Statistics Department, Research Findings, 19 (Home Office 1995).

HENHAM, R., 'Dangerous Trends in the Sentencing of Mentally Abnormal Offenders' (1995) 34 *Howard Journal of Criminal Justice* 10–18.

—— 'Making Sense of the Crime (Sentences) Act 1997' (1998) 61(2) *Modern Law Review* 223–35.

HERBST, K., and GUNN, J. (eds.), *The Mentally Disordered Offender* (Butterworth-Heinemann 1991).

HILLIS, G., 'Diverting Tactics' (1993) 89 *Nursing Times* 24–7.

—— *Birmingham Diversion Services* (Report to the Forensic Services Management Team 1993).

HODGINS, S., *Crime and Mental Disorder* (Sage 1993).

HODGSON J., 'Vulnerable Suspects and the Appropriate Adult' [1997] *Criminal Law Review* 785–95.

HOFFMAN, A., 'Living With Your Rights Off' (1977) 5 *Bulletin of the American Academy of Psychiatry and Law* 18.

HOGGETT, B., 'What is Wrong with the Mental Health Act?' [1975] *Criminal Law Review* 677–83.

—— 'The Mental Health Act 1983' [1983] *Public Law* 172–90.

—— *Mental Health Law* (Sweet & Maxwell 1990; rev. edn. 1996).

HOLLOWAY, J., and SHAW, J., 'Providing a Forensic Psychiatry Service to a Magistrates' Court' (1992) 3 *Journal of Forensic Psychiatry* 153–9.

—— 'Providing a Forensic Psychiatry Service to a Magistrates' Court: A Follow-up Study' (1993) 4 *Journal of Forensic Psychiatry* 575–81.

HOSTY, G., and COPE, R., 'The Outcome of Psychiatric Recommendations to Courts' (1996) 36(2) *Medicine, Science & Law* 163–6.

HOWLETT, M., and LLOYD, A. *Monitor: The Journal of the Zito Trust* (Zito Trust 1997).

HOYLE, C., *et al.*, *Evaluation of the 'One Stop Shop' and Victim Statement Pilot Projects* (Home Office 1998).

HUCKLE, P. L., 'A Survey of Sentenced Prisoners Transferred to Hospital for Urgent Psychiatric Treatment over a Three-Year Period in One Region' (1996) 36(4) *Medicine, Science & Law* 37–40.

HUCKLESBY, A., 'Remand Decision Makers' [1997] *Criminal Law Review* 269–81.

HUGHES, G., 'Trends in Guardianship Usage Following the Mental Health Act 1983' (1990/91) 22 *Health Trends* 145–7.

HUGHES, G. *et al.*, 'Diversion in a Culture of Severity' (1998) 37(1) *Howard Journal of Criminal Justice* 16–33.

HUMPHREYS, M. *et al.*, 'Restricted Hospital Orders: A Survey of Forensic Psychiatrists' Practice and Attitudes to their Use' (1998) 9(1) *Journal of Forensic Psychiatry* 173–80.

HUWS, R., *et al.*, 'Prison Transfers to Special Hospitals since the Introduction of the Mental Health Act 1983' (1997) 8(1) *Journal of Forensic Psychiatry* 74–84.

HYLTON, J. H., 'Care or Control' (1995) 18(1) *International Journal of Law & Psychiatry* 45–59.

INGLEBY, D. (ed.), *Critical Psychiatry: The Politics of Mental Health* (Penguin 1981).
—— 'Mental Health and Social Order' in S. Cohen, and A. T. Scull (eds.), *Social Control and the State* (Basil Blackwell 1985).
JAFFE, P. G., 'Diversion in the Canadian Juvenile Court: A Tale of Two Cities' (1985–6) 37 *Juvenile and Family Court Journal* 59–66.
JAMES, A., 'The Criminal Justice Act 1991: Principal Provisions and their Effects on Psychiatric Practice' (1993) 4 *Journal of Forensic Psychiatry* 286–94.
JAMES, D. V., and HAMILTON, L. W., 'The Clerkenwell Scheme: Assessing Efficacy and Cost of a Psychiatric Liaison Service to a Magistrates' Court' (1991) 303 *British Medical Journal* 282–5.
—— 'Setting Up Psychiatric Liaison Schemes to Magistrates' Courts: Problems and Practicalities' (1992) 32 *Medicine, Science & Law* 167–76.
—— 'A Court-Focused Model of Forensic Psychiatry: Abolishing Remands to Prison?' (1997) 8 *Journal of Forensic Psychiatry* 390–405.
—— ' What Demands do Those Admitted from the Criminal Justice System Make on Psychiatric Beds? Expanding Local Secure Services as a Development Strategy' (1998) 9 *Journal of Forensic Psychiatry* 74–102.
JAMESON, J., 'The Care Programme Approach: A Descriptive Study of its Use among Discharges from the Southsea Acute Psychiatric Unit (1996) 20(9) *Psychiatric Bulletin* 550–2.
JEFFERSON, T., and WALKER, M., 'Ethnic Minorities in the Criminal Justice System' [1992] *Criminal Law Review* 83–95.
JONES, G., 'The Use and Effectiveness of the Probation Order with a Condition for Psychiatric Treatment in North Wales' (1989) 20 *Cambrian Law Review* 63–82.
JONES, J., *et al.*, 'An Investigation of the Personality Characteristics of Mentally Disordered Offenders Detained under the Mental Health Act' (1998) 9(1) *Journal of Forensic Psychiatry* 58–73.
JONES, K., *A History of the Mental Health Services* (Routledge & Kegan Paul 1972).
—— 'The Wrong Target in Mental Health?' (1977) *New Society* 3 March 438–40.
—— ' Society Looks at the Psychiatrist' (1978) 132 *British Journal of Psychiatry* 321–32.
—— ' The Limitations of the Legal Approach to Mental Health' (1980) 3 *International Journal of Law & Psychiatry* 1–15.
—— 'Scull's Dilemma' (1982) 141 *British Journal of Psychiatry* 221–6.
—— *Asylums and After: A Revised History of the Mental Health Services* (Athlone Press 1993).
JONES, R., *Mental Health Act Manual* (Sweet & Maxwell 1996).
JOSEPH, P. L., 'Mentally Disordered Offenders: Diversion from the Criminal Justice System' (1990) 1 *Journal of Forensic Psychiatry* 133–7.
—— 'Mentally Disordered Homeless Offenders: Diversion from Custody' (1990) 22 *Health Trends* 51–3.
—— *Psychiatric Assessment at the Magistrates' Court* (Home Office 1992).
—— 'Diversion Revisited' (1992) 3(2) *Journal of Forensic Psychiatry*, Editorial.
JOSEPH, P. L., and POTTER, M., 'Diversion from Custody, I. Psychiatric Assessment at the Magistrates' Court; Diversion from Custody; II. Effect on Hospital and Prison Resources (1993) 162 *British Journal of Psychiatry* 325–30, 330–4.
JOSEPH, P. L., and FORD, J., 'A Psychiatric Bail Bed in a Residential Sick Bay: A One-Year Pilot Study (1995) 6 *Journal of Forensic Psychiatry* 207–17.

KAMMERLING, R. M., and O' CONNOR, S., 'Unemployment Rate as Predictor of Rate of Psychiatric Admission' (1993) 307 *British Medical Journal* 1536–9.

KAUL, A., 'Interim Hospital Orders: A Regional Secure Unit Experience' (1994) 34 *Medicine, Science & Law* 233.

KELLEHER, M. J., and COPELAND, J. R. M., 'Compulsory Psychiatric Admission by the Police: A Study of the Use of Section 136' (1972) 12 *Medicine, Science & Law* 220–4.

KENNEDY, M, *et al.*, 'Commissioning Services for Mentally Vulnerable Defendants' (1997) *Legal Action*, October, pp. 27–9.

—— 'Supported Bail for Mentally Vulnerable Defendants' (1997) 36(2) *Howard Journal of Criminal Justice* 158–69.

KENNEDY, N. M. J., 'Training Aspects of the Birmingham Court Diversion Scheme' (1992) 16 *Psychiatric Bulletin* 630–1.

KENNEDY-HERBERT, J., and GEELAN S. D., 'Bail and Probation Hostel for Mentally Disordered Offenders in Birmingham' (1998) 37(1) *Howard Journal of Criminal Justice* 112.

KILGOUR, J. L., 'The Prison Medical Service in England and Wales: A Commentary from the Director of the Prison Medical Service' (1984) 288 *British Medical Journal* 1603–5.

LAFOND, J. Q., and DURHAM, M. L., *Back to the Asylum: Future of Mental Health Law and Policy in the United States* (Oxford University Press 1994).

LAING, J. M., 'The Mentally Disordered Suspect at the Police Station' [1995] *Criminal Law Review* 371–81.

—— 'Mentally Disordered Offenders and their Diversion from the Criminal Justice Process (unpublished Ph.D. thesis, University of Leeds, 1996).

—— 'The Police Surgeon and Mentally Disordered Suspects: An Adequate Safeguard?' [1996] 1 *Web Journal of Current Legal Issues.*

—— 'Sentencing Mentally Disordered Offenders' (1997) 147 *New Law Journal* 1313–14.

—— 'The Likely Impact of Mandatory and Minimum Sentences on the Disposal of Mentally Disordered Offenders' (1997) 8(3) *Journal of Forensic Psychiatry* 504–5.

—— 'Mentally Disordered Offenders: Sentencing Policy under the Crime (Sentences) Act' 1997 (1998) 9(2) *Journal of Forensic Psychiatry* 424–34.

—— 'A Change of Direction in the Disposal of Mentally Disordered Offenders: The Impact of the Crime (Sentences) Act 1997' (1998) 38(3) *Medicine, Science & Law* 1–9.

LAING, R. D., *The Divided Self: An Existential Study in Sanity and Madness* (Penguin 1990).

LANHAM, D., 'Arresting the Insane' [1974] *Criminal Law Review* 515–28.

LART, R., *Crossing Boundaries: Accessing Community Mental Health Services for Prisoners on Release* (Policy Press, University of Bristol 1997).

—— 'The Wessex Project: Meeting the Mental Health Needs of Prisoners' (1998) 115 *Prison Service Journal* 20–1.

LAWTON, F., 'Psychiatry, Criminology and the Law' (1965) 5 *Medicine, Science & Law* 132–9.

LEIGH, A., *et al.*, *Deaths in Police Custody: Learning the Lessons*, Police Research Series, 26 (Home Office Police Research Group 1998).

LEIGH, L., *Police Powers in England and Wales* (Butterworths 1985).

LEVEY, S., and HOWELLS, K., 'Accounting for the Fear of Schizophrenia' (1994) 4 *Journal of Community & Applied Social Psychology* 313–28.

LEVEY, S., 'Dangerousness, Unpredictability and the Fear of People with Schizophrenia' (1995) 6 *Journal of Forensic Psychiatry* 19–39.

LEWIS, A., 'Psychopathic Personality: A Most Elusive Category' (1974) 4 *Psychological Medicine* 133–140.

LEWIS, P., 'Shall We Ask for a Psychiatric Report?' (1979) 143 *Justice of the Peace* 518–20.

—— *Psychiatric Probation Orders: Roles and Expectations of Probation Officers and Psychiatrists* (Cambridge, Institute of Criminology 1980).

LIEBLING, A., and KRAMP, H., *Suicide Attempts in Male Prisons*, Home Office Research Bulletin, 36 (Home Office 1994).

LITTLECHILD, B., 'Reassessing the Role of the Appropriate Adult' [1995] *Criminal Law Review* 540–5.

—— 'An end to "inappropriate adults" ' (1998) 144 *Childright* 8–9.

LOCKE, T., *New Approaches to Crime in the 1990s* (Longmans 1990).

LONGFORD, Lord, *Punishment and the Punished* (Chapmans 1991).

—— *Prisoner or Patient?* (Chapmans 1992).

Lord Chancellor's Department Best Practice Advisory Group, *Mentally Disordered Offenders* (London 1992).

LOWE, N., 'All in the Mind? '(1995) 139 *Solicitors Journal* 658.

LOWE-PONSFORD, F. L., and BEGG, A., 'Place of Safety and s. 136 at Gatwick Airport' (1996) 36 *Medicine, Science & Law* 306–12.

McCONVILLE, M., *et al.*, *The Case for the Prosecution* (Routledge 1991).

McCORD, W., and McCORD, J., *The Psychopath: An Essay on the Criminal Mind* (Insight 1964).

McGOVERN, D., and COPE, R., 'The Compulsory Detention of Males of Different Ethnic Groups with Special Reference to Offender-Patients' (1987) 150 *British Journal of Psychiatry* 505–12.

MACKAY, R. D., 'Psychiatric Reports in the Crown Court' [1986] *Criminal Law Review* 216–25.

—— 'The Decline of Disability in Relation to the Trial' [1991] *Criminal Law Review* 87–97.

—— 'Capping the Length of Detention of Mentally Disordered Offenders', Paper presented to the Fulbright Colloquium on Penal Theory and Penal Policy (University of Stirling 1992).

—— *Mental Condition Defences in the Criminal Law* (Clarendon 1995).

MACKAY, R. D., and KEARNS, G., 'The Continued Underuse of Unfitness to Plead and the Insanity Defence' [1994] *Criminal Law Review* 576–9.

MACKAY, R. D., and MACHIN, D., *Transfers from Prison to Hospital: The Operation of Section 48 of the Mental Health Act 1983* (Home Office 1998).

McKITTRICK, N., and EYSENCK, S., 'Diversion: A Big Fix?' (1984) 148 *Justice of the Peace* 377–9, 393–4.

MACROWAN, R., 'The Supervised Discharge of Mentally Ill People from Hospital' (1994) 50 *The Magistrate* 71.

MAHENDRA, B., 'Public Policy Rules' (1998) 148 *New Law Journal* 374.

MARSHALL, L., *Review of the Development of the Court Diversion Scheme* (Community Health, Sheffield 1993).

MARTIN, F. M., *Between the Acts: Community Mental Health Services 1959–1983* (Nuffield Provincial Hospitals Trust 1984).

MASON, T., and JENNINGS, L., 'The Mental Health Act and Professional Hostage Taking' (1997) 37(1) *Medicine, Science & Law* 58–68.

MATTHEWS, W. G., 'Pre-Trial Diversion: Promises We Can't Keep' (1988) 12 *Journal of Offender Counselling, Service and Rehabilitation* 191–202.

MENEZES, P. R., *et al.*, 'Drug and Alcohol Problems among Individuals with Severe Mental Illness in South London' (1996) 168 *British Journal of Psychiatry* 612–19.

MILL, J. S., *On Liberty* (Parker 1859).

MILLS, B., Victim's 'Influence on the Criminal Justice System' (1995) 51 *The Magistrate* 83, 99.

MOHAN, D., *et al.*, 'Developments in the Use of Regional Secure Beds over a 12-Year Period' (1997) 8 (1) *Journal of Forensic Psychiatry* 321–35.

MOKHTAR, A. S. E., and HOGBIN, P., 'Police may Underuse s. 136' (1993) 33 *Medicine, Science & Law* 188–96.

MONAHAN, J., 'John Stuart Mill on the Liberty of the Mentally Ill: A Historical Note' (1977) 134 *American Journal of Psychiatry* 1428–9.

MOORE, M. S., 'Some Myths about "Mental Illness" ' (1975) 32 *Archives of General Psychiatry* 1483–97.

MORTIMER, A. M., 'Changes in the Use of the Mental Health Act 1983 Four Years from its Inception in Leeds Eastern Health Authority' (1990) 30 *Medicine, Science & Law* 309.

MOTT, J., 'Police Decisions for Dealing with Juvenile Offenders' (1983) 23 *British Journal of Criminology* 249–62.

MULVANY, J., 'Professional Conflict and the Sentencing Process: The Case of the Hospital Order' (1995) 18(1) *International Journal of Law & Psychiatry* 101–15.

MUNRO, M. A., and FRASER, K. A., 'New Provisions for the Mentally Disordered Offender: The Use of Sections 35, 36 and 38 in Two Regional Secure Units' (1988) 28 *Medicine, Science & Law* 227–32.

MURRAY, K., 'The Use of Beds in NHS Medium Secure Units in England' (1996) 7(3) *Journal of Forensic Psychiatry* 504–524.

MUSTILL, Lord, 'The Mentally Disordered Offender: A Call for Thought' (1992) 3 *King's College Law Journal* 1–28.

NEMITZ, T., and BEAN, P., 'The Use of the Appropriate Adult Scheme (A Preliminary Report)' (1994) 34 *Medicine, Science & Law* 161–6.

—— 'The Effectiveness of a Volunteer Appropriate Adult Scheme' (1998) 38(3) *Medicine, Science & Law* 251–7.

NEWMAN, C. (ed.), *Promoting Care and Justice: Report of the Mental Health Foundation Regional Conferences on Improving Services for Mentally Disordered Offenders* (Mental Health Foundation 1994).

NOBLE, P., 'Mental Health Services and Legislation: An Historical Review' (1981) 21 *Medicine, Science & Law* 16–24.

O'GRADY, J., 'The Complementary Role of Regional and Local Secure Provision for Psychiatric Patients' (1990) 22 *Health Trends* 14–16.

O'GRADY, J. *et al.*, 'The Provision of Secure Psychiatric Services in Leeds: i. A Point Prevalence Study; ii. A Survey of Unmet Need' (1992) 24 *Health Trends* 49–50, 51–3.

ORMROD, R., 'The Developing Relations Between the Law and the Social Sciences' (1964) 4 *British Journal of Criminology* 320–31.

ORR, J. H., 'The Imprisonment of Mentally Disordered Offenders' (1978) 133 *British Journal of Psychiatry* 194–9.

OSLER, A., 'Mentally Disordered Offenders' (1991) 47 *The Magistrate* 161–2.

PALERMO, G. B., SMITH, M. B., and LISKA, F. J., 'Jail versus Mental Hospitals: A Social Dilemma' (1991) 35 *International Journal of Offender Therapy and Comparative Criminology* 97–104.

—— 'Jail versus Mental Hospitals: The Milwaukee Approach to a Social Dilemma' (1991) 35 *International Journal of Offender Therapy and Comparative Criminology* 205–16.

PALMER, A., 'Carnage in the Community' (1994) *The Spectator*, 7 May, 9–10.

PALMER, C., 'Still Vulnerable After All These Years' [1996] *Criminal Law Review* 633–44.

PARKER, E., 'Mentally Disordered Offenders and their Protection from Punitive Sanctions: The English Experience' (1980) 3 *International Journal of Law & Psychiatry* 461–9.

PARKER, E., and TENNENT, G., 'The 1959 Mental Health Act and Mentally Abnormal Offenders: A Comparative Study' (1979) 19 *Medicine, Science & Law* 29–38.

PARKIN, A., 'Caring for Patients in the Community' (1996) 59 *Modern Law Review* 414–26.

PARKINSON, L., *Conciliation in Separation and Divorce* (Croom Helm 1986).

PEARSE, J., and GUDJONSSON, G., 'How Appropriate are Appropriate Adults?' (1996) 7(3) *Journal of Forensic Psychiatry* 570–80.

PEARSON, G., *et al.,* 'Crime, Community and Conflict: The Multi-Agency Approach', in D. Downes (ed), *Unravelling Criminal Justice* (Macmillan 1992).

PEAY, J., 'Mental Health Review Tribunals and the Mental Health (Amendment) Act' [1982] *Criminal Law Review* 794–808.

—— 'Offenders Suffering from Psychopathic Disorder: The Rise and Demise of a Consultation Document' (1988) 28 *British Journal of Criminology* 67–81.

—— 'Mentally Disordered Offenders' in R. Morgan *et al.* (eds.), *The Oxford Handbook of Criminology* (Oxford University Press 1994).

PERLIN, M. L., 'Back to the Past: Why Mental Disability Law "Reforms" Don't Work' (1993) 4 *Criminal Law Forum* 403–12.

PETCH, E., 'Mentally Disordered Offenders and Inter-Agency Working' (1996) 7(2) *Journal of Forensic Psychiatry* 376–82.

PIERZCHNIAK, P., *et al.*, 'Liaison between Prison, Court and Psychiatric Services' (1997) 29 *Health Trends* 26–9.

PORPORINO F. J., and MOTINK, L. L, 'The Prison Careers of Mentally Disordered Offenders' (1995) 18(1) *International Journal of Law & Psychiatry* 29–44.

POTTER, K., 'Cries for Help' (1995) *Police Review*, 10 February, 24–5.

PRINS, H., The Butler Committee Report: Community Care Aspects' (1976) 16 *British Journal of Criminology* 181–3.

—— *Offenders, Deviants or Patients? An Introduction to the Study of Socio-Forensic Problems* (Tavistock 1980).

—— 'Mad or Bad? Thoughts on the Equivocal Relationship between Mental Disorder and Criminality' (1980) 3 *International Journal of Law & Psychiatry* 421–33.

—— 'Attitudes Towards the Mentally Disordered' (1984) 24 *Medicine, Science & Law* 181–91.

—— *Dangerous Behaviour: The Law and Mental Disorder* (Tavistock 1986).

—— 'Literature Review: Understanding and Managing Insanity: Some Glimpses into Historical Fact and Fiction' (1987) 17 *British Journal of Social Work* 91–8.

—— 'Mental Abnormality and Criminality: An Uncertain Relationship' (1990) 30 *Medicine, Science & Law* 247–57.

—— 'The Diversion of the Mentally Disordered: Some Problems for Criminal Justice, Penology and Health Care' (1992) 3 *Journal of Forensic Psychiatry* 431–43.

—— 'Keeping the "Mad" out of Prisons' (1994) 50 *The Magistrate* 114–15.

—— 'Is Diversion Just a Diversion?' (1994) 34 *Medicine, Science & Law* 137–47.

—— 'All Tragedy is the Failure of Communication: The Sad Saga of Christopher Clunis' (1994) 34 *Medicine, Science & Law* 277–8.

—— *Offenders, Deviants or Patients?* 2nd edn. (Routledge 1995).

—— 'Can the Law Serve as the Solution to Social Ills? The Case of the Mental Health (Patients in the Community) Act 1995' (1996) 36(3) *Medicine, Science & Law* 217–20.

PURCHASE, N., *et al.*, 'Evaluation of a Psychiatric Court Liaison Scheme in North London' (1996) 313 *British Medical Journal* 531–2.

RANDALL KROPP, P. *et al.*, 'The Perceptions of Correctional Officers Toward Mentally Disordered Offenders' (1989) 12 *International Journal of Law & Psychiatry* 181–8.

REED, J., and LYNE, M., 'The Quality of Health Care in Prisons: Results of a Year's Programme of Semistructured Inspections' (1997) 315 *British Medical Journal* 1420–4.

RESWICK, J., 'Waiting for Treatment: An Audit of Psychiatric Services at Bullingdon Prison' (1995) 6(2) *Journal of Forensic Psychiatry* 305–16.

Revolving Doors, *The Management of People with Mental Health Problems by the Paddington Police* (Revolving Doors Agency 1994).

RICHARDSON, G., *Law, Process and Custody: Prisoners and Patients* (Weidenfeld and Nicolson 1993).

RIX, K. J. B., *et al.*, 'Recorded Psychiatric Morbidity in a Large Prison for Male Remanded and Sentenced Prisoners' (1994) 34 *Medicine, Science & Law* 324–30.

ROBERTS, C., *et al.*, 'The Supervision of Mentally Disordered Offenders: Work of Probation Officers and their Relationship with Psychiatrists in England and Wales' (1995) 5 *Criminal Behaviour and Mental Health* 75–84.

ROBERTS, N., *Mental Health and Mental Illness* (Routledge & Kegan Paul 1967).

ROBERTSON, G., *The Role of Police Surgeons*, Royal Commission on Criminal Justice Research Study, 6 (HMSO 1993).

ROBERTSON, G., *et al.*, *Mentally Disordered Remand Prisoners*, HO Research and Statistics Department Research Bulletin, 32 (HMSO 1992).

—— 'A Follow-up of Remanded Mentally Ill Offenders Given Court Hospital Orders' (1994) 34 *Medicine, Science & Law* 61–6.

—— *The Mentally Disordered and the Police*, Research and Statistics Department, Research Findings, 21 (Home Office 1995).

—— 'The Entry of Mentally Disordered People to the Criminal Justice System' (1996) 169 *British Journal of Psychiatry* 172–80.

ROESCH, R. *et al.*, 'Mental Health Research in the Criminal Justice System' (1995) 18(1) *International Journal of Law & Psychiatry* 1–14.

ROGERS, A., and FAULKNER, A., *A Place of Safety: MIND's Research into Police Referrals to the Psychiatric Services* (MIND 1987).

ROGERS, R., and BAGBY, M. R., 'Diversion of Mentally Disordered Offenders: A Legitimate Role for Clinicians?' (1992) 10 *Behavioural Sciences & the Law* 407–18.

ROLLIN, H. R., *The Mentally Abnormal Offender and The Law* (Pergamon 1969).

ROMILLY, L. *et al.*, 'Limited Duration Restriction Orders: What Are They For?' (1997) 8 (3) *Journal of Forensic Psychiatry* 562–72.

ROSE, N., 'Unreasonable Rights: Mental Illness and the Limits of the Law' (1985) 12 *Journal of Law & Society* 199–218.

—— *Law, Rights and Psychiatry*, in Rose, N. and Miller, P. *The Power of Psychiatry* (Polity, 1988).

ROSE, N., and MILLER, P. (eds.), *The Power of Psychiatry* (Polity 1988).

ROTH, M. and BLUGLASS, R. (eds.), *Psychiatry, Human Rights and the Law* (Cambridge University Press 1985).

ROUGHTON, A., *An Investigation into the Operation of Section 136 of the Mental Health Act 1983 in the West Midlands* (West Midlands Police 1994).

ROWLANDS, R. *et al.*, 'Diverted to Where? What Happens to the Diverted Mentally Disordered Offender' (1996) 7(2) *Journal of Forensic Psychiatry* 284–96.

SAMUELS, A., 'Mental Illness and Criminal Liability' (1975) 15 *Medicine, Science & Law* 198–204.

—— 'Prosecution and the Public Interest' (1987) 151 *Justice of the Peace* 361–2.

—— 'Hospital Orders without Conviction' [1995] *Criminal Law Review* 220–2.

SANDERS, A., 'The Limits to Diversion from Prosecution' (1988) 28 *British Journal of Criminology* 513–32.

SARUP, M., *An Introductory Guide to Post-Structuralism and Postmodernism* (Harvester Wheatsheaf 1988).

SAVAGE, S. P., *et al.*, 'Divided Loyalties? The Police Surgeon and Criminal Justice' (1997) 7(2) *Policing & Society* 79–98.

SAVOURNIN, R., *et al.*, 'The Brixton Diversion Project: Evaluating a New Service for Mentally Disordered Offenders' (1993) 91 *Prison Service Journal* 20–4.

SCHEFF, T. J., *Being Mentally Ill: A Sociological Theory* (Aldine 1984).

SCHWARTZ, M., 'Glidewell Report: Reviewing the CPS' (1998) *Legal Action*, August, p. 9.

SCOTT, J., 'Homelessness and Mental Illness' (1993) 162 *British Journal of Psychiatry* 314–24.

SCOTT, P. D., 'Punishment or Treatment: Prison or Hospital?' (1970) 2 *British Medical Journal* 167–9.

—— 'Has Psychiatry Failed in the Treatment of Offenders?', The Fifth Denis Carroll Memorial Lecture (Institute for the Study and Treatment of Delinquency 1975).

—— 'The Butler Committee Report: Psychiatric Aspects' (1976) 16 *British Journal of Criminology* 178–81.

SCULL, A. T., *Decarceration: Community Treatment and the Deviant: A Radical View* (Prentice Hall 1977).

—— *Museums of Madness: The Social Organisation of Insanity in Nineteenth Century England* (Allen Lane 1979).

—— (ed.), *Madhouses, Mad-doctors and Madmen: The Social History of Psychiatry in the Victorian Era* (Athlone 1981).

—— 'Museums of Madness Revisited' (1993) 6 *Social History of Medicine* 3–23.

SHAH, S. A., 'Mental Disorder and the Criminal Justice System: Some Overarching Issues' (1989) 12 *International Journal of Law & Psychiatry* 231–44.

SHAPLAND, J., and BELL, E., 'Victims in the Magistrates' Courts and Crown Court' [1998] *Criminal Law Review* 537–46.

SIM, J., *Medical Power in Prisons: The Prison Medical Service in England 1774–1989* (Oxford University Press 1990).

SIMPSON, A. W. B., 'The Butler Committee Report: The Legal Aspects' (1976) 16 *British Journal of Criminology* 175–8.

SIMS, A. C. P., and SYMONDS, R. L., 'Psychiatric Referrals from the Police' (1975) 127 *British Journal of Psychiatry* 171–8.

SMITH, J. C., and HOGAN, B., *Criminal Law* (Butterworths 1996).

SMITH, R., *Trial by Medicine: Insanity and Responsibility in Victorian Trials* (Edinburgh University Press 1981).

—— 'Disorder, Disillusion and Disrepute; History of the Prison Medical Services' (1983) 287 *British Medical Journal* 1521–3, 1786–8.

—— *Prison Health Care* (BMA 1984).

SNOWDEN, P., 'A Survey of the Regional Secure Unit Programme' (1985) 147 *British Journal of Psychiatry* 499–507.

—— 'Regional Secure Units: Arriving but under Threat' (1987) 294 *British Medical Journal* 1310–11.

SOMMER, R., and OSMOND, H., 'The Mentally Ill in the Eighties' (1981) 10 *Journal of Orthomolecular Psychiatry* 193–201.

SPENCER, J. N., 'Reviewing the CPS' (1998) 162 *Justice of the Peace* 22–4.

STAITE, C., and MARTIN, N., 'What Else Can We Do? New Initiatives in Diversion from Custody' (1993) 157 *Justice of the Peace* 280–1.

STAITE, C., *et al., Diversion from Custody for Mentally Disordered Offenders* (Longmans 1994).

STARMER, K., 'Mental Health and the Bill' (1998) *Legal Action* 8–9.

STEADMAN, H., 'Attempting to Protect Patients' Rights Under a Medical Model' (1979) 2 *International Journal of Law & Psychiatry* 185–97.

STEGHART, P. (ed.), *Human Rights in the United Kingdom* (Pinter 1988).

STERN, V., *Imprisoned by our Prisons* (Unwin Paperbacks 1989).

STONE, N., 'The Decline and Fall of the Psychiatric Probation Order' (1994) 158 *Justice of the Peace* 380–81, 402–4.

STREET, R., *The Restricted Hospital Order: From Court to the Community*, Home Office Research Study, 186 (Home Office 1998).

SZASZ, T. S., *The Myth of Mental Illness: Foundations of a Theory of Personal Conduct* (Paladin 1972).

TENNENT, G., *et al.*, 'Is Psychopathic Disorder a Treatable Condition?' (1993) 33 *Medicine, Science & Law* 63.

TEPLIN, L. A., & PRUETT, N. S., 'Police as Streetcorner Psychiatrist: Managing the Mentally Ill' (1992) 15 *International Journal of Law & Psychiatry* 139–56.

THOMAS, D. A., 'Sentencing the Mentally Disturbed Offender' [1965] *Criminal Law Review* 685–699.

—— *Current Sentencing Practice* (Sweet & Maxwell).

—— 'Crime (Sentences) Act 1997' [1998] *Criminal Law Review* 83–92.

THOMAS, T., 'Supervision Registers for Mentally Disordered People' (1995) 145 *New Law Journal* 565–6.

—— 'The Continuing Story of the Appropriate Adult' (1995) 34 *Howard Journal of Criminal Justice* 151–7.

THORNTON, P., *Public Order Law* (Financial Training Publications 1987).

THOROLD, O., 'The Review of the Mental Health Act 1959: A Legal Comment' (1979) 19 *British Journal of Criminology* 263–7.

TOMISON, A., 'McNaughton Today' (1993) 4 *Journal of Forensic Psychiatry* 369–71.

TONAK, D., 'Mentally Disordered Offenders and the Criminal Justice Act 1991' (1992) 39 *Probation Journal* 99–102.

—— 'Mentally Disordered Offenders' (1993) 157 *Justice of the Peace* 332–3.

—— and CAWDRON, G., 'Mentally Disordered Offenders and the Courts: Co-Operation and Collaboration of Disciplines Involved' (1988) 152 *Justice of the Peace* 504–7.

TOOTH, G. C., and BROOKE, E. M., 'Trends in the Mental Hospital Population and their Effect on Future Planning' (1961) 1 *The Lancet* 710–13.

TRUMAN, C., and KEYES, S., *Commissioning Services for Offenders with Mental Health Problems: Measuring the Performance of Court-Based Psychiatric Schemes* (Mental Health Foundation 1997).

TUCKER, D., 'Victim's Rights?—Wrong' (1991) 141 *New Law Journal* 192–4.

UNSWORTH, C., *The Politics of Mental Health Legislation* (Clarendon 1985).

—— 'Law and Lunacy in Psychiatry's Golden Age' (1993) 13 *Oxford Journal of Legal Studies* 479.

VASS, A., *Alternatives to Prison: Punishment, Custody and the Community* (Sage 1990).

VERDUN-JONES, S. N., 'Sentencing the Partly Mad and the Partly Bad: The Case of the Hospital Order in England and Wales' (1989) 12 *International Journal of Law & Psychiatry* 1–27.

WADHAM, J., and MOUNTFIELD, H., *Blackstone's Guide to the Human Rights Act 1998* (Blackstone 1998).

WALKER, N. D., *Crime and Insanity in England,* i. *The Historical Perspective* (Edinburgh University Press 1968).

—— *Sentencing: Theory, Law and Practice* (Butterworth 1985).

—— 'Butler *v.* Criminal Law Revision Committee and Others' [1981] *Criminal Law Review* 596–601.

—— 'X *v.* The United Kingdom' (1982) 22 *British Journal of Criminology* 315–17.

—— (ed), *Dangerous People* (Blackstone 1996).

WALKER, N. D., and McCABE, S., *Crime and Insanity in England,* ii. *New Solutions and New Problems* (Edinburgh University Press 1973).

WASHBROOK, R. A. H., 'The Psychiatrically Ill Prisoner' (1977) 1 *The Lancet* 1302–3.

WASIK, M., 'The Crime (Sentences) Act 1997: Part I—Changes to Custodial Sentences' (1998) 162 *Justice of the Peace* 36–9.

WASIK, M., and TAYLOR, R., *Blackstone's Guide to the Criminal Justice Act 1991* (Blackstone 1994)

—— *Blackstone's Guide to the Criminal Justice and Public Order Act 1994* (Blackstone 1995).

WATSON, S., 'Changes in the Use of Psychiatric Reports in Magistrates' Courts' (unpublished M.Phil. thesis, University of York 1986).

WATSON, W., and GROUNDS, A. (eds.), *The Mentally Disordered Offender in an Era of Community Care: New Directions in Provision* (Cambridge University Press 1993).

WATT, F., *et al.*, 'The Prevalence of Psychiatric Disorder in a Male Remand Population: A Pilot Study' (1993) 4 *Journal of Forensic Psychiatry* 76.

WATTIS, J. P., *et al.*, 'Use of Guardianship Under the 1983 Mental Health Act' (1990) 30 *Medicine, Science & Law* 313.

WELLER, M., *et al.*, 'Psychosis and Destitution at Christmas, 1985–1988' (1989) 2 *The Lancet* 1509–11.

WELLER, M., and SOMERS, A., 'Differences in the Medical and Legal Viewpoint as Illustrated by R. v. Hardie (1991) 31 *Medicine, Science & Law* 152.

WESSELY, S., and TAYLOR, P. J., 'Madness and Crime: Criminology versus Psychiatry' (1991) 1 *Criminal Behaviour and Mental Health* 193–228.

West Midlands Police, *Diversion at the Point of Arrest: Interim Report* (July 1993).

West Yorkshire Police Authority, *Policing Plan for West Yorkshire 1995–96* (WYPA 1995).

West Yorkshire Probation Service, *Probation Works and Everyone Benefits Annual Report 1993–94* (WYPS 1995)

WEXLER, D. B., 'Putting Mental Health into Mental Health Law' (1992) 16 *Law & Human Behaviour* 27–38.

WHITE, S., 'The Criminal Procedure (Insanity and Unfitness to Plead) Act 1991' [1992] *Criminal Law Review* 4–14.

WICKHAM, T., *A Psychiatric Liaison Service for the Criminal Courts* (Social Work Monographs, Norwich 1994).

WILLIAMS, C., 'New Bail Powers for Custody Officers' (1995) 145 *New Law Journal* 685–6.

WIX, S., 'Keeping on the Straight and Narrow—Diversion of Mentally Disordered Offenders at the Point of Arrest' (1994) 1 *Psychiatric Care* 102–4.

WOLFF, G. *et al.*, 'Community Attitudes to Mental Illness' (1996) 168 *British Journal of Psychiatry* 183–90.

WOODSIDE, M., 'Probation and Psychiatric Treatment in Edinburgh' (1971) 118 *British Journal of Psychiatry* 561–70.

—— 'Psychiatric Referrals from Edinburgh Courts' (1976) 16 *British Journal of Criminology* 29–37.

WOOTTON, B., (assisted by V. G. Seal and R. Chambers), *Social Science and Social Pathology* (Allen and Unwin 1959).

—— 'Diminished Responsibility: A Layman's View' (1960) 76 *Law Quarterly Review* 224–39.

—— 'Psychiatry, Ethics and the Criminal Law' (1980) 136 *British Journal of Psychiatry* 525–32.

—— *Crime and the Criminal Law: Reflections of a Magistrate and Social Scientist* (Stevens & Sons 1981).

WRIGHT, M., 'Victims, Mediation and Criminal Justice' [1995] *Criminal Law Review* 187.

ZAPF, P. A., *et al.*, 'An Examination of the Relationship of Homelessness to Mental Disorder, Criminal Behaviour and Health Care in a Pre-trial Jail Population' (1996) 41 *Canadian Journal of Psychiatry* 435–40.

REPORTS

Crown Prosecution Service, *Annual Report 1992–93* (HMSO 1993).

—— *Annual Report 1993–94* (HMSO 1994).

Law Commission, *Mentally Incapacitated Adults and Decision Making: An Overview*, Consultation Paper,119 (HMSO 1991).

Mental Health Act Commission, *First Biennial Report 1983–1985,* Session 1984–5 HC 586.

—— *Second Biennial Report 1985–1987* (HMSO 1987).

—— *Third Biennial Report 1987–1989* (HMSO 1989).

—— *Fourth Biennial Report 1989–1991* (HMSO 1991).

—— *Fifth Biennial Report 1991–1993* (HMSO 1993).

—— *Sixth Biennial Report, 1993–1995* (HMSO 1996).

—— *Seventh Biennial Report, 1995–1997* (HMSO 1997).

MIND, *Diversion from Custody and Secure Provision: A MIND Summary Policy Consultation Document on Mentally Disordered Offenders* (MIND, 1996).

NACRO, *Briefings and Criminal Justice Digests* (NACRO 1990–8).

—— *The Resettlement of Mentally Disordered Offenders* (NACRO 1991).

—— *Revolving Doors: Report of a Telethon Inquiry into the Relationship between Mental Health, Homelessness and the Criminal Justice System* (NACRO 1992).

—— *Mentally Disturbed Prisoners at Winson Green* (NACRO 1993).

—— *Diverting Mentally Disordered Offenders from the Criminal Justice System in Kirklees* (NACRO 1993).

—— *Working with Mentally Disordered Offenders—A Training Pack for Social Services and Others Dealing with Mentally Disordered Offenders* (DoH/NACRO 1994).

—— *Risks and Rights* (NACRO 1998).

NACRO Mental Health Advisory Committee, *Community Care and Mentally Disturbed Offenders*, Policy Paper 1 (NACRO 1993).

—— *Diverting Mentally Disturbed Offenders from Prosecution*, Policy Paper 2 (NACRO 1993).

—— *Diverting Mentally Disturbed Offender from Custodial Remands and Sentences*, Policy Paper 3 (NACRO 1994).

—— *Mentally Disturbed Prisoners*, Policy Paper 4 (NACRO 1995).

—— *The Resettlement of Mentally Disturbed Prisoners*, Policy Paper 5 (NACRO 1995).

NACRO Penal Affairs Consortium, *An Unsuitable Place for Treatment: Diverting Mentally Disordered Offenders from Custody* (NACRO 1998).

NACRO, Young Offenders Committee, *Diverting Young Offenders from Prosecution*, Policy Paper 2 (NACRO 1992).

OFFICIAL PUBLICATIONS

General Reports

DHSS/Department of Health and Home Office

DHSS, *Revised Report of the Working Party on Security in NHS Psychiatric Hospitals* (HMSO 1974).

—— *Consultative Document Review of the Mental Health Act 1959* (HMSO 1976).

—— *A Review of the Mental Health Act 1959* (HMSO 1976).

—— *Care in Action: A Handbook of Priorities for the Health and Social Services in England and Wales* (DHSS 1980).

—— *Mental Health Act 1983: Memorandum on Parts I to IV, VIII and X* (HMSO 1987; rev. edn. DoH/Welsh Office 1998).

—— *Community Care: Agenda for Action* (DHSS 1988).

DHSS/HO, *Offenders Suffering from Psychopathic Disorder: A Joint Consultation Document* (HMSO 1986).

—— *Report of an Interdepartmental Working Group of Home Office and DHSS Officials on Mentally Disturbed Offenders in the Prison System in England and Wales* (DHSS/HO 1987).

DoH, *Mental Health in London: Priorities for Action* (DoH 1994).

—— *The Health of the Nation—Building Bridges: A Guide to Arrangements for Inter-Agency Working for the Care and Protection of Severely Mentally Ill People* (DoH 1995).

—— *The Health of the Nation, Building Bridges Executive Summary* (DoH 1996).

—— *The Protection and Use of Patient Information*, HSG(96) 18 (DoH 1996).

—— *The Patient's Charter Mental Health Services* (DoH 1997).

—— *The Spectrum of Care: Local Services for People with Mental Health Problems* (DoH 1997).

—— *Modernising Mental Health Services: Safe, Sound and Supportive* (Department of Health 1998).

—— *Partnership in Action: New Opportunities for Joint Working between Health and Social Services* (DoH 1998).

—— *Inpatients Formally Detailed in Hospitals under the Metnal Health Lgislation and Other Legislation* (DoH 1999).

DoH, *The Future Organisation and Delivery of Prison Health Care* IISC 1999/077 (DoH 1999)

DoH, *Draft Outline Proposals Scoping Study Committee Review of the Mental Health Act 1983 April 1999* (DoH 1999).

DoH/HO, *Report of the Department of Health and Home Office Working Group on Psychopathic Disorder* (DoH/HO 1994).

DoH/Prison Service, *Joint Prison Service/NHS Executive Working Group Report on the Future Organisation of Prison Health Care* (DoH 1999)

DoH Social Care Group, *Services for Mentally Disordered Offenders in the Community: An Inspection Report* (DoH 1997).

DoH/Welsh Office, *Mental Health Act 1983: Memorandum on Parts I to VI, VIII and X* (HMSO 1987; rev. edn. DoH/Welsh Office 1998).

—— *Mental Health Act 1983 Revised Code of Practice* (HMSO 1999).

HM Inspectorate of Probation, *Probation Orders with Requirements for Psychiatric Treatment Report of a Thematic Inspection* (Home Office 1993).

HO Circular 66/1990, *Provision for Mentally Disordered Offenders* (Home Office 1990).

—— *The Sentence of the Court: Handbook for the Courts on the Treatment of Offenders* (HMSO 1991).

—— Circular 29/1993, *Community Care Reforms and the Criminal Justice System* (Home Office 1993).

—— Circular 18/1994, *The Cautioning of Offenders* (Home Office 1994).

—— *Confidential Inquiry into the Homicides and Suicides by Mentally Ill People* (HMSO 1994).

—— Circular 12/1995, *Mentally Disordered Offenders: Inter-Agency Working* (Home Office 1995).

—— Circular 52/1997, *Crime (Sentences) Act 1997: Provisions Amending the Mental Health Act 1983* (Home Office 1997).

HO Circular 54/1997, *Implementation of Crime (Sentences) Act 1997* (Home Office 1997).
—— Circular 55/1998, Keeping victims informed of developments in their case (Home Office 1998).
HO/NACRO/Mental Health Foundation, *The NACRO Diversion Initiative for Mentally Disordered Offenders: An Account and an Evaluation* (Home Office 1994).
Lord Chancellor's Department Best Practice Advisory Group, *Mentally Disordered Offenders* (Home Ofice 1992).
Ministry of Health, *Working Party on Special Hospitals* (HMSO 1961).
Office for National Statistics, *Psychiatric Morbidity Among Prisoners in England and Wales* (ONS 1998).
Office of Population Censuses and Surveys, *County Report 45: West Yorkshire* (HMSO 1993).
Report of the Inquiry into the Care and Treatment of Christopher Clunis (HMSO 1994).
Home Office, *Speaking up for Justice: Report of an Interdepartmental Working Group on the Treatment of Vulnerable and Intimidated Witnesses in the Criminal Justice System* (Home Office 1998).

HM Chief Inspector of Prisons and Prison Service Reports

Annual Reports of HM Chief Inspector of Prisons (Home Office 1980–98).
HMCIP, *HM Prison and Young Offender Institution New Hall* (Home Office 1992).
—— *HM Prison and Young Offender Institution Moorland* (Home Office 1994).
—— *HM Prison Leeds* (Home Office 1995).
HMP Doncaster: Report of a Full Inspection by HM Chief Inspector of Prisons (Home Office 1996).
Reports on the Work of the Prison Department/ Prison Service Annual Reports (Home Office 1970–98).
HM Inspectorate of Prisons for England and Wales, *Patient or Prisoner? A New Strategy for Health Care in Prisons: A Discussion Document* (Home Office, 1996).
HM Prison Service, *Report of the Director of Health Care for Prisoners April 1992–March 1993* (HM Prison Service 1994).

Statistical Bulletins

DoH, *In-Patients Formally Detained in Hospital under the Mental Health Act 1983 and Other Legislation, England: 1984–1989/90*, Statistical Bulletin 2(7)92 (DoH 1992).
—— *In-Patients Formally Detailed in Hospital under the Mental Health Act 1983 and Other Legislation, England: 1987–88 to 1992–93*, Statistical Bulletin 1995/4 (DoH 1995).
—— *In-Patients Formally Detained in Hospital under Mental Health Act 1983 and Other Legislation, England: 1989–90 to 1994–95*, Statistical Bulletin 1996/10 (DoH 1996).
——*In-Patients Formally Detained in Hospital under Mental Health Act 1983 and Other Legislation, England: 1991–92 to 1996–97*, Statistical Bulletin 1998/01 (DoH 1998).
Home Office, *The Ethnic Origins of Prisoners*, Statistical Bulletin, 21/94 (Home Office 1994).
—— *Statistics of Mentally Disordered Offenders: England and Wales 1993*, Statistical Bulletin 01/95 (Home Office 1995).
—— *Statistics of Mentally Disordered Offenders: England and Wales 1994*, Statistical Bulletin, 20/95 (Home Office 1995).

—— *The Prison Population in 1994*, Statistical Bulletin, 08/95 (Home Office 1995).
—— *Restricted Patients: Reconvictions and Recalls by the End of 1995: England and Wales*, Statistical Bulletin, 1/97 (Home Office 1997).
—— *The Prison Population in 1996*, Statistical Bulletin, 18/97 (Home Office 1997).
—— *Statistics of Mentally Disordered Offenders in England and Wales 1996*, Statistical Bulletin, 20/97 (Home Office 1997).
—— *Summary Probation Statistics England and Wales 1997*, Statistical Bulletin, 12/98 (Home Office 1998).
—— *Statistics of Mentally Disordered Offenders 1997*, Statistical Bulletin 19/98 (Home Office 1998).
Probation Statistics England and Wales 1993 (Home Office 1994).

House of Commons and Command Papers

Royal Commission on the Care and Control of the Feeble-Minded (HMSO 1908) Cd. 4202.
Royal Commission on Lunacy and Mental Disorder (HMSO 1926) Cmd. 2700.
Royal Commission on the Law Relating to Mental Illness and Mental Deficiency (HMSO 1957) Cmnd. 169.
Report of the Departmental Committee on the Probation Service (HMSO 1962) Cmnd. 1650.
Ministry of Health, *A Hospital Plan for England and Wales* (1962) Cmnd. 1604.
—— *Health and Welfare: The Development of Community Care* (1963) Cmnd. 1973.
Report of the Committee of Inquiry into Allegations of Ill-Treatment of Patients and Other Irregularities at the Ely Hospital, Cardiff (HMSO 1969) Cmnd. 3975.
Report of the Farleigh Hospital Committee of Inquiry (HMSO 1971) Cmnd. 4557.
DHSS, *Better Services for the Mentally Handicapped* (1971) Cmnd. 4683.
Report of the Committee of Inquiry into Whittingham Hospital (HMSO 1972) Cmnd. 4861.
Report on the Review of Procedures for the Discharge and Supervision of Psychiatric Patients Subject to Special Restrictions (HMSO 1973) Cmnd. 5191.
Interim Report of the Committee on Mentally Abnormal Offenders (HMSO 1974) Cmnd. 5698.
DHSS, *Better Services for the Mentally Ill* (HMSO 1975) Cmnd. 6233.
Report of the Committee on Mentally Abnormal Offenders (HMSO 1975) Cmnd. 6244.
DHSS, *Review of the Mental Health Act 1959* (HMSO 1978) Cmnd. 7320.
Report of the Review of Rampton Hospital (HMSO 1980) Cmnd. 8073.
DHSS, *Reform of Mental Health Legislation* (HMSO 1981) Cmnd. 8405.
Royal Commission on Criminal Procedure (HMSO 1981) Cmnd. 8092.
Punishment, Custody and the Community (HMSO 1988) Cm. 424.
Caring for People: Community Care in the Next Decade and Beyond (HMSO 1989) Cm. 849.
Supervision and Punishment in the Community (HMSO 1990) Cm. 966.
Report of a Review by HM Chief Inspector of Prisons for England and Wales of Suicide and Self-Harm in Prison Service Establishments in England and Wales (HMSO 1990) Cm. 1383.
Prison Disturbances: April 1990 Report of an Inquiry by the Right Hon LJ Woolf and His Honour Judge Tumim (HMSO 1991) Cm. 1456.

Home Office, *Custody, Care and Justice: The Way Ahead for the Prison Service in England and Wales* (HMSO 1991) Cm. 1647.

DoH, *Health of the Nation (A Strategy for Health in England)* (HMSO 1992) Cm. 1986.

DoH/HO, *Review of Health and Social Services for Mentally Disordered Offenders and Others Requiring Similar Services* (HMSO 1992) Cm. 2088.

Government Response the Health Committee Fifth Report, Session 1992–3 (HMSO 1993) Cm. 2333.

Government Response to the Health Committee Sixth Report, Session 1993–4 (HMSO 1993) Cm. 2334.

Royal Commission on Criminal Justice (HMSO 1993) Cm. 2263.

DoH/OPCS, *The Government's Expenditure Plans 1995–1996 to 1997–1998* (HMSO 1994) Cm. 2812.

Home Office, *Criminal Statistics England and Wales 1993* (HMSO 1994) Cm. 2680.

DoH, *Government's Expenditure Plans 1996–1997 to 1998–1999*, Session 1996–7 Cm. 3212.

Home Office, *Criminal Statistics England and Wales 1995* (HMSO 1996) Cm. 3421.

DoH, *Departmental Report: Government's Expenditure Plans 1997–1998 to 1999–2000*, Session 1996–7 Cm. 3612.

Home Office, *Criminal Statistics England and Wales 1996* (HMSO 1997) Cm. 3764.

—— *No More Excuses: A New Approach to Tackling Youth Crime in England and Wales*, Session 1997–8 Cm. 3809.

—— *Annual Report 1998: Government's Expenditure Plans 1998–1999*, Session 1997–8 Cm. 3908.

DoH, *Departmental Report: Government's Expenditure Plans 1998–1999*, Session 1997–8 Cm 3912.

Report of the Review of the Crown Prosecution Service 1998, Session 1997–8 Cm. 3972.

The Report of the Committee of Inquiry into the Personality Disorder Unit, Ashworth Special Hospital (HMSO 1999) Cm 4194.

HMCIP, *Annual Report 1994–95*, Session 1994–5 HC 760.

—— *Annual Report 1995–96*, Session 1996–7 HC 44.

Crown Prosecution Service, *Annual Report 1996–97*, Session 1997–8 HC 68.

The 1996/1997 Annual Report of the Police Complaints Authority (1997/98) HC 95.

HM Chief Inspector of Constabulary, *Annual Report 1996–1997* Session 1997–98 HC 246.

Prison Service, *Annual Report 1995–96*, Session 1997–98 HC 247.

Home Office, *Report of HM Chief Inspector of Prisons 1996–1997* (Home Office 1998) HC 763.

Select Committees

Health Select Committee, *Fifth Report on Community Supervision Orders*, Session 1992–3 HC 667.

—— *Sixth Report on Community Care: The Way Forward*, Session 1992–3 HC 482.

—— *First Report: Better Off in the Community?* Session 1993–4 HC 102.

Home Affairs Select Committee, *First Report on Remands in Custody*, Session 1983–4 HC 252.

Social Services Select Committee, *Second Report on Community Care with Special Reference to Adult Mentally Ill and Mentally Handicapped People*, Session 1984–5 HC 13.

—— *Third Report on the Prison Medical Service*, Session 1985–6 HC 72.

—— *Eleventh Report on Community Care: Services for People with Mental Illness and Mental Handicap*, Session 1989–90 HC 664.

Index